Visual Perception and Action
in Sport

Visual Perception and Action in Sport

A.M. Williams, K. Davids and J.G. Williams

Taylor & Francis
Taylor & Francis Group
LONDON AND NEW YORK

First published 1999
by Spon Press, an imprint of Routledge
2 Park Square, Milton Park, Abingdon, Oxon, OX14 4RN
Reprinted 2000
Transferred to Digital Printing 2005
Simultaneously published in the USA and Canada
by Routledge
270 Madison Ave, New York NY 10016

Spon Press is an imprint of the Taylor & Francis Group

© 1999 A.M. Williams, K. Davids & J.G. Williams

Typeset in Sabon by
The Florence Group, Stoodleigh, Devon

British Library Cataloguing in Publication Data
A catalogue record for this book is available
from the British Library

Library of Congress Cataloguing in Publication Data
Williams, A. M. (A. Mark), 1965–
    Visual perception and action in sport / A. M. Williams,
    K. Davids, J. G. Williams.
    p. cm.
    Includes bibliographical references and index.
    ISBN 0–419–18290–X
    1. Sport–Psychological aspects. 2. Visual perception.
I. Davids. K. (Keith), 1953– . II. Williams, J. G. P.
    (John Garrett Pascoe) III. Title.
GV706.4W55 1999
796'.01'9–dc21   98–25207
                CIP

ISBN 0 419 18290 X   (pb)
ISBN 0 419 24800 5   (hb)

Printed and bound by Antony Rowe Ltd, Eastbourne

Contents

Prologue

This book is primarily about information, in particular the information necessary for athletes to perceive in order to succeed in sport. In the past few decades there has been increasing recognition of the role of perception in successful sport performance (for a review, see Williams, Davids, Burwitz and Williams 1992). There has been increasing recognition that athletes are dependent on a constant supply of accurate and reliable information from the environment while performing complex movements. Information is needed to perform complex actions such as when balancing on the floor or on a gymnastics beam, when running towards a target (such as a long jump take-off board), when intercepting a projectile and when recognising the pattern formed by a defensive line-up in team ball sports. Typically, research has demonstrated a close link between perceptual pick-up of these information sources and successful performance in sport. From a more practical viewpoint, there has been considerable emphasis on the skill of acquiring and interpreting environmental information, particularly under the severe time constraints experienced in sport. For example, athletes, coaches and teachers show an implicit understanding that effective performance in high level sport requires a range of perceptual, technical, psychological and physical skills. Clearly, the quality of a performer's actions cannot be divorced from the appropriate perception of important environmental events, objects and surfaces.

More specifically, this book is about the information which is perceived by the human visual system and the way that it is used to support actions in sport. By limiting our analysis to visual perception, it should be clearly understood that we do not mean to imply that non-visual sources of information are irrelevant or unnecessary for athletic performance. On the contrary, in the nine chapters which make up this book, we have taken many opportunities to demonstrate the wonderful flexibility of successful athletes who are capable of making sense out of the inputs from the different sensory systems as goal-directed behaviour unfolds in sport.

There has been growing awareness that the visual system provides us with an extraordinarily complex variety of information. It has been known for some time that most of the information that we receive and use to plan our actions comes from the visual system. Information from the visual system tends to dominate the inputs from the other sensory systems. Cutting (1986) has pointed out that 'it is largely through vision that we know our environment and our physical place within it' (p. 3). Schmidt (1988) has called it the 'most critical receptor system for supplying information about the movement of objects in the outside world' (p. 147). Recently, there has been increasing recognition that much previous research on visual perception has undersold the diversity of the roles played by the visual system. Indeed, Milner and Goodale (1995) have argued that most previous research in the visual sciences has assumed a single function of vision: that is the provision of knowledge of the structure of the world. For them, the emphasis has been almost exclusively on the input side of the visual processing system and has ignored the fact that the visual system has evolved to support 'effective and adaptive behavioural output' (p. 6). This has been somewhat of a problem given that sport scientists, amongst others, have generally been most interested in the relationship between visual perception and actions in natural environmental contexts.

A number of scientists have suggested that this problem has occurred because of the well established scientific tendency, dating back to earlier this century, to categorise the sensory systems on the basis of anatomical structure (e.g. see Smyth 1984; Lee 1978). They have indicated how James J. Gibson (e.g. 1979) considered this distinction to be dysfunctional. Almost twenty years ago Gibson (1979) highlighted the idea that the sensory systems should be distinguished in terms of their functions for picking up and utilising information. For Gibson (1979: 1) this functional distinction implied different roles for vision which, in his seminal text, he framed in almost mundane questions for visual perception theorists to answer:

> How do we see the environment around us? How do we see its surfaces, their layout, and their colours and textures? How do we see where we are in the environment? How do we see whether or not we are moving and, if we are, where we are going? How do we see how to do things, to thread a needle or drive an automobile?

As Milner and Goodale (1995) point out, the error in much traditional research on the psychology of perception has been to treat 'vision purely as a perceptual phenomenon' (p. 13). It is a fallacy to study visual perception separately from action because of its significant role in planning, developing, guiding, steering, overseeing and tuning ongoing movement activity (see Lee 1978). As this book purports to show, the remediation of such an error has important implications for our understanding of visual perception and action in sport.

In our 1992 review paper (i.e. Williams *et al.* 1992) we made the point that, in debates over the different theoretical approaches to the study of visual perception and action in sport, a substantial contribution may be made by sport scientists. It was our belief that the many natural tasks of sport exemplify important vehicles for the empirical study of visual perception and action. This book represents a natural progression from the position taken in that review article and we have attempted, as far as possible, to focus attention on the rich diversity of sport-related research studies which have informed our understanding of visual perception and action. It is quite simply divided into three sections. In the first section we start by providing an overview chapter of the theoretical basis for the traditional cognitive theory of perception and action. In this introductory piece we present the philosophical and theoretical basis for the dominant traditional model of perception and action: namely the information processing approach. For many readers in the sports sciences this introduction will provide them with a firm grasp of the backdrop to much of the traditional empirical research which we evaluate in later chapters. In particular, it sets the scene for the remaining four chapters which form Section A of the book. In these chapters, the information processing perspective on visual perception and action is examined stage by stage. Chapter by chapter, we explore the processes of attention, anticipation, decision-making and visual search. Additionally, Chapter 3 provides some neurophysiological background for the material in this section.

In Section B, we adopt a different viewpoint by examining in some detail the prevailing theoretical models of the ecological approach to perception and action. In the ecological approach, the issues raised by the narrow definition of visual perception emphasised in traditional psychological theories are overcome. Of relevance to the study of movement behaviour in sport contexts, according to Bruce, Green and Georgeson (1996), is the argument that 'an ecological framework has helped us to understand aspects of human action that were largely ignored by traditional approaches to human perception' (p. 287). As can be seen in the two chapters of Section B, this has necessarily meant employing an interdisciplinary perspective on visual perception and action. Exciting ideas and conceptual developments from mathematics, physics and biology are interpreted and their implications for ecological theories of perception and action discussed. We have attempted, as far as reasonably feasible, to keep to a minimum the mathematical formalisms which underpin modelling in the ecological framework. The emphasis is very much on providing the reader with a solid conceptual basis for making sense of the sport-related research. In Chapter 6, Gibson's (1979) theory of direct perception is elucidated after an analysis of some of the proposed weaknesses of the indirect approach to visual perception. In Chapter 7 the paradigms of modern science which inform the Dynamical Systems perspective on perception and action are outlined in some depth, before discussion of the empirical literature which models the movement system as a complex dynamical system.

Finally, in Section C, we bring together some of the most recent theories of skill acquisition which have more than a passing relevance to the study of visual perception in sport. Whereas the main emphasis in Sections A and B is to help the reader gain a clear understanding of various theoretical positions, in Section C we spend some time discussing the implications for practice in sport. We start in Chapter 8 by taking a detailed look at the Specificity of Learning hypothesis which examines whether visual information remains increasingly important for all levels of learners. In effect, what we are doing in the first part of the chapter is to ask whether visual information remains a significant constraint on learning as experience in a specific task develops. Later in Chapter 8 we move on to integrate this emphasis on visual information as a constraint on skill acquisition with more recent work from a dynamical systems perspective on other constraints on learning and development. We pose the question whether coaches and teachers can gain any benefit from manipulating the informational constraints on the learner to produce transitions in skill level. In the concluding chapter of Section C, we overview several approaches to observational learning including the visual perception perspective of Scully and Newell (1988).

In this book the accent is on the relationship between theory and practice. A consistent theme to emerge from most chapters is that in the study of visual perception and action, an integration of theoretical knowledge and practical expertise should underpin pedagogical activity in sport. We make the point that most sport practitioners, whether implicitly or explicitly, retain a model of the learner and performer which tends to form the basis for planning and organising practice activities. This book invites readers to (re)consider the models which they typically utilise in their sports and physical activities. To a large extent many of the practical examples discussed in the various chapters have been driven partly by the empirical research studies which currently form the basis of the theoretical arguments overviewed, and partly by the interests of the authors. It will be noted that much, but not all, of the work has been conducted on ball skills and other interceptive actions. The lack of emphasis on research involving other relevant sport-related skills warrants an apology and an invitation. First, we apologise if we have omitted to mention certain types of sport-related tasks. Second, we hope that this book can act as an invitation to readers to experience some of the excitement that we have had in the past decade undertaking research in visual perception and action in sport.

Acknowledgements

Once upon a time, a long time ago, four academics decided to write a book together. What seemed a like a relatively straightforward jaunt turned into a long and eventful journey which strained the mathematical skills of the writers. On the road, four were promoted to more responsibility, four turned into three, one left the country, one got married and five children appeared!

Writing this book has been a labour of love and an important goal for each of us. Its completion has depended enormously on the attention, interest and energy of so many people. In the first instance, without the drive and enthusiasm of our respective co-authors, allied to no little expertise and a constant supply of ideas, the conception and realisation of this book would not have been possible. To each other we say: 'Journey's end: can we go by train next time?' To our metamorphasising publishers, E & FN Spon, we say: 'Thanks for being patient: our next journey won't be so long!' To the friends and colleagues who contributed to earlier drafts of the chapters including Chris Button, James Cauraugh, Luc Proteau, Mark Fischman, Nicola Hodges, Aidan Moran, Geert Savelsbergh, Mark Scott, Bob Singer, Janet Starkes, Gail Stephenson and Joan Vickers, we say: 'Thanks for your help: may our paths cross again soon.' Finally, our journey would never have been completed without the love and support of our respective friends and families. To this end, we include some personalised sentiments to express our gratitude.

Mark Williams: To my mother Beti, brother Nigel and to Meirion, who were instrumental during the initial stages of this journey and have always been supportive: 'Diolch yn fawr!' To my parents-in-law Chris and Peter, who provided the refreshments along the way: 'Cheers: just one more for the road!' To my children Thomas and Mathew, who joined me at various stages on the journey, I'm not sure how I found the time (or the energy!), but: 'Thanks for keeping my feet on the ground and your fingers off the keyboard!' Finally, to my wife Sara, this book is dedicated to her love and devotion: 'Thanks for putting up with me (or without me!)'. For her patience and understanding, I express my deepest love and appreciation.

Keith Davids: To my parents Jan and Eric in Brisbane: 'Thanks for always being there when I needed you.' To my brothers and sister, Brian, Jon, Nick, Pat and Jenny: 'It's a long way from Forest Gate!' Next, without the (grand)parental dedication of Bob and Sheila (world-class babysitters), I would still be on the road. All roads lead to the Fat Cat in Sheffield and thanks to colleagues who contributed through discussion there: particularly Timothy Taylor (LL), Raoul Oudejans, Reinoud Bootsma, Jeff Summers, Simon Bennett, Mike Court and Martin Tayler. But, at the end of the journey, this book could never have happened without the support of my family, the ultimate self-organising system. To my wife Anna: 'Darling, you are IT!' and my children, Michael (He Who Sweeps) and Jake, Charlie and India Rose (They Who Make a Mess): 'You showed me that the edge of order and chaos is a truly beautiful place . . .'.

John Williams: However independent a person considers themselves to be, all of us need assistance of some kind. I take this opportunity to thank friends who helped me contribute to this project.

Mark and Keith my 'long-range' co-authors (we didn't meet face-to-face during the actual writing of the book), I hold you in the highest esteem, not only for your knowledge but also for your perseverance. It is not easy to communicate cogently with a grumpy old man who was weighed down with administrative baggage even when assisted (sometimes shielded) by electronic communications. Thanks for hanging in there guys!

To Parveen and 'PBC' who stimulated and mentored my neuroscience interests a long time ago in 'Beautiful BC'. And, even longer ago, Wilf, a model teacher who understood well the process of learning by observation and communicated it so effectively, you have been an inestimable influence on me. I am eternally grateful.

Last, and certainly not least, my family – Mary, Amy, Greg, Lee, Mark, and my parents, Kath and Herb – you are always a source of inspiration, support, and a fountain of ideas. Heartfelt thanks!

Forewords

Every once in a while a book is written that is truly set apart from traditional ventures. Unfortunately, an academic publication rarely makes a major breakthrough in terms of substance as well as style of presentation. Many professors have earned a reputation for being non-creative and non-challenging, as well as generally wordy and boring in presenting scientific matter oriented to educating the reader.

Such is not the case here! I truly looked forward to the opportunity of previewing this informative book and have not been disappointed in the least. True, the contents are of personal interest to me anyway. Nonetheless, the authors demonstrate a great ability in organizing and presenting exciting new developments with regard to understanding visual perception, attention, anticipation, decision-making and skilled movement in dynamic sport settings in which there is uncertainty of an opponent's intentions and actions, and a need to make fast and accurate decisions and movement responses. In addition, material is presented that describes the development of skill in making purposeful movements within particular environments.

The blending of contemporary research and theory with practical implications is demonstrated throughout each of the chapters. It is as if the authors followed the dictum of superb chefs preparing gourmet meals: to generate quality and appetizing substance, and to make it appealing and aesthetically pleasing to the senses. The ingredients for an unusual, complicated and tasteful meal are a great challenge for the gourmet chef. Likewise, the authors of this book have accepted the challenge of presenting and offering alternative conceptual models and sophisticated research for the explanation of visual perception action behavior. Part of the book is dedicated to the traditional cognitive, information-processing approach in which the computer metaphor has served as the basis for so much research since the 1950s. The other part offers more contemporary alternative models, generally subsumed under the rubric, ecological psychology, or the perception–action coupling framework. Putting it simply, the argument pits motor program, computational, and hierarchical-control theorists against those who advocate a dynamic, psychobiological, neural network, and body–environment interaction approach.

The reader is provided with rich nourishment from both theoretical camps as well as detailed analyses of pertinent research. On the one hand, enlightenment is the goal. On the other hand, confusion as to which propositions are most defensible and therefore most believable can result. Perhaps the major objective is awareness – awareness of the state of science related to understanding the dynamics of visual perception and action in sport settings as well as of theories that have guided research directions in this area. A thought came to me as I reflected on the contents of the book. An under-appreciated observation is that legitimate science is now being associated with sport. For years, many thought that sport performers and performance were not worthy of serious scientific scrutiny. Yet the study of skilled behaviors in reactive, time-constrained situations containing uncertainty is a compelling and legitimate area of focus for sport scientists as well as others concerned with these behaviors in various occupations, such as flying and driving vehicles, and in military operations.

The vast array of perspectives presented should stimulate researchers to initiate follow-up investigations, especially with an attempt to formulate more creative methodologies that involve tasks and testing under the most ecologically valid conditions. Throughout the book conservative interpretations and implications are made about existing research findings as a result of obvious limitations and constraints associated with the research itself. With continual technological breakthroughs and a greater number of scholars interested in understanding more about the topics presented in this book, we can be optimistic about the future.

Finally one might ask, 'What does it all mean?' What guidelines can be offered to coaches, athletes and anyone serious about improving movement skill? Are there tangible and practical suggestions? Will they contrast considerably with what is going on at present, and therefore make a big difference in outcomes, considering efficiency and effectiveness of training protocols? In other words, what do the contents of this volume bring to the table for those who desire cook-book, easy-to-follow prescriptions about how to train and prepare for events?

Throughout the book as well as in specific chapters, the authors try to provide pragmatic insights as to how learners and performers might benefit from the current state of knowledge on visual perception and action. Possibly, this is the most delicate issue addressed, and the most difficult to resolve. Speculations are offered. However, until a number of considerations are resolved between the two theoretical camps, and research protocols are advanced considerably, we may not yet be in a good position to make startling commentaries that might directly benefit athletes and others engaged in performance situations requiring skilled movement execution. Having said this (I learned this phrase from my English colleagues!), the authors are to be commended for taking risks in suggesting potential real-world applications.

In closing, I must say that my experience in reading this book has been exceptionally rewarding – from an intellectual as well as an enjoyment perspective. The theme is exciting. The depth of treatment of the various topics is perfect and the examples from various sport situations help to bridge research and practical interests. The book will serve many purposes and will be of value to scholars as well as educators in all parts of the world.

Robert N. Singer
Department of Exercise and Sport Sciences
University of Florida
Gainsville
USA

In the great diversity of sports one is fascinated by athletes demonstrating highly skilled and well coordinated behaviour. One of the most remarkable aspects of this highly skilled performance is that athletes seem to be able to exhibit their skills in a variety of circumstances. To reach such high levels of performance and flexibility often takes years of learning and practice. An important characteristic of skilled performance is the precise tuning of the action to the changing circumstances of the environment. Visual perception is indispensable in this respect. A second important characteristic of highly skilled performance, and indeed of any successful performance, is that all the components (e.g. muscle, tendons, joints) of the motor apparatus of the human body have to be controlled and coordinated. The books deals with these issues in a very legible way and elaborates upon the role of information in the coordination and control of sports skills, especially with regard to the nature of the visual information that lays the basis for perception and action. It demonstrates the usefulness of new approaches like the ecological psychological approach to perception and action and dynamic systems approach to sport sciences. Basic knowledge of how information, movement and skill level interact for the realisation of successful performance is provided. In my view, this book is an excellent starting point in the search for this fundamental knowledge. Also, answers are provided to more practical questons based on empirical findings. However, the contents are not only of interest to sport scientistts but also for students and researchers with interest in visual perception, skill acquisition, rehabilitation, kinesiology and movement science.

Geert J.P. Savelsbergh
Faculty of Human Movement Sciences
Vrije Universiteit
Amsterdam

Section A

Cognition in action

In Section A, we begin our journey by exploring the cognitive psychology interpretation of how the precise fit between visual perception and action is obtained as well as its implications for research and practice in sport (for detailed introductions, see Davids *et al.* 1994; Williams *et al.* 1992). It will be seen that in cognitive psychology the computer metaphor is dominant, with the mind viewed as an information processing device. The computational interventions of mind into the processes of perception and action have led to cognitive theories being labelled 'indirect'. It has been argued that the world cannot be known directly, but only through a stored representation of it in our minds. Due to the perceived inadequacy of the sensory systems, the assumption from this perspective is that the interventions of mind into the processes of perception and action need to be quite detailed. After a review of the theoretical and philosophical bases of the established cognitive approach to perception and action in Chapter 1, the focus of the remaining chapters in this section will be on the key processes of the information processing model, namely: attention, visual search, anticipation and decision-making. Moreover, Chapter 3 provides a neurophysiological background to this material by looking at the transfer of visual information from the retinas of the eyes through to the primary visual cortex and beyond. The main emphasis in many of the chapters presented in this section, as well as elsewhere in the book, will be on expertise in sport. This does not undervalue the importance of research work which has adopted clinical or developmental perspectives, for example, but merely reflects the propensity towards expertise research within the sports sciences. For example, sport psychologists have been interested in the study of expert performance as a window for understanding the acquisition of skill in sport. Knowing what essential attributes distinguish skilled performers from their lesser skilled counterparts provides a principled basis for determining what types of practice are most likely to be beneficial for enhancing the development of expertise. In this way, the knowledge generated by sport psychologists from expertise research can be of immediate relevance to the key issues of training, testing and talent identification routinely faced by sports scientists, coaches and practitioners. When sport psychologists study experts, it can also be valuable in evaluating the explanatory power of theories and models of expertise developed in other domains (Williams and Davids 1998a). Finally, in combination with information from the other sub-disciplines of sports science, such endeavours can provide some insights into the factors limiting high level sports performance (Abernethy 1993).

1 Indirect theories of perception and action

An overview

INTRODUCTION

A gymnast accelerates her legs towards the lower asymmetric bar and precisely times the beat to take advantage of reactive forces to facilitate her upward swing. A wheelchair basketballer modulates the forces on the wheels of his chair to arrive in front of the basket at the same time as the pass from his team-mate. These anecdotal descriptions of skilled actions in sport have one important thing in common: they exemplify the significant spatio-temporal demands on the top-class athlete in complex and dynamic environments. These demands, highlighted daily in the sports media, have been more precisely quantified in scientific analyses. In ball games such as baseball and tennis, projectile speeds of between 36 and 46 ms^{-1} have been recorded (Glencross and Cibich 1977; Bahill and LaRitz 1984). The time windows afforded performers in high-level sport are typically measured in thousandths of a second (ms). For example, Regan (1986) has demonstrated how cricket batsmen often have only 230 ms to cope with late fluctuations in the flight of a ball approaching at 150 kilometres per hour (kph). Yet, skilled performers are capable of the most extraordinary precision in matching the spatio-temporal constraints of their sports and activities. For instance, long jumpers can accurately hit a 20-cm take-off board at the end of a 40-m run-up at speeds of around 10 ms^{-1} (Hay 1988). Additionally, Bootsma and van Wieringen (1990) have illustrated the consistency of bat control in national-level table-tennis players by calculating the variability in timing the initiation of an attacking forehand drive. Astonishingly, they found that typical values for timing variability in the stroke were between 2.03 and 4.72 ms. The theme of this book is that, in order to satisfy these task constraints, the sport performer is heavily dependent on the visual system to provide much of the information for perceiving and acting.

A major question posed in this book is: How do skilled performers match the severe spatio-temporal constraints imposed on their behaviour by the rules and events of sport and physical activities? More specifically, how do skilled athletes perceive visual information from highly dynamic and complex environments in order to perform such exquisitely timed and consistent actions? Although these are not the only questions arising in this book, a significant aim is to examine the main theoretical explanations for the processes of visual perception and action in relation to sport performance. From our own experiences in watching and playing different types of sport, we have come to realise that skilled athletes typically exhibit a 'close fit' between their actions and immediate environmental demands. They seem to be able to consistently reproduce stable patterns of coordinated activity under severe competitive pressure. Yet, their actions cannot be described as stereotyped. Their movements appear to be subtly varied and coordinated to the sudden changes in their environments. In other words, there is a fine balance between persistence and change in the movements of skilled athletes. For example, high-level tennis players are able to improvise and produce the appropriate version of the forehand drive to suit the exact circumstances of performance. This was noted long ago by Bartlett (1932) who reasoned that during tennis performance 'When I make the stroke I do not . . . produce something absolutely new, and I never repeat something old' (p. 202). Of course the need for persistence and change in skill performance is not just a challenge for performers in more dynamic sports such as ball games. Even athletes in more static sports, such as archery, clay-target shooting and golf, are required to perform under differing conditions which prohibit the use of stereotyped movement patterns.

In attempting to understand how visual perception and action support movement behaviour in sport, we will not merely limit ourselves to highlighting the evidence from top class sport performance with a sense of awe. We will also look at relevant empirical work on the perception and action systems of novice performers and children. In contrast to the functional levels of persistence and change typically shown by experts, learners seem to be in a continuous state of near 'skeletomuscular anarchy'. Many of their movements may be characterised as 'pointless'. More specifically, their movements bear little relation to environmental demands and lack consistency early in learning. Moreover, as skill begins to develop, a slight change in the conditions of performance can leave learners clinging inflexibly to what has hitherto been learned. It is almost as if they are performing their actions in a kind of vacuum, which contrasts strikingly with the refined adjustments of the expert performer. The old cliché, 'a little learning is a dangerous thing', seems most appropriate at intermediate levels of performance because there is not enough of the functional kind of variability in movement behaviour shown by the skilled performer. Understanding the development of the visual perceptual and action systems can provide us with important information with which to underpin teaching and coaching behaviour. For example, the planning and organisation of practice sessions is often implicitly based on a theoretical model of how the learner acquires skill (see Handford, Davids, Bennett and

Button 1997). We believe that the acquisition of an explicit framework for the development of skill in visual perception and action requires an understanding of the theories and evidence discussed in this book. Important questions for practitioners include: How can we make sense of the qualitative and quantitative differences which we observe in the movements of experts and novices in sport? What kind of theory of perception and action is required to provide an adequate account of the need for persistence and change during sport performance?

Categories of theories for studying perception and action

Theories of perception and action fall into two broad categories: structural and phenomenological. Beek, Peper and Stegeman (1995) argue that the former focuses on dedicated structures and mechanisms underlying movement behaviour. The latter focuses on the development of laws and principles without reference to the mechanisms and structures of the human body. That is, the functional properties of the movement system may be described in different ways. One way is to examine the structure of the mechanisms and processes underlying the functionally specific properties which pertain to the movement systems of different biological species, whilst another way is to model the functional properties of movement systems at a general abstract level of theory without recourse to neurophysiological detail.

Perhaps due to the lack of sophisticated technology, the phenomenology of cognitivism has dominated motor behaviour theories for over half a century. Principles of the cognitive perspective have emphasised the self-regulation of movements with reference to anthropomorphic concepts such as schemas, programmes, representations and traces (e.g. see Schmidt 1988; Jeannerod 1993). Many issues have been raised with this conceptual approach to the control of human movements. These include the problem of how the many degrees of freedom of the human motor system[1] are regulated by an internally represented algorithm (see Bernstein 1967) and how the motor plan copes with the ongoing interaction between the motor system dynamics and the energy fluxes surrounding the system (Kelso, Holt, Rubin and Kugler 1981; van Gelder and Port 1995).

THE ROLE OF VISUAL PERCEPTION IN MOVEMENT BEHAVIOUR

Perception involves detecting and interpreting changes in various forms of energy flowing through the environment such as light rays, sound waves and neural activation (Bruce, Green and Georgeson 1996). The environmental changes which can be perceived from these energy flows over space and time are used to support the goal-directed actions of the athlete. For example, a netballer needs to be able to detect and interpret the light information which reflects from the surface of the ball as a common task, such as a two-handed catch, is organised. When performing this basic task in netball, she needs precise information to locate the ball in space ('where' information) at a specific point in time ('when' information). Spatio-temporal information regarding the approaching object must be acquired early so that the appropriate components of her skeletomuscular system (i.e. muscles of the trunk and joints in the arms and shoulders) may be coordinated in time. In many other ball games, the catcher also needs to be aware of late deviations in flight due to added complications such as spin, swerve or drag effects.[2] Furthermore, the visual perceptual systems of the netballer support the balance and postural control necessary as she organises the two-handed catching response (Lee and Lishman 1975; Forssberg and Nashner 1982). They also allow the skilled team games player to recognise patterns in the formation of the opposing players so that the two-handed catching action may be integrated into a tactical sequence of play.

Visual perception: elaboration and definition

From the above discussion, it is clear that the study of visual perception and action in sport is related to the athlete's need to perceive the spatio-temporal structure of environmental information in order to successfully perform actions (Bootsma 1988; Fitch and Turvey 1978; Lee 1980a; Turvey 1990). This is not to deny that other forms of sensory information are important, it is just that visual information is the source upon which we rely most (Lee 1978; Cutting 1986). Cutting (ibid.) points out that decomposing the word 'information' signifies that it means 'to instil form within'. Visual perception may be understood, therefore, as the process of picking up environmental information which instils form (of objects, surfaces, events, patterns) within a perceiver. Since we perceive a three-dimensional world with a two-dimensional projection device (the retina), it follows that geometrical form is that which is instilled in the observer. Geometrical abstractions are picked up and projected on to the retina to represent the external world. In this sense, the human visual system may be viewed as a 'geometry-analysing engine' (ibid.: 4). Cutting (ibid.) proposed that visual perception is 'the study of mapping from perceptible external objects, through optic information that represents them, to the observer who uses that information'. There are some key terms from the above description to note as precursors to later discussions dealing with the theoretical and philosophical bases of perception and action (see Chapters 6 and 7). These are: the geometrical basis of vision; the representation of optical information and the use of optical information to support the actions of observers. These are key issues which are expanded upon in some detail later.

Much of the previous theoretical work purporting to explain the nature of perception and action in complex environments has come from psychology. As Bruce *et al.* (1996) have argued, the psychological level of analysis is necessary to support the meagre neurophysiological data on the mechanisms of the central nervous system (CNS) underpinning perception and action. The support comes in the form of theoretical modelling which allows scientists to test their hypotheses regarding the functioning of perception and action systems. However, theories never exist in a vacuum. There are always significant social and philosophical ideas which influence how scientists formulate their models of phenomena in the natural world. As we have shown elsewhere, there is presently a state of confusion in the literature on perception and action (see Williams *et al.* 1992). The main argument concerns the extent to which perception of the environment is constructed by the knowledge of an individual or is unmediated by past experience. This has been characterised as the difference between top-down or conceptually driven theories (indirect perception) and those which are bottom-up or data-driven (direct perception) (see Gordon 1989; Bruce *et al.* 1996; Eysenck and Keane 1995; Williams *et al.* 1992). There has been an extensive debate regarding the theoretical model which best explains the nature of perception and action. For sport and exercise scientists, a basic understanding of the philosophical basis and the historical development of differing perspectives on perception and action is necessary because of the contrasting positions expressed in the literature. Without this background information, sports and exercise scientists would be unable to comprehend or contribute to the current debate. In Chapters 1 and 6, the theoretical basis of the current debate between indirect and direct approaches to the study of the perception–action relationship is reviewed. The implications for the study of movement behaviour in sport provide the specific backdrop for the discussion of key issues. Additionally, the emerging potential of an integrated approach which emphasises significant aspects of both schools of thought is highlighted.

PHILOSOPHICAL AND THEORETICAL UNDERPINNINGS OF THE INFORMATION PROCESSING APPROACH

After the second world war cognitive psychologists adopted a 'process-oriented' approach in which the main focus of study became the unobservable and hypothetical mental processes, such as perception, attention and memory, which were believed to mediate between the sensory reception of ambiguous stimulus information and movement response (e.g. see Neisser 1967; Marteniuk 1976; Neumann and Prinz 1990; Williams *et al.* 1992). Cognitions can be defined as 'any knowledge, opinion, or belief about the environment, self, or behavior potential that an individual might possess' (Silva and Hardy 1984: 80). From the traditional perspective, perception and action are determined by cognitions of the specific context of action: in our case sport settings.

In the ensuing chapters of Section A detailed analysis of these information processing activities is provided. The cognitive approach to the study of perception and action in sport has undoubtedly been most productive in terms of empirical output (e.g. see Whiting 1969; Starkes and Deakin 1984; Abernethy 1987a; Starkes 1987; Garland and Barry 1990). For this reason, it is considered to be the 'established' or 'traditional' perspective in the study of human movement (Fodor and Pylyshyn 1981; Beek and Meijer 1988; van Wieringen 1988). Generally, the research literature has supported the notion that perceptual skill is a significant component of proficiency in sport, particularly for fast activities such as driving, flying and ball games (Abernethy 1987b; Williams *et al.* 1992).

In the study of perception, an important philosophical issue has been the way that the stimulus properties of the environment are sensed and perceived. How do we gain knowledge of our world so that our actions are intentional and successful? One of the hallmarks of consciousness in biological organisms is intentionality. For our actions to have intent they have to be purposefully directed towards objects in the environment.[3] Obviously, behaving with intent in a rule-governed, social context like sport requires considerable understanding of the environment. That is, in order to engage in intentional behaviour in sport one needs to interpret precisely what is going on in the world. The cognitive perspective on the perception–action relationship has been dominated by the Cartesian school of philosophy which emphasises that the reality which we perceive is a kind of mental reconstruction of the environment (for more detailed treatments of the philosophical basis of cognitive theories of perception, see Shaw and Bransford 1977; Gordon 1989). Information processing activities underpin the development of internal models of the world to support actions. These models or representations are known in some areas of the psychology literature as cognitive knowledge structures (e.g. see Williams *et al.* 1992; Starkes and Allard 1993). Their role is to act as a type of reference base for the planning and organisation of behaviour in the performance of complex human activities found at work, in sport and the arts.

The representational mind

This capacity of the mind to represent the world internally has been compared to the way that a digital computer works. The way that a computer processes information and can represent it within the system in the form of a symbolically coded language has been used as a metaphor for mental processes. Typically, in cognitive science it has been believed that people attain knowledge composed of symbols which represent external objects in the mind (e.g. see Edelman 1992; van Gelder, in press).

Cognition involves manipulating these symbols in an abstract and rule-governed manner according to a syntax. Operating according to these rules is known as computation. Like a computer, it is argued, the mind 'reads' symbolic representations semantically. We rely on symbolic representations in order to carry out goal-directed activity. This is the essence of cognitivism. The basis for this computational modelling is rooted in Newell and Simon's (1976) Physical Symbol System Hypothesis (see Steier and Mitchell 1996). They argued that an important characteristic of intelligent behaviour is the capacity to manipulate physical symbols. Their hypothesis was that the symbols used in the encoding language used to represent concepts and programmes in a digital computer 'are in fact the same symbols that we humans have and use everyday in our lives' (Newell 1980: 136). In other words, like computers, humans are physical symbol systems. This is how the concept of the representational mind could be physically substantiated. The task for cognitive scientists is to specify the physical symbol systems which constitute the human mind or, in other words, 'that constitute systems of powerful and efficient intelligence' (ibid.: 136).

Traditional theorising on perception and action in humans has emphasised the representation and communication of information in the cognitive system, rather like a hierarchical control system in the engineering sciences (e.g. Kelso 1992). A major characteristic of control engineering theory is that it posits rules or algorithms for controlling system output. A major assumption is that biological nervous systems operate in the same way as robotic or engineering control systems (Carello, Turvey, Kugler and Shaw 1984). The role of the perceptual systems has been conceptualised as providing the necessary stimulus for the 'release' of a specific programme of action or as contextualising a symbolic movement representation, once initiated. In this sense, the processes of visual perception may be likened to a series of computations on the raw sensations registered on the retina during sport performance (see Williams *et al.* 1992). The basic cognitive science model of perception, that ambiguous sensory cues are compared with information stored in memory before output from the system can occur, has led to the popularisation of the computer metaphor for explaining perception and action in human behaviour.

In planning a motor response, cognitive psychologists have argued that skilled performers use internally represented knowledge to:

- attend to relevant sources of environmental information and to ignore the less relevant cues;
- search the visual field in a systematic and skilful way;
- anticipate events in time-constrained sports before they actually happen;
- verify the impoverished information which their perceptual systems receive from the environment (see Figure 1.1).

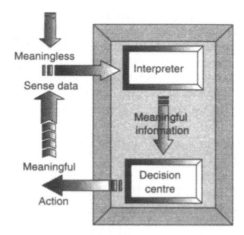

Figure 1.1 The Constructivist approach to perception. Note that meaning is attributed to essentially meaningless information by an internal representation
of reality which helps us to infer what is going on in the environment.
(Adapted from O.G. Meijer (1988) *The Hierarchy Debate: Perspectives
for a Theory of Movement Science*, Amsterdam: Free University Press.)

The construction of perception

This philosophical approach argued that inferential support was necessary
for adequate perception of environmental stimuli because of the ambiguous
nature of sensory input. Helmholtz (e.g. 1925) in the last century proposed
that, in between sensing and consciously perceiving events or objects in the
environment, there was an unconscious, supportive role for the knowledge
of the individual. For example, when a fell runner (a runner who specialises
in running over hills and mountains for extended periods of time) sees a
potential route feature (such as an obstacle or a gap between rocks) in the
environment, a retinal image of the signal is received (see Figure 1.2).

Cognitive psychology holds that we are unable to make much direct
sense of the route feature without the intervention of hypothetical processes
which, effectively, reconstruct reality in our heads. Thus, perception is a
process of constructing meaning and, by inference, can never be direct.
The resulting ambiguity for our fell runner is resolved by the indirect
perception of what a route feature means. The task of reconstruction
involves important cognitive activities such as remembering (the act of
attempting to stereotype, on the basis of long term memory, a stimulus
representation) and attending (scrutinising some and ignoring other parts
of the environment). These processes are dealt with in greater detail later
in this section, but at this stage it needs to be noted that the indirect
perception approach places a significant emphasis on the cognitive
processes which precede motor output.

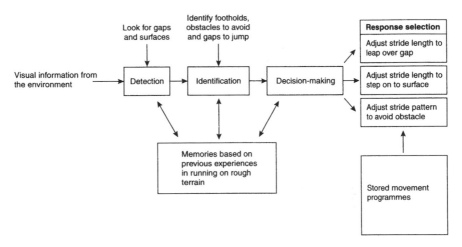

Figure 1.2 A generic information processing model which shows how athletes may use internal representations of the environment and of movements to maximise mental capacity for strategic planning and decision-making of a higher order.

Marr's (1982) computational approach to visual perception

A theory of visual perception which exemplifies the computational approach is that of Marr (1982). He proposed a psychological theory which built on existing neurophysiological knowledge about how the visual system works. An abstract retinal image was seen as a starting point for the processes of visual perception. Marr's view of the sensory stimulation from the optical field is more elaborate than the approach of Cutting (1986) which we mentioned earlier. An abstraction needs to be described in more and more detail for it to inform an observer. According to Marr (1982), a series of four representations helps us to elaborate the structure of the light stimulation sensed from the environment into a percept. These symbolic representations were called 'sketches'. Raw and unrefined primal sketches of the light structure in the environment are gradually built up and a '2½D' sketch provides us with a basis for action from our own point of observation. The final '3D' stage of computation allows an observer to identify an object via the use of stored representations of the world. For Marr, therefore, visual perception concerns a series of explicit computational stages in which retinal stimulation is gradually developed into perception of an object. In the model, the computational burden on the observer is reduced by having only the final stage involve a conscious comparison of an object image with its representation in memory. The primary stages of visual perception, leading up to the '3D' stage, are all constrained by more primitive features of the environment and do not need to be consciously controlled by the performer.

The influence of the philosophical ideas of René Descartes may be seen in the hierarchical nature of most cognitive psychology models of the perception–action relationship (see Descartes 1978). The machine metaphor has been adopted because the mind is viewed as the organ which controls a dependent physical system (the body). In early accounts of movement behaviour by information processing theorists, the physical components of the system were seen as merely subservient to the commands issued by the higher levels of the system (e.g. Marteniuk 1976). Perception may, therefore, be studied separately from action, given this emphasis. When reading the literature on perception and action in sport, a useful exercise for the reader is to attempt to ascertain the philosophical basis of the many different empirical studies under discussion. It will become readily apparent that the Cartesian notion of mind–body dualism currently dominates sport-related research on perception and traditional attempts to model motor behaviour.

Neural networks and visual perception

Recently, there has been a burgeoning interest in models of visual perception which emphasise the capacity of the neurons of the brain to link together in networks or patterns to interpret environmental information. According to Bruce *et al.* (1996), in these cognitive neuroscientific explanations 'the representations of the world are expressed in terms of activities in neuron-like units, rather than in terms of the construction and storage of abstract strings of symbols' (p. 233). The relative activity of the neurons as they connect with other neurons provides the basis for visual perception. The patterns of activity in the networks of neurons correspond to percepts. A description of an environmental feature such as the edge of the beam for a gymnast performing a routine would be provided in the brain as a pattern of connections between specific groups of neurons. Bruce *et al.* (ibid.) point out that these connectionist models of visual perception have a number of advantages over traditional information processing models. These include a better correspondence with existing neurophysiological evidence, the capacity for parallel processing and a greater potential for explaining how learning occurs through pattern formation and associative weighting. Their analysis of the current literature on connectionist models of visual perception reveals that virtually all of the work has been conducted on the processes of pattern recognition and object identification. A primary example of a connectionist model of visual perception is Marr and Poggio's (1976) algorithm for the perception of stereopsis. Some of the data emerging from these studies are quite exciting and promise a reasonable future. For example, a comparison of the performance of computerised neural network algorithms for pattern and object recognition processes shows good association with human skill levels. However, the technological development and mathematical modelling of such networks have been slow and their capabilities are relatively limited at present. Most of the work is currently focused on computer-controlled monitoring of automated production processes in industry and the development of security in electronic communications systems. At this stage, it is not clear how well connectionist models will generalise to the study of the goal-directed behaviour of dynamic, biological organisms moving in natural environments. The implications of this type of modelling for the study of visual perception and action in sport contexts are also not fully understood at this time. This is because there have been very few attempts to apply connectionist principles to the study of the relationship between the perceptual and action systems. A more detailed overview of this perspective is provided in Chapter 4.

REPRESENTATIONAL ACCOUNTS OF MOVEMENT ORGANISATION

Earlier we presented the rationale for the indirect approach to planning a movement. It was clear, from this perspective, that perceptual skill underpins skilled action. In this section, we briefly outline the main principles behind the established indirect accounts of movement organisation. It is not our intention to provide a detailed analysis of the main theories of motor learning and control in the cognitive school. The theories which emerged from this school of thought (e.g. Adams's (1971) closed loop theory, motor programming theory and Schmidt's (1975) Schema theory) have all been well documented elsewhere (e.g. see Schmidt 1988; Proctor and Dutta 1995). Rather we will concentrate on examining the relationship between the perceptual and action systems in such a group of theories.

The information processing approach to motor performance began to take off at the end of the 1960s (e.g. see Fitts and Posner 1967; Keele 1968; Adams 1971). Typically, cognitive scientists attempted to explain how action was constrained with reference to a motor programme or a 'higher order servomechanism' represented within the CNS (Kelso 1981; Newell 1985). Persistence and change in movement behaviour was explained through the use of centrally-located representations of the commands for an action and the use of feedback loops ensured that these actions were sensitive to sudden changes in dynamic environments (for a review, see Kelso 1981; Swinnen 1994).

The prototypical model for a movement representation in cognitive psychology is hierarchical in its structure. The internal representations are believed to contain more or less detailed instructions to regulate movement behaviour, perhaps including the forces, relative phasing and durations of the muscular contractions necessary (e.g. see Schmidt 1988). These representational accounts attempted to explain motor control, that is, how the movement system was organised and controlled by the brain and other components of the CNS. An important stimulus for the conceptualisation of pre-programmed motor commands to the motor apparatus was the work on the neurophysiology of locomotion in sub-human species (e.g. Grillner 1975). For example, Shik and Orlovsky (1976) proposed an automatic system for locomotion in cats and dogs involving central structures of the CNS and peripheral feedback mechanisms. They noted research which showed that, in some animals, the onset of locomotion could be stimulated not by perceptual information but by electrical activation of supraspinal structures. Ablation of parts of the higher centres of the CNS did not seem to hinder locomotion as long as the animals did not have to start the movement or avoid obstacles in their path. The automaticity of the system was enhanced by data showing that the sequence of joint movements in the swing and stance phases appeared fixed. The stability of the sequence remained even though variables such as parameters of the step, the amplitude of joint movements and the speed of locomotion changed considerably. The authors argued that this evidence demonstrated the 'special connections' (p. 467) which exist between the different joints of a limb during locomotion. Neurophysiological evidence from work with cats and dogs also revealed an important role for spinal automatisms called central pattern generators (CPGs). These are groups of neurons co-operating as a network at the spinal level of the CNS which provide a rhythmical neural output to act as a stimulus for locomotion. Some early cognitive theorists viewed these fixed sequences and the work of CPGs as potential evidence for the role of motor programmes in fundamental actions (see Kelso 1981; Reed 1988). Evidence that the speed of locomotion in the cats and dogs was directly controlled by varying the muscular forces in the propulsive phase of stance, rather than increasing the frequency of stepping, compounded the view of centralised movement control (Shik and Orlovsky 1976).

An initial point of discussion in the historical development of cognitive explanations of movement control was the specific or general nature of the representations (see Keele 1968; Schmidt 1975). For example, Kelso (1981) pointed out that these early definitions of a motor programme (e.g. Keele 1968) underwent rapid revisions due to criticisms that the concept of a movement representation invoked (i) was too rigid; (ii) involved storage problems due to its specificity; and (iii) would have implied an enormous computational burden for the brain. Motor programming theorists were forced to emphasise that the specific commands for an action were not stored in the CNS. Flexibility in contextualising action to sudden environmental changes would have been difficult with such a prescriptive movement representation. Later research reconceptualised the composition of programmes to contain more abstract information, such as the goals of the performer (e.g. 'travel over a barrier rather than under' or 'intercept an object rather than move the hand out of the way'). This more abstract definition allowed for different effector systems to be fitted to the commands (e.g. in soccer the same programme for interception could be theoretically implemented to contact a ball with hands, head or foot).

Moreover, the importance of perceptual information for modifying and adapting ongoing behaviour, exemplified in more dynamic sport contexts such as motor racing, ball games, fell running and water-skiing, could not be denied. For example, in locomotion on a treadmill, step frequency and duration of the stance phase could be modulated by changing the speed at which the belt operated. Gradually, the centralist–peripheralist debate became less polarised and Schmidt (1975, 1988), in his Schema theory, developed a theoretical model of a more generalised motor programme which showed how perceptual systems cooperated with stored movement representations to regulate behaviour. As Meijer (1988) noted, the important aspect of Schmidt's model is that the 'motor programme is not *a priori* given, it has to be re(written) time and time again. Both external and internal conditions are taken into account, and opportunity is provided for feedback not only to correct for minor errors in the execution of the programme but also to enable the organism to write better ones' (p. 8). As we shall see in Chapter 8, such arguments about the specificity or generality of the characteristics of sensorimotor representations have recently resurfaced in theoretical arguments on the specificity of the relationship between the information that needs to be present during learning and in transfer to novel situations (e.g. see Proteau 1992). We will pick up this argument in Chapter 8 and examine the theoretical and practical implications of the specificity versus generality issue in the context of perceptual information for motor skill acquisition in sport.

INFORMATION PROCESSING RESEARCH ON PERCEPTION AND ACTION IN SPORT

Many theoretical advances in psychology emerged from the rise to ascendancy of the information processing paradigm. These included the notion of central intermittency (Craik 1948), the perceptual moment hypothesis (Stroud 1955; Shallice 1964) and the foundation of the serial processing idea, the single channel hypothesis (Welford 1952). In this section, we will use the context of interceptive actions in ball games to describe some of the key ideas of the information processing approach to perception and action.

Some of the most important ideas in this respect were proposed by Poulton (1957 1965). He argued that two types of predictive information were necessary for successful performance of interceptive actions, such as catching. First, receptor anticipation information is obtained on the time of arrival of a ball at the catching hand. Receptor anticipation processes are used when performers have a clear view of an object during its approach. Successful interceptive actions are dependent upon a series of complex differentiations involving 'snapshots' of velocity and distance cues from ball flight which are related to past memories of similar events. In information processing accounts of timing behaviour, it is traditionally argued that the observer derives time-to-contact (Tc) from a number of physical variables during the relative approach (see Bruce *et al.* 1996; Gordon 1989; Savelsbergh 1990). These variables include distance, velocity and size information from an object, surface or individual. Extensive experience in a situation allows the observer to develop an internal algorithm to compute the value of each variable in extrinsically timing an action. For the computations, it is argued that the observer needs knowledge about the size of an approaching object before perceived information about velocity and distance can be scaled into the algorithm for computing Tc. The observer indirectly computes Tc by dividing the object's momentary distance from the eye by its current velocity or d / v (Tresilian 1991). Knowledge about object size is acquired through specific experience in a particular performance setting and is symbolically represented somewhere in the memory component of an information-processing system. Thus, the more information stored in memory about the interceptive task, the more likely it is that timing behaviour will be successful. Because expert performers have access to expansive knowledge bases which are specific to particular sport domains, it has been argued that they only need a limited amount of information from the environment to construct valid perceptions of events. Consequently, Savelsbergh, Whiting and Pijpers (1992) noted that, in the study of catching behaviour, the main questions during the past three decades have 'reflected concern about "the amount" of information necessary upon which to make decisions rather than the "nature" of that information per se' (p. 3). This was the rationale behind the manipulation of viewing time of a ball (in particular the extent and the location of viewing time along the flightpath) as an experimental variable in many catching studies (e.g. Whiting *et al.* 1970; Whiting and Sharp 1974; Sharp and Whiting 1975). The crucial questions revolved around (i) how much information needed to be present in the information processing system during successful catching performance; and (ii) the exact point in time when that information needed to be accessed by the performer's perceptual systems.

Second, after the performer has interpreted important cues on the velocity and position of the ball, the next prediction concerns when to initiate the movement. Knowledge of the temporal duration of an interceptive action, such as a batswing or a reach-to-catch, allows a performer to correctly predict when to initiate the movement. Cognitive theorists argued that extensive practice of a movement allows it to be included in a repertoire of programmed actions in the high-level athlete (e.g. Tyldesley and Whiting 1975; Franks, Weicker and Robertson 1985). It is important to note that the successful selection of the correct movement programme is dependent on skilled perception of ball flight characteristics.

Abernethy and colleagues (e.g. Abernethy 1981, 1987a, 1987b; Abernethy and Russell 1984) have pointed out that the time constraints of fast ball sports are so restrictive at the highest levels of performance that it is not feasible to readily modify the duration of parts of the movement (e.g. quicken one phase of a biphasic batting action). This type of variability would increase the programming demands upon the performer. Rather, the skilled athlete is one who 'buys' time by exploiting the advance signals emitted by the movements of opponents for decision-making and preparation of a response. Skill in rapid interceptive actions, such as catching and hitting a ball, is based upon the ability to detect and interpret perceptual information through a comparison with an internalised memory structure based on past experiences in similar situations. Top class players have developed highly sophisticated models of the world which allow them to predict events and to select pre-programmed sequences of movements specifically designed to carry out interceptive tasks. This explains why skilled athletes never seem to merely react to unexpected events, but appear to operate in the future. They use an 'anticipatory mode' of action (Whiting, Alderson and Sanderson 1973).

Consider the example of a cricket fielder attempting to intercept a ball hit by a batsman. An information processing perspective suggests that internal cognitive mechanisms provide the skilled fielder with a sound basis for interpreting very early signals from ball flight, often from advance movements of the batsman in preparing to play a stroke (see Chapter 4). Knowledge of the state of the game also provides information on the strategic options for the batsman, since information processing psychology is dominated by the view of the skilled performer as a rational decision-maker. It is believed that experienced performers form situational probabilities of events to plan actions in advance. In time-constrained environments, the ability to detect and interpret early cues allows the catcher to quickly prepare the appropriate movements to carry out the interceptive task, because the signals from later ball flight are redundant and carry little additional information. Furthermore, the ability to programme basic postural and orientational movements in addressing the approaching ball is believed to 'free' the attentional mechanisms of the expert fielder to focus on more sophisticated cues regarding what to do with the ball once it has been intercepted. For example, whilst less skilful fielders need to monitor response-produced feedback on the position of the arms and hands in order to get them into the right place at the correct time, expert catchers can use peripheral vision to check whether the ball, once intercepted, needs to be thrown to the wicketkeeper's end or not.

Keep your eye on the ball?

The example above seems to question whether skilful games players need to fixate the ball for the whole of its flight as demanded by the coaching edict: 'Keep your eye on the ball!' Even now the advice of most coaches of ball games is to keep your eye on the ball – regardless of expertise. But is this appropriate? Rather, at critical moments, experts seem to be able to switch attention between important, alternative sources of environmental information such as the position of opponents and team-mates and the location of surfaces and targets. The first attempt to adopt a rigorous, experimental approach to this question was by Hubbard and Seng (1954). They employed a highly innovative strategy to examine whether professional baseball batters needed to watch the ball for the whole of its flight in order to strike it successfully. They pointed out that top class sport performers often exhibited visual defects as measured on clinical tests. It seemed that perceptual skill was the basis of batting excellence – a combination of visual ability and extensive experience in sport. In order to test this assumption, they filmed the batting performance of 29 professional batters during practice. Through careful positioning of the camera and the use of a large mirror they were able to record the whole duration of 70 pitches from release of the ball to the strike of the bat. Despite some individual differences, the data seemed to suggest that skilled batters only needed to foveally track the ball up to 2.4–4.5 m from the bat. No further head or eye movements were recorded after this point. Furthermore, the batters seemed to reduce the scope of the motor-control problem by gearing the step before strike to the release of the ball from the pitcher's hand. That is, step duration was regulated by pitch velocity. Faster pitches induced shorter steps and slower balls warranted longer steps. What is the significance of this behaviour by skilled batters? This strategy had the effect of allowing the duration of the swing to be kept remarkably constant and independent of ball speed.[4]

From the point of view of the present theoretical discussion on indirect perception, the lack of late eye and head movements could be taken to indicate that extensive practice allowed professional batters to develop an internal representation of the event in order to use early cues from the action of the pitcher and the flight of the ball predictively. Later stages of ball flight were redundant due to the knowledge of the batters on the characteristics of various types of pitch. More recent work by Bahill and LaRitz (1984) has provided some support for the early findings of Hubbard and Seng (1954) by demonstrating that baseball pitches often reach a level of velocity which exceeds the tracking capabilities of the eye movement system (for further information, see Chapter 5 on visual search patterns in sport). Yet, baseball batters are capable of the most exquisite timing. For many psychologists these findings indicated the important role of knowledge founded on past experiences in supporting perception in such time-stressed circumstances. The approach taken by Hubbard and Seng (1954) was at least three decades ahead of its time since it examined the receptor anticipation abilities of skilled athletes and recorded changes in components of batting action *in situ*. Their approach looked at qualitative changes in movement behaviour over the whole time course of the interceptive task, which differs greatly from the typical reliance on outcome measures in the cognitive laboratory.

Although the study by Hubbard and Seng (1954) has been described as 'classical' (Bootsma and Peper 1992), it may be more precisely acknowledged as 'classically descriptive'. Hubbard and Seng (1954) did not attempt to provide any theoretical explanation for their findings. The study was atheoretical in the sense that the authors were driven by a practical problem: Do skilled athletes keep their eyes on the ball all the time during interceptive actions? There was little attempt to integrate the findings into a theoretical framework on the nature of the perception–action relationship. Only in hindsight have researchers interpreted the data from specific theoretical perspectives. From a cognitive viewpoint, the athletes seemed to be reducing the degrees of freedom of the motor system (i.e. the different parts of the skeletomuscular apparatus which are free to vary at any instant) by programming the motor response of the batswing. This strategy, based on years of repetitive drills and systematic practice, means that the skilled athlete can reproduce a consistent and highly reliable response under varying spatio-temporal constraints. In Chapter 6, we shall discuss how, utilising the framework of direct perception, Fitch and Turvey (1978) argued for an alternative explanation. Clearly, in order to achieve the objective of providing a theoretical explanation of motor control during interceptive actions, an entire programme of research was needed. Just over a decade later such a coherent effort was instigated at the University of Leeds in England by Whiting and associates.

How long do you need to watch a ball to catch it? The work of Whiting and colleagues

An important influence on the research programme of Whiting and colleagues (e.g. Whiting 1968, 1969, 1970; Whiting, Gill and Stephenson 1970), was the perceptual moment hypothesis (Stroud 1955; Shallice 1964). This approach viewed the athlete as a discrete processor of ambiguous cues requiring indirect confirmation and interpretation by relating these signals to an internal representation of performance. According to Savelsbergh *et al.* (1992), a major issue raised by extrapolating theoretical ideas on the perceptual moment hypothesis to the study of ball skills concerned the minimum amount of information needed to support successful interceptive actions. Earlier theoretical work in experimental psychology had identified periods of between 40 and 200 ms as appropriate for information processing purposes (Stroud 1955; Shallice 1964) and it was not clear whether these values would extrapolate to sport contexts. This question was investigated by using the occlusion technique (for more detailed reviews, see Savelsbergh *et al.* 1992; Williams *et al.* 1992). The technique allowed experimenters to light up a ball as it travelled towards the catcher for short periods of time (in the order of milliseconds) in a totally dark room. The earliest studies in this research programme (e.g. Whiting 1968) provided support for the seminal findings of Hubbard and Seng (1954), that success in interceptive actions did not depend on the performer tracking the ball with the foveae of the eyes for the whole duration of flight. Later studies attempted to verify the existence of critical time periods for processing ball flight information and particularly when these critical time periods were most informative (e.g. Whiting et al. 1970; Whiting et al. 1973; Sharp and Whiting 1974; Whiting and Sharp 1974). Although there was a large amount of individual variation in catching performance in their study, Sharp and Whiting (1974) provided evidence for a critical viewing period of 80 ms to support successful one-handed catching. Certainly, viewing periods of less than 60 ms resulted in poorer catching performance. However, the use of the occlusion technique placed an inordinate emphasis on the less representative processes (in ball games) of perceptual anticipation (Poulton 1957 1965), which subjects used in conjunction with past memories to perceptually construct parts of occluded ball flight. A significant constraint on the behaviour of the subjects of Sharp and Whiting (1974) was the total time for which they could use the processes of receptor and perceptual anticipation. There was a clear preference, where feasible, for receptor anticipation strategies. It was also not possible to separate the influences of both the viewing periods and the occlusion periods to attribute an effect on catching behaviour. Savelsbergh et al. (1992) pointed out that the covarying viewing period and occlusion periods during flight were inextricably confounded.

Generally, the results from several studies in the programme showed that the longer the ball was foveally tracked, the more successful was catching performance (e.g. Whiting et al. 1970; Sharp and Whiting 1974; Whiting and Sharp 1974). Most of the studies found that the greatest number of catches were made under full lights conditions where no flight cues were occluded. Even skilled catchers caught more balls under the full lights conditions than in any of the occluded conditions (Whiting et al. 1970). It is unclear why this should be the case given the evidence for motor programming of the response component which may be interpreted in the data of Hubbard and Seng (1954). The development of a highly consistent response format could be viewed as desirable in a discrete task such as one-handed catching since it would allow the performer to allocate attentional resources elsewhere in the environment.

How much consistency was there in the catching actions of the subjects involved in the occlusion paradigm? Unfortunately, the reliance on simple outcome measures such as the number of balls caught or located with the palm of the hand, prevented a more detailed analysis of the effects of visual degradation of the environment on movement quality. Self-report data from subjects themselves indicated that different movement strategies were used in conjunction with receptor and perceptual anticipation processes. In other words, within the methodological framework created in these studies, the period of 80 ms may have been useful in allowing subjects to cope with the task constraints imposed by the occlusion paradigm. However, given 'normal' constraints on the visual system during interceptive actions in receptor anticipation tasks, little evidence was provided on how performers organised their movement responses.

The operational timing hypothesis

The issue of motor programming in sport contexts was specifically addressed by Tyldesley and Whiting (1975) in a study of expert table tennis players. They argued, like Hubbard and Seng (1954), that inordinate levels of consistency in the output side of the perception–action relationship meant that performers only needed to attend to the input and decision-making components of performance. Their argument was that 'operational timing', a means of reducing the temporal uncertainty in somewhat predictable environments by practising an action until it is highly consistent in duration, could reduce the processing demands on the performer to that of 'input timing' only. Input timing refers to the performer's ability to compute velocity and distance information from ball flight characteristics in order to correctly predict the initiation time of an action with a known temporal duration. Developing the ideas of Keele (1973), Tyldesley and Whiting (1975) argued that timing could come about through the 'timed issue of muscular commands' in the form of 'consistent motor patterning' (p. 173). Expert performers, capable of a high level of motor programming due to intensive practice, seem to 'know' the precise duration of a programme, with the result that a degree of freedom is freed up in the perception–action relationship in complex environments. In other words, for highly skilled athletes, the initial processing demands of 'operational' and 'input' timing have been reduced to the latter. Empirical support for their theorising came from a comparison of the movement characteristics of groups of novice, intermediate and expert table tennis players during performance of the forehand drive to a designated target area on the table. Displacement and velocity profiles of movements were obtained by filming performance (400 Hz) in relation to a standardised feed (see Figure 1.3).

The data, presented in Figure 1.3, showed that both experts and intermediates were capable of reproducing a high level of spatial and temporal precision and consistency in the forehand drive. The main difference between the two groups is that, although the intermediate performer is capable of a high level of consistency, the differences in the movement patterns over time are of a spatial and temporal nature. However, for the experts, the movement patterns were so replicable that the problem of playing the shot seems reduced to solely one of timing. This is because,

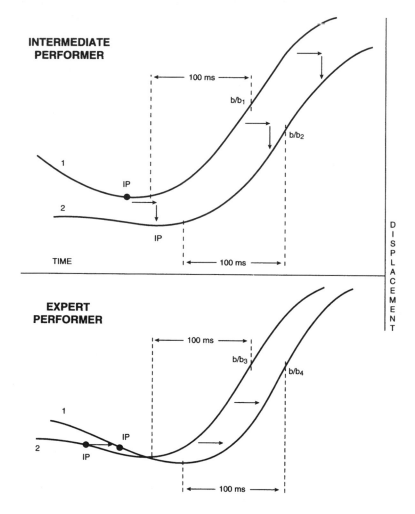

Figure 1.3 Movement displacement profiles over time for intermediate (top graph) and expert (lower graph) table tennis players performing a forehand drive to a standardised feed from a projection machine. The data are indicative of a high level of repeatability in the movement patterns of both groups of subjects. Note, however, that the more extensive practice of the expert affords a greater level of consistency for the temporal and spatial configuration of the drive at the initiation point (IP) and point of bat–ball contact (BB) – unlike the intermediate who is merely temporally consistent in reproducing both points. Novice data, not reproduced here, showed little consistency of either a spatial or temporal nature. (Source: Tyldesley, D. and Whiting, H.T.A. (1975) 'Operational timing', *Journal of Human Movement Studies* 1: 172–7.

at the key points of movement initiation and bat–ball contact, the displacement differences between trials were negligible. However, these are skilled performers since the operational timing variability for both the more experienced groups was in the order of 4 ms. The authors noted that, for these groups, 'Though the initiation location and time may differ, the completed pattern always lasts a uniform length of time and the sequential subsections are always arranged proportionally through time' (ibid.: 176). Novices, on the other hand, showed none of the spatio-temporal precision of their more practised counterparts, resulting in much poorer performance in the speed and accuracy of their movements. According to Tyldesley and Whiting (1975), the result of a high level of task practice is that 'the expert will be faced solely with a problem of temporal prediction of when to start a movement sequence which has been planned in its entirety in advance' (p. 176). An additional benefit is that, as skill develops, the conscious processing requirements typically involved in gaining adequate input timing information is moved to a very early portion of flight, thus freeing up the perceptual mechanisms 'to smooth out minor output disturbances' (p. 174) in the ongoing response and for strategic planning.

These data are useful in allowing us a glimpse of the qualities of skilled behaviour over the time course of a movement. The approach taken by Tyldesley and Whiting (1975) was ahead of its time in the sense that kinematic data were provided on the spatio-temporal structure of a sport-related movement over time. At that time the general tendency was to rely on outcome data which said little about the quality of movement as it unfolded. However, the influence of engineering models on the information processing approach is apparent in the assumption that movement repeatability is a clear end goal of practice even in highly changeable and dynamic tasks. It is clear that the cognitive basis of the study led the authors to view the small variability in the performance of the intermediate and expert groups as the result of 'noise' in the CNS or perturbations within the environment. The implicit idea was that increased practice would help to reduce this undesired variability to a level that could be adequately dealt with by the peripheral feedback loops operating in key muscles and joints. Although many other investigators have used the data presented here as evidence of the ability to prepare movements in advance as skill level increases, Tyldesley and Whiting (1975) themselves were more reticent. They argued that

> It is tempting to equate the consistent, replicable movement patterns required, with open loop control, but this assumption is not justified by the experimentation described. . . . In fact, programmed control in man has largely defied scientific proof, and its presence is inferred from movements psychologically defined as 'ballistic'.
>
> (p. 174)

As we shall see in Chapters 6 and 7, other scientists view the variability showed by top-class athletes in a far more positive light.

SUMMARY AND CONCLUSIONS

In this chapter we focused attention on the theoretical and philosophical basis of the traditional perspective on perception and action. We noted that the main influences on this approach to modelling human movement behaviour were from the engineering and computer sciences. Control engineering theory proposes the development of rules or algorithms for controlling system behaviour. Typically, therefore, cognitive scientists have attempted to explain ordered movement with reference to internalised knowledge structures and motor programmes represented within the CNS. These mechanisms have been invoked to explain how the skeletomuscular system is controlled by the mind (Newell 1985). The role of the perceptual systems has been conceptualised as providing the necessary stimulus which acts to 'release' an appropriate programme of action or to contextualise a movement representation. Information processing activities are thought necessary since the visual system's provision of geometric abstractions from the environment requires elaboration by our knowledge of the world. This constructive process is believed to be the chief responsibility of the mind which was seen as a kind of computer. Indirect accounts of perception suggest that large amounts of moment-to-moment computations are required 'to build elaborate symbolic descriptions from primitive assertions' (Bruce *et al.* 1996: 223). Movement representations for regulating behaviour are an important feature of the indirect approach to perception and action. The role of the perceptual systems is also apparent in movement planning and organisation. As Swinnen (1994) points out, gradually over the years cognitive explanations of motor control have become refocused on 'how central commands and sensory information cooperate to produce skilled action' (p. 234). Clearly, then, these studies suggest that a major feature of top-class performance is the high level of consistency of movement behaviour despite the informational demands of dynamic sport contexts.

An interesting question concerns the best way to practise in order to achieve such high levels of timing precision and movement consistency whilst maintaining the flexibility to adapt to different conditions. What kinds of information need to be present during practice for athletes to successfully learn a movement skill? For example, because previous research has shown that one does not have to watch the ball for the whole of its flight, and that movements may be pre-programmed, should coaches implement strategies encouraging athletes to look at other relevant sources of information late in ball flight? Alternatively, is there any value in the strategy employed by some athletes in enhancing the amount and quality of feedback information available during practice (e.g. through the use of mirrors and other such training aids)? What does research tell us about a practice strategy of performing movements blindfolded in order to increase sensitivity to proprioceptive information? These are relevant questions for coaches and athletes and some answers are forthcoming in Chapters 8 and 9. Meanwhile we will continue our detailed analysis of the information processing approach to perception and action in sport by decomposing the system into stages of relevance. The first stage to be examined in Chapter 2 is that of attention.

2 Attention in sport

INTRODUCTION

Attention is viewed as one of the most popular and complex areas of psychology (Parasurman 1984). In support of this contention, a vast amount of theoretical work on attention has been undertaken under controlled laboratory conditions. Several authors have also highlighted the importance of attention to skilled sports performance (e.g. Boucher 1992; Nougier *et al.* 1991). Yet, thus far, there has been a paucity of applied research which has examined the attentional mechanisms underpinning sports performance. Historically, when attention has been studied from an applied perspective, it has been in industrial and military contexts rather than the sport setting (see Stelmach and Hughes 1983). Furthermore, theoretical development in the sport and exercise sciences has been restricted by the use of non sport-specific paradigms such as dichotic listening techniques. This approach requires participants to follow separate auditory messages presented to the right and left ear simultaneously via headphones. Such laboratory-based paradigms, as well as the absence of research involving athletes, have weakened the applicability of this research to sports performance.

From a cognitive psychology perspective, the term attention is used to refer to three different processes. First, the construct of attention has been postulated to explain the selectivity of attention (i.e. focused attention). Second, it relates to our ability to distribute attention across several concurrent tasks (i.e. divided attention). Third, it refers to our state of alertness or readiness for action. Selective attention is viewed as 'the preferential detection, identification, and recognition of selected stimulation' (Woods 1990: 178). It is the process by which certain information is processed whilst other information is ignored. An example is the skilled baseball batter's ability to focus only on pertinent aspects of the pitcher's delivery action while disregarding extraneous information. Selective attention is involved at some level in almost all tasks, since even if the subject only attends to one visual or auditory cue, proprioceptive and interoceptive inputs simultaneously compete for attention (Woods 1990).

The second meaning of the term attention relates to the fact that skilled performers can regulate their mental resources or capacity across several concurrent actions. Consider the skilled racing driver who changes gear at a difficult hairpin bend while scanning the upcoming road layout and monitoring the position of opponents in the rear view mirror. This ability to perform two or more tasks concurrently distinguishes between controlled and automatic processing (Schneider, Dumais and Shiffrin 1984). Controlled processing is slow, effortful, attention demanding and under conscious control. For example, a golfer uses controlled processing in selecting the appropriate line and weight of shot into the green (Boucher 1992). In contrast, automatic processing is fast, effortless and not under conscious control (i.e. non-attention demanding). The skilled golfer is likely to process information automatically whilst playing a drive shot off the tee. Clearly, sports require a combination of both automatic and controlled processing. In some situations performers function in a 'reflexive', automatic manner, but in others, they are required to make decisions and process information consciously (Boucher 1992; Nougier, Stein and Bonnel 1991). The ability to rapidly and effectively switch between these different modes of processing is viewed as an important characteristic of expertise (Keele and Hawkins 1982). The third usage of the term 'attention' denotes our state of alertness or 'preparedness' for action. Typically, research in this area has examined the effects of alertness and arousal on sports performance (for a review, see Gould and Krane 1992).

In this chapter, we restrict our discussion to research and theory which have examined the importance of focused and divided attention during sports performance. Since sports performance requires attentional selectivity and the ability to perform two or more skills concurrently, understanding more about these processes is important to sport and exercise psychologists, coaches and athletes alike. In the first part of the chapter, various cognitive theories are reviewed with particular reference to fixed, flexible and multiple resource models of attention. As well as explaining why and how attention is limited, these theories address the issue of selective attention by highlighting the fact that enhanced selectivity results in a reduction in the attentional capacity or resource required to perform the task. Throughout this section we attempt to discuss the relevance of these models to visual selective attention in sport. Thereafter, we present a more recent 'action-based' approach to attention by considering Neumann's selection-for-action model. This approach is conceptually very different from the traditional cognitive models discussed above since limitations in performance are more closely coupled with the control of action rather than the analysis and interpretation of sensory information. In the second half of the chapter, we provide an overview of the research that has examined the importance and development of automaticity in sport. We highlight some of the characteristics of automaticity and suggest, with reference to contemporary theories, how it could be developed with practice. Since the ability to perform tasks automatically is an important characteristic of skilled performance the focus here, as in other parts of this chapter, will be on the relationship between automaticity and motor expertise. Finally, we conclude by focusing on the implications of research and theory for coaching and instruction and highlight some avenues for future research endeavour. Before progressing, readers should note that a single chapter cannot completely cover the broad and active field of attention. Other worthwhile reviews of attention have recently been completed by van der Heijden (1992), Kramer, Coles and Logan (1996) and Pashler (1996).

COGNITIVE MODELS OF ATTENTION AND THEIR RELEVANCE TO SELECTIVE ATTENTION IN SPORT

In Chapter 1, we examined how cognitive psychology considers the sports performer to be a processor and user of information. It was shown that cognitive processes may be regarded as a series of hypothetical stages during which unique transformations are performed on incoming sensory information (Solso 1995). These hypothetical processing stages which occur between signal and response include perception, memory, decision-making and attention. In this section, we compare and contrast four different cognitive perspectives on attention. First, we review undifferentiated fixed capacity theories of attention. These models suggest that the human performer has a fixed central capacity to process information and that performance decrement occurs if this capability is exceeded. Second, we review the research on flexible capacity theories. These models consider that the performer has a limited central processing capacity, but the capacity is viewed as having some flexibility based on the requirements of the task. Third, we present more recent multiple resource theories which view attention as a pool of separate resources each with its own capacity and designed to handle specific types of information processes. Finally, we touch upon some recent theorising which views attention as a set of neural networks carrying out particular functions. Where possible, within the constraints of current research, we attempt to draw implications for visual selective attention in sport.

Fixed capacity theories

These theories assume that there is a fixed capacity for processing information and that performance will deteriorate if this capacity is exceeded by the requirements of the task. The performers' capacity can be viewed schematically as a large circle as shown in Figure 2.1. In this figure, a basketball example is used to illustrate the fixed capacity notion. The

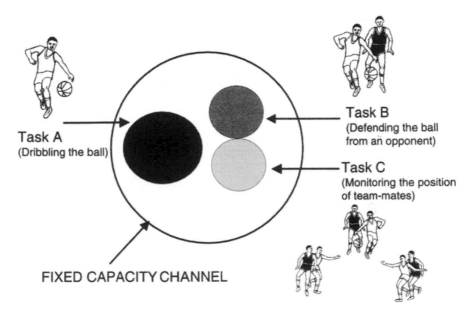

Figure 2.1 How three different tasks (e.g. dribbling a basketball while shielding it from an opponent and scanning the display for available passing options) can be performed simultaneously provided that the attention requirements do not exceed the fixed capacity channel. Clearly, the attention demands of these tasks, and consequently the size of the three shaded areas, varies enormously between players and from one situation to another. As long as all of the smaller shaded areas fit into the larger circle then the tasks can be performed effectively.

tasks of dribbling the ball down the court (Task A) while simultaneously defending the ball from an opponent (Task B) and monitoring the positions of team-mates (Task C) are seen as small circles. Provided these smaller circles fit into the larger circle representing the fixed capacity channel then the performer will be able to perform all three tasks effectively. In contrast, if the area of the three smaller circles exceeds that of the larger circle then a decrement in performance on one or more of these tasks would occur. For beginners, the task of dribbling is likely to require nearly all of the available processing space. On the other hand, the skilled player has reduced the attentional demands of dribbling and is able to simultaneously shield the ball from an opponent and assess the available passing options without attentional deficits.

Although several fixed capacity models exist, they differ only in terms of the time, or stage within the information processing model, that selection of relevant input occurs (Gopher and Sanders 1984). The models hypothesise that at some stage in the information processing chain a bottleneck or selective filter occurs that restricts the amount of information that can be attended to at any one time. The earliest theory proposed by Broadbent (1958) suggested that this bottleneck occurs during the stimulus categorisation phase of information processing. An alternative view was proposed by Treisman (1964), in which she agreed with Broadbent (1958) that the bottleneck was located at an early stage within the information processing model, but thought that the function of this selective filter was more flexible than had earlier been suggested. Rather than blocking out information the filter acted as an attenuator which amplified some inputs and weakened others. Other authors proposed that all incoming stimuli received some simple automatic and subconscious analysis for meaning, with only those items that are deemed to be pertinent receiving further processing (e.g. Deutsch and Deutsch 1963; Norman 1968; Keele 1973; Kantowitz 1974). These models argued that it is the most significant information which captures attention in order to produce a specific response. Deutsch and Deutsch (1963) and Norman (1968) suggested that the selective filter lies between perceptual analysis and response selection, whereas Keele (1973) and Kantowitz (1974) placed this bottleneck within the response programming stage.

In sport, probably the most popular of these fixed-capacity theories has been Norman's (1968, 1969) pertinence model. Norman proposed that all signals arriving at the sensors pass through an early stage of analysis performed by physiological processes (termed the stimulus analysing mechanism). The parameters extracted from these processes are used to determine where the representation of the sensory signal is stored in memory. Consequently, all sensory signals excite their stored representation in memory. Norman believed this sensory analysis was performed subconsciously with no demand being placed on the performer's limited processing capacity. At the same time as this sensory analysis, an examination of previous signals located in long term memory occurs (right-hand side of the model shown in Figure 2.2). This process establishes, based on past experience and contextual information, a class of events deemed to be pertinent to the ongoing analysis. The model implies that through learning, a performer builds up a vast reservoir of experience that can be used to interpret events encountered in situations similar to those previously experienced. The representation most highly excited by the combination of sensory and pertinence inputs is then selected for further analysis and specific attention.

Norman argued that through experience the performer knows the important contextual cues within the display. The recognition of these cues establishes probabilities or expectations that a certain outcome will occur. In sport, this enhanced task-specific knowledge base means that there is much redundancy within the perceptual strategy of the expert (for a more detailed discussion, see Chapters 4 and 5). The skilled performer knows the important information within the display and can focus attention

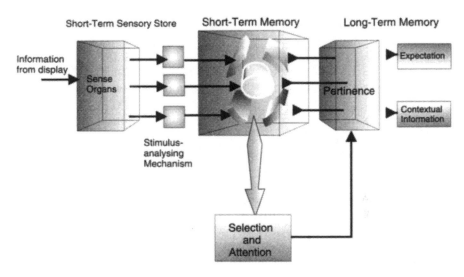

Figure 2.2 Norman's (1968, 1969) pertinence theory of selective attention. Selection depends on both the quality of the sensory input and the performer's cognitive knowledge base. (Adapted from Norman, D.A. (1969) *Memory and Attention*, New York: Wiley.)

on the relevant and ignore the irrelevant sources of information. Knowledge built up through experience reduces the amount of information that needs to be processed thereby decreasing the speed of response (see Starkes and Allard 1993). In Chapter 4, we examine this explanation further by demonstrating that skilled sports performers make more effective use of contextual information (e.g. advance visual cues) and expectation (e.g. situational probabilities) in anticipation and decision-making.

As an example, consider an attacking situation in soccer where the ball is played behind the defence into a position on the right wing with the opportunity to cross the ball into the penalty area from the goal-line. The covering defender or 'sweeper', along with the other defensive players, will be recovering back towards goal. In Norman's approach, the sweeper would be visually coding information from the display and the most important inputs, selected by the stimulus-analysing mechanisms, would reside temporarily in short-term memory. Simultaneously, the experienced sweeper would be making use of past experiences to establish expectations and probabilities of certain events occurring. The context in which the event occurs would be important in order to establish pertinence for a particular class of events. For example, in the above situation there is a relatively high probability of the cross being driven hard and low into the 'prime target area' between the goalkeeper and the retreating defenders along the edge of the six-yard box (Hughes 1994). Furthermore, the performer is likely to be making use of contextual cues such as the attacker's approach to the ball, preparatory stance, and early part of the kicking technique in order to anticipate ball direction (Williams and Burwitz 1993). In addition, the runs and movements of other players are assumed to be important sources of contextual information (Williams, Davids, Burwitz and Williams 1994). This combination of information derived from expectations and contextual cues then excites in memory the most pertinent or important event(s) to which attention may be allocated. The interaction of sensory information and past experience allows the performer to select and attend to the most important and informative areas of the display.

In Chapters 3 and 4 we review some of the research which has examined proficiency-related differences in visual attention and perception using 'hardware' (data-driven processes) or 'software' (conceptually driven processes) paradigms popularised by the computer metaphor of the human mind (see Chapter 1). Norman's model has frequently been referred to in this body of research since it distinguishes between these two processes (see Abernethy 1987c). The left-hand side of the model represents differences in the hardware components of the sensory systems (i.e. the quality of the visual system in picking up sensory information), whilst the right-hand side highlights the importance of symbolic representations or software knowledge structures in perception (i.e. the selection, processing, encoding and retrieval of information from memory).

Flexible capacity models

Flexible capacity theorists propose that fixed capacity approaches are too rigid and inflexible, arguing instead for a more flexible approach to the allocation of attention (Glencross 1978; Schmidt 1988; Magill 1993). For example, Kahneman (1973) believed that capacity should not be considered as fixed since it changes as the task requirements change. He proposed that as the difficulty of two simultaneous tasks increases, more capacity is made available until it is exceeded. Kahneman viewed attention as a general pool of effort which can be distributed to several concurrent activities based on the allocation policy of the individual and the characteristics of the tasks. Kahneman's model of attention is shown in Figure 2.3.

In Figure 2.3, the box containing the wavy line represents the available attention capacity. This depicts the general pool of limited resources which is available at a particular moment. The wavy line suggests that the arousal level of the individual influences the capacity available to perform the task. Kahneman (1973) argued that as task difficulty increases, the individual's level of arousal will increase, which in turn increases the capacity available. Eventually, when the attentional requirements of the task begin to exceed maximum capacity, decrements are seen in one or more of the simultaneously presented tasks. That is, interference occurs. It is, therefore,

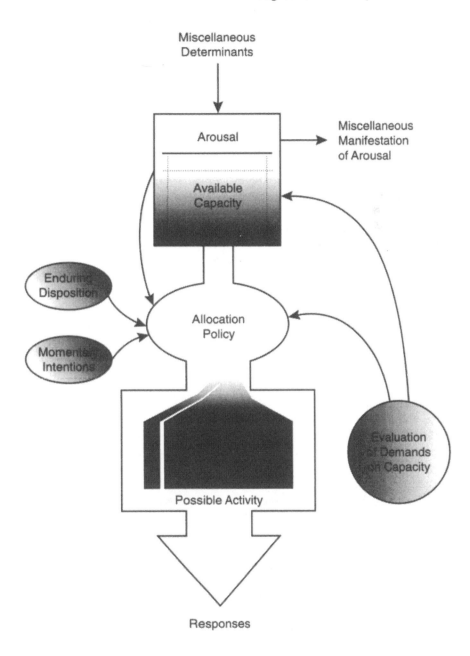

Figure 2.3 Kahneman's (1973) flexible capacity model of attention. (Adapted from Kahneman, D. (1973) *Attention and Effort*, Englewood Cliffs NJ: Prentice Hall).

apparent that if performance decrements are not to occur, then the available attention should not be exceeded. With this in mind, the efficient allocation of attention or selective attention plays a very important role within the model.

This relationship between attention and arousal was initially proposed by Easterbrook (1959). He suggested that under conditions of low arousal the sport performer has too broad a focus and picks up both relevant (e.g. position of team-mates and opponents) and irrelevant cues (e.g. movements of the crowd or the referee). As arousal increases, the performer's attention begins to narrow (see Landers 1982; Landers, Wang and Courtet 1985; Rose and Christina 1990). At some optimal point, attentional narrowing blocks out the irrelevant cues and allows the relevant cues to remain. If arousal increases still further, attention continues to narrow and relevant cues will be filtered out, causing a deterioration in performance (for a review, see Proctor and Dutta 1995). It is likely that a high state of arousal also impairs the process of discrimination (ability to distinguish relevant from irrelevant stimuli) thus reducing further the ability to focus on relevant external stimuli (Broadbent 1971).

Kahneman suggested that this 'allocation' policy is determined by two main factors. The first factor influencing selectivity is called 'enduring dispositions' which are rules of involuntary attention, such as the allocation of capacity to novel signals, to any object (e.g. racing car appearing in the rear-view mirror) in sudden motion, or to a very intense stimulus such as a sudden loud noise (e.g. call from a team-mate) or a flash of light (e.g. an imprudent photographer's flashlight on the tennis court). These enduring dispositions are viewed as automatic orienting responses where the performer's attention is attracted towards anything unusual or different in the environment (Martens 1987). Second, momentary intentions are viewed as being important in attentional selectivity. These are instructions given to an individual such as 'watch the ball or a certain player', or 'listen to the covering defender or coach'. These instructions have been referred to as developing the performer's 'mind-set' (ibid.). For example, through experience, or coaching, performers can develop a mindset to be alert to certain cues in the environment. Developing appropriate mindsets or enduring dispositions is crucial since knowing the correct cues to attend to, and what the potential distracters are, can substantially improve the anticipatory skills of the performer. Clearly, there is much similarity here with what Norman termed the 'pertinence' factor. That is, the performer allocates visual attention on the basis of past experience in terms of pertinence and contextual information.

Multiple resource theories

Later developments tended to move away from the single central mechanism approach advocated by fixed or flexible capacity theorists (see

Allport 1980; McLeod 1977; Navon and Gopher 1979; Wickens 1980 1984). Alternatively, multiple resource theories suggest that attention should be conceptualised as several individual resource pools each with its own capacity and designed to handle certain kinds of information processes. The approach argues that performance depends on different resources which are limited in quantity (Logan 1985). Tasks that are more difficult require more resources, allowing fewer to be available for other concurrent tasks. Interference and performance decrement occur only when two tasks share common resources. Figure 2.4 provides a simplified representation of multiple resources theory. Here two resources are identified. Tasks A and B both compete for common resources and therefore can

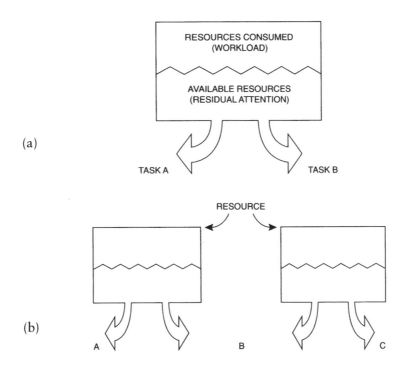

Figure 2.4 (a) represents the relation between two tasks which share the same resources. Here, the resources demanded by the task (workload) do not exceed the available attentional resource (i.e. there is residual attention); (b) highlights a situation where interference may occur. Tasks A and C use separate resources and therefore draw upon different attentional pools. That is, increases in the difficulty of one of these tasks will have little effect on performance of the other. Task B, however, shares resources with both A and C and will compete with each leading to performance decrement if the capacity of the resource pool is exceeded. (Source: Wickens, C.D. (1984) 'Processing resources in attention', in R. Parasuraman and R. Davies (eds) *Varieties of Attention*, New York: Academic Press.)

interfere with each other. Tasks A and C do not, and can be time-shared quite efficiently. According to Abernethy (1993a), the task for researchers is one of isolating the specific, special-purpose modular subsystems which comprise the resource pool. A key point is that no special selection mechanism is proposed to account for attentional selectivity in this approach. Selection is viewed simply as the process of allocating resources.

One line of research has proposed that resources for information processing are grouped into three categories (Wickens 1992) (see Figure 2.5). These categories include those responsible for input and output modalities (vision, limbs, audition, speech), the stages of information processing (perception, decision-making, response output) and the codes of processing information (verbal codes, spatial codes). Foveal and peripheral vision have also been suggested as different resource systems (Wickens 1989). When two tasks utilising the same resource are attempted they would be affected by the underlying capacity limitation resulting in interference effects and performance decrements. However, when two difficult tasks are attempted which require different resources, capacity would not be exceeded and performance levels would be sustained. Interestingly, autonomous visual mechanisms for the pick-up of time-to-contact information have also been proposed as an example of a resource module (see McLeod, McLaughlin, Nimmo-Smith 1985).

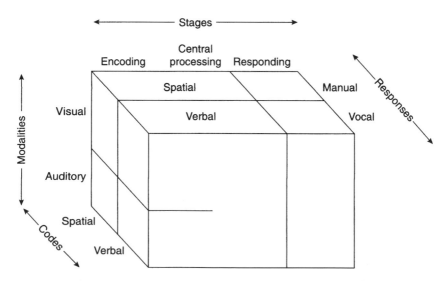

Figure 2.5 Diagram representing some of the resource pools and their proposed interactions. Tasks that are closer together in Wickens' (1984) three-dimensional model are assumed to share similar resources, and consequently, there will be greater interference between them. (Source: Wickens, C.D. (1984) 'Processing resources in attention', in R. Parasuraman and R. Davies (eds) *Varieties of Attention*, New York: Academic Press.)

In sport, therefore, the hockey player would be able to run with the ball while shouting out instructions to a team-mate because these tasks use different output modalities. Similarly, the squash player would be able to visually monitor the position of her opponent while executing the appropriate stroke since different input and output modalities are required. This is not always the case, however, as demonstrated by the novice performer's inability to execute these tasks concurrently without performance decrement. Proponents of this approach argue that although these tasks do not share input and output resources they may be sharing other resource systems, such as the stages or codes of information processing, that can account for the task interference seen in the novice performer (for a detailed review of the evidence supporting a multiple resource model of attention, see Wickens 1992).

This is one of the main criticisms of multiple resource theories. Because interference effects can always be accounted for on the basis of the dimensions of resource similarity between tasks, the model is not parsimonious. Since there may be an almost infinite number of these resource systems the model can account for nearly all of the empirical evidence collected. The model can therefore never be proved incorrect (Allport 1989). It is always possible to define another resource to account for the data. Wickens (1989) argues that the model must be made more parsimonious by setting fairly strict criteria as to what dimensions may actually be labelled resources (for a further review of the limitations of this approach, see Barber 1989 and Neumann 1985).

Perhaps the biggest problem with both resource and capacity theories of attention, however, is the apparent reluctance of sport and exercise psychologists to test the theoretical propositions within sport-specific contexts. Although these models have been around for some time now, there is still a paucity of research which purports to examine their relevance to the allocation of attention in sport. Whether the dearth of empirical research reflects the difficulties involved in developing realistic sport-specific paradigms to examine the differing theoretical propositions, or rather is a result of a perceived lack of applicability of these models to sports performance remains to be seen. Regardless, we are clearly at the stage where we need to make more significant progress in our understanding of the specific attentional mechanisms underlying sports performance.

Networks of attention

A more satisfactory global perspective on attention may be provided by recent developments in cognitive science based on parallel distributed processing or connectionist models (see Rumelhart and McClelland 1986; Rumelhart 1989). The approach originates from neurophysiology and our understanding of how neurons function within the brain (Anderson 1990).

A connectionist model involves a neural network of processing units or nodes that are connected by links. These nodes represent abstract elements over which meaningful patterns can be defined. Control is distributed at a more local level with each node being aware only of the output from the nodes to which it is connected. Nodes simply receive input from one or more other nodes and, based on this input information, they compute an output value which is transmitted to other connected nodes. The system is seen as being inherently parallel in that several nodes can carry out their computations at the same time. It is the pattern of connectivity between nodes which constitutes what the system knows and determines how it will respond. Each node constrains the others and contributes in its own way to the global observable behaviour of the performer (Rumelhart 1989).

Rumelhart (1989) suggests that knowledge structures are modified through experience by changing the patterns of interconnectivity between nodes. He suggests that with increasing levels of expertise performers develop new connections, lose some of the existing connections and modify the strengths of connections which already exist. In this way, the system exhibits plasticity in the sense that the pattern of interconnections is not fixed but rather undergoes modifications as a function of experience. This organisation offers a mechanism for learning by suggesting that changes in the activations of elements and the strengths of links occur with practice. The development of automaticity and enhanced attentional selectivity may therefore result from a strengthening of these connections between nodes (termed 'weights'). A higher weight means that a stronger signal was received along a connection with less resistance. Thus, the system is seen as a more efficient and constantly evolving or adaptive neural network.

Visual networks

Posner and Raichle (1994) propose that there are three neural networks involved in the control of visual attention. Using evidence from studies employing mental chronometry, positron-emission tomography (PET) and magnetic resonance imagining (MRI) techniques, they argue for the existence of a network for visual orientation, an executive attention network, and a vigilance network. Within the visual orientation network, the posterior parietal lobe acts to release attention from its current focus and directs the midbrain to move attention to another display area, while the thalamus selects the contents of the attended area that are to be given priority for processing by the executive attention network. Once attention has shifted to a new location and the visual information has been prioritised, the executive attention network then brings the object into conscious awareness. This network includes the recognition of an object's identity and the realisation that the object fulfils a sought-after goal. Finally, a vigilance attention network is responsible for maintaining a sustained state of awareness and alertness on a task or goal. The vigilance system influences the other networks by increasing the efficiency of the visual orienting network and suppressing ongoing activity in the executive attention network. This process is thought to ensure that a subjective state of consciousness is achieved such that the performer is both alert and free of conscious activity. An interesting discussion of the relevance of these networks to visual attention in sport is provided by Vickers (1996).

CONTEMPORARY MODELS OF ATTENTION: AN ACTION-RELATED APPROACH

Common to the models discussed above, has been an emphasis on auditory rather than visual selective attention and a disregard for the relationship between attention and action. A criticism has been that attention has nearly always been conceptualised as being related to the analysis and interpretation of sensory information rather than to the control of action (Neumann 1987). More recently, developments have marked the emergence of a more action-related theoretical approach to attention (see Allport 1987 1989; van der Heijden 1990 1992; Neumann 1990). Foremost amongst these developments has been Neumann's (1987, 1990) functional view of visual selective attention.

Neumann's 'functional' view of attention

The basic assumption of Neumann's approach focuses on the functional relationship between limited capacity and selective attention. He suggests that it is the selectivity of *action* that explains why capacity is limited, contrary to the traditional view that selection is needed due to the restricted capacity to process information. Selective attention is required because of physical limitations that require performers to select between alternative or competing actions. These physical constraints necessitate that performers select the most relevant information to control action. Competing actions and competing ways of carrying out an action need to be inhibited, and competing information must be prevented from gaining access to action control (Neumann 1990). In this approach, concurrent tasks can be performed provided they are controlled by a common action plan (e.g. running to catch a cricket ball). It is not perception but action, and not the capacity of the central information-processing system, but the capacity of the body that makes selection necessary. Selection is selection-for-action (Allport 1987).

Neumann (1990) distinguishes between two types of selection problems in action control. The first is termed the 'effector recruitment' problem. This occurs because of the scarcity of effectors within the human system. Consequently, effectors must be recruited in such a way that no mutually incompatible actions are attempted. For example, catching and throwing a ball at the same time causes problems since these two actions are physically incompatible. He suggests that in order to overcome this problem the system needs mechanisms of behavioural inhibition which can legislate between competing action tendencies. Shallice (1978) refers to this as selection of the 'dominant action system'. Neumann suggests that once the effectors have been selected all other inputs are then blocked such that only one action plan at a time can have access to the effector system. Allport (1987) argues that the problem the human performer faces is one of temporal priority. Since the same action system or effector mechanisms cannot be used concurrently the dilemma becomes one of selecting which category or mode of action, from the assortment of possible actions, has to be given temporal priority (ibid.).

The second selection problem is termed 'parameter specification'. This occurs when an intended action can be carried out in many different ways, but to execute it accurately, only one of these options must be selected at any one instant. In the motor control literature this is referred to as 'motor equivalence' (see Davids, Handford and Williams 1994). The problem is one of determining which of the possible parameter specifications to put into effect. For example, in a rugby game there are numerous potential targets to which a selected action can be directed depending on whether the player is attacking or defending. A player can kick, pass or run with the ball, or, alternatively, he may be forced to ruck, maul or tackle. The problem for the performer is one of deciding which goal to act upon at a certain moment in time (i.e. the problem of where the action is now to be directed (Allport 1987)). According to van der Heijden (1992), this form of selection is brought about by selective attention and operates within the constraints set by the task and in cooperation with expectations and intentions. This process ensures that skill parameters are assigned unequal values such that no two parameters can be assigned to the same task at the same time. The essence of Neumann's approach is that competing action tendencies have to be suppressed whether the information that provides the specification stems from the environment or is retrieved from memory. This argument is obviously different from capacity based theories which have assumed that selectivity is necessary for capacity reasons (e.g. to allocate scarce resources or to protect the limited capacity system from overloading).

Neumann (1990) suggests that at least part of the selection is done by using appropriate sensory information from the environment. That is, some selective process is necessary to map a relevant informational cue from the optic array on to the appropriate control parameter for action (Allport 1989). Sensory information constrains the set of alternative actions competing for effector recruitment as well as the set of alternative ways to carry out a selected action. This process is seen as the functional requirement of selection-for-action (ibid.).

A pertinent source of sensory information for action control could be Lee's tau variable for specifying time-to-contact information. For example, in Chapter 6 we note that Lee, Lishman and Thompson (1982) suggest that long jumpers control the timing of their approach run on the basis of the optical variable tau which is defined as the inverse of the rate of expansion of the take-off board on the retina. Neumann's suggestion is that this information automatically constrains the parameter specifications required to complete the action successfully. Although he suggests that some degree of computation may be required during the passage of information from retina to motor output, there is more than a passing empathy with the work of Gibson (1979) and others on direct perception (see Chapter 6). Neumann (1990) suggests that this information need not be categorised, stored or represented in memory prior to using it for action control. Neumann highlights three important characteristics of his selection-for-action approach:

- there is some variable (e.g. optical parameter tau) that specifies the required parameter(s)
- this parameter specification is achieved subconsciously and does not require attentional processes
- these parameter specifications are either innate or can be acquired through extended practice.

Taken together, these properties suggest that this type of selection-for-action takes place within, and is controlled by, specific control structures, or skills (Neumann 1990). These control structures specify the action's parameters partly by internally generating the relevant motor commands and partly by using environmental information. In short, they translate specific stimulus properties into specific action parameters (i.e. perception–action cycles). The processing of stimuli within such a control structure is itself highly selective. However, this selectivity is not the work of a selection mechanism that exists in addition to the control structure; rather this structure itself provides the required selectivity. Stimulus properties that are not directly coupled to motor output through specific connections within a control structure simply cannot be processed by this control structure. Neumann suggests that no mechanisms are needed to prevent what cannot be done. In this sense, there are many similarities with the parallel distributed processing or neural network approach discussed earlier. Nodes which are not connected in a neural network cannot affect the pattern of connectivity which determines action response (see Chapters 1 and 4).

Neumann's approach has a distinct ecological flavour since he proposes that attentional selectivity results from the discovery and development of direct links between perceptual (informational) and action (control) variables. Moreover, Neumann argues that selection and action cannot be properly understood in isolation. Selection mechanisms have evolved to cope with action control such that, once an action has been selected, it cannot be disrupted by other actions until it has run its course. The selected action requires certain subprocesses or structure for its completion and preventing some other action from using them would ensure that the selected action would have a good chance of being completed and its goal satisfied. Such an approach recognises the co-evolution of performers and their environment and pursues a doctrine of animal–environment reciprocity as its guiding principle.

In Neumann's approach, a tennis player with a momentary intention to play a passing shot or a volley, perceives much stimulus information in parallel during the initial stages resulting in the selection of a specific action. Once this response has been selected, competing processes are prevented from occurring, or can occur with great difficulty. Interference between two simultaneous tasks occurs *not* because attention (as a capacity or resource) is needed in order to perform various processes. Rather, interference occurs because an action has already been selected, and these other processes are completely or partially blocked. Thus, capacity limitations result from the selection problems involved, rather than the other way around.

A criticism of Neumann's approach, however, is that it does not specify a mechanism to explain how information constrains selection. Neumann's suggestion is that it is a biological mechanism which has evolved for benefit of the species and, consequently, is functional in nature. Perhaps a more informative interpretation is provided by Schoner's model of intrinsic dynamics and behavioural information from a dynamical perspective (see Chapter 7). Schoner (1994) argues that constraints continually inform the dynamics of the system such that the emphasis is as much on cooperation as on competition between the different patterns of coordination. The suggestion is that environmental information constrains or attracts the dynamics of the movement system into the required action pattern.

Thus far, we have reviewed various theories which attempt to provide an explanation for the allocation of attention in sport. In the next section, we turn our attention towards the development of automaticity in sport.

AUTOMATICITY AND SKILLED PERFORMANCE

Some characteristics of automaticity

As the novice becomes more skilled there is a dramatic improvement in performance. For example, when learning to parallel turn in skiing attention may be initially directed towards several aspects of technique, such as the positioning of the skis and ski poles, the forward lean of the trunk, the distribution of body weight on uphill and downhill skis, the angle of the knees and the rotation of the trunk. It is likely that novice skiers will have to consider each of these individual parts as they perform the skill. Consequently, performance will be rather awkward and not as smooth and efficient as that of skilled skiers. As novices becomes more proficient, they are likely to stop thinking about the individual parts of the turn. Rather these components will be grouped together as larger parts so that the entire action becomes much more coordinated and efficient. At this stage, attention may be focused only on the placement of the downhill ski pole or the imminent terrain of the slope. The rest of the action is carried out effortlessly without consciously thinking about any particular aspect of the technique. These changes equate to a reduction in the amount of attention which has to be devoted to the technique. This progression enables attentional resources to be allocated to other concurrent activities and to the development of more refined performance strategies (Glencross 1978). Moreover, if skilled skiers think too much about what they are doing as they ski down a difficult black run, they may find that there is a deterioration in performance (Baumeister 1984; Gallwey and Kriegal 1977). From a cognitive perspective, directing conscious attention to the various parts of the skill may disrupt the established motor programme controlling the action. This results in an over reliance on conscious feedback mechanisms or a shift towards a different mode of control during the task leading to what is referred to as 'paralysis by analysis'.

Many researchers have suggested that a possible explanation for the expert's more polished performance could be that as a result of prolonged practice some processing activities cease to make demands on attentional resources (e.g. Abernethy 1993a). Following extensive practice, skills can be performed 'automatically' requiring restricted conscious attentional demand. Fitts and Posner (1967) originally referred to an autonomous or automatic stage of learning. There has been some disagreement about the best definition of automaticity, but several researchers have drawn a distinction between conscious and subconscious processes (e.g. Shiffrin and Schneider 1977; Schneider, Dumais and Shiffrin 1984). Conscious procedures are referred to as controlled processes. They are regarded as being slow, of limited capacity, requiring attentional resources, and can be used flexibly in changing circumstances. Examples include the tennis player selecting the type of serve to play against her opponent or the golfer selecting the appropriate club to play his approach shot into the green. Subconscious mechanisms are referred to as automatic processes. They suffer no capacity limitations, are fast, parallel in nature and non-attention demanding, and are difficult to modify once they have been learned. For example, while executing the tennis serve or golf approach shot, skilled players are likely to be employing subconscious processes. According to this distinction, automaticity results when the performer moves from conscious to subconscious processing. It implies that skills can be performed with a reduced attentional demand, thereby conserving attention for other important tasks.

Assessing automaticity in sport: the dual-task paradigm

An approach which has been used to examine how effectively skilled performers divide attention between two competing tasks is the dual-task paradigm (for a review of this methodology, see Abernethy 1988a, 1993a). The approach is based on having participants perform two tasks simultaneously. The task for which assessment of attention demand is required is referred to as the primary task, whereas the secondary task provides the performance measure from which primary task demand is derived. That is, the decrement in performance observed when responding to the secondary task under dual-task compared with single-task conditions is taken as an indication of the attentional demands of the primary task. Poor secondary task performance would be expected to accompany a difficult (i.e. attention demanding) primary task. For example, Parker (1981) examined the concurrent performance of a ball catching and throwing task (primary task) and a peripheral vision detection task (secondary task) using groups of highly skilled, average and less skilled netball players. The primary task required the players to complete as many passes to a designated target and return as many catches as possible in a 30-second period. The secondary task involved detecting the illumination of lights located in the periphery. This dual-task approach was designed to closely replicate the demands of the actual game situation where players are required to catch and throw the ball while monitoring the positions of team-mates and opponents. The results, highlighted in Figure 2.6, show that there were no differences in primary task performance between the three groups of players. However, there were decrements in performance for all groups when they were required to perform primary and secondary tasks simultaneously. Even the most highly trained players had difficulty maintaining performance when pressurised by concurrent task demands. Nevertheless, performance on the secondary task was sensitive to skill level with the highly skilled group making significantly fewer detection errors than the less skilled players. The assumption is that the highly skilled players needed less attention capacity or resource to perform the primary task. The advantage for the skilled performer is that in a competitive situation ball catching and throwing is less attention demanding, thereby enabling visual attention to be directed towards scanning the display for suitable passing opportunities. Comparable findings have been obtained by Tenenbaum *et al.* (1994) in a study involving the recall of structured game situations as the primary task and a handball bouncing task as the secondary task.

The dual-task approach has also been employed to examine the attentional demand on performers during the preparatory stages of performance.

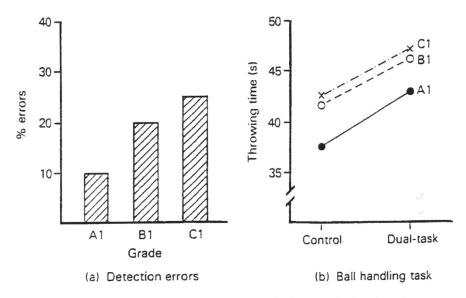

(a) Detection errors   (b) Ball handling task

Figure 2.6 The results from Parker's (1981) study showing dual-task performance across skill groups. Diagram (a) shows that the A1 (high skilled) group performed much better on the detection (secondary) task than the B1 (average) and C1 (low skill) groups. The differences in primary task (ball throwing and catching task) performance between groups are highlighted in diagram (b). These differences were not significant. (Source: Parker, H. (1981) 'Visual detection and perception in netball', in M. Cockerill and W.W. MacGillivary (eds) *Vision and Sport*, Cheltenham: Stanley Thornes.)

For example, Rose and Christina (1990) examined the attentional demands of pistol shooting using groups of elite, sub-elite and novice shooters. The primary task consisted of a precision-shooting activity, while the secondary task involved making a manual response to an auditory probe presented at various times during the period leading up to the shot. The results showed that the probe reaction time increased as shot time approached for the three groups of participants indicating a corresponding increase in attentional demand. The interesting finding was that there was a much greater decrement in performance on the secondary probe for the elite compared with the novice shooters. In particular, these differences were most pronounced at the aiming stage where the relatively skilled groups tended to miss significantly more probes than novices. The authors interpreted this latter finding to indicate that the skilled performers focused their attention more intently on task relevant cues at this stage than the novice shooters.

A similar approach was used by Castiello and Umiltá (1988) to examine how the attentional demand alters during the performance of a return of serve in volleyball and tennis. In one study, the primary task involved the reception of a volleyball serve whereas the secondary task involved a vocal response to an auditory signal. The results showed that reception of the 'floating' serve placed a greater attentional demand on the performer than did the 'jump' serve. Castiello and Umiltá (1988) suggest that the floating serve is less predictable than the jump serve since the trajectory of the ball can change markedly during flight, thus requiring more visual attention. Another interesting finding was that the attentional demand increased as the ball passed over the net, reaching its maximum when the ball was about to be received. In a second study, the attentional demands of athletes attempting to return the tennis serve were examined. Since the participants' response to the auditory probe was significantly higher under dual-task compared with single-task conditions, it was concluded that all component stages of the skill were attention demanding. Moreover, as in the volleyball serve, the period immediately prior to the initiation of the return stroke required most attention.

Davids (1988) made similar conclusions based on the results of a study which examined developmental differences in the allocation of attention during a two-handed ball catching task. In this study, subject groups ranging between 10 and 20 years of age were required to perform a two-handed catch and simultaneously process a peripheral visual signal presented either early in, in the middle of, or late in the flight of the ball, thus simulating many typical interceptive actions in ball game situations. Table 2.1 shows a significant increase in the mean number of ball catching and peripheral detection errors across the three portions of flight. These differences are most pronounced in the younger age groups as highlighted by the substantial increase in peripheral detection errors during the late (i.e. final 50–90 msec) segment of flight. Figure 2.7 indicates the type of

Table 2.1 The results from Davids' (1988) study showing the mean number of errors per subject on ball catching (BC) and peripheral vision (PV) task components in each segment of ball flight. (Source: Davids, K. (1988) 'Developmental differences in the use of peripheral vision during catching performance', *Journal of Motor Behavior*, 20(1): 39–51.)

Age group in years	Segment of ball flight			Task component
	Early	Middle	Late	
10	3.65	3.2	3.9	BC
	2.2	2.1	6.2	PV
12	1.95	2.1	2.45	BC
	1.5	1.9	4.65	PV
16	0.9	0.4	0.7	BC
	4.65	1.65	2.2	PV
20	0.2	0.05	0.2	BC
	1.1	1.2	1.5	PV

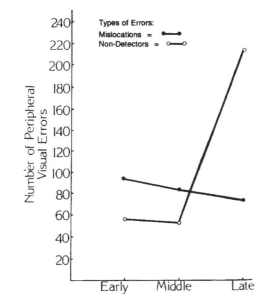

Figure 2.7 The results from Davids' (1988) study showing the types of errors made across the three segments of ball flight by all groups. (Source: Davids, K. (1988) 'Developmental differences in the use of peripheral vision during catching performance', *Journal of Motor Behavior* 20(1): 39–51).

errors made in each segment across groups. The greater attention demanded during the late segment of flight is clearly highlighted by the increased number of non-detections during this phase of catching. Comparable findings have been observed when dual-task procedures have been used to examine the attention demands during self-paced tasks (e.g. manual aiming). These studies suggest that attention is required at the initiation and at the end of the movement, whereas the middle portion of the task may be performed in a fairly automatic mode (e.g. Ells 1973; Glencross 1980; Posner and Keele 1969).

Although it is common to classify one task as primary and the other as secondary in dual-task situations, this designation is not necessary. Instructions can emphasise equal weighting to both tasks. This approach is valuable if the researcher is more interested in understanding the ability of participants to switch attention between concurrent tasks rather than assessing the attention demands of the primary task. Such an approach has been used successfully by Leavitt (1979) to examine the attention demands of skating and stick-handling in ice hockey. Ice-hockey players of varying levels of playing experience were required to skate and/or dribble a puck under four experimental conditions. These included skating only, skating while identifying geometric figures displayed on a screen, skating while dribbling or stick-handling a puck, and skating while dribbling a puck and identifying geometric figures. The dependent variable of interest was skating speed. The results showed that players with over 7.9 years' playing experience could perform more complex tasks such as skating, dribbling and visual identification concurrently without subsequent decrement in skating speed. Yet, the skating skills of players under 11 years of age (5.4 years' playing experience) were not automated enough to enable these skills to be performed simultaneously without a comparable deficit in skating speed. Smith and Chamberlin (1992) obtained similar results using groups of novice, intermediate and expert soccer players. Their findings showed that adding a cognitively demanding task during a soccer dribbling test caused a decrement in performance, the amount of decrement decreasing as the level of expertise increased.

An important characteristic of successful dual-task performance is the performer's ability to rapidly switch visual attention from one area of the display to another. Flexibility of attention is typically defined as the ability to quickly disengage, move and engage attention on various locations in space (Tenenbaum and Bar-Eli 1995). Much of the work on attentional flexibility in sport has been based on the work of Posner and colleagues (e.g. Posner and Snyder 1975; Posner, Snyder and Davidson 1980). Posner's cost–benefit approach uses differences in reaction time (RT) to a stimulus at expected (cued) and unexpected (uncued) positions to index the orientation of attention towards the expected position. A faster RT at cued locations reflects an 'attentional benefit', whereas slower RT at uncued locations is termed 'attentional cost'. The cost–benefit ratio determines the attentional effect or flexibility displayed by the subject. Nougier, Ripoll and Stein (1989) used this approach to examine the attentional strategies employed by groups of expert and novice boxers, archers and pentathletes. The results showed that skilled performers were equally as fast when required to respond to cued or uncued locations. They were able to optimise the distribution of attention, thus increasing the benefits and decreasing the costs of the attentional processes. The results confirmed their hypothesis that skilled performers are characterised by greater attentional flexibility enabling them to more effectively shift visual attention from one cue to the other (see also, Castiello and Umiltá 1992; Nougier *et al.* 1991). The ability to rapidly shift attention between concurrent tasks is likely to be an important characteristic of skilled performance. For example, a soccer player who gets caught in possession of the ball by an opponent may suffer from a failure to alternate attention swiftly enough between the skills of receiving the ball, scanning the display for available passing options and passing the ball (Moran 1996). An alternative explanation is that skilled athletes are able to distribute attention more effectively over multiple locations resulting in a smaller degree of commitment to a single target location (Nougier, Azemar and Stein 1992; Enns and Richards 1997).

In summary, the performer's ability to call upon task-specific knowledge and procedures automatically is crucial in sport. However, the development of automaticity should not be viewed as a distinct category, but rather as a continuum of varying degrees with the speed of processing and interference indicating the relative position of two tasks along this continuum (Anderson 1992; Cohen, Servan-Schrieber and McClelland 1992; Logan 1985). Processes that are regarded as being automated are still susceptible to some amount of interference and attentional demand (Cohen *et al.* 1992). This is confirmed by the absence of empirical evidence to suggest that skills are performed entirely attention free (see Stelmach and Hughes 1983; Jonides, Naveh-Benjamin and Palmer 1985; Neumann 1987). Even after extensive practice two difficult tasks can never be performed concurrently without some degree of mutual interference occurring.

Automaticity in sport: a theoretical backdrop

With regard to perception and action in sport, Schmidt (1987) suggests that automaticity results from a strengthening of the relationship between these processes. These changes in the perception–action relationship are assumed to result from the refinement of several mechanisms. First, it is believed that practice leads to a shift in the subject's reliance on different sources of sensory feedback. One suggestion is that practice leads to a greater reliance on kinaesthetic rather than exproprioceptive information (Fleishman and Rich 1963). Several research studies have indicated that experts are less affected by the loss of visual proprioception than novice performers, suggesting that experts are able to make more effective use of articular proprioception during motor control (e.g. Smyth and Marriot 1982; Bennett and Davids 1995).

Second, although there is some conflicting evidence (e.g. see our discussion of the work of Proteau and colleagues in Chapter 8), experts are thought to make less use of feedback-based processes during movement control due to a transition from closed-loop to more open-loop control (Pew 1966). Practice leads to the development of motor programmes which are: (i) 'comprehensive' in the sense of controlling and coordinating more degrees of freedom; and (ii) capable of controlling behaviour for a longer duration. The idea is that stored within the motor programme are all the movement commands required for controlling the action (Schmidt 1988). These are recalled and invoked prior to movement initiation such that the entire sequence is 'run-off' automatically without conscious attention demand. Automaticity therefore implies that the motor programme becomes increasingly responsible for a greater number of the sequential parts of movement (Lee and Swinnen 1993).

Third, automaticity may result from an improvement in error detection capabilities due to enhancement of the perceptual trace or recognition memory (see Schmidt 1988). Adams (1971) referred to this as the shift from a 'verbal-motor' to a purely 'motor-stage'. At this latter stage, performers demonstrate an increased ability to detect and correct their own errors based upon an internalised reference of correctness (see Schmidt and White 1972). Adams (1971) suggested that automaticity results from a reduction in the number of verbally mediated or conscious error corrections required during movement. A reduction in attention demands may also ensue from an increased role for subconscious or reflexive correction processes in motor control. Performers may become less reliant on conscious error correction processes and more reliant on reflexive closed-loop control mechanisms such as monosynaptic stretch reflexes, long loop reflexes, reflex reversals and triggered reactions (for more detailed coverage of these mechanisms, see Schmidt 1988). These mechanisms, which are rapid and subconscious, would reduce the attentional requirements of movement control. Coupled with this may be an increased capacity to more effectively use feedforward mechanisms (i.e. efference copy or corollary discharge), thus preparing the system for the receipt of upcoming sensory information.

Finally, Schmidt (1987) suggests that automaticity develops because patterns of sensory information can be detected quickly and accurately. They seem to 'trigger' appropriate actions without much mental effort. The ability to recognise patterns of sensory information results from the development of a pattern recognition capability which enables performers to 'chunk' information into larger, integrated and more meaningful wholes (see Williams and Davids 1995). The advantage of this ability to chunk stimulus information is that a number of stimuli, previously processed independently and serially, can be processed as one stimulus group, concurrently and in parallel. The empirical evidence which highlights the skilled performers' superior ability to recall and recognise structured patterns of play is reviewed in Chapter 4. This pattern recognition ability not only speeds up processing because more can be taken in at a glance, but the patterns of stimuli can be more easily interpreted. Chunking eases the processing burden on the athlete and allows other tasks to be accomplished. Moreover, the experts' enhanced ability to chunk task-specific information may be coupled with an improvement in stimulus-response (SR) compatibility. Following extensive practice, the relationship between a particular stimulus (e.g. initiation of a short-pitched ball in cricket or a drop shot by an opponent in badminton), and a response (i.e. avoidance or hooking action by the batsman in cricket or movement towards the net to retrieve the drop in badminton), become more 'compatible' resulting in more rapid actions (see Proctor and Reeve 1990).

Another theory which attempts to explain why prolonged practice leads to automaticity was proposed by Logan (1988). He suggested that: (a) every time a stimulus is encountered and processed a memory trace of that particular stimulus–response relationship is stored; (b) continued practice with the same stimulus leads to the storage of more and more information about the stimulus and its respective response alternatives; (c) this increase in task-specific knowledge leads to rapid and efficient retrieval of relevant information as soon as the appropriate stimulus is presented; (d) consequently automaticity is based on the efficiency of retrieval of knowledge from memory. Performance is viewed as being automatic when retrieval is based on 'single-step direct-access' of information from memory. According to Logan (ibid.), in the absence of practice the task of responding appropriately to a stimulus requires thought and the application of rules. However, prolonged practice leads to an increase in the knowledge base which subsequently permits rapid retrieval of relevant information and fast action.

This approach has much in common with Anderson's (1983) Active Control of Thought theory (ACT) presented in Chapter 4. In Anderson's theory, knowledge is initially encoded in a declarative format and then converted into a series of task-specific production rules (i.e. procedural knowledge). This is referred to by Anderson (ibid.) as 'knowledge compilation'. Anderson suggests that through processes of learning and what he terms conflict resolution, the strength of these specific production rules increases with practice such that they can be retrieved more effectively from long-term memory when required. In this approach, automaticity occurs, first, because there is a reduction in the number of production rules required to complete the task, and, second, because the process of knowledge compilation creates production rules that overlap less with other concurrent tasks (see Anderson 1992).

A criticism of these approaches is that they seem to lack the flexibility of more recent cognitive interpretations based on parallel distributed processing or neural networks. The suggestion that specific memory traces are stored every time a stimulus is encountered and processed seems to invoke problems of novelty (How are novel tasks performed?) and storage (Where does the performer store these specific memory traces?). Earlier in this chapter, we suggested that the parallel distributed processing (PDP) approach views the human performer as a system where processing occurs through the interactions of a large number of simple, interconnected processing units or nodes. These units are organised into modules or neural networks such that each network contains several processing units. The patterns of connectivity which determine what each network represents are not controlled by an executive; rather control is distributed at a more local level with each node being aware only of the input from the nodes to which it is connected. Processing in this approach occurs by the propagation of activation among the units within each neural network, via weighted connections. The knowledge that governs processing is stored in the weights of the connections. With increasing levels of expertise, performers develop new connections, lose some of the existing connections and modify the strengths (i.e. weights) of already existing links. The argument is that

the development of automaticity results from a strengthening of the connections between nodes (for a more detailed review of the PDP approach
to automaticity, see Cohen *et al.* 1992). An example of such modelling is
provided by Schneider and Detweiler's (1988) connectionist/control architecture. This model simulates a shift from controlled to automatic processing in visual search tasks by bypassing a central control structure. Initially,
the control structure modulates the transmission of information between
and within processing regions by attenuating some units and prioritising
others. However, with practice the connections between input and output
units are strengthened so that the appropriate output units become activated
by the input without intervention from the control structure.

FROM THEORY TO PRACTICE: DEVELOPING
AUTOMATICITY AND SELECTIVE ATTENTION IN SPORT

A fundamental objective of training and coaching is the reduction of the
attentional demands required to produce a particular outcome. A reduction in the attentional resources required for task-performance would
enable attention to be used for refining performance strategy and tactics
(Glencross 1978). Wickens (1989) highlights three techniques which are
available to the coach when attempting to develop automaticity. These
are dual-task and part-task training programmes and adaptive instruction.
Dual-task training involves practising several tasks simultaneously such as
shielding a ball from an opponent in basketball while dribbling and looking
for available passing options. Part-task training involves practice on some
subset of task components as a prelude to the practice or performance of
the whole task. Wickens (ibid.) suggests that training each of these components separately (i.e. shielding, dribbling and visual scanning) does not
give an opportunity for the emergent time-sharing skills to be practised.
Research has demonstrated that when participants transfer to a dual-task
condition, those who have also been trained under a dual-task condition
learn the skill better than participants who have received training on each
component task by itself (e.g. Damos and Wickens 1980; Connelly,
Wickens, Lintern and Harwood 1987). Participants who are part-task
trained fail to learn the time-sharing skills required to coordinate the
component activities.

However, because effective learning depends upon attention it can be
argued that part-task training may be more beneficial with novice
performers. Since the learning process requires attention, attempting to
learn a task which in itself is attention demanding may result in no attention being left for skill acquisition. Attention overload could therefore
result in error-ridden performance and, eventually, a reduction in the performer's motivation to learn. This suggests that components should be
trained in part, rather than in whole (however, for an alternative theoretical

argument, see Chapter 8). Such an approach may be particularly useful with beginners or low aptitude learners (see Wightman and Lintern 1985). A similar argument exists for using adaptive training, a technique in which the difficulty of a task is gradually increased as its performance is mastered.

Wickens (1989) proposes that if the task to be learnt contains consistencies – repeated sequences of events – learners will benefit more from part-task or adaptive training. That is, when the characteristics to be learnt are part of the task, and the task itself presents very complex information processing demands, then there will be some benefit in initially slowing or breaking down the task into simpler parts. The inherent danger of both adaptive and part-task training is that at the easier levels participants may learn habits that need to be unlearned at the more difficult levels (for further criticisms of this approach, see Chapters 6 and 8). Research is needed to increase our understanding of how to break up tasks in an appropriate and meaningful manner and to help coaches choose a suitable adaptive level for initial skill learning.

Since sports contain consistent and repeatable performance characteristics, both part-task and adaptive techniques have been used frequently within coaching. For example, when coaching the skills of ball control and dribbling in soccer, opponents are only introduced once the players have mastered these basic techniques and they have become at least partially automated in nature. The skill is broken down into its constituent parts in order to reduce the attentional demands of the situation. The child is first taught to control the ball so that attentional capacity can be released to concentrate on dribbling and running with the ball. Opponents may be introduced gradually depending on the ability level of the performer (i.e. adaptive training). The use of cones or static opponents might be considered useful intermediary steps before progressing to more realistic dynamic learning contexts. Similar progressions are evident in squash where shots may first be practised without the ball. The difficulty of coaching exercises can then be increased by introducing the ball, using a self-feed approach, followed by feeding from the instructor, continuous solo and pairs practices, pressure training and finally conditioned games (for some good examples, see McKenzie 1992). Gradually, more movement and pressure can be built up so that the player can be placed under similar pressure as in the game situation, or even more. This type of approach, where coaching routines start at an easy level and then build up in movement and pressure, can be used in teaching almost any complex skill. The skill may be decomposed and practised under increasing levels of difficulty until the most important aspects of skill execution have become automated (for more detailed discussion of the use of dual-task and part-task training techniques, see Chamberlin and Lee 1993; Proctor and Dutta 1995). Research is required to improve understanding of the principles behind optimal task decomposition.

Empirical support for adaptive training as a method of skill instruction has been provided by Leavitt (1979) using a variation of the protocol presented earlier (see pp. 47–48). In this study, ice-hockey players were asked to either skate only, skate while identifying geometric figures displayed on a screen, skate while dribbling or stick-handling a puck, or skate while dribbling a puck and identifying geometric figures. The control condition required subjects to perform each task using a regular sized ice-hockey puck, whereas in the experimental condition a much larger puck was used. Leavitt suggested that using a larger puck would reduce the attentional demands of the task thus increasing skating speed. The results confirmed this initial hypothesis with skating performance in the large puck condition being significantly better than the control condition. Therefore, by changing certain characteristics of a skill, the attentional demands can be reduced in order to facilitate learning. Reducing the attentional demands of one aspect of the skill enables additional attention to be devoted to other areas of skill development.

The ability of the coach to direct the learner's attention to relevant sources of attention is also an important part of the learning process. The coach should help performers to develop 'mind-sets' or expectations regarding which cues to attend to and which ones to ignore. For example, research presented in Chapter 5 suggests that consideration of important information can aid anticipation and prediction. Cues can be emphasised using film-based training programmes (e.g. Burroughs 1984; Christina, Barresi and Shaffner 1990; Williams and Burwitz 1993) or by highlighting important information during training such that they stand out from background distractions (see Maschette 1980). This latter approach can be achieved by using colour coding schemes to represent key cues. For instance, if the ball toss is an important cue in the tennis serve then an opponent can wear a brightly coloured glove or wristband to draw the learner's attention to this area of the display (ibid.). Similarly, the racket head can be painted with a bright colour so that the learner can easily pick out relevant racket angles as the ball is struck (for further information on improving anticipation in sport, see Abernethy and Wollstein 1989; Maschette 1980; Williams and Davids 1994). Coaches should begin by introducing only a few key cues as aids to guiding selective attention. Thereafter, more of these anticipation cues should be progressively introduced in line with the increase in skill level of the performer. As certain aspects of performance become automated this enables more of the performers attention to be devoted towards cue recognition and usage.

Finally, coaches should attempt to increase awareness of important internal cues related to performance. For example, the appropriate allocation of attention is important to ensure that the relevant feedback is attended to following task execution. A useful technique is to ask the performer what the movement felt like and how well he or she performed. This type of approach constrains the learner to engage in processing movement information and in the self-detection of errors during the period immediately after performance (see Swinnen 1990; Swinnen, Schmidt, Nicholson and Shapiro 1990). That is, it forces the learner to selectively attend to the sensory feedback and to subjectively evaluate it relative to the immediate response. An alternative approach is for the coach to direct the learner's attention towards the most important sensory information prior to movement. Statements requiring learners to concentrate on the feel of the movement are common within coaching practice as they draw explicit reference to the importance of this aspect of the task to skill acquisition. It is therefore important that the coach ensures that the learner focuses on the most significant sources of intrinsic feedback in order to facilitate the learning process.

SUMMARY AND FUTURE DIRECTIONS FOR RESEARCH EXAMINING ATTENTION IN SPORT

In this chapter we reviewed research and theory on attention with the aim of highlighting how attentional processes operate within sport. In particular, we focused on the importance of selective attention and automaticity to sports performance. Several different theoretical models were discussed in attempting to explain the mechanisms involved in the allocation of attention in sport. Fixed capacity models suggest that the allocation of attention is attributed to a special mechanism or filter located at various stages within the information processing model, whereas flexible allocation theories propose that attentional capacity is more flexible depending on the specific requirements of the task. These theories propose that past experience enables the performer to select and attend to the most important and informative areas during performance. An alternative theoretical approach was provided by multiple resource theory which suggests that attention is based on separate resource pools, each with its own capacity and designed to process distinct sources of information. In this theory, no special selective attention mechanism is proposed, rather selection is viewed simply as the process of allocating resources. Finally, we reviewed Neumann's (1987) action-based account of attention which proposes that selective attention is independent of all capacity or resource considerations, but that selectivity is needed for the control of action. Neumann argues that interference occurs for functional reasons, through the blocking of input information when a specific action has been chosen.

In view of the protracted history of research in this area, however, the limited nature of our existing knowledge about attention in sport is disappointing. As we have mentioned elsewhere in this chapter, a significant problem is that sport and exercise psychologists appear reluctant to test these theoretical propositions within sport-specific contexts. The reductionist philosophy that has underpinned experimental work in cognitive psychology appears to have weakened the applicability of these theoretical frameworks to the allocation of attention in sport (Abernethy 1993a). The majority of the research on selective attention has employed novel tasks with unpractised participants, preventing them from drawing on past experiences and contextual information which appears to be an essential part of attentional allocation (Logan 1985). Furthermore, most of the laboratory-based testing procedures require non sport-specific responses such as pressing a button in response to a tone. Poor stimulus response compatibility can affect the simple relationship between the amount of information to be processed and the capability to process it (Burns and Dobson 1984). A key issue is that most of the early work on attention was carried out in the laboratory with an ergonomics or human factors flavour. Clearly, we need to examine whether these models can explain performance in more dynamic and sport-related situations.

Perhaps another significant concern, given the emphasis of this book, is that much of the research has depended heavily on findings from dichotic listening paradigms relying on auditory input rather than visual input. Neumann, van der Heijden and Allport (1986) suggest that researchers should concentrate on developing separate models of selection for different sense modalities. They base their arguments on a number of fundamental differences between visual and auditory systems. First, they suggest that the gross and obvious structural differences between the eye and the ear makes it unlikely that comparable selection processes function. Visual information is already spatially sorted such that an image of the visual scene is presented on the retina. In contrast, sounds from different sources are not spatially coded at the sensory periphery since they require extensive processing beyond the sense organs. Auditory information is presented as one single acoustic pattern consisting of all stimulus information. Clearly, the selection problem in these conditions is very different. In vision, Neumann *et al.* (1986) suggest that the principal problem is one of choice, deciding which of the many areas of the display to select, whereas, in audition the problem is one of signal–noise separation, in other words, isolating the information to be selected from the acoustic pattern.

Second, they suggest that optical information is continuously available from all visible surfaces. The visual world has a nested structure with units at many hierarchical levels. For instance, the rugby player sees the playing stadium, the field of play, the structure and organisation of the opposing team, the structure of their forwards and backs, the positioning of individual players and the ball. The sensory information arriving at the eye is hierarchically organised and provides comprehensive and complete coverage of the visual array. In contrast, task-specific auditory information is neither continuously available, nor does it cover all parts of the environment. Auditory stimuli are only produced when something happens (i.e. there is movement by the basketball player, the bat strikes the ball or the ball is kicked). Thus, sound patterns are divided into natural units corresponding to such events. The rugby player's visual world has the complicated multi-level structure described above, while his auditory world may consist of a call from a team-mate, the crunch of the tackle, the pushing of the scrum or the roar of the crowd. These events may have a complex temporal structure, but they are not embedded in the same coexistent hierarchy characteristic of the visual world. Finally, Neumann *et al.* (1986) suggest that the high mobility of the eyes enables them to actively explore the environment, whereas, in hearing there is no 'listening around' component comparable to the 'looking around' function involved in visual search. In hearing although the mobility of the head contributes to gross acoustic localisation, peripheral movements are hardly used for exploratory purposes.

These differences in the physical and functional properties of the eye and ear imply that the theoretical treatment of visual and auditory attention may need to be markedly different. These dissimilarities suggest that vision and audition have disparate functions in controlling action in sport. Since visual information is both continuously available and more adaptable to various search processes, it can provide a more complete representation of the environment than sound. As we shall see in Chapter 6, vision can play a crucial role, for example, in guiding locomotion and in catching or striking a moving ball. Neumann *et al.* (1986) suggest that auditory information is usually not suited for guiding the execution of an action itself. However, they do suggest that it may serve as a signal to initiate a new action. For instance, the sound of the tennis ball on the racket may signify the type of shot played by an opponent, or the approaching sounds of an attacker in soccer may determine whether a ball should be headed clear rather than brought under control.

In the second half of this chapter, we focused more specifically on automaticity. We distinguished between controlled and automatic processes and presented several examples to illustrate the importance of automaticity to skilled sports performance. From a cognitive perspective, it appears that automaticity in sport results from the development of, and increased access to, an enhanced task-specific knowledge base. This knowledge base results in an increased ability to detect task-relevant information, a strengthening of the mappings or connections between input and output variables, and an enhanced ability to more efficiently organise movement information into higher order units or chunks.

Many issues need to be addressed in attempting to improve our understanding of automaticity in sport. Due to the difficulties of manipulating and controlling the variables necessary to facilitate our understanding of the learning process, motor behaviour research has tended to use simple laboratory-based tasks with tight experimental control but poor ecological validity. Future research should attempt to examine the development of automaticity within more ecologically valid performance contexts. Particularly useful approaches would be to assess dual-task performance at various stages of practice and to develop longitudinal research programmes to examine the development of automaticity over prolonged periods of practice. These types of studies would give important information on the interactive relationship between practice and automaticity. Geurts and Mulder (1994) have successfully used such an approach in a clinical context to examine the attention demands in balance recovery following lower limb amputation. Such an approach could also be used to verify the effectiveness of dual-task and part-task training techniques as methods of developing automaticity in sport. This could be done by measuring dual-task performance at various stages during training. Innovative coaches may also find use for dual-task methodologies in skill assessment and talent identification (Abernethy 1993a).

Finally, another promising research direction for the study of attention in sport is provided by the marriage of psychology and physiology. For example, psychophysiologists have begun to examine the relationship between physiological measures such as the electroencephalograph (EEG), event-related potentials (ERPs), contingent negative variations, positron emission tomography (PET), pupil diameter and heart-rate variability and various attentional states (for a review, see Wickens 1992). Sport psychophysiologists have studied attention by monitoring cortical and autonomic responses during athletic performance. For example, EEG studies have indicated that elite marksmen display cortical lateral asymmetry during shooting performance suggesting that they employ different attention control strategies compared with novice marksmen (e.g. Hartfield, Landers and Ray 1984, 1987; Salazar, Landers, Petruzzello, Crews, Kubitz and Han 1990; Landers, Han, Salazar, Petruzzello, Kubitz and Gannon 1994). Similarly, ERPs, which are averaged brain responses to a series of 'time-locked' stimuli, have also been examined as indices of attention. ERPs reflect transient changes in the brain's electrical activity that are 'evoked' by certain information-processing events (see Rugg and Coles 1995). For instance, Zani and Rossi (1991) showed reliable differences between clay-pigeon shooters specialising in either trap or skeet in the early latency N2 component (elicited by rare and unexpected events) and the late latency P300 component (reflecting the operation of attention) of ERP. Such findings show that elite athletes develop attentional strategies (styles) specific to their sport. Cardiac deceleration, which is assumed to be indicative of an external focus of attention, has been associated with attentional states prior to the event in archery, shooting and putting (see Boutcher and Zinsser 1990; Landers, Christina, Hartfield, Doyle and Daniels 1980; Wang and Landers 1988). Another approach which may offer exciting possibilities is the use of neuro-imaging techniques involving PET. The PET scanner can be used to detect changes in blood flow in localised cerebral regions. These measurements of blood flow are proposed to indicate the extent of cognitive activity in various brain regions. In future, such imaging techniques may provide multiple pictures of brain activity during the performance of sports tasks.

Nonetheless, psychophysiology is still in its infancy and there remains uncertainty in measuring, defining and describing electrophysiological phenomena. Future research must endeavour to establish, unambiguously, the relationship between the physiological changes observed during performance and attentional processes. So far, the collection of physiological measures has been limited to static sports such as rifle shooting and archery. However, recent advances in technology should allow for the accurate measurement of physiological variables in more dynamic sports. Further multidisciplinary research of this nature is clearly needed to help clarify the complex relationship between attention and sports performance. In particular, much could be gained by coupling covert measures of attention such as ERPs with more overt behavioural measures of performance such as eye movement registration and the recording of movement kinematics and/or kinetics (e.g. electromyography, various motion analysis systems).

3 The visual system hardware: Sport functional properties

INTRODUCTION

The human performer is effectively a moving platform (trunk) with manipulative devices (arms and legs) operating with a 'smart' processor (the brain and central nervous system). Some 30% of the processor is dedicated to visual information (Hubel 1988). Humans conduct their daily activities in a dynamic, cluttered environment within which survival depends heavily on visually processed information. If vision is disrupted or somehow impaired, even the simplest of tasks becomes laborious. In sport, where participants and objects frequently move on complex and rapid trajectories, the need for efficient vision is paramount. The fact that some sports performers can control a volleyball spiked at speeds approaching 160 kph producing angular velocities greater than 500 degrees per second or, as in baseball, strike a small, hard ball (23 cm in circumference) moving at similar speeds with a round bat (20 cm in circumference), often projecting the object further than 360 metres, is fascinating to both spectators and scientists alike.

This fascination has provided the impetus for sport and vision scientists to investigate how such apparently complex tasks are accomplished, whether such skills can be acquired through practice, and particularly, whether skilled performers possess some 'natural advantage' over their less skilled counterparts. Predictably, much of their effort has concentrated on the optical apparatus, notably, the eyes and the oculomotor musculature. These sensory organs provide us with information regarding the dynamics of sport and are generally referred to as the 'visual hardware'. This chapter delineates the hardware and draws conclusions on its significance in sports action. Initially, we outline the structure and physical characteristics of the visual system from the eye through to the visual cortex. The existing sport-specific research is then critically reviewed and the main implications of these findings for performance are discussed. Throughout these sections we examine whether skilled performers are characterised by superior visual hardware and whether visual function can be improved through specific visual training programmes.

Before progressing, the most commonly used terms in this area of research are highlighted in Table 3.1. Moreover, a visual health and performance screening device designed to profile the visual abilities frequently used in sport is presented in Table 3.2. This screening device has been published as a Sports Vision Manual by the International Academy of Sports Vision (see Planer 1994).

THE VISUAL SYSTEM AND SPORTS PERFORMANCE

The importance of vision to the sports player is self-evident. In some sports, such as baseball, the constraints of competent play apparently exceed the known operational capability of the visual system (e.g. see Bahill and LaRitz 1984). In other activities, such as ice hockey goaltending, a player's view of critical events may be severely impaired, yet performance is often no less than amazing. Plainly, sports action requires much more than the ability to 'see'. The apparent paradox of having to see, yet perform competently without being able to see well, has brought about a division of emphasis in research into the role of vision in sporting action. On the one hand, there are those who suppose that performance, particularly in high speed ball games, is a function of the quality of the individual's visual system. On the other hand, there are those who contend that perceptual skill is more a function of the expert knowledge gained through experience than the quality of the system that registers the various signals. The motivation for the second position has been generated by lack of evidence for the suppositions of the first. The two viewpoints are often referred to as 'hardware' (system quality) and 'software' (knowledge structures) perspectives (for an extended discussion, see Abernethy 1987b; Starkes and Deakin 1984; Williams *et al.* 1992). Specifically, hardware factors are taken to be 'physical differences in the mechanical and optometric properties of the visual system' and software factors as cognitive differences 'in the analysis, selection, coding, retrieval, and general handling of the available visual information' (Abernethy 1987b: 8).

The emphasis in this chapter is on the visual hardware, whilst in Chapters 4 and 5 we turn our attention towards the cognitive or software characteristics underlying skilled perception. In practice, however, this polarisation within sports vision research is artificial because of the obvious interdependence of hardware and software elements. Plainly, humans have evolved an intricate visual system which acts as the substrate for highly developed percepts of action rooted in knowledge. Performance in sports is dependent upon acceptable integrity of both elements. Perhaps it is because the hardware of the visual system is tangible, well researched in its own right, and the 'wiring' fairly well known, that this is a logical point at which one would begin to study the role of vision in sport.

Table 3.1 Explanations of the most common terms used in sports vision. (Source: Planer, P.M. (1994) *Sports Vision Manual*. Harrisburg, PA: International Academy of Sports Vision.)

Explanation of visual abilities

VISUAL ACUITY (STATIC)
This is the ability to resolve various sizes of letters or objects at various distances from the observer. This can be measured using the standard acuity tests which yield the commonly spoken of visions of 20/20, 20/30, 20/50, etc. While not extremely important in isolation in sports, nevertheless, athletes should have at least 20/20 to 20/15 acuity for most sports activities. Acuity with both eyes together should be better than each eye tested separately. Deficits in this ability can cause the athlete to be unable to see and recognise small objects clearly and rapidly.

VISUAL ACUITY (DYNAMIC)
This is the ability of maintaining precise clearness while the athlete and/or the object or place the athlete is looking at is in motion. Deficits in this ability can affect timing and depth perception.

CONTRAST SENSITIVITY
This is the ability of the athlete to discriminate detail in a higher field of view. As the brightness and colour of background areas approach that of the object the athlete is following, contrast of the object from the background becomes less and less. Deficits in this ability could make it difficult for the athletes to 'pick-up' and 'stay-on' any object that needs to be followed. The athlete would be slow to notice and have a tendency to lose balls, pucks, people, etc. once they are noticed.

COLOUR VISION
This is the ability to rapidly and accurately recognise the various colours in the spectrum. Special coloured glasses or contact lenses may in some instances help in colour discrimination. Some diseases and medications can have adverse affects on colour discrimination. Usually the deficits are inherited. Deficits in this ability can make it difficult for athletes to 'spot' a receiver, distinguish one of their team members from one of their competitors, and to follow accurately a moving object in their field of view.

EYE MOVEMENT (OCULAR MOTILITY)
This is the ability to accurately 'team' the two eyes together so they perform as one, and holding this 'oneness' as the athlete looks from place to place and/or follows a moving target, whether the athlete and/or the target is in motion or stationary. Deficits in this ability can affect all judgements of spatial orientation, depth perception, and the need for immediate clear, single vision for all objects of regard in the field of view.

FOCUS FLEXIBILITY (ACCOMMODATION)
This is the ability that allows the athlete to rapidly change focus from one point in space to another without excess effect. Focusing and converging (turning the eyes as a team inward to follow an incoming ball, puck, person, etc.) and diverging (turning the eyes outward as a team to follow an outgoing ball, puck person, etc.) all work together. Deficits in this ability can force the athlete to use excess effort in the convergence/divergence systems, thus slowing down the athlete's ability to quickly and accurately follow an incoming or outgoing object.

Table 3.1 Continued

Explanation of visual abilities

FUSION FLEXIBILITY (BINOCULARITY)
This is the ability to rapidly and accurately fuse the two images from the athlete's eyes into one image, and to have the eyes work as a team to maintain this 'oneness' in all areas of gaze. Deficits in this ability can cause the athlete to experience double vision, have difficulty accurately following objects and people in the field of view and misjudge directions and distances during competition.

DEPTH PERCEPTION (STEREOPSIS)
This is the ability to rapidly and accurately utilise the fused images from the athlete's eyes to judge distances and spatial relationships from object to object or place to place during sporting activities. This ability is intimately related to Eye Movement and Fusion Flexibility abilities. Deficits in this ability can cause athletes to misjudge where objects (balls, pucks, etc.) are in relation to other objects (themselves, other athletes, the basket, base, etc.).

VISUAL REACTION TIME
This is the time required to perceive and respond to visual stimulation. Involved in this ability, is the ability of the athlete to utilise auditory (sound) information to assist any visual stimulation. Deficits in this ability can cause athletes to be slow to respond to actions occurring during sporting activities.

CENTRAL PERIPHERAL AWARENESS
This is the ability of athletes to pay attention to what is in front of them (central) yet to be aware of, and use, that which is to the sides of (peripheral to) where they are looking without having to move their eyes from the object of regard. Deficits in this ability can cause athletes to see things/people in the sides of where they are looking, and very often to be distracted from where they are looking by things/people to the sides.

EYE–HAND–BODY COORDINATION
This ability involves the integration of the eyes and the hands/body as a unit. The eyes must lead and guide the motor (movement) system of the body. Deficits in this ability can affect all levels of performance that require movement of the athlete, racket, bat, ball, etc.

VISUAL ADJUSTABILITY
This is the ability to be flexible enough to rapidly adjust and guide the body's motor responses quickly and accurately, while having surroundings/environment change. It is the act of being 'tuned into' body responses, even though the demands of the situation vary. It is how long it takes to adjust the visual system's abilities to the varying environment so that the system can help guide the necessary responses. Deficits in this ability can slow the responses of the athlete considerably and make any responses that are attempted be unpredictable and inconsistent.

VISUALISATION
This is the ability to mentally imagine and visualise situations, actions and responses that can and do occur during sporting activities, modify them to be more efficient and correct, and then be able to use this information during actual play situations now, and in the future. Deficits in this ability can hinder the athlete's correct responses to various game situations that occur. They will make it difficult for athletes to learn from mistakes they and/or others might make during athlete competition.

Table 3.2 The Visual Health and Performance Assessment form published by the International Academy of Sports Vision. (Source: Planer, P.M. (1994) *Sports Vision Manual*. Harrisburg, PA: International Academy of Sports Vision.)

```
┌──────────International Academy of Sports Vision──────────┐
│              Visual Health and Performance Assessment     │
│                                                           │
│   Name_____   Visual Correction_____  │
│   Birth Date_____                           │
│   Sport/Team _____                           │
│   Position_____   Date of Assessment_____  │
│                                                           │
│   PERFORMANCE SCALE                                       │
│                                                           │
│   Superior                                                │
│   Above Average                                           │
│   Average       - - - - - - - - - - - - - - - - - -       │
│   Ineffective                                             │
│   Needs Immediate                                         │
│   Attention                                               │
│                                                           │
└───────────────────────────────────────────────────────────┘
```

VISUAL ABILITIES: Eye Health; Visual Acuity (static); Visual Acuity (dynamic); Contrast Sensitivity; Color Vision; Eye Movement (ocular mobility); Focus Flexibility (accommodation); Fusion Flexibility (binocularity); Depth Perception (stereopsis); Visual Reaction Time; Central-Peripheral Awareness; Eye-Hand-Body Coordination; Visual Adjustability; Visualization

* Refer to back for definitions

SUMMARY

☒ Evidences of deficiencies in the following areas were found:

☐ Eye health
☐ Visual acuity (Static)
☐ Visual Acuity (Dynamic)
☐ Contrast Sensitivity
☐ Color Vision
☐ Eye Movement (Ocular Mobility)
☐ Focus Flexibility (Accommodation)
☐ Other

☐ Fusion Flexibility (Binocularity)
☐ Depth Perception (Stereopsis)
☐ Visual Reaction Time
☐ Central–Peripheral Awareness
☐ Eye-Hand-Body coordination
☐ Visual Adjustability
☐ Visualisation

RECOMMENDATION

☐ No future enhancement is required at this time. A re-evaluation is recommended
☐ Referred to appropriate health care provider
☐ Protective sports specific eye wear should be worn during sports competitions for
☐ restoring clarity of seeing
☐ protection of the eyes
☐ Contact lenses should be worn during sports competition for restoring clarity of seeing and to allow a larger peripheral field of view
☐ Special purpose lenses should be worn during competition
☐ A program of Sports Vision Enhancement therapy to provide the opportunity to enhance deficient visual abilities to the level necessary to assist the athlete toward performing up to higher potential
☐ Other

In examining the functional characteristics of the visual system in sport, it is necessary to understand the interplay between optical properties, operational capacity, and the environmental demands placed upon the system. Therefore, in the next section, we take you on a journey from the external visual world to the visual receptors of the retina, through the major visual pathways to the primary visual cortex and beyond. The optics, 'wiring diagrams', and certain functional properties of the visual system are now fairly well known due to the resourceful collation of neuroanatomical, neurophysiological, engineering, lesion and clinical studies. However, as the authoritative researcher Hubel (1988) clearly documents, increments in knowledge are relatively slow and there remains a lack of exact neurophysiological understanding of visual perception even at a rudimentary level.

Anatomy

The visual system comprises three principal structures within the CNS and a myriad of other connections which enable 'seeing' to become 'perceiving'. Figure 3.1 schematises the three structures relative to the environment and events within it, in this case, a baseball player catching the ball. The basic idea of this illustration is to show the relationship between a sports action, which is heavily dependent on visual information about the object as it moves within the environment, the position of the eyes and brain within the skull at the cross-sectional level of the visual pathway (Figure 3.1a – MRI section), and representation of the object at the cortical level (Figure 3.1b). In Figure 3.1c, visual processing is traced from rudimentary 'sense-data' (the object within the optic array) to become 'perceived-data' (e.g. the baseball's features, trajectory). Ultimately, this information is further transduced and used for muscular contractions (for reaching and grasping the ball). Depicted are the eyes (peripheral organs of vision), lateral geniculate nuclei (mid-brain 'way-stations' for processing located within the thalamus), the optic chiasm (cross-over paths which enable sense data received on the retina of both eyes to be integrated as a complete image), and visual centres in the cortex (areas of detailed processing usually referred to by earlier authors as areas 17 (primary visual cortex), 18 (prestriate cortex) and 19 (inferotemporal cortex), but also labelled in other ways (see Hubel 1988)).

The eye

The eyes are the peripheral organs of vision and the primary sensory outpost of the brain. They operate in a complementary and conjugate (i.e. both eyes move together) fashion and serve as the pick-up point of light reflected from objects in the optic array. This is accomplished by means of a sensitive and precisely adjustable, transparent lens system which has

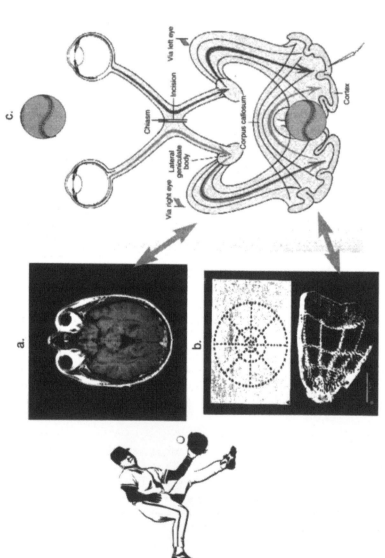

Figure 3.1 This illustration shows the pattern of neural activation in the visual cortex as influenced by the stimulus material (upper section). The anatomical components which enable seeing to become perceiving comprise multi-layered, multi-laned pathways from eyes to brain. The catching action depicted above left is heavily dependent upon vision and perception-in-action. The MRI section (a) is the approximate level at which the pathway (c) is located. The upper image of (b) is stimulus material and the lower image the pattern of neural activation in the visual cortex. (Source: Tootell, R. (1982) 'Deoxyglucose analysis of retinotopic organization in the primate striate cortex', *Science* 218: 902–4.)

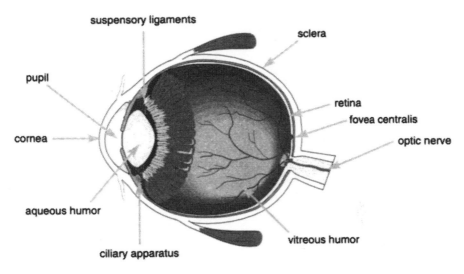

Figure 3.2 Cross-sectional view of an optic chamber.

evolved a structure comprising protein molecules for catching photons and bending light rays (Land and Fernald 1992). The main features of the human eye, depicted in horizontal section, are shown in Figure 3.2.

When the eyes are directed within the visual array, the optical arrangement produces a 'replica' of the environment in the form of an inverted, two-dimensional image upon a 'screen' of light sensitive cells termed the retina. The retina is an exceptional device which translates light into nerve signals permitting us to see under a very wide range of conditions of illumination, colour and focus. Figure 3.3 shows that reflected light arriving at the retina is translated into neural signals via five different layers of cells: receptors, horizontal cells, bipolar cells, amacrine cells and retinal ganglion cells. Notice that the retina is 'inside-out' in the sense that the light reaches the receptor layer only after passing through the other four layers. Then, once the various receptors are activated, the neural message passes back out through the retinal layers before reaching the retinal ganglion cells, whose axons project across the retina, and leaves the eye via the optic disk. There are two different receptor types in the retina. Cone receptors are responsible for high-acuity (fine-detailed) colour vision, whilst rod receptors are sensitive to light and motion but lack colour and detail. These differences between photopic (cone) and scotopic (rod) vision are due to the convergence of rods and cones on the underlying retina ganglion cells. Rods have a many-to-one mapping with retinal ganglion cells, whereas it is not unusual for a single cone receptor to converge on a single retinal ganglion cell (see Pinel 1993).

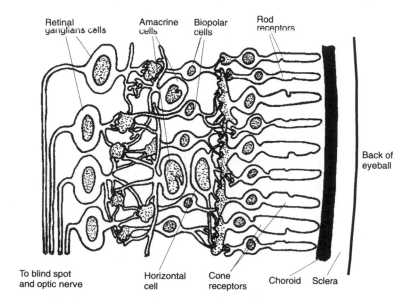

Figure 3.3 Cellular section of the retina showing the five different layers of cells. (Adapted from Pinel, J.P.J. (1993) *Biopsychology*, Massachusetts: Allyn and Bacon).

The visual retina

The sharpness with which the detail of objects such as form and contour can be seen is referred to as visual acuity: the resolving qualities of the eye (Blundell 1984). It can be argued strongly that the attainment of task-specific acuity is the prime purpose of the human visual system. Nowhere is this more apparent than in sport. The image on the retina is formed as a result of the refractive surfaces of the cornea and lens whose curved surfaces act much like a convex glass lens. The cornea is responsible for some two-thirds of the optical power whereas the lens is mainly concerned with adjustments of focus (Land and Fernald 1992).

The retina is functionally organised so that the maximum resolution of spatial detail can be obtained at a point when objects in the environment are fixated. This area of 'clear vision' is the fovea. It can be seen in Figure 3.2 that the fovea is effectively a tiny 'pit', with a high concentration of neural receptors, accounting for a very small part of the whole retinal surface (approximately 1–2 degrees of visual angle) (Zeki 1993). The major objective of the human oculomotor system is to adjust line-of-sight so that the fixation point and fovea correspond (see also Chapter 5).

Various methods are used to assess acuity, such as reading rows of different size letters on the familiar Snellen Eye Chart, determining the 'minimum separable distance' of two lines or reporting the 'minimal visible' width of a line discriminable from a homogeneous background. Although most of these methods are somewhat contrived, they readily convey the importance of seeing clearly whether it be in everyday activities, the workplace or sports. Whatever the circumstances, impaired acuity is disruptive and people go to great lengths and expenditure to rectify any shortcomings. Berman (1995) reports that sports enthusiasts in the USA spend in excess of $300 million per year on optical goods specifically related to sports activities. Much of this 'investment' is aimed at supporting and maintaining visual clarity.

Acuity is not uniform across the entire retinal surface. Only the fovea is specialised for enhanced acuity and is used for the inspection of detail. Figure 3.4 shows that this area contains a dense distribution of cone receptors whose operation is maximal only in well-illuminated conditions. A dramatic decrement in acuity occurs with increasing angular distance from the fovea. Performance falls to 50% at 2.5 degrees of arc, 25% at 7.5 degrees, and 4% at the extreme periphery (Ruch 1965). As an approximate guide, the width of the thumb with the arm fully extended covers roughly 2 degrees arc. Thus, in practice, much of the athlete's optic array lacks crisp resolution. In contrast, rod receptors predominate in the peripheral retina (see Figure 3.4). As a consequence of these physical differences, the fovea is specialised for fine discrimination, detail and colour vision and the periphery for motion detection and vision under low levels of illumination.

Prompt alterations in focus are required when gaze on objects shifts from far (6 m) to near (10 cm) or near to far to avoid blurring of the image. This process is referred to as 'accommodation' and is achieved by the eye's internal musculature (i.e. ciliary process) changing the convexity of the lens. The combined action of lens and pupil make a substantial contribution to the acquisition of clear retinal images. Decline in accommodative power is progressive from relatively early in life, yet is typically unnoticed until reading is affected usually between age 40 and 50 years and referred to as 'presbyopia'. Plainly, accommodative plasticity is an important operational requirement for competent participation in virtually all sports which demand numerous and rapid shifts of far-to-near and near-to-far focus often over lengthy time periods.

Eye movements

The requirement for the human eye to rapidly and consistently resolve environmental objects in sharp detail by way of a relatively small, yet highly sensitive area (i.e. the fovea) set within two optical chambers which, in turn, are set frontally inside orbits in the skull requires an elaborate movement system. As a result, the eyes have evolved as spheres with an intricate musculature to facilitate movement. In turn, the visual system is inextricably coupled with the head/neck and balance control systems (e.g.

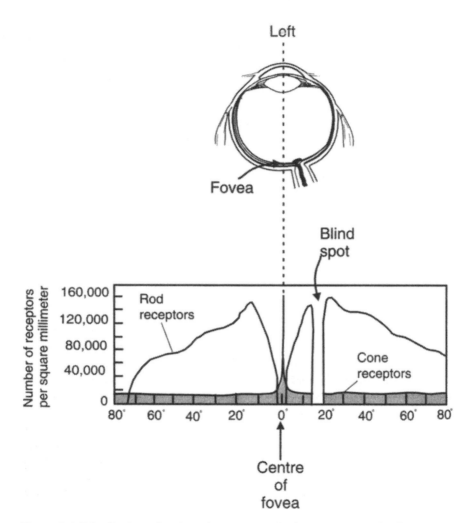

Figure 3.4 Distribution of rods and cones over the human retina. The figure highlights the number of rod and cone receptors per square millimetre in
a horizontal slice through the fovea and blind spot of the right eye as
a function of the angle (distance) from the fovea. (Adapted from Pinel,
J.P.J. (1993) *Biopsychology*, Massachusetts: Allyn and Bacon).

vestibular apparatus) which are tuned to keeping the performer in touch
with environmental events as depicted earlier in the example of baseball
catching.

   Each eyeball is moved by six extrinsic, striated muscles which are inner-
vated by three cranial nerves. The neuromuscular arrangement which
enables the eyes to move and acquire environmental information is schematised in Figure 3.5. In effect, the musculature rotates the eyeballs around

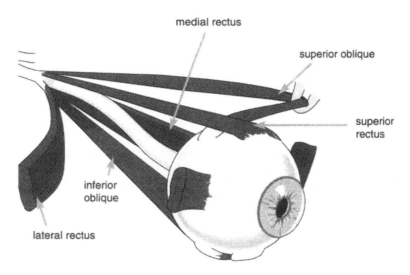

medial rectus

superior oblique

superior rectus

inferior oblique

lateral rectus

Figure 3.5 The extraocular musculature responsible for eye movements.

four axes, namely, horizontal (visual axis), transverse, vertical and oblique. This system enables the eyes to fixate objects within a circular area of diameter equal to about 100 degrees of visual angle. Rotations to left and right are approximately equal though vertical-upward are more restricted (40 degrees) than vertical-downward (60 degrees) (Ruch 1965). Eye movements, therefore, involve precisely coordinated orchestration of opposing muscles in order to move the eyeballs in unison. Fundamental visual system research classifies four main types of eye movement and several sub-classes (Carpenter 1988). These classifications of eye movements are reviewed in greater detail in Chapter 5. However, a sports example is included here to briefly explain the basic characteristics of the four main classes of eye movement.

Consider the soccer goalkeeper observing the field of play within which his opposite number has gathered the ball and is preparing to kick the ball downfield. The observer's gaze and visual focus is momentarily directed at the other keeper some 80 metres distant with head and eyes still. Next, the observer quickly scans the opponent's options. With the whole field of play in view and critical events, as yet at a distance, this would be achieved with rapid eye movements referred to as 'saccades'. Such movements can be very rapid and are used to redirect the eyes quickly from one point to another in the visual array. The saccadic mechanism enables the visual system to foveate and, thus, extract maximum detail from the environment.

Let's assume that the opposing keeper elects to kick long to the right winger, moving the ball with high trajectory over a distance of about

40 metres. The observer 'tracks' the path of the ball towards its intended target. This would be achieved using 'pursuit' eye movements. In contrast, to saccades, these are relatively slow movements which almost always involve head movements and are usually limited to speeds within the range of 60 to 100 degrees per second. Interestingly, Bahill and LaRitz (1984) report velocities which are twice this order of magnitude for baseball batters although these values are still too slow to track a high speed pitch which may reach angular velocities in excess of 500 degrees per second. This type of movement is invoked by the velocity of a moving target whereby the eyes 'catch' the object and keep pace with its motion by transforming target velocity information to 'drive' the oculomotor system.

Suppose that the player receiving the ball inside the observing goal-keeper's half of the field dribbles down the right flank to the goal-line and quickly crosses the ball back to a striker positioned some 4 metres from goal who shoots first time at the target. The defending goalkeeper's eye movements (and bodily movements) would, initially, have 'tracked' ball–player movement then rapid eye–head–body movement would have occurred to keep pace with the sudden change in the ball's position from side to front of goal requiring immediate re-setting of the eyes in synchrony with head and limb transfer. This extremely important type of movement is referred to as 'nystagmus'. Nystagmus is a product of the collaboration of visual and vestibular systems to effectively stabilise the eyes during head movements thereby minimising the motion of the image of a fixed object on the retina. There are sub-classifications for nystagmus movements and a substantial research literature dealing with their function and properties which is beyond the scope of this chapter (for a review, see Rosenbaum 1991).

Lastly, the goalkeeper needs to use the visuomotor control system effectively to prevent a goal being scored. We assume that this player has positioned directly in line with the fast moving ball approaching at head-level. This situation would bring about a kind of fronto-parallel tracking whereby the eyes move toward each other (i.e. inward rotation) as the object looms. These are termed 'vergence' eye movements.

Plainly, a great deal of collaboration between all classes of eye movements is required to make this a functionally efficient system, particularly with respect to the function of dynamic visual acuity to be discussed later. Thus, interaction between all of these movements during everyday tasks and sports actions is quite common.

Sense data to information

As already indicated, the principal 'biological' purpose of the visual system is visual perception which is the transformation, organisation and interpretation of reflected light supplied to the brain through visual sense modalities (eye movements subserve this purpose). A system which produces controlled movements such as saccades and pursuit movements of the eyes must use a control mechanism which implies some kind of 'interpretation'. The pathway from the optic array to the visual cortex which is an integral part of the interpretative process was traced in Figure 3.1. The burning question for visual and perceptual scientists is: 'How is reflected light transduced to become a percept?' Despite high quality research spanning some forty years, we still do not have a comprehensive answer to this question. Although the 'wiring diagrams' (neuroanatomy) and certain functional characteristics (neurophysiology) have been thoroughly described (see Hubel 1982, 1988; Hubel and Wiesel 1977; Nakayama 1985; Stone, Dreher and Leventhal 1979), the link between these and the processes of visual perception has only been addressed in relatively recent fundamental research (Goldman-Rakic 1988; Livingston and Hubel 1987).

A brief synopsis of the findings is presented here with the aid of the schematic representation provided in Figure 3.6, which depicts the layers (lamina) of the pathway from eye to brain. At the outset, it should be noted that what follows is a very general description drawn from a body of published papers of a number of research groups who have concentrated on the retina-geniculate-striate pathway. As Milner and Goodale (1995) point out, this is only one of two major eye-to-brain pathways in mammals. The other is the retinotectal projection which plays a prominent role in control of saccadic eye movements as well as being connected to the premotor and motor nuclei in the brainstem and spinal cord. Also, there are a number of less well-studied though no less important projections such as that to the accessory optic system (see Simpson 1984). These pathways have been implicated in processing the 'optic-flow' information which subsequent research may reveal to be highly important in sport action.

The central feature of Figure 3.6 depicts the retina-geniculate-striate pathway. This is the 'information highway' which carries neural signals from the retina via the lateral geniculate nuclei (LGN) to the primary visual cortex. Even a schematic representation is sufficient to convey that this is a complex communications network which is geared to 'making sense' of the environmental layout and all that happens within it. Consideration of the pathways, their origins and destinations, begs the question: How does 'seeing' become 'perceiving'? Despite great advances following the outstanding research undertaken by Hubel and Wiesel which led to the Nobel Prize in 1981, a solution to this puzzle remains some way off. Some background information is required to comprehend the current state of affairs. However, before progressing it is worth noting that much of the information comes from studies of mammals, such as the cat and various types of monkey. Certain authors are not entirely convinced of the functional equivalence of the visual system pathways of humans and some primates (e.g. see Shapley 1990).

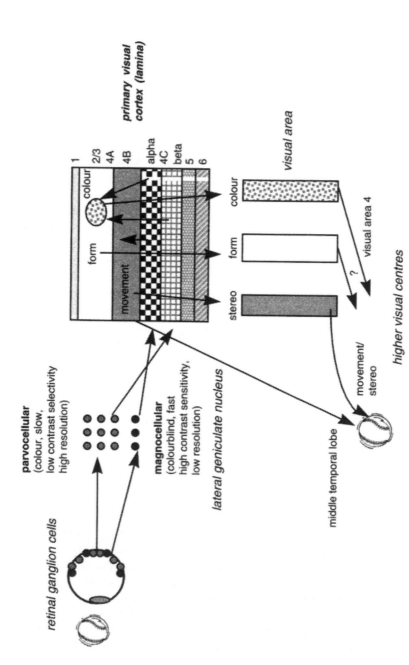

Figure 3.6 Schematic representation of the retino-geniculate-striate pathway from the retina to higher visual areas in the cortex. (Acapted from Livingston, M.B. and Hubel, D.H. (1987) 'Psychophysical evidence for separate channels for the perception of form, color, movement, and depth', *Journal of Neuroscience* 7: 3418–68.)

Seeing-to-perceiving

One of the earliest attempts to describe 'seeing-to-perceiving' at the most rudimentary level was by Hubel and Wiesel (1979). They advanced what is termed the S/C/H model. This model explained how the visual system interprets information in a primitive fashion and, in the process, delineated the functional anatomical architecture of the visual cortex showing patterns of ocular dominance and stimulus orientation. Their assertion was that very little 'processing' takes place at the retinal or geniculate (mid-brain) levels apart from sensitivity to differences in illumination. However, a convergence of connections from the relatively homogeneous geniculate cells on to cortical cells results in differentiation into three types of cell which possess unique receptive fields and stimulus properties, as well as directly influencing one another. These were labelled 'simple' (S) cells with small receptive fields and responsive to light slits and lines, which 'drive' 'complex' (C) cells with large receptive fields responsive to bars and edges and orientation specific, in turn driving 'hypercomplex' (H) cells characterised by sustained firing responses to moving lines. The impression gleaned from Hubel and Wiesel's reports was that of a functional hierarchy of information processing which increased in detail as it passed deeper into the brain until rudimentary feature detection resulted.

Shortly following Hubel and Wiesel's assertions, Stone, Dreher and Leventhal (1979) put forward a somewhat different explanation which they termed the Y/X/W model. This argued for functionally distinct cell types at the retinal level projecting *in parallel* to the cortical level with very little intermingling. The authors asserted that 'X' cells, high resolution types concerned with visual acuity, concentrated around the fovea and projected directly to the striate cortex (Area 17),[1] 'Y' cells with fast conducting axons and specialising in movement discrimination projected direct to visual cortical areas 17 and 18, and 'W' cells possessing large receptive fields, slow conducting axons and performing an 'integrating' function projecting to areas 17, 18 and 19, but having a strong influence in the latter area of the visual cortex. In this version of vision, little was said about processing at the cortical level itself.

Despite the usual ebb and flow of criticisms that routinely move between research groups, the notion of parallel pathways and specialised processing along the length of the visual pathway was tacitly accepted. This stemmed from neuroanatomical study of the projections from retina to cerebral cortex which show distinct layering and, within this, clear large (magno) and small (parvo) cellular subdivisions resulting in two specialised 'lanes' of the visual information highway which are referred to as the 'magnocellular' and 'parvocellular' projections (see Merigan and Maunsell 1993; Milner and Goodale 1993). The parvocellular layers are designed for high spatial acuity or resolution and colour sensitivity, but are relatively slow

and insensitive to changes in illumination levels. In contrast, magnocellular neurons are relatively fast, contrast-sensitive and colour-sensitive
and responsive to motion detection. These two subdivisions represent
specialised functional streams of information that are separated within the
LGN and remain separated at the level of the primary visual cortex
(Livingston and Hubel 1987).

From the standpoint of information processing, the idea is that channels begin at the retinal level and remain segregated up to the highest
levels of the visual cortex. These pathways are said to subserve specific
visual functions as outlined by Livingston and Hubel (1987). Interestingly,
the notion of two variants of visual perception has been around for some
time (for example, see Held and Schlank 1959) as has the notion of two
cortical visual systems supporting visual perception (see Trevarthen 1968;
Schneider 1969). Initially, it was thought that the parvo- and magnocellular streams remained separated beyond the primary visual cortex. For
example, Ungerleider and Mishkin (1982) proposed that visual pathways
projecting from the primary visual cortex to other cortical regions could
be divided into two relatively independent 'streams' of visual processing.
According to their original account, the dorsal stream which runs from
the striate cortex to the posterior parietal cortex is involved in the perception of movement and spatial location (i.e. Where is it?), while the ventral
stream which runs from the striate cortex to the inferotemporal region is
involved in the recognition of objects (i.e. What is it?). Since there appear
to be some functional similarities between the ventral and dorsal streams
and the underlying parvo- and magnocellular layers, Livingstone and Hubel
(1987) proposed that the visual system consisted of two independent and
parallel inputs that begin at the retina and remain segregated up to the
highest levels of the visual cortex. Merigan and Maunsell (1993) critically
examined some of the evidence which was claimed to support the notion
of parallel processing and indicated that there appears to be far more
integration between the main pathways than has hitherto been acknowledged. It appears that the dorsal stream, although largely magnocellular
in origin, also contains a significant, if small, parvocellular input, whilst
the ventral stream receives as much input from the magno- as the parvocellular system. Moreover, Goodale (1993) suggests that the dorsal stream
receives inputs from the superior colliculus as well as the LGN. The superior colliculus is known to be intimately involved in the control of saccadic
eye movements (Sparks and Mayes 1990) and in the coordination of eye,
head and postural movements (Kandel, Schwartz and Jessell 1991). This
viewpoint on the extensive integration of pathways is shared by Milner
and Goodale (1995), two researchers who have recently made a significant contribution to knowledge of the integrated action of perceptual and
visuomotor systems.

Perception-in-action

In several very important papers for students of visuomotor control, Goodale and Milner have proposed a rather different account of the functional significance of the 'two visual systems' (see Goodale *et al.* 1991; Goodale and Milner 1992; Goodale and Servos 1996; Goodale 1993; Milner and Goodale 1993). In their recent book, Milner and Goodale (1995) provide evidence, mostly from studies which have examined the effects of brain damage on reaching and grasping in monkeys and humans, to argue that the dorsal and ventral streams subserve different visual functions. They suggest that the ventral stream is critical to the visual perception of objects while the dorsal root mediates the required sensorimotor transformations for visually guided actions directed at those objects. That is, the ventral stream permits the formation of perceptual and cognitive representations which embody the enduring characteristics of objects and their spatial relations with each other, whereas transformations carried out in the dorsal stream, which utilise the instantaneous and egocentric features of objects, mediate the control of visuomotor actions. Furthermore, they contend that neither stream works in isolation but they engage in extensive orchestration (see Figure 3.7). The extent of such interaction is clearly exemplified in the anatomical flow diagram of Figure 3.8. In sum, they propose that this distinction ('what' versus 'how') captures more appropriately the functional differences between the ventral and dorsal pathways rather than the distinction between object and spatial vision ('what' versus 'where').

For Milner and Goodale (1995), understanding the actual interactive processes, schematised in Figure 3.8, is one of the central concerns in modern neuroscience. The principal difference in Milner and Goodale's account is that the interplay of the dorsal and ventral streams subserves action (output) rather than interpretation (input). A basic summary of their version of the integrated action of perceptual and visuomotor systems contains the following:

- quasi-independence of two visual streams for processing perception and action;
- essential co-operation of dorsal and ventral streams as input to appropriately programmed and coordinated action;
- early transfer of 'high-level' information between the two streams;
- dorsal stream specialised for 'on-line' control of bodily movement relative to task object;
- ventral stream 'tags' (attends to/identifies/recognises) goal objects within visual array;
- a higher-level praxic (skilled action) system (according to Kimura (1993) possibly based in the left parietal lobe) which accesses the products of the ventral stream's processing, collates, and instructs the relevant visuomotor system for the task.

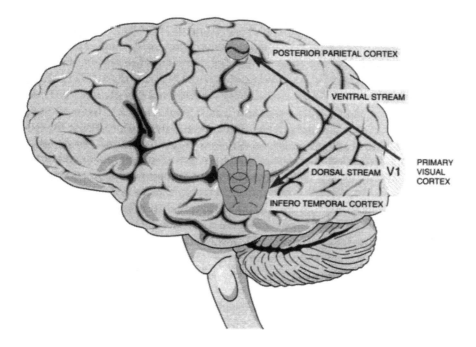

Figure 3.7 Two main streams of visual processing in the cortex. According to Milner and Goodale (1995), the ventral stream to the posterior parietal area plays a major role in object recognition and the dorsal stream to the inferotemporal region is involved with the 'on-line' control of goal-directed action as depicted by the object (baseball) and the catching action (ball–glove relationship). Despite the apparent independence of the two streams, coordinated action is dependent upon a higher degree of cooperation between the two pathways.

In view of the current debate between direct and indirect theories of perception (see Chapters 1 and 6), their arguments are certainly intuitively appealing since they suggest that visual information may be processed differently depending on the needs and intentions of the performer. When athletes are required to attach meaning and significance to objects and events in the world (e.g. recognition of a pattern of play in basketball or a specific information cue in sailing) the ventral root may predominate. That is, the ventral pathway is used to acquire knowledge about an object without necessarily implying that the object will be acted upon. In contrast, the dorsal root may be primarily employed during the visual control of goal-directed actions (e.g. reaching and grasping, catching). In such contexts, the visual control of action refers to the acquisition and use of sensory information in order to perform an action.

Finally, in a more applied vein, Trachtman and Kluka (1993) collated parallel information-processing research findings from several visuomotor

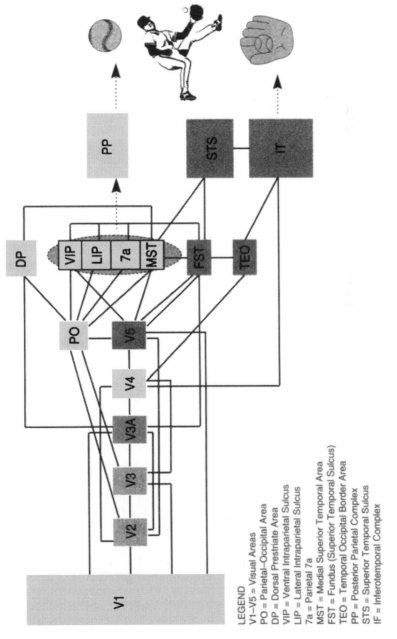

LEGEND
V1–V5 = Visual Areas
PO = Parietal–Occipital Area
DP = Dorsal Prestriate Area
VIP = Ventral Intraparietal Sulcus
LIP = Lateral Intraparietal Sulcus
7a = Parietal 7a
MST = Medial Superior Temporal Area
FST = Fundus (Superior Temporal Sulcus)
TEO = Temporal Occipital Border Area
PP = Posterior Parietal Complex
STS = Superior Temporal Sulcus
IF = Inferotemporal Complex

Figure 3.8 Simplified wiring diagram of interconnectivity of visual cortex pathways leading to the dorsal and ventral projections which subserve object identification and control of action. (Adapted from Milner, D.A. and Goodale, M.A. (1995) *The Visual Brain in Action*, Oxford: Oxford University Press.)

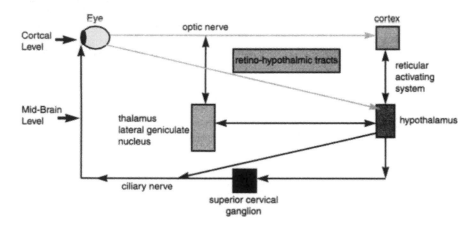

Figure 3.9 The inter-relationship between central and autonomic nervous system links in visual system processing. According to Trachtman and Kluka (1993), the parallel processing of visual information is facilitated by the numerous connections between retina, optic nerve, visual cortex and mid-brain centre all of which play an essential role in the regulation of movement. (Adapted from Trachtman, J.N. and Kluka, D.A. (1993) 'Future trends in vision as they relate to peak performance in sport', *International Journal of Sports Vision* 1–7).

behaviour areas to relate the sport functional characteristics of central vision (focal) and peripheral vision (ambient) to the known properties of the parvo- and magnocellular subsets of the visual system pathway; the 'seeing-to-perceiving' pathway represented in Figure 3.9. Table 3.3 summarises the relationship between sport-functional ability and visual system process.

Rather than limit their analysis to specific visual pathways, Trachtman and Kluka (1993) describe an extensive web of neurochemical relationships for vision within the whole nervous system. They speculate that, through the parvo and magno systems, 'accommodation' (i.e. change of focus via the ciliary muscles in order to view clearly near and far objects) is the link between cognitive and non-cognitive functions. Also, that autonomic nervous system control of accommodation facilitates links between central and peripheral processes. Trachtman and Kluka assert that outputs from the ciliary system which are required for accommodation go to both cortex and mid-brain centres which subserve central and peripheral vision. This connection enables the parallel processing necessary when both central and peripheral systems operate simultaneously, as they often do in sports action. The network of connections is depicted in Figure 3.9. Among the processes identified in the link between accommodation (controlled by the autonomic nervous system), and central and peripheral vision is a feedback loop between the retina and hypothalamus. Trachtman and Kluka

Table 3.3 Central and peripheral vision mechanisms relevant to sports action. (Adapted from Trachtman, J. N. and Kluka, D. A. (1993) 'Future Trends in Vision as they relate to Peak Performance in Sport', *International Journal of Sports Vision*, 1–7.)

Foveal (Focal) and Peripheral (Ambient) Vision Mechanisms and Visual Abilities	
Peripheral vision	ambient/magno
Reaction time	ambient/magno
The brightness of objects	focal/parvo
The clarity of objects	focal/parvo
The ability to focus on an object	both
The ability to shift focus from one object to another	focal/parvo
The ability to track an object	focal/parvo
The ability to fixate on an object in space	focal/parvo
The ability to locate an object in space – monocularly/binocularly	focal/parvo
The ability to concentrate visually with minimum tension	ambient/magno
The ability to concentrate visually without raising the thresholds of other senses	ambient/magno
The ability to coordinate vision with other senses	ambient/magno
The ability to coordinate vision with other ANS functions	ambient/magno
The ability to make texture judgements	focal/parvo
The ability to make fine depth judgements	focal/parvo
The ability to make gross depth judgements	ambient/magno

Focal and Ambient Characteristics

Focal vision	Ambient vision
conscious	subconscious
central 1–2 degrees	entire visual field
high spatial frequencies	low spatial frequencies
identification (what is it?)	localisation (where is it?)
body and photoreceptor	body and spatial orientation
gross movement control	fine movement control
bright light	dim light

Characteristics of the Magnocellular and Parvocellular Systems

Magno	Parvo
peripheral	central
noncognitive	cognitive
depth	texture
movement	shape
colour deficient	colour sensitivity
low luminance	high luminance
large receptive fields	small receptive fields
high contrast sensitivity	low contrast sensitivity
low spatial frequencies	high spatial frequencies
respond faster	respond slower
transient response	sustained response

(1993) contend that fibres within three distinct retinohypothalamus tracts supply different types of visual information to three separate areas of the hypothalamus. Furthermore, they present research to suggest that covariations in size of visual field and reaction time can accompany alterations in sympathomimetic activity. Several examples are provided to explain how knowledge of these processes could be employed to improve performance in certain sports; for example, they suggest that relaxation of the accommodative system can expand the peripheral visual field, and that accommodation training can bring about changes in colour perception as well as an improvement in the foveal fixation of objects in space. The implications of these assertions for the effective use of vision in sport awaits further research.

VISUAL HARDWARE AND THE FUNCTIONAL DEMANDS OF SPORT

Sports players, journalists and fans frequently discuss and debate the reasons for the superior performance of successful players. This is particularly true of sports in which the object can move at very high velocity and has to be caught, stopped or controlled in some manner. Baseball, cricket, tennis, badminton, ice hockey and pelota are some of the ball games which provide rich examples of such action. Not surprisingly, sports 'experts' refer to players having 'a great eye', 'superb vision', 'excellent peripheral vision'. Such statements imply superior visual hardware and probably provided the impetus for sports vision research, which has a fairly lengthy history.

The earliest, and perhaps most famous, professional articles are those connected with vision and performance in baseball (Abel 1924; Fullerton 1925). Fullerton (1925) reported on the visual performance of the famous player Babe Ruth, who was assessed at Columbia University in New York using tachistoscopic presentations and flash cards. Ruth's eyesight was said to be 12% 'faster' than an ordinary person and the reason for his exceptional hitting ability. Since then research has focused on three major issues, namely, to confirm the propositions: that athletes have superior visual abilities compared with non-athletes; that athletes possess superior visual abilities compared with ordinary athletes; and that selected visual abilities can be enhanced with training which, in turn, would bring about an improvement in athletic performance. These propositions are still alive and research continues, but the precise role played by vision in sport remains controversial.

An overview of the research perspective relating to vision in sport can be gathered by referring to Cockerill and MacGillivary (1981), Hitzeman and Beckerman (1993), Sherman (1980) and Loran and MacEwen (1995). However, the outstanding impression gained from these writings and various reports of research is the huge void between meticulous fundamental research into the elaborate substrate of the visual system itself and the complexity of the sports environment in which such a system actually functions. Furthermore, much of the research which has investigated hardware issues has been ill-conceived, poorly designed and piecemeal. Experimental studies involving careful manipulation of sport-specific vision variables are rare. As indicated, individual difference studies predominate and many of these have sought to compare rather generically defined groups of subjects, whereas the visual demands within sport can range from minimal through to close to the edge of supposed operational capability.

Although the 'hardware' versus 'software' dichotomy is somewhat arbitrary, it could be argued that *clarity of vision* lies predominantly in the hardware domain. That is, hardware factors relate most to the reception (i.e. sensation) of visual information, whereas software factors play a more dominant role in subsequent perception (Abernethy 1987b). Plainly, the purpose of much of the human visual anatomy exists to enable humans to see clearly so that they can gather the information necessary for taking appropriate courses of action. In the following section, we examine the relationship between visual function and the demands of the specific sports context. In essence, this is the major issue for that body of sports vision research which inclines towards a hardware account of performance.

Sport-specific visual acuity

Visual acuity refers to the clarity with which the eyes can discern detail in the optic array (Blundell 1984). Within the sporting environment, the optic array and the performer within it may be relatively static, as in the case of the rifle shooter lying prone some distance from a concentric circle target. Alternatively, the circumstances may be dynamic as when a football quarterback is being rushed by the opposing defence and is seeking to pass to receivers who are running various routes downfield. Furthermore, virtually everything in sport occurs in a three-dimensional layout. Two-dimensional situations are virtually non-existent. The rifle shooting example in which telescopic optical devices are used to zoom to the target is perhaps alone in this respect. Whilst it is clear that the efficient extraction of essential information from the optic array facilitates effective action, the requirement for high order acuity varies greatly both within and between sports (see Gardner and Sherman 1995).

Static visual acuity (SVA)

Most of the studies undertaken and the principal issues on this topic are covered in reviews by Blundell (1985), Hitzeman and Bekerman (1993) and Sanderson (1981). Typically, the research findings are equivocal concerning individual differences in athletic status and trainability. For example, Blundell (1982) tested the SVA of championship, intermediate and novice tennis players using the Snellen Eye Chart. Results showed that championship players were superior to the beginners, but not the intermediates. In contrast, Sherman (1980) found that 15% of players in the NFL and 20% of players in the NBA had poorer than average acuity. Similarly, a major survey at a recent Winter Olympic Games by the optical manufacturing company Baush and Lomb showed that 12.5% of athletes had below average SVA (Loran and MacEwen 1995).

Examination of the extant research reveals serious validity issues. A prominent shortcoming is that relatively few instances in sport logically correspond with the clinical or laboratory assessment techniques that have been used to determine static visual acuity (see Planer 1994). Whilst extrapolation from such rudimentary measurement of vision processes may be plausible, one is hard-pressed to believe in a relationship between performance on a static lettered chart and the dynamic three-dimensional layout of the sports environment. Even in relatively stable environmental circumstances, such as penalty shooting in soccer, field hockey or basketball, the optic array is far more detailed.

This viewpoint gains some support from a recent study by Applegate and Applegate (1992), who examined the effects of varied static visual acuity on basketball foul-shooting performance in male subjects aged 12–17 years. They reported no significant decrement in performance when wearing positive spherical lenses which produced the effect of systematically blurring both ring and backboard from 6/6 to 6/75 acuity. In a camera simulation of the array shown in the manuscript, the deteriorated display of the target is hardly discernible. Absolutely clear vision is apparently not a critical issue at this level of performance for this type of skill. This point is supported by an anecdote from the outstanding player, Michael Jordan. He is reported to occasionally shoot foul shots with his eyes closed during competitive play and comment to 'rookie' players, 'Welcome to the NBA!' In what might be termed a 'performer-static'–'environment-static' context which is rather rare in sport, visual acuity demand will depend on the precision requirements of the task. Thus, the rifle marksman requires high resolution of target whereas the vision requirements for the rugby goal-kicker are much less stringent.

Dynamic visual acuity (DVA)

In a great many everyday tasks, and virtually all sports, there is relative motion between the person and the visual scene. That is, either the person or the object(s) of interest is moving, and, frequently, both are moving at the same time. Such circumstances regularly demand that a performer be able to resolve detail in dynamic situations. This ability is referred to as dynamic visual acuity (DVA) (Miller and Ludvigh 1962). As early fundamental research amply demonstrates, DVA is not a straightforward derivative of static acuity (Barmack 1970). Naturally, more complex environmental circumstances such as those found in many sports demand the engagement and coordination of visual subsystems to realise the goal of acuity. As Sanderson (1981) points out, dynamic visual acuity is initially dependent upon the effectiveness of combinations of eye movements to 'catch' and foveally register the mobile event so that target detail can be resolved. Hoffman, Rouse and Ryan (1980) indicated that DVA testing is a generic, composite evaluation of a person's ability to release fixation from one target to another, perform accurate saccadic movements and accurate tracking movements, and maintain fixation on an object. Also, the individual must be peripherally aware of a target, its movement and location. Added to this, perceptual capabilities are necessary: namely, figure-ground discrimination, form discrimination, visual closure, visual memory and, possibly, visualisation. As Sanderson (1981) comments, early DVA assessment (e.g. see Burg 1966) placed emphasis on identification of target position rather than discrimination of object detail (i.e. efficiency of the oculomotor mechanism as opposed to acuity per se). However, the apparatus used for testing DVA in more recent studies apparently improves the validity of the method (e.g. see Long and Riggs 1991; Solomon, Zinn and Vacroux 1988).

Fundamental research has demonstrated only a modest correlation between static and dynamic acuity which diminishes considerably with increases in target velocity (Morrison 1980). Because of the inherently dynamic nature of many sports, vision researchers have argued that DVA rather than SVA is the more pertinent performance attribute and have studied its role using a variety of paradigms. Much of this work builds on studies carried out in connection with driving and flying skills (e.g. see DeKlerk, Eernst and Hoogerheide 1964; Miller and Ludvigh 1964). An excellent perspective on this topic in the context of sport is provided by Sanderson (1981).

The main thrust of research has been to differentiate criterion groups of sports players. Unfortunately, researchers have often elected to study sports in which the demand for high-level dynamic visual efficiency is rarely necessary. For the most part, the development of research hypotheses have not been well argued and may be the reason for contradictory and confusing results. For example, Beals *et al.* (1971) reported a relatively high and significant correlation (r = 0.76) between basketball field shooting accuracy and DVA, yet Morris and Kreighbaum (1977) found no differences between the DVA scores of high and low ability women volleyball and basketball players. Starkes (1987) found no significant DVA differences in a comparative study of national, varsity and novice field-hockey players. Plainly, many of the comparisons and relationships sought in such studies are far too generic; specialised positional play often engenders specific visuomotor skills. When the visual demands of the sports in question are considered in detail, it is clear that sometimes dynamic visual competence is crucial to successful performance and often it is non-critical.

In a logical, well-reasoned and soundly designed series of experiments, Sanderson and Whiting (1978) and Whiting and Sanderson (1974) examined the relationship of DVA to the performance of adults in one-handed catching (a skill for which DVA is viewed as an important requirement). In their procedure, subjects were instructed to catch a tennis ball projected directly at them from a machine at an average velocity of 10 ms^{-1} on a consistent trajectory arriving at shoulder height. The experiment comprised a variety of conditions which limited the catcher's view of the ball's trajectory.

The researchers reasoned that competence in DVA, as demonstrated by subjects' accuracy in reporting the *position* of a gap in a circular target (Landolt Ring), which moved at various angular velocities across their visual field, would correlate positively with catching performance. The results of several studies provided support for the prediction. That is, DVA and catching competence were related under the majority of treatment combinations and, most frequently, at the highest angular velocity.

The most consistent observation from DVA research is that acuity performance deteriorates with increase in target object velocity. This has important ramifications for those who participate in sports in which the object, be it puck, ball, shuttlecock or clay-pigeon, can move at high velocity. In their work with aircraft pilots, Miller and Ludvigh (1962) distinguished between 'velocity-resistant' and 'velocity-susceptible' individuals. The former group were said to show relatively slow decrement in target discriminability with progressive increases in an object's angular velocity relative to the latter group. Elaborating on this notion, Sanderson (1981) suggested that susceptibility to object velocity could be a potent source of individual differences in high-speed ball game performance and proposed that good ball game players would be 'velocity-resistant' (see Figure 3.10).

Discussing earlier empirical work (Whiting and Sanderson 1974; Sanderson and Whiting 1978) which was not specifically designed to test the 'velocity-resistance' hypothesis, Sanderson (1981) contended that these studies provide general support for the assertion that good ball-catchers are velocity-resistant. The reason for this is difficult to articulate, but he advances the view that the underlying reason for velocity-resistance may well be the capacity to maintain information processing under less than optimal conditions, notably, the motion of an object on the retina. It seems surprising that the notion of 'velocity susceptibility' in relation to performance in high-speed ball games has not attracted further attention from researchers.

If DVA is such a vital component in high-speed sports, the question arises as to whether performance results from some genetic endowment in hardware or if adaptations in performance can be achieved through practice. Early research with aviators suggested that practice was only

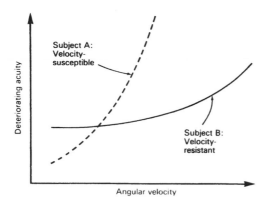

Figure 3.10 Individual differences in dynamic visual acuity as hypothesised by Sanderson (1981). Note that performance at low angular velocities may not be predictive of susceptibility or resistance at higher angular velocities. (Source: Sanderson, F.H. (1981) 'Visual acuity and sports performance', in M. Cockerill and W.W. MacGillivary (eds) *Vision and Sport*, Cheltenham: Stanley Thornes.)

beneficial for those with high initial ability (Miller and Ludvigh 1957, 1964). Despite numerous anecdotal reports, well-conducted research into the trainability of DVA in relation to sports action is virtually non-existent.

Although sports action has not necessarily been the primary interest of the investigators, some meticulous recent research has been undertaken into normative functions for DVA (Long and Penn 1987) as well as age-related changes (Long and Crambert 1990). Also, basing their premise on the observation that earlier null findings for DVA trainability resulted from highly selective subjects, Long and Rourke (1989) have reported a highly significant training effect. Furthermore, the most marked improvement in DVA performance was for those subjects with initially poorer performance – a result which was diametrically opposite to earlier work.

Conventional assessment of DVA requires that a subject's head is fixed or in some way restrained from moving during the data collection procedure. Because such constraints are rare in 'real' sport, applied vision researchers are sceptical of the practical value of such data even though stillness of the head relative to the torso is a well-emphasised coaching point in many high-speed ball games. Long and Riggs (1991) responded to this criticism and examined DVA training effects with free-head viewing in a sample of college students which included a sub-group of college athletes. The athletes included baseball, ice hockey, tennis and soccer players who were selected on the premise that those activities possessed a greater requirement for DVA compared with swimming and track events. The findings were virtually the same as those of an earlier study involving fixed-head viewing. That is, DVA performance improved significantly following a modest period of training. Those subjects with the lowest DVA scores initially improved most. No significant differences were found between athletes and non-athletes. This latter finding suggests athletes can benefit from DVA training although, as the authors emphasise, the exact relationship of DVA performance to specific sports action has yet to be elucidated.

Despite the logical importance of DVA to sports players, there have been fewer studies than might be expected as well as a diminution in published work during the past twenty years. The Committee on Vision of the National Research Council (1985), perhaps aiming its comments at automobile driving, cited DVA as a visual measure that exhibits considerable promise as an emergent technique for assessing a component of visual performance that has been generally overlooked by traditional tests. Also, in a more recent review which directly addresses sports vision issues, Hitzeman and Beckerman (1993) assert that DVA is an area of sports vision that deserves more study. It is rather bewildering that so few sound research projects have been carried out in the area of DVA when sports and vision scientists agree on the importance of this dimension. Pioneer researchers such as Burg, Ludvigh and Miller realised its importance and prepared the ground over thirty years ago, and their lead was taken and applied in the sports skill context in the early 1970s by John Whiting's inventive research group at the University of Leeds, England. Unfortunately, during the past twenty years, advances in knowledge about DVA in sports action has progressed very little, if at all.

Additional hardware issues

Up to now in this section, what has been termed 'sport-specific acuity' has been addressed as a composite issue. Recall that it was argued earlier that the problem for the sport and exercise scientist interested in the role of the visual hardware is essentially that of understanding the dynamic stereoacuity operation of the performer in particular sporting instances. Nonetheless, researchers have examined and reported upon some specific, and obviously related, topics. A selection of these are discussed below.

Contrast sensitivity function

A popular topic attracting much recent attention, though tackled some time ago by Brown (1972a, 1972b), is the study of contrast sensitivity function (CSF) which relates to the visual system's capacity to filter and process object and background information under varying conditions of illumination. CSF is measured in several ways, some of which require expensive instrumentation (see Kluka *et al.* 1995; Planer 1994). Several studies have reported that athletes from various sports in which the object often moves at high velocity (e.g. volleyball, softball, baseball) possess superior CSF compared to age-matched controls or non-athlete groups (see Hoffman *et al.* 1984; Kluka *et al.* 1995). Plainly, CSF is an integral element of dynamic stereoacuity in sport actions. However, criticisms have been levelled at the reliability of the assessment process (see Hitzeman and Beckerman 1993). In addition, even the most sophisticated measuring instruments such as the Optec 2000 (for a description, see Kluka *et al.* 1995) assess CSF using static stimuli. It is debatable whether static performance can be extrapolated to the inherently dynamic playing environment found in many sports. Consequently, Kluka *et al.* (1995) have called for sport-specific research which addresses the issues of object velocity, object contact position and ambient lighting variability.

Stereodepth/stereomotion

Stereodepth refers to the ability to distinguish binocularly the relative depth of objects in the optic array, the extent to which one object appears to be nearer than the other (Ogle 1964). This capacity, which includes the highly sport-relevant stereomotion, has been studied intensively from a fundamental processes perspective (see Poggio and Poggio 1984; Regan *et al.* 1986; Regan, Frisby, Poggion, Schor and Tyler 1990). This work has revealed a separate binocular processing system for 'motion-in-depth' detectors as distinct from static-depth detectors. Furthermore, separate visual pathways have been defined for movement of objects both away from and towards subjects as well as sensitive and 'blind' retinal locations for motion-in-depth processing. These findings articulate with the parallel-processing evidence from neurophysiology introduced earlier in the chapter and, from a practical standpoint, the notion of 'velocity resistant' versus 'velocity susceptible' individual differences discussed in connection with DVA performance. Perhaps superior fast ball-game athletes (e.g. batters, returners-of-serve, goal-tenders) possess higher capacity motion-in-depth detectors?

A number of sport-specific studies have been undertaken to compare criterion groups on their stereodepth perception ability (usually 'athlete' versus 'non-athletes'). Although the expectation in such studies was that the athletes would exhibit superior depth perception, the findings have typically been equivocal. For example, Miller (1960) tested 162 subjects from five sports (volleyball, basketball, fencing, swimming and gymnastics). Expert and intermediate performers demonstrated superior depth perception compared to a group of novice subjects, whilst there were no differences between the expert and intermediate groups. Similarly, Blundell (1984) found significant differences in depth perception between championship tennis players and both intermediate and beginner groups. However, Isaccs (1981) was unable to show any relationship between depth perception and basketball shooting performance.

Cockerill and Callington (1981) provide a summary and critical review of this research, the main thrust of which still applies at the present time. The major thrust of their critique relates to the validity of the assessment of binocular depth perception as judged by the criterion put forward by Miller (1960). Miller (1960) suggested that the most reliable indication of a person's depth perception in a given situation is by assessment in that situation, or on a test in which the situation is closely approximated. In the numerous studies reviewed by Cockerill and Callington (1981), laboratory or clinical evaluations (see Planer 1994) were used to measure stereoacuity in manner which, at best, seems only vaguely related to the context of sports action. For example, the most frequently adopted procedure, the Howard–Dolman test, requires subjects to align two vertical rods in an illuminated box. Distance (error) between the rods is taken to be representative of depth perception. Reflection on the dynamic relationships of objects and persons in most sporting environments would lead the majority of people to conclude that such an assessment has questionable validity. Clearly, sport is not a pastime that involves aligning two vertical rods at a point in space, rather it is an environment where perception and estimation of depth are constantly changing with the rapid movements of players and objects. Moreover, the Howard–Dolman apparatus is purported to measure stereopsis (i.e. the ability to perceive depth on the basis of retinal disparity); however, the subject is not limited to binocular cues since it is possible to use monocular cues such as motion parallax and gradient cues from the illuminated box material (Starkes and Deakin 1984). It appears, therefore, that this test is not a strict measure of stereodepth, but rather requires subjects to employ a combination of monocular and binocular depth perception cues. In many ways this may actually provide a more realistic representation of depth perception in sport since performers typically employ several information cues when perceiving depth. This may particularly be the case over longer distances (i.e. greater than optical infinity, approximately 6 m) where the use of binocular cues such as retinal disparity is likely to be minimal (Whiting 1969). In these instances, performers are likely to rely on a number of other monocular and binocular cues to perceive depth.

Concerns about the validity of stereodepth perception measures have been expressed by Hitzeman and Beckerman (1993). Although a test called the 'dynamic stereopter' has been developed using baseball batters as subjects (see Solomon *et al.* 1988; Zinn and Solomon 1985), the velocity of the moving object employed in this procedure (i.e. circular targets moving at 1 mph) contrasts starkly with a 140-kph fastball pitch. Further developments in instrumentation and research are awaited with interest.

Peripheral vision (field of view)

Enthusiasts, coaches and players describing the performance qualities required in sport frequently refer to the importance of peripheral vision in team games such as soccer, basketball and ice hockey. Peripheral vision refers to the ability to detect and react to stimuli outside of foveal vision. In an earlier section of this chapter, we showed that the foveal region which is responsible for detailed visual acuity accounts for only 1–2 degrees of arc or about 1% of the total surface of the retina in both horizontal and vertical planes. Also, recall that there is a sharp decrement in acuity as the stimulus moves away from the fovea with resolution reduced to 50% at 2.5 degrees of arc and to 4% at the extreme periphery. If the sports player wishes to foveate an object or event, the usual sequence is that the eyes are stabilised within the head, then, the head moves to fixate the object or scene. As described earlier, humans have developed a complex and relatively proficient repertoire of eye movements to keep pace with environmental events. However, a common occurrence during games play is for the performer's foveal vision to be occupied whilst events happen simultaneously in the periphery. For example, recent research has indicated that in time-constrained situations (e.g. 3 vs 3 situation on the edge of the penalty area) skilled soccer players fixate the ball in foveal vision while using peripheral vision to monitor the positions of team-mates and opponents in the periphery (Williams and Davids 1997). Similarly, in karate kumite and kickboxing performers appear to fixate central regions of the display (i.e. head, chest) whilst using peripheral vision to pick up information from outlying areas (i.e. arm and leg) regarding the initiation of their opponent's attack (Williams and Elliott 1997; Ripoll et al. 1995). Thus, the operational characteristics of peripheral vision become important in dynamic sport contexts. Sports and vision scientists have addressed such questions as, 'How important is peripheral vision?', 'What are its roles?' and 'How effective is it?'

With respect to the first question, research suggests that peripheral vision provides the performer with both exteroceptive (information regarding external events) and proprioceptive (information with regard to the orientation of the body) information. In Chapter 5, we provide a detailed overview of the role of peripheral vision in the visual search process. This research indicates that performers can use peripheral vision to extract information from the display as well as to determine the next fixation location. Furthermore, research indicates that peripheral vision provides the performer with information regarding body and spatial orientation (i.e. visual proprioception). For example, Sivak and Mackenzie (1992) describe the relative contributions of central and peripheral processes to the performance of fundamental motor actions such as pointing, reaching and grasping. They cite various experimental studies which have manipulated the extent to which peripheral vision could be used during reaching and grasping to assert that central vision is specialised for responding to the spatial pattern of the object whereas peripheral vision deals with response to location and movement. Similarly, the importance of peripheral vision in providing proprioceptive information has been demonstrated by those studies which have highlighted a decrement in performance when the peripheral vision of an effector is occluded. For example, studies by Smyth and Marriott (1982), Fischman and Schneider (1985) and Barfield and Fishman (1991) indicate that visual proprioception of the intercepting limb is important during tasks such as ball catching and controlling a ball in soccer (see also Chapter 8).

However, it is important to distinguish between the terms 'field of view' and 'visual field'. Field of view or stimulus field refers to the maximum visual arc or angle at which subjects can detect a stimulus presented in the visual periphery (Smythies 1996). This measure is normally recorded using a test such as the Hamblin Perimeter. This apparatus requires subjects to detect a stimulus light(s) positioned at various points within the field of view, whilst maintaining fixation on a central reference point. Typically, subjects are able to detect a signal within a visual arc of 160 degrees vertically and 200 degrees horizontally (Harrington 1964). This measure is regarded as a structurally defined hardware component. In contrast, the visual field (or what has also been called the perceived field) relates to the exact range of peripheral awareness during sports performance (Smythies 1996). This is not fixed but varies largely according to the task the athletes are concurrently performing in central vision (the so-called 'foveal load'), and the level of stress, fatigue or arousal the performer is experiencing. The perceived visual field, which is likely to be dependent at least in part on more cognitive or software factors, is typically assessed using dual-task paradigms (see Chapter 2). In this section, we will restrict our discussion to the research which has examined skill-based differences in the field of view.

As with most topics within the sports vision area, there is a severe shortfall in information on the field of view and its role in sports performance. Nonetheless, researchers pursuing answers allied to the other two questions posed above, have carried out studies with an 'applied' focus. A particular interest has been the general proposition that 'athletes' possess a larger field of view when compared with 'non-athletes'. Although there have been few studies which have explored this comparison, the weight of evidence provides some tentative support for the proposition of athlete superiority in this context. For example, Stroup (1957) found a relationship between field of view and basketball performance. Similarly, Williams and Thirer (1975) found significant differences between a mixture of American football players, fencers and players of various racket sports (athletes) and non-athletes in assessments of field of view in both the horizontal and vertical meridian. Also, Blundell (1982) obtained some interesting findings when examining the peripheral sensitivity of championship, intermediate and novice tennis players to the colours red, white, blue, yellow and green. Results showed that championship players had significantly broader field of view than the other two groups for the colours white and yellow only. He concluded that skilled performance in tennis necessitates the development, or pre-existence, of superior peripheral vision. This extended field of view for the colours white and yellow could allow championship players to more effectively monitor the position of their opponent on court thus enabling them to judge passing shots accordingly.

More broadly, in sports which are dynamic and involve rapidly moving information sources where peripheral visual awareness is patently necessary (e.g. team ball games), an interesting question is whether peripheral visual competence is position specific. This derives from the notion that players who perform certain roles such as the central midfield player in soccer or a 'pivot' in basketball are compelled to use peripheral vision more effectively than those whose position demands that they spend less time facing the whole playing area. Cockerill (1981) tested this proposition by comparing the right and left horizontal field of view of field hockey players who played in left wing, central and right wing positions. There were no differences between the criterion groups and several lines of argument were marshalled to explain why this should be the case. Much of the reasoning for the non-significant findings was weak. For example, it was stated that the subjects fell within a relatively narrow age band which limited the opportunity for differences (peripheral vision has been shown to be subject to an age effect). Another suggestion was that no subject held particular advantage over another because none had received specific peripheral visual training or experience. However, one plausible argument for the null findings relates to research by Low (1943, 1946) which suggests that peripheral vision is subject to practice and training effects. Cockerill's subjects were tested in the off-season; thus, any differences attributable to positional play or advantage relative to non-athletes may possibly have receded. The effects of training and practice on peripheral vision has received scant attention from sports vision researchers, but would be a topic worth revisiting.

Although some studies have been successful in identifying differences, an almost equal number have indicated no differences in field of view between skilled and less-skilled performers (see Cockerill 1981; Williams and Horn 1995). This general lack of consensus may be related to the method employed to measure peripheral visual function and to our earlier distinction between field of view and visual field. That is, it may be that the experts do not necessarily possess larger field of views (i.e. visual hardware), but rather they possess larger visual fields which they are able to employ more effectively during performance. A good deal more experimental research is required to clarify this distinction and the functional relationship between these two components of peripheral vision.

SUMMARY AND FUTURE DIRECTIONS

This chapter attempted to outline the structure and physical characteristics of the visual system from the retina of the eye to the visual cortex and beyond. Initially, we showed how light enters the eye via the various sensory receptors located in the retina. We highlighted the physical and functional characteristics of cone receptors (primarily located around the fovea) which are responsible for high acuity, colour vision and rod receptors (primarily located in the periphery) that are sensitive to light and motion. Thereafter, we traced the transmission of neural signals from the retina via the retina-geniculate-striate pathway into the primary visual cortex. It was shown that this pathway from retina to visual cortex can be differentiated into two specialised 'lanes' of processing referred to as 'magnocellular' and 'parvocellular' projections. Parvocellular layers are designed for high spatial acuity and colour-sensitivity, whilst magnocellular neurons are contrast- and colour-sensitive and responsive to motion detection. It was originally thought that these two subdivisions represented specialised functional streams of information that remained separated up to and beyond the primary visual cortex. The proposal was that the magnocellular pathway protracted from the primary visual cortex to the posterior parietal cortex (ventral stream) and was involved in the perception of movement and spatial location, while the parvocellular pathway extended from the primary visual cortex via the dorsal stream to the inferotemporal cortex and was involved in the recognition of objects. However, recent work by Milner and Goodale (e.g. 1995) indicates that there is far more integration between these pathways than originally suggested. They argue that the ventral stream may be critical to visual perception of objects, whilst the dorsal root mediates the required sensorimotor transformations for visually guided actions directed at those objects. The argument is that this distinction ('what' versus 'how') captures more appropriately the functional differences between the two pathways rather than the original distinction between object and spatial vision ('what' versus 'where').

In the second half of the chapter, we examined the relationship between visual function and the demands of the specific sports context. In particular, we examined whether skilled performers are characterised by superior visual hardware and whether visual function can be improved through visual training programmes. Some of the visual abilities discussed included static and dynamic visual acuity, contrast sensitivity, depth perception and peripheral vision. It appears that the research evidence is fairly equivocal, suggesting that skilled performers do not necessarily possess superior visual hardware compared with their less skilled counterparts. Certainly, it is apparent that no single oculomotor parameter adequately accounts for expert–novice differences in visual perception. However, much of the research has been poorly designed and lacks applicability to the complex sports environment in which the visual system actually functions. Future research should attempt to develop better designed and controlled studies which employ more accurate and realistic measurement techniques. For example, recent technological advances in instrumentation such as the sensitive devices used by Kluka *et al.* (1995) in the study of contrast sensitivity function and Trachtman (1995) in the analysis of accommodative microfluctuation, when used in conjunction with sound research design, offer much promise. Also, since sport is typically performed under temporal constraints and varying levels of physiological stress, attempts should be made to examine visual function under more realistic test conditions. It may be that skilled performers do not possess superior visual hardware under sterile laboratory conditions, but that expert–novice differences may arise when speed as well as accuracy of response is measured and/or when visual function is tested under varying levels of physiological fatigue (e.g. see Williams and Horn 1995).

Finally, we were left with the issue of the extent to which visual performance of various kinds can be modified by experience and/or specific visual enhancement training. This area has recently attracted significant interest from sports vision specialists. Their argument is that inefficient or inconsistent visual abilities can be improved through specific visual training programmes (e.g. Coffey and Reichbow 1995). However, although there have been a few promising studies (e.g. Kluka *et al.* 1996; Long and Riggs 1991; Worrell 1996), the problem for sports vision specialists is that there is typically a lack of empirical evidence to support their ideas. There is hardly any evidence to show that visual training does improve visual function and, more importantly, there is no evidence to suggest that the improvements which may be observed on clinical tests transfer to an improvement in performance on the sports field. Until the validity of these visual enhancement programmes are endorsed through empirical rather than anecdotal evidence, sports optometrists and vision scientists should be cautious about venturing beyond the provision of visual performance screening and vision correction services.

4 Anticipation and decision-making in sport

INTRODUCTION

During the last two decades there has been a significant increase in the amount of research examining skill-based differences in anticipation and decision-making in sport. Early research compared skilled and less skilled athletes on a myriad of sensory and information processing abilities such as reaction time, visual acuity, depth perception, colour vision and peripheral field of view (e.g. Blundell 1985; Cockerill and Callington 1981; Isaacs 1981). In Chapter 3, we concluded that although the relationship between these 'hardware' properties and sport skill may be intuitively appealing, the evidence supporting such a link is rather tentative. Moreover, in Chapter 1 we indicated that cognitive psychologists consider that anticipation and decision-making are mediated by knowledge structures stored in memory. The suggestion is that expert sports performers possess a more elaborate task-specific knowledge base than novices. This premise appears to have been supported by research which has examined expert–novice differences along more cognitive or 'software' dimensions. Experts have been found to differ from non-experts in the amount and type of knowledge they possess and in the way that this information is used in anticipation and decision-making. From a motor behaviour perspective, research adopting this more cognitive focus has addressed questions such as: Do experts encode and retrieve game-structured information more effectively than novices? Are skilled athletes able to detect and locate objects within the visual field faster and more accurately than less skilled performers? Are experts able to make better use of contextual information in anticipating future actions? Are experts able to make effective use of situational probabilities within the anticipation process? Do skilled athletes make faster and more accurate decisions? How do performers make decisions in sport? How do these skills emerge as a function of practice or experience?

This chapter reviews the research examining skill-based differences in anticipation and decision-making in sport. In the first instance, we focus on anticipation and skilled sports performance. We begin by reviewing evidence to suggest that skilled performers are able to encode and retrieve sport-specific information more successfully than their less skilled counterparts. It is suggested that this ability enables them to recognise and recall patterns of play more effectively, thus enhancing anticipation. Next, research is presented which demonstrates that experts are able to detect and locate objects of relevance within the visual field more quickly than novice performers. The argument is that this ability enables them to quickly locate important objects such as the ball from background distractions, thus reducing response time. We continue by reviewing the research examining advance cue utilisation in sport. It appears that skilled performers are able to use contextual information available prior to the event to facilitate anticipation. Also, we examine the importance of situational probabilities or 'expectations' in the anticipation process. In the second half of the chapter, we present evidence to show that skilled performers have better decision-making skills than their less skilled counterparts. Research suggests that the expert's superior decision-making is due to an enhanced cognitive knowledge developed through performing in sport rather than a by-product of experience or skilled observation. Clear differences are demonstrated in the nature of the knowledge bases available to experts and novices. Since the emphasis throughout this chapter is on expert–novice differences, a theoretical framework is then provided for understanding the nature of expertise in sport by drawing upon production systems models of cognition and more recent neural network models. Finally, some directions for future research work are highlighted. We begin, however, by examining some of the key issues involved in anticipation.

ENCODING AND RETRIEVAL OF SPORT-SPECIFIC INFORMATION

The ability to encode and retrieve task-specific information is assumed to be an important component of anticipation in sport. Encoding refers to how information is transferred into a form that can be stored in memory, whereas retrieval refers to the way information in memory is accessed in order to respond to the task in hand (Eysenck and Keane 1995). The ability to encode and retrieve sport-specific information has been examined through paradigms imported directly from the study of expertise in cognitive psychology. The two most commonly used approaches are the recall and recognition paradigms.

Recall paradigm

The seminal work in cognitive psychology was carried out by de Groot (1965) using skilled chess players. When chess masters were shown a game configuration for intervals of 5 to 10 seconds, they were able to recall the position of chess pieces almost perfectly from memory. In contrast, this ability dropped off very rapidly below the master level, from a recall accuracy of 93% to a value of 51% for club players. Comparable results where obtained by Chase and Simon (1973a, 1973b) who included a control condition where chess pieces were arranged randomly on the board rather than in a structured fashion. In this condition, there were no differences between a Grand Master, A level and Club player. This finding demonstrated that the expert's superior recall on the structured chess stimuli could not be attributed to hardware differences in visual short term memory capacity (see Frey and Adesman 1976). Chase and Simon (1973a) concluded that chess masters' superior recall was due to a more advanced task-specific knowledge base and more rapid and efficient retrieval of this information from memory. The interaction between skill and stimulus information has since been demonstrated in numerous other domains (see Gilhooley and Green 1989).

In sport, the recall paradigm has typically been used to examine whether expert athletes exhibit the same cognitive advantage demonstrated by experts in other domains. Subjects have typically been shown a static film-slide of a particular action sequence for a very short period of time. Immediately after, they have been required to recall as accurately as possible the positions of each player viewed on the slide. Recall performance has then been determined by the degree of correspondence between the presented and the reconstructed player positions. The initial research was conducted by Allard and colleagues at the University of Waterloo (e.g. Allard 1982; Allard and Burnett 1985; Allard, Graham and Paarsalu 1980). Allard *et al.* (1980) compared groups of basketball players and non-players on a task which required subjects to recall the position of attacking and defensive players from a 4-second view of a schematic slide. These slides included structured (i.e. attacking patterns of play) and unstructured (i.e. time-outs or turnover situations) game conditions in basketball. Subjects were required to place response magnets on a magnetic scaled representation of a basketball court to represent attacking and defensive players. The results supported the earlier findings of de Groot (1965) for master chess players, namely, that basketball players were superior to non-players in the recall of structured slides. Recall of unstructured information was similar for both groups. The differences in recall accuracy across groups are highlighted in Table 4.1.

The expert's ability to encode and recall structured information has since been demonstrated in American football (Garland and Barry 1990, 1991), ballet (Starkes, Deakin, Lindley and Crisp 1987), field hockey (Starkes and Deakin 1984; Starkes 1987), basketball (Millsagle 1988), gymnastics (Vickers 1988), rugby (Nakagawa 1982), snooker (Abernethy, Neal and Koning 1994a), figure skating (Deakin and Allard 1991), handball (Tenenbaum, Levy-Kolker, Bar-Eli and Weinberg 1994), volleyball (Bourgeaud and Abernethy 1987) and soccer (Williams, Davids, Burwitz

Table 4.1 Mean number of players recalled accurately per trial for basketball players and non-players for both structured and unstructured slides. (Source: Allard, F., Graham, S. and Paarsalu, M. L. (1980) 'Perception in sport: basketball', *Journal of Sport Psychology*, 2: 14–21.)

	Structured	*Unstructured*
Players	8.0	5.8
Non-players	5.3	6.5

and Williams 1993a; Williams and Davids 1995). The interpretation is that skilled perception is dependent on an enhanced sport-specific knowledge base which enables performers to encode and retrieve information more effectively from memory. This knowledge base enables them to recode the visual display into fewer, larger 'chunks' of information that can be more easily remembered and then decoded to reproduce the original pattern (Egan and Schwartz 1979; Ericsson and Chase 1982).

This 'chunking' hypothesis was supported by Allard and Burnett (1985) who presented basketball players and non-players with schematic diagrams of basketball situations. Subjects studied the diagrams for five seconds and then recalled as much of the play as they could using a coloured marker. Subsequent attempts were made using different colour markers to highlight the recall strategy adopted. It was assumed that information encoded within one 5-second view of the board would represent the size of each chunk of information stored by subjects. The results showed that the non-players required more views of the diagram (3.88 compared to 2.42) and accurately recalled fewer elements of information on each occasion (3.81 compared to 4.93 for the expert players). Findings showed that experts are able to take in more information in a single glance than less skilled players because their knowledge allows them to chunk or group information into larger and more meaningful units. Grouping the discrete stimuli in this manner can result in emergent features that are not evident if the stimuli are viewed in isolation. That is, their ability to chunk items (i.e. players' positions) into larger and more meaningful units (i.e. patterns of play) enables them to recognise a developing pattern of play early in its initiation, thus facilitating anticipation.

Recognition paradigm

The recognition paradigm was initially used by Charness (1976, 1979) to examine the incidental learning of game configurations in chess. In sport, subjects are presented with similar information to that used in the recall paradigm. Typically, half the slides or film sequences presented have already been viewed by the subject, whereas the remaining half have not been viewed previously. A performance score is determined by the accuracy with which the information presented earlier is recognised correctly.

The seminal sports-related work was conducted by Allard *et al.* (1980). In this study, subjects were presented with a series of 80 slides containing both structured and unstructured trials, and were required to recognise the slides which they had viewed in the earlier recall task. The results showed that skilled players were significantly more accurate than non-players in recognising structured slides only. It appears that skilled basketball players encode task-specific information to a deeper and more meaningful level, thus facilitating the recognition of particular patterns of play. Similar findings have been obtained in American football (Garland and Barry 1991) gymnastics (Imwold and Hoffman 1983), snooker (Abernethy *et al.* 1994a) and soccer (Williams *et al.* 1993a; Williams and Davids 1995).

The use of these recipient (Wilberg 1972) or imported (Bunge 1967) paradigms to examine skilled perception in sport has recently been criticised by several authors (e.g. see Williams *et al.* 1992; Abernethy, Thomas and Thomas 1993; Abernethy, Burgess-Limerick and Parks 1994b). Their first concern relates to the use of static filmslides to portray dynamic sport activity. The argument is that slides do not provide a realistic basis for examining perception in sport since motion may be an integral component of the pattern recognition process (c.f. Johansson 1973, 1975; Cutting 1978). This argument was supported by Bourgeaud and Abernethy (1987) who found that the experts' superior recall performance was only observed when slides were substituted by more realistic video presentation of volleyball action sequences. Also, these static action 'snapshots' do not provide a view of the game which is representative of the player's perspective during actual play. Typically, shots are taken from an elevated position looking down on the action (e.g. Millsagle 1988) or are schematic representations of play (e.g. Allard and Burnett 1985; Garland and Barry 1991; Salmoni 1989). Moreover, these paradigms only measure the accuracy of recognition and recall. The skilled games player must not only encode and retrieve information accurately, but must also perform in 'time pressure' situations. This makes it imperative that players are able to recall and recognise patterns of play quickly as well as accurately. Another issue is whether the experts' superior performance on these paradigms is a by-product of their greater task experience and familiarity rather than a direct cause of their task-specific expertise (Abernethy *et al.* 1993; Allard and Burnett 1985). Experts spend time reading and thinking about the game, watching others play, discussing the game with others and imagining themselves performing (see Mahoney and Avener 1977). The crucial issue is whether performance on these recall and recognition paradigms is actually related to skilled performance.

These concerns were recently addressed in a series of studies by Williams and colleagues (Williams *et al.* 1993a; Williams and Davids 1995). Williams *et al.* (1993a) presented subjects with dynamic and realistic soccer action sequences using a large (3 m^2) video projection screen. These action sequences were taken from professional and university soccer matches and were filmed from a position behind the goal in order to obtain a view most representative of a central-defensive player's position in the game. The structured trials contained offensive patterns of play ending with a shot at goal or a pass into the attacking third of the field, whereas the unstructured trials included sequences such as players walking on and off the field, teams warming up prior to a match, or a stoppage in play whilst an injured player received treatment. Following each 10-second action sequence, experienced and inexperienced soccer players were required to recall players' positions by entering a schematic representation of a player on a computer-generated image of a soccer field. This was considered a more sensitive measure of recall performance than used previously since error values were presented in computer screen pixels. Findings supported previous research with the inexperienced players having larger recall errors than the experienced players on the structured trials only.

Williams and Davids (1995) used the same procedure to examine recall performance in groups of soccer players who were matched on experience (e.g. number of competitive matches played, amount of training undertaken, degree of coaching they had been exposed to, and number of matches watched both 'live' and on television), but differed in their respective skill levels (i.e. amateur/recreational players compared with semi-professional players). The objective was to determine whether experts' superior recall performance is a by-product of experience or a characteristic of expertise (see Abernethy *et al.* 1993, 1994b; Allard 1993; Starkes 1993). A control group of physically disabled spectators was also tested to examine whether experienced 'watchers' with no experience of playing soccer exhibited a comparable soccer-specific knowledge base to experienced 'players'. The results, highlighted in Table 4.2, showed that the high-skill (semi-professional) group demonstrated superior recall performance compared with the low-skill (amateur) players on the structured trials only. Although there are reservations because of the difficulties involved in assessing the quality of practice that each group has undertaken (see Ericsson, Krampe and Tesch-Römer 1993; Ericsson 1996), the results suggest that the experienced players' superior performance on these cognitive tasks is a constituent of skill rather than a by-product of experience or exposure to the task. Experienced high and low-skill soccer players possessed a more extensive cognitive knowledge base than the experienced physically disabled spectators suggesting that experience of playing soccer promotes the acquisition and retention of soccer-specific declarative knowledge. Similar findings were obtained in a study examining the speed and accuracy of recognition of soccer action clips. Subjects were presented with 28 film clips (structured and unstructured), half of which were presented in the earlier recall study and half of which had not previously been viewed. Results showed that the high-skill group recognised previously viewed film clips

Table 4.2 Mean group performance scores for the experienced high-skill, experienced low-skill and physically disabled groups on the recall test. (Source: Williams, A.M. and Davids, K. (1995) 'Declarative knowledge in sport: a byproduct of experience or a characteristic of expertise?', *Journal of Sport and Exercise Psychology*, 17(3): 259–75.)

Group		Structured stimuli	Unstructured stimuli
Experienced High Skill (n = 12)	M	167.66	148.86
	SD	10.21	15.18
Experienced Low Skill (n = 12)	M	184.40	150.87
	SD	16.23	11.45
Physically Disabled Spectators (n = 12)	M	204.27	159.52
	SD	23.45	13.08

* Note: Values in screen pixels

faster and more accurately than the less skilled and physically disabled control groups. Finally, a regression analysis technique was employed to show that subjects' performance on a film-based anticipation test could be successfully predicted from their performance on the recall and recognition tests. Performance on the recall test had the highest standardised regression coefficient indicating that this variable was the strongest predictor of anticipatory performance. This finding confirms the hypothesis that the ability to recall structured patterns of play is an important component of anticipation in team games such as soccer and basketball (c.f. Allard *et al.* 1980; Williams *et al.* 1993).

SIGNAL DETECTION: SPEED OF DETECTING AND LOCATING OBJECTS OF RELEVANCE IN THE VISUAL FIELD

Sports such as cricket, baseball and volleyball require that subjects selectively attend and react to very basic information such as ball position. The signal detection approach is used to examine whether skilled performers are better at detecting the presence or absence of a particular object within a visual display. In this paradigm, subjects are presented with brief exposures to structured and unstructured sport-specific stimuli. Allard and Starkes (1980) required subjects to detect the presence of a volleyball in tachistoscopically presented slides of game and non-game situations. In the test, slides were presented for 16 ms and subjects were required to verbally indicate quickly and accurately whether or not a ball was present in the display. The purpose of this study was to confirm the earlier finding, using the recall paradigm in basketball, that skilled players are more sensitive to structured game information. In a series of five experiments, players were

Table 4.3 Mean detection accuracy (P(A)) and voice response time (VRT). (Source: Allard, F. and Starkes, J.L. (1980) 'Perception in sport: Volleyball', *Journal of Sport Psychology*, 2, 22–33.)

	P(A)		VRT (ms)	
	game	*non-game*	*game*	*non-game*
Players	0.877	0.878	917	928
Non-players	0.882	0.855	3007	3001

Note: P(A) is a response accuracy measure which is a non-parametric analog to d´.

found to respond much faster than the non-players to both game and non-game situations. No differences in response accuracy were found between groups. The results from one of these studies are highlighted in Table 4.3.

Expert volleyball players' superior performance on both structured and unstructured slides contradicted earlier research in basketball using the recall paradigm. The strategy adopted by volleyball players seemed to involve a rapid visual search for the ball while ignoring game structure or context. The suggestion is that search strategy may have been under 'target' rather than 'context' control (see Neisser 1967). Allard and Starkes (1980) suggested that fast ball sports such as volleyball, baseball, cricket and tennis require players to ignore much of the game structure present in the display and to concentrate instead on 'detecting' ball position. In contrast, invasive team games such as soccer, field hockey, rugby and basketball require skilled chunking. This 'fast visual search' versus 'structure analytically oriented' argument is intuitively appealing since sports differ considerably in their speed and complexity (Allard 1982). Support for this argument was provided by Starkes (1987) who replicated the Allard and Starkes (1980) study using national, varsity and novice field hockey players. The results showed no differences between the groups for perceptual accuracy or decision speed, suggesting that rapid visual search for the ball is not a major task constraint on skilled hockey players.

However, it is unlikely that sports can be classified discretely into 'chunking' or 'focusing' categories. A more plausible argument is that a perceptual continuum exists with primarily structure-oriented tasks at one end (e.g. American football) and fast visual search tasks at the other (e.g. baseball, cricket). Further support for such a continuum was provided by Bourgeaud and Abernethy (1987) who used the recall paradigm to investigate whether skilled volleyball players demonstrated superior recall as well as signal detection ability. The results supported previous research using the recall paradigm with the skilled group showing superior performance on the structured trials only. Expert volleyball players show superior chunking *and* focusing ability when compared with less skilled players. This suggests that skilled performance in many sports is not based on a single unifying strategy, but rather requires that performers exhibit a range of perceptual strategies. Further research is required to determine the exact perceptual demands of different sports such as netball, lacrosse, waterpolo and handball. Since sports may present individuals with different task constraints, this suggests that specific visual training programmes are needed in order to appropriately develop perceptual performance in sport.

As well as problems regarding poor stimulus presentations and unrealistic response measures, there have been some specific criticisms of the signal detection approach. For example, as we saw, tachistoscopic presentation of filmslides have been as brief as 16 ms in certain studies (e.g. Allard and Starkes 1980). Clearly, such transient 'snapshots' are far removed from the type of dynamically-evolving perceptual display that subjects are presented with in real-life situations. In tachistoscopic presentations, subjects are unable to use relevant contextual cues to anticipate the arrival of a ball in advance. Although some situations in sport require that subjects respond quickly to an unexpected stimulus (e.g. the goalkeeper who is unable to see the ball through a crowd of players), generally performers see the action sequence evolve and are able to make use of contextual information and situational probabilities to anticipate future ball destination.

ADVANCE CUE UTILISATION

Much research has investigated the relationship between advance cue utilisation and anticipation in sport. Advance cue utilisation refers to an athlete's ability to make accurate predictions based on contextual information available early in an action sequence (Abernethy 1987a). The ability to make predictions upon partial or advance sources of information is what Poulton (1957) referred to as perceptual anticipation. Perceptual anticipation is essential in sport because inherent limitations in the performer's reaction time and movement time would result in decisions being made too late to provide an effective counter (see Glencross and Cibich 1977). Several techniques have been used to examine advance cue usage in sport. These are logically divided into laboratory- and field-based approaches (Abernethy 1987a). The typical laboratory paradigm has involved using film to simulate the visual display that performers are confronted with during play. The most popular techniques have been the film occlusion approach and the reaction time paradigm. In the film occlusion approach, the duration and nature of the display is externally controlled and constrained by the experimenter, whereas in the reaction time paradigm response time or viewing time is under subject control and is allowed to covary with response accuracy. In contrast, field-based approaches have embraced a more ecological emphasis by measuring performance directly using techniques such as high-speed film analysis and liquid crystal occlusion glasses.

Laboratory-based approaches

Temporal occlusion

The temporal occlusion approach involves filming the appropriate display (e.g. the serve in tennis or the penalty flick in field hockey) from the competitor's customary perspective. The film is then selectively edited at different points to provide the subject with a varying extent of advance and ball flight information. This film is then played back to subjects using a repeated trials design with the subject being required to predict the end result of the sequence observed.

Jones and Miles (1978) initially used this paradigm to investigate whether tennis players and non-players could successfully anticipate the direction of an opponent's serve. Three different temporal occlusion periods were used: 336 ms after the impact of the ball on the racket (condition A), 126 ms after impact (condition B) and 42 ms before impact (condition C). Subjects included county or international tennis players, club level players and undergraduate students with no tennis experience. Subjects reported their perceptual predictions by indicating where they thought the ball would land on a diagrammatic representation of the service court area which was divided into three sections. The results showed that there were significant differences between the players and non-players in conditions B and C, whilst no differences were found in condition A. Table 4.4 indicates that the differences between groups were greater in condition C, when more potential information was withheld. Furthermore, the results indicated that the players scored significantly better than chance (i.e. 33.33% success rate) in condition C, signifying that skilled tennis players are able to effectively use information available prior to ball/racket impact in the tennis serve.

In a related study, designed to examine the visual cues used in ice hockey goalkeeping, Salmela and Fiorito (1979) required subjects to observe filmed sequences of a player executing a series of ice hockey shots. The film clips included the ice hockey player's approach to the puck and his preparatory actions up to the point of occlusion. Three temporal occlu-

Table 4.4 Mean percentage accuracy scores for each group across the three temporal occlusion conditions (±SD in parenthesis). (Source: Jones, C.M. and Miles, T.R. (1978) 'Use of advance cues in predicting the flight of a lawn tennis ball', *Journal of Human Movement Studies*, 4, 231–235.)

	Condition A *336 ms after impact*	*Condition B* *126 ms after impact*	*Condition C* *42 ms before impact*
Experts	75.40 (12.93)	78.41 (12.61)	42.38 (26.18)
Intermediates	78.30 (9.70)	75.00 (16.77)	38.06 (16.30)
Novices	74.35 (12.56)	68.75 (15.35)	27.01 (12.66)

sion periods were used in the study; these were 500, 333 and 166 ms prior to the puck being struck by the attacker. On viewing the film clips, subjects were required to verbalise into which of the four corners of the goal the puck was believed to be directed. Immediately after answering, subjects indicated their degree of response confidence on a 1–5 Likert scale, in both the horizontal and vertical axes. Four gradations of response success were used: 'total success' (TS) for when the correct corner was selected; 'horizontal success' (HS) involved a correct side (i.e. right or left) but incorrect height (i.e. top or bottom) decision; 'vertical success' (VS) was an incorrect side but correct height decision; and 'no success' was where both the side and height decisions were incorrect.

Table 4.5 shows the distribution of response alternatives as a function of the temporal occlusion period. The overall pattern of responses across the three occlusion periods differed from the chance distribution (i.e. 25% in each category) which would have arisen if the subjects had guessed at random. The data demonstrated that the ice hockey goalkeepers were able to make effective use of information available prior to the puck being struck. Table 4.5 indicates that the subjects were more successful in predicting shot side rather than height. This finding suggests that very powerful differential cues are available in the horizontal, as compared to the vertical plane. Support is provided in Table 4.6 which shows that the subjects were more confident in the horizontal rather than in the vertical plane. Subjects' confidence in their response also decreased with the increase in occlusion period. Yet, even at the 333 ms occlusion period the level of confidence was quite high indicating that the subjects felt that they could successfully perform using these early visual cues. This finding suggests that experts are very confident in their ability to make accurate decisions in sport situations. Chamberlin and Coelho (1993) argue that this may be an important discriminating characteristic between experts and novices. They suggest that novices lack the confidence of experts and are more careful in making a decision, preferring instead to acquire more information before making a response. The argument is that experts are not necessarily better at detecting and using advance sources of information, but rather are more

Table 4.5 Distribution of response alternatives across the three temporal occlusion periods. (Source: Salmela, J.H. and Fiorito, P. (1979) 'Visual cues in ice hockey goaltending', *Canadian Journal of Applied Sport Sciences*, 4, 56–59.)

Occlusion Period	Degree of Success			
	Total Success	Horizontal Success	Vertical Success	No Success
– 166 ms	345	217	147	107
– 333 ms	304	214	173	125
– 500 ms	295	235	146	140

Table 4.6 Subject confidence in goalkeeping predictions based on a 5-point Likert scale for slap and wrist shots as a function of occlusion period and type of shot. (Source: Samela, J.H. and Fiorito, P. (1979) 'Visual cues in ice hockey goaltending', *Canadian Journal of Applied Sport Sciences*, 4, 56–59.)

Type of shot		Occlusion Period	
	166 ms	*333 ms*	*500 ms*
		Horizontal Plane	
Slap shot	4.0	3.9	3.7
Wrist shot	4.3	4.1	3.7
		Vertical Plane	
Slap shot	3.5	3.3	3.2
Wrist shot	3.9	3.8	3.2

confident in making their decisions based on this partial information (for some contradictory evidence, see Tenenbaum, Levy-Kolker, Sade, Liebermann and Lidor 1996).

The finding that performers make fewer errors when predicting horizontal compared with vertical direction has been demonstrated in other sports (see Abernethy 1990b; Abernethy and Russell 1987a; Isaacs and Finch 1983; Salmela and Fiorito 1979; Williams and Burwitz 1993). Williams and Burwitz (ibid.) required subjects to observe filmed sequences of five different players taking soccer penalty kicks. Subjects viewed the player's preparatory stance, approach run and kicking action up to the point of occlusion. Four temporal occlusion periods were used: 120 ms (condition 1) and 40 ms (condition 2) before the player kicked the ball, at impact (condition 3) and 40 ms after impact (condition 4). Two groups of experienced and inexperienced players viewed the penalty kicks on a video projection screen. Subjects were required to indicate to which of the four corners of the goal the ball was to be directed. The results presented in Table 4.7 showed that the experienced players exhibited superior performance only under the shortest durations (i.e. pre-impact viewing conditions). Table 4.8 shows that the majority of errors (mean across all occlusion conditions = 61.8%) were associated with incorrect height judgements, whilst only 25.71% of errors were due to incorrect side predictions. Further analysis of Table 4.8 indicates that there was a marked improvement in height judgement only after initial ball trajectory had been viewed (condition 4). The implication is that soccer goalkeepers should anticipate the correct side prior to the ball being kicked, while prediction of the correct height could be made after viewing the initial portion of ball flight just prior to breaking ground contact in the diving phase.

An alternative explanation may be that the greater horizontal prediction accuracy noted in these studies is a by-product of the typical

Table 4.7 Mean percentage of correct responses for experienced and inexperienced goalkeepers across the four temporal occlusion periods (±SD in parenthesis). (Source: Williams, A.M. and Burwitz, L. (1993) 'Advance cue utilisation in soccer', in T. Reilly, J. Clarys and A. Stibbe (eds) *Science and Football II*, London: E & FN Spon.)

	Condition 1 120 ms prior impact %	Condition 2 40 ms prior impact %	Condition 3 at football impact %	Condition 4 40 ms after impact %
Experienced players	51.00 (15.13)	62.66 (12.89)	82.66 (9.55)	83.33 (7.88)
Inexperienced players	39.33 (14.22)	54.00 (15.18)	78.00 (12.20)	85.33 (5.62)

two-dimensional film display used to represent the player's customary view of play. The loss of dimensionality may make it difficult for subjects to accurately estimate depth, or alternatively, it may cause them to alter their habitual performance strategy. Field-based research is required to examine whether this finding is an experimental artefact or whether the same pattern of cue usage is observed when subjects are presented with 'real life' three-dimensional displays.

Encouraged by the success of these studies, numerous researchers have attempted to determine whether experts in other sports are able to make effective use of information available prior to the event. The expert's ability to use advance visual cues has been shown in field hockey (Starkes 1987; Lyle and Cook 1984), cricket (Abernethy and Russell 1984; Houlston and Lowes 1993) tennis (Isaacs and Finch 1983; Goulet, Bard and Fleury 1989; Tenenbaum *et al.* 1996), volleyball (Souliere and Salmela 1982; Widmaier 1983), squash (Abernethy 1990a) badminton (Abernethy and Russell 1987a; Abernethy 1988c) and soccer (Patrick and Spurgeon 1978; Jackson 1986).

Table 4.8 Variations in error type, as a proportion of total error made, across all four conditions for both groups combined. (Source: Williams, A.M. and Burwitz, L. (1993) 'Advance cue utilisation in soccer', in T. Reilly, J. Clarys and A. Stibbe (eds) *Science and Football II*, London: E & FN Spon.)

Response Category	Condition 1 120 ms prior impact %	Condition 2 40 ms prior impact %	Condition 3 at football impact %	Condition 4 40 ms after impact %
Incorrect height	71.23	67.00	68.35	40.62
Incorrect side	17.36	26.91	25.64	32.91
Height and side Incorrect	11.41	6.09	6.51	26.47

Event occlusion

A limitation with the temporal occlusion approach is that it only provides information regarding the time of extraction of important visual cues. The approach does not tell us about the nature of the anticipatory cues the performer uses in the anticipation process. However, these questions can be addressed by combining temporal occlusion with spatial or event occlusion procedures. The event occlusion approach involves presenting the subjects with a consistent time course of events across trials while selectively occluding specific cue sources for the duration of the trial. The argument is that the accessibility of a cue and the time at which it becomes available influences the performer's perceptual strategy (see Abernethy 1985). Thus far, relatively few researchers have combined temporal and event occlusion techniques when investigating cue usage in sport. The main reason for this may be because the question that this paradigm addresses (i.e. Which areas of the display provide the most informative visual cues?) is assumed to be more effectively answered using a visual tracking technique (Chamberlain and Coelho 1993). However, in Chapter 5 we highlight the advantages of using event occlusion techniques to corroborate data obtained via an eye movement registration system.

The majority of research using event occlusion in sport emanates from Abernethy and colleagues at the University of Queensland (e.g. Abernethy 1988c, 1990b; Abernethy and Russell 1987a). For example, Abernethy and Russell (1987a) presented expert and novice badminton players with a film display of a provincial-level player executing a series of badminton strokes. In one experiment, five different temporal occlusion periods were used: 167 ms prior to racket-shuttle contact; 83 ms before impact; at impact; 83 ms after contact; and a control condition where the subjects viewed the complete trial. Subjects were required to indicate on a schematic representation of the court the intended destination of the shuttle. The results showed that experts were better at predicting the future destination of the shuttle under all occlusion conditions except the control condition. The expert advantage was greatest in the period from 167 ms to 83 ms prior to the player striking the shuttle suggesting that this period is particularly crucial for extracting pertinent anticipatory cues. In a second experiment, each trial was occluded at impact and different cue sources were masked for the duration of the trial. These included: the racket and arm; racket only; face and body; lower body; and a control condition involving an irrelevant background feature. The argument was that if an important visual cue such as the racket is occluded then there will be a marked decrement in performance compared with the occlusion of an irrelevant control condition. The results showed that the critical anticipatory cues in badminton are provided by the racket and the arm holding the racket. When visibility of these cues was occluded, prediction error for experts and novices increased above that exhibited for the control condition, suggesting that they made an important contribution to antic-ipation in badminton.

Reaction time paradigms

An alternative to the film occlusion approach is the reaction time paradigm. In this approach, the length of time available to view the display is under subject control and is allowed to covary with response accuracy (see Abernethy 1985). Abernethy and Russell (1984) used this paradigm to examine anticipation in cricket. Groups of skilled and less skilled batsmen were required to make response selection decisions from filmed sequences of the run-up and delivery action of two medium-pace bowlers. The results showed that highly skilled batsmen were more accurate in their shot selec-tion, with these decisions being frequently made over shorter viewing times. Similarly, Williams *et al.* (1994) used this approach to examine anticipa-tion in 11 vs 11 offensive simulations in soccer. Groups of experienced and inexperienced players viewed 10-second film clips of attacking patterns of play in soccer. On viewing each pattern of play, subjects were required to verbalise quickly and accurately the area of the field to which the pass would be played. Table 4.9 shows that experienced players were much quicker than the inexperienced players in anticipating future pass destina-tion. No differences between groups were found using a verbal or a com-puter-based measure of response accuracy. The reaction time paradigm has also been used successfully in volleyball (Coelho and Chamberlin 1991; Handford and Williams 1992), baseball (Paull and Glencross 1997) and soccer (Helsen and Pauwels 1992, 1993; Williams and Davids 1998b).

   Although these paradigms have been successful in identifying differences in anticipation in sport, they have received much criticism. This has included the loss of image size and dimensionality when using small-screen television monitors and the absence of realistic movement-based response measures. Also, the loss of other sources of sensory information such as

Table 4.9 Mean group performance scores for experienced and inexperienced soccer players on the 11 vs 11 anticipation test. (Source: Williams, A.M., Davids, K., Burwitz, L. and Williams, J.G. (1994) 'Visual search strategies in experienced and inexperienced soccer players', *Research Quarterly for Exercise and Sport*, 65(2): 127–35.)

Group		CRT (ms)	RT (ms)	VRE (%)	CRE (pixel)
Experienced	M	494.6	9219.6	16.1	103.5
(n = 15)	SD	134.0	404.9	11.1	52.8
Inexperienced	M	405.0	9742.7	16.9	87.0
(n = 15)	SD	85.5	417.7	11.6	51.7

Note: CRT = choice reaction time; RT = response time; VRE = verbal responce error; CRE = computer response error.

audition may have detrimental effects on anticipation in sport (Cobner 1981; Takeuchi 1993). For example, Takeuchi (1993) found that when subjects were deprived of auditory information when playing tennis there was a marked decrement in performance. This observation indicates that multisensory information is used in an adaptive manner when playing tennis. This argument is discussed in greater detail in Chapter 9.

A number of specific problems exist with film occlusion studies. First, many of these studies have presented subjects with action clips from only one performer (e.g. Abernethy and Russell 1987a; Jones and Miles 1978; Salmela and Fiorito 1979). The possibility that there may be certain idiosyncrasies in this performer's technique, which may make it easier or harder to predict event outcome, makes it difficult to draw widespread conclusions from these studies.

Second, when using film occlusion techniques the experimenter needs to have some preconceived ideas concerning what cues are important and when they are needed. This may lead to a situation were some important sources of information are excluded from the outset or there may be a lack of correspondence between the temporal occlusion periods used and the time available in the field situation for the performer to extract the cues necessary for response selection. The problem is exaggerated as skilled performers may use more than one cue at a time making the interpretation of the results of single temporal and spatial occlusion procedures difficult. The problem is that numerous conditions are needed to isolate cue usage within a narrow range.

Third, Sperling (1963) suggests that visual information is retained in short-term memory for some time after the occlusion of the stimulus. Consequently, it may be that subject performance on the occlusion task may not be directly related to the film occlusion time used, but rather to the total time course of available information (i.e. the occlusion period plus the duration of iconic persistence). That is, because a response is not required immediately, visual information can be held for delayed processing in laboratory tasks. It is therefore important that realistic time constraints are imposed on subjects to replicate the demands placed on performers in real-life situations. These arguments suggest that reaction time paradigms may be more realistic than film occlusion techniques when assessing anticipation in sport. Alternatively, it may be that a backward masking condition should always be used when brief visual stimuli are employed (for an example, see Starkes, Allard, Lindley and O'Reilly 1994).

Finally, a common problem with these film-based techniques is that they fail to provide performers with any contextual information prior to the response situation (Chamberlain and Coelho 1993). Research has tended to isolate the performance context by removing the environmental (i.e. the action that has gone before or the type of shots/actions preferred by their opponent) or situational information (e.g. score, innings, playing time left) normally available to the performer (McPherson 1993a). In the game situation, the tennis player may soon realise that her opponent always serves to the backhand, or the soccer defender quickly determines that the opposing player is predominately right-footed and always wants to dribble in this direction. Paull and Glencross (1997) showed that decision-making was significantly improved when subjects were provided with *a priori* contextual information in baseball. It was found that knowing the strategic context decreased decision time and reduced the errors in predicting the final position of the pitch over the plate. Later in this chapter we review further evidence indicating that prior knowledge regarding stimulus probability has a significant effect on anticipation in sport (e.g. Alain and Proteau 1977, 1980; Coley and McPherson 1994).

Arguments for increasing the ecological validity of the investigative paradigms employed are now increasingly familiar in the sport and exercise sciences (see Williams *et al.* 1992). The argument is that the more closely the experimental protocol replicates the natural task then the greater will be the expert advantage over the novice (Abernethy *et al.* 1993). Abernethy *et al.* (ibid.) argue that simplistic or contrived laboratory tasks may negate experts' advantage by:

- removing from the task the experiential basis for their advantage;
- introducing potential floor or ceiling effects in the measurement process;
- causing experts to function differently either by denying them access to information they would normally use, or by causing them to use different information to solve a particular problem.

In a recent study, Williams, Davids and Burwitz (1994) examined the importance of using a movement-based response paradigm to examine anticipation in sport. Experienced and less experienced soccer defenders viewed 1 vs 1 and 3 vs 3 soccer offensive sequences on a large video projection screen. The action sequences were filmed from the perspective of a covering defender. In one condition subjects were required to verbally indicate their response, whilst a second condition required them to physically respond to the same action sequences by moving as if to intercept the ball. The results showed that experienced soccer players were quicker at responding whether they were asked to reply either verbally or by movement response. However, when each group's decision times were compared across the two experimental conditions some interesting effects were observed. In the verbal response condition, the experienced group responded 38 ms faster to the 1 vs 1 simulations and 315 ms to the 3 vs 3 situations. However, these differences were much greater in the movement response condition with the expert advantage being 205 ms and 350 ms for the 1 vs 1 and 3 vs 3 simulations respectively. Therefore, the experienced group's advantage was increased by 167 ms in the 1 vs 1 situation and 35 ms in the 3 vs 3 simulation when using a movement-based rather than a verbal response protocol. No differences were observed in response accuracy across the two conditions. These results indicate that the more closely the experimental task replicates the real world the greater the expert's advantage over the novice. The greater discrimination observed with the movement-based paradigm may be a result of the improved stimulus–response compatibility under the more realistic conditions. That is, the life-size visual image and movement-based response is much more compatible with the skilled player's customary response in the game situation. This results in more rapid access to, and retrieval of, task-specific information stored in memory (see Proctor and Reeve 1990). Another interpretation may be based on Milner and Goodale's (1995) distinction between the use of vision for perceptual discrimination and identification purposes and the role of vision in the control of action (see Chapter 3). Historically, perceptual psychology has only employed discrimination tasks which require no action component, whilst performance in real-world contexts involving a movement-based response may involve the two different visual cortical pathways.

Field-based approaches

Notwithstanding the above criticisms, laboratory-based approaches have successfully provided the experimenter with rigorous control over the test environment. However, there is a need for replication and verification of these laboratory findings within the actual performance setting. Thus far, too few studies have ventured outside the bounds of the laboratory.

High-speed film analysis

Howarth, Walsh, Abernethy and Snyder (1984) used a high-speed film analysis technique to examine anticipation in squash. Rally sequences were filmed at a rate of 100 frames/second from a position above the court during matches between two high-skill (A grade) and two low-skill (D grade) competitors. An anticipatory movement was defined by the experimenters as the first displacement of the receiver's body in the direction necessary to intercept the oncoming stroke. Viewing time was regarded as the time necessary to make a perceptual assessment of the environment and to reach an appropriate decision. Viewing time was estimated to end at a point in time 200 ms prior to the initiation of the first anticipatory movement. This was taken as the inherent visual latency time over which visually-based corrections could be executed (McLeod 1987).

The results showed that the overall speed of the game (as measured by the average time between successive strokes) was similar for both skill groups. However, Figure 4.1 shows that the high-skill players made their initial anticipatory movements significantly earlier than their less-skilled counterparts. The high-skill players made an anticipatory movement in the

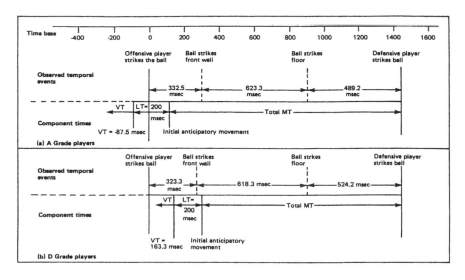

Figure 4.1 A temporal comparison of the initial anticipatory movements for high-skill (A Grade) and low-skill (D Grade) squash players. (Source: Howarth, C., Walsh, W.D. Abernethy, B., and Snyder, C.W. Jr. (1984) 'A field examination of anticipation in squash: Some preliminary data', *Australian Journal of Science and Medicine in Sport* 16: 7–11.)

correct direction on average 112.5 ms after the offensive player struck the ball, whereas the low-skill players did not make preparatory movements until some 250 ms later. When the 200 ms visual reaction time latency period was subtracted from the point of initial movement initiation to estimate viewing time, distinct perceptual differences between the two groups emerged. The negative viewing time value for the high-skill players (VT = −87.5 ms) indicated that these players were dependent upon advance visual cues for the determination of their initial anticipatory movement. In contrast, the average viewing time of 163 ms for the less-skilled players suggested that their initial decision to move was based on information arising after the offensive player's stroke was executed, but prior to the ball hitting the front wall. These findings provide support for the high-skilled player's greater anticipatory capability using a field-based paradigm.

Visual occlusion techniques

Another interesting field-based study was conducted by Day (1980). In this study, Day attempted to replicate Jones and Miles's (1978) approach by using a visual occlusion helmet to mask vision at the point of racket–ball contact in tennis. Subjects were positioned on the baseline facing an opponent who was instructed to play forehand shots at random to any position on the singles court. Visual occlusion was achieved by an electronic shutter which was triggered by a pressure switch positioned on the racket used by the striking player. The results supported the findings from earlier laboratory-based studies by demonstrating that skilled tennis players were able to make accurate predictions based on pre-contact cues. Day's (1980) results confirmed earlier suggestions that subjects were more successful in making lateral rather than depth predictions. This finding indicates that depth prediction seems to rely much more upon information processed during the initial portion of ball flight. Furthermore, this suggests that the increased difficulty experienced by subjects when attempting to estimate depth might not necessarily be an artefact of the use of a two-dimensional film medium (e.g. Salmela and Fiorito 1979; Williams and Burwitz 1993).

Recently, liquid crystal occlusion techniques have been used to assess visual cue usage in field-based situations. Starkes, Edwards, Dissanayake and Dunn (1995) used such glasses to control visual exposure in a field experiment of temporal occlusion. Expert and novice volleyball players viewed and estimated the landing position of 12 volleyball serves in each of three visual occlusion conditions (i.e. pre-contact, contact and post-contact). Subjects observed the serve up to the point of occlusion, after which they were required to place a marker on the floor to indicate where they believed the ball had landed. The dependent measure was radial error of subjects' estimation of the landing position. The results showed that skilled players were better overall at predicting the landing position of a serve, and all subjects had more accurate predictions when they had the information provided by the server's contact with the ball and flight information from the serve. Although no attempt was made to distinguish between lateral and depth errors, the results supported previous research using more traditional film-based approaches (e.g. Wright, Plesants and Gomez-Meza 1990). The use of liquid crystal occlusion glasses would appear to provide researchers with an opportunity to move away from the laboratory to test situations with more realistic perceptual information sources. Moreover, Starkes *et al.*'s (1995) suggestion that this methodology may allow ongoing assessment and training of advance cue usage in 'live-model' situations requires further investigation.

Although the results of these field-based studies support previous laboratory-based work, there are a number of methodological concerns. With regard to high-speed film techniques, the process of identifying when the anticipatory movement begins is problematic and involves some degree of experimenter subjectivity in determining response initiation. Moreover, this approach views the performer as an essentially linear and serial processor of information. Decision-making is seen as a discrete process whereas, in fact, it is likely to be more of a continuous cumulative process with early differentiated aspects of the movement response being frequently commenced before final response selection, and usage of all available cues is completed (Miller 1982). This could therefore have the effect of making the viewing time appear shorter than is actually the case.

The use of McLeod's (1987) visual reaction time latency has also been criticised by Bakker, Whiting and van der Brug (1990). In McLeod's (1987) study, skilled cricket batsmen faced a bowling machine on an artificial wicket which had dowel rods spaced a few centimetres apart and laid parallel to the line of flight of the ball. If the ball landed between the dowels, it would continue on a straight path through to the batsman. However, if the ball struck the batting mat in the vicinity of a dowel it would change direction unpredictably to the left or right. Cinematographic analysis of three international batsmen showed reaction times similar to those obtained in traditional laboratory studies. Specifically, no evidence could be provided for stroke adjustments occurring in less than 190 ms after the bounce of the ball. Bakker *et al.* argue that the cricket batsmen in this situation were confronted with a choice rather than a simple reaction time situation. This 200-ms value would therefore provide an overestimate of the actual latency period. Furthermore, they argue that the movement of the cricket bat involves considerably more inertia than the simple finger movement involved in traditional laboratory-based paradigms. Consequently, establishing the precise value of the latency period may be contaminated by the mass of the implement to be wielded. Also, recent evidence suggests that although minimum visual reaction time delay in choice situations may be around 200 ms, it is possible that under certain conditions it can be considerably quicker (see Chapter 6 on perception–action coupling). This may particularly be the case in situations where stimulus information is continuously rather than suddenly available (for a review, see McLeod and Jenkins 1991).

Finally, the use of visual occlusion techniques in sport settings raises several concerns. For example, occluding vision during performance may cause subjects to rely on different sources of information from those which they would normally use in the game situation. Furthermore, by occluding vision at critical times this technique prevents the subject from physically responding to the action thereby restricting researchers to using verbal response measures. Although liquid crystal goggles have recently increased experimenter control and flexibility over visual occlusion, they have also increased concern regarding ethical and safety issues (see Milgram 1987). If future research can overcome these problems, liquid crystal occlusion techniques may provide the sport and exercise scientist with some promising avenues for future research work.

SITUATIONAL PROBABILITIES AND ANTICIPATION IN SPORT

As well as their enhanced ability to extract task-specific contextual information from the display, research suggests that skilled performers are able to make use of expectations or situational probabilities to facilitate anticipation in sport. Early research was carried in the laboratory using choice reaction time paradigms. These studies demonstrated that reaction time is directly proportional to the amount of 'uncertainty' or information present within a display (e.g. Hick 1952; Hyman 1953). Moreover, it has been suggested that the performer can significantly reduce this level of uncertainty through practice (see Mowbray and Rhoades 1959). An argument is that experienced performers can use their superior knowledge base to dismiss many events as being 'highly improbable' and can attach a hierarchy of probabilities to the remaining events (Gottsdanker and Kent 1978). In this way, sports performers can reduce uncertainty regarding 'what' event will occur (i.e. event uncertainty) and 'when' it will happen (i.e. temporal uncertainty).

The majority of work examining the importance of situational probabilities in sport has been conducted by Alain and colleagues at the University of Montreal (Alain and Girardin 1978; Alain and Proteau 1977, 1978, 1980; Alain and Sarrazin 1990; Alain, Lalonde and Sarrazin 1983; Alain, Sarrazin and Lacombe 1986). Alain and Proteau (1978) attempted to examine the extent to which defensive players in various racket sports made use of situational probabilities to anticipate the shots available to their adversaries. The decision-making behaviour of squash, tennis, badminton and racketball players was studied in the game situation by filming some of the rallies, allowing subjects to view the film, and then asking specific questions regarding shot selection during the rally. Players were asked to comment on the subjective probabilities they had assigned to their opponent's shots. In order to achieve this, players had to classify perceived stroke probability into either 10%, 30%, 50%, 70% or 90% confidence levels. Also, they were asked whether their movements in specified directions were guided by their anticipations based on these subjective probabilities. From the filmed sequences, the player's initial movement in the direction required to return the stroke was measured to provide an index of anticipatory behaviour (i.e. the degree to which each return stroke was guided by anticipation).

Figure 4.2 shows that the higher the probability that defensive players subjectively attributed to an event, the higher the proportion of anticipatory movements. Players evaluated the probabilities of the possible events that could occur and then used this evaluation to maximise the efficiency of subsequent behaviour. Alain and Proteau (1978) suggested that initial anticipatory movements were guided by the performer's expectations with subsequent corrective or confirmatory movements being made on the basis of current information or contextual cues. In Figure 4.2, there is a sharp increase in the proportion of anticipatory movements when the subjective probability shifts from 0.5 to 0.7. This suggests that a threshold value of 70% certainty exists before anticipatory action is taken by the performer (see also Proteau and Alain 1983).

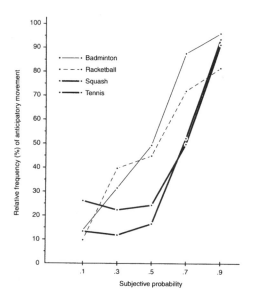

Figure 4.2 The relative frequency of anticipatory movements as a function of the subjective probability the performer assigned to an event. (Source: Alain, C. and Proteau, L. (1978) 'Etude des variables relatives au traitement de l'information en sports de raquette', *Canadian Journal of Applied Sport Sciences* 3: 27–35.)

Alain and Girardin (1978) suggested that one of the major sources of information used when assigning shot probabilities could be the on-court positions of both players. They tested this argument by examining how racketball players of varying ability levels manipulated the amount of uncertainty conveyed by their shots. The study involved a detailed film analysis of A-, B- and C-level racketball matches. The amount of uncertainty conveyed by players' shots was computed from a frequency count of the number of times that each type of shot was used when the two players were in the same positions on the court. The results showed that the amount of uncertainty associated with each shot did not increase as a function of the skill level of the player. This suggests that presenting an opponent with maximum uncertainty is not the prime consideration in the shot selection process. This finding is surprising in view of our understanding of the importance of situational probabilities to anticipation in sport (Whiting 1979). Alain and Proteau (1978) suggested that the results may have been due to the type of sport examined. Racketball is a sport where power and speed may make redundant the need for an uncertainty-based attack strategy. Perhaps the more common approach is to adopt a strategy of striking the ball as hard as possible in order to reduce the time available to an opponent. Such an approach would eliminate the need to adopt a strategy of maximising uncertainty to increase an opponent's response time.

Although an uncertainty-based approach may not be used extensively by skilled racketball players, it is still interesting to note that not all shots carried the same probability of occurrence. For example, backcourt shots were found to convey much greater uncertainty than frontcourt shots. This indicates that knowledge of event probabilities does play some role in facilitating anticipation in racketball.

An alternative approach to examine the importance of subjective probabilities in sport attempts to simulate the game situation by presenting objective event probabilities to subjects using a laboratory-based choice reaction time task. For example, Alain and Proteau (1977) required subjects to move to their right or left side in order to strike a ball suspended from the ceiling. Subjects were required to move in response to two stimulus lights arranged on the backhand and forehand side respectively. Subjects' reaction times and movement times were measured under varying conditions of stimulus probability ranging from 0.1/0.9 to 0.9/0.1. Figure 4.3 shows that the only conditions under which reaction time performance was statistically different from that observed when the events were equiprobable were the 0.9/0.1 and 0.1/0.9 probabilities (c.f. Proteau and Dugas 1982; Proteau and Laurencelle 1983). This suggests that if attacking players have the option of presenting their opponents with one of two possible strokes, they can use their preferred shot 80% of the time and the opponent would not react faster than if both shots were equiprobable.

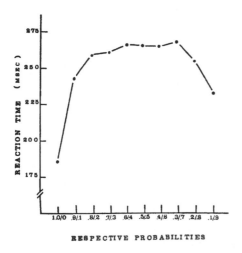

Figure 4.3 Reaction time values as a function of the respective probabilities assigned by performers to two events. (Source: Alain, C. and Proteau, L. (1977) 'Perception of objective probabilities in motor performance', in B. Kerr (ed.) *Human Performance and Behaviour*, Banff, Alberta.)

This probability 'threshold' of 90% is higher than the 70% (0.5/0.7) value from Alain and Proteau's (1978) field-based study. An explanation may be the difference between providing objective probabilities and having subjects formulate their own subjective probabilities based on past experiences (Abernethy 1987b). Research suggests that subjects place more weight on self-acquired information rather than externally provided information as supplied in the laboratory task (Singer 1980; Singer and Gerson 1981). Another reason to explain the conservative strategy used by subjects could be that in the laboratory task they were not forced to complete their response within a limited time period (Alain and Proteau 1978). Consequently, the subjects may have decided that there were no positive benefits to be gained by attempting to react quickly, while responding incorrectly would be classed as a failure. In support of this interpretation, recent studies have demonstrated that the performer's reaction time is based on the interaction between subjective probability and the time available to complete the response (Alain and Sarrazin 1990; Alain *et al.* 1986; Proteau, Levesque, Laurencelle and Girouard 1989). Performers are more likely to adopt a strategy of relying on situational probabilities in situations where the speed of response is paramount.

Finally, Dillon, Crassini and Abernethy (1989) suggest that the conservative strategy used by the subjects in Alain and Proteau's study may be an artefact of using fully between-subject designs. That is, each of the stimulus probability data points in Figure 4.3 are derived from a different group of subjects. The problem is that such a design does not partial out any between-group differences in baseline reaction time, thus contaminating the data. They suggest that research should either use within-subject designs or should attempt to partial out between-group differences in reactivity by computing reaction time difference scores (i.e. scores reflecting the difference in reaction time between the low and high frequency stimulus events experienced by each group). They used this latter technique to examine the effect of situational probabilities on a reaction time task which required subjects to perform a forehand tennis stroke in response to a right visual stimulus and a backhand stroke to a left visual stimulus. The results showed a significant increase in reaction time difference values when the probability differences reached 0.7/0.3. This indicates that the subjects adopted a less conservative approach to decision-making than suggested by earlier analyses based on absolute reaction time (e.g. Alain and Proteau 1977).

Although there is a paucity of research purporting to investigate the importance of subjective probabilities in sport, the evidence which does exist clearly suggests that players make use of these probabilities to guide their perceptions. The ability to perceive the most likely shot or pass to be made by an opponent focuses the expert's attention and reduces considerably the amount of uncertainty within the display. From a practical perspective, this suggests that players and coaches should make systematic analyses of the respective probabilities of certain shots or play options favoured by different opponent's. If players can be taught to selectively prepare their strategic responses on the bases of prior knowledge of non-equiprobability in their opponents' play, then this approach could facilitate anticipation in sport (Dillon *et al.* 1989).

To summarise so far, we have demonstrated that expert sports performers are characterised by superior perceptual skill. When compared with novices from within their domain of expertise, experts are known to be faster and more accurate in recognising and recalling patterns of play, are able to detect objects of relevance such as the ball from back-ground distractions, are superior in anticipating the actions of their opponents based on contextual information and are more accurate in their expectation of what is likely to happen given a particular set of circum-stances. In the next section, we turn our attention to decision-making in sport.

TACTICAL DECISION-MAKING

Theoretically, the expert's ability to encode and retrieve sport informa-tion efficiently and accurately should be extremely valuable in decision-making. Wickens (1992) argues that skilled decision-makers have three advantages over their less-skilled counterparts. First, they are able to select the most relevant cue(s) from the display based on perceptual chunking (i.e. more effective processing of contextual information). Second, they have a greater repertoire of possible hypotheses and possible actions stored in long-term memory and are better able to calibrate their decisions to current probabilities and risks (i.e. more extensive knowledge of situa-tional probabilities). Third, they display a tighter coupling between cue recognition, hypothesis formation and decision-making outcomes (i.e. improved stimulus–response compatibility based on recognition and matching processes). In sport, therefore, the skilled netball player has direct rules which determine that if a particular pattern of play is recog-nised, a certain action is most effective when the action is part of a large store of such actions in long-term memory (for a more detailed theoret-ical backdrop, see our discussion of Anderson's ACT* theory later in this chapter). Chase and Ericsson (1981) argue that practice and training leads to the strengthening of this relationship between the encoding structure, retrieval structure and relevant retrieval cues, resulting in faster and more accurate decisions.

Despite the perceived importance of decision-making in sport, there is a paucity of empirical research to verify the experts' enhanced decision-making capabilities. In one study, Thiffault (1980) used five groups of ice hockey players differing in age, experience and skill level. Players were presented with filmslides representing actual game situations. The players viewed each slide for a limited amount of time and had to decide quickly and accurately whether the most appropriate response was to dribble, shoot or skate. The correct response for each slide had previously being assessed by ten hockey experts, whilst the dependent variable was voice reaction time. The results showed that all three independent variables (age, experience and skill level) significantly affected decision-making.

Similar designs have been used to examine tactical decision-making in basketball (Bard and Fleury 1981) field hockey (Starkes and Deakin 1984) and soccer (Helsen and Pauwels 1988, 1992, 1993; McMorris and Graydon 1996). Starkes and Deakin (1984) presented national, university and novice field hockey players with filmslides of game situations. Subjects were required to verbally indicate quickly and accurately whether the correct decision for the player with the ball was to shoot, dribble or dodge. Slides had previously been screened by three university coaches to determine the most appropriate response in each situation. The results showed that the national players made more accurate decisions than either university or novice players. No differences were found in decision time.

Helsen and Pauwels (1988, 1992, 1993) have recently used more realistic paradigms to examine decision-making in sport. Helsen and Pauwels (1993) presented expert and novice players with a dynamic, life-size film display of various tactical situations in soccer. These simulated game situations had been selected from international matches and then realistically acted on 16 mm film by expert soccer players. Subjects viewed the action sequence evolve on screen until the ball appeared to be played back towards them by one of the attackers on film. Subjects were then required to physically respond, as if they were in the game situation, either by shooting the ball towards the goal, passing to a teammate or dribbling past an opponent or goalkeeper. The results showed that the expert soccer players had faster initiation, ball contact and total response times and were more accurate in their decisions than the novice players.

A significant criticism of much of the research on decision-making in sport is that it is primarily descriptive in nature and consequently, makes a relatively limited contribution to theoretical explanation within the area. Another criticism is that this work does not facilitate our understanding of the knowledge structures underlying decision-making in sport (McPherson 1993a). Although the research highlights the perceptual strategies employed by experts as well as their enhanced decision-making capabilities, it does not increase our understanding of *what* information is used in decision-making and *how* the underlying knowledge structures are developed as a result of practice. Such information is crucial to coaches and practitioners when attempting to develop sport-specific decision-making. Next, we present some of the research that has attempted to address these limitations.

DECLARATIVE AND PROCEDURAL KNOWLEDGE IN SPORT

The knowledge-based paradigm

The knowledge-based paradigm was introduced into the study of cognition by Anderson and others (e.g. Anderson 1982; Chi and Rees 1983) and more recently has been adapted to measure expertise in sport (French and Thomas 1987; McPherson and Thomas 1989). This approach attempts to describe more precisely the knowledge structures underlying skilled performance. Thus far, experts have been shown to possess a more complete and highly differentiated memory store. Anderson (1987) suggests that there are two important sources of knowledge, namely, procedural and declarative knowledge. Procedural knowledge enables us to know 'how to do' something (e.g. how to play a forehand volley in tennis or an overhead clear shot in badminton). In contrast, declarative knowledge refers to our knowledge of facts relevant to a specific task (i.e. knowing 'what to do' in a situation).

A number of studies have distinguished between these different types of knowledge in a sports performance context (e.g. French and Thomas 1987; French, Spurgeon and Nevett 1995; McPherson and French 1991; McPherson and Thomas 1989; Thomas, French and Humphries 1986). Moreover, several studies have attempted to examine how the knowledge structures underlying decision-making develop as a result of practice and instruction. For example, French and Thomas (1987) examined the contribution of basketball knowledge (declarative) and specific basketball skills (procedural) to the development of skilled decision-making and overall basketball performance. Subjects included groups of high- and low-skilled 8–10- and 11–12-year-olds. They completed a basketball knowledge test designed to assess each player's declarative knowledge, whilst basketball shooting and dribbling skills tests were taken as measures of procedural knowledge. An observational instrument was designed to assess the children's performance during an actual game. This was used to evaluate their control of the basketball, their decision-making accuracy and their ability to execute the chosen skill. The results showed that the skilled children in both age groups possessed more basketball knowledge, scored higher on the shooting skills test and demonstrated better performance in actual game situations. This indicated that both cognitive and motor skills contribute to the development of children's basketball skills. Further support for this contention was provided by a canonical correlation analysis which indicated that performance on the knowledge test was related to the decision-making component of basketball performance, while performance on the dribbling and shooting skills tests was related to the control and execution aspects of performance.

In a further study, French and Thomas (1987) attempted to determine whether there was an increase in children's declarative and procedural knowledge over the course of a season. The basketball knowledge test and both skill tests were administered to the 8–10-year-old players both at the beginning and at the end of the season. Analysis of game performance indicated that the subjects' ability to control the basketball (i.e. catch the ball) and to make accurate decisions improved over the season. The mean pre-season performance scores were 87% for control, 67% for decisions and 68% for execution, while the post-season percentages were 96% for control, 83% for decisions and 72% for execution. Performance improvements were also noted on the basketball knowledge test. However, the subjects' performance on the two skills tests remained relatively constant over the season. These findings suggest that young basketball players may acquire declarative knowledge quicker than they can improve the procedural aspects of performance. That is, children may learn what to do in certain basketball situations faster than they can acquire the motor skills to carry out the actions. Furthermore, the study indicated that the increase in basketball knowledge was a significant predictor of decision-making ability at the end of the season. This confirms the suggestion that the development of a sport-specific knowledge base plays an important role in decision-making.

The finding that children learn what decisions are appropriate during the game faster than they acquire fundamental basketball skills has been questioned by McPherson and French (1991). They suggested that these results may have been due to the greater emphasis placed on cognitive skills during practice and games. An overemphasis on motor skill development may result in players with good technique but poor strategic knowledge of the game, whereas too much instruction on strategy and decision-making may produce players who know what to do but do not possess the necessary motor skills. To examine this assumption, McPherson and French (1991) required sixteen novice tennis players to undertake a 14-week programme of instruction. During the first 7-week block, instruction consisted of a traditional fundamental skill approach in which skill development preceded instruction on strategy and decision-making. Subjects were initially taught factual tennis knowledge (e.g. rules, strokes, scoring), followed by motor skill instruction (e.g. forehand, backhand, serve, volley) and then finally combination drills and actual singles play. The second 7-week block of instruction focused on the development of singles strategy (decision-making) and response execution (motor skill development) in actual game situations. Subjects' declarative knowledge was examined at the beginning (pre-test), middle (mid-test) and end (post-test) of the 14-week instruction course using a multiple choice tennis knowledge test. A tennis skill battery was used to assess groundstoke (backhand and forehand) and serve skill, whilst an observational instrument was used to record service play (i.e. serve skill) and game play following the serve (i.e. backhand and forehand ground strokes) during actual game situations.

Table 4.10 Mean scores and Newman-Keuls post-hoc comparisons for the knowledge and skills tests for pre-, mid- and post-tests. (Source: McPherson, S.L. and French, K.E. (1991) 'Changes in cognitive strategies and motor skill in tennis', Journal of Sport and Exercise Psychology, 13: 26–41.)

	Pre-test (1)		Mid-test (2)		Post-test (3)		F^a	Contrasts^b		
	M	SD	M	SD	M	SD		1 vs 2	2 vs 3	1 vs 3^c
Service play										
Control	87.3	17.3	98.7	4.4	100.0	0	n.s.	n.s.	n.s.	
Decision	24.8	27.4	34.0	21.0	74.9	21.0	12.92**	n.s.	18.97**	
Execution	13.4	24.7	24.4	21.7	43.0	21.2	5.38	n.s.	n.s.	13.90**
Game play										
Control	49.5	27.6	67.8	30.0	77.0	17.3	4.35*	n.s.	n.s.	9.15*
Decision	28.1	17.8	51.8	26.4	84.8	14.6	32.81**	109.33**	29.35**	
Execution	15.9	13.7	30.0	22.6	38.9	13.0	7.94**	n.s.	n.s.	22.33*

a 2,20 df for overall test; b 1,10 df for each contrast; c only contrast 1 vs 3 was significant
* $p < 0.05$; ** $p < 0.01$.

Table 4.11 Mean percentage of successful responses and Newman-Keuls post-hoc comparisons for service and game play components of performance for pre-, mid- and post-tests. [Source: McPherson, S.L. and French, K.E. (1991) 'Changes in cognitive strategies and motor skill in tennis', *Journal of Sport and Exercise Psychology*, 13, 26–41.)

	Pre-test (1)		Mid-test (2)		Post-test (3)			Contrasts[b]	
	M	SD	M	SD	M	SD	F[a]	1 vs 2	2 vs 3
Knowledge	46.3	8.7	56.5	9.2	59.0	12.0	14.40**	17.81**	n.s.
Forehand	14.8	5.2	22.6	4.7	19.7	6.4	10.41**	18.77**	n.s.
Backhand	12.3	8.2	19.3	5.2	20.5	5.1	8.13**	7.07*	n.s.
Serve	9.1	5.6	11.3	4.7	12.8	3.7	n.s.	n.s.	n.s.
Volley	14.6	6.0	16.0	2.8	17.5	2.9	n.s.	n.s.	n.s.

a 2,20 *df* for overall test; b 1,10 *df* for each contrast.
* $p < 0.05$; ** $p < 0.01$.

Table 4.10 indicates that knowledge and groundstroke skill (forehand and backhand) improved over the first 7-week instruction period, whereas no progression was noted over the second instruction block. Table 4.11 indicates that there was a significant improvement in decision-making ability for both service and game play components of performance over the second 7-week teaching block. These findings support a specificity of training argument. Improvements in fundamental motor skills and tennis knowledge were greatest when these components were stressed within the instruction program, whereas decision-making ability and skill execution improved when emphasis was placed on these components during game play situations.

In a second experiment, thirteen subjects took part in a similar tennis instruction programme. During the first half of the course, subjects received instruction on game strategy and tactics. The instruction programme was designed to integrate declarative and procedural knowledge regarding decision-making and response execution in a game situation. Much less time was devoted to fundamental tennis skill and factual knowledge. In the second half of the programme, subjects refined response selections and motor skills in game situations. The results showed a significant increase in declarative knowledge (i.e. knowledge test) over the initial 7-week block, whereas there were no improvements in motor skills across this same instruction period. However, analysis of service play and game play following the service demonstrated significant improvements both in decision-making and skill execution over the second half of the course. The implication is that direct instruction is required to develop fundamental motor skills in tennis, whilst cognitive aspects of performance such as decision-making are improved regardless of whether practice is skill or strategy oriented.

Verbal protocol analysis

An alternative approach to examining players' cognitive knowledge and how this influences decision-making has involved using structured and unstructured interview techniques (see Ericsson and Simon 1980). This approach may involve using verbal report protocols or think-aloud interviews to explore the breadth, depth and diversity of the knowledge base of experts and novices (e.g. Abernethy *et al.* 1994a; Cote, Salmela, Trudel, Baria and Russell 1995; Russell and Salmela 1992; McPherson 1993a, 1993b, 1994). Such an approach can provide deeper and more detailed information than the typical perceptual and memory tests described in previous sections. McPherson and Thomas (1989) used these techniques to determine what high- and low-skill tennis players were thinking about during service, backcourt and net game situations. Subjects were interviewed while viewing a diagram representing their position and their opponent's position on the tennis court (situation interviews), and on a point-by-point basis during actual game play (point-by-point interviews). In the situation interviews, players were asked to indicate what and how they would use knowledge in each specific instance, whereas in the game situation they were asked to respond to the question 'What were you thinking about while you were playing that point?'. Subjects' verbal reports were coded to determine the content and structure of knowledge used in decision-making in each situation.

The content of the knowledge base was assessed according to the number of concepts, the number of different concepts and the quality of each concept. A concept was defined as a unit of information related to response selection in tennis. Three different concepts were identified: condition, action and goal concepts. Condition concepts were defined as units of information that specified when or under what circumstances to apply a particular action to achieve a goal (i.e. an opponent's position on court, current score in the game or an opponent's weakness). An action concept referred to the action or actions required to produce goal-related changes in a game situation (i.e. this can include statements such as hitting the ball deep or rushing to the net). Finally, goal concepts reflected the means by which the game was won (i.e. winning points in tennis) or indicated the purpose of an action selected. An example of the interaction between action, goal and condition concepts is shown in Figure 4.4. In this example, the goal of winning the point (goal concept) can be achieved by playing a high lob (action concept) to the opponent's weak backhand (condition concept).

The structure of knowledge was represented by the number of connections between concepts and the linkage of concepts. Connections were classed as any word (if, when, or, and) or phrase (so that) connecting two concepts. The linkage of concepts was coded if two or more concepts

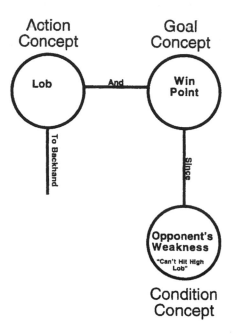

Figure 4.4 An example of the links between action, goal and condition concepts. (Source: McPherson, S.L. (1993a) 'Knowledge representation and decision-making in sport', in J.L. Starkes and F. Allard (eds) *Cognitive Issues in Motor Expertise*, Amsterdam: Elsevier Science.)

were connected within one phrase or sentence. For example, in Figure 4.4 there are three connections and two linkages.

The situation interviews revealed that the high-skill tennis players generated significantly more condition and action concepts. No differences were evident in the number of goal concepts between groups. With regard to knowledge structure, high-skilled players possessed a greater number of connections and linkages between goal, condition and action concepts. The high-skill players were more sophisticated in knowing when or under what conditions to apply particular actions. Also, the actions selected by the high-skill players were more appropriate and tactical in nature. Comparable findings were obtained from the point-by-point interviews during actual game situations. These interviews indicated that the high-skill group were more effective in executing the action selected. That is, they could execute the response they selected more often than novices. Finally, the results showed that the high-skill group were better at monitoring their performance and using self-regulation strategies to detect errors.

These findings demonstrate that high-skill performers revealed knowledge representations in which concepts were more complex and sophisticated. In addition, these concepts were more associated, reflecting causal or linked relations among concepts. In contrast, the low-skill players indicated that they knew the goal structure of the game but were unable to generate the detailed condition and action concepts required to success-fully perform the skill. The results also showed that during game play low-skill players generated the same number of total concepts, however the tactical content and structure of these concepts was what separated high- from low-skill players.

In conclusion, research using these knowledge-based approaches has shown that experts have a more extensive and richly structured knowl-edge base which they are able to use effectively during game situations. Furthermore, the expert's superior decision-making ability is not only due to the development of an enhanced declarative knowledge base, but also to a well-developed procedural knowledge base. Experts' are more aware of 'what to do' and 'how to do it' resulting in more specific and compe-tent problem-solving. They are able to represent problems at a deeper, more principled level than novices, solving problems through the use of concepts, semantics, and principles rather than through reliance on superficial, syntactic elements of the problems. In contrast, the novice performer's declarative and procedural knowledge base is less developed, resulting in a more generalised, inefficient approach to problem-solving.

Although these knowledge-based paradigms have considerable value as a method of examining knowledge representation in sport, there are several methodological assumptions which need to be addressed. For example, Abernethy *et al.* (1993) have highlighted a number of concerns with the use of this approach to study expertise in sport. First, they argue that there is much ambiguity in the meaning of procedural knowledge in the motor domain. Is procedural knowledge strictly knowledge used in the actual production of the selected action, or is it knowledge of how to select the correct course of action (as in the cognitive domain)? They argue that in high-strategy sports, procedures could be used in decision-making (e.g. when an opponent is deep in the back court area in badminton an error could be forced if the attacking player plays a drop shot to the front court area) or movement execution (e.g. keep the head and knee over the ball when playing a pass along the ground in soccer). The majority of research has referred to procedural knowledge as the processes used in decision-making, resulting in comparatively limited attention to the movement execution element of expertise. This problem highlights the inadequacies in using different knowledge production taxonomies to examine expertise. Furthermore, the numerous knowledge-based models and taxonomies which exist appear to be quite arbitrary in nature. These tend to be derived from the researchers' representations of the problem rather than from empirical observation and natural law (Abernethy *et al.* 1993).

Second, Abernethy *et al.* (1993) argue that these paradigms place too strong an emphasis on verbal reports as the principal source of data. They argue that much of the knowledge that performers use in decision-making is subconscious or implicit in nature, thus making it difficult to gain direct verbal access to these cognitive processes. Self-report data, they suggest, may be no more than a rational reconstruction of the strategy used from a third person perspective, varying little from the position occupied by the experimenter. Subjects merely verbalise the type of approach that they would expect other performers to use, rather than the strategy that they actually used to solve the problem presented. According to Abernethy *et al.* (1994b) self-reports may be particularly fallible in situations where movement execution is of principal concern. This is because movement execution may be essentially automatic and below the level of metacognitive or conscious awareness (Abernethy *et al.* 1993; Magill 1993). Despite these criticisms most cognitive psychologists agree that, if used properly, verbal reports can provide valuable insight into the cognitive processes involved in problem-solving and decision-making (see Ericsson and Simon 1993; Green 1995; Le Plat and Hoc 1981; White 1988).

A final concern relates to the tendency to directly link expertise with an increase in knowledge of the rules and concepts underlying performance in the sport concerned. Abernethy *et al.* (1993) suggest that this relationship may not necessarily be causal in nature. There is some evidence to suggest that experts behave intuitively rather than analytically, making decisions that cannot be described through procedural rules (Dreyfus and Dreyfus 1986). Interestingly, this argument suggests that these approaches may be more suitable for describing what is termed 'routine' rather than 'adaptive' expertise. On this note, since the emphasis throughout this chapter has been on identifying and explaining skill-based differences in anticipation and decision-making in sport, we now attempt to provide a stronger conceptual framework for this work by reviewing two cognitive theories of expertise.

EXPERTISE IN SPORT: A COGNITIVE PERSPECTIVE

Several theories exist to explain how the experts' superior knowledge base is acquired and used in sports performance. Among the most popular are the Active Control of Thought (ACT*) model developed by Anderson (1982, 1983, 1987) and the Parallel Distributed Processing (PDP) or neural network approach championed by Rumelhart and McClelland (1986).

Anderson's ACT* theory

Anderson's ACT* model was initially developed to examine expertise in more cognitive task domains; however, the theory appears to have a conceptual depth which may provide a theoretical framework for studying sports performance. Anderson (1983) suggests that human cognition is based on a set of condition–action links called productions. These productions are responsible for initiating appropriate actions under specified conditions. For example, if the condition specifies some sensory pattern (e.g. a short-pitched ball in cricket), and if elements matching these patterns are in working memory, then the production initiates the appropriate response (e.g. hook shot or avoidance action by the batsman). A production is what McPherson and Thomas (1989) termed an 'IF . . . THEN . . . DO' statement (i.e. condition–action link) with execution of the specified action contingent upon instantiation of the stated condition.

An ACT* production system consists of three different memories: declarative, production and working. Declarative memory consists of information about 'what to do', whereas production or procedural memory contains knowledge regarding 'how to do' something. We have already shown that both of these knowledge bases are important to skilled performance. Working memory contains the current information to which the system has access. It consists of information retrieved from long-term declarative memory as well as temporary information amassed from encoding processes and the action of productions.

In Anderson's theory, highlighted in Figure 4.5, several processes are identified. As indicated at the bottom of the diagram, the performer has

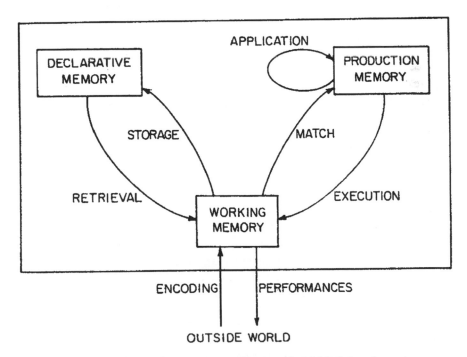

Figure 4.5 The ACT* production system framework, highlighting the major structural components and their interlinking processes. (Source: Anderson, J.R. (1983) *The Architecture of Cognition*, Cambridge MA: Harvard University Press.)

two links with the outside world. Encoding processes deposit sensory information from the environment in working memory, whereas performance processes convert commands in working memory into behaviour or actions by the performer. Likewise, working memory is linked to declarative memory through processes of retrieval and storage. Storage processes are used to create new permanent records of the contents of working memory and to increase the strength of existing records stored in declarative memory. The retrieval process retrieves information from declarative memory. The match process, highlighted on the right-hand side of the model, informs the production memory of the conditions present in working memory. Execution processes involve the transfer of the appropriate production rules required for a behavioural response to working memory. This entire process of production matching followed by execution is referred to as production application. Notice the arrow called application cycles which goes back into the production memory box. According to Anderson, this reflects the fact that new productions are learned by studying the outcome of existing productions. The outcome of the action response informs the performer of the appropriateness of the existing production. In this sense, the performer learns by doing.

An important aspect of the ACT* theory is that expertise is developed by the transition from control by declarative knowledge to control by procedural knowledge. Anderson (1983) argues that initially all incoming knowledge is encoded declaratively. These declarative encodings are accessed step-by-step by a procedure subject to capacity limits and under conscious control (e.g. verbal propositions are used). Here performance requires the maintenance in working memory of task components and their relationships. With practice, a production system develops that replaces the interpretative application with productions that perform the behaviour directly without conscious awareness. The production system represents task-specific procedures in long-term memory which are activated without requiring knowledge about the procedures to be retrieved into working memory. In effect, this results in a reduction in the number of production rules required to complete the task. This dropping out of consciousness of declarative knowledge is consistent with the cognitive views of automaticity discussed in Chapter 2.

Declarative knowledge is transferred into procedural knowledge through the process of knowledge compilation. This is a gradual process which enables errors in procedural information to be corrected over practice. Knowledge compilation has two subprocesses of composition and proceduralisation. Composition combines a sequence of productions into a single production which achieves the same end. This speeds up the knowledge compilation process by creating new operators that embody the sequences of steps used in a particular problem domain. Proceduralisation removes clauses in the condition of a production that require matching from long-term memory via working memory. That is, it builds versions of the production that do not require declarative information to be retrieved from working memory. The required declarative knowledge is simply built into the production rule. This is a significant advantage to the expert performer because it leads to an increase in the capacity that is available in working memory for other task-related activities (for a discussion, see Allard and Burnett 1985).

Once a production set has been created it is then tuned (i.e. made more appropriate and efficient for the task in hand) through subprocesses of generalisation, discrimination and strengthening. The generalisation process results in the development of more flexible productions such that they are more widely applicable in different situations. Discrimination processes restrict the use of a production only to instances where it will be successful. The strengthening process refers to enhancement of the production rule with repeated application so that the time taken to apply it diminishes. This process allows better rules to be reinforced and poor rules to be weakened. Finally, the actual selection of a production rule is determined by a competition among production rules in which they compete for the activation of the sensory elements to which they match. This competition will result in stronger productions being selected over weaker ones.

The successful development of these production systems illustrates the important role that the proceduralisation of knowledge plays in skilled performance. From a practical perspective, it is therefore important to examine the most efficient methods of developing these production systems in sport. Anderson (1983) suggests that new productions are learned by studying the outcome of existing productions. Performing a task (i.e. proceduralisation or the 'action' component of the production system) promotes the acquisition and retention of specific declarative knowledge. It is important to note however that strictly speaking, in ACT* theory, 'actions' refer to cognitive rather than motor actions. Therefore, the statement 'performing the task' relates only to the response selection component of performance. Consequently, strict application of ACT* theory to the study of motor expertise is complicated because in sport 'performing the task' could refer to either the selection of a movement or its execution (for a more detailed discussion, see Abernethy *et al.* 1993; McPherson 1994).

Another critical question for those interested in developing expertise in sport is how knowing and doing are related. This question was recently addressed in an article by Allard and Starkes (1991). They reviewed a study by Parker (1989) which attempted to determine whether the expert's enhanced declarative knowledge is actually a component of skill or rather a by-product of experience or exposure to the task. Groups of hockey players, coaches and spectators were required to sort photographs of game phases into conceptual categories (e.g. counterattacks, defensive strategies and tactical ploys). The results showed that fans were less able to identify the play highlighted on each picture, resulting in differences across groups in assigning pictures to categories. The expert players and coaches were able to use their existing knowledge developed through playing the game to interpret what was shown in the pictures, while novice subjects who watched lots of hockey, but had limited experience of playing, sorted only on the basis of information present in the picture. The implication is that declarative knowledge is a constituent of skill rather than a by-product of the time spent in a particular domain. That is, knowing facilitates doing.

Allard and Starkes (1991) suggest that if knowing and doing are linked then this link should work both ways such that doing should also facilitate knowing. Williams and Davids (1995) examined the importance of the doing–knowing link in the development of declarative knowledge in soccer. This study involved testing groups of experienced players and physically disabled experienced spectators on soccer-specific recall, recognition and anticipation tests. The experienced players had played an average of 650 competitive soccer games and watched less than 50 live matches, whereas the experienced soccer spectators had viewed an average of 600 soccer matches, but had never played soccer. The assumption was that the skilled soccer players would demonstrate an enhanced cognitive knowledge base because the doing aspect of performance facilitates knowing. The experienced soccer players showed better recall, recognition and anticipation performance than the physically disabled group. The results from the recall study are presented in Table 4.2. The main difference between the two groups was that the physically disabled subjects had acquired experience purely by spectating, while the soccer players had gathered experience through performing. In other words, the subjects were comparable with regard to their soccer experience but differed in the way that this experience had been accumulated. Findings suggest that knowing and doing are linked such that not only does knowing influence doing but also that doing facilitates knowing. The argument is that knowing how to perform a particular skill 'provides more "hooks" on which to hang new declarative knowledge' (Starkes and Deakin 1984: 123).

These studies show that skill in knowing and skill in doing are important aspects of performance. However, Allard and Starkes (1991) suggest that knowing and doing are not linked directly by 'IF . . . THEN . . . DO' relationships. Instead, they argue that knowing and doing can be influenced independently (c.f. McPherson and French 1991). Not only do experts have large declarative and procedural knowledge bases but they are also more adaptable in the way that these knowledge bases are linked. They suggest that 'it is the flexibility in linking, rather than the establishment of stable links, that is vital for successful motor performance' (Allard and Starkes 1991: 150).

Although Anderson's work provides a plausible theoretical background to explain skilled decision-making in sport, Holyoak (1991) suggests that the research evidence supporting a production systems or symbolic representation account of cognition is somewhat contradictory. He suggests that these theories with their emphasis on specialised production rules through knowledge compilation provide an explanation of what he terms 'routine expertise' (i.e. solving of familiar or routine problems quickly and accurately), but are unable to explain how experts are able to invent new procedures to respond within unpredictable situations. This type of proficiency, which is based on a deeper conceptual understanding of the task, he refers to as 'adaptive expertise'. Holyoak (ibid.) suggests that this type of expertise can be better explained by a more recent theoretical approach based on PDP.

Parallel distributed processing: a neural network model

The PDP or neural network approach attempts to develop models of cognition from a knowledge of neural processing. The approach originates from neurophysiology and our understanding of how neurons function within the brain (Anderson 1990). This perspective is also referred to as connectionism because it is concerned with ways of connecting neural elements together to account for higher-level cognition.

The important distinction between this model and Anderson's ACT* theory is that connectionism presents an analysis whereby cognitive representations are held as distributed patterns of activity across a set of processing units rather than as symbolic representations stored in some 'specific' address in memory. When information is not being used, patterns of activation are not stored as data structures and are not present in the system. As suggested by Tienson (1990), 'the only symbols ever present in a connectionist system are active representations' (p. 392). Memory is not viewed as a collection of explicit traces stored at identifiable addresses, but rather as a set of potentialities across an entire network of processing units (Bruce *et al.* 1996). These processing units are viewed as abstract elements which define a meaningful pattern of activity (Shadbolt 1988). All processing is carried out directly by these units without any higher-level or executive control being involved. The set of units and their connections are typically referred to as a neural network. The number of units, their pattern of connectivity and their interactions with the environment are collectively termed the cognitive architecture (McClelland 1989).

Units are simple processing devices which become activated based on input from the environment and from other units. It is the actual pattern of connectivity between these units which reflects what the network represents. For example, the recognition of a curve ball in baseball would trigger off a different pattern of activation between these units compared with the detection of a particular pattern of play in basketball or rugby. Units interact by transmitting signals to their neighbours. The strength of their signals and therefore the degree to which they affect their neighbours are determined by the level of activation of each unit. The level of activation is determined by the weights assigned to the connections between

units. Weights may be either positive or negative corresponding to exci-
tatory (i.e. receiving unit becomes active when the sending unit is activated)
or inhibitory (i.e. receiving unit becomes inactive when the sending unit
is activated) connections. The knowledge that governs processing is stored
in the weights of the connections. Learning occurs through the adjustment of these weights with processing activity (Cohen *et al.* 1992;
McClelland 1989; Rumelhart and Todd 1993). This is what Tienson
(1990) refers to as 'getting your weights changed' (p. 387). This can be
achieved by three processes: developing new connections, losing existing
connections and modifying the strengths of connections that already exist
(Rumelhart 1989).

In many ways, neural network models appear to display characteristics
that make them similar to the non-linear, self-organisation models
discussed in Chapter 7. First, these models are computationally non-linear
with the characteristics of the output pattern being modelled by the layers
of hidden units connecting input and output units (for a discussion, see
Churchland 1989). Second, neural networks exhibit principles of attractor
dynamics whereby the system attempts to move into the most natural and
comfortable mode of computation (Jeannerod and Marteniuk 1992). For
example, initially there is much activity, with units sending and receiving
signals repeatedly. However, in time the system settles into a stable configuration or attractor phase that constitutes a virtual solution to the
problem posed (for an example, see Massone and Bizzi 1989; Jordan
1990). The important point is that, rather like a non-linear dynamical
system, a neural network settles into a solution rather than this solution
being calculated via some symbolic structure. The calculations are not
based on some logarithmic formula, but rather are an inherent aspect of
the system (Jeannerod and Mackenzie 1992). The principal difference
between the theories is that connectionist models suppose that the nervous
system is the exclusive level of explanation for action, while dynamical
models also propose that the organisation of an action is constrained by
components and processes at the level of the action system (e.g. coordinative structures) and at the level of the environment (e.g. laws of
perceiving and acting) (see Schmidt and Fitzpatrick 1996).

A schematic representation of a typical multilayered neural network is
provided in Figure 4.6. In this model, there are three layers of interconnected processing units or nodes with each unit in the network being
connected to every unit at the adjoining level. There is an input to each
unit from the stimulus pattern, and an output or response which is
expressed as a pattern of activation across the units in the output layer.
Input units may also receive stimuli from units within the system,
and output units can send feedback to units within the system (Tienson
1990). When a pattern is presented to the network, the system's response
is determined by that pattern's profile of activation across the input units
and by the strengths (or weights) of the connections within each of the

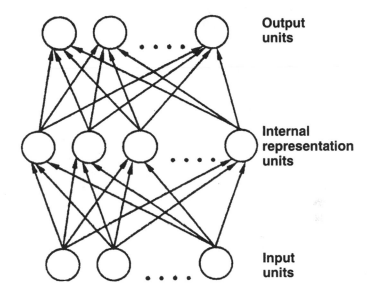

Figure 4.6 An example of a simple multi-layered neural network. (Adapted from Masson, M.E.J. (1990) 'Cognitive theories of skill acquisition', *Human Movement Science* 9: 221–39.)

intervening layers in the system. The pattern of activation moves from the input layer, through the internal representation tier (i.e. what is called the hidden layer) and then on to the output layer. At each of these layers, the activation received by each unit is the sum of the unit's activity multiplied by the weight on the connection between that unit and the unit within the previous layer.

In such a network, stimulus information enters the system at the input level thus creating a particular pattern of activation. This pattern of activation determines what the system is representing at any time. In sport, this pattern could represent an opponent playing a forehand drive in tennis or a boast shot in squash. The pattern of activation at the input level is computed and then transformed into a value which represents the activation level in the hidden layer. Further computations then occur before a response such as a crosscourt return stroke in tennis or a frontcourt drop shot in squash is propagated to the output level. The eventual response to the stimulus pattern is determined by the weight or strength of each of the connections within the system. Initially, it will be somewhat accidental if the system produces the correct output for a given input. However, through experience, weights are adjusted algorithmically layer by layer back through the system as a function of each weight's contribution to the error (Tienson 1990). Adjustments are made to connection weights to ensure that the observed output patterns produced by the network coincide more closely with the desired output patterns. This procedure entails comparing the actual output pattern to the desired pattern and computing the size of the error in each unit. The amount of deviation or error is then used to calculate the extent to which the connection weights attached to the unit must be changed. In this way, the system evolves a set of correction weights that enables it to settle into a stable configuration that constitutes its solution to the problem posed (ibid.). Clearly, there is a profound difference between this approach and more traditional approaches such as Anderson's ACT* theory. The neural network model assumes that knowledge is acquired through the tuning of connections as they are used in processing, whereas the symbolic viewpoint suggests that information is formulated and stored as declarative facts (Rumelhart 1989).

Research addressing the plausibility of the connectionist approach has expanded dramatically in recent years. Much of this work has been inter-disciplinary in nature, being conducted by psychologists, physicists, computer scientists, engineers and neuroscientists (Rumelhart 1989). Although there has been some research conducted by those interested in motor behaviour (e.g. Bullock, Grossberg and Guenther 1996; Jordan 1990; Jordan and Rosenbaum 1989; Kawato 1993; Requin, Riehle and Seal 1993), the plausibility of the connectionist approach as a theoretical explanation for expertise in sport has not been adequately addressed. This is disappointing since the advantage of having small units of knowledge operating in parallel (i.e. a neural network) rather than having larger units of knowledge operating individually (i.e. compiled rules) may provide a more logical explanation for the skilled performer's greater flexibility and adaptability (Holyoak 1991).

SUMMARY AND FUTURE RESEARCH DIRECTIONS

Our aim in this chapter was to review research examining anticipation and decision-making in sport. Since the majority of research work in this area has examined skilled-based differences in anticipation and decision-making, the emphasis throughout the chapter was on expertise in sport. We showed that when compared to novices from within their domain of expertise, expert sports performers are known to: (a) be faster and more accurate in recognising patterns of play; (b) be able to quickly and accurately detect and locate objects of relevance in the visual field; (c) be superior in anticipating the actions of their opponents based on advance visual cues; (d) have superior knowledge of situational probabilities; (e) make more appropriate tactical decisions; (f) possess deeper and more structured knowledge of both factual and procedural matters; and (h) possess superior self-monitoring skills. Based on contemporary cognitive theories such as Anderson's ACT* theory and neural network modelling, we showed that experts have a larger and more highly differentiated cognitive knowledge base which expedites skilled performance in sport.

Although the research presented in this chapter illustrates the impressive breadth of knowledge on anticipation and decision-making, much research needs to be undertaken before we have an adequate picture of the processes underlying skilled performance in sport. Thus far, the majority of research has adopted the expert–novice paradigm to examine differences in anticipation and decision-making. This paradigm typically involves exposing expert and novice performers to a single laboratory-based task which purports to measure the particular parameter under study (Abernethy *et al.* 1993). However, there are several criticisms which need to be addressed if knowledge is to be advanced.

First, previous research has relied too heavily on recipient paradigms borrowed from cognitive psychology. It has been a consistent theme throughout this text that sport and exercise scientists should now move away from these imported paradigms and develop paradigms which more adequately reproduce the demands on performers in sport. Although contemporary research has attempted to use more realistic stimuli and response measures (e.g. Helsen and Pauwels 1993; Williams *et al.* 1994, Williams and Davids 1998b), there still appears to be an over-reliance on contrived or simplistic laboratory tasks. However, the recent explosion of measurement technology should enable researchers to move towards more ecologically valid paradigms. Many researchers now have at their disposal advanced measurement technology such as three-dimensional motion analysers, force transducers, high-speed video, eye movement registration systems and liquid crystal occlusion glasses. These systems enable researchers to acquire more sensitive and reliable measurements and to move closer to conducting research in natural settings without losing experimental control (Abernethy *et al.* 1993).

Notwithstanding the challenges involved in developing more realistic paradigms, an argument exists for the more extensive use of qualitative (i.e. structured and unstructured interview techniques) and idiographic (i.e. single-case study designs) approaches in the investigation of expert–novice differences in anticipation and decision-making in sport. Employing such approaches would provide a richness and depth of knowledge which can not be generated through the exclusive use of quantitative, nomothetic (i.e. between-group) approaches. Combining different approaches will help to maximise our understanding of skilled performance in sport. To illustrate this promising new direction in the study of sport expertise, a study by Russell and Salmela (1992) employed both qualitative and quantitative methods within a single case-study design to examine how an international cyclist perceived, and planned strategies for, typical problems which confronted him in competition.

A second concern relates to the definition of the expert group. In one study, experts may be international performers whereas another study may use university players as their expert subject sample. The classification of an expert appears to be quite arbitrary in nature varying considerable from one study to another. This lack of consistency makes it difficult to compare findings or observations across research studies, thus restricting generalisations about anticipation and decision-making in sport (Abernethy *et al.* 1993). Some researchers propose that it takes at least ten years of intensive practice to become an expert in any domain (e.g. Bloom 1985; Hayes 1985; Ericsson *et al.* 1993). However, Sternberg (1996) points out that the relationship between amount of practice and performance is not linear and that some individuals fail to progress despite years of practice within their particular domain. The implication is that sport and exercise scientists should develop more universal criteria as to what constitutes an expert. Ericsson and Charness (1994) suggest that a more objective term 'expert performance' should replace the rather diffuse construct of expertise. They define expert performance as consistently superior performance on a specified set of representative tasks for the domain in question. This approach suggests that the hallmark of expertise is the capacity to reliably reproduce a high standard of proficiency in a given sport.

Alternatively, Chamberlain and Coelho (1993) suggest that it may be more appropriate to classify experts and novices based on their anticipation or decision-making ability rather than on their current performance level, which entails an interaction between perceptual and motor skills. The argument is that having two groups of subjects consisting of high- and low-ability decision-makers would tell us more about expert decision-making in sport compared with groups of high- and low-ability performers. They suggest one way of separating groups based on anticipation or decision-making ability would be to use a behavioural assessment instrument to assess performance during actual game play (for an example of such an assessment instrument, see French and Thomas 1987).

Another related problem arises in the selection of the control group of novice subjects. This is generally comprised of subjects with little or no experience in the sport. The problem with using such control groups is that they differ from the expert group both in terms of skill level and in task familiarity (i.e. experience on the task). This makes it difficult to determine whether differences in performance between groups are due to experts' greater ability or rather to their increased familiarity with the task environment. Several researchers have recently suggested that a more logical control group would involve subjects with comparable amounts of experience but poorer task performance (e.g. Abernethy *et al.* 1993; Allard *et al.* 1993; Chamberlain and Coelho 1993; Starkes 1993). Such control groups would enable us to determine whether the expert group's superior performance is a characteristic of expertise or a by-product of the subject's experience on the task. Thus far, this type of control group has been rarely employed in the sport science literature (for exceptions, see Starkes, Deakin, Lindley and Crisp 1987; Williams and Davids 1995).

Another advantage of using such control groups is that they enable researchers to determine the relative importance of initial ability compared with experience on the task in the development of anticipation and decision-making skills. By directly manipulating skill and experience levels researchers could determine how much of expert performance can be attributed to the individual abilities that the subject brings to the task compared with training and experience (Starkes 1993). The relative importance of innate abilities compared with 'deliberate' practice to skilled performance is currently a topical area in cognitive psychology (see Ericsson and Charness 1994; Ericsson *et al.* 1993; Ericsson 1996).

A common problem in measuring anticipation in sport has been that studies have typically only measured performance on one task using single dependent measures. Additional insights could be gained by combining several methodological approaches (e.g. recall, recognition, eye movements, verbal reports and think-aloud protocols) in order to have multiple dependent measures of performance (McPherson 1993a). The use of multiple dependent measures has several advantages. First, differences may not exist on a particular component when that element is measured in isolation, whereas it may be significant through its interaction with other components of skilled perception. Second, such an approach recognises that skilled performance is dependent on multiple perceptual attributes ranging from optometric and perimetric characteristics to more cognitive abilities such as recall and recognition. Therefore, a multitask approach provides a more detailed and comprehensive analysis of the perceptual characteristics underlying skilled performance in sport. Although there have been some promising attempts to use multitask approaches to examine skilled perception (see Starkes 1987; Helsen and Pauwels 1993; Williams and Davids 1995), this type of research strategy has not been extensively used in the sport and exercise sciences.

The existing database on anticipation and decision-making has been characterised by one-off studies rather than coherent research programmes. That is, research has tended to use a 'shot-gun' approach whereby subjects from one sport have been examined on a single task. Future research needs to be more systematic by conducting persistent studies on performers from one sport or by examining the same characteristic across a range of different sports (Abernethy *et al.* 1993). An example of such a research programme has been conducted by Williams and colleagues (Williams *et al.* 1993, 1994; Williams and Davids 1995, 1998b) who have examined perceptual skill in soccer using recall, recognition and reaction time paradigms. They found that the perceptual strategy underlying decision-making is dependent on the type of task that performers are presented. These findings suggest that a more detailed analysis of anticipation in a particular sport necessitates the use of multiple paradigms with the same group or groups of subjects. Similarly, attempts to examine recall ability across different sports has resulted in some interesting conclusions regarding the perceptual requirements of each sport (for a discussion, see pp. 103–4). Since there appears to be much potential for training skilled perception using video simulations (see Chamberlain and Coelho 1993; Starkes and Lindley 1994), much more systematic research programmes are required to determine the specific perceptual requirements of each sport.

Finally, there is a need for more longitudinal rather than cross-sectional research to determine how anticipation and decision-making skills develop over considerable time and practice. Although there are several logistical problems with longitudinal designs (see Abernethy *et al.* 1993), such research is required if we are to determine the most appropriate instructional interventions that influence the development and maintenance of expertise across the life span (Housner and French 1994; McPherson 1994). One approach is to follow performers over the course of a season to determine changes in knowledge and skill level over a period of time (for an example, see French and Thomas 1987). Perhaps an initial analysis using large groups of subjects could be followed by more detailed analyses of a smaller number of subjects or only a single subject (Housner and French 1994). Certainly, a single case-study approach would allow deeper and more meaningful analyses of the factors which impact on the development of skilled perception and decision-making in sport. Another approach could be to incorporate age rather than experience or skill level as an independent variable in cross-sectional designs (for an example, see Abernethy 1988c). Regardless of the methodology used, it is only by measuring changes in knowledge structure and skill development over protracted periods of time that we can attempt to determine the factors underpinning skilled perception and decision-making in sport (French and Nevitt 1993).

In concluding, it is important that future work in this area should endeavour to adopt a stronger theoretical focus. Previous research has often being criticised for being too descriptive and lacking in theoretical explanation. Although descriptive research is an essential step towards improving our understanding of anticipation and decision-making in sport, it should not be seen as a substitute for understanding. Understanding, as Abernethy *et al.* (1993) suggest, is a step beyond description resulting in the development of a conceptual or theoretical framework for the explanation and prediction of skilled anticipation and decision-making in sport. Since there now exists a substantial literature base within this area, researchers should ensure that future work is more theoretically driven and that concerted efforts are made to link existing descriptive work to theoretical premises (for a more detailed discussion, see Abernethy *et al.* 1993; 1994b). It is an indication of the maturity of this area of study that we are now ready to move the field beyond description and towards explanation.

5 Visual search strategy in sport

INTRODUCTION

In many sports, performers have to make rapid decisions in a complex and constantly changing environment. For example, games players must act on the basis of information presented by the ball, team-mates and opponents (Williams *et al.* 1994). These decisions must be made under pressure with opponents trying to restrict both the time and space available to perform. In Chapter 2, we suggested that effective performance in such contexts requires that players focus their attention only on the most relevant or crucial sources of information. That is, knowing 'where' and 'when' to look are important aspects of skilled performance. The way in which performers continually move their eyes to focus on selected areas of the display has generated significant interest in recent years. It has been known for some time that the visual search patterns displayed by the expert are not conducted in a random manner, but are based on deliberate perceptual strategies (Bard and Fleury 1981). Eye movements are controlled by a search strategy which enables the performer to make more efficient use of the time available for analysis of the display.

This chapter examines the role of visual search strategy in sport. Initially, we highlight the type of eye movements used during sports performance and critically review some of the techniques used to measure these eye movements. Since visual search data have frequently been used to make direct implications regarding skill-based differences in selective attention, we continue by investigating the relationship between visual fixation and selective information pick-up. Several assumptions and limitations in inferring a direct relationship between visual fixation (i.e. 'looking') and selective attention (i.e. 'seeing') are highlighted. Next, a theoretical background to the control of search strategy in sport is provided by drawing upon contemporary theories in cognitive psychology. The existing sport-specific research is critically reviewed and the main implications of these findings to performance are outlined. In subsequent sections, we review some alternative methods for assessing visual search processes in sport and examine whether visual search strategy can be enhanced through the development of sport-specific training programmes. Finally, some suggestions are provided for future research within this area.

EYE MOVEMENTS IN SPORT

Performers confronted with the task of picking up relevant information in sport engage in the process of visual search. For example, consider a skilled basketball player such as Michael Jordan. While dribbling the ball down the court, he will be acquiring information from the ball, the basket and the positions of team-mates and opponents before deciding on a passing option. To achieve this, he must make small and rapid eye movements to shift informative areas of the display from the periphery of the visual retina, where resolution is poor, to the fovea (see Chapter 3). Therefore, the visual search process involves using vision to acquire information from the environment in order to determine what to do in any given instance (Magill 1993).

The fovea covers around 1–2 degrees of the central area of the retina and it receives the clearest and most sharply focused image (Zeki 1993). This area is composed entirely of cone receptors which, because of their one-to-one relationship with the bipolar and ganglion cells found in the next nuclear layer in the retina, enable the mediation of fine visual acuity (Sivak and MacKenzie 1992). Cones transduce light waves from the environment into electrical impulses which are subsequently transmitted to the brain for interpretation. The clarity of the visual image decreases gradually as the stimulus moves into the parafovea, which covers some 10 degrees of visual arc (Pinel 1993), and rather more rapidly in the periphery which extends up to 160 degrees vertically and 200 degrees horizontally (Harrington 1964). In Chapter 3, we showed that visual clarity decreases due to the reduction in concentration of cone cells and the increase in rod receptors in the parafovea and periphery. Rod receptors are more sensitive to light and motion, but because of their many-to-one mapping with the underlying ganglion cells, lack the ability to pick up both detail and colour. Therefore, to view moving objects with the greatest clarity the performer must continually adjust the positioning of the fovea of the eyes.

The two-visual system and visual search strategy

In the visual search process, it is assumed that an object is initially detected within peripheral vision, which provides information concerning 'where it is'. The object is then identified or perceived by bringing the stimuli into the more sensitive foveal region of the retina, which provides information regarding 'what it is' (Trevarthen 1968). The detection of stimuli within the periphery is generally assumed to be subconscious or non-attention demanding (i.e. 'preattentive'). However, this does not preclude the fact that peripheral vision can also be used consciously during the visual search process (see Williams and Davids 1998b). In contrast, the foveal stage of performance is assumed to be conscious or attention demanding and is termed the 'attentive' stage of the visual search process (e.g. Neisser 1967). Following the above rationale, to accurately and rapidly identify the swerve of a cricket ball, or recognise an attacking play in netball, the sports performer must continually adjust the position of the eyes to maintain optimum visual clarity (Davids 1984). In Chapter 3, we provided an illustration to highlight the types of eye movements commonly employed in a task like soccer goalkeeping. In this section we elaborate on this earlier discussion by providing more detailed coverage of the most commonly employed eye movements, namely, saccades, smooth pursuit tracking and the vestibular–ocular reflex.

Saccadic eye movements

In Chapter 3 we showed that eye movements are achieved via six pairs of small extraocular muscles which are attached to the eyeball. These muscles enable the eye to move, thus bringing images of objects of interest on to the sensitive foveal region. The most frequent eye movements in time-constrained contexts such as sport appear to be saccades. These are conjugate eye movements (i.e. both eyes move in the same direction together) which are responsible for the rapid jumps that bring a new part of the visual field into foveal vision (Carpenter 1988; Rosenbaum 1991). In sport, a performer may use saccadic eye movements to scan quickly from one player to another or from a ball to a target such as a golf hole or a basketball hoop. Therefore, saccades are rapid movements of the eyes to a new fixation point, enabling another informative area of the display to be fixated.

Research suggests that there is a dramatic decline in visual sensitivity *during* saccades (Ditchburn 1973; Festinger 1971; Massaro 1975). That is, visual information cannot be acquired during saccadic eye movements. This reduction in visual sensitivity, referred to as saccadic suppression, can be explained by either central or peripheral limitations (see Williams, Davids, Burwitz and Williams 1993b). Theoretically, because of the suppression of information processing during saccadic eye movements, a search strategy which involves fewer fixations and, consequently, a reduced need for saccadic eye movements is assumed to be more effective (Williams *et al.* 1994). A more selective and efficient search pattern would involve fewer fixations of longer duration enabling more time to be spent analysing stimuli rather than using saccadic eye movements to search through a display. Practically this assumption has not always being corroborated by the research findings. This is an important point and is discussed in greater detail later in this chapter.

Visual fixations

The purpose of saccadic eye movements is to shift the image of an informative area of the display from the peripheral retina to the more sensitive fovea. However, since visual sensitivity is reduced markedly during saccades, researchers have studied the fixations which separate eye movements. That is, as far as visual search research in sport is concerned, the 'pause is mightier than the move' (Mackworth 1976: 174). Visual fixations enable the performer to stabilise an informative area of the display, such as a ball or a player in foveal vision, enabling more detailed processing to occur. The duration of the fixation period has been assumed by researchers to signal the relative importance and complexity of the display area to the observer. The more information which has to be processed, the longer the fixation duration (Just and Carpenter 1976). For this reason, fixation duration varies markedly depending on the nature and difficulty of the task and on the type of visual display presented to observers (see Abernethy 1988b; Abernethy and Russell 1987a). In sport, relatively high fixation durations (850–1500 ms) have been reported in complex viewing circumstances in team games like soccer (Williams *et al.* 1994; Williams and Davids 1998b), whilst values as low as 100 ms are typical for highly practised performers or those reviewing familiar stimuli such as in golf putting (Vickers 1992).

Pursuit tracking eye movements

Smooth pursuit movements enable the eyes to track slow-moving targets within the visual field, such as the ball or an opponent, so that a stable retinal image may be maintained. For example, if you follow the path of your finger, whilst keeping your head fixed, as it slowly crosses your visual field you will be using smooth pursuit eye movements. The maximum velocity of these eye movements is around 100 degrees/sec, although the eye's tracking ability begins to deteriorate at an angular velocity greater than 30 degrees/sec (Rosenbaum 1991). Thus, the success of the visual system in achieving a stable retinal image depends on the speed of the moving target which the eyes are required to follow (Sekuler and Blake 1990). Pursuit eye movements are therefore restricted to situations such as following the target in clay pigeon shooting, watching the ball after a shot in golf, following a floating serve in volleyball, or tracking the movements of a distant player on the rugby field. Generally, however, the rapid changes in the visual array typical of most fast sports, such as squash and ice hockey, makes it difficult to visually follow an object using pursuit-tracking eye movements (Haywood 1984). At excessive speeds, it has been demonstrated that experienced sport performers do not attempt to track a ball during its entire flight path but instead use saccadic eye movements to predict the future position of the ball (e.g. Bahill and LaRitz 1984;

Hubbard and Seng 1954; Ripoll 1991). Therefore, most investigations of visual search strategies in sport have tended to concentrate on saccadic rather than pursuit-tracking eye movements. From a more practical viewpoint, the inability of the performer to maintain visual fixation during rapid ball flight clearly contradicts the common coaching dictum of 'keep your eye on the ball'. Perhaps this recommendation may be more to do with maintaining a stable head and body position during skill execution than with the need to extract operational information from the ball.

Vestibular–ocular reflex

The vestibular–ocular reflex functions to stabilise gaze and ensure clear vision during head movements. Primarily, it serves to maintain visual clarity during dynamic sport situations. For example, the ice hockey player attempting to pick up information from a team-mate or opponent can achieve this either by initiating saccadic eye movements to bring the player into foveal vision or, alternatively, by keeping the eyes fixed but moving the head. The vestibular–ocular reflex comprises a number of structures, located within the inner ear, which register motion of the head within each movement plane (Rosenbaum 1991). These structures enable the performer to produce compensatory eye movements much more rapidly (about 16 ms) than changes associated with the use of the visual system alone (about 70 ms) (Leigh and Zee 1991). Therefore, the head, body and oculomotor control system function as one closely coupled system during skilled performance (Guitton and Volle 1987).

Although the vestibular–ocular system appears important in sport, relatively little research has examined the interaction between head and body movements in sport contexts. This may be primarily due to technical problems with eye movement registration systems which have restricted their use in dynamic situations. These problems have typically constrained researchers to using a fixed-head approach where subjects have been required to hold their head as still as possible during testing. Nevertheless, recent research has demonstrated an important functional relationship between head and eye position in aiming and throwing activities (e.g. see Bard, Fleury and Paillard 1990; Ripoll, Bard and Paillard 1986; Guitton and Volle 1987; Schmid and Zambarbieri 1991). These studies suggest that during aiming at far targets, such as a basketball hoop, the eyes move prior to the head. The head then follows because of its greater inertia, with the eyes localising the target first and visual discrimination commencing immediately upon fixation even though the head is moving (Gauthier, Semmlow, Vercher, Pedrono and Obrecht 1991). Clearly, further innovative research is required to increase our understanding of the complex relationship between head, body and eye movements in sport contexts. For example, it would be interesting to examine how the interaction between head, body and eye movements alters as a function of the constraints of the task and subject skill level in various sports. Understanding these complex relations could give us insights for teaching learners how to pick up visual information during sports performance.

EYE MOVEMENT REGISTRATION TECHNIQUES[1]

There are several techniques currently available for measuring eye movements (see Leigh and Zee 1991). The most popular procedure in motor behaviour has been the head-mounted corneal-reflection method. This technique is based on the principle that the reflection of a beam of light placed in front of the cornea forms a near image behind the surface which can be recorded on to video. The reflection of this light source on the central portion of the cornea is assumed to be a function of eye position and, therefore, the point of fixation. A change in the point of fixation changes the position of the cornea, which can be picked up by the corneal-reflection system. The most commonly used systems in sport settings over the last few years have been the NAC Eye Mark Recorder and the ASL Series 4000 systems.

NAC Eye Mark Recorders[2]

With the NAC system the primary visual image is obtained by means of a head-mounted video camera which continuously records the field of view. Two light emitting diodes (LED), placed at the lower end of the head-mounted system, send light into the observer's eyes providing a direct image on the cornea. The light reflected from the cornea is picked up by adjustable mirrors in two small cameras fitted on to each side of the eye goggles. The mirrors are adjusted by calibration so that the reflection point corresponds to the observer's fixation point within the visual field. These signals are then transmitted to a camera controller and generate separate image signals representing both right and left eyes. The respective signals are then superimposed by means of an external processing unit on to the video image of the display which is recorded for further analysis. During testing, when subjects move their eyes, the virtual image made by the LED lamp on the cornea is put in motion by the movement of the eyeball, thus indicating the section of the display being fixated. The system provides data in terms of X and Y coordinates which can be interpreted to provide data on the location, duration and order of subjects' fixations.

ASL Series 4000 eye movement measurement systems[3]

The ASL is a video-based monocular system that works by detecting the position of the pupil and the corneal reflex (reflection of a light source from the surface of the cornea), in a video image of the eye. The relative position of these features is used to compute eye line-of-gaze with respect to the optics. The corneal reflex is measured by the reflection of a small helmet-mounted light source from the surface of the cornea in a similar manner to the NAC system. An advantage of the ASL system is that it also measures the position of the pupil, thus enabling accurate measurement of visual fixation with respect to the helmet, even if the helmet slips on the head. This represents a major advance since the system is robust enough to enable data to be collected in realistic field-based circumstances without the need for frequent recalibration (see Figure 5.1). Displacement data from the pupil and cornea are recorded by a small camera, processed by computer, and superimposed as a cursor on the scene camera image to highlight the point-of-gaze. The reflected image of the light source from the corneal surface is represented as moving cross-hairs or cursor on a scene monitor. These are subsequently analysed to produce data on fixation location, duration and order.

Problems with eye movement registration systems

Historically, there have been numerous problems with the use of eye movement registration systems in sport. These have included difficulties with the measurement range and accuracy, calibration and set-up time, subject discomfort during testing and the time required to analyse the data using

Figure 5.1 A schematic representation of the ASL 4000SU system being used to collect data during simulated 3 vs 3 situations in soccer.

frame-by-frame video analysis. The major difficulty experienced by many researchers has been the need for frequent recalibration of these systems following minor postural adjustments by the subject. This problem, in particular, has prevented their use within realistic experiments involving movement-based response measures. However, recent technological advances have provided important improvements which have increased their utility within sports-based contexts. For example, these systems are now more comfortable and less invasive for the subject, more accurate, easier to calibrate and more tolerant of head and body movements. Also, advances in computer technology have reduced the time required for data analyses with a number of semi-automated and automated procedures now available to analyse eye movements. For example, these systems can now be incorporated with magnetic head tracking devices which enable simultaneous recording of head and eye movements. The combination of information regarding eye fixations, head position and key locations in the image being viewed by the subject allows visual point-of-gaze to be determined automatically via on-line data analysis packages. This procedure also enables the researcher to examine the interaction between head and eye movements during dynamic performance contexts.

Regardless, there are still problems with these systems. The NAC system does require some recalibration when excessive head and postural movements are involved. This presents problems when conducting field-based work where subjects are required to produce a movement response. Furthermore, because the system has only a manual adjustment procedure for parallax error it is poorly equipped for dealing with real-life activities when objects are moving towards, or away from, the subject. This reduces its application within tasks such as ball catching and striking. The problem of visual parallax is reduced in the ASL system because a reflection of the visual field from a head-mounted visor, rather than that from the scene camera, is processed. Yet, this procedure is not exemplary since it can reduce the brightness and clarity of the recorded camera image making subsequent analysis difficult. Moreover, neither system works particularly well when used outdoors in direct sunlight. Exposure to strong sunlight constricts subject pupil size and weakens the intensity of the infrared light source, thus complicating calibration and data collection procedures. The NAC system also needs to be used in association with a driver/control unit which is strapped to the subject's back restricting movement. Additional problems, such as the lack of agreement between the left and right eye marks, and the loss of linearity in the response of the subject's eye mark for eye movements across the entire range of the visual field should also be acknowledged. Despite these difficulties, NAC systems have been used in a variety of contexts and, to date, are the most prevalent eye movement recorders within sports-based research programmes (for an example, see the work of Bard and colleagues reviewed later in this chapter).

Problems with the ASL system include a 25-m trailing lead which has to be attached to the performer's waist. Although, the performer may find this restrictive, its effect has been minimal when used in tasks such as golf putting (Vickers 1992) and ice hockey shooting and goal tending (Vickers, Canic, Abbott and Livingston 1988). The system is not as sensitive as the NAC system with data being collected at 50 frames per second (PAL system) compared with the NAC capability of 600 frames per second. However, calibration is a relatively simple procedure and, because data are sampled from both the pupil and corneal reflex, the system is robust and does not require frequent recalibration. Planned improvements include the development of a daylight shooting unit, higher sampling capabilities, a smaller and more portable system (Model 501 Eye Tracking System) and a telemetry-based control unit. The ASL system appears appropriate for use in sport contexts offering an unlimited field of view and free head and body movements (for an example, see the work of Williams and colleagues reviewed later in this chapter).

VISUAL SEARCH STRATEGY AND SELECTIVE INFORMATION PICK-UP

The visual search literature suggests that fixation location and duration characteristics are indicative of the perceptual strategy used by the performer to extract meaningful information from the display. That is, fixation characteristics are taken as representing the approach used by the observer to extract specific information (Abernethy 1985). Fixation location is assumed to reflect the important cues used in decision-making, whereas the number and duration of fixations (i.e. search rate) are presumed to reflect the information-processing demands placed on the performer. For example, this approach has been used by Abernethy and Russell (1987b) in badminton, and Goulet *et al.* (1989) in tennis.

However, these assumptions have been subjected to a number of challenges. First, visual orientation, as implied from fixation characteristics, may not be directly related to information extraction (see Abernethy 1988b; Davids 1984; Williams *et al.* 1993). It may be possible to fixate an object without extracting specific information (Papin, Metges and Amalberti 1984; Stager and Angus 1978). This has frequently been referred to as the difference between 'looking', which implies fixation on the fovea, and 'seeing' which implies information processing or cue extraction (Abernethy 1988b; van der Heijden 1986; Neumann *et al.* 1986) – for example, the sensation of staring at the television without actually watching or concentrating on what is happening on screen.

Second, subjects are able to relocate attention within the visual field without making distinctive eye movements to change the point of fixation (see Jonides 1981; Abernethy 1988b; Remington 1980; Sanders and Houtmans

1985; Williams and Davids 1997, 1998b). It is possible to 'look' at one point in the field but extract information from the periphery. For example, a basketball player may fixate on the ball, or the player in possession of the ball, but may be picking up information from peripheral vision regarding the movements of players around the court. Similarly, in karate kumite, performers may fixate on a central point such as their opponent's head or chest, but may be picking up information from the movements of the limbs in anticipating the direction of their opponent's attack (see Williams and Elliott 1997). From a practical perspective, such search strategies are often encouraged by coaches as deception strategies. For instance, keeping one's gaze fixed on one point makes it difficult for an opponent to anticipate the destination of a pass or impending attack. Wright and Ward (1994) argue that shifts in visual attention can be goal- or stimulus-driven. Goal-driven or endogenous shifts in attention are initiated voluntarily and are assumed to be driven by the subject's need to pick up information cues from the periphery. In contrast, stimulus-driven or exogenous shifts in attention are initiated reflexively in response to unexpected or abrupt-onset cues in the environment. Current research indicates that stimulus-driven shifts in attention are closely coupled to visual saccades, whilst goal-driven shifts of attention may occur independently of saccadic eye movements (Jonides 1981; Yantis and Jonides 1990; for a review, see Egeth and Yantis 1997; Wright and Ward 1994). The argument is that athletes may be able to shift attention independently of eye movements during sports performance (for an example, see Castiello and Umiltá 1992). These shifts in attention have been shown to occur without the loss of input information normally associated with saccadic eye movements (Abernethy 1985).

The above issue is an important one within contemporary eye movement research and it is an area where further investigation is required. For some time it has been known that information processed through peripheral vision plays an important role in perceptuo-motor performance (e.g. Davids 1984; Paillard 1980; 1982; Williams *et al.* 1992; Williams and Davids 1997, 1998b). Perhaps, fixations simply provide the most appropriate reference points for picking up and organising information from the periphery (Rockwell 1972). Without doubt, there is a need for innovative research which evaluates the specific role of peripheral vision within the visual search process. At present it seems appropriate to concur with Broadbent's (1982) suggestion that eye movements may reinforce selectivity, yet it can occur without them.

Third, the suggestion regarding fixation duration is that it signifies the importance of the display area being fixated (Gould 1973). The assumption being that a longer fixation duration represents foveation on a crucial information source (Groner, McConkie and Menz 1985). However, data on fixation duration obtained via eye movement recording procedures are confusing since they represent both cognitive processing time and the time required to determine the next fixation location and initiate the ensuing saccade (Abernethy 1985). This is referred to as the oculomotor period. Therefore, long fixation durations could be indicative of either cognitive or oculomotor delay problems (ibid.). Moreover, recent research in the vision sciences has challenged the proposed relationship between fixation duration and cognitive processing by indicating that the distribution of fixation duration is not normally distributed, as would be predicted from a cognitive perspective, but is positively skewed implying that fixation duration is intrinsically a stochastic process in which fixations are terminated randomly in time by saccades (for a more detailed explanation, see Harris, Hainline, Abramov, Lemerise and Camenzuli 1988; Harris 1989). Clearly, it would be difficult to explain this termination at a cognitive level. The proposition is that scan characteristics, namely the distributions of fixation duration, fixation location and saccade magnitude, can be related to each other and the stimulus by a low-level mechanism that depends on non-foveal retinal stimulation (Harris 1989). For example, as retinal image size increases, more non-foveal retina is stimulated, which raises the probability of a saccade being triggered, thus decreasing average fixation duration. That is, saccades emerge to terminate fixations when peripheral stimulation is integral to the viewing conditions. This suggests that the implicit relationship between fixation duration and information processing may not be as parsimonious as initially presumed. Interestingly, fixation duration findings appear to account for much of the conflict in the evidence examining expert–novice differences in sport and ergonomics. This variability may be due, in part, to the problems highlighted above but may also be due to methodological limitations and differences in the nature and type of task presented to subjects.

A COGNITIVE PERSPECTIVE ON VISUAL SEARCH STRATEGY IN SPORT

Traditionally, it has been assumed that visual search strategies are determined by task-specific knowledge structures stored symbolically in long-term memory. It is argued that through learning a performer builds up an immense knowledge base of experience which can be used to interpret events encountered in circumstances similar to those previously experienced. These knowledge structures direct the performer's visual search strategy towards more important areas of the display based on past experience and contextual information. For example, recall Norman's (1968, 1969) pertinence-based model highlighted in Chapter 2. This model suggests that skilled sports performers have acquired knowledge of the most informative aspects of the display as a result of their sport-specific experience. These experiences produce specific knowledge structures (i.e. what Marr (1982) termed 'visual prototypes') that are stored in long-term memory and which direct performers to fixate on the more pertinent or informative areas of the display (for an interesting discussion of how such visual prototypes may relate to visual search strategies during the interpretation of road traffic situations, see Wierda and Maring 1993). In other words, their visual search strategy is controlled by this knowledge which has been developed over years of training, coaching, playing and observing. This enhanced knowledge base means that there is a large amount of cue redundancy within the expert's search strategy. The expert knows which are the most informative areas of the display and, consequently, can ignore areas of low information content. Figure 5.2 highlights a typical cognitive model of visual search with selective attention as the mediating process between preattention and foveal or focal attention.

One popular cognitive theory about how certain cues in the environment are selected is Treisman's feature integration theory (see Treisman 1985, 1988). This theory suggests that during the visual search process we initially recognise objects on the basis of their different sensory features such as colour, orientation, size or movement. These features are detected automatically or subconsciously with no attention demand. At this level of processing, the visual scene is organised or categorised into potential objects for more detailed perceptual analysis. That is, these cognitive maps become the basis for further visual search processes when the task requires that specific cues must be identified. For example, the hockey player might categorise the red colour of her opponents' shirts, separating them from her team-mates' green shirts, so that the respective positions of team-mates and opponents can be identified. The key to the identification process

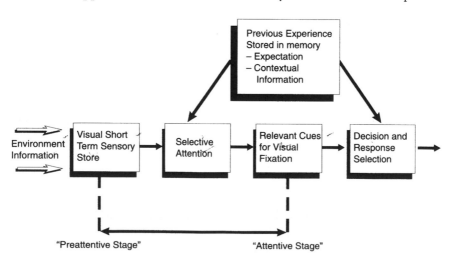

Figure 5.2 A typical cognitive model of visual search strategy with selective attention as the mediating process between preattention and focal or foveal attention. (Adapted from Abernethy, B. (1988b) 'Visual search in sport and ergonomics: Its relationship to selective attention and performer expertise', *Human Performance* 4: 205–35.)

is the formation of cognitive maps which contain information related to the different values of each feature. Thus, performers would have a feature map for colour or for orientation enabling them to distinguish between different colours (e.g. red, blue, green) or distinct types of movements (e.g. vertical, diagonal, horizontal). Attention is required to locate and combine features to define specific objects. This selection occurs by focusing attention on a 'master map' of features stored in long-term memory. When attention is focused on a particular location in the master map, it enables automatic retrieval of those features active in that location for comparison with the information present in the different feature maps. Hence, conscious perception depends on the matching of information held in feature maps with descriptions of objects/events stored in a recognition network or master map within long-term visual memory (for an alternative theoretical framework, see Chapter 8).

SPORTS-BASED RESEARCH

Visual search research using static slides

The research programme initiated by Bard and colleagues at Laval University in Canada was the first to investigate systematically differences in visual search strategy in sport (e.g. Bard and Carriere 1975; Bard and Fleury 1976, 1981; Bard, Fleury and Carriere 1976). These studies typically investigated the differences in search strategies which occurred when subjects were presented with schematic slides of sport situations. For example, Bard and Fleury (1976) examined the search patterns of five expert and five novice basketball players while viewing typical offensive game situations. Subjects were required to verbalise quickly and accurately whether they would respond by shooting at the basket, dribbling or passing to a specific team-mate. Whilst viewing the slides, subjects' visual search patterns were recorded using an NAC eye movement registration system. The dependent variables were decision time and the frequency and location of visual fixations. The results showed no significant differences in decision time between the two groups, although there was a trend towards the experts having faster response times. The eye movement data indicated that significantly fewer fixations were used prior to a response by expert basketballers ($\underline{M}$ = 3.3) than novices ($\underline{M}$ = 4.9). Also, differences were found in the distribution of visual fixations to selected areas of the display. Novices fixated primarily on a receiving team-mate when deciding to pass, while experts fixated additional sources of information such as the position of the nearest defender and the space available between the defender and basket. Finally, the results indicated that the number of fixations required prior to responding coincided with the level of complexity presented within the slide display. As the level of complexity increased both groups required more fixations prior to responding than in the less complex situations. This finding has subsequently been supported by several studies, suggesting that search rate may be a function of the uncertainty presented in the display (e.g. Bard and Fleury 1981; Tyldesley *et al.* 1982).

In Tyldesley *et al.*'s (1982) study subjects were presented with static slide presentations of a soccer player taking a penalty kick. Groups of experienced and inexperienced players were required to anticipate penalty kick direction by pressing one of four response keys representing four alternative shot directions (high/low, left/right). On presentation of the slides, subjects were required to depress the appropriate directional key as quickly and accurately as possible. Results showed that the experienced players responded significantly faster than the inexperienced players to the soccer-specific stimuli. Moreover, visual search data revealed that when viewing a right-footed player strike the ball, the experienced players did not fixate on either the supporting leg or any part of the left side of the body. Their scanning behaviour was more structured and consistent than the novices with fixations being restricted to the right side of the body and the shooting leg. Also, the inexperienced players had a fixation time which was typically 26.6 ms longer than their experienced counterparts, interpreted as highlighting their difficulty in picking up information from the display. Finally, both groups required more fixations before responding in the four-choice task, where subjects had to decide on height and side of the shot, than in the two-choice situation in which they had to select the correct height or side only. When subjects had to decide between all four corners of the goal (the most demanding task circumstances) they needed at least two fixations before responding. A high proportion of first fixations (60%) were directed at the hip and almost 30% at the legs, feet and ball. Second fixations tended to be directed at the shoulder region. The findings are highlighted in Figure 5.3. These data were construed as evidence for a search strategy which began in the lower half of the body then moved to upper body regions. This suggests that skilled goalkeepers may initially determine the direction of the penalty kick based on advance information arising from the hip and lower leg regions, whereas the height of the kick is determined subsequently from the kicker's upper body or the initial portion of ball flight. Support for this search strategy has been provided by Williams and Burwitz (1993) using retrospective verbal reports (see p. 175). In practical terms, the results suggest that goalkeepers can acquire advance information regarding penalty kick direction from the hip, lower leg and trunk regions. More specifically, it appears that the angle of the hip at ball contact appears to be particularly important (Williams and Burwitz 1993). For a right-footed kicker, the 'opening' of the hips may suggest that the ball is about to be played to the goalkeeper's left, whereas a penalty played to the goalkeeper's right may be characterised by a more 'closed' or central orientation of the penalty

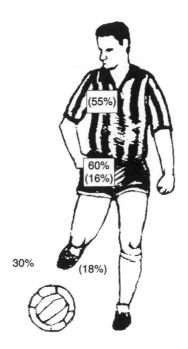

Figure 5.3 The results of Tyldesley *et al.*'s, (1982) study indicating the percentage of first and second (in parenthesis) fixations to respective areas of the display during the four-choice reaction time task. (Adapted from Tyldesley, D.A., Bootsma, R.J. and Bomhoff, G.T. (1982) 'Skill level and eye movement patterns in a sport-orientated reaction time task', in H. Rieder, H. Mechling and K Reischle (eds) *Proceedings of an International Symposium on Motor Behaviour: Contribution to Learning in Sport*, Cologne: Hofmann.)

taker's hips relative to the goalkeeper. Interestingly, penalty takers should note the fact that these information cues are more pronounced when penalties are struck with the inside of the foot.

Research using dynamic film presentations

There have been attempts to replace the static presentation of stimuli via slides with more dynamic film tasks. For example, Bard and associates examined visual search strategies and cue utilisation in national- and club-level gymnastic judges (see Bard, Fleury, Carriere and Halle 1980). Subjects were instructed to evaluate a film of two national-level gymnasts performing compulsory balance beam routines and two optional routines. The baseline for errors was derived from an evaluation of the four routines by an expert judge prior to the experiment. Although the more experienced judges exhibited 27% fewer fixations than the less experienced group, the results were not significantly different. The lack of statistical significance may have been due, in part, to both the small number of subjects per group (N = 4) and the large variability in the number of fixations used by the novice judges. Differences were evident in the distribution of fixations to respective areas of the display. Experts fixated more on the upper body of gymnasts (head and arms), while novices focused on the legs. Bard *et al.* (1980) suggested that these differences may have been due to the novice group's experience in judging non-expert gymnasts who generally make more foot and leg placement errors than skilled gymnasts. Additionally, the novice judges detected only half the number of errors when compared to the expert group, although this difference in performance was not statistically significant. These findings suggest that judges should fixate more on the head and arms rather than the leg region when evaluating gymnastic performance.

More recent research has coupled these more dynamic film displays with movement-based response measures. Helsen and Pauwels (1992, 1993) investigated the search patterns employed during tactical decision-making in soccer. Expert and novice players were presented with a near 'life-sized' film display of soccer action sequences. Film clips included simulated offensive situations involving a restricted number of players (e.g. 3 vs 3, 4 vs 4) and 'set play' conditions (e.g. free-kicks). At a specific moment, the ball appeared to be played by one of the attackers on screen in the direction of the subject. The subject, who had a ball placed by his feet, was then required to respond quickly and accurately by shooting at goal, passing to a team-mate, or dribbling around the goalkeeper/ opponent on screen. Dependent variables included movement initiation time, ball–foot contact time, total response time and response accuracy. Visual search data were collected on the number, duration and location of fixations.

Expert players had significantly quicker movement initiation times, ball/foot contact times and total response times, and they were more accurate in tactical decision-making. It was suggested that the expert group's superior performance was due to their enhanced ability to recognise structure and redundancy within the display, resulting in more efficient use of search time. This hypothesis was supported by the eye movement data which revealed that expert visual search patterns were more economical with fewer fixations on different areas of the display. Experts were more interested in the positioning of the 'sweeper' and any potential areas of 'free' space, while non-experts searched for information from less sophisticated sources such as other attackers, the goal and the ball. These differences appeared to be related to the expert's more refined awareness and functional understanding of the strategic role of the 'sweeper' in providing defensive cover (Helsen and Pauwels 1993). The mean number of fixations and fixation duration per trial are highlighted in Table 5.1.

Table 5.1 The mean number of fixations and fixation duration for the expert and novice players whilst viewing offensive situations in soccer. (Source: Helsen, W. and Pauwels, J.M. (1993) 'The relationship between expertise and visual information processing in sport', in J.L. Starkes and F. Allard (eds) *Cognitive Issues in Motor Expertise*, Amsterdam: Elsevier Science Publishing, pp. 109–34.)

Group		Number of fixations	Fixation duration (ms)
Experts	M	1.71	471.07
	SD	0.28	49.33
Novices	M	2.24	444.64
	SD	0.34	65.69

Williams *et al.* (1994) derived comparable conclusions from their investigation of visual search strategy and anticipation in 11 vs 11 'open play' situations in soccer. In this study, subjects were required to anticipate ball direction from filmed soccer sequences presented on a large 3 m² video projection screen. The action sequences were filmed directly from professional and semi-professional matches and included more complex 'open play' situations than previously employed (i.e. Helsen and Pauwels 1992, 1993). The matches were filmed such that the entire width of the playing field could be viewed on screen thus providing a visual display which was representative of a central defensive player's view of play. The results indicated superior anticipatory performance by experienced soccer players in comparison to a group of less experienced players. Furthermore, visual search data showed that the inexperienced players fixated more frequently on the ball and the player passing the ball, whereas the experienced players fixated more on the positions and movements of players 'off the ball'. The experienced players' more extensive search strategy was highlighted by a greater number of fixations of shorter duration on significantly more locations per trial. These findings are presented in Table 5.2. Also, the typical search profiles employed by the experienced and inexperienced players are represented schematically in Figure 5.4.

Table 5.2 Mean number of locations, fixation duration and number of fixations per trial across groups in the 11 vs 11 soccer situations. (Source: Williams, A.M., Davids, K., Burwitz, L. and Williams, J.G. (1994) 'Visual search strategies in experienced and inexperienced soccer players', *Research Quarterly for Exercise and Sport*, 65(2): 127–135.)

Group		Number of fixation locations	Fixation duration (ms)	Number of fixations
Experienced	M	4.46	933.94	10.30
(n = 10)	SD	0.25	99.34	0.97
Inexperienced	M	3.87	1163.16	8.72
(n = 10)	SD	0.39	206.26	0.94

Figure 5.4 A schematic representation of the visual search strategies employed by experienced and inexperienced soccer players when presented with simulated 11 vs 11 situations. Subjects were required to anticipate the area of the field where the player highlighted inside the black square would make his pass. The lighter shaded area represents the typical area scanned by an experienced player. The distributed nature of the search pattern shows that expert players were more aware of the positions and movements of players 'off the ball'. The darker shaded area represents the typical scan area covered by a novice. The search strategy is much more closely distributed around the player in possession of the ball suggesting that novice players are more guilty of 'ball watching'. (Adapted from Williams, A.M. and Davids, K. (1994) 'Eye movements and visual perception in sport', *Coaching Focus* 26: 6–9.)

The higher search rates demonstrated by the experienced group in this study contradicted previous research (e.g. Helsen and Pauwels 1992, 1993). Williams *et al.* (1994) suggested that a search strategy which involved periodically scanning back and forth from the ball to informative areas of the display, such as the runs of the attacking players, was regarded as being more advantageous than fixating on the passing player or ball alone. This more extensive search strategy ensures that defenders are aware of a number of sources of information including the location of the ball, their own position in relation to pitch markings such as the edge of the penalty area, the movements of key offensive players attempting to penetrate the spaces between and behind defenders and the positions of team-mates attempting to defend critical areas of the field (e.g. Hughes 1995). The extensive number of perceptual information sources, located disparately across a large area of the field, constrains the experienced observer to utilise more fixations of shorter duration. The potential benefits of adopting such a strategy in team games may exceed the disadvantages of the increased saccadic suppression involved with high search rates.

A similar hypothesis would account for differences in the findings of Bard, Guezennec and Papin (1981) and Hasse and Mayer (1978) in fencing and Ripoll (1989) in table tennis. Hasse and Mayer (1978) used a laboratory-based visual reaction test and observed significantly longer fixation durations for expert fencers. In contrast, Bard *et al.* (1981) used more realistic circumstances involving competitive duelling. They found that higher search rates were apparent for superior performers in this more field-based fencing task. Likewise, Ripoll (1989) found significantly higher search rates for skilled table tennis players under real match conditions compared with practice or drill situations (see Ripoll 1991). Such contradictions in search rate have been common within the research literature (see Abernethy 1988b). Theoretically, experts would be expected to have lower search rates because of the reduced information-processing load or because they require less sensory input to create a coherent perceptual representation of the display (Abernethy 1990a). As we stated earlier, this expectation has not always been supported by research findings from sport and ergonomics. This inconsistency is due, in part, to the difficulty in comparing directly between research studies because of differences in the operational definition of a fixation and in the sensitivity of the eye movement system used (Abernethy and Russell 1987b). Further, problems arise because of the nature and difficulty of the task, the type of visual display presented to observers, and the experimental description and instructions given prior to testing (for more detailed review of the limitations involved in measuring search rate in sport, see Abernethy 1988b).

Inconsistency may also occur because subjects use different search strategies in specific situations. For example, games players may be characterised by higher search rates when attempting to recognise patterns of developing play, such as a team's attacking or defensive structure, whilst lower search rates may be employed in more specific, time-constrained contexts involving a restricted number of players (i.e. defensive 3 vs 3 situations on the edge of the penalty area). Perhaps, as we suggest in greater detail in Chapter 8, the constraints of the task or situation lead to the emergence of a particular visual search pattern. In a recent study, Williams and Davids (1998b) attempted to address this issue by comparing the search strategies observed in typical sub-group (i.e. 3 vs 3) and individual (i.e. 1 vs 1) task contexts with those obtained previously in the 11 vs 11 simulations. In the 3 vs 3 soccer simulations, subjects imagined themselves as a covering defender or sweeper. Each sequence included two defenders marking two offensive players and a defensive midfield player marking an offensive midfield player. Subjects viewed each pattern of play and had to anticipate the offensive midfield player's pass. Subjects moved either right, left, forwards or backwards in response to each sequence. In the 1 vs 1 condition, subjects imagined themselves as a challenging defender.

Table 5.3 Mean fixation duration, number of fixations, and frequency of alternation of fixations between the player in possession of the ball and other areas of the display per trial across groups in the 3 vs 3 simulations. (Source: Williams, A.M. and Davids, K. (1998b) 'Visual search strategy, selective attention, and expertise in soccer', *Research Quarterly for Exercise and Sport* 69(2): 111–29.)

Group		Fixation duration (ms)	Number of fixations	Frequency of alternation of fixations
Experienced	M	865.83	4.17	1.03
(n = 12)	SD	145.22	0.62	0.39
Inexperienced	M	973.50	4.02	1.04
(n = 12)	SD	151.67	0.90	0.20

Each sequence involved an offensive player dribbling the ball directly towards them. Subjects anticipated whether the attacker would dribble past them on their right or left side. Initiation time (IT), movement time (MT), response time (RT), and response accuracy (RA) were the dependent variables. Also, visual search data were recorded using an ASL 4000SU corneal reflection system to obtain information on search order, fixation location, fixation duration and number of fixations. The experimental set-up used in these simulations is highlighted in Figure 5.1.

The results showed that the experienced players were better at anticipating pass direction in the 3 vs 3 simulations. They had faster ITs and RTs than the inexperienced group, whereas no differences were evident in MT or RA. However, the visual search data showed that there were no differences between groups in fixation duration, number of fixations, fixation location or search order. The mean values for some of these dependent measures are presented in Table 5.3.

The experienced players also demonstrated superior anticipation in the 1 vs 1 simulations. They had quicker RTs and higher RA, whilst no differences were observed in IT or MT. Visual search data revealed that the

Table 5.4 Mean fixation duration, number of fixations, and frequency of alternation of fixation between the hip and lower leg and ball regions across groups. (Source: Williams, A.M. and Davids, K. (1998b) 'Visual search strategy, selective attention, and expertise in soccer', *Research Quarterly for Exercise and Sport* 69 (2): 111–29.)

Group		Fixation duration (ms)	Number of fixations	Frequency of alternation of fixations
Experienced	M	1104.6	2.60	0.28
(n = 12)	SD	332.4	0.83	0.20
Less Experienced	M	1555.0	1.90	0.11
(n = 12)	SD	673.6	0.72	0.17

experienced players employed more fixations of shorter duration and fixated more on the hip region. Also, differences were found in search order with experienced players alternating their fixations more frequently between the ball and hip regions, indicating that these areas were important in anticipating an opponent's movements. The mean values for fixation duration, number of fixations and search order are shown in Table 5.4.

Analysis of the different search rates employed across the three simulations (i.e. 11 vs 11, 3 vs 3, 1 vs 1) supported the initial hypothesis by indicating that search characteristics are determined by the constraints of the individual task (see Tables 5.2, 5.3 and 5.4). For example, in the 11 vs 11 simulations the experienced players employed a search strategy which comprised more fixations of shorter duration. This more extensive search strategy is advantageous in the 11 vs 11 context because defenders have to be aware of an extensive number of perceptual information sources, located disparately across a large area of the field. This, in effect, constrains the experienced observer to utilise more frequent fixations than in the sub-group context (i.e. 3 vs 3). The task constraints, as expressed by the number of perceptual information sources, are less severe in the 3 vs 3 simulations resulting in a greater emphasis on the role of peripheral vision (for data confirming the involvement of peripheral vision in the visual search process, see pp. 178–9 and p. 172). In these situations, perceptual skill involves accurately 'anchoring' the visual system in order to diffuse attention according to the specific requirements of the task. Skilled defenders pick up information from the player in possession of the ball while simultaneously monitoring positional changes of play in the periphery. This type of approach has several advantages. First, the saccadic eye movements which separate each foveal fixation are inactive periods of information processing, thus in time-constrained circumstances a search pattern with fewer foveal fixations may be regarded as a more efficient search pattern. Also, it is much faster to switch attention from one area of the display to another covertly using peripheral vision rather than eye movements (see Nougier *et al.* 1991; Posner and Raichle 1994). Second, research suggests that we can use peripheral vision to process movement related information more rapidly than foveal vision (Milner and Goodale 1995). Finally, in the 1 vs 1 situations, observers need highly precise information from motion invariants provided by changes to key joint angles to specify information on direction, velocity and force of locomotion in dribbling. Since the hip and lower leg–ball regions appear to provide the significant information in these situations, performers need to fixate on these areas to pick up the key motion invariants. This type of information can be provided only poorly by the peripheral visual system, therefore constraining the observer to use foveal vision most of the time.

These findings have important implications for training visual search strategy in sport. When defenders are attempting to determine the opposition's general offensive structure, such as in the 11 vs 11 film sequences, higher search rates would be required so that they are aware of the movements and positions of a large number of players. In these instances, the area of play may be too large for defenders to rely on peripheral vision to pick up information from team-mates and opponents; instead players are constrained to move the eyes to foveate important areas of the display. A higher search rate, relative to the inexperienced defender, may also be required in 1 vs 1 situations in order to pick up key information from various motion invariants such as the orientation of the hip, knee and foot relative to the ball. In contrast, in situations involving a restricted number of potential information sources lower search rates may be required, thus enabling subjects to use non-foveal retinal stimulation (i.e. parafovea and periphery) to extract task-specific information. Since there is evidence to suggest that information can be picked up in peripheral vision more quickly than in foveal vision (see Millner and Goodale 1995), this approach may be particularly important in time-constrained circumstances. Similar arguments have been proposed by Ripoll (1991) who suggested that a difference between experts and novices is that the former direct their gaze to a position in which many events can be viewed integratively during one single eye fixation (i.e. synthetic analysis), whilst novices gaze at events according to their chronological order of appearance (i.e. analytic analysis).

Finally, many other studies have identified differences in visual search strategy using film-based methods. For example, proficiency-related differences have been noted in tennis (Singer, Cauraugh, Chen, Steinberg and Frehlich 1996; Fleury, Goulet and Bard 1986; Goulet *et al.* 1989; Ritzdorf 1983), volleyball (Handford and Williams 1992; Neumaier 1982; Ripoll 1988), baseball (Shank and Haywood 1987) and French boxing (Ripoll, Kerlirzin, Stein and Reine 1995). These studies have demonstrated differences in the allocation of fixations to selected areas of the display and, generally, have indicated some disparity in search rates between skill groups.

Field-based research findings

The progressive development of more ecologically valid experimentation has resulted in a number of studies examining visual search behaviour within field rather than laboratory settings. Although technical limitations in eye movement technology have generally restricted research to tasks where the observer is relatively stationary, there have been some promising studies. Bard and Fleury (1981) required expert and novice ice hockey goalkeepers to respond to a 'live' model performing a slap shot or sweep shot on the ice. Results showed that expert goalkeepers initiated their response much sooner than novices regardless of the type of shot performed by the offensive player. Analysis of visual fixations as the shot took place, demonstrated that the goalkeepers concentrated mainly on the stick and

Table 5.5 The distribution of visual fixations to the stick and puck areas across groups for the sweep and slap shots as a percentage of total viewing time. (Source: Bard, C. and Fleury, M. (1981) 'Considering eye movement as a predictor of attainment', in I.M. Cockerill and W.W. MacGillvary (eds) *Vision and Sport*, Cheltenham: Stanley Thornes.)

	Experts		Novices	
	Stick	Puck	Stick	Puck
Slap Shot	71	29	30	70
Sweep Shot	60	40	87	13

the puck. However, there were major differences in the distribution of visual fixations between the groups of subjects suggesting the relative importance of the stick and the puck to decision-making. Experts allocated 65% of their fixations to the stick during both types of shot, whereas novices utilised a distinct visual search strategy for slap shots and sweep shots. When faced with slap shots, 70% of their fixations were concentrated on the puck and 30% on the stick; however, for a sweep shot 87% of fixations were addressed to the stick and 13% to the puck. These findings are highlighted in Table 5.5. Bard and Fleury concluded that the experts preferred to anticipate the flight of a shot using cues from the stick's orientation and movement speed, while beginners tended to make the same decisions only after the puck had been struck. This conclusion supported the results of previous studies based on film occlusion techniques (e.g. Salmela and Fiorito 1979).

Field-based methods have also been employed by Petrakis (1986, 1987) to investigate the search strategies used by tennis and dance teachers. Petrakis (1986) required expert and novice coaches to view a 'live' tennis player perform both forehand drive and service shots. Eye movement data revealed that the expert group had more fixations on the hip region for the forehand drive. On the service, experts concentrated on the upper body and the racket, while novices fixated the head and racket areas only. No differences were found in search rate between the two groups. This non-significant finding may be due to the small sample size used in the study (N = 6) since there was a trend towards shorter fixation durations for the expert coaches. Comparable findings were reported when expert and novice coaches were required to view 'live' performance of a dance composition (Petrakis 1987). The novice coaches fixated on the arms, hips and legs, while the experts focused on the head, arms and legs (see also Bard *et al.* 1980). In addition to the small number of subjects used in both these studies, criticisms arise because the coaches were not required to provide evaluative feedback on the model's performance after each trial. Since search strategies are situation specific (Williams *et al.* 1993), and are affected by instructional set (Yarbus 1967), there could be a substantial bearing on the scan patterns employed. Furthermore, both studies indicated much variability in search strategy between groups. Such large variability may have masked proficiency-based differences or, alternatively, suggests that factors other than visual search strategy contribute to being a skilled coach.

In a more recent field-based study, Vickers (1992) compared the visual strategies of low-skilled (i.e. high-handicap) and high-skilled (i.e. low-handicap) golfers performing a series of 3 m putts. Significant group differences emerged in the number and duration of fixations during the preparation, backswing/foreswing and the follow-through phases of putting action. High-skilled golfers used 27.8% fewer eye movements per putt than the lesser skilled group (mean of 16.4 compared to 23) and tended to fixate on different locations of the display. Specifically, during the preparation phase the high-skilled golfer fixated for longer on the ball and the target, whereas the less skilled player watched the putter head. During the critical backswing/foreswing component of putting, the low-skilled golfer made almost twice as many eye movements, to varied locations, than the other group. The low-skilled group exhibited shorter fixation durations on the ball and a greater propensity to watch the club at the apex of the backswing, which contrasted with the high-skilled golfer who was more selective in the use of fixations tending to concentrate more on the ball. During the contact phase the more skilled group tended to fixate under the ball as the club head made contact. Finally, the data showed that there was a greater probability of a successful putt if the subjects fixated on the ball during the backswing/foreswing phase and on the surface under the ball as the club head made contact. This finding relates well to coaching advice to keep the head and line of gaze stable during stroke execution (Palmer and Dobereiner 1986).

Another promising approach has been to assess the subject's gaze behaviours while simultaneously recording the subject's actions using video film. This can be achieved by using a digital effects mixer to interface an external video camera (focusing on the subject's actions) with the head-mounted scene camera on an eye movement recorder (focusing on the subject's point-of-gaze). This approach offers many exciting possibilities since it permits us to examine the relationship between perception (as inferred from point-of-gaze) and action (as determined by the subject's physical movements) in real-world contexts. Such an approach has been employed by Vickers (1996a, b) using the basketball free throw, Vickers and Adolphe (1997) during the return of serve in volleyball, and Williams, Singer and Weigelt (1998) during service return in tennis. Vickers (1996a, b) examined the gaze behaviours of elite and near-elite basketball subjects as they performed successful and unsuccessful free throws. The split-screen image was used to divide the basketball free throw into four distinct phases: namely, the preparation, pre-shot, shot and flight phases. Six fixation locations were identified from the head-mounted scene image: the ball, subject's hands, front hoop, middle hoop and backboard. Data were then coded to obtain information on fixation location, search order and the number and duration of fixations across the four phases for successful and unsuccessful free throws.

Expert free throwers exhibited less frequent head movements, fewer visual fixations and a longer fixation on the basketball hoop during the preparation and pre-shot phases. Moreover, they showed a longer 'quiet eye' duration than near-experts. Quiet eye duration was defined as the period of time from fixation on the target to the first observable movement of the hands into the shooting action. In contrast, once the movement was initiated experts moved their visual fixation away from the target earlier, while they employed more fixations and eye blinks with a higher incidence of head movements during the shot and flight phases. Vickers (1996) proposed that the higher blink rate may be used to suppress interference from the moving hands and ball in the visual field. To explain these findings, she proposed a location-suppression hypothesis to explain high levels of performance in aiming tasks such as the basketball free throw. In this hypothesis, a long fixation duration is initially required on

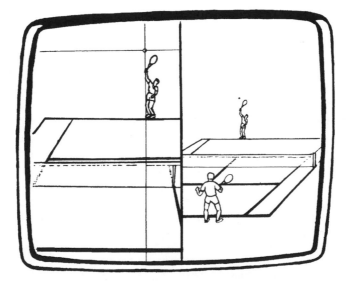

Figure 5.5 The split-screen approach used by Williams *et al.* (1998). The right side of the screen shows the image from an external scene camera highlighting the subject's movements during the return of serve. The left side of the screen illustrates the typical point-of-gaze data obtained from an eye movement registration system employing a head-mounted scene camera. Position of gaze is shown by the cross-hairs. (Adapted from Williams, A.M., Singer, R.N. and Weigelt, C. (1998) 'Visual search strategy in "live" on-court situations in tennis: An exploratory study', in A. Lees and I.W. Maynard (eds) *Science and Rackets*, vol. II, London: E & FN Spon.)

the target location (i.e. basketball hoop or backboard). In the second impulse phase, movement should be initiated slowly for fixation to be maintained. Finally, during the execution phase, fixation offset should occur early, followed by a suppression of vision to avoid interfering visual input during task execution. Future research is required to verify whether this location-suppression hypothesis extends to other far aiming tasks such as archery, snooker or dart throwing.

Figure 5.5 shows the typical scene observed by Williams *et al.* (1998) using the split-frame video technique to assess the visual behaviours employed by a group of skilled tennis players as they prepared for and executed the return of serve. Players fixated on the arm, shoulder and racket regions prior to the initiation of the serve. Thereafter, with the exception of one player who fixated on the server's racket, subjects followed the ball to the apex of the toss by employing either pursuit tracking or saccadic eye movements. The greatest variation in visual behaviour was observed during ball flight, where players either maintained fixation on the ball via pursuit tracking eye movements or made no attempt to foveally track the ball, but rather employed a predictive saccade to move their point-of-gaze to the expected ball bounce area. Those who employed pursuit tracking during the initial ball flight period maintained fixation on the ball after it bounced until on average 150–200 ms (2–4 m) before ball–racket contact, whereas players who employed predictive saccades did not attempt to fixate the ball after it bounced, but rather fixated in the general vicinity of ball–racket contact. Further research is required to examine the relative effectiveness of these approaches during the return of serve in tennis.

Further field-based studies have been conducted in ice hockey goal-keeping and shooting (Vickers *et al.* 1988), ball catching (Emes, Vickers and Livingston 1994), table tennis (Ripoll 1989; Ripoll, Fleurance and Cazeneuve 1987), pistol shooting (Ripoll, Papin, Guezennec, Verdy and Philip 1985) and rock climbing (Dupuy and Ripoll 1989). These studies have generally demonstrated the expert's ability to employ perceptual resources more efficiently. Such studies highlight the progressive development of more ecologically valid approaches.

Criticisms of previous research work

An important criticism of earlier studies is the use of static slide presentations to represent dynamic sport situations. It is now well known that dynamic displays provide subjects with different information than do static displays, and that objects in motion are far more informative than those at rest (Cutting 1978; Johansson 1973). For example, Tyldesley *et al.*'s, (1982) study used slides of a soccer player 10–50 ms prior to kicking the ball. This prevented subjects from using pertinent information from the approach run, preparatory phase and much of the time period immediately prior to and after ball contact. These stages could provide crucial information when attempting to anticipate ball direction in soccer (Williams and Burwitz 1993). Similarly, the static slide presentations used in Bard *et al.*'s (1981) study prevented subjects from viewing each pattern of play as it developed on screen. That is, subjects were unaware of what had happened in the game prior to the situation presented on slide. The absence of temporal, directional and sequential movement information regarding each pattern of play may influence search strategy in such tasks (c.f. Bourgeaud and Abernethy 1987).

Although studies using dynamic film tasks have many advantages over slide-based protocols, there are still several difficulties. For example, it is not particularly clear what effect the reduction in image size and dimensionality has on visual search performance. There have been few attempts to compare visual search strategies between sport-related stimulus conditions in which subjects are faced with dynamic, 'life-sized', three-dimensional models and the two-dimensional images presented on small monitors. In one such study, Abernethy (1990a) required subjects to predict the direction and force of a squash player's stroke under two conditions. In one condition, subjects were presented with 32 different strokes presented on film, whilst in a second condition they were required to predict an opponent's stroke direction using a 'live' model. The results indicated some differences between search strategies in the two settings with increased fixations upon pre-contact ball flight cues and slightly slower search rates being evident in the field setting. However, these differences were not marked and, overall, the findings from the two studies were very similar, thus providing a modicum of validity for film-based research studies.

Also, it is not clear whether the search strategies observed under 'contrived' laboratory conditions provide an accurate reflection of subjects' visual behaviour within realistic field-based situations where motivation, anxiety and emotion may affect performance (c.f. Abernethy 1987a). For example, research suggests that high levels of anxiety lead to a narrowing of the perceptual field (i.e. peripheral narrowing), thus effectively impairing the possibility of information pick-up via peripheral vision (Bacon 1974; Landers, Wang and Courtet 1985). Theoretically, if the ability to extract information via the periphery is reduced this may increase the importance of foveal vision in the visual search process, thus elevating search rate. Subjects may compensate for the reduction in information extraction via peripheral vision by increasing the frequency of foveal fixations to peripheral areas of the display. It may be that search rate exhibits an inverted 'U' relationship with anxiety. As anxiety increases there may be a comparable increase in the size of the functional visual field, allowing subjects to use peripheral vision to extract task-specific information. This may reduce the need to use foveal vision to extract information from the display leading to a corresponding reduction in search rate, whereas at the other extreme, high levels of anxiety may result in a narrowing of the peripheral visual field, thus producing higher search rates.

The effects of anxiety-provoking circumstances on visual search strategy were recently examined by Williams and Elliott (1997). Expert and novice martial artists were required to physically respond when presented with a life-size filmed display of three male karateka performing ten different karate techniques. Eye movements were recorded using an ASL 4000SU system to obtain data on fixation location, search order and the number and duration of fixations. However, the important manipulation in this study was that subjects were required to perform under low and high anxiety conditions. Anxiety was manipulated by the introduction of a competitive environment and through the selected use of ego-stressors. The Competitive State Anxiety Inventory-2 (Martens, Burton, Vealey, Bump and Smith 1990) was used to ensure that two distinct levels of cognitive anxiety were created. The results showed that under the high anxiety condition both groups of subjects employed more fixations to a greater number of locations per trial compared with the low anxiety condition. Also, there was a reduction in the amount of time subjects spent fixating central areas of the display (i.e. head and chest) and an increase in the time spent fixating on peripheral locations (i.e. shoulders, arm/fist, leg/foot). The results supported the initial hypothesis since anxiety had a mediating effect on the breadth of cues attended and on the amount of time spent fixating on peripheral areas of the display. The suggestion is that search strategy is constrained by the subject's ability to extract information through peripheral vision (i.e. peripheral narrowing).

Another significant criticism of current research has been the focus on perception to the exclusion of action. Recent theorising in ecological psychology suggests that perception and action should be viewed as a mutually interdependent, cyclical process where what is perceived is tightly constrained by previous actions which, in turn, are affected by perception (see Chapter 6). The development of research protocols which allow sensory and motor systems to function in an integrated manner during perception is a necessary step towards ecological validity in the study of eye movement behaviour. In fact, there has been little work which has directly compared eye movement data in situations with and without an action component. There is a need to carry out similar experiments in both laboratory and field situations to observe the similarities and differences between these conditions. Such experiments would provide important information as to the effects of decoupling perception and action on the visual search processes. If visual search strategy is affected by the decoupling of the normal functional links between perception and action, this would question the validity of much previous research within the area.

With regard to this latter issue, Ripoll (1991) has recently distinguished between semantic and sensorimotor visual function. The role of semantic visual function is to identify and interpret the environmental display that the performer is confronted with, whilst sensorimotor visual functioning is concerned with the actual execution of the motor response. Interestingly, the existence of two separate visuomotor channels within the visual cortex has been proposed by Milner and Goodale (1995). They conclude, based on an extensive review of neurophysiological and behavioural research, that separate cortical pathways are responsible for visual identification and the visual control of action (for a more detailed discussion, see Chapter 3). Clearly, in open sports such as hockey, volleyball and netball high-level performance demands the coordination of both these visual functions. Thus far, the majority of research has only really addressed semantic visual function in sport. Therefore, to obtain a more complete representation of visual behaviour in sport, research should attempt to develop protocols which adequately simulate both the semantic and somatosensory characteristics of the task. The work of Vickers and colleagues (Vickers 1996a, b; Vickers and Adolphe 1997) and Williams *et al.* (1998) using the split-screen approach provide positive examples of this type of work.

Some conflicting evidence with regard to fixation location

Despite the fact that the majority of visual search research has demonstrated differences in fixation location between groups some conflicting evidence has been reported. For example, Abernethy and Russell (1987a 1987b) found no significant differences in search strategy between groups of expert and novice badminton players using an eye movement recording approach. However, differences in information extraction and cue usage were found in the same context using an event occlusion technique (see Chapter 4). This approach involved presenting subjects with the same film display as used in the visual search study but with selected aspects of the display occluded for the duration of the trial (e.g. the player's racket, racket and arm, trunk or head). The assumption was that removal of the most important cue source(s) would result in the greatest decrement to performance in comparison to the full display condition. The experts were Commonwealth Games players and the novice group comprised undergraduates. Subjects viewed 16 mm film clips of a badminton player executing a series of strokes. Following presentation of each trial, they were required to note down, on a scaled representation of a badminton court, the probable landing position of the shuttlecock. Analysis of the scanning strategies of the players, using a corneal-reflection technique, revealed no statistical between-group differences in the allocation of fixations to selected areas of the display. Both groups fixated primarily on the performer's racket and arm, with additional fixations being directed towards the head, trunk and lower body. Furthermore, there were no significant differences in the number and duration of fixations between groups.

However, the results of the event occlusion study indicated a number of significant differences between groups (Abernethy and Russell 1987a).

This approach revealed that experts were able to make better use of advance visual cues in anticipating shuttle direction and relied more on visual cues emanating from the arm/racket region. That is, the occlusion of the arm/racket area produced the greatest decrement in performance. These discrepant findings suggest that, although the two groups fixated on similar areas of the display, substantial differences in the ability to extract meaningful information were apparent. For example, when the eye movement data (Abernethy and Russell 1987b) are related to the findings on event occlusion (Abernethy and Russell 1987a), experts demonstrated the capacity to elicit more sophisticated and refined cues from the racket arm than novices although there were no differences in fixation distributions to this area of the display. This suggests that, although both groups fixated the racket and supporting arm for equal periods of time, only the experts were able to extract the information required for effective task performance. Therefore, the discriminating characteristic between experts and novices may not be related to differences in visual search strategies, but instead may be due to differences in the ability of performers to *use* the available information (Abernethy and Russell 1987b).

Similar conclusions were made by Williams and Davids (1998b) in a follow up to the study described earlier in this chapter. In this study, an attempt was made to examine the relationship between visual search strategy and selective attention in 3 vs 3 and 1 vs 1 situations using an event occlusion technique. In the 3 vs 3 simulations, a video-based occlusion technique was used to obscure information 'pick-up' from areas other than the ball/ball passer, while in the 1 vs 1 situations, a similar approach was used to mask the dribbler's head and shoulders, hips, or the lower leg and ball region. The results showed that masking areas other than the ball/ball passer affected the experienced players' performance in the 3 vs 3 situations more than the less experienced group, thus indicating that they extracted more information from these areas of the display. However, the experienced players demonstrated superior performance under both occluded and full vision conditions, suggesting that they were also able to extract better quality information from the ball/ball passer. Therefore, although no differences were observed in the earlier eye movement study (see pp. 161–4), the experienced players were able to more effectively extract information from other display areas using peripheral vision, and to extract better quality information per fixation. The different visual occlusion conditions employed in the 1 vs 1 situations are highlighted in Figure 5.6. The results showed that occluding the dribbler's hips and the lower leg and ball region did not affect the experienced players' performance more than the less experienced players. Although the earlier

Figure 5.6 The event occlusion conditions employed for the 1 vs 1 simulations: (a) head and shoulders; (b) hips (i.e. above the knees and below the mid-chest region); (c) lower leg (i.e. below the knees) and ball region; (d) an irrelevant area of the display.

study involving an eye movement registration technique had suggested that the experienced players extracted more information from the hip region, this did not directly relate to differences in selective attention. The suggestion is that the experienced players were able to acquire similar information from other (non-occluded) areas of the display, or that they fixated on the hip region because it was the most appropriate position to 'anchor' foveal vision whilst they employed peripheral vision to extract task-specific information. These findings clearly highlight the advantages of integrating eye movements with more direct measures of selective attention.

COMPLEMENTARY PARADIGMS FOR ASSESSING VISUAL SEARCH STRATEGY

In this chapter we have shown that visual orientation, as implied from fixation location characteristics, may not be directly related to information extraction. If attention can be relocated within the visual field without making distinctive eye movements to change the point of fixation then it presents a significant problem when attempting to interpret eye movement data. Also, the possibility that sport-specific information can be obtained from peripheral, as opposed to central or foveal vision, further obscures interpretation. Some caution must therefore be exercised when inferring cue usage and information extraction without substantiating eye movement data with complementary measures such as film occlusion techniques, verbal report data and point-light displays.

Film occlusion techniques

Contemporary research has demonstrated that the film occlusion approach has much potential as a method of assessing cue usage in sport (see Chapter 4). When establishing the important information cues, and the time at which they become available, there is a need to integrate both event and temporal occlusion procedures. The temporal occlusion technique involves filming the appropriate environmental display, such as the service action of a tennis player, from the opponent's on-court perspective. The film is then selectively edited at different points in order to give the subject variable extents of advance and ball flight information (e.g. occluded prior ball–racket contact, at impact, or following contact). The film is then played back to subjects using a repeated trials design, with the subject being required to report perceptual judgements as to the eventual landing position of the ball. This approach addresses the amount of time needed to select the information required to make a correct response. The event occlusion approach involves selectively occluding specific cue sources for the duration of the trial (see Abernethy 1985). The assumption is that if performance is worse when a particular area or information source is occluded then it can be inferred that this region is important for successful task performance. The scale of performance decrement is linked to the systematic removal of specific information sources via spatial occlusion techniques (for a more detailed review, see Abernethy 1985). Film occlusion techniques have been used successfully by Abernethy in badminton and squash (e.g. Abernethy 1990a, 1990b; Abernethy 1988c; Abernethy and Russell 1987a, 1987b) and by Williams and Davids (1998b) in soccer.

Verbal reports

Thus far, few researchers have examined visual behaviour and cue usage in sport using verbal report procedures. This approach requires subjects to verbalise the area of the display which they consider particularly informative. Consequently, a more direct measure of attentional allocation and information extraction is provided (Bainbridge 1990; Ericsson and Simon 1993). Data can be collected either concurrently, during performance, or retrospectively following completion of the task (Green 1995). Despite these advantages, few studies have used verbal protocols to examine visual attention during performance. Furthermore, there have been even fewer attempts to validate eye fixations with supporting information based on verbal reports.

Retrospective studies

Williams and Burwitz (1993) used a retrospective technique to identify cue usage by soccer goalkeepers during a penalty kick. The results showed that the primary sources of information used by experienced goalkeepers included the position of the penalty-taker's hip, and the angle of the trunk and foot prior to ball contact. Interestingly, these data concurred with eye movement data obtained in an earlier study by Tyldesley *et al.* (1982), suggesting a positive relationship between verbal reports and eye fixations. A retrospective approach has also been used in other sport contexts. For example, Buckholz, Prapavesis and Fairs (1988) examined cue usage in filmed tennis simulations by requiring subjects to indicate the areas of the display which were most informative in anticipating the direction of their opponents' strokes (see also Tenenbaum, Levy-Kolker, Sade, Liebermann and Lidor 1996). Several important visual cues were successfully identified from the verbal report data. The findings are summarised in Table 5.6.

Abernethy (1990b) reported conflicting findings when subjects were required to identify the relative importance of seven anticipatory cue sources in squash. The racket and the arm holding the racket were found to be the most important cues for anticipating stroke direction and depth by both expert and novice subjects. However, although this finding supported the implications drawn from an earlier film occlusion study, generally, the results failed to demonstrate any differences between groups

Table 5.6 Cues used to predict passing-shot type (down-the-line, cross-court, lob) based upon information available prior to racket-ball contact (pre) and up to the point of contact (at) for the tennis forehand. (Source: Buckolz, E. Prapavesis, H. and Fairs, J. (1988) 'Advance cues and their use in predicting tennis passing shots', *Canadian Journal of Sport Sciences*, 13: 20–30.)

	Forehand Passing-shot Type					
	Down the line		Cross court		Lob	
Pre		At	Pre	At	Pre	At
Advanced						
Body position (closed stance) 68%		Racket position (open racket face) 71%	Racket position (closed racket face) 100%	Body position (open stance) 100%	Body position (leaning back) 100%	Body position (leaning back) 100%
Other 58%		Body position (closed stance) 70%	Contact point (early and out in front) 100%	Contact point (early and out in front) 100%	Racket position (low racket head) 100%	Racket position (low racket head) 100%
Racket position (open racket face) 25%		Other 66%	Body position (open stance) 75% Other 75%	Other 100%	Other 75%	Other 75%
Intermediate						
Situation (phase of play) 71%		Other 66%	Racket swing (moving across player's body) 100%	Contact point (early out in front) 100%	Body position (leaning back) 100%	Body position (leaning back) 100%
Body position (closed stance) 70%		Body position (closed shoulders) 50%	Body position (open stance) 81%	Other 36%	Racket position (racket head drops) 100%	Racket position (racket head drops) 100%
Body position (closed shoulders) 50%		Situation (phase of play) 20%	Other 30%		Other 57%	Other 33%
Other 66%						

Percentages indicate the prediction accuracy of the associated cue.

in the importance of different cue sources. There were no differences between groups either overall or on specific cue sources. It appears that the verbalisation data provided little assistance in determining the source of the expert–novice differences discovered in the film task.

The utility of using verbal reports to identify differences in cognitive processing in such contexts has been questioned by some authors (e.g. see Le Plat and Hoc 1981; Nisbett and Wilson 1977). The argument is that verbal reports may be contaminated by subject biases and *a priori* expectations, and may be no more accurate than a rational reconstruction of events from a third person perspective. That is, retrospective reports may be corrupted by the subject's attempts to 'tidy up' what actually happened, or to rationalise what occurred (Green 1995). Similarly, Nisbett and Wilson (1977) argue that subjects are sometimes unaware of the existence of a stimulus that influenced task performance and, in some situations, are even oblivious to the response made. Much of the knowledge used by performers is subconscious and may therefore be difficult to articulate within verbal report procedures.

Concurrent verbalisation protocols

However, most cognitive psychologists agree that, if used appropriately, verbal reports can provide valuable insights into higher mental processes (Brinkman 1993; Ericsson and Simon 1993; Green 1995). Ericsson and Simon (1993) suggest that verbal reports are valid providing that certain principles are adhered to in the experimental procedure. They argue that, wherever possible, concurrent verbal reports should be collected and analysed. This procedure enables subjects to verbalise the information they are currently processing in short-term memory (Ericsson and Oliver 1989). With retrospective reports, the information may no longer be available in short-term memory, but has to be retrieved from long-term memory. Since retrieval from long-term memory is fallible, this can result in important sources of information being omitted or redundant information being included (e.g. see Brinkman 1993; Russo, Johnson and Stephens 1989). Furthermore, with retrospective reports it is difficult to distinguish information attended to during the task from information acquired or used after (or even before) the completion of the task (Green 1995).

Concurrent verbal reports have been successfully utilised by Vickers (1988) with elite, intermediate and novice gymnasts. She found a relationship between subjects' eye fixations of slides of gymnastic displays and their verbalisations about each sequence following a retention period. Both verbal report and eye movement data revealed that skilled gymnasts fixated on different areas of the display than less skilled gymnasts. However, more importantly, the results showed that the gymnasts' verbal identification of important body cues was found to be 70.4% consistent with their eye movement data.

Similarly, a concurrent verbalisation protocol was used by Williams and Davids (1997) to examine the relationship between eye movements (i.e. 'looking') and concurrent verbal reports (i.e. 'seeing') in two different performance contexts. In one study, subjects reacted to 11 vs 11 soccer simulations, whilst in a second study they had to respond to 3 vs 3 soccer situations. Each study involved two experimental conditions: (i) visual fixations were recorded using an eye movement registration system; (ii) subjects were required to continuously verbalise their visual fixations whilst viewing the film sequences. To reduce the amount of information which needed to be verbalised, the viewing screen was divided into three areas: 'box' – ball/ball passer; 'right' – right side of the screen; 'left' – left side of the display. The results demonstrated many similarities between verbal reports and eye movements as methods of assessing the locus of attention in the 11 vs 11 situations. For example, there were no differences between the two methods in identifying the location of visual attention and/or fixation. The eye movement data indicated that the less experienced group spent more time fixating inside the box area than the experienced group, whilst the verbal report data provided supporting evidence to suggest that the less experienced players expended more time extracting information from this area of the display. That is, the less experienced players appeared to be guilty of 'ball-watching'. Moreover, both methods showed that the experienced group spent more time visually fixating on, and attending to, other areas of the display such as the positions and movements of players (c.f. Williams *et al.* 1994). This suggests that the experienced players considered areas other than the box (i.e. ball/ball passer) to be more informative. Therefore, both eye movements and verbal reports provided valid measures of selective attention in these situations.

Differences were observed between verbal reports and eye movements when identifying the locus of visual attention in 3 vs 3 situations. The eye movement data indicated that there were no differences in the distribution of visual fixations to selected areas of the display. According to this method, subjects fixated primarily on the 'box' (i.e. ball/ball passer) with infrequent fixations to the right or left of the screen. However, the verbal report condition showed that the experienced players distributed their attention evenly between the box, and the right and left side of the screen. In the verbal report condition, the experienced players were attending to information inside the box area for a shorter time period ($\underline{M}$ = 50.9%) compared with the eye movement condition ($\underline{M}$ = 72.45%). The suggestion is that, although the experienced players were visually fixating inside the box area, they were using peripheral vision to extract information from other areas of the display. They seemed able to use the box as a visual 'pivot' or central reference point while simultaneously scanning peripheral vision for the positions and movements of players. This more extensive search strategy was highlighted by the fact that 71.44% of their verbal comments involved a change in the locus of attention compared with only 58.44% for the less experienced players. There were no differences between eye movements and verbal reports for the less experienced players. They made less use of peripheral vision preferring instead to use foveal vision to extract information from the ball or the player in possession of the ball. These findings supported earlier research which used a film occlusion technique to mask information pick-up from areas other than the ball/ball passer (see p. 172). In sum, these studies show that the validity of eye movement recording as a method of determining differences in selective attention is dependent, at least in part, on the subject's level of experience and the type of task undertaken.

Point light displays

The use of point light displays to examine perceptual processes was popularised initially by Johansson (1973, 1975) and then more recently in the gait-perception work of Cutting and colleagues (Cutting 1978; Cutting *et al.* 1978). This technique involves the presentation of either film, live or computer simulated displays consisting of the motion of light points representing the displacement-time histories of the joint centres and key kinematic landmarks in the opponent's action. This technique has been used successfully by Abernethy and Packer (1989) to examine cue usage in squash. In this study, squash players of different skill levels were required to make perceptual judgements regarding the forthcoming direction and force of an opponent's stroke from a filmed 26-point light display. Although some reduction in prediction performance was evident when the display was degraded to a point light source (indicating at least some role for contour and background information), both groups were able to perceive the important kinematic information needed to predict shot direction and force. Thus, there appears to be a close link between perceptual skill and the kinematic properties of the display being viewed (see Chapter 9). Abernethy (1993b) suggests that this technique can be used to effectively derive the key invariants involved in perception in sport. The argument is that by manipulating the point light display researchers can identify the important joint-centre representations needed to preserve prediction accuracy. Evidence of a reduction in prediction performance when a certain point light is occluded will highlight this cue or light source as one that the subject normally uses when predicting an opponent's stroke. In such a way the researcher would be able to determine both the important cues used in anticipating stroke prediction and the time at which these become pre-eminent during the anticipation process. Although such an approach has many similarities with film occlusion techniques, the possibility of using computer simulated models may offer a less time-consuming and hence more productive technique for determining cue usage in sport (for an interesting discussion, see Abernethy 1993).

TRAINING VISUAL SEARCH STRATEGIES IN SPORT

Earlier in this chapter we raised the issue of whether the perceptual refinement of the expert sports performer can be explained by differences in the search strategy employed or, alternatively, by the quality of information extracted. Clearly, the answer to this question has significant implications for the design of visual training programmes in sport. Researchers have suggested that knowledge of the most pertinent or informative areas of the display is crucial to successful performance (e.g. Bard and Fleury 1981; Ripoll 1988). In contrast, others have argued that it is not the allocation of attention which is important but the ability to establish a meaningful relationship between the information extracted and subsequent behaviour (e.g. Abernethy 1990a, 1990b; Abernethy and Russell 1987a, 1987b; Goulet *et al.* 1989). They question the utility of training programmes which attempt to improve performance solely by focusing on informative areas of the display without highlighting the critical relationship between important display features for the learner. For example, merely directing the tennis player to fixate on the opponent's racket, or the gymnastic judge to focus on the gymnast's upper body may not in itself facilitate performance. As well as highlighting expert search patterns as models of perceptual performance, training programmes should include tasks which contribute towards the development of a comparable knowledge base upon which visual search strategies may be based. Training programmes should attempt to explain what these areas of the display mean and what effect they have on subsequent performance.

For example, in soccer this could be achieved by the use of attack versus defence 'phase play' where coaches can stop play and highlight informative areas of the display and their importance within developing play. Also, awareness of player positions could be enhanced by 'one-touch' and 'silent' soccer games (see Taylor 1992). These practices could be used to encourage players to direct their attention toward the movements and positions of players 'off the ball', thus developing anticipation. Similarly, in tennis, coaches should teach players the relationship between specific racket head angles and resultant stroke direction (c.f. Abernethy and Wollstein 1989; Maschette 1980). However, coaches should recognise that highlighting relevant cues to performers makes the link between perceptual information and action response explicit. Extensive practice is then required to make the use of these sources of information more implicit or subconscious, thus requiring less of the performer's attention.

An alternative technique may be to use video-based training programmes to highlight the links between important display cues and eventual outcome (e.g. see Burroughs 1984; Christina, Barresi and Shaffner 1990; Haskins 1965; Singer, Cauraugh, Chen, Steinberg, Frehlich and Wang 1994; Tayler, Burwitz and Davids 1994; Williams and Burwitz 1993). By stopping the video at specific times and requiring the learner to specify what will result from the action, links can be drawn between various information cues and eventual action outcome. Certainly, these studies have been successful enough to illustrate the practical utility of such training programmes in sport. For example, Christina *et al.* (1990) found that a linebacker's decision-making skills could be improved via the use of a video-based training programme. Similarly, Williams and Burwitz (1993) showed a significant improvement in anticipatory performance when the relationship between important postural cues and eventual penalty-kick placement were highlighted to a group of novice soccer goalkeepers. However, despite the success of these video-based simulations very few studies have included a transfer task to examine whether training facilitated performance in a real game context (for an exception, see Adolphe, Vickers and Laplante 1997). Clearly, appropriate transfer tests need to be developed which would enable researchers to examine whether these improvements transfer back to the game situation. Perhaps an approach would be to assess actual pre- and post-training performance by videotaping game play prior to and after visual training. However, since it would be difficult to control the game situations presented to subjects, perhaps a combination of set sequences and actual game play would prove a more appropriate measure of performance (for a more detailed discussion regarding issues of video simulation and transfer, see Chamberlain and Lee 1993; Starkes and Lindley 1994).

Regardless of whether video or 'live model' training methods are used, coaches should begin by introducing only a few key cues as aids to anticipation. Thereafter, more of these anticipation cues should be progressively introduced in line with the increase in skill level of the performer. In other words, as certain aspects of performance become automatic, requiring less attention to be devoted to technique execution, more of the performer's attention can be devoted towards cue recognition and usage (Williams and Davids 1994).

Finally, when players have reached a high level of performance, coaches should encourage them to be inventive and resourceful so that some misleading cues are included in their performance repertoire, thus making it difficult for opponents to anticipate their actions (Maschette 1980). For instance, if players can use the same preparatory acts when executing similar shots then this may mislead an opponent into an inappropriate response. This type of deception is particularly common in tennis serving and in overhead shots in badminton.

SUMMARY AND FUTURE RESEARCH DIRECTIONS

Our aim in this chapter was to examine the role of visual search strategy in sport. Initially, we suggested that the importance of eye movements in sport is to bring informative areas of the display into foveal vision. The fovea covers 1–2 degrees of central vision and is the area of highest visual clarity. It is responsible for object identification and discrimination, whilst peripheral vision is responsible for object location. The assumption is that objects are initially detected in peripheral vision and then brought into foveal vision for subsequent identification. The main eye movements used in sport are saccades and pursuit tracking. Saccades are rapid movements of the eyes which bring areas of interest into foveal vision. Pursuit tracking occurs when the eyes follow a slow-moving object in the visual field. Thereafter, we summarised some of the limitations involved in assuming a direct relationship between visual fixation and selective attention. It was suggested that visual fixation may not be directly related to information extraction and, further, that attention may be relocated within the visual field without making distinctive eye movements to change the point of fixation. A theoretical backdrop was then provided by suggesting that search strategies are controlled by task-specific knowledge structures stored in memory. These knowledge structures are developed as a result of previous experience of similar and related situations. We then reviewed current research examining proficiency-related differences in visual search strategy in sport. The research suggests that experts and novices fixate different areas of a given display, implying differences in cue usage. Additionally, skill-based differences were found in both the fixation duration and the total number of fixations required during task performance. However, these findings were not conclusive with higher search rates being demonstrated by experts in certain situations and lower search rates in others. Also, contradictory evidence was presented indicating that perceptual differences may not be related to visual search strategy, but rather to the use made of the available information. Finally, we examined some of the alternative techniques available for assessing cue usage in sport. It was argued that verbal reports, film occlusion techniques and point light displays may provide alternative and/or complementary methods to eye movement recording.

Although we have continually highlighted avenues for future research effort during this chapter, we finish by highlighting some specific areas of interest. First, future research should continue to develop more ecologically valid paradigms to examine visual search strategy in sport. In particular, there is a need to develop protocols whereby eye movements are collected within 'real-world' performance contexts. Eye movements must be collected within meaningful and realistic situations where athletes are allowed to function naturally, as they would within their natural habitat. The research covered in this chapter clearly highlights this progressive and much needed move towards enhanced ecological validity in visual search research. Furthermore, recent advances in eye movement recording should make it easier for sport and exercise scientists to use eye movement registration techniques within intact sports situations. Initially, we need to carry out similar experiments in the laboratory and on the field in order to examine similarities and differences between these conditions (c.f. Ripoll 1991). Important questions here would be: Does the use of a film display eliminate certain visual and auditory cues which are normally crucial in the 'live' situation? How does moving around the environment alter the visual search strategy used? (In other words, does what we see depend on where/how we move?)

Since visual fixation is not always directly related to information extraction, future research should attempt to combine eye movement registration with parallel measures of information pick-up such as verbal report or event occlusion techniques. These methods would provide additional evidence regarding expert–novice differences in the allocation of attention and/or in the quality of information extraction. Similarly, researchers should attempt to increase our understanding of the role of peripheral vision in the visual search process. The occlusion of aspects of foveal and/or peripheral vision during task performance may give some indication as to their respective role within sport. For example, recent technological developments have enabled corneal-reflection principles to be used to occlude specific features of the visual field during eye movement recording in sport. This method enables stimulus presentation to the fovea, parafovea and periphery to be continuously and dynamically controlled. That is, occlusion of the fovea would enable researchers to identify the relative importance of information pick-up from the peripheral visual field alone. Such an approach offers an exciting and productive avenue for visual search research in sport.

Further research is required to examine the interaction between head and eye movements during performance. For example, when rapidly changing the point of visual fixation from one area of the display to another (i.e. from the position of a defensive player to that of the basket or an offensive team-mate in basketball) subjects can keep the head fixed but use saccadic eye movements to alter the point of fixation, keep the eyes fixed but move the head to bring the object of interest on to the fovea, or hold the head and eyes fixed but move the trunk to fixate the desired object. Thus far, we have only a limited knowledge of the different reaction modes and strategies used by subjects. It may be that experts combine head and eye movements more effectively during skill execution. Clearly, the functional significance of these individual differences and their predictive value for performance would be an interesting area of study. A variation on the same theme is the use of eye–head or image–retina visual systems during coincidence–anticipation performance (e.g. see Haywood 1984).

Finally, there is a dearth of research which has attempted to determine the visual search patterns employed during the skill learning process. For example, what do subjects look at when observing a demonstration of a skill to be learned? How do visual search patterns in such contexts differ as a result of the learner's age and level of ability, the nature and/or complexity of the task or the verbal instructions given by the demonstrator? Since appropriate visual behaviours would appear to be a necessary prerequisite to successful skill learning in the majority of sports skills, what are the differences between good and poor learners in such contexts? These are interesting theoretical and applied issues which could be addressed via the recording of visual search behaviours during skill acquisition.

Section B

Perception and action

In Section A, a traditional model for perception and action, the information processing approach, was introduced and analysed. Recently, this established framework for understanding perception and action has been criticised by scientists rejecting the person–machine metaphor of cognitive science. Broadly speaking these researchers are working within the ecological framework and propose different phenomenological models to explain perception and action. In Section B, we examine some of the main ideas behind the ecological approach to perception and action. Perhaps the defining characteristic of this perspective is the level of analysis chosen to study behaviour. It places less stress on the internalised knowledge structures or executive regulators which form an integral part of traditional information processing theories. Rather the goal is to integrate theories and tools from psychology, biology and physics to gain an understanding of how an organism functions successfully in its environment. According to ecological theorists, the study of the relationship between perception and action should be aimed at 'phenomena within the organism-environment synergy rather than within the organism per se' (Beek and Meijer 1988: 160). This emphasis on the coordination that exists between a biological organism and its natural environment recognises that they have evolved together as a functional system. In the words of Kugler and Turvey (1987: xii):

> Ecological Science, in its broadest sense, is a multidisciplinary approach to the study of living systems, their environments and the reciprocity that has evolved between the two ... Ecological Psychology ... [emphasizes] the study of information transactions between living systems and their environments, especially as they pertain to perceiving situations of significance to planning and executing of purposes activated in an environment.

Within ecological psychology there are various subclasses of models. Beek and van Wieringen (1994) have identified at least three distinct theoretical positions in the ecological camp[1] (see also Beek, Peper and Stegeman

1995; Michaels and Beek 1995). These are: (i) the direct approach to perception and action (as advanced by proponents such as Lee (1980a, b), Bootsma (1988) and Warren (1990); (ii) the dynamic patterns approach of Kelso, Schoner and colleagues (e.g. Kelso 1995; Schoner 1994); and (iii) Kugler and Turvey's (1987) thermodynamic theory of perception–action cycles.

In this section of the book, we will observe that the specific positions of these theoretical groups differ only slightly in explaining how the perceptual and action subsystems support goal-directed behaviour. As explained elsewhere (e.g. Davids *et al.* 1994; Turvey 1990), their research efforts are galvanised by the attempt to resolve important issues on perception and action raised by Bernstein (1967) and Gibson (1979). Michaels and Beek (1995) propose that a common feature of these theoretical approaches is that they emphasise the 'circular relations' that exist between the perceptual systems and the action systems. This proposal echoes Cutting's (1986) argument that a complete understanding of human perception entails not only being able to describe what is perceived by an individual, but also how the act of perception is achieved and acted upon.

Whereas some of the theorists in the ecological camp prefer a physical and mathematical description to explain the coordination of actions with environmental events, others argue that an important issue concerns how the structure and function of a biological system have been shaped by evolutionary pressures (see Turvey and Fitzpatrick 1993). The emphasis is on the specialised relationship between the perception–action subsystems which has evolved for all biological organisms (Turvey 1990). In the course of evolution these subsystems have become tailored to a specific environment. Therefore, the focus of perception and action in human behaviour is on the 'Organism–Environment fit'. Other terms used to describe this relationship in the ecological literature include 'mutuality', 'coalition' and 'synergy'. van Wieringen (1988: 88) has summarised the sphere of study as the 'complementarity and reciprocity between the organism and environment'.

The list of theoretical influences on the ecological approach, outlined above, should not be considered exhaustive. There are many other ideas in biology, physics and the neurosciences which are beginning to gain acceptance in the movement sciences. These include stimulating theoretical work on the neurobiology of pattern formation in the brain by Edelman and colleagues (e.g. Edelman, 1992; Spoorns and Edelman, 1993), and the model of Newell (1986) on the role of constraints and coordinative structures in the self-organisation of movement. However, although the subtle differences between the camps are very real for the researchers within them, there are only slight differences in orientations and priorities, and it is extremely difficult to completely disentangle the theoretical strands within the ecological camp. For example, Newell (1985) agreed that his conceptualisation of constraints on the emergence of coordination was informed by the thermodynamic interpretations offered by Kugler, Kelso and Turvey (1982: 295), but 'without necessarily invoking the theoretical position advanced by this group ... although ... I am sympathetic to this theoretical position'.

In Chapters 6 and 7, we shall seek to understand some of these theoretical positions and what they mean for perception and action in sport contexts. Chapter 6 will start with an overview of some recent criticisms of the traditional information processing approach. We continue by examining the philosophical, theoretical and empirical bases of the major challenge to traditional theories of perception: Gibson's (1979) theory of direct perception. In Chapter 7, we overview the dynamical systems approach to movement coordination with particular emphasis on attempts to solve what is referred to as Bernstein's (1967) degrees of freedom problem.

6 Direct perception and action

INTRODUCTION

In Chapter 1, we noted that a fundamental question in visual perception is how rudimentary 'meaningless' sensory information arriving at the eye is translated into 'meaningful' visual information. Helmholtz (1925) had previously argued that the ambiguous sensory stimulation provided by an information cue needs to be progressively upgraded into a percept which is recognised and interpreted by the mind. This description is based on a model of mind–body dualism which underpins theories of perception and action in cognitive science, advocated originally by distinguished philosophers such as Aristotle, Plato and Descartes. Dualism provided the ideological basis for traditional cognitive psychology. The job of cue elaboration or information derivation is carried out by special cognitive processes and internalised devices, sometimes called knowledge structures or symbolic representations. These mental entities are considered particular to human beings (Blumberg and Wasserman 1995). They have the role of conveying meaning and understanding of the world to a perceiver from the static snapshots of the environment provided by the visual system (see Figure 6.1).

The indirect propositions have a more modern expression in the work of Marr (1982) in Artificial Intelligence. In Chapter 1, we saw that he modelled visual perception as a computational process in which sensory information from an object in a basic form, the so-called 'primal sketch', is received, elaborated and transformed into a highly developed perceptual pattern with reference to a representation of an image of it in memory. We outlined the main historical influences on cognitive science as the philosophical theory of indirect realism, and the engineering and computer sciences. We saw how, consequently, cognitive psychology has tended to eschew the biological and physical sciences in modelling human motor behaviour (Prinz and Neumann 1990).

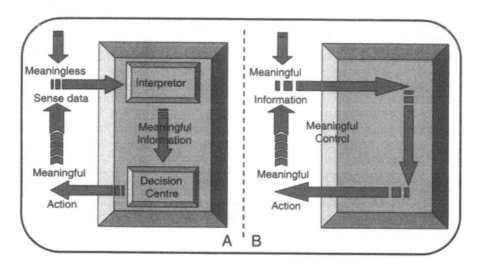

Figure 6.1 Indirect and direct conceptions of the relations between perception and action. (Adapted from Meijer, O.G. (1988) *The Hierarchy Debate: Perspectives for a Theory and History of Movement Science*, Amsterdam: Free University Press.)

Why minds are not like computers

The ecological approach is a radical alternative to this traditional perspective on perception and action. The established philosophical view implies that 'mind', located somewhere in the higher centres of the CNS, is composed of a special substance which is not governed by the physical laws of matter (Edelman 1992). The major criticisms of the accepted view are that: (i) the human brain is too dynamic to be a computer; and (ii) psychologists have been guilty of idealising the mind rather than considering it within the framework of physical biology. In fact, the Turing machine, which provided the formal basis for the original development of computer systems, has been described as an ideal mathematical object (Carello, Turvey, Kugler and Shaw 1984). Therefore, it cannot be applied to the study of organic material like the brain without reference to the physical laws and biological constraints which influence its behaviour.

A fundamental issue concerns the cognitive tradition of accepting the existence of internalised representations as control mechanisms for the perceptual and action systems, *a priori* to scientific investigation.[1] Just because an algorithm can be written for a machine to act as a sensing device, this does not constitute an explanation for perception and action in biological systems. For direct realism theorists, a major task is the development of more lawful explanations of behaviour like perception and action. To achieve this objective, one needs to understand the concept of mind from the framework of physical biology. This alternative approach relies on biological and neurophysiological accounts of how the brain and other higher centres of the nervous system actually function during perception and action. Note that such an approach, far from requiring science to 'mortgage scientific understanding' (Kelso 1995), would permit it 'to remain in the black' as it were (see Fitch and Turvey 1978). A necessary step in this direction would be to develop a theory of the human mind which has a biological rather than an engineering basis – a theory which allows mind to be 'embodied' (Edelman 1992).

An understanding of cognition which is critically dependent on neural processes, can be gained from Edelman's (1987, 1992) Theory of Neuronal Group Selection (TNGS). Edelman (ibid.) produced a persuasive interdisciplinary argument, encompassing data and theory from philosophy, biology, physics and the neurosciences, rejecting the notion of mind as a computational, symbol-representing device. His main argument is that the traditional information processing approach lacks relevance to biological organisms. In fact, current evidence shows little support for the idea that the brain's structure permits an analogy with the computer.[2] The problem for Edelman (ibid.) has been the Cartesian tradition that matters of consciousness are the responsibility of the mind. A fundamental assumption of TNGS is that thoughts, emotions and actions should be considered, not as stored coded structures, but as softly assembled neural patterns arising within the CNS (i.e. the connections between neurons are emergent and not rigidly hardwired).

The main tenet of TNGS is that the brain is a dynamic organ containing many interconnecting neurons, which are selected into variant groups due to genetically and environmentally imposed constraints. In a highly plausible connectionist account, Edelman (1992) proposes that thoughts, emotions, ideas, beliefs, images and actions are merely the neural traffic between the billions of neurons in the CNS. Some of the neuronal cells in the brainstem are responsible for sending chemical neurotransmitters around the brain, with the role of strengthening the probability of connections between neuronal groups at the time of occurrence of a functional behaviour, such as an idea or an action. For example, if a gymnast practising a movement achieves the desired coordination pattern, then the network of neurons combining at the time of success will be strengthened (selected). The neural network patterns connected with less successful manoeuvres are less likely to be selected. Gradually, more functional connections are selected over time as the individual successfully negotiates environmental objects, surfaces and events during behaviour. Thelen and Smith (1994) point out that Edelman's (1992) connectionist account of the neurophysiological basis of cognition, perception and action is 'entirely harmonious' with the general principles of dynamical systems theory in the ecological approach. In this unified view of mind and body, it is clear that selection is imposed in the brain, by the brain, and that there is a significant role for individual exploration in searching for functional patterns of cognition, perception and action. This theme of search, exploration and discovery in perception and action will constantly reappear in Chapters 6, 7 and 8.

A computational approach to perception and action, therefore, creates a gap between the cognitive subsystem and other important subsystems such as the CNS and the body–environment system (van Gelder and Port 1995; van Gelder, in press). An explanation of perception and action promoted by theorists such as Edelman (1992), Kelso (1995) and van Gelder and Port (1995) accounts for this gap by 'embedding' cognitive processes within a deep understanding of the neurophysiology of the CNS and the dynamics of the performer–environment context. An exciting prospect envisaged by Goldfield (1995), amongst others, is of a unified theoretical framework for the study of perception, action and cognition in which the same dynamical principles can account for behaviour at different levels of analysis including the neurophysiological, behavioural and social levels. Moreover, as Newell and van Emmerik (1990) argue, such an encompassing account would superimpose itself on the different timescales bordering previous distinctions between evolutionary, ontogenetic and perceptual levels of analysis in the study of human behaviour. These ideas are also pursued within Chapters 6, 7 and 8.

So far, we have focused on the philosophical and theoretical differences between traditional and alternative accounts of perception and action. In Section B, we will present support for a model of the sports performer as a complex, 'open' biophysical system, rather than as a type of computer which can process information and rely on internally-stored programmes of movement behaviour. Prominence will be given to a theoretical standpoint demonstrating formally how perceptual information acts as a major constraint on the precise form adopted by the movement system during goal-directed behaviour. In order to pursue the argument that representations do not mediate our dealings with the world, we need a non-traditional theoretical description of the concept of information. Such a reconceptualisation needs to be framed in a theory of perception with a keener appreciation of our biological inheritance. One such approach is that of James Gibson's (e.g. 1979) theory of direct perception.

GIBSON'S ECOLOGICAL PSYCHOLOGY

Do human beings need internally-represented, expert systems to help us to make sense of our world? Gibson's (1979) radical proposition was that we do not. He theorised that a lawful relationship exists between the properties of the environment and the structure of surrounding energy distributions, implying that perception is specific to sensory information. The layout of the environment imposes a rich spatio-temporal order upon surrounding energy flows, particularly the crucial source – optical energy.[3] Light reaches the eye after having been reflected off surfaces and objects in cluttered and busy environments. Light is reflected in straight lines and exists in a highly structured distribution called an array (ibid.). Light carries information for an observer because it has dense structure which is specific to the observer and his or her habitat. It is not reflected uniformly in natural environments. Numerous elements (e.g. material composition, texture and angular interconnections of surfaces) alter the flow. So, not only is there ordered flow in light energy (invariants), but there are also perturbations to the flow (variants). These perturbations help us to perceive the motion of objects travelling in the environment, the layout of surfaces and our own ego-motion. From an evolutionary perspective, the slants and angles of the textured elements of the environment perturb the flow of light rays in meaningful ways for animals which have been purposefully adapted to live in specific niches (see Figure 6.1). The continuous availability of information for pick up by purpose-designed perceptual systems is an important element of ecological explanations of goal-directed behaviour in which there is little recourse to computation by physical symbol systems (see Chapter 1).

Perception, action and the problem of intentionality

In this part of Chapter 6, we shall present the main arguments of ecological psychology for rejecting the traditional notion that perception is mediated. Traditionally, it was believed that a 'homunculus' (literally, a little person in the brain) was needed to interpret the neurophysiological signals received on the retina, at the ear or by the proprioceptive system. Such mediated perception then allows us to pursue our intentions towards perceived objects by relying on the homunculus to relate this sensory information to our mental representations of the world. A difficult question is: Who interprets the sensory information of the homunculus? Surely, there would be an infinite regress that would just push the problem of perception deeper into the unknown recesses of the mind?

Gibsonian theorists have highlighted the relationship between perception and action as direct and cyclical. They are mutually interdependent activities which cannot be studied separately (Michaels and Carello 1981). According to Gibson (1979), a lawful account of perceiving and acting in dynamic contexts should be based on a theory of a mutually constraining relationship between animals and their environments. In the direct perception camp, invariants and affordances are key concepts. Invariants are higher order properties from the surrounding energy flows which remain constantly available for pick-up, despite transformations associated with observers and the environment. That is, despite continuous changes to energy distributions surrounding a performer, the higher order invariants remain available to provide meaning. Gibson (1979) argued that humans perceive invariants as affordances for action. In sport, balls invite actions such as hitting, catching, throwing and avoiding, whilst gaps afford traversing in different ways and barriers afford leaping, stepping and hurdling. Affordances, therefore, are invitations to act within specific contexts (ibid.). We will take a more detailed look at this important ecological concept later in this chapter.

Turvey (1986) argues that 'mundane intentional behaviour' (p. 153) such as locomotion through gaps or interceptive actions, occurs through biological organisms using their unique frame of reference to direct their actions in relation to important objects. In sport, for example, a performer's frame of reference for intentional behaviour within a dynamic environment is constructed with reference to his or her own limb magnitudes, body morphology and physiological metabolism. That is, the perception of affordances for intentional actions in a sport context is constrained by an individual frame of reference encompassing the relationship between the environment and the performer. This relationship implies that the performer and environment can be best understood as a system. For example, a cross-country runner needs information expressed in a unique frame of reference which can specify the affordances of an upcoming obstacle in the terrain. How far away is it at current approach velocity? Given the current state of the mechanical and metabolic systems, can it be jumped over or does it need to be stepped on? A runner needs information on the state of the environment which is specified in a dynamic frame that is uniquely relevant to his or her current capacities, abilities and body dimensions. An individual reference frame is updated regularly over the life cycle as an organism goes about its daily business. An objective frame measured in arbitrary units, such as seconds or metres, will be less useful to a dynamically changing organism because it is static. From a computational perspective with an objective reference frame, a young child or novice learning to catch in different types of ball games would need to commit to memory the values of various significant physical variables related to ball shapes, sizes, textures and masses. This would incur a significant cognitive burden for the learner, without the guarantee of success. For a biological organism, in which the perceptual and action systems have evolved in a highly integrated way, how would such a static system requiring the interpretation of standardised measurements have evolved? From a direct perception viewpoint, an active organism needs information on the actions afforded it, scaled in current body-relevant units (such as arm lengths or step lengths) (e.g. Warren 1990; Warren, Young and Lee 1986; Savelsbergh, Wimmers, van der Kamp and Davids, in press).

The conclusion is that a cognitive subsystem, predicated on representations, computations and other such concepts of the information processing paradigm, is unnecessary and irrelevant in the study of intentionality in biological systems. Rather, the focus of study should be on how animals typically produce a tight fit between the environment and their actions. A mechanism proposed to explain the 'fitness' of successful animals is the evolutionary sensitivity of their perceptual systems to the energy flows available as informational constraints on their behaviour[4] (Riccio and Stoffregren 1988; Warren 1990). We propose in this book that a key source of energy available as information for perception and action is optical energy.

Information for perception and action

The theory of direct perception deals with the problem of visual perception by emphasising optic flow patterns. Gibson (1979) rejected the constructivist claims that the retinal image is only the 'starting point' for visual processing. He suggested that the optic array specified at the eye contains abundant information over time and space that allows the actor to directly and unambiguously perceive the layout and properties of events within the environment. In contrast to the constructivist theory, the ecological approach to perception claims that there is much more information potentially available in sensory stimulation than previously believed. Ecological psychology suggests that ambient light arriving at the eye has structure and is highly complex and potentially rich in information. Gibson maintained that this optic array contains veridical, or invariant, information such as motion parallax, texture density gradients and gradient of image size which conspicuously specifies the layout of objects in space (see Bruce *et al.* 1996).

In ecological psychology, information is unambiguous and contrasts strongly with indirect accounts of stimuli to be embellished. The specificational nature of this unambiguous information forms the crux of direct perception. This quality contributes to what Turvey (1992: 111) has termed a 'realist theory of knowing'. It does not need 'epistemic mediators' or 'internalised knowledge structures' in the brain to make sense of the world (Fitch and Turvey 1978). Rather it is believed that information as higher order invariants, such as optic variables specifying affordances, is picked up directly through the perceptual search activities of an animal.

Optic variables

Applications of Gibson's (1979) theory of direct perception to the study of visual perception and action in sport requires an understanding of the differences between physical variables and optic variables for describing the information available to support movement behaviour. Physical variables refer to the properties of surfaces and objects in the environment which can be measured in an objective frame of reference which is external to the individual (see Todd 1981; Turvey 1986). As proposed earlier, a reference frame for the environment perceived in physical variables can be calibrated in arbitrary metrical units such as metres or yards and seconds or minutes. For example, the important physical variables in sport environments include the size of a hurdle facing the approaching athlete, or the momentary distance a ball is from the fielder in cricket and its velocity of approach. This calibration frame may be useful to a scientist attempting to take standardised and objective measures of physical phenomena, but an actor wishing to perform actions in relation to these objects and surfaces requires information in a more meaningful and instantaneously relevant frame.

Optic variables, on the other hand, refer to the properties of the light reflected in a lawfully structured way from important surfaces and objects and which are available for pick-up by all organisms equipped with a visual system. Optic variables come in many forms and include information on texture and density gradients from the layout of the environment, the direction of motion of an object, the distance from the observer it will pass and even the time until it contacts the point of observation (e.g. Lee 1976; Gibson 1979; Todd 1981; Michaels and Oudejans 1992). Since they are calibrated within a unique frame of reference for an observer and the environment as a system, optic variables are characterised by the action possibilities or affordances they offer each individual (Gibson 1979). Information specifying these affordances is available in the invariant and rich spatio-temporal patterns in the light playing on the retina of a uniquely positioned observer. In the observer's natural habitat, there exists an invariant relationship between the properties of important surfaces and objects and the spatio-temporal structure of the optical information reflected from them. These invariants can be exploited by performers as reliable sources of information which are directly available to support actions in their natural environments. That is, the actions of a performer can be tightly geared to these informational invariants. When a performer moves, a specific translational optic flow or pattern of light intensity is created which is reflected on to the retina from surfaces and objects near and far. The specificity of the optic flow allows the performer to rely on the dynamic patterns of retinal light reflections for supporting actions. The advantage that optic invariants have over physical variables is that when confronted with surfaces and objects with novel physical properties such as unique sizes, textures and heights, a performer can still pick up their affordances thereby specifying the necessary actions.

Affordances for perception and action

Fitch and Turvey (1978) argue against a theory of perception based on 'animal-neutral' descriptions of information in traditional physics (e.g. light reflected from an object such as a ball is measured in units such as photons). An ecological account of perception emphasises that information is perceived in 'animal-relevant' terms (i.e. what it offers, invites or demands of the performer in terms of an action). Gibson (1979) under-lined the fundamental flaw in cognitive theories of perception when he stated that 'psychologists assume that objects are composed of their qual-ities . . . what we perceive when we look at objects are their affordances, not their qualities' (p. 134).

As we stated earlier, affordances represent possibilities for action in a sport context and here we will refer to a volleyball movement to exem-plify what we mean. Affordances are at the same time objective (i.e. they are phenomenal) and subjective (i.e. they invite a specific action from the performer which is dependent on individual biomechanical characteristics) (Fitch and Turvey 1978). A volleyball in flight is not perceived in terms of its dimensions, colour, density or distance away. It is perceived in terms of its affordances for action (e.g. a volley, a dig or a smash). The lawful structure of the light waves reflected from a ball travelling along a partic-ular flight path specifies the action which is afforded a player. Along another flight path the optic structure would differ. The difference in the optic structure stipulates a different affordance for the performer. Thus, in the direct perception approach, a volleyball delivered at a certain height affords digging, whereas a ball at a higher trajectory affords volleying. There is no physical standard prescribing this choice for each player. The individual's frame of reference will specify the affordance uniquely to each player. According to Gibson (1979), this information need not be stored in some form of memorial code, or representation, but is consistently and directly available as a consequence of the richness of information contained within the optic array. The learner is not burdened with the task of devel-oping symbolic memory structures through training, observational modelling and match play. Instead, the perceptual systems become progres-sively more 'attuned' to the invariant information in the environment through direct experience in realistic practice and match play. The infor-mation picked up becomes more subtle, elaborate and precise with task-specific experience. Contrary to a popular misconception, Gibson (1979) did not deny the possibility of the existence of cognitive processes such as reminiscence, expectation, dreaming and imagery; nor did he suggest that memory did not have a role at all in perception. Rather, his view could be interpreted as suggesting that the performer–environment relationship was the appropriate scale of analysis for examining the rela-tionship between perception, action and cognition. Therefore, the traditional emphasis was wrong in looking for all the answers at the cogni-tive level of the human movement system.

Gibson (1979) stated that the concept of affordances provides a powerful way of combining perception and action: 'within the theory of affor-dances, perception is an invitation to act, and action is an essential component of perception' (ibid.: 46). The important implications for sport and exercise science research is that only in experiments where percep-tion and action are coupled together, with subjects relatively free to move within a realistic environment, will the smartness of evolutionary-designed perceptual mechanisms come into play (see Runeson 1977; Milner and Goodale 1995). This view of research design is in direct contrast to cognitive theories where perception and action are seen as being functionally independent and generally are studied as separate research topics (e.g. see Section A).

The ecological emphasis on the performer–environment relationship signifies that the world may be directly perceived by an organism with the result that perception and action can become tightly coupled. Turvey (1990: 941) best summarises the key argument by suggesting that:

> Information in the ecological approach refers to specificity between the structured energy distributions available to a perceptual system and the environmental and movement properties causally responsible for that structure.

To summarise so far, perception is the act of directly picking up the invariants in the environment which specify events, structures, surfaces, objects and the layout for the purpose of goal-directed activity (Gibson 1979). Affordances for action in an environment are specified within a unique frame of reference for each individual. Descriptions of the state of the environment can only ever be 'frame dependent' because affordances are perceived in relation to relevant properties of an individual including the scale of his or her body dimensions (e.g. limb sizes), morphological structure (e.g. skeletal bone densities) and metabolism (Turvey 1986). Therefore, a mutually constraining relationship exists between intentionality, perception and action within an ecological frame of reference for each individual.

PERCEPTION–ACTION COUPLING

Transformations to the optic array, as an animal moves around its specific habitat, can be coupled to the forces used to generate the movements so that detailed, specificational information sources, as invariants, are available to constrain behaviour (see Warren 1990). The idea that movement creates information which, in turn, constrains further movements is known as perception–action coupling (see Figure 6.2). As Gibson (1979) argued, 'We must perceive in order to move, but we must also move in order to perceive' (p. 223). The idea of perception–action coupling is fundamental to ecological theory and contrasts strongly with the traditional idea that the action systems passively depend on the information provided by the perceptual systems for movement organisation.

The notion that regularities in the optic flow field can constrain movement behaviour was demonstrated in early experiments on balancing in

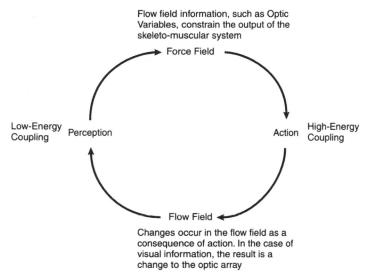

Flow field information, such as Optic
Variables, constrain the output of the
skeleto-muscular system

→ Force Field

Low-Energy
Coupling

Perception

Action

High-Energy
Coupling

Flow Field ◄

Changes occur in the flow field as a
consequence of action. In the case of
visual information, the result is a
change to the optic array

Figure 6.2 How perception–action coupling works. Through learning, one or a
few informational invariants in the optic flow field become coupled
with free parameters of the action system to form a control system.
Information flows can be used to control movements in an adaptive
manner. As the performer moves, the information flows are altered
creating more information to steer the ongoing action. (Adapted from
Kugler, P.N. and Turvey, M.T. (1987) *Information, Natural Law and
the Self-Assembly of Rhythmic Movement*, Hillsdale NJ: Erlbaum).

children and adults (Lee and Lishman 1975). In a purpose-built room,
with a fixed floor and moveable walls, considerable postural sway was
induced in subjects by moving the walls slowly forwards or backwards.
The direction of sway was dependent on the direction the walls were
moved. Subjects were compensating for what they perceived as forward
or backward ego-motion signified by the changes in the visual flow field.
In this experiment, it was shown that when the surrounds were moved,
the subject 'unconsciously and unavoidably "corrects" posture' (ibid.: 162).
Body sway and postural adjustments were driven by oscillations in the
walls of around six millimetres, implying a high level of sensitivity to
the visual surrounds. This example of a simple coupling of the force field
(i.e. musculature for orientation in space and balance) to the optic flow
field (i.e. ambient visual field) led Lee and Aronson (1974) to characterise
their subjects as visual puppets whose behaviour was *driven* by visual
information. Empirical support for the 'on-line' regulation of action
provides the basis for ecological ideas about perception–action coupling.
Since energy distributions, in the form of optic and acoustic variables, are
continuously available, it follows that this rich source of information is
freely available for pick-up by any observer with intact sensory systems.

Perception–action coupling in sport contexts

The continuous availability of optic variables suggests that they can be used to modify precisely actions right up until the threshold for neural activity in the CNS, the so-called visuomotor delay. This idea contradicts traditional cognitive theorising on the process of perception which is considered as being completely constrained by mediated stimulus information. In many cognitive laboratories, the processes of perception and action have been decoupled and not studied together (for a review, see Williams *et al.* 1992). The design of laboratory-based tasks in the cognitive paradigm, with their emphasis on reaction time measures as dependent variables, resulted in values of around 200 ms being proposed for the visuomotor delay between stimulus onset and the initiation of a motor response (see Newell 1980; McLeod 1987).

From an ecological view, however, the pick-up of information is seen as 'an act, not a response, an act of attention, not a triggered impression, an achievement not a reflex' (Gibson 1979: 33). Clearly, a value of around 200 ms for a visuomotor delay does not fit well with idea of on-line visual regulation for instantaneously adapting ongoing actions. In fact, it has been argued that demonstrations of visuomotor delays in the order of 50–100 ms for movements of around one second, would provide crucial support for the proposal that action is based on on-line visual regulation. In the literature on perception and action in sport, there are many recent studies which can be interpreted to provide support for perception–action coupling via the notion of on-line visual regulation of action. These have looked at a range of dynamic actions including gymnastics tumbling, baseball batting, table tennis strokeplay and the volleyball spike (e.g. Bardy 1993; Matsuo and Kasai 1994; Sardinha and Bootsma 1993; Bootsma and van Wieringen 1990). In this chapter we shall focus in detail on the findings of the study by Bootsma and van Wieringen (1990) as the key exemplar, because it was the original attempt to examine on-line regulation which is widely cited in the ecological psychology literature.

Bootsma and van Wieringen (1990) criticised previous research which postulated visuomotor delays of around 200 ms as artificial. They drew a crucial distinction between the role of visual information to initiate a movement, typically required in reaction time studies, and its regulatory role in adapting, steering and guiding ongoing movements in the real world. They pointed out that a study of subjects leaping to punch a dropping ball by Lee, Young, Reddish, Lough and Clayton (1983) found visuomotor delays between 55–130 ms in a movement taking around 700 ms for completion. The implication is that periods of around 200 ms for visual information processing could not be justified outside the laboratory, particularly during natural actions when visual information was used primarily to adapt and modify ongoing movement. The study of expert table tennis players by Bootsma and van Wieringen (1990) is regarded as providing a high degree of support for the concept of perception–action coupling, even in movements like the forehand drive taking less than 200 ms for completion. Five national-level table tennis players (age range 18–24 years) were required to perform forehand drives towards a target area 25 × 25 cm across the net. In table tennis, the spatio-temporal constraints are very severe. Mean angular velocities of the bat of around 800 degrees per second were found at the point of contact with a ball, with SDs of 5.2 degrees per second. This window of variability equates to 6.5 ms for a successful contact to accurately drive the ball on to the target area at high velocity. How do expert table tennis players manage to cope with these tight spatio-temporal constraints? The data showed lower variability at the point of bat–ball contact compared with the point of stroke initiation, particularly for the direction of travel of the bat during the stroke (see Figure 6.3).

This finding makes sense because table tennis players perform in a dynamic context and need to impart a high level of force to the ball in a controlled manner, because of the spatial constraints of the task imposed by the table boundaries. This is exactly the type of finding that would be predicted if experts were engaging in ongoing visual regulation of action right up until a small visuomotor delay. The higher timing variability at the movement initiation point was interpreted as contradicting the evidence for motor programming of the forehand drive by Tyldesley and Whiting (1975) which we overviewed in Chapter 1. How could subjects base their timing of the action on 'knowing' the duration of the drive when there was greater temporal variability at movement initiation?

Bootsma and van Wierigen (1990) argued that their finding of decreasing variability towards the point of bat–ball contact indicated that the small amount of observed inter-trial variance was functional in allowing performers to compensate for minute variations in conditions at the

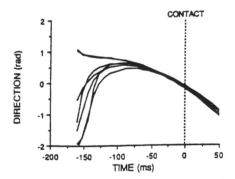

Figure 6.3 The compensatory relationship between the perceptual systems and action systems exemplified in sport: (Source: Bootsma, R.J. and van Wieringen, P.C.W. (1990) 'Timing an attacking forehand drive in table tennis', *Journal of Experimental Psychology: Human Perception and Performance* 16: 21–9.)

beginning of the stroke. The co-dependency of the perceptual and action systems meant that overall performance could be varied as conditions dictated in a dynamic context like a table tennis match. The basis of perception–action coupling in this study of expert table tennis players was that each subsystem could continuously compensate for the other, depending on the nature of the covariation between movement duration and initiation time for the movement. Compensatory variability is a functional type of variability. It is a means by which skilled performers in dynamic environments can produce a tight fit between the action system and the task goal at the all-important endpoint of execution by ongoingly modulating movements on the basis of perceptual information. Such variability between trials should be viewed as compensatory because early movement initiations would be locked to slower drives and later ones to faster drives.

Support for this interpretation was evident in the negative correlations found between the time before contact that the drive was initiated and its mean velocity and mean acceleration. This type of relationship would be predicted as individual players speeded up or slowed down a stroke, depending on how much time they had available. When the drive was broken up into a first and second part, the higher negative correlations for the first part with mean velocity suggested that adaptations were taking place from trial to trial. Evidence for intra-trial variability was provided in two subjects by the finding of lowest levels of movement variability (estimated by the coefficient of variance) during the middle to late components of the movement, and not the earliest parts, suggesting that these 'subjects were still altering their movement during execution' (Bootsma and van Wieringen 1990: 27). On top of this, visuomotor delays of 105–122 ms were calculated for four subjects reflecting the idea that players are able to pick up regulatory information at a relatively late stage of performance. There are a number of reasons why these findings make sense. First, in a dynamic sport like table tennis the initiation point of the drive will never be the same between trials. Second, if the basis of perception–action coupling is correct (that the important parts of an action are the initiation point and endpoint), then how the movement system solves the problem within the rule-based context of sport is more or less irrelevant (Latash 1996). However, later in an action, the potential range of variability in contributing subsystems will be lower due to the task constraints.

These findings are harmonious with the Gibsonian view of the cyclical relations between perception and action. Actions create perceptual information which supports further (corrective) action to ensure the accuracy of a movement. The overall conclusion by Bootsma and van Wieringen (1990) was that even in expert performers 'consistency is . . . a matter of degree. Before dismissing the (small) trial-to-trial variations in movement execution parameters as "noise", one has to make sure that such variations do not serve functional purposes' (p. 27). For some movement scientists, this conclusion does not go far enough. Latash (1996) has even argued that the difference in initial conditions inherent to all types of movement makes 'different trials of one task actually different tasks, and it is not surprising that the human problem-solving apparatus comes to different solutions' (p. 278). Therefore, the negative correlations associated with on-line adaptations during the forehand drive in the study of Bootsma and van Wieringen (1990) is probably a regular feature of many sport tasks waiting to be empirically verified.

In the remainder of this chapter, we examine other data to exemplify further how optic variables can provide the specificational information for perception–action coupling in sports performance. It will become clear from the ensuing overview that most work on the nature of optic variables has been conducted on predictive visual timing behaviour. The perception of time-to-contact (Tc) when there is relative approach between an observer and an environmental object or surface of importance has received the most attention (e.g. see Todd 1981; Tresilian 1990, 1991, 1993, 1994a, 1994b, 1995). There is a body of work on optic variables demonstrating how athletes satisfy the severe spatio-temporal constraints of common sport-related tasks like interceptive actions. A striking feature to be noted from these empirical findings is that precise timing is not just the preserve of elite athletes.

THE ROLE OF OPTIC VARIABLES DURING INTERCEPTIVE TIMING

Satisfying spatio-temporal constraints in sport

Savelsbergh and Bootsma (1994) point out that three task constraints need to be satisfied for successful performance of interceptive actions in sport. Performers need to: (i) ensure that they contact a desired object (typically a ball or surface) in the environment; (ii) contact it with the intended velocity; and (iii) contact it with an intended spatial orientation to satisfy the (usually severe) accuracy requirements of the task. To satisfy these constraints, athletes need to perceive Tc information so that the limb segment or implement intended to carry out the interception is moved into the right place at the right time (Bootsma and Peper 1992). Lee (1980a) has termed this capacity to precisely coordinate the movements of the whole body or parts of the body in relation to important external events, objects and surfaces as extrinsic timing. We highlighted in Chapter 1 how extrinsic timing is dependent on the observer being able to perceive the ratio of the distance (*d*) at which an object is currently located and the velocity (*v*) of its relative approach. This *d/v* ratio provides the observer with Tc information about when a collision will occur. We have already seen from the study of the forehand drive in table tennis the tight spatio-temporal constraints involved in high level sport. There is other relevant work on fine timing in sport. For example, in cricket it has been demonstrated that expert batsmen have only a time window of 4 ms to contact a ball with a backward glance (McLeod 1987).[5] In selecting this stroke, the margin of error (estimated by the standard deviation (SD) around the mean time taken to perform the action) is minimal since the frontal plane of the blade of the cricket bat ($\approx$ 10 cm in width) is turned almost 90 degrees to deflect the ball past the wicket keeper. Yet, skilled cricketers can successfully perform this delicate stroke against fast bowling at speeds of around 40 ms^{-1}. Another study of catching a ball projected at 10 ms^{-1} demonstrated the temporal consistency with which skilled games players can execute complex technical skills in dynamic settings (Alderson, Sully and Sully 1974). During the grasp phase of one-handed catching, a similar low level of inter-trial variability in timing was observed (SD = 15 ms).

Extrinsic timing is not just a problem for ball games players. It remains a problem for any athlete negotiating important surfaces and objects during relative approach at considerable velocity. For example, skilled ski jumpers were filmed as they timed the upward thrust at the point of take-off in order to maximise the height of the jump (see Lee 1980a). The mean approach velocity at the take-off point for 14 Olympic standard ski jumpers was calculated at around 90 km/h and the upward thrusting movement, from a crouching approach position, was initiated at a mean time of 194 ms before take-off. The timing precision at the point of execution of the thrust phase of the jump was exemplified by very low levels of intra-individual variability (SD = 10 ms).

Precise levels of timing are not achieved at the expense of accuracy. In the study by Bootsma and van Wieringen (1990), national-level table tennis players could hit a 25 cm $\times$ 25 cm diameter target across the net with a 75% success rate. There was no compromise in speed since the mean ball velocity was 17 ms^{-1}. Novices on the other hand attained a percentage accuracy of between 17.5 and 20% only. After 1,600 practice trials the accuracy score increased to around 37.5% (Bootsma, Houbiers, Whiting and van Wieringen 1991). Ball velocity during the novices' forehand drive was not even half the value for the expert group. As we noted earlier, the all important point in the task was the point of bat–ball contact. The low level of timing variability by national-level table tennis players was a function of the ratio of the rate of change of direction of the bat (around 16 rads/s^6) and the SD of the direction of travel of the bat at contact (a remarkable 0.05 rads/s). Therefore, when converted to temporal units, the average timing variability required of the experts was an astonishing 2–5 ms.

Timing and 'ordinary people'

For Lee and Young (1985), this extraordinary demonstration of timing precision 'suggests that visuo-motor systems have evolved which are particularly efficient at detecting time to contact and gearing actions to the information' (p. 2). The implication is that people may be able to exploit a sensitivity to optical information when they need to time their responses to extrinsic targets.

What evidence is there for this view? To answer this question, one needs to review the studies of timing behaviour in human infants and naive subjects with little task-specific practice. For example, von Hofsten (1983) videotaped five infants aged between 34 and 36 weeks as they reached towards a brightly coloured object travelling in a circular path in the horizontal plane at velocities of either 30, 45 or 60 cm per second. In all, 144 reaches were analysed to show a surprising level of accuracy and timing precision. Only 17 of the trials resulted in the target being completely missed by the infants. In the slowest target velocity condition, the mean timing error was only 9.4 ms in an average reaching time of 550 ms. For targets moving at 45 cm s⁻¹, with a faster average reach time of 479 ms, the systematic error dropped to a mean of 4.4 ms.[7] These data from infants support the suggestion that *smart* (i.e. purpose-designed) perceptual mechanisms are tuned to the optical variables continuously available for pick-up from the environment to support timing behaviour (Runeson 1977). Furthermore, this level of timing precision is not just a function of the relatively slow velocities used in von Hofsten's (1983) work with infants. McLeod, McLaughlin and Nimmo-Smith (1986) asked non-games players to strike vertically dropping squash balls with paddle bats towards a designated target area. A high level of consistency was soon reached by the subjects in this novel task with SDs of 10 ms found in 90% of trials and 5 ms in 50% of trials. McLeod and Jenkins (1991) have argued that these data suggest that 'ordinary people, without any particular practice' (p. 286) can produce fine timing.

To summarise so far, in Chapter 1 we outlined the computational approach to visual timing which emphasises the role of memory and symbolic representations of stimulus properties acquired through extensive practice. However, data from real-world sport tasks reviewed above, points to the facility with which information on the time of relative approach of an object and surface can be picked up and used for timing actions in dynamic contexts, by children and 'ordinary people'. It seems that with relatively little experience or practice, subjects are able to gear their actions tightly to environmental objects and surfaces during relative velocities. It is possible that sport performers are able to take advantage of the fundamental basis of visual timing in demonstrating a high level of precision in many interceptive actions. Can a traditional account of perception and action provide a plausible explanation of these estimates of interceptive timing capacities in humans? In the following section, we proceed by discussing some problems with the traditional view of timing behaviour, followed by an overview of the ecological alternative.

PROBLEMS WITH TRADITIONAL ACCOUNTS OF PERCEIVING TIME-TO-CONTACT (Tc)

A number of serious questions about the traditional theoretical approach to the perception of Tc have been raised by Tresilian (1991, 1995). A major issue concerns the amount of computation involved in the traditional perspective. A computational approach to predictive timing requires much cognitive processing effort, with the possibility of errors being introduced due to the number of steps involved in judging Tc through comparing retinal snapshots. Moreover, although some investigators have previously interpreted their experimental findings from an indirect perspective, Tresilian (ibid.) argues that such conclusions are not warranted. The types of tasks used in these studies can be questioned because (i): they were not behavioural; and (ii) they involved perceptual anticipation processes rather than the more typical receptor anticipation processes involved when performing natural tasks (see Poulton 1965).

Curiously, for such an established explanation of extrinsic timing, information processing theorists have never provided a principled account of how d/v is obtained. Tresilian (1991: 870) points out that:

> Although this method for obtaining Tc information is frequently cited as an alternative to a tau-based account, no fully worked out distance divided by velocity scheme is to be found in the literature. What needs to be specified is precisely what perceptual information about real-world distances and velocities might be used to compute Tc.

Furthermore, as was evidenced in the computer simulation experiments of Todd (1981), Tc estimations are possible even when observers do not have access to absolute values of distance and velocity information for processing. Why should such a computational system have evolved if optic variables are available to be picked up for free? One possibility is that a computational strategy may operate solely in abnormal perceptual conditions (e.g. static or degraded) in which observers cannot pick up normally available optical sources of information to support action.

Another issue with an indirect perspective is the view that skilled performers can rely on internalised movement representations for timing behaviour. In Chapter 1, the notion of 'operational timing' was proposed to describe how skilled and semi-skilled table tennis players were able to reduce the temporal variability of initiation of the forehand drive to within 4 ms. The argument was that they had reduced the spatio-temporal problem to one of timing alone through the development of a motor programme for the forehand drive. Through extensive practice the operation time of the programme was reduced to a stable level which became 'known', and the problem became one of deciding when to 'launch' the motor programme. We have already seen data from Bootsma and van

Wieringen (1990) which calls into question the interpretation of a low level of variability at the movement initiation point for a forehand drive. Furthermore, even without this empirical observation, how do infants and 'ordinary people' demonstrate such reliable extrinsic timing skills? It does not seem feasible that infants and subjects with such little practice would have developed the motor programmes to use operational timing in the interceptive tasks described earlier (see McLeod *et al.* 1985; von Hofsten 1983). In summary, it seems artefactual to assume that predictive timing requires the performer to compute the values for a host of physical measures from ball flight (e.g. size, distance from performer, velocity and acceleration), before selecting a generalised motor programme for an action, parameterising it with these sources of information, and then launching it at the correct time.

The ecological alternative for predictive timing is next reviewed. From this perspective, interceptive actions are some of the most fundamental skills (Lee and Young 1985; von Hofsten 1987). We will overview the argument that judging Tc with important objects and surfaces, using an individual-specific frame of reference calibrated in body-relevant units, may be an innate capacity to be exploited from an early age by sports performers. We will examine Lee and Young's (1985) hypothesis that the visual mechanism may not have evolved beyond the first order. That is, actions may be timed on the basis of neural pattern formation on the retina, providing information to directly specify the ratio of the current distance of a surface or an object to the current velocity of approach to the performer.

ECOLOGICAL ACCOUNTS OF PERCEIVING TIME-TO-CONTACT

Ecological psychology has re-emphasised the biological basis of human movement behaviour and has focused attention on the *qualitative nature* of the information used to support activity. How animals create and exploit the information sources available in the surrounding energy flows during goal-directed actions, remains an ongoing issue for direct perception and action theorists. The logic of the ecological perspective on the perception–action relationship has been neatly summarised by Bootsma and Peper (1992: 289):

> In terms of the evolutionary pressures that have acted upon almost all visually equipped species, it makes sense that an observer confronted with an unknown approaching object does not have to rely on esti-mates of distance and velocity based on ambiguous cues (or worse, have to wait until binocular information becomes available), but is able to directly perceive the time remaining until collision, and hence act accordingly.

This argument builds on Lee's (1980b) earlier proposal that visual details about the physical size and shape of an approaching object were less important than changes to the patterning of light in the optic flow since these physical variables (rather than optic variables) provided 'purely exterospecific information . . . of little functional value to an animal.' (p. 175).

OPTIC VARIABLES FOR Tc IN SPORT: THEORETICAL DEVELOPMENT AND EMPIRICAL SUPPORT

Ecological theories for the direct perception of Tc have three main pillars of support (see Bootsma and Oudejans 1993; Tresilian 1995), and in the following sections we will address research from each of these strands. First, the mathematical basis of ecological models of timing has been developed to provide a formal argument supporting the idea that, in principle, optic variables can specify the relationship between perception and action (e.g. see Lee 1976; Lee and Young 1985; Tresilian 1990, 1991, 1993). Second, computer simulation tasks have provided empirical support because it is relatively easy to experimentally control potential confounds such as physical variables like distance, velocity and size of objects to be perceived (e.g. see Bootsma and Oudejans 1993; Schiff and Detwiler 1979; Schiff and Oldak 1990; Todd 1981). Finally, evidence comes from investigations involving actual movement responses by subjects in behavioural studies (e.g. see Bootsma and van Wieringen 1990; Lee, Lishman and Thompson 1982; Lee, Young, Reddish, Lough and Clayton 1983; Savelsbergh, Whiting and Bootsma 1991; Savelsbergh, Whiting, Pijpers and van Santvoord 1993; Warren, Young and Lee 1986). The aim of these studies has been to show that actions in a variety of tasks, such as striking an object, are geared to optical information directly available from the structure of the environment. These studies are important within the context of this book because many have been conducted in sport settings exploring the perceptual and movement behaviour of skilled athletes *during* task performance as a vehicle to verify Gibsonian ideas. Later in this chapter, we will look at some prime examples of behavioural studies of actions such as catching tasks and locomotion towards a surface target in space (exemplified through the approach phase of long jumping).

Mathematical modelling of tau

Tresilian (1991) points out that the optic variable denoting time-to-contact, originally called 'tau' (conventionally denoted by the symbol τ) by Lee (1976, 1980a, 1980b, 1990), is the 'paradigm example' of research on optic variables in direct perception. The original equations were formulated in a geometrical analysis by Lee (1976). He demonstrated that optical information specifying the spatio-temporal information necessary to intercept or avoid an oncoming object may be obtained, in principle, directly from the environment as argued by Gibson (1979). Basically, Lee (1976) showed that: Tc(t) = Tau(t), assuming a constant approach velocity of the object.

Keep in mind that the mathematical modelling we are about to discuss shows that:

$$\text{Tau} = \frac{\text{Angular separation of any two image points of the object}}{\text{Rate of separation of the image points}}$$

Over the years, Lee (1976, 1980a, 1980b, 1990) drew attention to the potential role of this instantaneously available source of optical information for interceptive timing behaviour in a range of movement systems (e.g. diving gannets, humming birds, locomotion in humans) and across a range of activities (e.g. hunting, landing on supportive surfaces, driving cars, intercepting static and dynamic objects). The optical variable τ is important for the study of visual perception and action in sport because 'it directly specifies when an object will be at the observer's present location' (Goldfield 1995: 154).

Many definitions of tau have been proposed in the copious theoretical work which followed the publication of Lee's (1976) original arguments and the underlying aim has been to show that the basic equation of *d/v* describing how Tc can be obtained, is directly available in the form of an optic variable. All the definitions emphasise the same principle that humans are sensitive to the rate of dilation of the solid angle provided by the approaching object on the retina. However, when reading about the concept of tau in the ecological psychology literature, one may experience a certain amount of confusion. This is due to the different definitions of tau which have been proposed, often in the same paper (for helpful discussions, see Bootsma and Peper 1992; Tresilian 1991, 1993, 1994). There has been some contention over how this solid angle is specified, and indeed, whether the evidence in favour of tau is as strong as originally believed. Below, we attempt to pick our way through the rich theoretical tapestry which has been composed in the perception literature ever since Lee's (1976) adaptation of the original mathematical arguments of the astronomer Hoyle (1957). Our aims are to provide an outline of the different definitions of tau, evaluate the research findings purporting to support the role of tau in interceptive timing, and finally to provide a critical analysis of current evidence on the validity of the concept.

Forms of tau: global and local information sources[8]

Recent understanding of the differences between Global and Local forms of tau owe much to Tresilian's (1990, 1991, 1993, 1994a, 1994b) re-analysis of the early ideas of Lee and colleagues. As Tresilian (1991) points out, tau has been defined by Lee and his co-workers (e.g. Lee 1976; Lee and Young 1985) in three qualitatively different ways. He identified the definitions of Lee (1976) and Lee and Young (1985) as Local Tau 1 and Local Tau 2, respectively. The definition of Lee (1980a) was termed Global Tau. All three definitions assume that an object is approaching with constant velocity in the original equations. Let us start with an analysis of the Global Tau variable available for pick-up as we move through the environment.

Global Tau

Global Tau refers to the rate of dilation on the retina of the angle between a visible point in the environment and the performer's focus of expansion (FOE) provided by locomotion through the environment. It can be formalised as:

$$\text{Global Tau} = \frac{r}{\dot{r}} = \frac{Z}{\dot{Z}} = Tc$$

In Figure 6.4, O = the point of observation, Z = distance information and R = the area between the FOE and the visible point in the environment.

In this account, the observer needs to be moving to generate optical outflow information. Lee and Young (1985) showed that humans moving directly ahead towards a uniform point in the environment are able to perceive flow field image vectors, composed of light reflected from environmental texture, radiating towards or away from the targeted point or

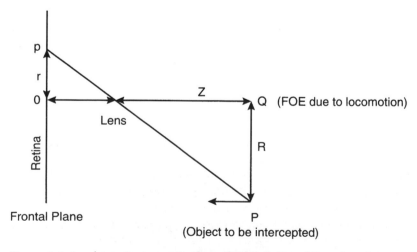

Figure 6.4 A schematic representation of Global Tau. Note that the convention is for physical variables to be coded in upper case letters and lower case letters are used to denote optic variables.

FOE. This outflow of information is a qualitative and macroscopic description of the structure of the optic flow field and constitutes an important source of information for visual timing. Lee's (1980a) definition of Global Tau makes use of the FOE in accessing Tc information. The constant flow of light information from visible points on rigid environmental surfaces and objects provides an instantaneous velocity field projection on the retinal surface. The instantaneous velocity field has been defined as 'a projection onto a two dimensional surface (the imaging surface) of the (instantaneous) velocities of the geometrical projection points on visible environmental surfaces ... As such it is an abstraction from the spatio-temporal variation in light intensity constituting actual stimulation' (Tresilian 1990: 224). Solid visual angles are provided with the apex of the geometrical points of light projected on the retinal surface and the base of the angle made up by light reflected from the surface contours of objects and texture elements during approach (see Gibson 1979).

During forward or backward motion, the translation of the velocity field projection results in the continuous flow of velocity vectors away from or towards the FOE. The rate of translation of the velocity vectors can provide an 'on-line' specification of Tc information which is continuously available to the observer (Tresilian 1990a). Essentially, the argument is that when a performer is approaching an important object (e.g. a ball) or surface (e.g. a take-off surface or barrier), distance information can be obtained directly from the image of the visible surface of the object or barrier which is projected on to the retina. If a performer is moving towards a surface at constant velocity, and can perceive an optic texture element (P) from it, then the *ratio* of the distance that P is from the centre of the expanding optical flow and the velocity with which P expands outward on the retina is called Global Tau. Whereas the missing dimension of depth is, in indirect accounts of perception, provided by an executive algorithm, this is not the case in direct theories. According to Lee (1976 1980a, 1980b) the missing depth dimension is available in an instantaneous temporal depth map created by the velocity vectors during translation to specify the distance of environmental points in temporal terms. Taking the point of observation as the X–Y plane, in principle it has been shown that the 'velocity scaled depth is the time remaining before an environmental point reaches the X–Y plane – the time-to-contact with this plane' (Tresilian 1990a: 226).

Global Tau does not require that the object to be intercepted is travelling towards the point of observation. The object merely has to be on a trajectory intersecting the frontal plane of the observer (see Figure 6.4). Kaiser and Mowafy (1993) have provided an experimental demonstration that even when there is no optical dilation of an object's image on the retina, Global Tau can provide Tc through the relative rate of expansion of the optical gap between the observer's line of sight and an approaching object (see also Tresilian 1991). They concluded that Global Tau was a relevant source of information in conditions where the dilation of an object's optical outline only happens at a late stage of the approach, for example in the last 200–300 ms before hand–ball contact in catching (see Savelsbergh *et al.* (1993) for supportive evidence later in this chapter).

Global Tau and the tau margin: an example from sport

How could sports performers make use of Global Tau information for interceptive timing? Consider the problem facing a steeplechase hurdler approaching a barrier. In theory, the steeple chaser could run towards the barrier using a visible point on it as the focus of expansion. A retinal image velocity field is available providing Tc information in the form of the rate of change of the velocity field vectors radiating outward from the visible point on the barrier. When tau reaches a critical value, a 'tau margin' is specified which steeplechasers can use to predict the moment to initiate the lift of the lead leg when bearing down on a barrier. Lee and Young (1985) have argued that a tau margin is an estimate, provided by optical information, of the time before contact of an important surface or object with the point of observation. This estimate is highly accurate when the velocity of the relative approach is constant since 'the tau margin decreases by 1 ms every millisecond, giving the actual time to nearest approach' (p. 4).

What is the benefit of tau margin information in dynamic interceptive tasks? Bootsma and van Wieringen (1990) earlier argued that it was useful in dynamic circumstances when compensatory variability between the perceptual and movement subsystems allows performers to adjust movements to different timing requirements. They showed that tau margin information was useful when it is not possible to start a movement (like a forehand drive in table tennis) from a standard position. One would not need to rely on a memory of the duration of a movement for accurate timing, since a movement could be initiated when tau reached a critical value during approach of an object or surface. The result is that in dynamic contexts there would be a reduction of a degree of freedom for the action system to control. To refer back to our steeplechase example, tau margin information permits steeplechasers to maintain relative movement invariance in lifting the lead leg on to the barrier at a critical approach value even when running at different velocities. Obviously, retinal images which dilate at a relatively faster rate specify an earlier movement initiation time (i.e. at a different critical value of tau) than slower retinal expansions. From a direct perception perspective, steeplechasers do not need to compute distance information and velocity information before using the ratio of the two physical variables in parameterising a generalised motor programme to lift the lead leg.

To summarise, the tau margin concept could be useful in explaining timing behaviour in many situations, including batting in baseball

(Hubbard and Seng 1954) and forehand driving by the intermediate and expert table tennis players of Tyldesley and Whiting (1975), which we discussed in Chapter 1. In a scientific sense, the direct perception explanation is a simpler one, making fewer assumptions. The timing information for these actions is available in the optic array.

The two forms of Local Tau

What happens in situations when we do not have access to global flow patterns of light? For example, when an observer is stationary there is no flow and no focus of expansion in the optic array. Consider the case of a ball travelling towards a stationary observer. Tresilian (1994) points to the literature on catching in the dark with luminous balls and argues that there is no global optical flow information available in these conditions. Yet, successful performance is still possible and comparable to performance in full light (e.g. Bennett and Davids 1996). Can optical information specify time-to-contact in these conditions as well?

Ecological psychologists have argued that, when an object approaches a stationary observer, the increase in size of the solid angle subtended by the object on the retina is non-linear (e.g. Lee 1976, 1980b). This effect is due to the magnitude of the solid angle being inversely related to the distance from the point of observation. The result is that over the initial portion of the approach the angle increases slowly. However, towards the end of the approach, the solid angle expands much more rapidly. This explosive expansion of the visual image of the object has been termed 'looming'. Explanations of tau in which the observer is stationary take advantage of this looming effect. For example, Tresilian (1991) has referred to an information source for timing which can be 'localised' to a specific object or surface area within the global flow of optical information. As we shall see, two different definitions of this local form of tau have been identified. We shall follow Tresilian's (1991) suggestion of differentiating between them by using the terms 'Local Tau 1' and 'Local Tau 2'.

Local Tau 1

It has been mathematically demonstrated that Local Tau 1 can be picked up from two visible surface points on an approaching object, as long as the distance between the points remains constant over the duration of the approach (Lee 1976). Assumptions are made regarding the constant velocity of relative approach and that collision is directly with the point of observation. The initial definition of Local Tau 1 means that the rate of dilation can be conceived as the rate of separation of the two points on a surface patch of the object to be intercepted. (see Figure 6.5). Formally, this can be expressed as:

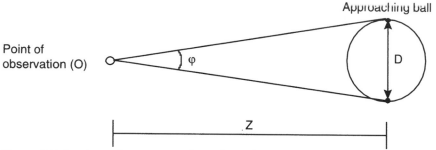

Figure 6.5 A schematic representation of Local Tau 1 after Tresilian (1991).

$$\text{Local Tau } 1 = \frac{\varphi}{\dot{\varphi}} = - \frac{Z}{\dot{Z}} = Tc$$

Local Tau 2

Another definition of local tau, again originating from Lee and Young (1985), states that it can be picked up from the inverse of the relative rate of dilation of the closed optical contour of an object image on the retina. This has been termed Local Tau 2 by Tresilian (1991) because it refers to an information source which can be localised to a specific object or surface area within the global flow of optical information.[9] In contrast to the earlier definition of Local Tau 1, Lee and Young (1985) suggested that the angle subtended by the object at the eye was provided by the surface area of the object A(t) (see Figure 6.6). In this definition Tau was formalised as:

$$\text{Local Tau } 2 = 2 \frac{A}{\dot{A}} = - \frac{Z}{\dot{Z}} = Tc$$

As with Global Tau, it is the rate of retinal expansion which directly provides temporal (not distance) information for athletes performing interceptive tasks.

To summarise, for Local Tau 1 to specify Tc, two points on the approaching object must remain a constant absolute distance apart over the time duration of the approach. On the other hand, to accept that Local Tau 2 provides Tc, the whole of the surface area of an object must remain constant and unchanged over the approach period. It is worth noting that the tau margin of an approaching object remains independent of the type of Local Tau which is used to provide the time-to-contact information.

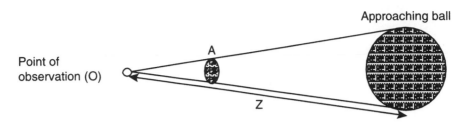

Figure 6.6 A schematic representation of Local Tau 2 after Tresilian (1991).

BEHAVIOURAL STUDIES OF OPTIC VARIABLES

In the previous section, we provided a brief outline of the theoretical development of the optic variable tau to exemplify research on optic variables in ecological psychology. We saw that the theoretical foundation of the research on tau is in mathematical modelling. But is this enough to meet the goal of a mature, principled account of perception and action? Some would argue that support from behavioural studies of optic variables is needed to achieve this scientific goal. For example, Yates (1979) warned scientists interested in the behaviour of living systems to be aware of the distinction between 'conceptual possibility and real possibility', and particularly that 'mathematical truths are very different from physical truths, and are not sufficient basis for modeling' (p. 57). We believe that sport-related tasks form a most natural context for the verification of ecological theories of perception and action. In this section, we continue by reviewing the body of sport-related work which contributes meaningful behavioural data to our understanding of the role of optic variables in sport. As will be seen, a range of activities has been studied. We have chosen to focus on some prominent examples including locomotion towards a target in space and one-handed catching.

Running to jump: the approach phase of long jumping

The long jump can be separated into four distinct phases, one of which is the run-up. Typically, coaches drill long jumpers to stereotype the footfall pattern of their approach run to ensure they hit the 20-cm take-off board accurately and with minimal disruption to velocity or posture at take-off (see Hay 1988). The goal of striking the take-off board with precision and speed is a major task constraint on the performer. Jumpers often attempt this goal by practising the run-up phase without jumping because of current coaching orthodoxy that such drills help to standardise the approach run. Theoretically, this type of practice is harmonious with the traditional view of developing a motor programme for a reliable and consistent gait pattern for use in changing performance conditions (e.g. Schmidt 1988).

If the athlete was using a motor programme for a consistent gait pattern during the approach, a relatively low level of footfall variability across trials would be predicted. However, research by Lee, Lishman and Thomson (1982) showed that the footfall placements over trials during the approach phase of three international long jumpers was actually much more variable than previously believed (see Figure 6.7). In their study, athletes built up a standard error[10] of footfall placement of 35 cm until they were five strides from the take-off board. Variability was then reduced over the final five strides to 8 cm, a value well within the 20-cm task constraint imposed by the width of the take-off board. Immediately prior to the take-off board, a high level of variability in footfall placement was typical (see Lee, Lishman and Thompson 1982; Hay 1988; Hay and Koh 1988). This was called the 'zeroing-in' phase by Lee, Lishman and Thompson (1982). The increase in variability during the zeroing-in phase was interpreted as indicating that the athletes were adjusting stride patterns to dissipate the variability of footfall placement accumulated in the early part of the run-up, termed the 'accelerative phase'.

The ability of the international jumpers to replicate their early stride pattern until just before the take-off board is remarkably consistent given

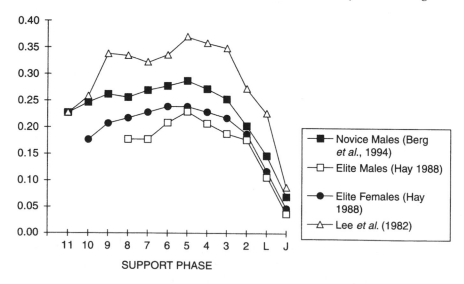

Figure 6.7 A reconstruction of the mean standard deviation of toe–board distance in the run-up for novices and elite long jumpers based upon Lee, Lishman and Thompson (1982), Hay (1988) and Berg, Wade and Greer (1994) (L = last; J = jump). (Source: Scott, M.A., Li, F.-X. and Davids, K. (1997) 'Expertise and the regulation of gait in the long jump approach phase', *Journal of Sports Science* 15(6): 597–605.)

a typical approach run of 35–40 m. Nevertheless, if the early stride pattern were to be maintained, there would be an accumulation of error in striking the take-off board and adjustments would be necessary in the 'zeroing-in' phase of the approach run. The original data by Lee *et al.* (1982) with three subjects were supplemented by the work of Hay and colleagues with a larger sample of international athletes (n = 47) (e.g. Hay 1988; Hay and Koh 1988). Hay (1988) also found evidence of a pattern of ascending and descending variability in foot placement across trials. In that study, the required stride adjustments were not spread evenly over the final five strides. More than 67% of the total adjustment was made during the final two strides. The notion of the reproducibility of a specific stereotyped pattern of gait is still rejected by these data from elite jumpers and is not consistent with the concept of a motor programme controlling the approach phase.

How then do skilled jumpers control the pattern of strides to hit the take-off board? Correlations between stride length and gait parameters suggested that only one parameter, flight time, was being adjusted by the athletes during the approach run (Lee *et al.* 1982). On the basis of this finding, Lee *et al.* (1982) proposed that the run-up was controlled by keeping flight time constant during the accelerative phase and by adjusting it to alter stride length during the zeroing-in phase. The correlation co-efficients for stride length and flight time remained consistently high, ranging between 0.70 and 0.99 across six run-throughs and six jumps for each of the three athletes. Lee *et al.* (1982) argued that the vertical impulse of the step was the most likely candidate for the kinetic parameter which athletes used to modulate stride length. It was believed that the vertical impulse was used to increase the flight time component of the stride without greatly affecting the other parameters of gait.

The large irregularities in the pattern of the last few strides were taken as evidence for a switch to a strategy of visual regulation by the athletes to enable accurate placement of their lead foot on the take-off board (Lee *et al.* 1982). The slope of the variability curve shown in Figure 6.7, was argued by Lee *et al.* (1982) to support the idea of two sub-phases of the approach run: an accelerative phase and a zeroing-in phase. It was also proposed that 'time-to-contact is specified directly by a single optical para-meter, the inverse of the rate of dilation of the image of the board' (Lee, Lishman and Thompson 1982: 456). However, this explanation now seems unlikely since this source of optical information would now be classified as the Local Tau of the take-off board during relative approach (Tresilian 1991). In principle, Local Tau specifies Tc most accurately when the approaching object to be intercepted is travelling directly towards the point of observation (i.e. the eye) at a stable velocity. Some have argued that the *approximation* of Tc provided by Local Tau may be appropriate for interceptive tasks in which the constraints of object velocity and distance from the eye are within tolerable limits (Wann 1996). In the long jump approach phase, these limits may well be exceeded since the task constraints result in the athlete's point of observation passing *over* the take-off board at relatively high velocities (see Hay 1988). Still, the remaining Tc to the take-off board during the approach run could be specified by Global Tau information from the inverse of the relative rate of dilation of the distance between the take-off board and the focus of expansion of the optic flow field (see Figure 6.4).

In the study by Lee *et al.* (1982), the result of switching to a sub-conscious visual regulation strategy by the elite athletes led to an estimated increase in the variance in footfall position of around 53% in the final few steps before the take-off board. Also worth noting is the 'funnel-shape' in the reduction of the estimated variance in footfall placement in the last five strides. We noted earlier that a similar distribution of the estimate of variance was found by Bootsma and van Wieringen (1990) in their study of the forehand drive of expert table tennis players. Compensatory variability during the long jump approach run may allow expert jumpers to make functional on-line adjustments in the stride pattern right up to a visuomotor delay before striking the board.

Is visual regulation an 'expert' strategy?

An important methodological point is that most previous studies of perception and action in sport have typically focused on groups of highly skilled athletes (e.g. Bootsma and van Wieringen 1990; Lee *et al.* 1982). Earlier we presented some data on interceptive actions suggesting that timing behaviour may have a fundamental basis because of the evolutionary design of the perception and action systems. In Gibsonian terms, an important question raised by these findings is whether organisms are innately sensitive to specific sources of environmental information. The studies of infants and 'ordinary people' performing interceptive actions indicated a remarkably high level of timing consistency in catching and striking actions. This theoretical question motivated some further relevant research on long jumping. The argument was that if sensitivity to on-line visual regulation has an evolutionary basis, then it would be expected that people with no experience of long jumping could exploit this capacity for visual regulation in approaching the take-off board. That is, it would be expected that novices would demonstrate distinct similarities in gait patterns as experts.

Berg *et al.* (1994) produced some evidence on this issue with a sample of subjects they termed 'novice male long jumpers'. They filmed 19 high school jumpers (age range 14–17 years) during competition and found an ascending–descending trend in variability of footfall placement during the run-up similar to that of Lee *et al.* (1982) with international athletes (see Figure 6.7). The maximum mean standard deviation in footfall placement across trials for subjects in the study by Berg *et al.* (1994) (SD = 29 cm) compared very favourably with the values reported in Lee *et al.* (1982) (SD = 35 cm). The slope of the curves in Figure 6.7 implies that the novice long jumpers also used a visual control strategy. Berg *et al.* (1994) interpreted these findings as suggesting that visual control emerged close to the important target for interception: the take-off board. This was around the fourth stride from take-off, a point in the run-up which was also integral to the visual regulation strategy of the elite males and females. The values for the subjects of Hay (1988) were 4.4 and 4.1 steps respectively (when corrected by Berg and Greer 1995). Berg *et al.* (1994) implied an innate basis for these remarkably comparable values by arguing that the 'manner in which gait is visually regulated in the long jump approach is less a specially trained skill than a natural means of controlling gait in this task' (p. 862). From an ecological perspective, the similarities in the shape of the data curves for 'novice' and 'elite' jumpers may be interpreted as support for the argument that interceptive timing is an integral part of the basic repertoire of animals evolved to locomote towards surfaces and gaps in the environment.

However, on closer analysis, the findings of Berg *et al.* (1994) are somewhat ambiguous. The data may be interpreted in two possible ways resulting in alternative, plausible hypotheses. Although classified as novices, their subjects had undergone an unspecified amount of task-specific training (see Berg and Greer 1995). Berg *et al.* (1994) reported a mean best performance of 5.23 m (SD = 0.14) for the 10 *poorest* jumpers in their study, with the 10 *best* performers displaying a mean of 6.25 m. Thus, although it could be argued that the sample of Berg *et al.* (1994) were novices *relative* to the elite athletes previously studied, there is still considerable overlap between their performances and those of the elite jumpers of Lee *et al.* (1982) whose best jumps ranged between 5.78 and 6.54 metres. The implication is that the limited amount of task-specific training had attuned the perceptual systems of the novices to the optical information available to regulate their approach strides to the take-off board. It still remained unclear, however, whether the similarities in movement patterns of the expert samples (Hay 1988; Hay and Koh 1988; Lee, Lishman and Thompson 1982), and the novices of Berg and colleagues (1994), were due to a fundamental sensitivity to optical information for the regulation of goal-directed gait or were the result of the task-specific attunement in the long jump run-up.

To examine this question Scott, Li and Davids (1997) studied the performance of a group of non-long-jumpers with no specific training. If visual regulation is an innate capacity for humans, then non-long-jumpers without a modicum of task-specific training in the long jump should show similar characteristics in goal-directed gait to their more skilled counterparts. However, it would be expected that the values of key stride parameters would differ in magnitude to those of experts, reflecting the lack of specific training by the non-long-jumpers. Data were collected on

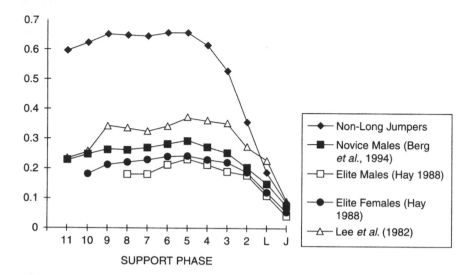

Figure 6.8 Mean standard deviation of toe–board distance in the run-up for non-long-jumpers, novices and elite long jumpers based upon Lee, Lishman and Thompson (1982), Hay (1988) and Berg, Wade and Greer (1994) (L = last; J = jump). (Source: Scott, M.A., Li, F.-X. and Davids, K. (1997) 'Expertise and the regulation of gait in the long jump approach phase', *Journal of Sports Science* 15(6): 597–605.)

male non-long-jumpers (age range 20–25 years). The mean best performance of their subjects was 4.39 m (SD = 0.41). This value was 84 cm and 1.86 m below that recorded for the means of the poorest and best jumpers respectively in the novice sample studied by Berg *et al.* (1994). Figure 6.8 illustrates a comparison of the previous research (i.e. data from Lee *et al.* 1982; Hay 1988; Berg *et al.* 1994) with the findings of the current investigation. There are three important features in Figure 6.8.

First, the non-long-jumpers did not display an ascending trend of variability during the initial portion of the approach. Instead they displayed a consistently high variability from the eleventh stride to the fourth stride from the take-off board. The second important feature is the maximum amount of variability for the non-long-jumpers (65 cm). This value is considerably larger than the values found in previous research. Lee *et al.* (1982) suggested that the increase in variability was due to small inconsistencies in stride length accumulating over the approach. After a relatively small amount of training, the beginners of Berg *et al.* (1994) showed the same pattern of increasing variability of footfall placement as more skilled jumpers until about four strides from take-off. Comparing the data from Scott *et al.* (1997) and Berg *et al.* (1994), it is possible to argue that, if the non-long-jumpers had received some training in using a consistent starting position, their maximum mean standard deviation would have been considerably lowered (see Hay and Koh 1988). Finally, the third, and most important, aspect of Figure 6.8 shows that, close to the take-off board, the non-long-jumpers displayed a descending trend of variability similar to that demonstrated by the elite and novice athletes. By the fourth-from-last stride, the variability exhibited a descending trend until the take-off. At the take-off board, the SD of footfall placement across trials was reduced to 9 cm, a remarkable feat which compares favourably with the elite group of Lee *et al.* (1982) who achieved a reduction to 8 cm. It seems that to guide the final phase of their run-up, the non-long-jumpers used a strategy of 'on-line' visual guidance. This descending pattern of variability provides support for the ecological explanations invoked previously (Lee *et al.* 1982; Berg *et al.* 1994). The current findings help to clarify Berg *et al.*'s (1994) ambiguous conclusion that the general descending trend of variability (indicative of visual regulation) is a fundamental strategy which is robust to task-specific training. The non-long-jumpers in the Scott *et al.* (1997) study had received no practice or coaching at the task and the data imply that the strategy employed to intercept the 20-cm target is one that has not been *specifically learned* to regulate gait in the approach phase. How else could these data be explained except to invoke the influence of a smart perceptual mechanism (Runeson 1977)?

Finally, when the data on absolute metrical distance are compared to the number of strides relative to the take-off board as the proposed onset of a visual regulation strategy, further support for the idea of perception–action coupling in goal-directed locomotion was received. The onset of the strategy of the visual adjustment of step length is constrained to appear at a body-scaled value relative to stride length in humans, around four strides from the board it appears. Due to individual differences, such as height, limb length, stride length, flexibility, strength and fitness, the absolute distance at which visual adjustment can occur seems to vary considerably. These data support the implication, raised at the start of this chapter, of a unique frame of reference being used to calibrate the affordance for jumping from the take-off board in humans. It seems that body-scaled units were preferred for all jumpers rather than an external frame provided by arbitrary measurements such as metres or yards (Turvey 1986).

In summary, studies examining the task of running to intercept a surface target in space, exemplified in the long jump approach, show that non-long-jumpers, novices and experts have a similar pattern of stride variability. Strong support is provided for Lee *et al.*'s (1982) hypothesis that the final phase of the long jump is under visual control. These data suggest that a strategy of visual regulation during approach is the same as that used during other forms of goal-directed gait in human experience (e.g. walking to place a foot on a kerb when road-crossing or negotiating support surfaces during fell running). The work with non-long-jumpers also concurred with previous research suggesting that the ability to success-fully perform interceptive actions may be a fundamental characteristic of human behaviour (e.g. Regan and Beverley 1978; McLeod and Jenkins 1991; von Hofsten 1987). Indeed, sensitivity to optical information such as looming has been shown in infants as young as ten days old (Bower, Broughton and Moore 1970).

Despite the intuitive appeal of the findings of Lee *et al.* (1982), the role of tau in predictive timing for striking the take-off board has never been directly verified. Indeed, much of the evidence on perception–action coupling discussed above, although consistent with the idea of tau providing Tc information, is descriptive and circumstantial. That is, the role of optic variables in providing Tc information for regulating gait can only be *inferred* from the data. However, Gibson's (1979) ideas about the *specificational* role of optical information logically suggests that a useful experimental strategy would be to perturb the structure of infor-mation flows in the environment so that instantaneous changes to the movement system would be manifested. This approach would provide stronger inference for the idea of 'on-line' visual regulation of action.

In the next section, we overview the progression of experimentation aimed at empirically supporting the crucial role of optic variables like tau in interceptive actions. It will become clear from our overview that the natural task of one-handed catching remains an impressive vehicle for theoretical development in ecological psychology. The body of work reviewed is an excellent example of how stronger theoretical inferences can gradually be drawn in a scientific programme which involves descrip-tion, manipulation of variables and the rigorous testing of experimental hypotheses.

Manipulation of the optic array in one-handed catching

In the task of one-handed catching, some predictable changes to observ-ables such as the kinematics of the grasp phase should be revealed, if the theory of perception–action coupling is valid. One-handed catching is a highly intricate skill since the optimal area for receiving the ball at the hand is very small – just above the palm and at the base of the knuckles (Alderson *et al.* 1974). Once the hand is spatially oriented in the correct line of flight, a major problem is the timing of the grasp action. Closing the fingers too early results in the ball hitting the knuckles, too late and the ball may rebound out of the palm. Recall from Chapter 1 that the margin of error for catching a ball travelling at a speed of 10 ms^{-1} has been calculated at around ±15 ms (Alderson *et al.* 1974). Because of these severe time constraints, anticipatory muscle responses must be implemented so that the maximum aperture of the catching hand occurs before the ball contacts the palm, and the finger joints be prepared for stabilisation against impact. Lacquiniti and Maioli (1989b) pointed out that 'the information which is presumably needed to trigger anticipatory responses with the appropriate timing relies on continuous sensory inputs providing instantaneous estimates of the time-to-contact' (p. 156). An important question is: What are the sensory inputs that skilled catchers use for predicting when to initiate the onset of the grasp?

One candidate is obviously the optic variable tau (e.g. Lee 1976, 1980a, 1980b). Logically, if tau is used to initiate an action, then perturbing the pick-up of tau should be manifested in changes to the kinematics of interceptive timing behaviour. This has been termed 'the alter-tau, alter-action' strategy (Michaels and Beek 1995).

Early work

There were some clues on this question in early work on one-handed catching (e.g. Sharp and Whiting 1974, 1975; Whiting and Sharp 1974), although only global outcome measures of catching success (such as number of balls caught or touched) were reported in that research programme. For example, in the study by Sharp and Whiting (1975), subjects were required to catch tennis balls in the dark due to an occlusion period of 200 ms immediately prior to hand–ball contact. Earlier viewing periods (in which the laboratory lights were suddenly illuminated) consisted of several different values ranging between 80 and 480 ms. It was noted that occluding the last 200 ms of flight always produced a lower mean catching score (expressed as a percentage ≈ 86%–87%) than in full-vision conditions (100%). Was the pick-up of Tc being perturbed? The data are only inferential and, although the evidence indicates that catching is dependent on visual information, the experiment did not show how it was used to support catching behaviour. Clearly, two important tasks for investigators using this strategy are: (i) the direct manipulation of the visual information used in controlling actions; and (ii) the kinematic profiling of adaptations to the patterning of the grasp action as a function of perturbations to the optic array.

Vision of the ball modulates kinematics of interceptive actions: Lacquiniti and Maioli (1989b)

Lacquiniti and Maioli (1989b) attempted to achieve both these goals by analysing the temporal constraints on a form of one-handed catching using electromyographic (EMG) and kinematic measurements as well as outcome measures. Subjects caught a ball of uniform weight (0.4 kg) dropped from different heights (0.4, 0.8, 1.2 m) with and without vision. In the vision condition, the final 100 ms before hand–ball contact was full of EMG preparatory activity in which the flexors and extensors of the catcher's arm were typically co-ordinating together. The opposite was generally true of the no-vision condition, although there was a lot of inter-trial variability. Statistical analysis revealed that mean EMG amplitude was significantly smaller in the no-vision condition compared wih the full-vision control for the final 50 ms before impact for six muscles of the arm. For example, a ratio of 30%:70% was calculated for the amplitude of EMG activity in the no-vision condition compared with full vision. Wrist and elbow kinematics also varied between the conditions. Without vision, changes to elbow and wrist joint angles were most pronounced 50–100 ms *after* impact. Peak angular displacement of the elbow and peak extension velocity were significantly larger at this time than with vision (1.3 times larger in the case of the first kinematic variable). Phase plane portraits were plotted for elbow and wrist angle changes by velocity. In vision, the movement had greater equilibrium and was more stable and less expansive. Without vision, the variability in the sum of wrist and elbow angular velocities was 1.23 times greater than in control conditions.

It seems that access to ongoing visual information allows catchers to use more efficient preparatory movements than when vision of the ball and arm is suppressed. However, although visual information from the ball was suppressed in one condition of this experiment, subjects may have been able to rely on other sources of information for timing the grasp action. For example, they could have used prior knowledge of ball flight and/or auditory information signalling when the ball was released for timing the stabilisation of the wrist and fingers against ball impact. Additional trials were conducted where these alternative sources of information were suppressed. In these conditions, an absence of anticipatory muscle responses, much smaller short latency bursts immediately after impact, as well as far greater and more prolonged variability in elbow and wrist angular displacement (1.81 times more variable than in control conditions) were observed. In these cases some catching errors were evident due to the failure to correctly time the grasp phase.[11] The data from these comparisons can be interpreted as support for the role of Tc information within the final 100 ms before hand–ball impact for successful perfor-mance of the grasp. These are precisely the sorts of behavioural findings to be predicted from the nonlinear, looming effect in the mathematical modelling of tau. When vision was not available, Tc information could not help the performer to prepare anticipatory muscle responses and there was a shift in emphasis to a more reactive mode of control in which medium and long latency reflexes (active 40–200 ms after ball–hand contact) stabilised the wrist and fingers after impact. In fact, Lacquiniti and Maioli (1989a, 1989b) were cautious about implicating the optic variable tau in timing the grasp phase during the vision conditions because the dropped ball was accelerating and was not in the direct line of sight of the inexperienced catchers. Both of these issues with original tau modelling have been addressed in more recent theoretical work in ecological psychology. They are discussed in more detail in the section on the provision of spatial and directional information by ecological optics later in this chapter.

EMG activity in the grasp initiated at a constant Tc: Savelsbergh, Whiting, Burden and Bartlett (1992)

At around the same time, Savelsbergh *et al.* (1992) looked at the role of tau in a behavioural study of four relatively experienced subjects catching balls projected directly towards them from a distance of 6 m. High-speed film analysis (200 Hz) and EMG data were used to examine the relationship between predictive visual information and the onset of muscle activation for the initiation of the grasp at three different ball velocities (11.9, 13.9 and 16.2 ms^{-1}). The logic was that if tau was being used to time the grasp, the activation of anticipatory muscle responses would be independent of ball velocity. Tau margin data for each subject were calculated during one-handed catching, operationalised as the time interval between the hand and the ball at the time of the initiation of finger closing in the grasp phase. Savelsbergh *et al.* (1992) found that the tau margins for the onset of the closing time for the fingers at different ball velocities were not statistically different. This finding suggested that EMG activity in the wrist and digital flexors and extensors was initiated at a constant time before ball–hand contact, rather than at a constant distance or time after ball projection. However, a power analysis and effect-size data were not reported in this study, despite the possibility that the lack of statistically significant differences could have been a function of the small subject sample. Furthermore, although these findings support the work of Lacquiniti and Maioli (1989a, 1989b) on the role of visual information in timing the grasp, no attempt was made to provide stronger support for tau by implementing an 'alter-tau, alter-action' strategy. That is, experimenters needed to perturb the ongoing pick-up of visual perceptual information such as the retinal expansion velocity of the approaching ball, if more rigorous support was to be forwarded in support of tau.

Altering-Tau, Altering-Action: Savelsbergh, Whiting and Bootsma (1991)

An important development in this respect came in an experiment with a pendulum-based interceptive task purporting to simulate the timing requirements of one-handed catching.[12] Savelsbergh *et al.* (1991) analysed several key kinematic variables of the grasp phase while experimentally manipulating the optic flow field. Earlier on in this chapter it was shown how direct perception theory would predict that the *relative* retinal expansion velocity of different-sized balls, attached to a hinged pendulum and approaching the observer at a constant velocity, would be the same irrespective of physical dimensions such as size. According to the original equations, during the approach of a ball towards the observer at constant velocity, at an instantaneous value of tau, the rate of retinal dilation provided by a small ball would be the same as the rate of retinal dilation of a large ball. What would happen to the parameters of the grasp if the rate of retinal expansion of an approaching ball was experimentally perturbed without the subjects' knowledge?

To answer this question, Savelsbergh *et al.* (1991) used small (diameter 5.5 cm) and large ball (diameter 7.5 cm) conditions to observe the kinematics of the grasp during one-handed catching. Optical structure, provided by the solid visual angle subtended by the area of the ball, was manipulated by using a third deflating ball condition. A balloon was inflated to a size of 7.5 cm to cover a small ball (5.5 cm diameter) and attached to the pendulum. As the balloon approached the catcher it was mechanically deflated without the subjects' knowledge, so that when it reached the catching hand it was the same diameter as the small ball. In effect, what Savelsbergh and colleagues attempted was a dissociation of the rate of retinal expansion of the image of the oncoming ball from the actual approach velocity in order to check which was the source of information that performers relied on to time the grasp. The deflating ball simulated the approach of a ball travelling at a lower velocity, and the data on the kinematics of the grasp in that condition demonstrated that Tc was consistently overestimated since the retinal expansion velocity of the image of the shrinking balloon did not match its actual velocity during approach (see Table 6.1). The authors argued that these data would be predicted if a tau strategy was preferred by subjects for timing behaviour in this interceptive task.

Table 6.1 Mean kinematic data on timing the grasp phase of a one-handed catch for three different balls with standard deviations in parenthesis. (Source: Savelsbergh, G.J.P., Whiting, H.T.A. and Bootsma, R.J. (1991) 'Grasping tau', *Journal of Experimental Psychology: Human Perception and Performance*, 17: 315–322.)

Hand Aperture at Moment of . . . (cm)	Large Ball	Small Ball	Deflating Ball	Alpha Level of ANOVA test
Initiation of Catch	8.84 (0.71)	8.33 (0.74)	8.8 (0.71)	$p < 0.001$
Maximal Closing Velocity	7.38 (0.8)	6.3 (0.68)	6.6 (0.76)	$p < 0.001$
Ball/Hand Contact	6.22 (1.1)	4.68 (1)	5.0 (1.1)	$p < 0.001$

Manipulating access to optical information during looming: Savelsbergh, Whiting, Pijpers and van Santvoord (1993)

In a more recent study Savelsbergh *et al.* (1993) extended these findings using a pendulum-based interceptive task to examine how timing of the grasp component was affected by the quality of informational support. They manipulated the nature and the amount of visual information available to subjects as the ball approached. The amount of viewing time was regulated with the use of perspex goggles attached to a computer-controlled timer. The timer could trigger an electrical current through the eye pieces of the goggles to make them turn opaque (rise and fall times of < 4 ms) as the subjects viewed the approach of the three different sized balls attached to the pendulum. Therefore, the time for which the ball could be seen was controlled by the experimenter. The results confirmed that movement time and the time of appearance of the maximal closing velocity of the fingers around the ball were varied instantaneously as a function of the amount and nature of available information for the group of good catchers[13] in their study. Grasp adjustments were different when subjects had 300 ms viewing time before ball–hand contact compared with 0 ms. In particular, the role of optical expansion information between 300–200 ms before ball–hand contact seemed to be most critical, precisely the time window before ball–hand contact for the pick-up of tau (e.g. Kaiser and Mowafy 1993).

To summarise, we have seen that a reasonable programme of work exists to substantiate the concept of perception–action coupling in sport-related tasks. The major focus of research of ecological optics for perception–action coupling has been on the role of the optic variable tau in timing behaviour. Many strong claims have been made for the primacy of tau in the perception of Tc information during a variety of actions such as locomotion towards a target and ball catching. On the face of it, there seems a prima facie case for the role of tau in interceptive timing in sport.

However, in the ecological psychology literature there have recently appeared a number of critical position papers, querying not only the strength of support for ecological concepts, but more seriously, the direction and extent of research on perception and action (e.g. see Michaels and Beek 1995; Summers 1998; Wann 1996). We would like to pick out for further discussion three major criticisms made in these stimulating reviews. First, it has been argued that the concept of tau has not made adequate theoretical development, has stayed in a rather limited form and has difficulty in generalising to the majority of interceptive actions in sport. Second, there seems to have been a lack of work on developing understanding of optic variables other than tau. Third, there appear to be serious methodological weaknesses in the research on this 'flagship' ecological concept. In the following section, we deal with the first two issues together, before tackling the third question mark over ecological psychology research on visual perception and action.

With regard to the first issue, two thorny problems remain as obstinate blemishes in the theoretical framework of tau. First, a common assumption of most experiments on the provision of Tc information by tau is that of constant velocity of approaching objects or individuals. However, many actions in sport, involving relative approach between individuals and surfaces or objects, include accelerations and decelerations. All ball games contain instances of non-constant projectile velocities, from the outfielder judging a dropping ball, to expert tennis serving and fast bowling in cricket with late kicks and sudden swerves in the ball's trajectory. Examples from other sports include the gymnast accelerating towards the vaulting horse, high diving and the Formula One driver decelerating for a chicane entry.

Second, many actions which have to be accurately timed do not involve head-on collisions as modelled in the original tau equations of Lee (i.e. 1976, 1980a, 1980b). Typically, many everyday actions in life make it impossible to use tau for timing relative approach. For example, when shaking hands, lowering oneself into a seat or crossing a busy road, one needs spatial information about where important surfaces or objects are located in the environment. Moreover, the original equations for tau could not explain, for example, how a squash player times a volley for a ball traversing the visual field or how a wheelchair basketballer judges the force required to manoeuvre the chair to intercept a pass between opponents. For greater explanatory power, therefore, the theoretical framework of ecological psychology needs to consider the *spatio-temporal* constraints on behaviour. How do the visual perception systems cope with the pick-up of spatial *and* temporal sources of optical information during action? These issues with current ecological modelling are of a complex, technical nature, possibly interesting only those readers with a specialist knowledge of this area. If you are content with a broad grasp of the issues in the modelling literature on tau, but wish to know more about the limitations of the existing research base, then proceed to p. 238.

THE 'WHERE' AND 'WHEN' OF ACTION: MODELLING OPTIC VARIABLES FOR THE PROVISION OF TIME AND SPACE

How does ecological psychology address the issue of timing in circumstances when one needs to judge the time to arrival of an accelerating/decelerating object or the distance an object will pass by? This is not an easy question to resolve since most of the research in the literature has focused on the task of judging *when* an object or surface, in conditions of constant velocity, will intersect the X–Y plane associated with the observer. As Bootsma (1988) indicated, timing behaviour in dynamic environments also involves judgements of *where* objects or surfaces, travelling at variable speeds, will be in relation to each other or the performer at any instance. In this section, we will review evidence in favour of Cutting's (1986) arguments that rich sources of information to support actions may be found in the 'geometric relations' existing between objects, individuals and the environmental surroundings. Cutting (1986) declared that the key to understanding these relations is to discover the rules which govern them. He went on to propose that the most influential of these rules were those of projective geometry and the laws of optics. In the following pages, it will become clear that much recent theoretical and empirical work on optic variables for spatial and relative distance information has followed Cutting's (1986) line of argument. To simplify things, we will start by highlighting some recent contributions to the ongoing research programme on optic variables for non-constant velocities. We will then move on to look at the evidence for the role of tau in non-head-on collisions, that is, the provision of spatial and motion direction information through ecological optics.

Recent extensions to modelling on tau: non-constant velocities and non-direct approaches

The constant-velocity strategy

As we said earlier, the provision of Tc information through optic variables assumes a constant relative approach velocity between a performer and an object or surface of importance (e.g. Lee 1976). Despite this limitation, there has been very little work aimed at ascertaining whether tau can be used in relative accelerative approaches (Lee and Reddish 1981; Lee, Young, Reddish, Lough and Clayton 1983). Therefore, by modelling constant approaches, the original equations on tau may only have exemplified the 'limiting cases' for the perception of Tc, rather than the most typical requirements for action in dynamic environments (Bootsma and Oudejans 1993).

One solution to the problem was promoted by Lee (1980a). He argued that when observers have to deal with non-constant velocities during relative approach they can opt to deal with the task as if velocity were constant.[14] When the relational velocity between an individual and a target is non-constant (i.e. involving accelerations and decelerations) then the tau margin can provide a mathematically less accurate, but nevertheless functional, approximation of time-to-nearest approach. This is because, as Bootsma and Oudejans (1993) indicated, the 'perceived tau-margin and the 'real' time to contact will converge as the event unfolds' (p. 1050). Therefore, it was argued, Global Tau information can provide a tau margin for initiating actions at accelerative approach velocities.

This was the proposition of Lee and Reddish (1981) in their analysis of diving gannets (*Sula bassana*) fishing at sea. The birds dive to intercept fish from a range of vertical heights (up to around 30 m) and use their outspread wings to accurately steer the dive through perturbing crosswinds. At the point of entry into the water, the wings have to be folded into a streamlined position to avoid the risk of injury. Film analysis suggested that a tau-based strategy was being employed by the birds, presumably using light reflected from the surface of the water to provide a focus of expansion for the optic flow field. The equation of motion which best fitted the data was not based on a computational strategy, in which information on physical values (e.g. height, distance, velocity of approach) were processed and compared with the previous experience of the birds. Rather, the heuristic of waiting until tau reached a critical margin value formed the likely basis for timing the folding of the wings by the birds. Further, Lee and Reddish (1981) suggested that a constant velocity strategy was being used by the diving gannets, despite their acceleration under the influence of gravity during the dive. The effect of implementing such a strategy, given the definition of the tau margin by Lee and Young (1985), would be for the birds to overestimate T_c with the surface of the water. The provision of an *overestimate* of T_c could be construed as functional since it permits a built-in time lag for any late perturbations or movements involved.

It has been argued that such a strategy would also be appropriate in dynamic sport contexts. There is some evidence that human subjects faced with the task of intercepting a dropping ball implemented a similar strategy to the diving seabirds. Lee *et al.* (1983) addressed the issue of timing information in non-constant velocity approaches during an interceptive sport-related task. They postulated that tau, and its time derivative, may implicitly register acceleration. They also considered the possibility of visual mechanisms which allow changes in acceleration to be taken into consideration when detecting T_c, although there is a trade-off to be made since more complex visual mechanisms may imply slower operations. Clearly, such a visual system is unlikely to have evolved for performance in highly dynamic, time-stressed environments. As an alternative they proposed that the visual system may not have actually evolved beyond the first order, signifying that humans probably time their actions on the basis of tau and are not sensitive to accelerations.

To test this hypothesis, Lee *et al.* (1983) required subjects to jump up and punch a falling ball which was accelerating under the influence of gravity. Interception of objects accelerating due to gravity is a task which occurs frequently in many ball games (e.g. fielding in the outfield in cricket and baseball, catching a hoisted 'up-and-under' in rugby or in soccer goalkeeping). Balls were dropped from three different heights (3, 5, 7.5 m), whilst the angles at the knee and elbow, on the side of the punching arm, were measured using potentiometers. The results showed that subjects guided their actions to the less accurate estimate of Tc provided by tau information from the ball instead of gearing their action to the actual acceleration of the ball. Therefore, as Lee *et al.* (1983) suggested, the visual system appears to be sensitive to first order temporal derivatives, such as tau.

In summary, the investigations by Lee and Reddish (1981) and Lee *et al.* (1983) provided support for the use of tau in interceptive actions when there is some relative acceleration between actor and environmental objects or surfaces. These data are useful because they underline the relevance of ecological approaches to the perception of Tc in real-world settings such as sport. Although the studies of Lee and Reddish (1981) and Lee *et al.* (1983) shed some light on the issue of non-constant velocities, they both involved a head-on approach. The question of how humans deal with perception of Tc in non-collision trajectories has been the subject of other studies.

Relative distance information

The earliest effort to model an optic variable for the provision of Tc in instances where an object is not directly approaching the point of observation, was made by Lee and Young (1985). They mathematically demonstrated that visual information specifying the tau margin between the actor's eye and the point of *nearest* approach of a moving object could, in principle, be available for pick-up in the optical flow field. However, this model was not empirically tested until the work of Bootsma on perceptual information for predicting the time at which an object would pass a point near to an observer (e.g. Bootsma 1991; Bootsma and Oudejans 1993). A series of mathematical equations showed how, in principle, it was possible for an observer to perceive an optical variable providing relative distance information for use during predictive timing behaviour. Using the example of ball catching, the model of Bootsma and Oudejans (1993) explains how Tc 'until a ball reaches any specified point' (Peper, Bootsma, Mestre and Bakker 1994: 591) in the environment is available for pick-up in the optic flow field. Bootsma's (1991) account showed that this source of predictive timing information can be lawfully specified by the relative rate of constriction of the optical gap between the ball and a designated target position in the environment (assuming constant velocity of approach as in the original tau equations and as long as there is no change in the optical image size). For example, when a basketball is being passed between one stationary opponent and another in the frontal plane of the observer, and the distance between the ball and the observer's eye does not change over time, then, in principle, the optical variable for the relative rate of constriction of the optical gap between ball and catcher can specify Tc of the ball at the hands of the receiver. The plausibility of this explanation assumes a smart perceptual mechanism (Runeson 1977) having evolved for directly picking up relative distance information.[15] A follow-up series of four computer simulation studies by Bootsma and

Oudejans (1993) provided some limited empirical support for this model. They demonstrated formally the availability of an optical variable which can reduce to tau when the optical gap between the point of observation and a moving object in space is 0 degrees. When the optical gap is greater than 0 degrees, the inverse of the relative rate of constriction of the optical gap between the object contour and any target position in space can be used for judging relative distance. To test these ideas, a forced-choice paradigm was used in four experiments by Bootsma and Oudejans (1993). The basic task was for 'well-practised observers' to decide which of two moving squares, located at opposite sides of a cathode ray tube, would arrive at a common mid-line first. The speed of approach of both squares was kept constant and the size of the square sides ranged from 8.5 to 9.5 cm. Time differences between the squares arriving at the common mid-line ranged between 10 and 200 ms. Subjects did not seem to base time-to-arrival judgements on the size differences between the squares, distance information nor velocity of approach. For example in the first experiment, the object with the smallest velocity when arriving at the mid-line was almost equally as likely to have been chosen by the subjects (on average 42.2% of the time).

These data appear to indicate that, in conditions where there is relative expansion of the retinal image of a ball which is not approaching the point of observation, then a *combination* of optical quantities can specify the movements required to intercept it at a nearby point in space. The relative rate of constriction of the optical gap between an object and a designated target specifies a first-order temporal relationship, similar to the relative rate of optical contour magnification in head-on approaches as demonstrated by Lee (1976). The implication is that different optic variables may be capable of specifying Tc as conditions in a dynamic environment change. The wider issue of whether different optic variables can be used to specify behaviour is known as 'multiple specificity' in the ecological psychology literature and will appear in several of the models that we will discuss below.

Predictive spatial information in the optic flow field

The previous theorising on tau focused on temporal information for judging when an individual or object will reach a target point in space. But what about the pick-up of spatial information? For example, how does the performer obtain optical information specifying the distance that an individual or object will pass by or where it will land? In the context of sport these instances are very typical. For instance:

- How does a backcourt volleyball player perceive how far away a ball is in deciding whether to implement a one-handed retrieval or a two-handed dig?

- How does a gymnast judge when to reach out and grab the bar during flight?
- How does a defender in soccer judge the distance to a dribbling opponent before initiating a slide-tackle?
- How do cricket slip fielders judge the direction and the distance that a ball will pass by to one side?

In these and similar circumstances, one needs optical information specifying predictive spatial information as well as Tc, because there are significant *spatio-temporal* constraints on movement behaviour. Peper *et al.* (1994) point out that there have been very few studies on predictive spatial information, and these have typically tended to focus on the specification of direction of motion (see Schiff 1965; Fitch and Turvey 1978; Regan, Beverley and Cynader 1979; Lee and Young 1985). Direction of motion information is needed by any athlete wanting to intercept a projectile, a surface or another player when moving through space. If an approaching projectile, surface or player is not on a collision course with an observer, direction of motion information is an important source for determining whether to move forward, backward or to the side to complete an interception.

Direction of motion information

An early study examining the optical information for the provision of direction of motion was by Todd (1981). He presented a mathematical analysis of the translation of a line segment connecting two points (*ab*) in 3-D space moving towards the point of observation, where the values of X, Y and Z temporal coordinates = 0. The motion of the segment *ab* was described purely in terms of optic variables defined with reference to a projection surface (i.e. the retina). Using substitutions and the quadratic formula, Todd demonstrated that TX (the horizontal distance in units of time before X = 0) and TY (the vertical distance in temporal units before Y = 0) were optically specified for all possible values of distance, velocity and acceleration. The ratio of TX and TY provides further information (the so-called Todd Numbers) on where an object will first contact the horizontal axis relative to the point of observation. When TX/TY = 1, the object was predicted to hit the horizontal axis at the point of observation. If TX/TY was < 1, then the object would land in front of the point of observation, and if TX/TY was > 1, the object's landing position would be beyond the centre of the horizontal plane referencing the point of observation.

Todd's mathematical model supports Cutting's (1986) argument that, in principle, the perception of geometric relations between objects can be used to form the basis of action. Potentially, this was an example of an ecological variable other than tau. It seems that performers could use an optic variable to specify the direction of motion required to make contact with an object in parabolic flight at the point of observation. An outfielder in cricket and baseball could, in principle, use this type of optical information to predict the direction of movement needed for intercepting a ball. However, despite the mathematical modelling, Todd's (1981) follow-up computer simulation tests found no reliable evidence for his theory. Therefore, stronger verification from behavioural studies was needed to confirm that outfielders in baseball and cricket could use optical invariants to judge motion direction in fielding a fast moving ball.

Predicting the direction of ball flight in interceptive actions

Fortunately, optical information for judging motion direction has been extensively studied with interceptive actions like ball catching. Oudejans, Michaels, Bakker and Davids (1996) highlighted that computational strategies for predicting the spot where a ball will land do not have much support in previous research. Rather, they argued, the fielder can use optic invariants. Although there have been many different terms to describe these optic invariants, it has been proposed that the basic strategy is to keep the optical displacement velocity of the midpoint of a ball's image constant on the retina resulting in a collision between the ball and the point of observation (Peper *et al.* 1994).

For example, Michaels and Oudejans (1992), examining the task of the outfielder running to intercept a fly ball, proposed an optical invariant which could be exploited in moving forward or backward to meet the ball. It was called vertical optical acceleration the (VOA) after Chapman (1968). In their mathematical equations, the optical height of a ball in flight is specified by the height of the ball at time *t*, divided by its distance from the catcher at *t*. The optical velocity of the ball, therefore, is simply a function of the influence of gravitational forces and the horizontal velocity of the ball (see Figure 6.9).

When a fielder is stationary and located at the correct spot to catch the ball then gravitational forces and the horizontal velocity of the ball are constant. It follows that VOA is also constant. That is, the VOA of the image of the ball on the retinal image plane has been cancelled out. If the fielder was too far underneath the ball, then VOA would be increasing on the retinal plane and corrective *backward* locomotion would be required. When the value of VOA is decreasing, *forward* locomotion is required until it reaches zero. By gearing his or her movements to cancelling out VOA, the fielder is effectively setting up the intersection of the ball and eye trajectories. Michaels and Oudejans (1992) argue that VOA does not provide the observer with either spatial or temporal information about where and when a ball will land at a spot nearby to guide their actions. It specifies only that should the existing spatio-temporal constraints (in the form of gravitational forces and current horizontal velocity) on the ball remain the same, the trajectory of the ball and the eye will meet.

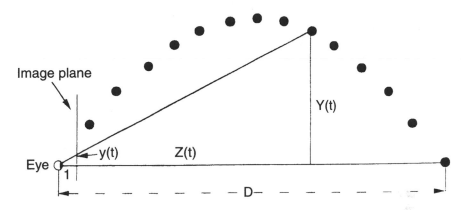

Figure 6.9 How cancelling out vertical optical acceleration can help outfielders catch a fly ball. (Source: Michaels, C.F. and Oudejans, R.R.D. (1992) 'The optics of catching fly balls: Zeroing out optical acceleration', *Ecological Psychology* 4: 199–222.)

Michaels and Oudejans (1992) made the point that the plane geometry of the optics in the stationary catcher can generalise to the more typical situation when there is relative movement between the fielder and the ball. Regarding the presence of VOA on the retinal image plane, their findings conveyed a straightforward message to the outfielder in cricket and baseball: move to lose it! These predictions were tested in three experiments, two behavioural studies and one computer simulation, of a fly ball catching situation. In the behavioural studies, subjects were asked to couple their actions to fly balls pitched at various heights above eye level (3–8 m) with horizontal travelling distances of 6–25 m. Zeroing out optical acceleration appeared sufficient for perception and movement to the correct landing position of the ball in both binocular and monocular circumstances. In the second experiment, it was apparent that information from the initial portion of the ball's trajectory alone was sufficient for perceiving its direction of motion. A ball-projection machine was used to prevent the use of optical invariants from the thrower's action, and the reaction time data and the acceleration curves for the catchers' movements showed a very rapid initial response with no changes once a direction for movement had been chosen. However, the data from the computer simulation study contradicted predictions,[16] possibly because the subjects were required to couple perceptions to *verbal* judgements of the simulated landing position of a small dot on the computer screen. Another perceived difficulty was that the dot representing the ball in the experiment on a computer monitor was kept a constant size during the approach, thus not providing retinal image expansion. These contradictions cast some doubt on the relevance of data from computer simulations of activities with severe spatio-temporal demands. Michaels and Oudejans (1992) suggested that their attempt to simulate on screen the optics of the task of catching a fly ball 'reveals some of the perils of a simulation study wherein one can find observers basing their verbal reports on variables that simply would not be effective for guiding action in the actual situation being simulated' (p. 218).

McLeod and Dienes (1993, 1996) have raised an important issue with the data from the study of direction of motion information by Michaels and Oudejans (1992). The latter's study was based on the ideas of Chapman (1968) who modelled the trajectory of a ball in flight on parabolic principles. Chapman (1968) argued that a ball travelling in the sagittal plane of the catcher would result in the projection of the ball rising in a linear fashion on the vertical image plane at the eye of the catcher. In other words, the tangent of α, the angle between the ball and the horizontal surface, measured at the point of observation, would increase linearly throughout the trajectory, with the acceleration being zero. Keeping the tan α near to zero would result in the catcher getting to the right place at the right time. In order for this strategy to succeed, the catcher must continually detect the sign (i.e. whether positive or negative) of acceleration of tan α. On the basis of this information, forward or backward movement adjustments can be made ongoingly to get the body to the correct spatio-temporal location.

However, McLeod and Dienes (1993, 1996) argued that this assumption is not valid in the real world because of the effects of factors such as wind resistance. As we noted in Chapter 1, aerodynamic drag effects could alter flight trajectory by as much as 40% (see Brancazio 1985). Therefore, running at a constant velocity to keep the acceleration of tan α at zero would not work because this strategy requires the fielder to know where and when the eye and ball trajectories would meet, *before* the consequences of wind resistance on the ball could be effected. McLeod and Dienes (1993, 1996) asked whether it is possible that an algorithm for judging where a ball will land could operate independently of wind resistance. They were effectively questioning whether Chapman's (1968) strategy[17] would actually get fielders close enough to the ball to catch it. They also noted that Michaels and Oudejans (1992) did not actually measure the running velocities of the subjects in their study. To test their ideas, McLeod and Dienes (1996) provided two experiments to manipulate the running movements of a fielder. Balls for catching were projected either further from or closer to the initial starting position and, secondly, the angle of projection was changed (from 45 to 64 degrees) to give the fielder more time to get to the place where the ball was falling. Would the fielders use the extra time to get into position early to catch the ball rather than rely on the acceleration of the angle of elevation of gaze to get them to the place where the ball would fall at the precise time of landing?

The data did not support Chapman's (1968) constant running velocity strategy. Rather, different running patterns were used as the fielders strove not to let the acceleration of angle of elevation of gaze deviate from zero. It seems that, due to wind resistance effects on a ball in parabolic flight, therefore, fielders need to constantly adjust running speed to keep the acceleration of the angle of elevation of gaze close to zero. This explanation for catching fly balls offered by McLeod and Dienes (1993, 1996) differs from that of Michaels and Oudejans (1992) because keeping the angle of elevation of gaze constant results in α needing to be kept within a range: greater than 0° and less than 90°. Thus, the fielders' speeds would vary between the time that a value for the angle of elevation of gaze was generated by the initial movements (α > 0°), and the appropriate trajectory of the ball was perceived (α < 90°). According to McLeod and Dienes (1996) the angle of elevation of gaze is used 'as the input to a servo that controls running speed' (p. 536). This may be interpreted as a form of perception–action coupling in which the detail of the running action required is not specified in advance but unfolds as the goal of catching the ball is achieved. The aim of the servo is to allow the fielder to get within 2 m of the dropping ball so that another optic variable (such as tau) can be picked up to allow the catching action to be completed. McLeod and Dienes found that in successful catches, the angle of elevation of gaze did not deviate much from zero until the final 240 ms of ball flight, a value which fits well with existing data on the time window for the looming effect provided by the optic variable tau.

This finding supports an important outcome from the study by Michaels and Oudejans (1992), namely that their subjects appeared to modulate their movements to keep the optical velocity of the ball constant up until 200–400 ms before ball contact. Subsequently, *other* optical variables to modulate the spatio-temporal patterning of reaching and grasping the ball would need to be picked up. Current research implicates optical variables such as tau and the relative rate of constriction of the optical gap between hand and ball. The timing of the onset of nonlinearity in the plots for optical height and horizontal distance (about 200–400 ms before the catch) found by Michaels and Oudejans (1992) coincides with existing reported values on the modulation of the reach and grasp phases of one-handed catching (i.e. 200–300 ms in the studies of Kaiser and Mowafy 1993; Savelsbergh *et al.* 1993; Bennett and Davids 1996). These findings suggest that multiple informational invariants can specify environmental properties to support perception–action coupling. It may be argued that actions could be broken down into sub-components supported by different optical invariants (Michaels and Oudejans 1992). The hypothesis that multiple optical invariants may be available to be picked up during the coordination of complex goal-directed activities like interceptive actions is an important area requiring further work.

To summarise so far, there are burgeoning empirical programmes of work attempting to discover other optic variables for regulating actions, despite the criticisms that many ecological psychologists have a fixation with the optic variable tau (see pertinent comments from Michaels and Beek 1995; Summers 1998). Research on the issues of non-constant velocities and non-direct approach have been discussed. Empirical work on the provision of optical invariants for spatial information has focused on the task of fielding fly balls as a relevant vehicle for theory development in ecological optics. Clearly, this is an important area for future work which has been identified in recent critical reviews as needing urgent attention. Next, we conclude our overview of recent criticisms of ecological psychology by looking at some perceived weaknesses with the optic variable tau.

SOME CRITICISMS OF THE EVIDENCE FOR THE ROLE OF TAU IN CONTROLLING ACTION

The studies on the provision of Tc through tau, examined earlier, inspired much confidence in the ecological camp that Gibson's notions of ecological optics and direct perception were correct. This conviction resulted in some fairly forceful statements on the role of the optical variable tau in perception–action coupling during interceptive actions. For example, we have already made note of Lee *et al.*'s (1982) forthright proposal for the role of tau in the visual regulation of gait to strike the take-off board in long jumpers. In the context of interceptive actions, Savelsbergh and van Emmerik (1992) argued that 'There is a wealth of evidence that shows that this optical variable is responsible for the control of action' (p. 447). Moreover, in the EMG analysis of the muscles of the arm during one-handed catching, Savelsbergh *et al.* (1992) proposed that their data on the timing of the initiation of the grasp phase provided 'unequivocal support' for the role of tau.

Recently, however, some important criticisms have been made by several leading figures in the field of motor behaviour, including some influential ecological theorists (e.g. see Michaels and Beek 1995). For example, from a wider perspective Summers (1998) has identified weakness and imprecision in the theoretical definition of key ecological concepts such as invariants and affordances. Of relevance to the present discussion on the optic variable tau, Wann (1996) has also raised some fierce criticisms concerning the evidence for the role of the optic variable tau, and more specifically the tau margin, in timing behaviour. Wann (1996) takes as his departure point the emphatic statements above on the role of tau in controlling action. The key message from Wann (1996) seems to be that theorists should not be too 'bullish' in their support for the tau margin hypothesis as the sole explanation for the timing of actions. His argument is that emphatic conclusions from the body of research on the role of tau for interceptive timing, such as the statement of Lee and Young

(1985: 12) that 'other possible explanations for the results could be ruled out', are currently unwarranted.

But why should the programme of research into the tau margin, which on the face of it has been principled and rigorous, be re-evaluated? The reason is that this stage of science is a natural part of the maturation of new theoretical perspectives which challenge traditional views. Early enthusiasm and exuberance with the revolutionary ideas give way to a sober assessment of the theoretical progress made and the potential for application for real-world tasks, hence the number of reflective reviews in the past few years (e.g. Davids *et al.* 1994; Michaels and Beek 1995; Summers 1998; Wann 1996; Williams *et al.* 1992). In this section of the book, this reflective mood is caught in our discussion of the perceived difficulties with the theoretical modelling and empirical support for the optic variable tau. To start with, there have been some expressions of concern with the original mathematical modelling (e.g. Tresilian 1994; Wann 1996). These criticisms have mainly focused on errors in perceiving Tc from tau margin information and the issue of an object which is not on a direct collision course with the eye.

Problems with the mathematical modelling

Wann's (1996) argument, that support for the tau margin in timing behaviour is 'ethereal', has been influenced by previous comprehensive criticisms from theorists such as Tresilian (1995).[18] In particular, as we noted earlier, the modelling on the provision of the tau margin has long suffered from the problem of the approaching object not travelling directly towards the eye. Tresilian (1991) points out that Lee's (1976) hypothesis of a tau strategy for initiating the braking of a car (i.e. tau must be less than 0.5 for adequate deceleration time) cannot work because it fails to take into account the front end of the car before the plane of the observer's eye. Thus, Z in the original equations should be modified to Z − d where d equals the distance from the object to the front end of the car. Tresilian (1991) examined the modelling in which the approaching object does not come towards the eye but rather to a point nearby (i.e. an arm's distance away). He provided a mathematical account demonstrating that Local Tau approximates very closely the time to nearest approach, provided that the distance (D) between the eye and the interception point is not large. Using values from Whiting and Sharp (1974) showing that the final 300 ms provides information for catching, Tresilian (1991) provides a geometrical analysis to estimate the temporal error involved in this approximation: 2.08 ms. This value is well within the range of the filmed studies showing SDs of 5–10 ms in world-class sports performances. However, at slow speeds the error creeps up dramatically: at 4 ms^{-1} it increases to 52 ms and under 1 ms^{-1} it is 800 ms. Therefore, the rate of change of direction of an object's image on the retina, rather than Local Tau, may be a better information source for timing an action to the point of nearest approach.

Although Bootsma and Oudejans (1993) derived a model for just these circumstances, Tresilian (1994a) criticised them for not mentioning that the rate of change of direction information over time is subject to significant errors when the distance between the eye and interception point is large. He argued that their derivation of the variable specifying the relative rate of restriction of the optical gap between object and surface allowed possible timing errors of up to 70 ms. Tresilian (1994a) pointed out that the mathematical arguments of Bootsma and Oudejans (1993) required that the optical gap between two targets be small. However, in cricket slip fielding, it is not atypical for a fielder to track and reach for a fast moving ball travelling along an angular trajectory of 20 degrees or more from the point of observation. For example, Tresilian (1994a) showed that if V were 8 ms^{-1} and D were 0.5 m, a timing error of 10 ms would pertain in the Bootsma and Oudejans (1993) model at a Tc of 100 ms (see Figure 6.10).

If Tc were to be increased to 500 ms, a value well within the experience of slip fielders, the timing error accrued in the optical gap model would be 60 ms. Tresilian (1994a) argued that the potential timing error is in the region of 10%–11% of the time window for action weakens the model of Bootsma and Oudejans (1993). It would be 'premature' (Tresilian 1994a: 157) to suggest that observers use the relative rate of restriction of the optical gap in cases of non-head-on approaches. On the basis of this geometrical analysis, Tresilian (1994a) proposed that the rate of change of direction of a visual target was a better alternative for predictive visual timing for a ball travelling some distance from the point of observation. In the case of tracking a ball in a game, optical texture is provided by background elements in the visual field. The rate of change of direction information can be provided as the target passes each texture element. When the distance between the interception point and the eye is small, the ball passes close to the head and Local Tau from the closed optical contour would suffice for timing. The main conclusion of Tresilian (1994a) was that a tau-based account of interceptive timing has significant problems in explaining the skill and flexibility of human timing in *all* environmental circumstances. Variables other than tau must be involved in timing, but a computational strategy was ruled out as too error prone and time consuming because it involves knowledge of the scale of object size. Again, we note the implication, this time made by Tresilian (1994a), that Tc could be specified by different optic variables as environmental conditions change.

Problems with laboratory-based methodologies

Some major criticisms of the research on tau concern the use of laboratory-based methodologies for the purpose of examining Tc judgements. The term

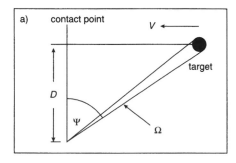

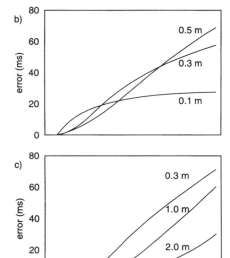

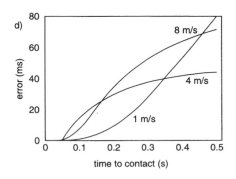

Figure 6.10 Tresilian's (1994a) comparison of the difference between actual tau margin and an approximation of the tau margin provided by Bootsma and Oudejan's (1993) equation. Tresilian (1994a) argued against the reliability of the equation. The top diagram shows the geometry behind the calculations: V = constant velocity of 2 ms^{-1}; D = 0.5 m. The two graphs below ((b) and (c)) show the timing errors that would accrue when D was varied. The last graph (d) shows the timing errors when D = 0.5 m and the different projectile velocities were used. (Source: Tresilian, J.R. (1994a) 'Approximate information sources and perceptual variables in interceptive timing', *Journal of Experimental Psychology: Human Perception and Performance* 20: 154–73.)

'laboratory-based', as used in the present discussion, refers to the use of classic methodologies of perceptual experimentation in cognitive science. These include the use of computer simulation tasks and film stimuli on flat-screen displays, and devices such as anticipation timers which tend to min-imise the interactive relationship between the perceptual and action systems.

In particular, the implications of using computer simulations for the study of visual perception and action represents an ongoing controversy in the ecological psychology literature. Michaels and Beek (1995) reminded us that the invariant energy patterns in the environment, continuously available as optical sources of information, represent affordances for actions. They argued that ecological psychologists have typically failed to exploit this principle of Gibsonian theory in designing research studies on perception and action. For them a major flaw in the design logic of some studies is the belief that 'because perception is about action, any (ecolog-ical) study of perception is de facto a study of action and any (ecological) study of action is de facto a study of perception. The unfortunate result is that perceptual experiments are treated as surrogates for action studies' (p. 260). This criticism echoes Milner and Goodale's (1995) argument that visual scientists have traditionally focused almost exclusively on the acquisition of knowledge about objects in studies of perception.

Of course, the reason why investigators opt for using computer simu-lations is their ease of use and the level of experimental control provided. Furthermore, Bootsma and Oudejans (1993) point to the often surpris-ingly high level of performance by the observer in many simulation studies (e.g. they reported 80% response accuracy in one experiment using their forced-choice task). However, the problem for tau researchers is that when these methodological paradigms are used in laboratory-based investiga-tions, they often produce outcomes which differ strikingly from the findings of behavioural studies of tau using natural tasks such as catching, hitting and locomotion. In particular, a lower level of performance variability is often seen when natural tasks are used. One reason for these differences may be due to the impoverished nature of the simulation displays (Bootsma and Oudejans 1993). Computer monitors present a two-dimensional display to subjects which may de-emphasise certain sources of informa-tion available in the optical structure of the environment (e.g. depth information, binocular invariants).

One interpretation is that the use of computer simulations weakens the case for tau in regulating interceptive actions because another optic invariant may be responsible for the superior performance observed in natural tasks. For example, Wann (1996) argued that studies of tau using flat screens do not allow binocular invariants to be picked up by the observer. Instead the information made available should be considered 'bi-ocular' because there is no stereoscopic information in the two-dimensional displays. Wann (1996) concluded that data from com-puter simulation experiments demonstrated that 'tau can be used for approximate TTC estimation, but not that it is a primary source of information in natural contexts' (p. 1031).

Tresilian (1994b, 1995) has also highlighted a number of key methodological differences between other laboratory-based studies (using traditional equipment like the Bassin Anticipation Timer) and natural interceptive actions such as one-handed catching. In the laboratory-based studies there has been a tendency to focus on coincidence anticipation tasks in which subjects have to typically predict when a (suddenly occluded) object/image would arrive at a designated target point. These motion prediction paradigms also emphasise *perceptual anticipation* processes, whereas in the study of natural interceptive actions such as one-handed catching, the emphasis is on *receptor anticipation* processes (see Poulton 1957; Williams *et al.* 1992). For example, in perceptual anticipation tasks subjects are permitted to see only a part of the trajectory of the object image on the computer screen. They are required to represent perceptually part of the approach trajectory of an object image in short-term memory to predict its time of arrival at a target location (e.g. see Todd 1981; Bootsma and Oudejans 1993). When a natural task such as ball catching is used, subjects are typically able to view the ball until it is received into the hands.

Thus, the typical constraints of motion prediction and natural interceptive tasks suggest that different control mechanisms may be employed by actors in the different conditions (see also Milner and Goodale 1995). For example, the slower velocities used in perceptual anticipation tasks (typically > 1 s) could permit the cognitive construction of the object/image trajectory. In natural interceptive actions, the execution times are far more brief (300 ms for one-handed catching at 10 ms^{-1} (Alderson *et al.* 1974)) encouraging the development of perception–action coupling (Tresilian 1995). In simulations, subjects usually underestimate Tc, with the amount of underestimation increasing with actual Tc[19] (e.g. see data from Schiff and Detwiler 1979; McLeod and Ross 1983; Schiff and Oldak 1990; Kaiser and Mowafy 1993). However, as evidenced by the data on timing from 'ordinary people' and infants, the large variability in estimation of Tc typically reported in simulation studies is often not present in natural tasks such as fast interceptive actions. Tresilian (1995) highlights the fact that 'the variability (standard deviation of response times) of responses in CA [coincidence anticipation] tasks is some five or six times greater than that observed in IAs [interceptive actions] performed under the same stimulus conditions' (p. 237; see also Bootsma 1989). This finding, particularly with the 'practised observers' and skilled catchers used in many studies of interceptive actions, calls into question the use of CA tasks for testing interceptive timing. It suggests difficulties with the development of perception–action coupling in CA tasks (see also Milner and Goodale 1995). Practice at an interceptive action should lead to decreased variability in performance as perception–action coupling is first established and then refined by the athlete (see Tresilian 1995).

Is tau used alone? Size arrival effects

Earlier in this chapter, we highlighted some fairly unequivocal statements from catching studies (e.g. Savelsbergh *et al.* 1991, 1992) attempting to provide empirical support for the role of tau in controlling action by manipulating the optic structure for catchers. We noted that this is a most complex task, and just when it seemed that the problem was cracked, some points of contention with the methodology and data in that programme of work have emerged. In particular, the confounding of object size with retinal expansion rate has led to questions about multiple ecological invariants supporting perception–action coupling.

In the data from Savelsbergh *et al.* (1991), presented in Table 6.1, an issue of concern is whether tau alone was adequate for controlling action or whether (an)other optic variable(s) may have been used in coordinating the configuration of the grasp. There have been some arguments that, in the data from the key study by Savelsbergh *et al.* (1991), the optic variable tau is inextricably confounded with ball size and/or binocular invariants as alternative sources of information for visual timing of the grasp (see Tresilian 1994b; Wann 1996). Analysis of the data in Table 6.1 on the mean hand aperture at the *onset* of the grasping action for all three balls, appears to show that the deflating balloon and large ball were treated similarly by the subjects (i.e. as evidenced by the hand aperture at initiation of the grasp: 8.84 cm for the large ball and 8.8 cm for the deflating ball). As the ball deflated during flight, two things become clear from the data: (i) the deflating ball came to resemble the smaller, rather than larger, ball; and (ii) the initial difference in hand aperture between the deflating and large ball (0.04 cm) had increased to 1.22 cm.

An alternative hypothesis which has recently been proposed is that the differing kinematic profiles associated with each condition were due to the different sizes of each ball, rather than the differences in Tc estimates provided. There is some evidence from computer simulations of self-motion in relation to an object image to 'leap over' that, despite the use of equal distances and velocities, temporal judgements appear to be biased by object size effects (e.g. DeLucia 1991; DeLucia and Warren 1994). The size effects were seen in earlier initiation times for larger objects compared to smaller ones, but only when the Tc values were > 700 ms. This finding implies that, whilst Tc can be provided by the optic variable tau, it is not the only means by which observers can perceive information for interceptive timing.

The data from the computer simulations of DeLucia and Warren (1994) have recently been replicated in a ball-grasping task under monocular and binocular viewing conditions by van der Kamp, Savelsbergh and Smeets (see van der Kamp, Vereijken and Savelsbergh 1996). When ball size was manipulated, it was found that subjects initiated the grasp earlier for larger balls under monocular viewing only, thus questioning the use of tau alone in those conditions. Furthermore, they found evidence of the initiation of the grasp at a constant Tc under binocular viewing and not in monocular conditions, thus implicating binocular invariants for the provision of Tc information. This question over the integration of information from different sources to provide estimates of Tc was supported by data on the timing of the grasp phase across ball conditions in the original study by Savelsbergh *et al.* (1991). The time of maximal closing velocity of the fingers for grasping the deflating ball was delayed under both monocular and binocular viewing conditions, relative to control conditions. However, the delay was about 5 ms in binocular conditions, but around 20 ms for monocular viewing. An obvious interpretation from these findings is that observers learn to perceive many different sources of information to guide visual timing behaviour, depending on the environmental circumstances. That is, tau may be one of a number of optic variables which contribute to the perception of Tc in the face of differing informational constraints in the sport context (see Wann 1996).

SUMMARY AND IMPLICATIONS

In this chapter we started by introducing some philosophical and theoretical issues with the computer metaphor which have undermined the long-standing dominance of the traditional cognitive approach to perception and its relationship with action. We then introduced the ideas of James Gibson on direct perception, focusing particularly on the pick-up of visual information. It was noted that the concept of information in indirect and direct perception is very different and the implications for action in dynamic and uncertain environments, typical of sport, were outlined. The optical variable tau was used as a 'paradigm example' (Tresilian 1991) of ecological ideas to examine how perception–action coupling could support goal-directed behaviour. Different versions of tau were highlighted and an outline of some of the sport-related research was provided using the context of interceptive actions as the chief exemplar for promoting understanding of motor behaviour from a direct perception perspective.

From a more practical standpoint, we reviewed evidence that humans may be sensitive to elements of the surrounding flow of optic information, through the evolution of purpose-designed, smart perceptual mechanisms for picking up certain optic invariants. Compelling evidence from human infants and adult learners showed a competent level of proficiency in tasks such as interceptive actions and locomotion towards targets in space to support these theoretical contentions. We raised the idea that, due to the innate sensitivity to the optic array, learners in sport could rapidly exploit invariants to underpin visual timing behaviour. Clearly, there is a need for more work to establish this argument. Particularly needed is research which looks at the design of practice environments so that perception–action couplings can be quickly confirmed and exploited by learners. One exciting possibility to be researched is how the use of salient materials, objects and colours in purpose-designed dynamic learning environments could help learners pick out invariants from the surrounding optic array. This approach could be beneficial at all levels of skill, but especially with young infants in dynamic learning environments. The data from the interceptive actions in infants showed the potential benefits of 'tuning up' the sensitivity of functional, smart perceptual systems. The issue of task structure and design and the effect on performance variability was highlighted in the observations of Tresilian (1995). In practical terms, more work on Global and Local Tau could help us to understand how the optic array may be best structured so that learners could pick up the most appropriate optic variable for producing sound timing in interceptive actions. Tresilian (1995) made some valuable comments on the substitution of perceptual sources of information for interceptive timing, introducing the idea of flexible learners switching between information sources as environmental conditions change. These are worth following up. A preliminary attempt is discussed in Chapter 8, where we will present data from a study of catching behaviour in young children showing the effects of manipulating informational constraints on learning.

There is another key point to be made concerning the organisation of practice conditions. For example, the data from the stride patterns of long jumpers clearly suggested the rapid benefits available to learners if they practised a strategy of visual regulation around four strides from the take-off board. Even with a relatively small amount of training (about 12 months' experience it seems) long jumpers can learn to exploit the optical information from the take-off board and surrounds to produce a highly accurate strike (around 9 cm variability in an approach phase of 30–40 m). There are question marks over the traditional tendency to break up sports performance into smaller chunks (the so-called whole–part–whole approach in teaching and coaching). The point to be made is that this technique could have the effect of decoupling perception and action at important phases of the task. Moreover, such an approach would prevent the differentiation of the visuomotor channels dedicated to the visual control of action (Milner and Goodale 1995). For example, the classic strategy of practising run-throughs without jumping after striking the take-off board is seriously questioned by the data from the learners in long jumping. Moreover, the use of trackside markers to help make the approach phase more consistent should be considered only to get the athlete to a point around four strides from the board when the visual regulation strategy can 'kick in'. A key question for sport and exercise scientists to tackle, therefore, is whether 'perception–action coupling' is an overarching principle for designing practice environments for learners. Currently, it seems that task decomposition occurs arbitrarily in coaching and teaching contexts without the benefit of theoretical guidance. Ecological psychology may be on the verge of correcting this weakness in traditional pedagogy. In Chapter 8, we look more closely at the issue of learning from an ecological perspective.

Finally, during the chapter we introduced some important questions regarding the multispecification of information for perception and action from the ecological approach. One implication to be drawn from the criticisms of the current state of ecological psychology is that investigators need to take a close look at the possibility that optic variables other than tau may be influential in constraining actions or whether optic variables may support behaviour in combinations (Summers 1998).

One current proposal made by Wann (1996) concerns a potential alternative to the tau margin in behavioural studies of relative approach under gravity, which he termed the zeta ratio (ζ ratio). The ζ ratio is a relative variable that can be used as a strategy to time approach under constant acceleration conditions. It has been defined as 'the instantaneous visual angle subtended by a fixated object, relative to the visual angle it subtended prior to dropping' (Wann 1996: 1036). It is an estimate which can be provided by a number of monocular and binocular sources of information. In order to use it, a performer needs merely to learn to initiate an action when the optic size (specified by ζ) of an important object, such as a dropping rugby ball, has increased by a critical proportion of the optic size at the zenith of its flight. Some investigators have pointed out that the ζ ratio could imply a role for inferential processes comparing a known object's size at two different points of its trajectory (e.g. van der Kamp *et al.* 1996). However, Wann (1996) suggested very little cognitive loading for the observer, other than learning to recognise the critical proportion of increase in the subtended visual angle at which an invariant motor pattern can be initiated (in the case of our dropping rugby ball, the initiation of the two-handed grasp action). Given the amount of time spent in practice, this may not be an intolerable burden for the athlete.

Finally, in this chapter, it is concluded that the task of discovering the optical variables used for perceiving information for regulating action represents a major challenge for ecological psychology in the coming years. The major issues would appear to be how optical sources of information can specify actions in the form of affordances and the relationship of this idea with the notion of visual information as a constraint on movement coordination. In our quest to come to terms with the missing specificational link between perception and action from an ecological perspective, we move next to a review of the dynamical systems approach to the relationship between visual perception and action.

7 Information and dynamics: The dynamical systems approach

INTRODUCTION

For Michaels and Beek (1995), the core problem for the ecological group is 'the coordination of activity with respect to perceptual information' (p. 259). In Chapter 6 the basis of perception–action coupling was discussed from the Gibsonian perspective of direct perception. Amongst other things, the role of the optic array in guiding the coordination of an athlete's movements with respect to task goals was emphasised. However, we concluded that it is currently not clear how optic variables *specify* the changes necessary to the action system during goal-directed behaviour. For instance, during interceptive timing, tau merely specifies the temporal initiation point for successful completion of an action. What is missing is the *specificational* link between optical information and the dynamics of the movement system.

With regard to this criticism, van Soest and Beek (1996) recently argued that the results of Bootsma and van Wieringen (1990), on the co-dependency between the perceptual and motor systems of expert table tennis players, need not be interpreted as support for perception–action coupling. They were not convinced that the idea of on-line visual regulation fitted with neurophysiological evidence of neural control loop latencies of 80–100 ms. That is, the perception–action system is simply not fast enough to operate on the basis of regulatory feedback in such time-constrained circumstances. Using the soccer kick as an example, they produced a feedforward dynamical model as an alternative control explanation in which a single 'neural activation pattern' could be tuned by visual information so that the movement system 'capitalizes on the inherent dynamical properties of the muscular and skeletal system' (van Soest and Beek 1996: 100). This approach to the coordination between perception and action subsystems portrays the movement system as a dynamical, self-organising system capable of operating flexibly in a variety of performance contexts.

Whilst the Gibsonian ideas of direct perception represented a solid starting point for reinterpreting perception and action, Turvey (1990) has argued that the study of movement coordination required a second round of theorising emphasising the main ideas of a dynamical systems view-point. The main emphasis of the second phase of theoretical and empirical work has been to find a solution to Bernstein's (1967) degrees of freedom problem. That is, how coordination can emerge in the movement system with its huge number of degrees of freedom, such as muscles, joints and limb segments. Muchisky, Gershkoff, Cole and Thelen (1996) suggest that the degrees of freedom problem can be resolved in the human movement system if we conceptualise it as a dynamical system in which coopera-tivity between the subsystems results in the 'reduction in the dimensionality of the original components to a more compact pattern' (p. 125).

In this chapter we analyse the main theoretical influences on the model of the human movement system as a complex, dynamical system (for detailed reviews see Yates 1979; Kugler and Turvey 1987; Kauffmann 1993, 1995; Clark 1995; Kelso 1995). Ideas from modern scientific para-digms such as chaos theory, complex systems theory and non-linear dynamics have been integrated to reshape our understanding of the func-tion of the perceptual and action systems in biological organisms (see Beek and Meijer 1988; Davids *et al.* 1994). A systems perspective is empha-sised and the organism–environment relationship remains the focus of study. An important question to start with is: What is meant by the term 'complex' in this scientific context? Furthermore, to enhance understanding of perception and action from a direct viewpoint: What can we learn from the study of complex systems in nature? Detailed answers to these ques-tions will emerge during the course of this chapter. At the outset, it is worth bearing in mind Webster's (1977) dictionary definition of a complex system in science as being composed of many interacting parts (Wallace 1996).

Our aims in this chapter are to look at how the cooperativity or coor-dination between the subsystems of the movement system emerges to produce goal-directed behaviour. We begin by introducing the philo-sophical and theoretical basis of the dynamical systems approach to movement coordination. We continue by examining how direct percep-tion theory can be unified with ideas from dynamical systems theory to provide a principled alternative to traditional theories of perception and action in human movement systems. We shall see that the dynamical systems approach to motor coordination has gained increasing popularity within the ecological camp during the last decade, and has developed into a plausible alternative to the computational perspective. However, as with the traditional computational paradigm, there is no unitary dynamical position taken by all scientists working within this new framework. As pointed out by van Gelder and Port (1995) 'dynamicists are a highly diverse group, and no single characterization would describe all dynami-cists perfectly' (p. 4). Our aim in this chapter is to provide an interpretation of a kind of 'standard dynamicist' position focusing on similarities, and shared ideas, tools and concepts.

THE THEORETICAL BASIS OF THE DYNAMICAL SYSTEMS PERSPECTIVE

The systems approach in science

In ecological theory, a 'systems' approach to studying human behaviour is taken. According to Clarke and Crossland (1985: 16) a systems approach is useful because:

> structures and configurations of things should be considered as a whole, rather than examined piece by piece. In a highly complex system like the human mind or human body all the parts affect each other in an intricate way, and studying them individually often disrupts their usual interactions so much that an isolated unit may behave quite differently from the way that it would behave in its normal context.

Systems in the natural physical world, then, are defined as elements that cohere together and interact with each other during behaviour. In the human movement system the elements are the many different, but integrated, subsystems of the human body which are instrumental in physical activity. These include the neural subsystem, perceptual subsystem and skeletomuscular subsystem. The coordinated dimension to the behaviour of a collection of microscopic elements (e.g. muscles and bones of the human body) signifies that changes in some parts of a system are dependent on what other parts are doing (van Gelder and Port 1995; van Gelder, in press). Historically, the systems perspective originated as a reaction to the empiricist tradition of attempting to reduce phenomena to their essence in order to study them in a controlled experimental setting. This form of reductionism has dominated science for centuries partly because the relatively low level of technology available for studying natural phenomena precluded work in 'real-life' contexts. However, it fails to recognise that the relationships between elements of phenomena in natural settings are characterised by great 'complexity'. As we stated earlier, this concept has a very specific meaning in modern science, and is an important part of the dynamical perspective. Next we consider its implications.

Complexity in biological systems

Complex systems exhibit many fundamental attributes including: many independent degrees of freedom (i.e. component parts) which are free to vary; many different levels to the system (e.g. neural, hormonal, biomechanical in the human body); non-linearity of behavioural output; capacity for stable and unstable patterned relationships between system parts to occur through system self-organisation (i.e. these systems can spontaneously shift between many coordinated states); and the ability of subsystem components to constrain the behaviour of other subsystems (see Yates 1979; Kugler and Turvey 1987; Kauffmann 1993, 1995; Kelso 1995). Examples of complex systems in the natural physical world include the weather, animal colonies including human societies, the economic markets and the human body. Note how these systems possess a huge number of *microscopic* components (e.g. molecules of vapour or individual organisms or specific muscles and joints). Also, note that the behaviour of the whole system is best understood at a *macroscopic* level in which the individual components combine together to form coherent patterns (e.g. a river, a colony of ants, or coordinated motor patterns). In other words, the way that the individual elements form recognisable patterns over space and time is far more relevant than what any individual element is doing at any one moment.

Complex systems as dynamical systems

The search for general laws to model the behaviour of these complex systems remains a fundamental task for dynamical systems theorists (e.g. Kauffmann 1993, 1995). Non-linear dynamics is a branch of mathematics which deals with the formal treatment of any system which is continually evolving over time, and which can, therefore, be modelled as a numerical system with its own equations of motion (Abraham, Abraham and Shaw 1990).[1] Non-linear dynamicists believe that there are only a few lawful principles which can explain the way that animate and inanimate systems change or maintain their states of behaviour, regardless of scaling characteristics or material structure of these systems. According to Haken and Wunderlin (1990: 1) 'the underlying mathematical structure of these characteristic transitions is universal, and does not depend on the detailed composition of the system.' As Muchisky *et al.* (1996: 123) point out, one of the strengths of the dynamical systems perspective is that the 'theory itself is content free and may thus be adapted to specific data, levels of analysis, or species'. Moreover, the primacy of dynamical principles to describe system behaviour at evolutionary, ontogenetic and perceptual scales of analysis is advocated because 'such principles describe systems ... that live in many different time scales' (Thelen and Smith 1994: xiii). To reiterate, complex, dynamical systems change between different organisational states (the dynamics), as internal and external pressures on them change (acting as information for the system). This process of change in different types of systems (even in simple and inorganic ones), operating at different time scales, can be described by the same abstract physical principles.

The application of the principles of non-linear dynamics to the study of complex, biological systems is feasible because, as Yates (1979) argued, biological systems are in essence physical systems. He stated that 'The ontological reduction of biology to physics claims that at the level of atoms and molecules living systems obey laws of physics (and chemistry) and have no new laws of their own' (p. 65). The laws governing the behaviour of biological movement systems are specific instantiations of more general physical laws, which the language of mathematics is used to formalise.

To summarise so far, we have been setting the scene for an analysis of human movement systems as complex, dynamical systems. We have observed that the underlying basis of the explanations for pattern formation in natural complex systems is 'model-independent'. The material components of complex systems are only of interest insofar as they may adapt the laws of physics for expression within special boundary conditions. These fundamental descriptions of behaviour are abstract and mathematical. As such, the principles which govern the behaviour of natural complex systems may be equally applicable to systems as wide-ranging as the body of a human athlete or the molecules of water forming a puddle. This is a most important idea which readers, particularly those nurtured from a traditional cognitive perspective, need to comprehend. As Kelso (1995) points out, the idea 'that the same principles are at work even though the stuff that is producing the patterns may be very different indeed' (p. 2), might seem a little strange, especially if one engages in rather radical thoughts such as: What does my brain have in common with a puddle of water?!

In the study of perception and action in sport, it is worth picking out two of the most important characteristics of complex, dynamical systems for more detailed discussion. These features have important implications for the construction of an ecological model of the human movement system as a pattern-forming, complex system.

SENSITIVE DEPENDENCE ON EXISTING CONDITIONS

The first important point to recognise is that complex systems are 'open' systems in the sense of being easily influenced by the energy flowing around them. Typically, 'open' systems are biological systems, such as a flock of birds, a school of fish, a colony of ants or movement systems. Biological systems are extremely sensitive to existing environmental conditions in which surrounding energy flows can act as constraints on system behaviour. An 'open' system has been described as a non-conservative system because it has variable amounts of kinetic energy dissipating around its components at any given moment (von Bertalanffy 1950). According to the second law of thermodynamics in physics, unless there is an effort to recycle or utilise the energy flowing around a complex system to sustain stability, everything will ground to a halt. In open systems the kinetic energy already within the system interacts with the instantaneously available forces in the environment (e.g. reactive forces, gravity, friction).

The result is that the energy which enters the system at any given moment could produce chaotic and unpredictable effects in system output. Therefore, stability is a problem for open, dynamical systems because of the potential for interaction between energy from the environment and the energy already within the system.

A good example of an 'open' system is the weather, whose behaviour is generally very difficult to predict more than a few days in advance. The problem is that a tiny change in the energy which *surrounds* a weather system can cause chaotic fluctuations in system behaviour on one occasion and have little effect at other times because the energy which exists *within* the system is never constant. Thus, if we were to characterise developing human movement systems as complex, 'open', non-conservative systems, it would mean that brief periods of stability were possible, depending on the constraints surrounding the system, although the long-term behaviour would be difficult to predict accurately (Clark 1995).

STABILITY IN COMPLEX SYSTEMS

Despite the abundance of support for the second law of thermodynamics, scientists have been puzzled by the surprising amount of order which exists in many complex, dynamical systems (Waldrop 1992; Kauffmann 1993, 1995). Recently, there has been increasing evidence of the effect of physical processes called 'self-organisation' (also called 'anti-chaos') in biological systems. They seem to have developed the capacity to use environmental energy to sustain stability for functional purposes (i.e. they have learned to prevent disorder from disrupting system stability) (e.g. see Clark 1995; Kauffmann 1993, 1995). It has recently been discovered that the 'openness' of a system to surrounding energy flows can prevent the slide towards disorder (e.g. Prigogine and Stengers 1984). Indeed, the energy flows may be seen as a kind of information acting on system behaviour to shape the patterns formed by the components. The enormous co-dependency between parts of a dynamical system provides the basis for self-organising and self-regulation. A major task for scientists, therefore, is to understand how complex, open systems take advantage of the physical processes of self-organisation to form new and ever more functional patterns which satisfy the constraints on their behaviour (Waldrop 1992).

Now that we have provided an overview of important concepts such as self-organisation and energy flows from theoretical physics and physical biology, we can look at the link with the processes of perception and action in movement systems. We continue by investigating the efficacy of the dynamical systems alternative to perception–action coupling in the Gibsonian perspective of direct perception (e.g. Bootsma and van Wieringen 1990; Savelsbergh *et al.* 1991). In relation to the specific theme of this book, we examine how environmental energy flows, in the form of optical information reflected from surfaces and objects, could help to channel the movement system into an ordered, patterned stability, in the face of a universal 'pull' towards disorder.

HUMAN MOVEMENT SYSTEMS AS COMPLEX, DYNAMICAL SYSTEMS

The application of non-linear dynamics to the study of perception, action and cognition in human movement systems has been called the Dynamical Hypothesis (van Gelder and Port 1995; van Gelder, in press). The application of ideas and analytical tools from non-linear dynamics to the study of movement systems emphasises the development of a general, abstract theory of coordination which 'is concerned with the stability, loss of stability, the variability, and the adaptability of coordinated movement patterns' (Beek, Rikkert and van Wieringen 1996: 1077). With reference to movement systems, the primacy of dynamical principles needs to be re-emphasised. The same abstract, mathematical basis can describe behaviour in all movement subsystems, at different time scales (see Figure 7.1). Such a theory satisfies

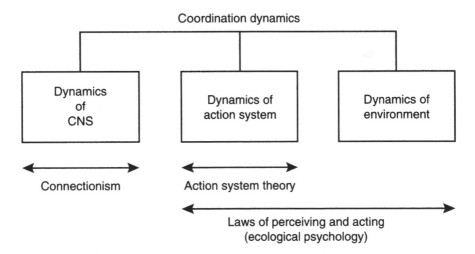

Figure 7.1 The primacy of the principles of dynamical systems theory across different levels of the performer–environment system. The principles seem to offer a solution for ecological concepts and issues such as perception–action coupling and Bernstein's (1967) degrees-of-freedom problem. There is also the possibility that dynamical systems theory can be integrated with ideas from Edelman's TNGS (see Thelen and Smith 1994). (Source: Schmidt, R.C. and Fitzpatrick, P. (1996) 'Dynamical perspective on motor learning', in H.N. Zelaznik (ed.) *Advances in Motor Learning and Control*, Champaign IL: Human Kinetics.)

the criticisms of computational accounts of mind by Edelman (1992) which we discussed in Chapter 6. Dynamical systems theory does not assign a single causal role to any specific subsystem for movement, cognition or perception. Indeed, it is difficult to separate the 'inextricable causal web of perception, action, and cognition' (Thelen and Smith 1994: xxii). A dynamical systems account rejects Cartesian dualism and insists on a unified, lawful framework for explaining movement coordination.

An important question is: How does order arise in a complex, dynamical system without recourse to a regulating agent which is external to the system? Evidence suggests that, despite the presence of numerous degrees of freedom, order is a characteristic of dynamical systems because most natural systems actually settle into relatively few preferred stable coordination patterns in goal-directed behaviour (Kauffmann 1993, 1995). In movement systems, Reed (1988) pointed out that while there are a huge number of movements and postures into which the movement system degrees of freedom can be configured, there are actually very few functional modes of action (he termed them 'action systems') which can be adopted during goal-directed behaviour. This is because biological systems, including movement systems, are not general-purpose devices. They may be better conceived of as special-purpose devices which operate according to relatively few general principles in fairly restricted environmental settings (Turvey 1990). This idea implies that biological systems are designed to inhabit particular environments and to perform specific tasks.

Empirical evidence for the relatively restricted number of preferred co-ordination states has been found in the movement science literature, for example in studies of quadruped gait (Warren 1988) and cascade juggling (Beek 1989a). This important idea was also demonstrated in a study of the development of one- and two-handed prehension movements in children (mean age: 4.4 years) and adults (mean age: 31.2 years) by Newell, Scully, Tenenbaum and Hardiman (1989). The task was to grasp ten different-sized cubes (range: 0.8–24.2 cm) with any combination of finger movements required to achieve the movement goal. When considered across two hands there are actually 1,013 possible combinations of fingers–thumb configurations which the subjects could have used to achieve the task goal. In fact, as theoretically predicted, the number of stable coordination patterns which formed the solutions to this movement problem were very few. It was found that only five grips accounted for 62% of the solutions used by children and 89% in the adult group.

PATTERN FORMATION IN DYNAMICAL SYSTEMS: ATTRACTORS

These functionally preferred states within complex systems are known as attractors in dynamical language. It has been shown formally that attractors act like 'magnets' for the behaviour of the many dynamic parts of the whole system. In a sense, they represent 'attractive' functional states for the system to settle into. The components of a complex system can, at least theoretically, interact to form rich, chaotically unpredictable patterns of behaviour. In reality, however, individual elements of the system spontaneously enslave or attract other components so that, typically, astonishing amounts of symmetry emerge in system behaviour (see Figure 7.2)

Figure 7.2 shows the huge reduction in the degrees of freedom of the complex system as it adopts a stable state of symmetry in an attractor region. The result is that, despite the potential for chaos, complex systems become highly ordered and coordinated when in an attractor state. This mathematical description of order in biological systems shows that they are highly specialised systems. Despite the many potential combinations

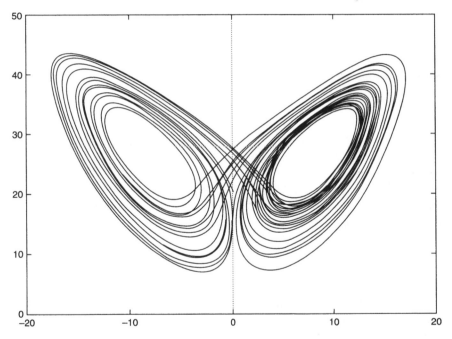

Figure 7.2 Order and variability in biological motion. Attractors can be described with equations of motion or can be graphically depicted to show the stability and instability in a complex system. Each line represents a behavioural trajectory of the system (in our case this would be a movement). Typically, more ordered stable systems show greater density and less spread between the trajectories. The attractors can be plotted with any two variables relevant to coordination in a complex system (e.g. relative velocity of two joints in the body). (Adapted from Davids, K., Handford, C. and Williams, A.M. (1994) 'The natural physical alternative to cognitive theories of motor behaviour: An invitation for interdisciplinary research in sports science?', *Journal of Sports Sciences* 12: 492–528.)

available to complex, dynamical systems in nature, they are composed of only a relatively small number of attractors which 'box in' the behaviour of a system (Kauffmann 1993, 1995).

Attractors have been defined by Kauffmann (1993: 177) as:

> a set of points or states in state space to which trajectories within some volume of state space converge asymptotically over time ... the different attractors constitute the total number of long term behaviours of the system. In due course the system winds up on one or another of its finite number of attractors ... the system becomes boxed into an attractor unless perturbed by an outside force.

Types of attractors

In a movement system, an attractor may roughly correspond to a state of coordination between the parts of the body which is functional in the sense that it is formed to achieve a desired task goal, such as locomotion, balancing, or reaching to intercept or kick an object. Kelso and Ding (1993) argue that attractors in movement systems are formed of 'an infinite number of unstable periodic orbits' (p. 304), meaning that amidst the symmetry there is a certain amount of variability to enhance flexibility (see Figure 7.2). This characteristic of attractors is important for movement systems because it can explain how consistency emerges alongside the minute levels of functional variability necessary for adaptive behaviour.

Beek *et al.* (1995) have summarised the four general types of attractor that are known. These are: (i) A point or equilibrium attractor which is a stable, single-valued state of the system variables. A practical example of a point attractor in a movement system could include a T-balance in gymnastics or an interceptive action with a very specific endpoint for the movement; (ii) A periodic attractor in which a set of system variables is revisited after a fixed time interval. The result is a stable orbit known as a limit cycle oscillator in which energy is periodically injected into the system to maintain its state. This description is particularly suited to the study of rhythmical movements such as juggling, cycling or other forms of locomotion; (iii) A quasi-periodic attractor which is not quite as stable as a limit cycle oscillator; (iv) A strange or chaotic attractor which is a set of state variable values without an immediately apparent spatio-temporal coherence but which remain within predictable long term boundaries. Although not all these types of attractors may be seen in movement behaviour, a key task for researchers is to identify attractors and the transitions between them in the movement system by varying parameters and observing qualitative and quantitative changes in behaviour.

Attractors in a dynamical landscape

To fully appreciate the relevance of attractors for system behaviour we need to get to grips with some of the other concepts of dynamical systems theory. Many wonderful descriptions exist and the outline below is indebted to the creativity of the biologist Stuart Kauffmann (1993, 1995) and the dynamical systems theorists Abraham *et al.* (1990). Here we provide a summary of some of the key ideas which could help the reader to understand a dynamical interpretation of the coordination problem in human movement systems.

Consider the following examples of highly integrated, dynamical systems in nature: the weather; a school of fish; a society of human beings; the human body. They are all made up of many subsystems which can interact with each other to produce changes in global system behaviour. A picture emerges of a system with its microcomponents all capable of incremental change, hence the term 'dynamical'. Imagine the difficulty in describing the behaviour of such a highly dynamic system at any particular moment. How could such a description be undertaken? A mathematically rigorous way is to break down the integrated system into its N component parts (the system variables) and to plot the global system's behaviour as these variables change over time – yielding an N-dimensional state space of coordinate points for each system variable. In the language of non-linear dynamics the state space of a system is the hypothetical totality of all the possible states of order which are achievable. In the study of the human movement system, the state space represents all the possible states of coordination into which the system's degrees of freedom can be configured. A state space therefore represents coordination potential in a movement system.

Over one small unit of time, the N-system variables of a dynamical movement system are all changing in value, often at different rates. As the variables of the system change, the path of these changes along the coordinate points can be plotted and a trajectory emerges in the hypothetical state space of the movement system. If you join the lines between the coordinate points (rather like a child's join-the-dots picture book) the changing trajectory describes the behaviour of the dynamical movement system in the form of a flow. Therefore, a dynamical system flows through the hypothetical state space composed of all its possible coordinate points. The process of self-organisation, which we examine next, takes the movement system to one region or another in the state space.

The state space can be visualised as a topological landscape with hilly, unstable peaks and smooth, stable hollows, around which a movement system could flow like a trickle of water (see Figure 7.3). The landscape has been described as a metaphor for development and change in a movement system, just like the computer is a metaphor for information processing models of human behaviour (Muchisky *et al.* 1996).[2] The

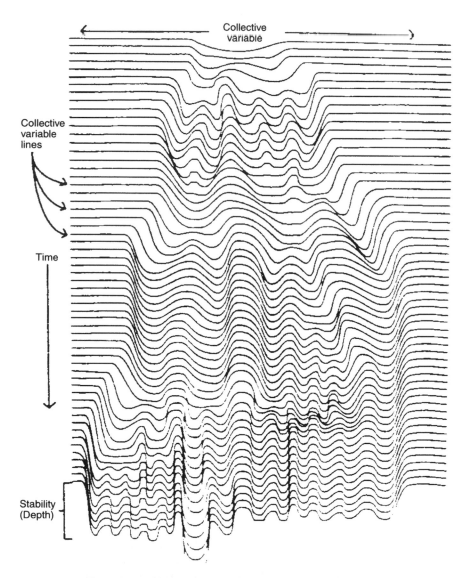

Figure 7.3 The perceptual-motor workspace as a dynamical landscape. A meta-
phorical description of the emergence of coordination as a movement
system flows dynamically through its state space seeking stability. The
deep regions represent attractor states in which the system achieves
coordination, whereas more shallow regions are less stable. (Source:
Thelen, E. (1995) 'Motor development: A new synthesis', *American
Psychologist* 50: 79–95.)

landscape metaphor is rigorous, with a strong mathematical basis, and exemplifies the dynamic, flowing, inherently unstable nature of movement systems. The state space landscape in the study of human movement co-ordination is composed of the many variables of the subsystems of the global neuro–perceptuo–motor system.

A key point is that the landscape for a dynamical system only ever offers temporary stability at most (Kauffmann 1993, 1995). Put simply, stability in dynamical systems is probabilistic. Dynamical systems are more or less likely to be stable depending on the nature of the internal and external constraints pressurising system stability at any instant. The type of stability that characterises dynamical movement systems, therefore, is a 'dynamic stability' (Kelso 1981). For example, unlike in the generalised motor programme theory, relational properties of a dynamical system, such as relative timing between system components, reflect stability rather than invariance (Kelso 1997). Variability in system dynamics, exemplified by fluctuations in stability, should not be considered as system 'noise', but as a functional property which allows the system to explore new states of order. At any instant, therefore, a dynamical movement system is either temporarily assembled into an attractor or is flowing to an attractor. Some less hilly regions of the landscape offer more stability to a dynamical movement than others. If the hollows are small and deep with relatively steep sides, they offer a stable region for the system to settle in, some-what like a marble rolling around an ashtray. In these regions of the neuro–perceptuo–motor landscape, the system requires low amounts of energy to sustain stability. These regions of the landscape represent funda-mental or well-practised skills which are relatively consistent, reliable and stable, such as standing, walking, reaching and grasping or any well-practised sport task, for that matter. The hilly or broadly flat regions are much more unstable and difficult for the flowing system to find a lasting foothold, consequently attractors require high levels of energy to be main-tained. These regions represent more complex skills which are being learned, such as running for an infant or one-handed catching for a young child. Although it is a general principle that preferred movements are located in regions which require optimal amounts of energy to sustain system stability, movement systems can also form attractors in the hilly, less stable, locations of the landscape. Novel or artificial movement patterns may emerge in these regions; for example, consider the types of activities employed in ballet, ice dancing, race-walking and synchronised swimming. It is much more costly in terms of energy and conscious intentionality for movement patterns to be sustained in the hilly locations of the neuro–perceptuo–motor landscape (Goldfield 1995).

Attractors in a perceptuo-motor landscape: an example from sport

The 'openness' of the human movement system allows it to adopt one of many possible movement trajectories in the landscape as a solution to a task problem. These radical ideas have been exemplified in a recent dynamical systems analysis of one-handed catching performance in children aged 8–10 years by Davids, Bennett, Handford, Jolley and Beak (1997). Tennis balls were projected by a ball machine to more and less successful catchers. Coordination between the degrees of freedom of the developing movement system was examined by calculating phase portraits for the relative velocity between the shoulder and elbow joints within the catching arm. Data from a successful (100% of balls were caught) and less successful (37% and 60% success rate) catchers are presented in Figure 7.4 (a–c). Each line represents a movement trajectory for an individual catcher over

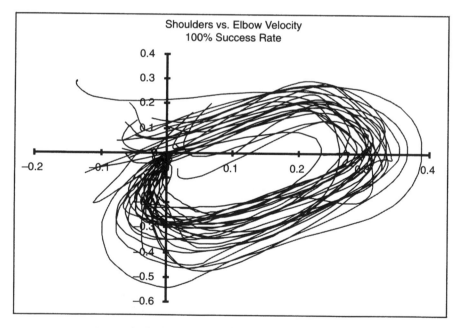

Figure 7.4a A phase portrait depicting the coupling of the elbow and shoulder joints of a successful catcher aged 10 years. The one-handed catching movement represents an attractor in which each separate line is a movement trajectory. Note that the lines are close together demonstrating stability in the movement. There is also some evidence of functional variability in that lines are not too tightly bound as would be seen with a very poor catcher with rigidly coupled movements. According to Kauffmann (1993, 1995), this attractor exemplifies a biological system operating in the complex régime on the border of chaos and rigidity in which there is the greatest chance for evolution into a successful system.

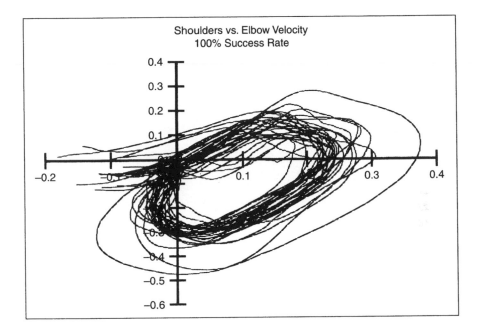

Figure 7.4b A phase portrait of a child aged 10 years learning to catch. There is too much instability in the attractor, exemplified by the spread of the movement trajectory. This movement system is operating in the chaotic régime in which behaviour is unpredictable. There is some slight evidence of pattern formation and the child may be making the transition towards the complex régime in which an appropriate balance between order and chaos exists.

30 trials. Pattern formation between the system degrees of freedom is apparent in the way that the movement trajectories are drawn towards the attractor region for one-handed catching. However, there is a relatively small level of variability present in the attractors. In the very successful catcher (100% success rate) an appropriate balance exists between the stability of the coupling of the elbow and shoulder joints, and the trial-to-trial variations in movements which are necessary to flexibly adapt to minute differences in ball flight due to the variation in projection.

Like successful biological species, sports performers need to adapt to their surroundings in order to succeed. The phase portraits of coordination between parts of the movement system in the successful catchers exemplify what some theoretical biologists call a system hovering in the complex régime located between the chaotic (completely unpredictable) and frozen (stereotyped) system state (e.g. Kauffmann 1993, 1995). From theoretical biology it has been shown that systems in the frozen régime

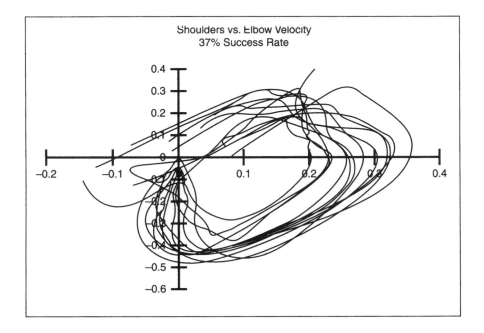

Figure 7.4c An attractor for a reasonably successful catcher aged 10 years. There is more stability to the pattern of the individual movement trajectories. The child is making the transition from the partially successful to the successful category. Comparison with the successful catcher shows that more stability is required between the shoulder and elbow joint relations. The variability shown by this catcher is not as functional as that shown by the successful child.

demonstrate a rigid coupling between system degrees of freedom. They are only capable of simple forms of stereotyped behaviour and will have to adapt to survive in dynamic environments. It has been argued that the complex régime offers optimal avenues for evolution or development in dynamical systems. In a behavioural context, success in catching is not based on repeating a stereotyped movement pattern, time and again. The catching data show how complex movement systems create and exploit variability in a functional manner during goal-directed activity (Thelen and Smith, 1994). This explanation offers an alternative to the perception–action coupling arguments of direct perception theorists (e.g. Bootsma and van Wieringen 1990).

The phase portraits for the two less successful catchers exemplify different stages in the development of catching skill. In the least successful catcher (37% success), there is too much variability in the movement trajectories over trials as exemplified by the greater spread of the trajectories in the attractor. Here is a movement system in the chaotic régime, in which behaviour is unpredictable. However, there is some stability appearing in the movement pattern as the child searches the task for a successful solution. In other words, this movement system is making the transition to the complex régime where there is an appropriate balance between stability and variability in system behaviour. This system will need to adapt by learning to freeze some of the important system degrees of freedom to stabilise behaviour or it will become extinct (in the sense of not being able to function in a ball game!). The attractor for the child who was reasonably successful (60% success rate) shows a movement system which is clearly making the transition to the complex régime. This catcher exhibits more stability than the least successful performer, with more relative instability than the more successful counterpart. Skilled (functional) behaviour, therefore, is about attaining the right balance between persistence and change in goal-directed activities like catching.

How does this functional form of variability emerge in skilled athletes? The answer is that skilled performers are able to exploit the full range of variability in the attractor parameters for a movement coordination pattern. That is, any one of the movement trajectories making up an attractor for a task, such as locomotion, provides relative stability for a dynamical movement system flowing into the region. During locomotion the 'openness' of the movement system allows it to precisely adapt to environmental conditions. Harnessing the energy flows in the environment can instantaneously constrain or pressure the movement system on to one or another of the movement trajectories depending on the conditions.

The underlying argument is that an account of perception and action which relies on symbolic representations fails to provide a principled basis for explaining the variability in movement behaviour. In the study of real-world movements, there is too much motor redundancy and variability in a movement system to support the idea of a representation controlling actions. For example, the same postural changes within a limb have been associated with varied patterns of neuro-muscular activity and different actions can result from the same movement patterns given a particular context of forces (Turvey, Fitch and Tuller 1982; Reed 1988). Shik and Orlovsky (1976) have previously reviewed evidence from studies of loco-moting quadrupeds showing how the patterning of neural signals within muscles of the same locomoting limb varies considerably more than the kinematic pattern of activity. They pointed out that 'The smaller variability of the kinematic pattern may be explained by the fact that the same mechanical result can be obtained by various combinations of muscle activities' (p. 468).

Therefore, the precise orbit (movement trajectory) of the attractor that the movement system settles into is best not prescribed beforehand. Rather, on its journey around the landscape of possible states of coordination, the dynamical movement system continuously self-organises (adjusts its state of organisation) as it comes under the influence of many variables and energy flows. As in the case of evolving species, a successful task solution for a perception–action system emerges under the instantaneous constraints on its behaviour. Clearly, self-organisation is an important part of a dynamical systems explanation of emergent movement coordination. In biology, it has been known for some time that complex systems can exhibit powerful self-organisation (e.g. see Kauffmann 1993, 1995), and we turn now to discussion of this key concept.

'ORDER FOR FREE': CONSTRAINTS AND SELF-ORGANISATION IN DYNAMICAL SYSTEMS

Recently, Beek *et al.* (1995) complained that 'the notion of self-organization is interpreted by some movement scientists as a kind of mystical ability, according to which movements come out of the blue. This is giving an incorrect ontological twist to the concept' (p. 577). The main point of their comment was to show that processes of self-organisation in the sciences of complexity have a substantial theoretical basis. Advances in mathematics, physics, chemistry, and evolutionary and theoretical biology have demonstrated how internal and external constraints on system behaviour can lead to pressure for system change and the emergence of spontaneous pattern formation. These theoretical developments have shown how order, available in nature 'for free', can be exploited by systems needing to adapt to changing conditions (Kauffmann 1993, 1995). The capacity to continuously form, and then adapt, patterns amongst system components provides movement systems with the flexibility needed in ever-changing environments. In an explanation of self-organisation processes in movement systems, therefore, the notion of constraints as pressures on system behaviour is most important.

Constraints on system behaviour

Self-organising dynamical systems achieve functional states of coordination only when under constraint. Constraints have been defined as boundaries or features which limit the form of a biological system engaged in a search for an optimal state of organisation (Kugler, Kelso and Turvey 1980; Newell 1986; Clark 1995). In this sense they have the effect of reducing the number of configurations available to a dynamical system at any instance. That is, constraints help to structure the state space of all possible configurations for a biological (movement) system. There are many classes of constraints which can affect the behaviour of a dynamical system and it remains an important empirical task to identify them. Constraints are specific to biological niches and can be found at many different levels of the system or the environment. At the level of a species, they are allied to selection as part of the optimising evolutionary process which guides biological organisms towards functionally appropriate behaviours in a particular niche or habitat (Kauffmann 1993, 1995). At the level of perception and action, constraints operate in the same way on the behaviour of movement systems during goal-directed activity (Goldfield 1995). That is, selected coordination patterns in the human movement system emerge under constraint as less functional states of organisation are destroyed.

The theoretical biologist Yates (1979) has provided a model for us to understand how the transition between states of organisation (known as order–order transitions) occur at the timescale of perception and action (see also Kugler, Shaw, Vincente and Kinsella-Shaw 1990). In biological movement systems, as energy flows in the environment undergo critical changes, 'a mode of marginally-stable behaviour emerges, and holds until an outside cue creates a transient switch state (a bifurcation), and the system moves into another marginally stable mode, entrained by the environmental cue' (p. 65). What this means, according to Yates (1979) is that 'many of the apparent command-control 'algorithms' of living systems actually reside in the interaction between the environment, and their plant structures. These interactions initiate the trajectories from one marginally-stable dynamic mode (out of a very limited set) to another' (p. 65). Therefore, structurally stable states of ordered behaviour or attractors are created or destroyed in association with critical variations in the perceptual field allowing the animal to switch to other stable modes of behaviour. The development of such models, according to Yates (1979) 'is likely to lead to the discovery that much animal behaviour, previously thought to be the province of mental states, is in fact the province of hydrodynamics/thermodynamics states and transitions' (p. 66–7). This description helps us to understand how the ecological concept of perception–action coupling can be instantiated in dynamical laws, a theoretical synthesis which Warren (1990) has pursued.

Warren's (1990) physical and informational constraints

The processes of self-organisation are similar in physical (inanimate) and biological (animate) systems. However, Warren (1990) has observed some important differences. The main difference is the 'openness' of biological systems to energy flows. Warren (1990) argued that the behaviour of biological systems is not deterministically driven by physical laws, unlike inanimate systems. The evolution of sensory systems in tune with their habitats allows biological movement systems the capacity to continuously adapt their behaviour to instantaneous internal and external changes. The process of transition between functional coordination patterns is guided by the information available to an animal with sensory systems. This capacity to be sensitive to environmental constraints dovetails with the emergence of order in a dynamical movement system. In skilled movement systems, the huge number of system degrees of freedom are compressed so that only a manageable few are free to self-organise. For Warren (1990), constraints and self-organisation are integral to a principled account of the coordination of a movement system with its environment.

Coordinative structures

Warren (1990) proposed that constraints on the behaviour of the movements system were either physical or informational. Coordinative structures or muscle synergies, acting as attractors, physically constrain the flow of the movement system in the dynamic landscape of action possibilities. Coordinative structures have been defined by Kay (1988) as 'an assemblage of many microcomponents ... assembled temporarily and flexibly, so that a single microcomponent may participate in many different coordinative structures on different occasions' (p. 344). They were proposed by Turvey (1977) as a solution to Bernstein's degrees of freedom problem. Any change in one component is automatically adjusted for in other system components without jeopardising the achievement of the task goal (see Figure 7.5). Flexibility in adapting to localised conditions is enhanced by the capacity of the microcomponents of a coordinative structure to vary in relation to each so that an action goal can be achieved.

Although the coordinative structure is an important part of an ecological alternative to motor programming theory, there is little evidence for its existence in movement behaviour. Some evidence for the existence of coordinative structures in sport-related contexts has been found in studies of aiming and interceptive actions. For example, the principles behind coordinative structure theory were exemplified long ago in a study showing how the wrist and shoulder movements of skilled pistol shooters were functionally covaried in order to achieve an accurate shot on target

Figure 7.5 The highly interconnected movement system as a complex, dynamical system. A change in one subsystem has implications for the global system state. Note how the system degrees of freedom become compressed (exemplified by the low number of strings) as coordinative structures are created. (Adapted from Kugler and Turvey 1987.)

(Arutyunyan, Gurfinkel and Mirskii 1969). More recently, using a two-handed catching task, Tayler and Davids (1997) assessed the support for an explanation of skilled performance from the coordinative structure perspective. Coordinative structure theory predicts a close temporal relationship between the hands in a bimanual task, even when each hand is required to move different distances (see Kelso, Southard and Goodman 1979; Kelso, Putnam and Goodman 1983). From a traditional programming perspective, it is emphasised that separate motor commands are issued for each limb to arrive simultaneously at the specified movement endpoint, leading to low temporal associations between them (e.g. Marteniuk and MacKenzie 1980; Marteniuk, MacKenzie and Baba 1984). The problem is that most previous empirical work on bimanual coordination has only used manual aiming tasks in which the hands started at the same location and moved to different target locations or have been constrained by experimenter instructions (e.g. see Swinnen, Beirinckx, Meugens and Walter 1991).

Tayler and Davids (1997) were able to examine performance in a real-world catching task in which the required bimanual coordination pattern was constrained, not by the spatial layout of the targets in a laboratory or by experimenter instructions, but by natural task constraints in the form of ball flight characteristics. Skilled catchers, standing upright with their hands on their thighs, caught tennis balls with two hands in three conditions. In condition 1, a ball was projected to the right shoulder area (left hand moved greater distance); in condition 2, a ball was projected to the centre of the chest area (both hands moved same distance); and, in condition 3, a ball was projected to the left shoulder area (right hand moved greater distance). An interesting question was whether the data would fit the coordinative structure model. Kinematic data (time to peak velocity, movement initiation time), indicating significant cross correlations between the left and right limbs in all three conditions, agreed with those of Kelso and colleagues (1979, 1983) on manual aiming (see Figures 7.6 a–c).

As can be seen from Figures 7.6 a–c, although the limbs of this typical subject moved at different speeds when each was required to move different distances, times to peak velocity showed strong associations, suggesting the constraining presence of a coordinative structure and rejecting the idea of independent programming of limb trajectories. However, from a dynamical systems perspective, the freezing of system parameters into coordinative structures is not enough because as Warren (1990) argues 'although the action is stable, it is also stereotyped and blind' (p. 34). Some parameters must be free to vary. Perceptual information acts to constrain the remaining system degrees of freedom so that localised solutions to coordination problems can emerge as internal and external conditions in system behaviour change. The way that the performer regulates the spatio-temporal behaviour of the few remaining system variables has been referred to as 'the heart of the perception-action coupling problem' (ibid.: 26).

(a) Velocity

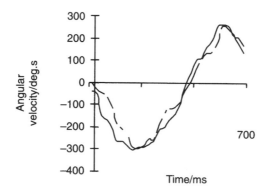

(b) Acceleration

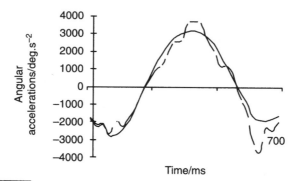

Figure 7.6a Velocity and acceleration traces for one catch performed in condition 1 by subject 3.

What needs to be understood is how variables of the energy flow fields (e.g. optic) are harnessed as information to regulate parameters of the movement system. The crux of the issue is that, whereas in inanimate systems a component in a field is driven towards attractors by the energy forces within the field itself, in animate systems, components are not as deterministically driven. A biological movement system 'uses the field as information' (ibid.: 28), as it moves through it, to organise its behaviour. What is needed, according to Warren is to bring together our understanding of the movement system as a dynamical system with that of ecological optics to attack the problem of perception–action coupling. Later in this chapter we discuss a similar proposal by Schoner (1994).

(a) Velocity

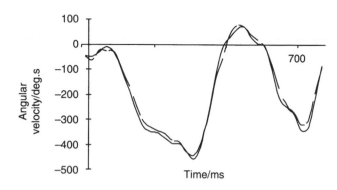

(b) Acceleration

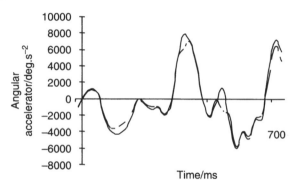

Figure 7.6b Velocity and acceleration trace for one catch performed in condition 2 by subject 3.

The language of dynamics: 'control parameters' and 'order parameters'

From the analyses by Yates (1979) and Warren (1990) it should be apparent that attractors are not permanently stored in the memory of the human movement system – a common misconception of those unfamiliar with dynamical systems theory. Rather, through the physical process of self-organisation, they spontaneously emerge and disappear as a consequence of changes in the surrounding energy flows acting as informational constraints on a dynamical system. In the following sections, we discuss how the physical process of self-organisation has been mathematically

(a) Velocity

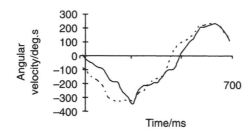

(b) Acceleration

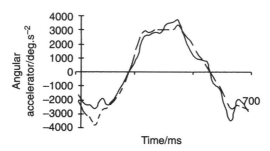

Figure 7.6c Velocity and acceleration trace for one catch performed in condition 3 by subject 3. (Source: Tayler, M.A. and Davids, K. (1997) 'Catching with both hands: An evaluation of neural cross-talk and coordinative structure models of bimanual coordination', *Journal of Motor Behavior* 29: 343–54.)

modelled by dynamical systems theorists to describe order–order transitions in movement systems.

The organisational state of the movement system can be more simply described with reference to 'order parameters' when it is in a state of order (i.e. assembled in an attractor). Order parameters are variables which can be used to describe the structural organisation of a complex dynamical system. In a such a highly integrated system, the order parameters of relevance will be those which describe the relations between system sub-components (Kelso 1995). Therefore, they are key essential variables for capturing the cooperation or collectivity between the components of a complex dynamical system. For example, in a movement system an important order parameter is the relative phasing of the limbs during different types of locomotion (Warren 1990). Due to their coherence with respect to system organisation, Kelso (1995) argues that order parameters act as 'functionally specific, context-sensitive informational variables' (p. 145), which simplify the structure of biological movement systems.

Order parameters, therefore, are variables which can be used to describe the order in attractor states in movement systems. But how does the system 'decide' which attractor to flow on to during its journey? This is a job for the 'control parameters'. Continuous changes in control parameters, like environmental information or oscillatory frequency of limb segments, most often are associated with little change in an order parameter. However, eventually, changes in the value of a control parameter can lead to significant and discontinuous changes in the overall pattern of the dynamical system (Warren 1990). This is why they have been termed 'control parameters' (Haken and Wunderlin 1990). The function of control parameters is to 'move' the system through the many potential patterns of coordination which are attractors in the landscape of all possible system states. A useful analogy for understanding the relationship between control and order parameters has been provided by Roberton (1993: 97). She argues that in the dynamical systems approach, qualitative change in motor patterns:

> is seen as a post hoc result of change in another variable, known in dynamical systems parlance as a 'control parameter' . . . (the latter is similar in concept to an 'independent variable' except that nature has no scientist manipulating the control parameter). When scaled past some critical value, the control parameter causes reorganisation of the dependent variable (known as the essential or collective variable) . . . An everyday example is the changes that occur in the state of H_2O molecules as temperature is increased: the macro 'states' shown by molecules form a 'developmental sequence' from ice to water to steam. No pre-programmed directions, either genetic or computed, are contained in the temperature-molecule system; yet, the changes are observable, predictable and ordered.

Self-organisation under constraint in movement systems

With regard to movement systems, the agenda for the ecological group has been straightforward. 'If it can be shown that (part of) motor control follows laws of self organization, then we will not have to look for any superior authority specifying the movement' (Meijer, Wagenaar and Blankendaal 1988: p. 519). This challenge has been met by Kelso and colleagues (e.g. Haken, Kelso and Bunz 1985; Kelso and Schoner 1988; Kelso, Ding and Schoner 1993; Kelso, Buchanan, DeGuzman and Ding 1993). Their work on rhythmic finger and limb movements has been proposed to exemplify how the coordinated output of human movement systems can be lawfully described through principles of self-organisation.

This group of researchers has always placed a great emphasis on providing empirical support for the abstract theoretical and mathematical modelling they have undertaken on movement systems as dynamical systems. For example, Kelso (1984) empirically demonstrated that co-ordination can emerge through the spontaneous interaction between elements of the human movement system. Utilising rhythmical and sequential index finger movements as an empirical vehicle, Kelso (1984) found evidence of self-organisation when subjects were required to coordinate the relative phase of the index finger movements in the left and right hands (see Figure 7.7a). The frequency of the rate of flexion and extension of each finger in the transverse plane was proposed as a control parameter by Kelso (1984). It has been recognised that order parameters are variables which describe the relations between system components. In this task it was argued to be the relative phase of the finger movements. Subjects always started with anti-phase finger movements and demonstrated a sudden involuntary shift to in-phase relations as the rhythmic frequency of the movements increased. Below a critical value of the frequency of finger movements, as can be observed from the EMG data (see Figure 7.7b), one finger could flex, while the other was extending. Beyond a critical value of the control parameter, both fingers could only flex or extend together.

This phase transition occurred despite no instructions being issued by the experimenter. Kelso (1984) argued that these two distinct modes of interaction between the components of the human movement system represented two attractor states in its intrinsic structure. This may be interpreted as an example of 'order for free' in the human movement system modelled as an open system. Further evidence for phase transitions as the movement system undergoes self-organisation has since been found in coordinations between hands and feet (Carson, Goodman, Kelso and Elliott 1995), arms and legs (Kelso and Jeka 1992) and even coordination between individuals (Schmidt, Carello and Turvey 1990).

'Non-specific' and 'specific' constraints on system dynamics

From the previous theoretical outline, the key characteristics of non-linear dynamical systems have been revealed as a number of qualitative changes in behaviour at the macroscopic level, regardless of the material composition of the system. These include the capacity for abrupt transitions between system states (known as bifurcation points), regions of stable system organisation known as attractors and the relationship between order parameters and control parameters in the emergence of coordination.

Schoner (1994) modelled the intrinsic dynamics of the movement system as a series of point attractors which the performer settles into during goal-

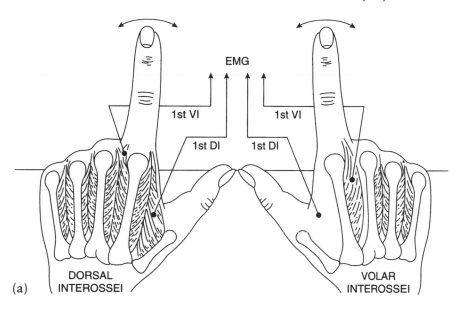

(a)

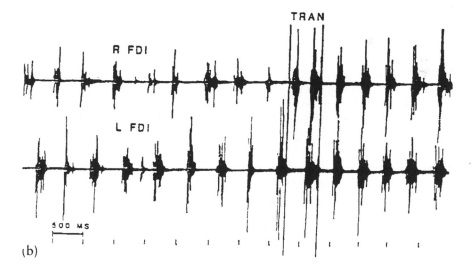

(b)

Figure 7.7 How two system states become one: self-organisation in the human movement system. Subjects were asked to oscillate index fingers in the transverse plane. At low oscillatory frequencies, two system states (anti-phase and in-phase relations) were evident. Above a critical frequency value (2.2 Hz) only one system state (in-phase) was possible. Positioning of the electrodes for EMG analysis is shown in (a), and in (b) inter-spersed potentials are abruptly aligned after around 4.5 s of movement activity. (Source: Kelso, J.A.S. and Schoner, G. (1988) 'Self-organiza-tion of coordinative movement patterns', *Human Movement Science* 7: 27–46.)

directed activity. He emphasised the role of the intrinsic dynamics of the movement system as an ensemble of attractor points 'tuneable' by surrounding environmental energy. Kelso, DelColle and Schoner (1990) propose that a tight fit between perception and action emerges because 'environmental information perturbs the vector field of the intrinsic dynamics, such that it attracts these dynamics to the required behavioural pattern' (p. 167). That is, the intrinsic dynamics of the movement system are incessantly shaped and modified ongoingly by constraints on the system. These constraints may be modelled as sources of 'behavioural information' because they continually inform the dynamics of the movement system. As we shall see below, sources of behavioural information which shape system dynamics during an action can include memorised information, intentions (see Davids, Button and Bennett, in press; Kugler, Shaw, Vincente and Kinsella-Shaw 1990) and perceptual information from flow fields such as vision, audition and proprioception (see Kelso 1994, 1995).

The type of control parameter described in the experiments of Kelso and colleagues is known in the dynamical systems literature to act as a 'non-specific' constraint on system behaviour (see Haken, Kelso and Bunz 1985; Kelso, 1995; Beek *et al.* 1995). In the example of the oscillating index fingers in Figure 7.6, the transition of the system from one state (anti-phase) to another (in-phase) was not an intentional act, since subjects were not instructed to switch. The transition from one attractor to another was spontaneous and emergent under a non-specific constraint. Non-specific sources of behavioural information can take the form of the energy flows and forces surrounding the movement system at any instant including auditory information, visual information and gravitational force fields. Because of the continual exposure to non-specific constraints, the precise form of dynamics required by the movement system to achieve a task goal cannot be prescribed in advance. In this sense they are emergent and spontaneous. Indeed, the actual dynamics of a particular movement contain the most relevant attractor points in the system and also incorporate the changes specified by behavioural information. For example, once an outfielder in cricket or baseball has the intention of locomoting from one place to another to intercept an ball, the spatio–temporal characteristics of a ball in flight act as a non-specific constraint on the precise dynamics of the movement pattern which emerges to solve the locomotion problem.

'Specific' constraints on the movement system include memories or the particular intentions of a performer to produce a specific form of co-ordinated movement. Kelso (1995) defined an intention in a movement system as 'specific information acting on the dynamics, attracting the system towards the intended pattern' (p. 141). Intentions act in the same state space as the movement system's order parameters by disrupting or sustaining the symmetry of the system's existing dynamics to attain specific task goals. In fact, Kelso (1995) viewed intention as an important source of behavioural information 'stabilizing or destabilizing the organisation' (p. 141) that already exists in the intrinsic pattern dynamics of the movement system. Intentionality, acting as a specific constraint on intrinsic dynamics, could allow the movement system to flow to attractors established in the hilly, less stable, regions of the perceptuo–motor landscape of coordination possibilities. To return to our outfielding example, the fielder can decide to intentionally constrain the dynamics of locomotion by 'showboating' to reach the interception point of the ball. There are many such examples of 'playing with flair' in sport which exemplify intentional constraints on the movement system.[3] The important point is that movement systems are not deterministic (closed conservative systems) which always have to settle into the most energy efficient movement pattern available. Being open and non-conservative (i.e. being able to sustain energy flows within), movement systems can be perturbed by a specific control parameter, such as memory or an intention, to flow to rockier, less stable regions of the potential landscape which require a higher energy input to sustain pattern symmetry.

To summarise, the movement system in a sport context makes its behavioural choices under the influence of non-specific (e.g. task, environmental) *and* specific (e.g. memories, intentions, organismic) constraints (Davids *et al.* in press). Apart from global intentions, such as when deliberately deciding to produce a specific movement pattern, it has been argued that the brain 'does not care' how the system degrees of freedom interact to produce goal-directed activity (Latash, 1996). At the level of the CNS a huge amount of trial-to-trial variability is apparent in the role of muscles and in the neurophysiological status of the movement system. It is neither interesting nor relevant what individual microcomponents of the movement system are doing during a hockey goalkeeper's dive to save a penalty shot, for example. As long as initial conditions and the movement endpoint are taken into account, there may be many different routes from one to another. In most instances, movement behaviour is emergent and is the product of a number of interacting variables, all pressurising the form of the movement system to a greater or lesser extent at the specific instance of performance.

EMERGENCE IN MOVEMENT SYSTEMS

From a dynamical systems perspective, therefore, attractors are coupled to behavioural information, in the form of specific and non-specific control parameters, to produce transitions from one state of system order to another. Could dynamical systems principles be used to explain order–order transitions in sport, for example in interceptive actions or locomotion?

Schoner's (1994) reanalysis of the empirical work on interceptive actions in ecological optics can be interpreted with the sport-related task of one-handed catching in mind. Like Warren (1990), Schoner (1994) argued that an important research avenue for ecological theorists was to integrate the ideas of ecological optics and dynamical systems theory. He proposed a mathematical model for the coupling of visual information to the intrinsic dynamics of the action system. It demonstrates how tau information can act to constrain system dynamics during interceptive actions. What we have done here is to apply Schoner's (1994) model·to the co-ordination of a one-handed catching movement.

The model proposes that two separate attractor states represent the key initial (wide hand aperture, fingers spread) and target (hand aperture narrowed, fingers closed around the ball) postures in one-handed catching. The intrinsic dynamics of the movement system, Schoner (1994) demonstrated, are coupled to visual information from the optic flow field. That is, the intrinsic dynamics of the system are modified ongoingly and instantaneously by behavioural information from ball approach during the transition between the initial and target postures. The rate of change of dilation of the retinal image of the ball differs for balls approaching with faster and slower velocities. Schoner's (1994) computer simulations imply that when the expansion rates are suddenly shifted between faster and slower flight times, the stable relative timing of the intrinsic dynamics, hand aperture in our example, is instantly altered. If a perturbation to flight resulted in a slower flight time, the shape of the dynamics is instantly adjusted to decrease the rate of closure of the hand aperture. The opposite is true if perturbations decrease flight time of the ball. Without the optic flow, a stereotyped motor pattern which is not constrained by behavioural information, from optical sources, will be triggered. It is worth noting that most cognitive laboratory paradigms tend to produce stationary environments which are devoid of flow – a feature which may explain why stereotyped motor patterns have been found in laboratory studies of motor programmes. In static environments, devoid of information flow, the intrinsic dynamics of the action system are stronger than the competing influences of the behavioural information. In real-life circumstances, the more constraints (in the form of sources of behavioural information) which contribute to the shaping of the intrinsic dynamics of the system, the greater the qualitative difference in the motor pattern used to achieve a task goal.

Order–order transitions in locomotion

In the previous discussion of the movement system as a dynamical system, it was clear that a non-specific constraint changing in scale, and leading to a qualitative change in system dynamics, can act as a control parameter for order–order transitions. Warren (1990) identified how order–order transitions in locomotion are dependent on changes in system behaviour at critical points of the control parameter–order parameter relationship. Typically, a small change in a critical control parameter, such as the oscillatory frequency of the limbs, has little effect on an order parameter, perhaps described by the relative phase of the limbs during walking and running. At bifurcation points (i.e. critical points at which the system changes its organisation), a small change in the control parameter will specify a dramatic shift in the order parameter, with significant consequences for system organisation. For instance, in quadruped locomotion the system may autonomously switch from an attractor for walking to an attractor for running as a function of a change in the oscillation frequency of the legs during stepping.

Warren (1990) argues that this model for order–order transitions at critical points in the gait of quadruped animals allows them to adopt the most energetically efficient pattern, given the momentary constraints on their action. These movement solutions represent attractors and typically occur at optimal points in the control parameter–order parameter relationship. Referring to previous research, Warren (1990) argued that, in most biological movement systems, the potential landscape of attractors for quadruped gait is composed of a limited number of solutions: patterns for walking, trotting, cantering and galloping only. Moreover, in the study of human gait patterns, it seems that the dynamic relationship between variables for timing and amplitude of lower limb movements permits only an eightfold range of walking speeds (Grieve 1968). Such a level of variability is functional in allowing the human movement system the capacity to adapt to local changes, within a more or less energy efficient range, without being overwhelmed by an inordinate number of potential task solutions. That is, during locomotion, human movement systems can search the landscape and quickly find a 'functional' attractor, as a physical constraint in the form of a coordinative structure.

To summarise so far, self-organisation in movement systems implies that skilled performers are able to substitute perceptual information and motor patterns to create goal-directed movement behaviour. Coordinative structures are formed as a kind of 'task-specific device' suited for specific performance circumstances. Movement systems 'soft-assemble' the solutions to movement problems (Kugler and Turvey 1987). That is, the parametric configurations of the (fuzzy) attractor can be instantaneously tuned to localised conditions. Next we explore the idea from dynamical systems theory that movement solutions are malleable, but highly structured, functional devices formed to achieve a specific task goal from the momentary resources available to a movement system.

Task-specific devices as tuneable movement solutions

Task-specific devices (TSDs) are formed when performers coordinate the components of the movement system into a functional and effective form of 'machinery' for achieving a particular task goal (Bingham 1988; Beek and Bingham 1991). According to Beek and Bingham (1991), task-specific dynamics is concerned with the 'goal-directed behaviour which reveals how properties of the environment and properties of the animal are related and temporarily organised into a special-purpose machine or task-specific device' (pp. 38–9). They emphasise that such an approach is necessary in understanding human action since 'Action is an intrinsically creative business. At any instant, generated states of the system are as likely to be novel as not' (p. 39).

Bingham (1988) argues that task-specific devices have a number of properties which make them particularly attractive to the development of a theory of human action. They are purpose-designed and thus take advantage of the smartness of the human neuro-skeleto-muscular system. They are dynamic in that the behaviour of the biological material which forms them (e.g. tendons, ligaments, muscles) varies considerably as a consequence of environmental conditions. The perceptual information which is used in the construction of TSDs varies considerably as conditions change and events unfold. They have the character of being determined and soft-assembled at the same time. What this means is that, once an optimal task solution emerges with exploratory behaviour, a performer may rely on it time and again under similar conditions. The coupling of perception and action through practice allows similar task solutions to be repeatedly soft-assembled from the available perceptual resources and biomechanical properties under certain environmental conditions.

To support this argument, Bingham, Schmidt and Rosenblum (1989) showed that in choosing between objects of differing weights and sizes to throw over long distances, subjects were highly consistent and individual in their perceptions of what constituted an optimal projectile. Furthermore, kinematic analyses of preferred throwing styles with objects of different sizes and weights showed abrupt transitions in the coordination mode used in the task. The solution of generating kinetic energy during the last 50 ms of the release phase by pre-stretching the long extrinsic tendons of the wrist and hand, rather than the strategy of transferring kinetic energy from the large muscle groups of the trunk and legs, was highly correlated with perceptions of projectile size and weight. The problem of grasping a projectile with greater mass led to an increase in the stiffness of the wrist joint which constrained subjects to the solution of using the second strategy outlined above. Follow-up kinematic analyses of the phase relations between the peak extension of the wrist joint and the peak extension of the elbow revealed an increasingly tight coupling for projectiles approaching preferred weight. These phase relations remained invariant across the preferred weight for individual subjects. Lighter and heavier projectiles showed that subjects assembled different patterns of coordination between the wrist and elbow joints to cope with the specific demands of the throwing task.

These data may be taken as evidence for the deterministic nature of TSDs in optimal conditions, although a novel task solution may be soft-assembled when conditions vary. Bingham (1988) argued that TSDs are designed so that a single or limited number of control parameters may influence the structure of an action. In the study of overarm throwing, the projectile mass appeared to be the control parameter constraining the dynamics of the action system. A key task for researchers is to identify the sources of information which may act as control parameters to structure TSDs. The perceptual systems seek out relevant information sources to support the goal-directed activity of the performer and remain sensitive to small changes in these variables so that the properties of the TSD remain dynamic. If important information sources momentarily become unavailable, such as when vision becomes occluded, the performer has the flexibility to rely on other control parameter values to construct the TSD.

How task-specific devices enhance performance flexibility: the case of ball catching

Recent research on catching suggests that environmental information sources (e.g. vision of ball, limbs, background structure) may be flexibly assembled into a task-specific device depending on the conditions of performance (e.g. Lacquiniti and Maioli 1989a, 1989b; Montagne and Laurent 1994; Tresilian 1995). This is not a new idea. Todd's (1981) data from a computer-simulation study supported the idea that 'Many important properties of environmental events are multiply specified' (p. 807). Also, Whiting and Savelsbergh (1992) coined the term 'flexible operating system' to denote how human performers could create a TSD from these multi-specified resources in a movement context. Whiting and Savelsbergh (1992) have never defined precisely what is meant by the term 'flexible operating system'. However, a synthesis of the ideas proposed by Todd (1981), Bingham *et al.* (1989) and Tresilian (1995) provides a clue by suggesting that skilled performers can substitute motor patterns and perceptual sources of information in assembling a TSD as informational constraints change. How strong is the evidence for these arguments? In this section we outline data emerging from a number of studies on catching behaviour which support the idea of the substitution of sensory information and motor patterns in TSDs as the performance constraints change.

Adapting task-specific devices to informational constraints

Whiting and Savelsbergh (1992) proposed that visual information is a key ingredient in the composition of a TSD soft-assembled by the performer. To support this idea, they pointed to previous research showing that catchers can perform successfully under various forms of visual constraint. Early qualitative evidence for this argument was provided by Whiting *et al.* (1970: 271) when they observed in their catching study that:

Under restricted (light) conditions the subjects moved the hand forward to the catching point and caught with a snatching movement whereas under the full lights condition there was a tendency to move with the ball as is done in catching in the normal games situation.

However, more quantitative data on the substitution of motor patterns and perceptual information have appeared in the literature on one-handed catching. Below we discuss the findings of three such studies.

One line of empirical evidence on this issue was provided in the study by Lacquiniti and Maioli (1989b) which was originally discussed in Chapter 6. In their study, subjects demonstrated a high level of sensory plasticity and motor flexibility, when they were asked to catch a dropping ball under differing visual informational constraints. In particular, their subjects became more reliant on medium and long latency reflexes (occurring around 80–200 ms after ball–hand contact) in the no-vision conditions to implement the finger grasp. In normal vision they used advance information from ball flight to prepare anticipatory muscle responses. When the dropping ball could be seen, finger flexion was activated prior to the arrival of the ball. In Chapter 6 we discussed the authors' argument that these movements may have been initiated on the basis of time-to-contact information provided by continuous access to sensory inputs, possibly the optic variable tau (see also Savelsbergh *et al.* 1992). Without vision, the authors proposed that subjects learned to rely on an estimate of the mechanical interaction between the ball and catching limb. In the absence of vision, the emergent solution to the catching problem was facilitated by perceptual substitution of proprioceptive information for visual information. Successful catching was supported by proprioceptive and cutaneous information from the wrist extensors and metacarpophalangeal joints on the basis of learning after one trial only in the dark. The ideas of sensory and motor substitution are supported by the 'drastically different' (Lacquiniti and Maioli 1989b: 150) electromyographic (EMG) and kinematic patterns which emerged to solve the same task problem of grasping the dropping ball in different visual conditions.

This strategy of manipulating the informational constraints on action has also been pursued in two other studies of catching. Savelsbergh *et al.* (1993) focused on the quality of the movements involved in one-handed catching under more and less stringent informational constraints. Unlike the Lacquiniti and Maioli (1989b) study, in which vision was either available or denied, the aim of their study was to 'explore the nature and amount of information in the optic array used by subjects required to carry out one-handed catching actions' (p. 148). Small, large and deflating balls were attached to a pendulum to manipulate the retinal expansion pattern based on the work of Savelsbergh *et al.* (1991). Liquid crystal goggles allowed the investigators to occlude parts of ball flight so that vision was denied 0, 100, 200 and 300 ms before the ball contacted the hand.[4]

The main concern in the Savelsbergh *et al.* (1993) paradigm was the ongoing adaptations to their actions by good catchers, as the informational constraints were changed during ball flight. The time of appearance of the maximal closing velocity (TAMCV) of the hand was significantly later for conditions when ball flight information was perceived up until 0 ms before ball–hand contact (TAMCV mean = 64 ms before) compared with when vision was only made available until 300 ms prior to contact (TAMCV mean = 39 ms before). Moreover, movement time (MT) was significantly longer when visual information was made available until 300 ms before hand–ball contact (MT mean = 170 ms) than when it was made available only 0 ms before contact (MT mean = 142 ms). The implication of these findings is that different types of movement strategies were being employed under different informational constraints. In particular, the data suggested a snatching action when visual information was not accessible in the final 300 ms of ball flight. When visual information was provided for the whole of flight, subjects seemed able to assemble a different, smoother, coordinated action. However, like the findings of Lacquiniti and Maioli (1989b), these data are from a semi-dynamic type of interceptive task which only approximated one-handed catching because the spatial position of the hand was fixed before ball release. The data are only suggestive and a detailed kinematic profile of the stability and variability in coordination patterns under spatio–temporal constraints is necessary to check the generality of these findings to a more natural catching task.

Bennett and Davids (1996) attempted to clarify whether emergent goal-directed behaviour was associated with a degree of variability in the kinematic patterns under changing informational constraints. As we noted earlier, the only other evidence on this issue was indirect and anecdotal in the form of self-report measures by Whiting *et al.* (1970). Good catchers in their study reported using a 'snatch type' of action in the dark. In full light, they drew the hand back smoothly to cushion the impact of the ball. However, these reported movement profiles have never been empirically verified in a quantitative analysis. The aim of the investigation by Bennett and Davids (1996) was to check whether subjects could substitute different motor patterns, as visual informational constraints changed, in order to achieve the same task goal.

To achieve this goal, they examined the movement kinematics of skilled catchers (n = 8) with an on-line motion analysis system as they caught balls projected towards them at 10.6 ms^{-1}. The informational constraints on performance were manipulated by requiring subjects to perform one-handed catches in two conditions. These were: in full light conditions; and in UV light conditions to prevent vision of the surrounds and body parts of the subject, leaving only the ball visible. In addition to the number of successful catches, data on the temporal characteristics of movement, such as initiation time (MIT) and movement time (MT), were recorded. Finally, kinematic data on peak velocity of the movement (PV), time to peak velocity (TPV), peak acceleration of the movement (PA) and time to peak acceleration (TPA) were also processed. The results clearly supported the idea of goal-directed movement patterns emerging under task constraints. While no differences in global catching performance were observed in the changing conditions, as predicted in previous work, significant alterations were noted in the movement characteristics. Both MIT and MT changed in the dark conditions (see Table 7.1). Subjects also exhibited a significantly greater PA and PV in the dark. It seems that in the dark, movements were initiated significantly later. In order to successfully achieve the task goal of catching the ball, subjects compensated for the later initiation time by reducing movement time. The reduction in movement time was achieved by an increased peak acceleration and peak velocity of the arm.

These data provide some evidence on the self-assembly of functional TSDs in response to novel conditions in a sport context. The main implication is that the skilled catchers were able to utilise information from multiple modalities to precisely satisfy the stringent spatio–temporal constraints of performance. The data beautifully demonstrate the highly flexible and emergent nature of expert performance. The emergent characteristic of skilled movement behaviour was highlighted by Newell (1996) as the instantaneous adaptability of the performer to variable organismic, task and environmental constraints pressurising the topology of the movement system. The findings from Bennett and Davids (1996) exemplify how, at the highest levels of skilled performance, athletes can precisely refine the coordination and control solution to the movement goal, even in the most dynamic conditions. Newell (1996) showed that the inspira-

Table 7.1 Means and standard deviations of the catching performance, kinematic and movement duration variables under differing informational constraints.

	Condition			
	FL		UVB	
	M	*SD*	*M*	*SD*
Catches	29.75	0.71	29.25	0.89
PA (ms^{-2})	22.7	5	27.3	1
PV (ms^{-1})	2.67	0.33	2.88	0.33
TPA (ms)	194	27	195	34
TPV (ms)	277	25	269	26
MIT (ms)	140	20	157	25
MT (ms)	340	20	320	25
FT (ms)	479	9	477	13

tion for his constraints-led perspective on the soft-assembly of skilled movement solutions was Bernstein's notion of dexterity. Newell's (1996) reminder was that 'skill, or as Bernstein would say, dexterity, is an ability to solve a motor problem – correctly, quickly, rationally, and resourcefully. Dexterity is finding a motor solution for any situation and in any condition' (p. 398). The data from the catching studies demonstrate the enormous value of Bernstein's (1967) insights to dynamical systems accounts of motor behaviour.

SUMMARY AND IMPLICATIONS

From the theoretical and empirical analysis we have presented, it has become clear that the processes of self-organisation in movement systems need not take on a 'mystical quality' as argued by Beek *et al.* (1995). In fact, they can be reasonably well understood through the experimental strategy of manipulating the informational constraints on behaviour and quantitatively observing adaptations in emergent movement patterns. Theoretically, we have reviewed the argument that movement systems have what may be termed a 'stability problem' rather than an 'invariance problem' as proposed in traditional cognitive accounts (Kelso 1997). Ideas from physics have been imported demonstrating that specific forms or patterns adopted by the molecular constituents of a system emerge as a solution to the pressures on its stability (Haken 1983, 1991). Pressures are imposed by key parameters at a macroscopic level.[5] When the parameters exerting pressure on the system change in value, the temporary symmetry adopted by the system could break up. A new solution (i.e. a new state of coordination) to the stability problem emerges. The temporary states of functional stability in the human movement system were identified as coordinative structures. As we observed, not all the system degrees of freedom are integrated into a coordinative structure. Those which remain outside are free to vary under the pressure of various forms of informational constraints in the environment, as actions are contextualised. For movement systems, this level of variability in system behaviour should be viewed positively, given the need for flexible adaptation in sport.

In the two chapters of Section B, we have suggested that a systems perspective is necessary to understand how a movement system coordinates its activity with environmental surfaces, objects and forces. In order to explain the failure of traditional accounts of movement control, Kugler and Turvey (1987) have highlighted Pattee's (1979) argument that animate systems interact with their environments in two modes: psychological and dynamic. Control systems theories have typically emphasised the psychological modes of explanation, and their dependence on the storage of symbolic information, to the detriment of the dynamical mode, with its capacity for energy fluctuation and dissipation within a complex system. In movement systems, Kelso (1994) argued that ' Information in the symbolic sense should be kept to a minimum. Not all the details of a particular process need to be encoded symbolically, symbols act more as a constraint allowing the dynamics to fully express itself' (p. 394). The dynamical systems approach provides a lawful account of coordination and control in motor behaviour illustrating how the performer learns to 'exploit reactive forces and other intrinsic biophysical properties during the control of movement' (Kelso 1994: 394). These properties represent 'the order for free' which is fundamental to biological self-organising systems (see Kauffmann 1993, 1995; Davids *et al.* 1994). Thus, in the search for mechanism, the analogy with automata is inappropriate for the study of human movement behaviour.

The ecological perspective suggests that coordinated motor behaviour represents patterns of neuromuscular activity which arise spontaneously to form 'task-specific devices' in the service of goal-directed behaviour. Experimental observations showed that temporary solutions to coordination problems are soft-assembled from the various informational constraints acting on the movement system. The view of the neuro-skeleto-muscular system as 'purpose-built', in which the perceptual systems, muscles, limbs and body segments have evolved in a integrated manner, facilitates this argument. The relevance of this argument for the design of motor behaviour research programmes is obvious. The behaviour of specific biological movement systems can only be properly understood in the environments which they typically inhabit. The argument for studying timing behaviour in sport with natural actions, therefore, seems insurmountable. One problem in the literature on predictive timing is that there are very few instances in sport when one needs to use the perceptual anticipation strategies which dominate computer simulation studies.[6] Typically, athletes have continuous access to perceptual information sources during sport performance which they use to guide and modify their ongoing behaviour. That is, they rely on on-line prospective control (Bootsma and Peper 1992). In the discussion of perception–action coupling in Chapter 6, we noted that movements create perceptual information for actors to use. Traditional laboratory tasks like that of coincidence anticipation do not allow special-purpose perceptual systems to operate according to their evolutionary design.

Although there has been much effort expended on showing that, in principle, dynamical accounts can explain the emergence and dynamics of states of coordination (e.g. see mathematical modelling in the work of Warren 1990; Bootsma and Peper 1992; Peper *et al.* 1994; Schoner 1994; Kelso and Schoner 1988), there is a need for more work on 'natural' actions in which the perception–action relationship can function normally. The material presented in Chapters 6 and 7 suggests that the sport sciences have an increasingly influential role to play in the development and evaluation of adequate accounts of movement coordination. Clearly, there is a need for more work using real-world behaviours, such as interceptive actions and other sport-related tasks, to further our understanding of the relationship between the perceptual systems and the action systems during goal-directed activity.

A key issue for sport science in future years concerns the relationship between intentionality and the physical laws governing pattern formation in complex, natural systems. The arguments have been eloquently summarised by Goldfield (1995) in stating that 'Action systems are held together by informational boundaries that are created by the intentions of the actor and by perceptual input' (p. 142). Intention functions as an exceptional boundary condition in accounts of human coordination in sport. In other words, it acts as a significant constraint on the emergence of coordination in the human movement system. The sport context, in general, represents an extraordinary boundary condition within the framework of the general physical laws describing the behaviour of biological systems. The argument is that human movement in sport contexts is lawful but that the specific application of these laws is dependent upon extraordinary constraints (i.e. those which may not apply to coordinated behaviour in other living systems). An overarching philosophical question is: Is sport an example of a special adaptation to its environment by the human species?

Finally, one of the most important tasks is to examine the nature of the relationship between intentionality and perceptual information in the development of perception–action coupling in sport. From what we have seen in Chapter 7, skill performance from a dynamical perspective involves the processes of assembling a fuzzy task-specific solution, exploring the free parameters of the assembled attractor and the selection of the most successful solutions to particular movement problems. Specific and non-specific control parameters act to constrain the free parameters of the movement system in sport. But, whilst the initiation and endpoints of a movement may be important for the brain to control, the dynamics of the movement pattern involved in getting from the beginning to the end may be more or less irrelevant (Latash 1996). Variability in movement patterns, seen from the dynamical perspective, has a more positive connotation than when seen from the traditional perspective which informs current teaching/coaching orthodoxy in sport. An important implication to emerge in the preceding theoretical discussion of the movement system as a dynamical system is that the role of the teacher or coach may be less prescriptive than previously believed. In the catching studies discussed earlier in this chapter, we focused on the experimental manipulations of the constraints on subjects revealed changes in coordination patterns. The question is: Is this an important role for teachers/coaches? Skill acquisition, as we shall detail in Chapter 8, involves the movement system engaging in spontaneous activity so that novel, and more appropriate, solutions to specific coordination problems can be assembled and tested. The role of teachers/coaches may be to create the practice conditions in which appropriate coordination patterns emerge under constraint and to direct the search of performers towards these optimal solutions. What evidence is there for the view of 'directed search' in learning? We turn to the question of skill acquisition in the remaining chapters of this book.

Section C

Skill acquisition in sport: Cognitive and dynamical systems perspectives

In this section of the book we explore some of the main implications of theoretical work on visual perception and action for the acquisition of skill in sport contexts. Any scientist interested in applications will instantly recognise the difficulties involved. Conducting studies on movement behaviour with real applications is not an easy task, nor is generalising fundamental research on basic movement principles. Whilst we have examined some reasonable sport-related investigations on anticipation and attention, and their association with visual search strategies in experts and non-experts, the weaknesses in methodologies and the conclusions drawn have been justly criticised (e.g. see McLeod and Jenkins 1991; Williams *et al.* 1992). Furthermore, one of the perceived weaknesses of the ecological approach is that, thus far, there is a paucity of work that has addressed issues related to skill acquisition (e.g. see Handford *et al.* 1997; Summers 1998). Discussions with colleagues around the world suggest that there are two main views on applying empirical research findings from perception and action to sport settings. From one position, there are those who argue: 'Don't even think about it! Come back when we have cracked the problems.' Others propose that ongoing tests of validity, generality and reliability of findings are essential for the development of sound theoretical modelling, otherwise years of empirical effort may have to be redressed. In this book the second position is adopted. We start by comparing the implications for skill acquisition and practice organisation of recent modelling from traditional and ecological perspectives.

8 The acquisition of movement coordination

INTRODUCTION

As a starting point for this chapter, we pick up a recent theme that practitioners in sport and exercise require a conceptual model of human motor performance as a basis for practical activities in skill (re)acquisition (Handford *et al.* 1997). A model of the human performer promotes an informed organisation of learning environments and more effective and efficient use of practice and therapy time. A point raised by our treatments of alternative theoretical perspectives on perception and action in earlier chapters is that the standpoint adopted by practitioners strongly influences their beliefs about the learner, the learning environment and the nature of their interaction. A key question, raised in Chapter 7, and reoccurring in the motor learning literature under different guises, concerns how the perceptual information to support actions changes with learning. In this chapter, we selectively examine some of the main implications from the traditional and ecological theories of perception and action for the acquisition of movement skill in sport contexts.

Traditional and ecological models of the development of skill in perception–action systems

In previous experiments on the role of perception and action in skill acquisition, the hypotheses, methodologies and interpretations of investigators have been directly influenced by the then dominant theoretical approach (Abernethy and Sparrow 1992). From Section A, it should be clear that the information processing approach to perception and action emphasises the development of internal representations for prescribing movement behaviour (for comprehensive reviews, see Schmidt 1982; Carello *et al.* 1984; Kelso 1995; Beek and Meijer 1988; Abernethy and Sparrow 1992; Williams *et al.* 1992; Handford *et al.* 1997). This popular view of skill acquisition has been established by researchers as the traditional model for practitioners working on skill (re)acquisition in sport and exercise settings (see Abernethy, Kippers, Mackinnon, Neal and Hanrahan

1997; Magill 1993; Schmidt 1991; Sharp 1992; Glencross, Whiting and Abernethy 1994).

As we pointed out in Chapter 1, a major concern in traditional theorising is the specific or general nature of the sensorimotor representations developed during skill acquisition. The historical question of specificity vs. generality has recently resurfaced in the context of the perceptual information for skill acquisition. For example, Proteau and colleagues (e.g. Proteau 1992; Proteau and Cournoyer 1990; Proteau, Marteniuk, Girouard and Dugas 1987) recently produced a comprehensive argument in favour of the specificity of information sources to facilitate skill acquisition. Contrary to previous skill acquisition models, the central prediction was that learning does not result in a shift in reliance away from one source of information towards another (e.g. vision to proprioception: see Fleishman and Rich 1963). Neither is it proposed that, with learning, the individual experiences a shift towards an open-loop mode of control from an initial closed-loop mode (e.g. Schmidt 1975, 1982). Rather, the emphasis in the specificity of learning hypothesis is on the continued and increasing importance of visual information with task experience. Established within the traditional information processing framework, this model of skill acquisition advocates the development of an internal, multimodal store of information to facilitate the anticipation and recognition of different sources of feedback during specific movements. In the first part of this chapter, we examine the applicability of the specificity of learning hypothesis to skill acquisition in sport.

In Chapter 7, we introduced the basis of the dynamical systems perspective to movement coordination. We outlined the radical implication of the dynamical systems perspective, that mental states, ideas, perceptions, memories, intentions, plans or programmes may be best conceived as dynamical, self-organising, macroscopic patterns formed by the constant interaction of the molecular components of the neuro-skeleto-muscular system. In the second half of this chapter, we build on these ideas to discuss how the acquisition of movement coordination may be understood from a dynamical systems viewpoint. We discuss the question instigated by Bernstein (1967): How is the complex, seemingly unmanageable, movement system changed into a simpler, 'user-friendly' apparatus for performing actions reliably and flexibly? We examine whether the answer to Bernstein's (1967) problem lies in the discovery and exploitation of physical constraints, such as coordinative structures, to compress the system degrees of freedom into a more manageable device. We ask what are the important informational constraints on the movement system during skill learning.

Skill acquisition in sport: the practical dimension

In previous chapters we highlighted research evidence suggesting that a major feature of skilled performance in sport is the high level of temporal and spatial consistency of movement behaviour despite the severe spatio–temporal constraints in performance contexts. There are many interesting questions raised by these empirical findings. For example, what are the best ways to acquire such high levels of timing precision and movement consistency whilst maintaining the flexibility to adapt to different conditions? What kinds of information need to be available during practice for athletes to successfully learn a movement skill? As we shall discover, these theoretical questions have a practical dimension. Many coaches and teachers share an intuitive belief in the strategy of manipulating access to the sensory information available during learning. In this chapter we hope to verify the theoretical relevance of such a strategy.

For example, because of the well-established finding that skilled games players do not have to watch an approaching ball all the time in order to intercept it, should coaches encourage athletes to search for other sources of environmental information late in flight? Additionally, is there any value in the strategy employed by some athletes in *enhancing* the amount and quality of feedback information available during practice (e.g. through the use of mirrors and other such training aids)? Also, what does research tell us about a practice strategy of *reducing* information content for learners. (For example, does performing movements blindfolded increase sensitivity to proprioceptive information?) The general question is: Should athletes simply be required to 'grind out' thousands of practice trials to develop movement skill, or are there strategies and procedures that teachers and coaches can implement to short circuit the long and arduous process of skill acquisition? These are relevant questions for coaches and athletes and some answers emerge in our ensuing analysis.

DON'T BE AFRAID OF THE DARK: THE SPECIFICITY OF LEARNING HYPOTHESIS

As stated earlier, for some time within the literature on motor learning there has been disagreement regarding the way that skill develops with practice (e.g. see Birch and Lefford 1967; Stubbs 1976). A primary issue centres around the relative contribution of central and afferent mechanisms during movement control. Traditionally, two lines of argument exist. First, some models have suggested that, with increasing task experience, subjects undergo a transference away from visual towards proprioceptive control of the relevant limbs during action (e.g. Fleishman and Rich 1963). The second proposal is that motor control develops from a closed-loop to open-loop mode over time (e.g. Legge 1965; Pew 1966; Schmidt 1988). The argument concerns whether, as skill develops, performers either switch to a reliance on proprioceptive feedback from visual information or experience a reduction in the need for any sensory information to regulate movement.

Proteau (1992) rejected the idea that increased expertise in a task results in a move from closed-loop to open-loop modes of control, as suggested in earlier motor behaviour research (e.g. Pew 1966; Keele 1968; Schmidt 1975, 1982). Rather, he argued that afferent sources of information remain crucial at all levels of performance and do not diminish in importance as learning progresses. Skilled performance is characterised by an increasing dependence on the *specific* sources of information available during learning. According to the specificity of learning hypothesis, as learning progresses, the relevant sources of information related to a movement task are presumed to become even more tightly integrated into a central movement representation. Problems are predicted to occur when performance conditions result in the appearance or disappearance of relevant sources of information which are or are not already part of the multimodal store. It is this aspect of the specificity of learning hypothesis which calls into question the manipulation of information as a pedagogical strategy.

Is vision always necessary for movement control in sport?

Sometimes athletes have to adopt a body orientation which occludes horizontal and vertical peripheral vision of relevant parts of the environment, such as the moving limbs and/or implements during sport. Examples include the javelin throw, the tennis volley, dribbling in soccer or basketball and squatting with heavy weights across the shoulders. In these types of tasks the performer often loses sight of the implement or ball and/or the working limb(s), in attempting to exert maximal force or to orientate the visual system to pick up environmental information such as defensive formations in team games. This effect was qualitatively described in the early investigations of Graybiel, Jokl and Trapp (1955). Skilled javelin throwers, wearing goggles to occlude peripheral visual information, did not throw as far compared with 'normal' vision conditions in which peripheral vision was available. They complained of not being able to see the tip of the javelin in peripheral vision. Additionally, when dribbling in soccer, basketball or hockey, less skilled players depend on visual feedback for correct positioning of the ball and foot/hand/stick.

In sport, a hallmark characteristic of skilled behaviour is the ability to adapt to dynamic environments (Schmidt 1991). As we highlighted in Chapter 6, being able to use whatever information sources are momentarily accessible enhances flexibility and affords greater control for the athlete. This belief has led many coaches to manipulate the quality and quantity of information available during practice so that athletes become attuned to different sources of information. For example, coaches attempt to direct attention to key sources of visual information for learners through the use of practice aids such as mirrors, photographs or video footage of performance. This approach is necessary because novice gymnasts, dancers and ice skaters, for example, are unable to interpret information from limb displacements, velocities or accelerations on the basis of proprioception alone. Additionally, beyond the novice stage, the use of training aids to heighten sensitivity to other non-visual sources of information by occluding vision of moving limbs is common in sport. An example of this approach includes volleyball players practising the block with a blindfold in order to focus attention on concurrent auditory and proprioceptive signals (Handford *et al.* 1997). Other coaches employ a strategy of inhibiting vision of the ball and/or moving limbs with artificial aids, purportedly to develop dribbling skill (see Figure 8.1).

Theoretically, Gibson (1988) argued that such strategies are useful during skill learning for several reasons. In particular, she proposed that a major role of a developing organism is to become more sensitive to the many relevant information sources surrounding it in order to produce a tight fit between its intentions and what the environment offers. As can be seen in Table 8.1, coaches and teachers seem to show an intuitive appreciation of this idea by altering, restricting and enhancing the quality and quantity of the perceptual information surrounding learners.

Surprisingly, the validity of such learning strategies in sport contexts has rarely been investigated. However, it is implicitly addressed by the specificity of learning hypothesis. In fact, the predictions of the specificity of learning model are quite clear on this issue. According to Proteau (1992) 'the withdrawal of one source of information used to develop the intermodal store leaves the individual with an incomplete reference store and causes a decrease in performance' (p. 97). The data to support this contention came from a series of studies with a manual aiming task. Subjects were required to perform an aiming movement with a stylus towards a 0.5 mm target situated directly in front of them (e.g. Proteau *et al.* 1987; Proteau, Marteniuk and Lévesque 1992). Typically, the series of experiments included some conditions in which vision of the moving limb and target was available, in comparison with other conditions when the (illuminated) target only was visible in a dark environment. On other

Table 8.1 Possible reasons for manipulating perceptual information in the environment during skill acquisition in sport.

- To increase sensitivity to other potentially useful sources of information for response organisation such as haptic, proprioceptive and auditory modes.
- As part of the learning process, to become less reliant on central vision for steering, orienting and guiding movements.
- To look away from the ball being dribbled or implement being handled to search for information to aid further response organisation and decision-making.
- In team games, to visually scan defensive patterns or check positions of team-mates for a pass when in possession of the ball.

Figure 8.1 Dribble aids are popular for learners in sports such as basketball or
football. They are worn like a pair of spectacles with a small protruding
surface immediately under each eye to prevent vision of the hand/foot
and ball when dribbling.

occasions, vision of the stylus and/or arm of the subject were also illuminated or eliminated (e.g. Proteau and Cournoyer 1990).

For instance, Proteau *et al.* (1987) examined the effects of amount of practice on the specificity of learning predictions. Practice at the task under 'normal' visual conditions (in which both the moving limb and target were seen) was either moderate (200 trials) or extensive (2,000 trials). Following acquisition, subjects were transferred to a condition in which the target only was visible without performance KR. The results showed that when vision of the responding limb was occluded, performance on the transfer test decreased. Subjects receiving most practice with vision of the limb and target were most vulnerable in the target-only conditions. The authors concluded that:

> the role played by visual information coming from the environment and the ongoing limb was still very important even after extensive practice at the task.
>
> (ibid.: 81)

Other results are, perhaps, more controversial in the light of experience in sport. Proteau, Marteniuk and Lévesque (1992) showed that even when visual information, not present during the acquisition phase, was *added* in the transfer phase, performance decreased. From this perspective there appears to be little empirical support for the strategies of coaches who manipulate information to direct athletes to seek different sources of information such as proprioception or audition. In fact, some of the data suggest that performance could actually be impeded by learners having to cope with the addition or subtraction of relevant sources of visual information during practice. Their studies led Proteau to conclude that:

> These results are in direct contradiction with any proposition suggesting that learning involves progressing from a closed-loop mode of control to an open-loop one, or progressing from a visually to a kinaesthetically guided movement.
>
> (Proteau 1992: 4)

HOW SPECIFIC IS THE SPECIFICITY OF LEARNING HYPOTHESIS?

Above we saw an example of a mismatch between theoretical modelling and experimental work on the one hand, and the intuitive beliefs of practitioners involved in training and coaching at the sharp end of action. So, how much store should we place on the specificity of learning hypothesis? Are coaches and teachers showing an intuitive faith in a method which does not actually work? In the following sections we examine the strengths of the arguments for and against the specificity of learning hypothesis. We will examine findings from some of the relatively few sport-related studies on the predictions of the specificity of learning hypothesis. We refer to the literature on ball catching and other sport tasks in addressing the validity of the main predictions. Within the framework of analysis for this book, we will limit our comments to studies on the role of visual information for movement control in sport.

Support for specificity of learning in sport-related tasks

This section highlights data from some studies on interceptive actions in sport which appear to support the specificity arguments. In Chapter 1, we noted that most previous experiments in the ball catching literature focused on the *amount* of information necessary for catching an approaching ball (e.g. Sharp and Whiting 1974; Whiting *et al.* 1970, 1973; Whiting and Sharp 1974). A typical finding was that performance is better in the full lights conditions compared to conditions where vision of the ball is occluded for parts of its trajectory. Consider, for example, the data from Whiting *et al.* (1970) on a group of skilled catchers who were selected for the study on the basis of having caught 100% of the balls in a pre-test (see Figure 8.2). There is clear evidence of a significant, quasi-linear relationship between the amount of time available to view the ball and catching performance.

Typical success rates of around 45%–50% were found under occluded conditions compared with 91%–100% under normal or close-to-normal visual conditions (e.g. Sharp and Whiting 1974, 1975; Whiting *et al.*

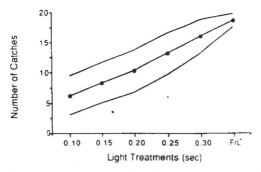

Figure 8.2 Number of catches by a group of skilled catchers as a function of viewing time. Mean data are represented by the circled line, standard deviations by the uncircled outer lines. The data clearly indicate that the longer the ball is viewed in flight the more successful the outcome. (Source: Whiting, H.T.A., Gill, E.B. and Stephenson, J.M. (1970) 'Critical time intervals for taking in flight information in a ball-catching task', *Ergonomics* 13: 265–72.)

1970). In order to successfully catch a ball, prolonged visual information of the ball was necessary even for the most skilful catchers in the experimental programme (see Whiting *et al.* 1973). This is exactly the type of finding predicted by the specificity of learning hypothesis. The data from occluded-vision–full-vision comparisons indicate that learners of interceptive actions should not be encouraged to monitor information from the environment while a ball is approaching. Continuous access to visual information from the ball is necessary to support successful catching behaviour during learning.

The screen paradigm

Further support for this argument appeared in the ball catching literature during the 1980s when researchers became interested in the *nature* of the visual information needed for successful performance. For example, the importance of vision of the catching arm and/or the last 200 ms of ball flight was examined using the 'screen paradigm' (e.g. see Smyth and Marriott 1982; Fischman and Schneider 1985; Diggles, Grabiner and Garhammer 1987; Rosengren, Pick and von Hosten 1988; Davids and Stratford 1989). Proteau (1992) has interpreted some of these data as supporting the predictions of the specificity of learning hypothesis. Initially, Smyth and Marriott (1982) argued that previous studies on ball catching had mainly emphasised the importance of visual information from the ball, and that the role of visual proprioceptive information for accurate limb positioning had been neglected. They studied the catching performance of 24 subjects of unspecified skill level under normal visual (NS) conditions and when vision of the catching hand was occluded by an opaque screen (OS). The OS occluded around 150–200 ms of the final segment of ball flight thus obscuring the fine orientation and grasp phases of ball catching as outlined by the classic analysis of Alderson *et al.* (1973) (see Figure 8.3 a,b).

Subjects received only 20 trials in each condition, but the results indicated that performance was significantly worse in the OS condition than the NS condition. The mean number of successful catches in the NS condition (17.5) suggested that the group were competent catchers under normal visual conditions. In the OS condition, the group mean had dropped to 9.21 catches. Analysis of the catching errors was by type (either an error in accurately positioning the arm in the line of flight or inadequate grasping with the fingers). The data showed more positional (183) than grasp (76) errors in the OS condition.[1] These data were reversed in the NS condition (18 positional vs. 42 grasp errors). In fact, subjects completely failed to contact the ball in 52% of all the position errors in the OS condition, whilst the value was 31% in the NS condition. These data support the predictions of the specificity of learning hypothesis. They show a large decrement in aligning the arm in the ball's flight path when a relevant

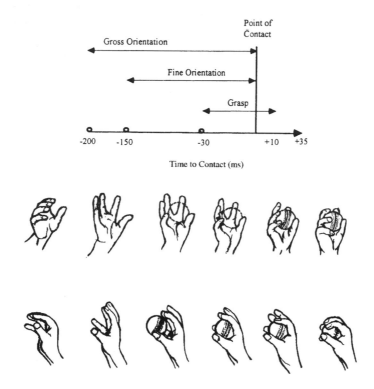

Figure 8.3 The phases of one-handed catching as outlined by the ciné film analysis (300 Hz) of Alderson, Sully and Sully (1974) with four competent games players. Balls were projected at 9 ms⁻¹. Note that negative sign indicates time before contact of the ball with the palm of the hand and positive sign signifies time after contact. (Adapted from Alderson, G.J.K., Sully, D.J. and Sully, H.G. (1974) 'An operational analysis of one-handed catching task using high speed photography', *Journal of Motor Behavior* 6: 217–26.)

source of information, presumably present during the acquisition of catching skill in this group, was omitted (see also Diggles *et al.* 1987).

Things that go bump in the night: the dark paradigm

A related issue, raised by the study of Proteau and Cournoyer (1990), concerns what happens when the information present during the skill acquisition phase is *successively* degraded or upgraded for the learner. For example, a coach might decide to occlude different limb segments of the body during learning to gradually help the athlete to become better attuned to proprioceptive information. Alternatively, there may be a progressive enhancement of the visual information that an athlete can use for learning, such as when a mirror provides vision of obscured limb segments during practice. Proteau and Cournoyer (1990) provided some evidence on the issue of successive degrading of information, using a manual aiming task with a stylus in an experimental design with more than one acquisition (i.e. after 15 and 150 trials) and transfer phase (i.e. early and late in transfer). This strategy, in a fully darkened laboratory with a luminous arm, stylus and target, permitted an analysis of skill acquisition in relation to the successive changes to the visual information present during the acquisition phases (i.e. manipulating information about the arm and stylus), compared with the transfer tests with vision of a target only in the dark. Their findings suggested that performers can rely on a number of different sources of visual information during performance, but that learning is better when there is a close and specific match between the different sources available in acquisition and transfer.

Support for this argument can be found in the ball catching literature in which different sources of visual information were occluded or illuminated in a darkened laboratory. For instance, by illuminating the ball and the wrist and finger positions on a glove for subjects to wear, in addition to six small luminous strips (2.54 cm) acting as an environmental reference frame, Rosengren *et al.* (1988) were able to successively degrade the amount of visual information in transfer. The critical assumption is that their subjects typically learned to catch under normal visual conditions. Subjects performed twelve trials in each of five conditions (full vision; ball only; ball and hand only; ball, hand and frame; and frame and ball only). Performance was significantly better under full light conditions than in any of the other treatments. There was a comparative reduction in performance of almost 50% between the full vision and both the frame conditions. However, the provision of an environmental frame alongside the hand and ball led to greater success than when information from the hand and ball or the ball only was available. It appears that producing a close match between the information available in acquisition and transfer results in successive increments in catching performance. From a practical perspective, the data imply that there is little to be gained from manipulating the information present during learning. Still, a question mark hangs over this conclusion because the study by Rosengren *et al.* (1988) did not actually employ a learning paradigm (i.e. examining the behaviour of a group of complete beginners at the task).

Nevertheless, similar findings were reported by Whiting, Savelsbergh and Faber (1988) and Savelsbergh and Whiting (1988) in their comparisons of one-handed catching when groups of skilled and unskilled performers were transferred to conditions in which environmental information was successively degraded. These studies are interesting in that they present the opportunity to compare the effects of occluding the arm by using a screen in normal lighting, in contrast to darkening the whole environment while illuminating the hand and/or ball. Do we see the same effect emerging from these related studies (the former was a pilot for the latter)?

Broadly speaking, some support emerged for the hypotheses of Proteau and colleagues, in that the greater the extent of the visual degradation of the environment, the greater was the reduction in catching performance. The findings mirrored those of Rosengren *et al.* (1988) showing detrimental effects of successively degrading the quality and quantity of visual information in the environment. For example, skilled catchers in the study by Whiting *et al.* (1988) caught significantly fewer balls in the dark when the ball only was illuminated compared with full-vision conditions. However, when information from the luminous hand was added to the luminous ball condition, the number of catches in the dark and full lights was not significantly different. Therefore, for a skilled catcher operating in a visually-degraded environment seeing one's hand is important, in line with the findings of Smyth and Marriott (1982). However, vision of the hand in the dark is not enough to enhance performance early in learning. For the unskilled group there were clear differences between performance in the full light and dark conditions in which the ball and hand were present. When positional errors were analysed, both skill groups found it difficult to correctly align the hand in the path of the ball in the dark. This finding suggests that the performance of skilled catchers reverts to a novice-like characteristic when vision of the hand and ball is occluded in the dark conditions.

It seems, from these findings, that information about the hand and/or ball alone is not enough to support successful positioning of the arm when no other environmental sources of information are present. Proprioceptive information alone is not adequate to achieve this task. This conclusion may be drawn because more positional errors were recorded in the dark for poor catchers when the hand was not seen (Savelsbergh and Whiting 1988), and for both good and poor catchers when vision of the arm and/or ball was occluded in full light (Whiting *et al.* 1988). The key point in support of the specificity of learning hypothesis is that, for both skilled and unskilled catchers, performance in the dark was always worse than in the normal light with a screen occluding the catching arm and/or ball. Exactly why this is so is unclear at this stage. It is possible that, in the dark, one is occluding more than just the visual information from the arm and ball. Background structure is also missing. There is some evidence to suggest that the quantity and quality of background texture present in the environment aids performance of different types of interceptive actions (e.g. Montagne and Laurent 1994).

Other data from Whiting *et al.* (1988) provide some evidence for the negative effects of the *addition* of visual information in transferring to the dark. Data from a novice group permitted a comparison of catching performance in the dark with and without vision of the hand in conjunction with the ball. An increased number of grasp errors were found in the dark when both hand and ball were visible compared with the ball-only condition. This finding could be viewed as a detrimental effect due to the addition of information in transfer. A reason for this effect, proposed by Whiting *et al.* (1988), was that adding information about the catching hand in the dark 'constitutes a distraction for this category of catchers' (p. 267).

To summarise so far, we have presented evidence from a series of studies by Proteau and colleagues which purport to show a specific relationship between the quantity and quality of visual information available in the skill acquisition phase, and performance in transfer when the information is either withdrawn or added. Data to support this argument from studies of one-handed catching were also discussed. The evidence can be interpreted as an example of transferring subjects from acquisition under full-vision conditions to conditions in which key information sources are occluded. Generally, some of the data may be taken to indicate that information from the ball is important for successful catching as well as visual feedback regarding positioning of the limb in relation to the background environment. In the next section, we look at some problematic data which are difficult to explain from the specificity of learning perspective.

LACK OF SUPPORT IN THE BALL CATCHING LITERATURE FOR SPECIFICITY OF LEARNING

We begin by re-examining the evidence from ball catching studies believed to support the propositions of the specificity of learning argument. Despite Proteau's (1992) argument that these data exhibited 'good support' (p. 76) for the main predictions, analysis of this body of work shows a number of anomalies which contradict the predictions of the specificity of learning hypothesis. The main argument raised is that some of the data question the generality of the specificity of learning hypothesis as it currently stands.

Evidence from occlusion studies

In the ball catching literature there are marked individual differences which contradict the specificity of learning propositions. Although it has been known for some time that watching a ball for longer usually produces better catching performance, it is not a necessity. For example, Whiting *et al.* (1970) looked at skilled catchers attempting to catch a ball when flight was illuminated for six different time periods in different conditions (see Figure 8.2). Recall that these were: 100, 150, 200, 250, 300 and 400 ms (full lights). The performance curve was almost linear but some individuals were capable of catching almost 50% of the balls under the 100 ms and 150 ms treatments. Moreover, it can be seen in Figure 8.2

that the difference in performance between the 300 ms and full lights condition amounted to only around 12%

Other data from Sharp and Whiting (1975) also suggest that vision may be an advantage but not a necessity for controlling movements. Subjects were provided with variable viewing periods (VP) of 80–480 ms. An occluded period (OP) always followed the VP and was varied in length between 200, 240, 280 and 320 ms. The OP included a CNS latency period of 200 ms during which it was believed that no further afferent information could be detected and used in controlling performance. VPs of 240, 280 and 320 ms produced an average catching success rate of 87.1%, and when this was increased to 400, 440 and 480 ms, the mean proportion of successful catches only rose to 87.6%. That is, under restrictive viewing conditions, the finding that performers were able to come within 12–13%, on average, of performance under full lights conditions seems to be robust. This is quite an interesting effect given the previous research suggesting that vision of the catching arm and hand seems necessary for successful performance. How is it that subjects were able to perform so well under restrictive viewing conditions? In the Whiting *et al.* (1970) study only skilled catchers, categorised on a within-task criterion measure, were used. It may be that these skilled performers were able to control the positioning of the arm and fingers during catching by substituting another source of information when visual information was made intermittently unavailable. Proprioception is the obvious candidate. The data contradict the assertion, regarding the informational support for precise limb displacement in space by Proteau (1992), that 'kinesthetic information is not sufficiently accurate to replace visually-based motor control' (p. 71). Quite clearly in some catching studies, the discrepancy between conditions in which vision is and is not available shows that, despite the manipulations, successful performance can be achieved by skilled performers.

Does skill level mediate the relationship between specificity of information during acquisition and performance?

From the results of manual aiming studies which have manipulated visual information from the environment and the limbs of a performer, it was argued that extensive practice does not result in less dependence on visual feedback for successful performance (e.g. Proteau *et al.* 1987; Proteau 1991). How typical is this finding in the sport-related research?

Fischman and Schneider (1985) used groups of softballers and baseballers as experienced catchers in one experiment and a group of non-softballers and non-baseballers as inexperienced catchers in a second experiment. In the first experiment on the skilled catchers with at least five years of competitive experience behind them, they found an effect for the occlusion of the catching limb in the predicted direction. Catching performance in a no-screen condition (NS) was better than performance in an occluded-arm condition (OS). However, the support for the findings of Smyth and Marriott (1982) was rather limited since the total proportion of positional errors in both conditions was only 2.99% of trials. In fact, there were only 5.56% positional errors in the OS condition compared with 38.13% for Smyth and Marriott (1982). Also, the catching success rate of the skilled catchers in the OS condition of Fischman and Schneider's (1985) study was 81.5% which compares favourably with the figure of 87.5% in the NS condition for Smyth and Marriott (1982).

In their second experiment with groups of unskilled catchers, Fischman and Schneider (1985) actually found a Screen x Error Type interaction. With inexperienced catchers it was claimed that occluding the catching arm hindered positioning but had little effect on the grasp. Further data on this issue were reported by Savelsbergh and Whiting (1988) who found no significant differences for the total number of successful catches made, the ability to position the arm, or the timing of the grasp, in a group of skilled catchers with and without vision. That is, on all three dependent variables, a group of poor catchers performed worse than the skilled subjects. The latter were presumably able to substitute other sources of information when vision was not available. Other evidence on this issue was presented by Whiting *et al.* (1988). They found no significant differences between the number of successful catches (out of 30) in normal vision ($\underline{M}$ = 29.29) and in the dark when the ball and hand were illuminated ($\underline{M}$ = 25) for the skilled group only. Moreover, in dark conditions, when either vision of the ball only or ball and hand was provided, there was a mean difference of 2.2 catches in favour of the latter condition for the skilled group. For skilled performers, adding information on the position of the hand benefited performance, clearly contradicting the specificity idea of stored information specific to the task underlying performance. A revealing comparison can be made between the means in the OS condition ($\underline{M}$ = 28), with background structure available and the dark condition ($\underline{M}$ = 25) with only the hand and ball illuminated. It appears that skilled subjects learn not to depend on visual information from the catching arm during practice, as evidenced by the high mean in both visual occlusion conditions. Also, the differences between the means suggests that environmental information, in the form of background structure, seems useful for successfully intercepting the ball. There was also a difference between the unskilled and skilled groups, for positional errors in the OS and the dark conditions when only the hand and ball were illuminated. It has to be said that these particular outcomes do not support the specificity of learning argument. It is not the deprivation of relevant visual information about the arm during catching which is important during learning, but the degradation of environmental information in general.

The results of these experiments give grounds for belief that vision of the catching limb is *helpful* for successful positioning of the arm in skilled catchers, but is *necessary* for unskilled performers. According to the

Table 8.2 Proportional (%) decrease in catching errors as a function of blocks of 20 trials. Note that * denotes a percentage increase since there was a doubling of catching errors between the first block of 20 trials and the second block under normal viewing conditions. (Source: Davids, K. and Stratford, R. (1989) 'Peripheral vision and simple catching: The screen paradigm revisited', *Journal of Sport Sciences* 7: 139–52.)

Trial block	OS	TS	NS
20–40	40	44	107*
40–60	20	35	44
60–80	6	13	27

predictions of Proteau and colleagues (1992) the data from relatively skilled catchers should have shown a greater decrement when compared with the novices in the OS conditions due to the more extensive practice they had undertaken (e.g. five years' experience in organised softball or baseball for Fischman and Schneider (1985)).

In fact, the notion of a greater specificity effect after extensive task practice was also questioned by Davids and Stratford (1989). They found a main effect for visual occlusion of the hand and arm, in that catching success rate in an OS condition was significantly worse than in TS (transparent screen) and NS conditions, but there was a definite improvement with task experience. The percentage decrease in catching errors by trials is illustrated in Table 8.2. Here we have compared the percentage reduction of errors in blocks of 20 trials. The mean number of balls dropped in the first 20 trials of the OS condition was 3.04. By 60–80 trials, the error mean had decreased to 1.37. Both skilled and unskilled catchers were improving catching performance in the OS condition after 60 trials without vision of the catching limb. For the skilled catchers the improvement in catching performance between the first 20 trials and after 80 trials amounted to 81%. Furthermore, the decrease in the total number of catching errors between 60 and 80 trials was fivefold for the skilled performers, whereas for the unskilled group it was threefold. These findings on performance under differing informational constraints present some difficulty for the specificity of learning proponents. One would not expect a gradual improvement in performance under conditions in which vision of the arm was occluded, particularly for the skilled group with a greater amount of previous experience of catching under full vision conditions.

VISION DURING MOTOR CONTROL: A NECESSITY OR AN ADVANTAGE?

Another problem is that some studies using the 'skill-differences' paradigm show little support for the specificity of learning hypothesis. Several studies of sport-related tasks such as tennis volleying (Davids, Palmer and Savelsbergh 1989), controlling a ball with the foot (Barfield and Fischman 1991) and powerlifting (Bennett and Davids 1995), have demonstrated no significant effects of transferring to a no-vision condition from a vision condition, particularly for skilled athletes. One possible reason for the lack of support for the specificity of learning hypothesis in these studies is that the spatio–temporal constraints in these sport tasks are not as restrictive as those found in manual aiming at a target of 0.5 mm. The need for visual regulation of action might be reduced as the task demands become less stringent (see Fischman and Mucci 1989). For example, in their study Davids *et al.* (1989) asked subjects to perform a forehand volley towards designated target areas of a tennis court whilst vision of the racket and arm was occluded with a screen in one condition (see Figure 8.4). In other conditions the arm could be viewed with and without a clear screen.

The results showed that groups of experienced and inexperienced tennis players could successfully perform a volley with appropriate speed and accuracy when vision of the racket and arm was occluded. A particularly difficult set of data from this study for the specificity of learning proponents concerns the findings from the experienced performers. Davids *et al.* (1989) suggested that a likely basis for the lack of a detrimental effect of transferring from a vision to a no-vision condition in the experienced group is an increasing reliance on proprioception as skill develops. That is, focal vision of the ball and peripheral vision of the racket and arm may be used to control movement up to a certain point in the ball's flight path. Thereafter, concurrent proprioceptive information from the arm may have allowed the athlete to get the racket's centre of percussion into suitable contact with the ball.

This argument would support the notion that vision may be best viewed as a considerable advantage that skilled performers have learned not to become dependent upon. They have become attuned to other sources of movement-related information for regulating performance. This explanation was later adopted in studies of soccer players and weightlifters by Barfield and Fischman (1991) and Bennett and Davids (1995) respectively. In fact, Bennett and Davids (1995) found that only highly skilled lifters could perform accurately in a squatting task when vision was occluded by a blindfold, compared with performance under normal visual conditions. Low skilled and intermediate groups of lifters needed visual information for both spatial accuracy and temporal consistency in the biphasic task. The authors argued that, as skill develops, there can be a shift in reliance to proprioceptive control. Observations by Proteau and Cournoyer (1990) on the discrepancy between the Y (main) axis and X (secondary) axis data in several of the manual aiming studies support this argument. They acknowledge that the regulation of behaviour on the secondary axis may have been due to a 'different mechanism than that

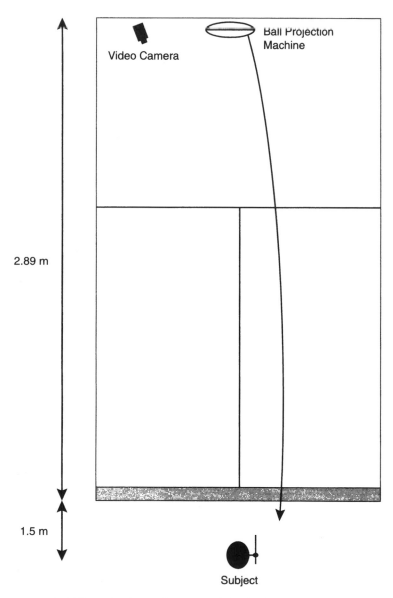

Figure 8.4 The experimental set-up of the study by Davids *et al.* (1989) on the
effects of occluding vision of the arm during an interceptive task in
racket sports. One half of a normal sized, indoor tennis court was
used and the subject's task was to perform volleys to standardised
feeds from a ball projection machine. Volleys were graded according
to criterion variables such as depth, height and angle. (Source: Davids,
K., Palmer, D.R.P. and Savelsbergh, G.J.P. (1989). 'Skill level, peripheral vision and tennis volleying performance', *Journal of Human
Movement Studies* 16: 191–202.)

used to control the ongoing movement on the main axis of the movement, and possibly employing other sources of information' (pp. 823–4). In all of the studies we have discussed so far, a notable feature is that performers were unable to rely on central vision to regulate movement during the entire action. The task constraints (particularly the object velocity in the interceptive tasks and the need for appropriate head orientation with a heavy weight on the shoulders in the powerlifting task) were very different from a manual aiming task in which the target and final trajectory of the hand remain in central vision.

The proposition that information from central vision becomes more important to subjects in an aiming task does not fit the data obtained by Bennett and Davids (1995). That is, according to competition-level performance criteria, skilled powerlifters showed a tendency to position the hips relative to the top surface of the thigh just as well when vision was taken away (see Figure 8.5 a,b).

These outcomes supplement the findings from the studies in the ball catching literature which show that the provision of 'homing in' information on the relative positioning of the hand and ball by central vision is not always necessary, particularly with skilled subjects (e.g. Fischman and Schneider 1985; Davids and Stratford 1989; Whiting *et al.* 1988; Savelsbergh and Whiting 1988).

What conclusions regarding the specificity of learning hypothesis can be drawn from the research just reviewed? We have shown that there are many anomalies in the data from studies specifically designed to test the ideas, as well as issues with the research which provides indirect support for the main predictions. These studies may be interpreted as suggesting that over-reliance on one type of feedback or an integrated store of information sources might not provide the flexibility required in dynamic, highly complex environments.

In the next section, we consider two other more recent lines of evidence to support our interpretation of the current state of the specificity of learning concept. First, alternative arguments proposed by Elliott and colleagues (e.g. Robertson, Collins, Elliott and Starkes 1994; Robertson and Elliott 1996, 1997; Elliott, Zuberec and Milgram 1994), from an information processing point of view, are discussed. A series of manual aiming and sport-related studies support the argument that a specific sensorimotor representation is not developed during learning. Rather, subjects develop and adapt their strategies for processing information during learning, thus allowing them to cope in transfer conditions in which important sources of information are added or taken away. Following this, we explore the relevance of a dynamical systems perspective which models learning as an exploration process in which the search for, and discovery of, emergent task solutions, is emphasised.

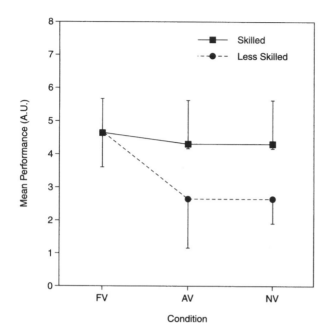

Figure 8.5a Performance of skilled and less skilled powerlifters in occluded and normal visual conditions of both practice and competition.

THE STUDIES OF ELLIOTT AND COLLEAGUES ON THE TRANSFER OF INFORMATION PROCESSING STRATEGIES

Recently, Elliott and co-workers (e.g. Robertson *et al.* 1994; Robertson and Elliott 1996, 1997; Elliott *et al.* 1994) have produced a body of evidence against the idea of the development of a specific sensorimotor representation during skill acquisition. Instead they proposed that the learner develops more general information processing procedures which transfer across many similar circumstances. That is, general skills for managing information are developed. Like us, Elliott and colleagues started by noting the outcomes of previous studies showing that movements can be effectively regulated even when there is an apparent reduction in environmental information. They supported their observations with a series of studies, employing the 'skill differences' paradigm with groups of ball catchers and gymnasts. They examined the prediction that the highly experienced groups of athletes would suffer greater performance decrements when visual information was manipulated.

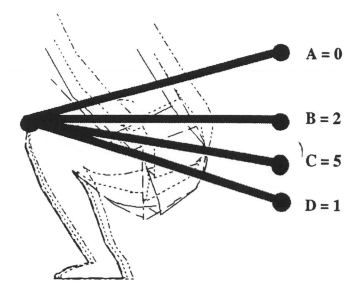

Figure 8.5b The subjects were graded by two experienced lifters according to the
criteria used in competition to judge successful lifts. (Source: Bennett,
S. and Davids, K. (1995) 'The manipulation of vision during the
powerlift squat: Exploring the boundaries of the specificity of learning
hypothesis', *Research Quarterly for Exercise and Sport* 66: 210–18.
Reprinted with permission of AAHPERD.)

For example, in a programme of four experiments, ball catchers were
allowed only intermittent access to visual information about ball flight
using a pair of liquid crystal goggles. Subjects were able to catch between
65% and 75% of balls, provided that the time between visual samples
did not exceed 80 ms (Elliott *et al.* 1994). Even when the time windows
for perceiving ball flight information was as low as 10, 20 or 30 ms,
performance was surprisingly good, compared with full vision conditions
in which the success rate approached 90%.

Further work was carried out on groups of experienced and inexperienced gymnasts performing a beam-walking task (Robertson *et al.* 1994;
Robertson and Elliott 1997). The task was to walk across the balance
beam as quickly as possible in a number of different visual conditions.
As well as no-vision and full-vision conditions, intermittent visual periods
of 80, 100, 120, 170, 250 and 500 ms were provided for the gymnasts.
As in the study by Bennett and Davids (1995) with powerlifters, it was
found that the experienced athletes outperformed (i.e. crossed the beam
faster than) their less experienced counterparts in all visual conditions. In
the no-vision condition, the inexperienced group suffered greater performance decrements than the experienced performers, contradicting the
specificity predictions. A follow-up study by Robertson *et al.* (1994) also

found that the experienced gymnasts crossed the beam just as quickly in the no-vision and full-vision conditions, although the task solution which emerged in each condition was quite different. The number of postural adjustments made in the no-vision conditions increased by around 400%–500%, implying a reversion to proprioceptive movement regulation. A further learning study with a group of novice gymnasts showed that after a few hundred practice trials in no-vision conditions over five days, vision remained an advantage but was no longer a necessity (Robertson and Elliott 1997). Without vision, some performance decrements were suffered as learners adapted to different sources of information to support performance. This was exemplified in the ball catching study. When visual information was degraded slightly through the use of intermittent viewing periods (Elliott *et al.* 1994), there was still a notable effect on catching performance (reduction from 90% to 65%–75%).

In contrast to the view of Proteau and colleagues, Elliott and co-workers argued that their results suggested that learning was a process of developing information processing strategies which could be employed across similar versions of the same type of task. Their explanation was that visual information provides the best basis for movement regulation and that learners try to make use of whatever visual information is available for performing a movement, rather than try to build a specific, symbolic sensorimotor representation. The data from the beam-walking study also led Elliott and colleagues to agree with the fundamental arguments of Proteau and co-workers in rejecting the idea that learning involves progressing from a closed-loop mode to an open-loop mode of movement control. However, the idea proposed by them was that, with learning, vision becomes less of a necessity for performance. Adequate levels of performance are possible when vision is degraded, although the movement pattern for achieving a task goal may be very different under visually degraded conditions.

To summarise, there is a large body of evidence to suggest that Proteau and colleagues were right to reject the idea of a transition from closed- to open-loop modes of control. Athletes become increasingly skilled at finding information to support their actions. However, contrary to the ideas of Proteau and colleagues, these sources of information do not need to remain exactly the same in practice and in novel performance conditions. Moreover, visual information is an advantage for athletes, particularly unskilled performers, not a necessity as implied by the specificity of learning hypothesis. It seems from the literature that there are grounds for believing that skilled performers become adept at substituting perceptual sources of information and motor patterns to achieve task goals. Moreover, coaches who intuitively manipulate the information present during learning are allowing athletes to experience non-visual movement regulation. Indeed, there is some evidence of an increased sensitivity to proprioceptive or auditory information in the appropriate practice environment. There is some agreement with this idea from the studies of

Elliott and colleagues. Their emphasis was on the acquisition of more general processing strategies for dealing with the information present during performance, rather than on the development of internal representations.

We began this chapter by overviewing exemplar data supporting one approach to skill acquisition from the traditional cognitive perspective. A number of discrepancies were noted in the data, and a major issue seemed to concern the generality of the main findings to tasks other than manual aiming. Issues like these have dogged the application of traditional cognitive ideas on motor control to the study of skill acquisition (for a review, see Handford *et al.* 1997). This state of affairs recently led Glencross, Whiting and Abernethy (1994: 33) to decry:

> the lack of advance in the understanding of motor skill acquisition that nearly a quarter of a century of motor control research has provided. Indeed a perusal of major contemporary textbooks on motor control and learning (Magill, 1989; Schmidt, 1988) suggests that we have not progressed much beyond the level of description in the motor learning field so that more important tasks of understanding and explaining the learning process have seldom been addressed.

Elsewhere, it has been argued that the study of natural real-world tasks as found in sport may require a different, more accommodating theoretical paradigm (see Davids, in press). In the next section we link together the ideas in Chapter 7 on dynamical systems theory with the earlier criticisms of representational accounts of skill acquisition (exemplified in this chapter by the specificity of learning hypothesis, but see Davids (in press) for a similar critique of another currently prominent cognitive account – the theory of deliberate practice (e.g. see Ericsson *et al.* 1993)). To achieve this goal, we build on the ideas developed in Chapter 7 to suggest how a constraints-led perspective may be a fruitful avenue for future research in the study of skill acquisition in sport.

CONSTRAINTS AND THE EMERGENCE OF MOVEMENT COORDINATION

Muchisky, Gershkoff-Cole, Cole and Thelen (1996: 123) have argued the merits of the dynamical systems approach for understanding the development of movement skill by proposing that:

> Dynamic systems provides an alternative, time-based, and continuous view of the gains and losses of development, equivalent to other theories in explanatory level, but. ... able to explain more data and generate novel and interesting predictions. Moreover, the theory itself

is content free and may thus be adapted to specific data, levels of analysis, or species.

For these authors, clearly, the fundamental issue is the relatively stable organisation of the movement system and the processes by which it changes over time. Bernstein (1967) himself emphasised the process of change over time in his seminal definition of the emergence of movement coordination. Coordination is viewed as 'the process of mastering redundant degrees of freedom of the moving organ, in other words its conversion to a controllable system' (p. 127). The basic problem is then: How does coordination emerge within and between the many different subsystems of the human motor system?

As we highlighted in Chapter 7, constraints are important influences on the coordination pattern emerging when any biological organism performs important functional, goal-directed activities in its natural habitat. A dynamical perspective on movement coordination contends that internal (e.g. the compositional structure of the body) and external constraints (e.g. visual information) act as pressures on the emergence of patterned relationships between the movement articulators during action.

Newell's (1986) theory of constraints

An influential theory of constraints in the study of movement coordination was proposed by Newell (1986). He argued that the major constraints are organismic, task-related and environmental, and that a triangulated effect guides the organisation of the free variables of the neuromuscular system into an attractor state during the course of goal-directed activity (see Figure 8.6).

Organismic constraints   refer to characteristics of the individual, such as height, weight, muscle-fat ratio, or how genetic predispositions affect the connective strength of synapses between parts of the brain to form cognitive states. Organismic constraints on movement behaviour can be found in the physical, cognitive and emotional subsystems, amongst others. In sport, customary patterns of thought, levels of practice, or defects in the visual system, can constrain the way that individuals approach a movement task. Organismic constraints represent relatively unique resources, such as emotional, anatomical and intellectual characteristics, which can be brought to bear upon a task problem. They may also act as limitations, such as lack of strength or flexibility or anxiety, influencing the intrinsic dynamics of the movement system of the athlete.

In Chapter 7, we made the point that the human system has many important subsystems (e.g. cognitive, emotional, perceptual, action, and so on), all of which develop at different rates during the lifecycle and which are interconnected as a dynamical system. At a specific point

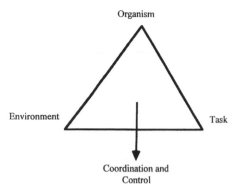

Figure 8.6 The emergence of coordination under constraint. The confluence of constraints on the performer pressure the form of the movement system. Note how such a theoretical emphasis supersedes traditional dichotomies in the motor behaviour literature, such as the phylogenetic/ontogenetic distinction or the nature/nurture controversy. (Adapted from Newell, K.M. (1986) 'Constraints on the development of coordination', in M.G.Wade and H.T.A. Whiting (eds) *Motor Development in Children: Aspects of Coordination and Control*, Dordrecht: Nijhoff.)

in developmental time, one or more of these subsystems can act as an organismic constraint on the global behaviour of the system. That is, in dynamical language, one or more subsystems are capable of acting as the executive by providing the key control parameter(s) to regulate behaviour on specific occasions. This idea was exemplified by Thelen (1983) in a study of the emergence of walking in infants. She argued that walking in infants depends on the development of up to eight subsystems – nearly all of which are related to the processes of perception and action. Due to the intertwined nature of these subsystems of performance, the rate at which one develops may hold back or limit the progression of locomotory skills in infants. This explanation for the onset of infant walking shows clearly why it is theoretically unsophisticated to focus solely on the perceptual processes of the performer in explaining skilled movement behaviour in sport, as traditionally argued (see Chapter 1).

Another example of a behavioural organismic constraint is a coordinative structure assembled to achieve a particular task goal (e.g. a movement pattern formed in the young child to maintain posture while reaching to intercept a ball in space). To exemplify the dynamical basis for understanding physical constraints in the human movement system, the Boolean network provides a useful model for describing both interconnectivity in the nervous subsystem, and the organisation of muscle groups and joints in the behavioural subsystem (see Goldfield 1995; Kauffmann 1993, 1995; Turvey 1990). Boolean networks are characterised by functional 'soft-assembly' (meaning that interconnections between parts are constantly changing and temporary rather than hard wired). Kelso (1995) beautifully captured this dynamic quality, apparent in all subsystems of the human movement system, by likening the neural subsystem to the surface of a river with constantly emerging and disappearing patterns and swirls. In a similar vein, the musculature of the human movement system, like coordinative structures, may be seen as soft-assembled during motor performance.

An important role of physical organismic constraints is to provide some stability within the dynamical movement system. In Chapter 7, we outlined the positive benefits of variability in the motor system. Clearly, there are also instances in sport where an athlete seeks to be as consistent as possible in a relatively static environment. Physical organismic constraints, like coordinative structures or neural networks, are instances of physical organisation emerging in the dynamical movement system to offset the negative effects of variability. Without physical constraints, the sheer potential for interconnectivity between the parts of the human movement system could overwhelm the performer by sending perturbations reverberating through the system to disturb the relative stability required in movement tasks like shooting, archery or darts.

Environmental constraints on goal-directed behaviour are found in the contexts of action. They can be particularised in the form of energy flows such as visual and auditory information surrounding the performer or in the socio-cultural contexts of sport behaviour (Clark 1995). In Chapter 7, we discussed how biological systems differ from physical systems because they are generally non-conservative (i.e. they are open to energy flows and have energy flowing within the system). The energy surrounding biological systems, such as movement systems, can act as an environmental constraint on emerging behaviour. A well developed model of a non-conservative biological system operating under environmental constraint is the nest-building behaviour of a colony of millions of African termites (e.g. see Kugler 1986). The pheromone secretions deposited by the insects bind together loose material into a solid mass for the nest. The building activity of the colony, and the precise form of the nest which emerges, is selected under the constraint of the pheromone.

These findings from biology imply that an important task for perception and action theorists is to develop a better understanding of the dynamics of environmental energy flows to which humans are sensitive. As we have stressed in Chapters 6 and 7, energy flows such as optical information, constrain emergent movement patterns and should not be underplayed by psychologists. Many of the empirical examples from ecological optics in Chapter 6, emphasising the visual regulation of action, may also be understood within the framework of environmental constraints. That is, optic variables, such as tau or vertical optical acceleration, could constrain the free parameters of a coordinative structure as a natural action unfolds in sport. From a dynamical perspective, coordination in a movement system is only completely understood in the midst of the 'stream of action' (Reed 1988). Coordination between parts of a movement system needs an 'environment of forces for its proper expression' (Turvey, Fitch and Tuller 1982: 239). Turvey (1990) argued that attempting to understand movement coordination separately from its environmental context of forces would result in the amplification of the degrees of freedom problem by this reductionist research strategy. Rather, what is needed in a theory of movement coordination is an explicit account of how attenuation of the degrees of freedom occurs as the 'multivariable movement system and its multivariable environment complemented each other, thereby constraining mutually their respective degrees of freedom' (p. 940).

Turvey's (1990) argument may be interpreted as a call for a greater emphasis on the performer–environment relationship as a system than has been evident in cognitive theorising. Turvey's (1990) argument picks up on the ideas of Bernstein (1967: 109) who proposed that

> the secret of coordination lies not only in not wasting superfluous force in extinguishing reactive phenomena but, on the contrary, in employing the latter in such a way as to employ active muscle forces only in the capacity of complementary forces. . . . The mastery of coordination must consist in the ability to give the necessary impulse at the necessary moment.

Task constraints are usually more specific than environmental constraints. They include an individual's goals, the rules of a sport, or an implement or tool to use during an activity. In sport, the achievement of the task goal remains paramount. Energy efficiency and safety considerations can often be subverted as performance circumstances change. Tactics and strategies also fall within this category. The result is that an individual's movement patterns may vary between performances, even in activities requiring a high level of consistency such as a gymnastic vault, a long jump approach run or a golf putt, simply because the tactical goals of the performer act as a powerful, intentional constraint.

An important point to note is that the *interaction* of the main classes of constraints on the neuromuscular system during goal-directed activity results in a search for an optimal state of coordination. The relative uniqueness of emergent movement solutions under constraint was emphasised by Newell (1985) when he argued that 'in principle, these constraints will determine the optimal coordination and control for a given individual in a given activity' (p. 305). Relevant states of coordination emerge from the attempts of the performer to satisfy the main constraints on behaviour. Since coordination is a concomitant fact of the constraints, rather than the result of an *a priori* prescription of commands to solve a motor problem (Kelso 1981), the role of exploration and search under constraint is important in a dynamical systems perspective on skill acquisition. We now turn our attention to the implications of these ideas for the process of skill acquisition in sport.

THE PROCESSES OF SKILL ACQUISITION IN SPORT: A CONSTRAINTS-LED PERSPECTIVE

The primacy of dynamics in a constraints-led perspective

The primacy of dynamical principles in a physical explanation for onto-genetic and phylogenetic development is consonant with Kauffmann's (1993, 1995) use of a similar emphasis to describe the process of evolution in biological systems. He proposed a process of 'search-and-refinement' in evolution in which biological systems are continually probing the boundaries of their stability to select better solutions to the problems of existence. These ideas of 'search plus selection under constraint' equate to the notion of 'chaos plus feedback' espoused by Turvey and Fitzpatrick (1993) for ontogenetic development. In sport, this exploratory process resembles the deterministic randomness which defines a chaotic system. As we shall see below, when we discuss the role of constraints on the emergence of skills, there are boundary limits to the states of coordination which can be attained during learning. The non-linearity of developmental change, in all the different timescales, is often emphasised by large-scale changes resulting from the instantaneous changes in the constraints on the form of a system. These transitions in movement form are followed by the exploration and fine-tuning of the details of adaptations to satisfy specific pressures on system behaviour in performance contexts. As we will argue later in this chapter, these radical views of development and change have some profound implications for coaches, teachers and therapists in sport settings.

Recently, these arguments have been allied to the ideas of Edelman (1992) on learning as selective pattern formation in the brain. A constraints-led perspective of skill acquisition indicates that, once a performer has identified a functional task goal, a process of random exploration results in an appropriate solution to the task, given the instantaneous constraints on the individual. The emergence of a movement pattern which succeeds in achieving a task goal results in the strengthening of neural pathways connecting different parts of the brain by a chemical neuro-transmitter acting as a 'value system'. The temporal synchrony between the successful achievement of a functional task goal and the diffusion of the neurotransmitter by the value system strengthens a pattern of neural connections as a neural attractor state. The successful network pattern is selected because of its functionality and becomes increasingly differentiated as practice progresses, whilst other less successful patterns stimulated during the random search are discarded. From the dynamical perspective the self-organisational process in skill acquisition, at the behavioural and neurophysiological level, can be deemed as 'selection under constraint' (Thelen 1995).

To summarise so far, the primacy of dynamics provides a lawful basis for understanding the development of coordination in a movement system, and signals the inadequacy of traditional distinctions between the acquisition of fundamental and voluntary movement behaviours (Goldfield 1995). Newell (e.g. Newell 1986; Newell and van Emmerik 1990; Newell and McDonald 1991) argued that adopting a constraints-led perspective cuts across this traditional dichotomy in understanding the development of movement skill. A univariate level of causality for change in system behaviour is rejected by a constraints-led perspective, in favour of the 'Simultaneous influence of multiple levels of causality' (Muchisky *et al.* 1996: 124). In dynamical movement systems, constraints can be equally imposed by the transmission of networks of genes predisposing patterns of connectivity in the neural subsystem, or by the pressures of the socio-cultural backgrounds of athletes learning sports skills. Traditional theories of motor control and learning, exemplified in the Specificity of Learning hypothesis, Schema theory or the theory of Deliberate Practice (e.g. Proteau 1992; Schmidt 1982, 1988; Ericsson *et al.* 1993), tell us little of the emergence of coordination. Due to the philosophical influence of control engineering theory, the major constraint in cognitive theories of motor behaviour is a prescriptive, symbolic sensorimotor representation of a movement adapted by feedback loops. In order to redress this perceived imbalance, Newell (1985) proposed a three-stage model of skill acquisition. The stages were: coordination, control and skill. In the following sections, we focus on Newell's (1985) model to discuss some of the implications of a dynamical systems perspective for practitioners in sport and exercise.

The emergence of coordination

Early in learning the athlete attempts to identify and establish basic relationships among the components of the dynamical movement system, assembling the appropriate relative motions among selected body parts in the construction of a goal-directed action. To achieve this aim, the athlete explores the perceptual–motor workspace in which the interaction with important environmental objects, surfaces and forces takes place. This involves a search for the borders of attractor regions in an attempt to reveal the geometric form of the 'landscape of possibilities' as the existing intrinsic dynamics compete with the demands of the task. The continuous collapse and rebuilding of unstable regions is a signature of early learning and often manifests itself in unpredictable and dramatic shifts in movement form (Newell, 1985; Newell *et al.* 1989, Schmidt *et al.* 1992; Scully and Newell 1985). The abruptness of changes depends on the degree of cooperation between the task demands and existing intrinsic dynamics of the movement system. If the intrinsic and required task dynamics cooperate closely, an existing attractor may require reparameterisation (attunement) and the attractor landscape does not alter significantly. This is a physical explanation for the process of positive transfer in skill acquisition. Or, a more continuous adaptation may occur as an existing attractor is destabilised during competition with another local attractor (negative transfer) and is absorbed into the new, more functional, system state. Alternatively, completely new attractor states may be developed, increasing the number of stable states and causing abrupt shifts in movement patterns (Zanone and Kelso 1994). This initial process may be viewed as a search for 'soft' assembly of body segments so that an approximate solution to the movement problem is realised before being fine-tuned.

Despite the inherently interactive nature of constraints, teachers or coaches should be aware that later in the growing child's learning experience 'anatomical constraints are less important and developmental progress may depend more on social or other environmental factors' (Muchisky *et al.* 1996: 124). Therefore, an important coping mechanism for dealing with anatomical constraints is that the coordination stage, particularly in younger athletes, is characterised by the temporary fixation or freezing of the degrees of freedom. The consequence is that movement around key joints tends to be severely limited. This feature of novice performance has been identified in a number of tasks including pistol aiming (Arutyunyan, Gurfinkel and Mirskii 1968, 1969), dart throwing (McDonald, van Emmerik and Newell 1989), handwriting (Newell and van Emmerik 1989), simulated skiing (Vereijken 1991; Vereijken, van Emmerik Whiting and Newell 1992) and soccer kicking (Anderson and Sidaway 1994). The rigid and inflexible functioning of young novices is obvious in the early phases of learning in many highly dynamic movements, such as the tennis serve or volleyball spike, requiring the organisation of multiple degrees of freedom. Newell and McDonald (1994) suggest that the severity of freezing is highly dependent on the task and the individual learner, and can be considered to reflect, at a behavioural level, initial conditions. An additional solution in this early stage may be to coordinate multiple degrees of freedom rigidly into close phase relations in an attempt to reduce control to a smaller number of 'virtual' degrees of freedom (Bernstein 1967). These coordinative structures are tuned to function specifically in each unique situation by environmental information.

Swimming provides an excellent opportunity to understand this idea. The independent actions of arm stroke and leg kick are required to be temporally linked either in-phase (breaststroke and butterfly) or anti-phase (freestyle and backstroke). Concomitantly, the arm stroke and leg kick are coupled together into additional phase relations, thereby further reducing the control problem. In support of this notion, van Ingen Schenau (1989) demonstrated the unique action of bi-articular muscles in the activities of jumping and cycling. Evidence was presented suggesting that these structures naturally act to impose anatomical constraints which optimise coordination of the segments in these movements. These examples show how a proper relation among the many degrees of freedom may be achieved through self-organisation governed by simple physical principles (Turvey 1990). The assembly of these temporary coordinative structures, leaving only a limited number of degrees of freedom unconstrained by muscle linkages, is the acquisition of 'coordination'.

Constraints and the acquisition of coordination: the learner as a novelist

What is proposed here is in sharp contrast to traditional approaches to early learning which emphasise verbalisation, active cognition and a dependency on feedback from external agents such as a coach. The proposition is that the learner should be free to explore motor system degrees of freedom rather than being shackled by what may be the artificial constraints imposed by a textbook approach (see Handford *et al.* 1997). The role of the coach/teacher in this context is to ensure the correct 'discovery environment' through the manipulation of task and environmental constraints in an attempt to guide exploration of the dynamics of the perceptuo–motor workspace. A practical implication of the 'search plus selection under constraint' theoretical ideas discussed in Chapter 7, and followed up in this chapter, is that, in a sense, coaching/teaching is about creating pressure for changes in the form of the dynamical movement system. If one uses the metaphor of a 'story' to conceptualise the skill acquisition processes in sport, then the end-state form (the skill) to be acquired by each individual is not prescribed at the outset, but is painstakingly and creatively written ongoingly. In such a 'self-reading and self-writing' dynamical system (Kugler 1986), practitioners have a major say in the development of the individual's unique storyline by creating localised pressures (as constraints) so that functional global system behaviour emerges from practice time. The implication is that there is a need for significant research programmes in the sport and exercise sciences to gain a broad understanding of how constraints shape the individual 'stories' of skill acquisition in different sport contexts.

What we are suggesting is that the set of possible movement solutions for a learner's task problem can be limited by the dimensions of the perceptuo–motor workspace imposed by the coach. Directed coaching may be defined as a very narrow search process, whereas, at the other extreme, random unguided discovery learning theoretically encompasses the whole workspace. Highly directed coaching does not allow learners to learn how to search. Completely random searching of the workspace would be time-consuming and possibly unsafe, and could lead to losses of confidence and motivation in learners. An important role of the coach, from this theoretical position, would be to support the search process by manipulating constraints so that exploratory activity occurs over an optimal area of the perceptuo–motor workspace.

If the boundaries of the perceptuo–motor workspace are too tightly constrained, alternative regions of stability in the landscape may be difficult to discover. Similarly, if the limits are too broad then multiple regions of stability may continually emerge and disappear as the learner searches indefinitely. The skill of the coach at this stage is to constrain the workspace appropriately, based on a knowledge of the parameters which influence successful coordination. The suggestion is that the interaction between coach and performer is minimised in the very early stages of learning so that the true dynamics (important controlling variables) of the movement task are revealed through discovery. In a soundbite, the key point is: Let the learner begin to write his or her own story. Direct coach intervention at this stage may well assist in the short-term assembly of coordinative structures as temporary solutions, but the ongoing process of establishing control may be delayed as a result of inappropriate (i.e. textbook and non-individualised) coordinations early on. In fact, the adoption of generalised 'textbook' approaches can be likened to the short-term solution of 'plagiarism' by the learner in our analogy of writing a story. In other words, the learner may come to rely on these 'neatly packaged' temporary solutions for immediate performance effects in specific environments. But, the unique relationships between movement subsystems, which influence long-term performance transfer to a variety of novel situations, will not be established early in learning. Recently, there has been increasing recognition of this type of strategy in teaching and coaching (e.g. see Balan and Davis 1993; Davis 1988). For example, Davids and Handford (1994) have advocated a 'hands-off' approach to coaching based on the idea of manipulating constraints. Thorpe (1996) has also reminded coaches that they must learn when to remain 'silent', and has warned against 'coach dependency' brought about by the over-reliance of athletes on coaches for solutions to performance problems. The message seems to be 'Don't let the coach write the story for you!'.

Some empirical support for these arguments is offered by an investigation exploring the resistance to stress of groups of learners on a golf-putting task (Masters 1992). Evidence was presented showing that a skill acquired in a discovery learning type environment was less likely to fail under pressure than one acquired through explicit knowledge. An ecological interpretation of these findings would suggest that the most stable dynamics of the skill were revealed through discovery learning. These dynamics were most resistant to the perturbing forces enforced by the organismic constraint of anxiety. The dynamical perspective on skill acquisition may also have profound implications for the prevention of long-term accu-mulative injuries in sport. These injuries are thought to result from early attempts to acquire techniques which are often anatomically inappropriate for particular individuals. The current debate amongst fast-bowling tech-nicians in cricket provides a clear example in sport (e.g. see Elliott, Hardcastle, Burnett and Foster 1992).

The emergence of control

Once the relationships between body parts and the coordination of action with environmental objects and surfaces have been established, the performer is faced with the challenge of discovering the laws governing their control. More specifically, the search is for a tighter coupling between body segment relations, previously assembled, and the forces generating goal-directed movement. This coupling now requires the performer to become perceptually tuned to the consequences of different combinations of forces (control variables) in order to channel the search of the move-ment dynamics (Fowler and Turvey 1978). Exploration of the workspace has perceptual consequences associated with it, which are thought to act directly to tune the movement system until the desired kinematic outcomes are attained and the set of task constraints are satisfied (see Fitch, Tuller and Turvey 1982). From an ecological view, perceptual search is neces-sary for picking up the informational invariants which specify affordances for actions. In the control stage, learners become attuned to higher order derivatives of movement displacement information, such as velocity and acceleration (see Cox 1991; Fuchs 1962; Schmid 1987).

Exploration and search in the control stage is facilitated if the coordi-native structures assembled in early learning are progressively released and allowed to reform into different configurations. This process is charac-terised by the unfreezing of movement system degrees of freedom so that they become more 'open' to reconstraining by a variable of the performer–environment system. Perceptual information generated by movement in the environment becomes critical as the performer attempts to control the newly released degrees of freedom. As learners becomes increasingly tuned to the perceptual consequences of particular movements, and their rela-tionship with stable regions of attraction, greater control over degrees of freedom is temporarily surrendered to certain variables specified by envi-ronmental information (e.g. optic variables). In this way, the various constraints formulate a coordinative structure which is task-specific and directly governed by perceptual information. Hence perception and action are interfaced. Control over movement using only a small number of envi-ronmentally specified parameters is not capacity-limited and so resolves the storage and novelty problems haunting more traditional approaches.

There is some evidence to suggest that the progressive increase in the number of independently controlled degrees of freedom exhibits directional trends. Studies on handwriting, dart throwing and soccer kicking reported that, as learning progressed, there appeared to be a shift in control from proximal to distal segments (for a review, see Handford *et al.* 1997). This finding may be considered to indicate control exerted at the level of task space rather than at the level of body space. In other words, as control develops, exploration of the performer–task dynamics is vital for success in goal-directed behaviour (Latash 1993). Bernstein (1967) offers a complementary explanation which assumes that there is some biomechanical advantage to be gained from such a directional change in coordination. Indeed, biomechanical analyses have shown that actions such as jumping and throwing, which require maximum velocity of the limb extremities, necessarily dictate that body segments with relatively large moments of inertia move first with low inertial segments following later, at higher angular velocities (van Ingen Schenau 1989).

It is likely that such a change of control strategy in favour of external parameters is not permanent and may regress, given situations where the motor problem becomes acute due to unreliable environmental information (e.g. poor lighting conditions during a cricket or tennis match, a slippery running surface, or the erratic flight path of a floating volleyball serve). Fluctuations in attractors for emotional states such as anxiety and arousal have also been shown to lead to diminished accuracy of information detection (Bootsma *et al.* 1992). Weinberg and Hunt (1976) also reported a reduction of sequential muscle activity in favour of an energy-expensive, inhibitive co-contraction of agonists and antagonists in highly anxious throwers.

Increases in muscle tension may be interpreted as efforts to refreeze degrees of freedom and to reorganise coordinative structures in an attempt to regain control. In a later study, Beuter and Duda (1985) considered the stepping performance of young males under low and high arousal conditions. Examination of selected kinematic characteristics revealed striking inter- and intra-individual differences in the patterns of ankle coordination between arousal conditions, while hip and knee joint dynamics remained relatively stable. It was concluded that the proximal (ankle) joint appears to be subjected to a different set of dynamical rules which are apparently influenced by arousal, thus supporting the regression hypothesis. Evidence that coordinative structures can be successfully reorganised is provided in a study of the rehabilitation of patients following stroke (Ada, O'Dwyer and Neilson 1993). Improvements in standing ability were reflected in transformations from irregular multiple peak to smooth single peak angular velocity profiles of the knee and hip after only 29 days of movement rehabilitation.

The interpretation offered here differs considerably from the traditional approach which proposes that an increase in the accuracy, consistency and efficiency of actions is a result of a more elaborate and refined prescription for movement. In the dynamical approach, the role of the coach is to encourage the performer to become aware of the perceptual conse-quences (visual, kinaesthetic and auditory) of movement without artificially constraining the degrees of freedom. To be effective, coaches/teachers should seek an understanding of the links between actions and the pres-surising perceptual variables in the sport environment. They should consider how to access these relationships through appropriate manipu-lation of constraints and practice design. That is, in order to assist in the releasing and reconfiguration process the coach must provide the performer with opportunities to further explore the perceptuo–motor workspace. This will not happen if the performer is suppressed into strict compliance with an explicitly defined movement pattern which does not emerge through discovery (Shaw and Alley 1985).

Given the influential role of information relating to movement kinematics/kinetics, it is apparent that augmented feedback concerning time displacement, joint angles, limb velocity and acceleration will be likely to benefit learners at this stage. This expectation of a dynamical systems account of skill acquisition has recently led to a resurgence of research interest in the area pioneered by Newell and colleagues (e.g. Newell and Walter 1981; Newell *et al.* 1985). However, several limita-tions, including the use of single-degree-of-freedom movements and an absence of any transfer or retention tests, restrict the application of the original findings to sport skill acquisition (see also Schmidt and Young 1991). More recently, a number of investigations using multi-degree-of-freedom, sport-related activities have also demonstrated an enhanced performance effect following feedback of this nature (Ayalon and Ben-Sira 1987; Broker, Gregor and Schmidt 1993; Hatze 1976; Mendoza and Scholhorn 1993; Sanderson and Cavanagh 1990). Unfortunately, the majority of these studies were aimed at performance optimisation rather than feedback per se and are consequently limited by similar design char-acteristics. The potential of this avenue of investigation is unclear at this time. However, findings by Vereijken *et al.* (1992) suggest that it may be more beneficial for the coach/researcher to seek a source of feedback infor-mation which more closely reflects the essential relationship between performer, environment and task.

The optimisation of skilled behaviour

When the laws which govern control have been discovered, the problem for the learner is to assign optimal values to the controlled variables. The use of the term 'optimal' by Newell (1985) connotes the idea that energy efficiency is a significant determinant of an emergent movement pattern and is 'an a priori organizing principle of coordination and control' (p. 304). 'Skill', or optimal organisation, arises when the components of the control structure are quantitatively scaled so that performers can utilise the reactive forces of the limbs for movement. Passive, inertial and mechanical properties of limb movements are then fully exploited. Coordinative structures become extremely stable and additional degrees of freedom are released increasing the number of controllable parameters and resulting in more functional variability and fluid movement (Bernstein 1967). For some movements, this increased fluency may allow performers to take advantage of elastic energy released by the tendons during muscle stretch–shortening cycles not previously stimulated. Thus, the acceleration phase of a limb following a change in direction may be increased as a result of reflex involvement, important for biphasic movements. For example, if the performer separates the two phases in the transition from the back swing to the down swing in a golf chip, there is no contribution to the acceleration of the down swing from the stretch reflex. However, smooth transition will bring these forces into play (see Schneider *et al.* 1989). With optimisation the movement now becomes highly energy efficient. Hence, intuitive comments, often based on subjective observation, that describe the execution of actions by elite athletes as appearing 'effortless' may be close to the mark. Additional important characteristics at the optimal level of skilled performance include instantaneous adaptations to minute environmental changes and the capacity to use information to predict future events (Newell 1996). These features were amply demonstrated in Chapter 7 by the data of Bennett and Davids (1996) on expert one-handed catching as informational constraints were varied.

In summary, Newell's (1985) model represents an exciting attempt to redefine the stages of skill acquisition based on dynamical systems principles and emphasising the constraints on the emergence of system behaviour. However, it needs much more experimental work to exemplify how the stages operate in sport-related behaviours. In this respect, the task for sport scientists is huge. In the next section we examine some initial data from two studies on the development of skill in young children which exemplify how constraints can affect the emergence of coordination patterns. These studies may be seen as examples of how different types of constraint influence the acquisition of skill in a natural sport task: namely, one-handed catching.

IMPLICATIONS OF A CONSTRAINTS-LED PERSPECTIVE FOR PRACTICE

Subsystem development as a rate-limiter on skill acquisition: the example of postural control and catching

When someone is learning to catch, stable attractor states emerge from the constraints imposed by the interaction of task, environmental and organismic components. Riccio (1993) suggested that the organismic goals and system components become nested and 'The goal-directed behaviour of the system constrains the way in which the goals of a component subsystem can be achieved, and vice versa' (p. 349). In the case of one-handed catching, a bipedal stance is usually required and the action is nested upon, and constrained by, the goal of maintaining upright posture. Raising the arm to align it in the flight path of the oncoming ball results in compensatory activation of lower leg muscles to stabilise posture, introducing potentially perturbing reactive forces into the 'nested' perception–action system for the interception task.

The question posed by Davids, Bennett, Court, Tayler and Button (1997) was: How do children learn to cope with such a stability problem during one-handed catching in an upright position? The early stages of learning involve assembling the system degrees of freedom required for the task into a functional unit or coordinative structure (Bernstein 1967). In the case of catching, the postural subsystem provides a stable foundation for the very sensitive grasp phase of the catching action. In early learning, the system's degrees of freedom are frozen to enhance stability. This can be seen in the coordination pattern described by the rather rigid and tightly coupled synchrony of the shoulder and elbow joints in the poor catcher who fails to intercept the ball (Figure 8.7a). This pattern emerges as compensation for the large amount of instability in the postural subsystem, exemplified in the dysfunctional levels of variability in angular accelerations of the knee and hip.

During skill acquisition, flexibility in the coordination of the shoulder and elbow joints emerges as the child searches the task. In our good catcher, the postural and reaching components of the system have become more cooperative. Now there is greater stability in the postural system which permits the reaching and grasping subsystem to explore functional levels of variability in intercepting the ball. From a Bernsteinian perspective, the nested subsystem's degrees of freedom have become unfrozen as the shoulder and elbow work independently to transport the hand to the right place at the right time (Figure 8.7b).

The hypothesis that the postural control subsystem could act as a rate-limiter for the development of catching skill in children aged 9–10 years was tested in a follow-up study by Davids *et al.* (1997). Groups of skilled and unskilled catchers were required to perform one-handed catches whilst standing in one condition and sitting down in another. The experimental logic was to freeze the postural subsystem's degrees of freedom, so that its rate-limiting constraints on catching performance were nullified. The data in Table 8.3 show clearly that with good catchers there were only marginal changes in performance between the conditions, indicating that postural control was not inhibiting catching performance. It is worth highlighting, however, that the minute, functional adaptations in posture seen immediately prior to the catch in Figure 8.7b were not permitted in the sitting condition, resulting in a decrement in performance. For the unskilled group, there are clearly some significant benefits in not having to contend with the perturbing forces of the postural support subsystem.

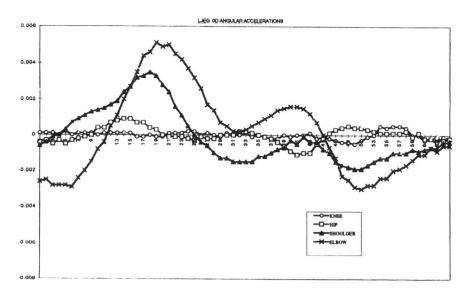

Figure 8.7a How a lack of movement variability can be dysfunctional: typical data on the angular accelerations of upper and lower body segments during one-handed catching performance from an unskilled catcher. Note the higher level of variability in the postural subsystem (as exemplified by the angular accelerations of the hip and knee joints), compared with the skilled catcher (Figure 8.7b). To compensate against the perturbations, the shoulder and elbow joints are rigidly coupled together.

In summary, approaching practice from a dynamical perspective offers a structure in which to define the limits and properties of the perceptuo–motor workspace with sound conceptualisation of the information being made available to the performer. From this perspective, practice is a continuous search for movement solutions in a perceptuo–motor workspace which is generated by the combined constraints of the learner, the environment and the task (Newell 1986; McDonald *et al.* 1995). The search

Table 8.3 Percentage success rate in one-handed catching in groups of good and poor catchers in conditions where the rate-limiting effects of the postural subsystem were present and negated. (Source: Davids, K., Bennett, S.J., Handford, C.H., Jolley, L. and Beak, S. (1997) 'Acquiring coordination in interceptive actions: An ecological approach', in R. Lidor and M. Bar-Eli (eds) *Proceedings of IXth World Congress in Sport Psychology*, Netanya, Israel: ISSP.)

	Standing	Sitting
Good catchers	75%	67%
(>50% Success)	+/–14.5%	+/–19%
Poor Catchers	18%	36.5%
(<50% Success)	+/–15%	+/–29%

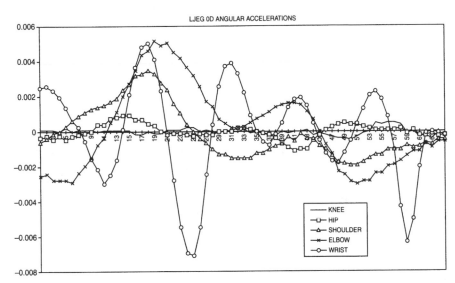

Figure 8.7b Typical data from a skilled catcher of the same age, showing how movement variability can be functional. The postural subsystem is inducing less perturbing forces into the action, with the knee and hip generally moving in-phase. In contrast, the shoulder, elbow and wrist joints are operating relatively independently, although they all come together for the point of hand–ball contact. Note that there is only a small lag between the acceleration traces of the elbow and shoulder joints for the movement duration. (Source: Davids, K., Bennett, S.J., Handford, C.H., Jolley, L. and Beak, S. (1997) 'Acquiring coordination in interceptive actions: An ecological approach', in R. Lidor and M. Bar-Eli (eds) *Proceedings of IXth World Congress in Sport Psychology*, Netanya, Israel: ISSP.)

process involves the adaptation and stabilisation of movement solutions from trial to trial without identical performance, a type of 'repetition without repetition' (Bernstein 1967; Vereijken and Whiting 1990). A significant feature which emerges from this approach is that the nature of the constraints which interact to form the movement problem dictate that each search, and eventually each solution, is individualised.

Data supporting the influence of constraints are apparent in the areas of motor development and motor control (e.g. see Kelso and Schoner 1988; for a review, see Thelen and Smith 1994). However, there have been very few attempts to manipulate the task constraints in sport contexts to examine the emergence of different patterns of coordination. In the sections below we discuss two further studies which can shed some light on how manipulating task constraints could affect the acquisition of skill in sport. First, we examine some recent data from a series of studies which have examined the visual behaviour of expert and novice defensive players in soccer during simulated attacking sequences of play (Williams *et al.*

1994; Williams and Davids 1998b). Second, we take a look at a stronger line of evidence from a study, involving an actual learning paradigm, of one-catching behaviour in children.

Self-organisation in movement systems: the example of constraints and the emergence of eye movement behaviour

Visual search strategies in sport were discussed in great detail in Chapter 5 and, traditionally, have been invoked as support for the internalised knowledge structures which high level athletes develop as a function of their extensive experiences in a specific sport context. As is clear in Chapter 5, these eye movement patterns are usually assumed to underlie the decision-making processes in sport performers and, as a reflection of superior knowledge, are typically found to differ between groups of more and less experienced athletes (see also Williams *et al.* 1993). The data we are about to discuss emerged as a pattern from a series of studies on skill-based differences in perception and action in soccer. Groups of inexperienced and experienced soccer defenders were asked to move in response to near life-size, filmed simulations of attacking patterns of play in 11 vs. 11, 3 vs. 3 and 1 vs. 1 sequences. Table 8.4 summarises data from three different simulation conditions (Williams *et al.* 1994; Williams and Davids 1998b).

The small-sided simulations represent the typical micro-states of soccer. As a consequence, 3 vs. 3 and 1 vs. 1 practices usually dominate in soccer coaching and training régimes (e.g. see Hughes 1994). The initial question of interest concerned the differences in visual search patterns between experienced and inexperienced defenders, although the research also highlighted some important intra-group differences across the different task conditions. In particular, it is worth noting how the values for search parameters change across conditions regardless of the influence of experience. In the full-sided context, the extensive number of perceptual information sources, located disparately across a larger area of the field, constrains the experienced observer to utilise more frequent fixations than in the micro-state contexts, typical of counter-attacking moves (here exemplified by 3 vs. 3 and 1 vs. 1 simulations). The task constraints, as expressed by the number of perceptual information sources, are less severe in the 3 vs. 3 and 1 vs. 1 conditions than in the 11 vs. 11 context and this results in a greater emphasis on the role of peripheral vision. Interestingly, fewer fixations of longer duration were noted for both groups in the 1 vs. 1 simulations than both the other simulations. The 3 vs. 3 and 11 vs. 11 offensive simulations both contained other players who were continuously adjusting their positions in order to present or prevent a passing option for the ballpasser. In the 1 vs. 1 conditions players needed information only from important limb segments of the dribbler. Clearly, there is not a simple linear relationship between the number of players

Table 8.4 The parameters of visual search in experienced and inexperienced soccer players. Note: The number of players involved in the simulations represents one of the constraints on the eye movement behaviour of the players in these defensive simulations.

Simulations	Skill Level	Mean No. Fixations	Mean Duration (ms)
1 vs 1	Experienced	2.6	1104.6
1 vs 1	Inexperienced	1.9	1555
3 vs 3	Experienced	4.17	865.83
3 vs 3	Inexperienced	4.02	973.5
11 vs 11	Experienced	10.3	933.94
11 vs 11	Inexperienced	8.72	1163.16

present in the simulation and the duration and number of fixations in the search pattern.

How are these data to be interpreted? From a dynamical perspective, the many components of the visual system define it as a complex system with redundant degrees of freedom. It may be viewed as having multiple states of stability. For example, information can be picked up through foveal vision and peripheral and parafoveal areas of the retina using saccades, fixations and smooth pursuit tracking techniques (see Chapter 5). Historically, there have been few attempts to examine the emergence of coordination in the visual system as a function of the constraints on the performer. As we saw in Chapter 5, cognitive accounts of perceptual skill in sport suggest that perceptual skill is dependent on intermediary knowledge structures which control the eye movement patterns necessary for picking up important cues from the environment. Such an explanation is clearly not plausible to explain how the search patterns for the inexperienced group of defenders (averaging only 65 matches over the previous four years) mirrored the changes of their more experienced counterparts (averaging more than 750 matches over 13 years). It is inconceivable that search patterns could be selected on the basis of a representation for the inexperienced players. Since the inexperienced group had not been taught to vary search pattern parameters, the logical conclusion is that these patterns emerged from the many interacting components of the visual system as a function of the differing task constraints.

But could the eye movements of the inexperienced players be stimulus-led rather than dependent on a prescriptive device? Data rejecting traditional cognitive ideas of visual search being stimulus-driven in inexperienced observers has been reported by Harris, Hainline, Abramov, Lemerise and Camenzuli (1988). They presented 149 infants (age range 14–246 days) and 11 adult students (age unspecified) with visual stimuli varying along many different characteristic dimensions. Their aim was to test the prevailing assumption in the literature that the key search characteristic of length of fixation duration was associated with stimulus complexity. The stimuli were varied in texture, structure, complexity and along a static–dynamic scale. The fixation distributions were similar among subjects, regardless of age and stimulus conditions. Their findings led the authors to exclude both a stimulus-driven explanation and the mediating role of higher mental processes. They concluded that the 'duration of a fixation is not set up ahead of time, but rather during the fixation. A given amount of processing time is not allocated for a fixation (by either stimulus features or some supervisory agent)' (p. 427). Harris *et al.* (1988) argued that during visual search a fixation duration is 'determined, at least in part, by nonfoveal retinal stimulation' (p. 420).

This observation concurs well with the data in Table 8.4. The fewest between-group differences in fixation duration existed in the 3 vs. 3 simulations suggesting that peripheral vision may have had a constraining influence on search parameters. The nature of perceptual information varied from offensive patterns in 3 vs. 3 and 11 vs. 11 simulations to motion invariants from key muscle–joint complexes (particularly the hip region) in the 1 vs. 1 conditions. It is plausible that foveal vision tended to dominate in the 11 vs. 11 and 1 vs. 1 tasks for different reasons. In the former context the simulation was 'awash' with movement and change of positions – too much important information to be partially processed by peripheral vision. In the 1 vs. 1 simulations observers needed highly precise information from motion invariants provided by changes to key joint angles to specify information on direction, velocity and force of locomotion in dribbling. Since the hip region appeared to provide the most sensitive information on intended direction in dribbling in the 1 vs. 1 simulations, the findings of fewer fixations and less frequent alternations of fixations than in the 3 on 3 conditions is to be expected. This finding fits well with current understanding of the role of lower limb joints in postural regulation. For example, Horak and Nashner (1986) found that hip mobilisation was more functional than regulation of ankle joints when rapid readjustments of the centre of gravity was required. In 3 vs. 3 and 11 vs. 11 simulations, the observer needed to pick up information from the dribbler on velocity and direction whilst simultaneously monitoring positional changes of players in the periphery. A different search strategy emerged from both groups, characterised by an increased number of fixations of shorter duration with more frequent alternations between perceptual sources.

Inter-group differences in the values for the different search parameters may be taken as evidence for the tighter coupling between the visual search pattern and the task constraints for the experienced performers (see Chapter 6 on perception–action coupling). For example, note that there is actually very little difference in fixation durations between 11 vs. 11 and 3 vs. 3 contexts for the experienced group, perhaps reflecting stable organisation in the visual system at the level of what Beek (1989b) calls 'the deep structure'.

In summary, the visual search pattern used in team games may be viewed as behaviour emerging due to the interaction between the task constraints and the many components of the visual system. More empirical work is needed to check whether visual search patterns are best understood as co-ordinated movement patterns which are self-organising and constrained by the nature and location of perceptual information sources, particularly those in the parafoveal and peripheral segments of the viewing scene (Harris *et al.* 1988). Whilst these data, using an expert–novice paradigm, provide a somewhat tentative body of evidence for self-organisation in the visual system under constraint, as we stated earlier, a stronger and more direct test would involve a study with a learning paradigm. Evidence for the role of constraints in the acquisition of sports skills is very rare. One amenable avenue for research on the manipulation of informational constraints during learning involves what Eleanor Gibson (1988) termed 'directed search'. She argued that the main objective of development is to discover the information which superimposes what the environment affords on the behavioural goals of the actor. Gibson's (1988) notion of directing the search of learners to find the perceptual invariants to support action is harmonious with the idea of manipulating informational constraints for skilled movement behaviour to emerge during learning in sport. Below we discuss a recent attempt to examine whether directed search could aid the acquisition of one-handed catching skill.

Manipulating task constraints: directing search in the perceptuo–motor landscape

A study on directed search was recently conducted on the catching behaviour of young, inexperienced catchers using the screen paradigm to occlude vision of the catching arm by Bennett, Davids and Button (1996). Data were obtained from a group of 24 children (mean age = 9.65 years; SD = 0.23). After pre-testing, each subject was randomly assigned to one of three experimental groups (n = 8) of equal catching ability (pre-test catching means for all groups = <10%). The subjects were required to learn to catch tennis balls with one hand under different visual informational constraints. One group (RV) learned to catch without vision of the catching arm during the skill acquisition phase of 120 trials and a second group (VA) had vision of the catching arm available during the whole learning phase. In transfer, subjects crossed over to the opposite condition in which vision of the arm was suddenly added or removed respectively. The data of interest to the present discussion emerged in a pre-test–post-test comparison of both groups' performance with that of a control group with vision available during acquisition *and* transfer (see Figures 8.8a and 8.8b). A number of dependent variables were measured including the number of successful catches, a performance rating on a 1–5 scale and the number of missed catches. Below we report data on the catching score scale adapted from Wickstrom (1983).

A significant group by test interaction was noted for the number of catches. The most important finding in respect to the present discussion is that, by the post-test stage, the group practising without vision of the arm caught significantly more balls than the other two groups ($p < 0.05$). Although Figure 8.8a shows that all groups improved between pre- and post-tests, these were not significant changes. The data lend support to the proposition that the children catching under restricted-vision conditions may have learned to substitute visual information of the catching limb with proprioception. That is, manipulating visual information available during learning may have led them to become better attuned to the proprioceptive information to regulate the position of the catching arm. This statement is justified by the reduction in the number of positional errors from Acquisition Phase 1 to Transfer Phase 2 (see Figure 8.8b).

In summary, the main findings from the learning study indicated that (i) there may be some positive residual effects of practice under one set of informational constraints on performance in another, and (ii) that learners can be guided towards relevant information sources, whether visual or non-visual, during practice. However, from these findings, it is not clear how the manipulation of informational constraints affects learning. Determining the sources of information available in practice that may benefit subsequent learning is an important challenge in future work (see also Michaels and Beek 1995). These data should not be construed as suggesting that, by manipulating the informational constraints, learners become more sensitive to one particular source of information only. Rather, it is more likely that the multimodal support for the intrinsic dynamics of the one-handed catching task is enhanced as a result of guiding subjects towards the relevant information sources (see Tresilian 1995). Recall our statements in the Prologue which underlined that experienced sport performers are able to use information from all sensory systems and are not just reliant on visual information for successful performance. The perceptual systems have been characterised as 'opportunistic' (Tresilian 1995: 239). Whatever information is instantaneously available for a perceiver can be picked up to get the job done in situations that are unfamiliar or when a previously developed perceptuo–motor linkage fails to activate. According to Tresilian (1995) 'Experience results in refinement of use and a 'homing in' on the most appropriate source(s) of information (i.e. those that satisfactorily get the job done)' (ibid.).

SUMMARY AND CONCLUSIONS

In this chapter, we have compared recent traditional and alternative theoretical approaches to skill acquisition. The ecological approach has

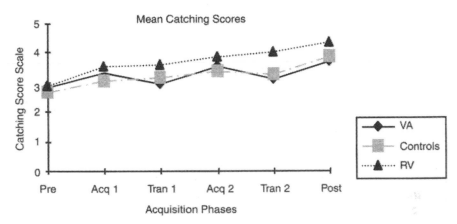

Figure 8.8a Removing vision of the catching arm during learning can help to direct the search of novice catchers.

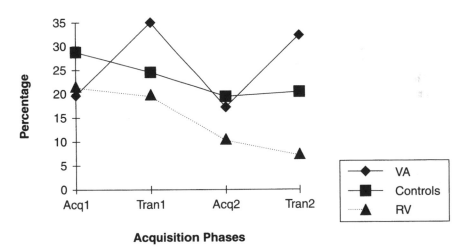

Figure 8.8b A reduction in positional errors over time: evidence that directing the search helped to attune learners to proprioceptive information. (Source: Bennett, S., Davids, K. and Button, C. (1996) 'The specificity of learning hypothesis and one-handed catching', *Journal of Sports Sciences* 14: 21–2.)

prompted a re-examination of traditional theorising (and supporting evidence) at a basic level and with particular reference to sport and exercise. The evidence we reviewed, supporting a knowledge-based, prescriptive model for complex skill learning, has been shown to have some serious limitations which affect the practical application of much of the current research-based knowledge. In Section B, the ecological approach was proposed as an alternative framework which is sympathetic to the teaching, coaching and study of skill acquisition in the highly dynamic environment which is modern sport. From the radical new perspective, skill acquisition may be characterised as the movement system (*qua* dynamical system) searching for relevant states of coordination as it engages in functional activity. It may be viewed as a process of 'hollowing' out a functionally appropriate attractor well into which the system can settle down during a task or activity. That is, skill acquisition may be a process of making a temporary state of coordination more resistant to the environmental forces which could perturb the stability of the system. Learning is the process of enhancing the temporary organisation of the system when it has found a useful niche in the landscape to settle into (e.g. Zanone and Kelso 1994). Such a description makes it clear that attractor wells for movements do not need to be stored or symbolically represented in the higher centres of the CNS.

However, despite methodological moves away from measures of performance outcome on relatively simple laboratory tasks, few attempts to investigate ongoing changes in movement patterns during the complete acquisition and learning of multi-degree-of-freedom skills are forthcoming. Although the embryonic stage of theoretical development presently restricts the scope for serious hypothesis testing, increased research effort is needed to evaluate the practical impact of the main tenets of an ecological perspective in sport. This remains an enormous challenge for sport scientists interested in skill acquisition from an ecological perspective.

Regarding practical applications, the ecological framework appears to offer an exciting, principled platform on which to formulate teaching and coaching strategies in sport. Recently, several comprehensive theoretical position statements on the implications of the ecological approach for movement skill acquisition have appeared in the literature (e.g. Smith and Thelen 1993; Balan and Davis 1993; Davids *et al.* 1994; Thelen and Smith 1994; Handford *et al.* 1997; Davis 1988). They suggest that the ecological approach offers sports scientists a unique invitation to understand the processes of skill acquisition in sport contexts. However, some researchers believe that there has been an imbalance of ecologically-inspired research favouring the development of theoretical and mathematical models such that processes of skill acquisition have been virtually ignored. For instance, Summers (1998) argued that the ecological perspective 'lacked a comprehensive theory of learning and development' and that 'a rigorous program of research' (p. 12) was required on these processes.

Whilst Summers (1998) may be correct in arguing that more empirical work is needed, many recent studies on the processes of skill acquisition from an ecological perspective have begun to emerge in the literature. In this chapter, we have highlighted several of these studies such as the work by Thelen and colleagues on motor development in children (e.g. Thelen and Smith 1994; Smith and Thelen 1993), and the recent research on how sports teachers and coaches may be guided in the design of practice conditions (e.g. see Handford *et al.* 1997). The empirical findings from these ongoing programmes of work have revealed a significant number of suggestions for the activities of coaches and athletes during practice. From this 'constraints-led perspective' the major issues of concern for pedagogists include: (i) getting a better understanding of the term 'discovery learning' and what it means to search, discover and exploit task solutions; (ii) understanding how to break down sport tasks for the purposes of practice, perhaps evaluating perception–action coupling as a guiding principle (see Milner and Goodale 1995); (iii) exploring the validity of ecological principles such as the affordances of body-scaled information and directed search for the design of practice conditions and learning environments; (iv) attempting to understand how pedagogists could channel the search activities of learners by manipulating the constraints in order that the influence of rate-limiters on skill development may be counteracted; (v) assessing observational learning as a strategy for acquiring sport skills from an ecological perspective; and (vi) focusing on the implications of ecological principles for the role of the coach in manipulating task constraints (Davids and Handford 1994; Handford *et al.* 1997). To summarise, we have outlined an agenda for sport scientists, working from an ecological standpoint, to attempt to integrate theoretical research and practical applications. These are by no means the only issues which need to be tackled by motor control specialists in the sport sciences. However, only when issues such as these have received a rigorous assessment, will the real impact of the ecological approach to motor behaviour become clear.

9 Observational learning in sport

INTRODUCTION

Observational learning refers to the tendency in humans to watch the behaviour of others and to adapt their own behaviour as a result of the experience. The medium by which learning through observation occurs is referred to as modelling – an ability which enables people to emulate the actions of others. The core process is imitation. At the rudimentary level, imitation involves two individuals: an observer who imitates and a model who is imitated. Imitation occurs when the observer's behaviour is more like the model's behaviour than it would have been had the observer not watched the model (Sluckin 1970). Vital to imitation, modelling and observational learning is perceiving. These will be the main terms used throughout this chapter. However, the reader should be aware that a wide range of closely related expressions may be encountered in the literature, notably, 'vicarious learning', 'social facilitation', 'mimicry', 'matched-dependent behaviour', 'allellomimesis', 'ideo-motor action' and 'copying'. These terms have been used by the various 'schools of thought' which have addressed the subject of observational learning. It should be noted that the terms and expressions are used with varying degrees of precision depending largely on the theoretical inclination of the numerous authorities in the area. For more detailed discussion of definition and taxonomy, reference should be made to Hill (1963), Aronfreed (1969), Sluckin (1970) and Whiting (1988).

Experience in sports coaching and competitive situations reveals innumerable instances in which the human tendency to model others occurs both intentionally and incidentally. Perhaps the most familiar situation is the 'formal' instructional setting in which a sports coach attempts to harness the athlete's imitative capability to ensure that the performer develops a clear idea of a given action and the pattern and feel needed to produce the movement. The usual approach is for the coach to communicate a desired action sequence by means of some combination of visual demonstration ('show') and verbal instruction ('tell') using a 'live' or symbolised model. Figure 9.1 uses the sport of baseball to provide an

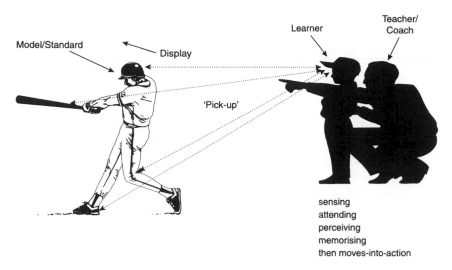

Teacher/
Coach

Learner

Model/Standard

Display

'Pick-up'

sensing
attending
perceiving
memorising
then moves-into-action

Figure 9.1 Observational learning in sport: basic conditions. The learner observes
a competent model and, in so doing, 'picks up' salient information
under the direction of a coach, teacher or significant other so as to
acquire an 'image-of-the-act' to be used in subsequent attempts to
emulate the model.

illustrative conceptual framework and summarise the processes as follows.
During observational learning, the learner/athlete views the actions of an
appropriate model with the help of a coach. Then, the learner attempts
to produce a version of the movements required to complete the task.
Practice coupled with guidance (which may involve further modelling)
is usually required until a criterion performance level is achieved. If
successful, the athlete becomes more like the model than he or she would
have been had the process not taken place. The potential benefits for
observational learning derived by way of imitation and modelling are
many and diverse. A concise description of the process is that of a multi-
faceted communication between persons providing simultaneously an
overall view of an action, focus for attention, movement syntax relative
to a goal and a performance standard. A significant aspect of modelling
is that learning time is reduced because a great deal of what is to be
learned can be accomplished in a single exposure to the model's action.
(For an extended discussion on the gains which can accrue from using
visual demonstration during instruction, see Mosston 1981.)

By no means all observational learning takes place in formal, instructional situations. Indeed it is probable that the 'instinct' to model and
become like others in our various social groups is so potent that the bulk
of our learning occurs without an express intention to learn. This phenomenon has been referred to as 'incidental learning'. This topic has received

some, though not much, attention from sport scientists, but is an area which must be taken into account in a comprehensive coverage of observational learning in sport. Those with a particular interest in this area should consult the seminal work of Postman (1964) and studies undertaken by Dickinson (1977, 1978) and Crocker (1983).

Finally, although the emphasis in this chapter is upon the observational learning of sports skills as specific motor acts, it should be noted that other changes in the learner can occur as a result of being exposed to a model. As well as adaptations in motor behaviour, new values, attitudes and motives can be acquired. Some of these facets interact in a complex fashion which will be discussed in later sections. Readers who are particularly interested in the influence of affective factors in observational learning should refer to Aronfreed (1969) for some foundation reading.

THEORETICAL PERSPECTIVES ON OBSERVATIONAL LEARNING

To return to the example given in Figure 9.1, readers might be considering exactly how a new behaviour is acquired. Clearly, direct, 'hands-on' experience (physical practice) is a necessary part of the process, but not before the learner has somehow been able observe an unfamiliar pattern of movements and produce a noticeably similar pattern with his or her own body for the first time. Is there a plausible explanation for the change in behaviour? Because imitation, modelling and observational learning play a central role in the behavioural repertoire of humans there is a lengthy history of theoretical reasoning and research on these topics and related variables. Over the years, considerable interest has been shown in providing answers to a range of questions from diverse theoretical viewpoints. Psychodynamic, developmental, cognitive, behaviourist and ecological approaches can all be found in an extensive literature on the subject. Bandura (1969, 1971, 1977, 1986), Yando, Seitz and Zigler (1978), Prinz (1984) and Scully and Newell (1985) provide comprehensive accounts on the topic from differing perspectives, whilst sketching in the historical background.

Although the study of sport and its constituent skills were not the focus of interest in early theoretical writing and empirical research on observational learning, brief mention will be made of the major themes because of their importance in building a conceptual framework for the area. The purpose here is to assist in the understanding and interpretation of contemporary research.

A useful starting point is the distinction in the literature between theories which are concerned with the process of 'learning to imitate' and 'using imitation to learn'; the example provided in Figure 9.1 involves the latter. Nonetheless, it is plain that people have to possess imitative capability before they can use it to learn. Unsurprisingly, much early theorising was concerned with the question of how imitation develops in early childhood. For those attracted to this area, Parton (1976) presents a very good critical review of the major theories (see also Abravanel, Levan-Goldshmidt and Stevenson 1976). Several significant points, to be discussed briefly, are detectable in the various theoretical accounts of learning to imitate which have been embodied into more recent, comprehensive theories. Moreover, some of the contemporary sports-based observational learning research has examined variables drawn from these areas. Because a major trend in both competitive and recreational sport is the increasingly early age of participation, early developmental considerations assume greater significance.

Early childhood development

Developing cognitive structures

Perhaps the best-known theory in which imitation plays a major role is the cognitive–developmental stage theory put forward by Piaget (1951). Rather than present details of how imitation is achieved, this theory emphasises the importance of the establishment of cognitive–representational structures early in life to enable complex activities to be learned at a later stage. This account with imitation as the enabling process is based on Baldwin's (1920) assertion that imitation plays a central role in memory development by assisting the brain to become a 'repeating organ' so as to permit recall and recognition of things past. From the neonate stage up to approximately the age of eighteen months, imitation ('accommodation') is the catalyst whereby organismic structures constantly change through interaction with the environment and lead to the development of cognitive structures which enable the individual to form internal representations of events. Although Piaget was less specific about imitation in older children, at which time it is evident that their imitative ability increases in accuracy and quality, it is clear that the establishment of this propensity early in life is a precursor to the acquisition of a rich repertoire of action, language and other behaviours. Both the chronological and developmental age of the individual in the examples suggest a 'readiness' beyond mere mimicry of the activities involved.

Movement-into-action

The problem of exactly how the imitation of action occurs is unresolved and remains a subject for further research. Piaget's account hints that there is an instinctive element, perhaps akin to 'imprinting', occurring very early in life whereby existing response patterns are triggered by external stimulation. Beyond this, a wide variety of ideas and notions have been advanced in an effort to explain the process. Within the examples given, several instances equivalent of this type of 'matching' seen in early child-hood would have been noticeable to an onlooker, notably: (a) repetitive matching of an infant's own responses as in the iteration of vocalisations or hand movement; (b) matching the action of another person when the infant has previously performed that action; as when a mother repeats a particular sound uttered by her child and the child matches the sound; (c) the matching of another person's action when that action is not part of the infant's existing vocabulary of actions such as when a mother waves a hand at her child and the child waves in response. Many attempted explanations for imitative matching stem from the behaviourist notions of conditioning and reinforcement (see Miller and Dollard 1941). However, although the behavioural modification witnessed in observational learning may be influenced by these factors, it is inevitable that perceptual–cognitive and motivational factors play a substantial role in the process. For this reason, recent theories possess a more comprehensive structure and have moved beyond the notion of imitation, modelling and observa-tional learning as merely matching 'follow-the-leader' behaviour, expressing a greater interest in examining and explaining the processes involved. A prime example of this is the two-factor model of early imita-tive development advanced by Yando *et al.* (1978) which emphasises the importance of the interplay between the observer's cognitive developmental level and that person's motivational system.

Motivation: curiosity, identification, competence

When learning sports skills, performers require an appropriate level of motivation. As might be expected, theorists and researchers alike have attempted to define the role of motivation in observational learning. Broadly speaking, this work has been expressed mainly through three fundamental psychological constructs, namely, identification, competence and novelty.

The term 'identification' possesses Freudian connotations and refers to seeking to be similar to another person for reasons of liking or accep-tance. Young sports players often refer to established athletes and coaches as their 'role-model': the person whom they are trying to emulate. However, research examining the link between identification and imita-tion has been plagued with definitional and methodological problems. For many, the construct is ill-defined and problematic. Nonetheless, any serious theory of observational learning which failed to consider mentor–learner relationships would be impoverished. Sport is a particularly rich source of examples of these connections. This area will be revisited later in this chapter.

Humans and other animals, especially the young, show high levels of activity, exploration, curiosity, manipulation and interest in novelty. It has been suggested by White (1959) that the purpose of such behaviour is to promote general effectiveness in dealing with the environment; the resultant feelings of competence or self-efficacy strengthens the ego. Sport is a prominent medium through which 'effectance' can be realised (see Bruner 1973). Clearly, a broad matrix of imitative, modelling and observational learning situations can arise within sports contexts. The quest for competence and personal significance may well be a motivational source for observational learning. For those with a particular interest in the developmental aspects of imitation and modelling in observational learning, the text by Yando *et al.* (1978) provides a good foundation.

Mainstream theories: mediation versus perception-in-action

Mediational interpretations: blueprints, images and schemata

As indicated above, early theory building and psychological interpretation germane to observational learning were founded on imitation research undertaken largely from a behaviourist perspective which focused predominantly on the effects of reinforcement and incentive variables (see Miller and Dollard 1941). Sheffield (1961) seems have been the first author to break from that emphasis and put forward a detailed, logical and concise explanation of the processes at work when a person is engaged in observational learning. The motive for his research and that of colleagues was to evolve a 'science of instruction' guided by the relevant aspects of a 'science of learning' (see Lumsdaine 1961, Chapter 31). Much of the foundation for this notion was based on research which focused upon the development and evaluation of effective instructional media for training armed forces personnel and industrial workers mainly in mechanical assembly tasks which required the fitting together of component parts in a given order. Sequencing of this kind is an important (though by no means the only) aspect of sport skill learning; coaches of gymnastics, ice skating, diving and trampolining will readily relate to this statement. The conduct and style of this early research does seem to have influenced significantly recent studies of modelling on topics in the motor domain.

Sheffield (1961) contended that perception and the direct link of perceptual processes to overt action play the key role in aiding a learner to produce the actions demonstrated by a model. He likened the process to that of assembling, say, an item of furniture from the constituent parts with the aid of a hard copy 'blueprint' which is used both to perceive the finished product and as a step-by-step check on progress during construction. The blueprint would be the teacher's demonstration conveyed and received as an image of the act (as depicted in Figure 9.1) and, presumably, held as a memory image which is manipulated as practice continues until perceptions of the action itself and perceptual memory coincide. Many instructional variables pertinent to visual demonstration and observational learning in the motor domain based on Sheffield's ideas were examined in a fairly rigorous manner over 30 years ago (see Lumsdaine 1961, 1962). Quite a wide selection of the instructional variables studied then have been taken up by motor skills researchers during the last decade or so. Some of these facets will be considered later in the chapter.

Similar in many respects to Sheffield's ideas, though much broader in scope, is Social Learning Theory (Bandura 1969, 1971, 1977). This is the explanation of modelling designed to account for the acquisition and modification of behavioural and social skills which has prompted most general psychological and motor behaviour research. Latterly, this commentary has been revised and consolidated to become Social Cognitive Theory (Bandura 1986): an all encompassing theory which incorporates many elements of the previously mentioned approaches. Some researchers have tested predictions which have implications for sports skills teaching and coaching (e.g. see Carroll and Bandura 1982, 1985, 1987, 1990).

It should be stressed that this theory did not originate or develop from an interest in sports or everyday motor skills. When the perspective of motor behaviour theory and research is considered, it seems that those who recognised the importance of modelling in motor skill instruction and wished to research pertinent observational learning issues discovered that Social Learning Theory was the only tenable explanation and source of hypotheses which was available at that time (e.g. see Martens, Burwitz and Zuckermann 1976). Furthermore, the motor learning theory of that period (Adams 1971), which centred around the notion of a cognitive 'reference of correctness', had much in common with both Bandura's and Sheffield's ideas. Subsequent motor learning–modelling research has remained – and still remains – close to the social cognitive interpretation (e.g. see Feltz and Landers 1977; Doody, Bird and Ross 1985; Carroll and Bandura 1990). In fact, almost tacit acceptance of some of the basic assumptions of Social Cognitive Theory may have limited the perspective of those interested in motoric modelling processes.

The central theme of Social Cognitive Theory (e.g. Bandura 1986) is that modelling influences lead to learning through an informative function. In the course of observing a model, a learner acquires 'symbolic' representations of the activity which serve to work together to aid subsequent production of the action. Four inter-related component processes are implicated in the eventually learned behaviour. These are: *attention* whereby the learner selectively attends to and extracts distinctive features of the modelled act which are modified by the individual's perceptual, past experience and current situational requirements; *retention* which facilitates memory of the observed act by reconstructing and transforming it using strategies such as labelling, coding and imagery; *motor reproduction* which uses symbolic representation ('blueprint') to guide overt performance that is refined with practice and self-correcting adjustments;

and *motivation* which affects performance by motivating the learner to execute the modelled response.

There is little doubt that Bandura's theory is the most complete and comprehensive explanation of modelling and the richest source of hypothesis testing for topics in the motor domain. However, several areas of Social Cognitive Theory are not well explained. For example, Bandura (1977, 1986) contends that the learner/observer selectively attends to spatial and temporal features of the model's performance and, in so doing, extracts and transforms these into a cognitive representation which acts as a guide to subsequent movement production. But, what is the nature of the cognitive representation? What is its form? Where does it reside? Precisely how does it help the learner to produce the required action? Most motor domain researchers who have tested predictions tendered by Social Cognitive Theory have examined the formation of the cognitive representation with some type of recognition memory test. It follows from this that the better the recognition performance, the better the cognitive representation and, in turn, the better the production of the modelled action (see Carroll and Bandura 1982, 1985, 1987, 1990). However, this argument hinges on the validity of the recognition–memory method as an index of cognitive representation.

Recognition testing involves physically confronting the learner with the previously observed action which raises the question of whether modelling is achieved via some internal mediational process or, alternatively, adaptive utilisation of vital information inherent in the model's action. In settings where modelling is at work, learners persistently seek to refresh their precept of what is to be achieved through recourse to the model's action. In this sense, the model is the 'representation' and desired movement patterns may be acquired by the learner more directly through a transactional process rather than by cognitive means, perhaps in the manner signalled in research on the kinematic specification of dynamics in person-and-action perception (see Runeson 1985; Runeson and Frykholm 1981, 1983). This has led some researchers to critically examine the process of perceiving whilst imitating and modelling. Some of this work is discussed in the next section.

Finally, on the 'representational' aspect, Annett (1982, 1985, 1986) has put forward several refined and thought-provoking ideas which merit careful consideration. He suggested three principal candidates for the cognitive representation, namely, 'images' (consciously experienced representations of actions which can be visual or kinaesthetic), 'criteria' (stored sets of conditions which have to be met in propositional form), or 'schema' (coherent conceptual frameworks built on experience which permit the interpretation of events). Also, as Annett (1982) succinctly points out, the visual-to-motor route is by no means the only effective pathway. In describing what are termed 'action prototypes' (movement patterns which seem to be controlled by verbal representations), he suggested that instructional experience informs that teachers often get a movement idea across using metaphor. For example, 'kick your legs like a frog' to elicit the often difficult-to-attain breaststroke kicking action in swimming. Likewise, auditory demonstrations are frequently used to good effect when the production of certain impact or force specifications are required to successfully accomplish a motor act, such as 'listen to the landing' when learning to absorb impact forces after jumping from a height.

Plainly, the current notion of a conceptual representation is highly generic and requires considerable clarification in the context of motor skill learning. The inception and application of theoretical ideas from a much broader base is necessary. The development of more inventive research protocols and measurement systems that permit insight into processes of skill learning seems to be a mandatory requirement.

Transactional interpretations: affordances, kinematic-specification-of-dynamics, invariant pick-up

Several authors have commented that Social Cognitive Theory lacks critical detail in its explanation of the operational characteristics of the attentional component and, particularly, the role of perceiving (e.g. Annett 1982; Scully and Newell 1985; Whiting, Bijlard and Brinker 1987; Williams 1982, 1985). Early in the elaboration of his theory (Bandura 1977), and reiterated later (Bandura 1986: 51), Bandura stated that, 'people cannot learn much by observation unless they attend to, *and accurately perceive*, the relevant aspects of modelled activities'. He proceeded to explain that learning an observed movement pattern is based upon the construction of a conceptual representation composed of symbolic codes of the behaviour which serves as an *internal* model for subsequent response production. No suggestion is offered as to the 'relevant aspects' of the observed movement sequences that are or might be extracted for construction of the conceptual representation. The very essence of modelling implies that crucial 'information' is, on the one hand, made available for an observer and, on the other hand, looked for by an observer in order to respond. Any theory which is so dependent on the process of perceiving to explain how an observer transforms visual input to motor output really has to attempt at least to spell out what is perceived. There seems to be little doubt that sports coaches and teachers would value such knowledge because they could put this to good use when designing their various instructional strategies.

Research by Williams (1985) and Whiting and colleagues (Whiting *et al.* 1987) attempted to discover the nature of the information that the learner abstracts from the model and uses to produce movement and action. Also, the research of Hoenkamp (1978) and Runeson and Frykholm (1981, 1983), mentioned previously, is relevant in this context. Much of this work is based on ideas developed from fundamental perceptual psychology research concerned with how humans perceive biological motion (see Johansson 1973; Cutting *et al.* 1978). The results indicate that for a relatively 'simple' movement and action, at least, an observer picks up 'invariant' spatial features (e.g. the arrangement of the limb segments) and temporal features (e.g. cadence of limb motion) which are available in the bodily motion of the model. These features afford or provide meaning for the observer and form the basis of a 'frame of reference' for the self-generation of a version of the action which was presented by a model.

Both Prinz (1984), using logical explanation, and Whiting *et al.* (1987), in discussing the results of research on imitation learning of simulated downhill skiing, incline to the view that invariant or 'categorical' properties inherent in a model's actions form the basis of a learner's attempts at movement production rather than some process of copying structural detail. Figure 9.2 depicts the task and comparison of adaptations in amplitude, frequency and fluency categories with and without a model. Part of this process may be 'self-organising' in the manner suggested by Vogt (1986) who explained that, when modelling limb movement, the organism seeks and 'tunes in' to a compatible response frequency afforded by the model. This process initiates a response and other elements which are necessary for continuity of motion are 'filled in'.

Similar arguments have been proposed by Scully and Newell (1985). They suggest that previous theoretical approaches have been solely concerned with the *how* of perception and action and, consequently, have failed to examine *what* visual information about action is picked up when observing human movement. Following Gibson's (e.g. 1979) theorising on direct perception (see Chapter 6), Scully and Newell (1985) argue that the visual system is able to perceive directly invariant information about the movements of body parts in relation to one another (i.e. topological characteristics of the relative motions). They dispute the need for symbolic coding or memorial representations to mediate between observing a modelled action and its reproduction. Simply, once perceived, this relative motion information, which is essential to movement coordination, acts as an informational constraint on the emergence of coordination.

For researchers in the motor behaviour area, one appealing aspect of this dynamic perspective of the modelling process is that it takes into consideration the first two stages of motor learning, namely, coordination and control. In fact, a major prediction of this perspective is that visual demonstrations are facilitatory at the coordination stage, but not the control stage. In other words, when the skill to be learned requires the acquisition of a new pattern of coordination, modelling effects will be found. For example, when viewing a demonstration of the serve in tennis, the learner may pick up information from the movements of the arm and racket in relation to each other and in relation to the movement of the trunk and legs. Scully and Newell (1985) argue that at the early

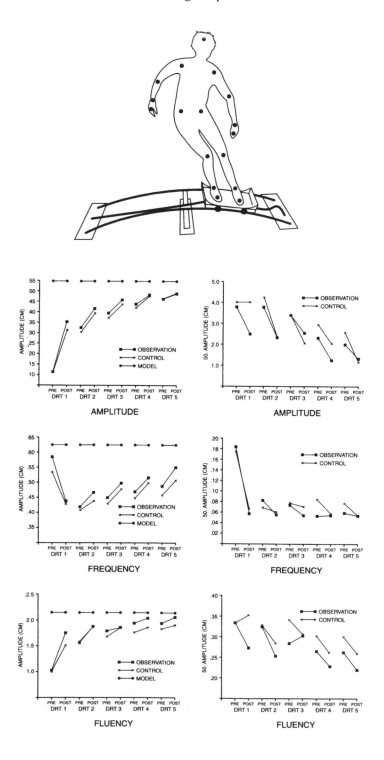

stage of learning, viz. the coordination stage, observing a model should help a learner to acquire a new coordination pattern by revealing critical information about the relationships among body parts. However, if the skill involves controlling an already coordinated or learned movement pattern, no modelling effects will be found. During this control stage, although the information about the appropriate scaling or parameterisation of relative motion can be perceived through demonstrations, such information might not be effective. For example, using a demonstration to show a soccer player how to perform an instep pass over 40 rather than 20 metres, or a golfer how to use a pitching wedge over varying distances, may be relatively ineffective since these involve employing the same relative motion pattern (the actual pattern of coordination does not change), but with changes to the 'scaling' of various control parameters (see Scully 1988). In such circumstances, Scully and Newell (1985) suggest that because movement coordination is subject to individual differences (e.g. anatomical and morphological constraints) optimal parameterisation can only be achieved through practice regardless of whether visual demonstrations are available or not. Clearly, research is required to test these theoretical propositions.

Some plausible coaching applications arising from the knowledge of how human motion is perceived will be addressed later. However, there is little doubt that a full explanation of how precepts of action are transformed into movements (an integral element of modelling) is still not available although vigorous pursuit of the answer probably began even before the well-known quest for an explanation for ideo-motor phenomena sought by James (1890). The answer remains at the level of elegant description and speculation in the writings of Prinz (1984) and Scheerer (1986). In truth, only modest progress has been made towards an understanding of motoric modelling processes for the most rudimentary actions in nearly one hundred years. A solution to the problem will probably be particularly elusive as far as complex coordinative actions are concerned (see, for example, some of the problems with 'mis-perception' of gymnastic actions in research by Daugs, Blischke and Oliver 1986 and the discussion section following research with simulated skiing by Whiting *et al.* 1987).

As indicated, modelling in motor skill acquisition involves observation of a model's action followed by production of the seen action at some

Figure 9.2 Imitation learning of simulated downhill skiing. The illustration shows a subject on a ski simulator. The spots are markers to be tracked by a system used to derive kinematic data for the subject's actions. This study of imitation learning compared performance (amplitude, frequency and fluency) with (graphs on the left) and without (right) the presence of a model. Information provided by personal communication with H.T.A. Whiting (1987).

point later in time. Experience tells us that humans can be quite exact modellers who can often produce, not only the sequential order of action, but also appropriate spatial, temporal and kinetic features effected through various modalities. Beyond the puzzle of perceptual processes arises the question of precisely how information is retained after it has been abstracted from the model's bodily actions. Inevitably, time elapses between observing and moving; thus memory is challenged. Most contemporary theorists assert that there is a requirement for some form of 'mental' activity or mediational process as a bridge between seeing and doing. As a consequence, perhaps a promising approach which attempts to combine competing theoretical perspectives into an 'integrated theory' has been proposed by McCullagh, Weiss and Ross (1989). This approach incorporates the reasoning of the 'direct' school of thought which stresses the autonomy of visual perception in motor skill modelling and the 'indirect' account which emphasises central representation of events as the principal process.

RESEARCH

The aim in this section is to link the findings from selected research studies which have been generated from the theoretical interpretations discussed above and consider the practical implications. To begin, a cautionary observation is issued. Although there has been a considerable amount of research into modelling processes and motor skill learning, the majority of these studies have examined the performance and learning of contrived and artificial tasks such as knocking down barriers (Doody *et al.* 1985; McCullagh and Caird 1990), completing facile locomotor sequences (Weiss and Klint 1987), a novel ladder climbing task (McCullagh 1986), a version of sign language/semiphore-like signalling (Carroll and Bandura 1982, 1985, 1987, 1990), computer games (Martens *et al.* 1976; Pollock and Lee 1992) and coincident–anticipation tasks claimed to be similar to a batting motion (Weeks 1992). Also, most of these studies draw conclusions from single-level outcome measures which seriously limit interpretation of the adaptive processes involved. For example, if a sport scientist wishes to develop a thorough understanding of how a child learns to catch a ball with one hand, a record of 'catches' and 'drops' as practice proceeds will inform that change has taken place but not why. Only comprehensive information on operation and adaptive changes occurring in the visuomotor system will permit the beginnings of insight as to how learning occurs. In the case of modelling, multi-level comparative analysis of model and learner under varied experimental conditions with 'real' motor skills is crucial. Contrived tasks and simplistic learning criteria are insufficient.

Despite this criticism a number of studies have made efforts to study authentic skills or sub-skills of common everyday or sporting actions using valid performance measures. These have attempted to examine the effects of modelling conditions in as realistic and comprehensive a manner as possible (see Jordan 1979 (dance steps); Williams 1985, 1989b, 1992, 1993 (overhand throwing action, gymnastic vault, one-handed catching, lifting action); Daugs *et al.* 1986; Blischke 1986; Fehres and Olivier 1986 (hurdling and gymnastic actions); Roach and Burwitz, 1986 (cricket batting strokes); Whiting *et al.* 1987 (simulated skiing); Wiese-Bjornstal and Weiss 1992 (underhand pitching); Hand and Sidaway 1992 (golf chip shot); Winfrey and Weeks 1993 (balance beam performance); Austin and Miller 1994 (golf swing); Herbert and Landin 1994 (tennis volley); Williams and Thompson 1994 (lifting action); Ramsey 1995 (field hockey receiving); Catina 1995 (powerlift squat action)). Pertinent issues for motor skill instruction are discussed below, bearing in mind the observation made in the prior section on theory that the majority of research has examined hypotheses derived from Social Cognitive Theory.

Developmental variables

As stated earlier, a great deal of children's learning is achieved by emulating the actions of other children and adults. Yando *et al.* (1978) cite numerous studies in support of their two-factor theory of imitation. This proposes that the imitative skill of an observer is dependent upon that person's cognitive representational skills which change with maturity and experience. Also, that children's modelling is strongly influenced by a developmental effect in the ability to attend to informational displays appropriately. It is well established that children are less adept at observing, selecting and interpreting environmental information than adults (Sugden and Connell 1979). Likewise, there is a strong age effect in reconstructing sequences of events during observational learning (Leifer, Collins, Gross, Taylor, Andrews and Blackmer 1971). Furthermore, Majeres and Timmer (1981) reported that young children tend to imitate motor skills at their own developmental level rather than above or below their current level of competence.

The research of Yando and co-workers has been the source of ideas for experiments on the developmental aspects of modelling in the motor skill domain. For example, Feltz (1982) using an adult model for the learning of a complex coordinative skill (balance-ladder climbing) revealed that the differences in modelling effects between college-age and elementary school-age female participants were attributable to the larger repertoire of motor abilities possessed by the older participants. She concluded that younger participants may need more practice time with the addition of verbal cues to enhance modelling effects.

Weiss (1983) compared the effects of 'silent' and 'verbal' adult models during the course of learning to put into a sequence already acquired basic multi-limb coordination skills (e.g. hop, gallop, skip) by young children. The performance of seven- and eight-year-olds was superior to that of the four- and five-year-olds. The older children did equally well with either model whereas the younger group required the verbal model to improve their performance. These findings were supported in a follow-up study (Weiss and Klint 1987) which, in addition, showed that girls performed consistently better than boys. Wiese-Bjornstal and Weiss (1992) replicated, and modestly extended, prior work arriving at broadly similar conclusions. It should be noted that the dependent measures used in these studies were 'sequence correctness' and 'form', but the actual derivation of the scores was not at all clear. It is well established that the process of scoring sequence correctness in memory studies is troublesome (see Harcum 1975; Summers 1977), yet this point seems to go unheeded in motor sequence research. Likewise, the derivation of measurements which accurately reflect movement 'form' has proved to be extremely difficult for motor skills researchers (see Whiting *et al.* 1987).

Clearly, the use of visual demonstrations within the motor skill instruction of children requires careful consideration with respect to the interaction of what is shown, who shows it, and the nature of any accompanying verbal directions. When considering verbal directions, it is noteworthy that Gallagher and Thomas (1986) reported that only adults can use provided or self-organised strategies to unorganised input. They found that children aged eleven years were able to apply an organisational strategy and transfer it to other circumstances only when the strategy was provided for them. Children aged seven years were unable to transfer organisational strategies to alternative situations even when the movement contexts were similar. At age five, recall of movements was not aided by the provision of organisational structure.

It is unfortunate that the tasks which were modelled by participants in most of these studies concentrated predominantly on the sequencing of already learned behaviour. Performance was measured by recall method. Whereas these paradigms permit conclusions to be drawn concerning visual memory for bodily actions many of them are, in effect, old-style memory experiments with different stimulus material. As a result, understanding of motoric modelling from a developmental perspective has not been substantially enhanced.

An exception is a recent study by Wiese-Bjornstal and Weiss (1992) which examined the effects of visual and verbal models on the learning of a softball throwing action in children aged seven to nine years. They used a kinematic analysis technique as well as a recognition test as a measure of the 'cognitive blueprint' of the action alluded to earlier (Sheffield 1961). It was found that the children's kinematic form (a composite of seven variables which included body angles, ball release angles and ball velocity) improved significantly to become more like the model following practice. The introduction of verbal cues dramatically increased participants' progress to approximate the model. Also, participants' recognition of modelled correctness of the action improved substantially (over 20%). Evidently, exposure to a model demonstrating a complex coordinative action, then practising to be like the model (the instruction given in this study), results in the learner being able to act and understand the action even at a relatively early age.

Research with an emphasis on perceptual processes has shown that older children (fourteen to fifteen years) recognised a throwing action presented as the relative motion of the wrist, elbow and shoulder joints (point-light format) as quickly and accurately as adults (Williams 1988). This adds to the evidence provided by Johannson (1973), Cutting and Kozlowski (1977), Bassili (1978) and Poizner, Bellugi and Lutes-Driscoll (1981) for other common actions and expressions, In a follow-up experiment, twelve-year-old participants accurately video-modelled a throwing action by producing the spatial arrangement of the throwing limb and responded appropriately to timing changes in the action (Williams 1989b) The results, presented in Figure 9.3, showed that older children are sensitive to abstract spatio–temporal features in modelled displays of this type of bodily action which may be used in the movement production process. The results go some of the way to understanding the type of information attended to, picked up and transformed to produce bodily motion.

Motivation

As indicated earlier, an understanding of the effects of motivational variables is essential to a comprehensive account of modelling and observational learning processes. Motor skills researchers have reported the results of some studies in this area. Both intrinsic and extrinsic incentives have been shown to facilitate the effects of modelling during motor skill acquisition (Bandura 1977; Yando *et al.* 1978). However, Feltz and Landers (1977) demonstrated that motivational cues provided by knowledge of the model's performance standard did not significantly influence performance.

An important instructional skill is the ability to establish and maintain a learner's confidence. Frequently, this includes the minimisation of apprehension brought about by the learning situation. Certain motor skill learning conditions are initially anxiety-producing and can diminish a learner's motivation to participate. For many individuals, the early stages of learning to swim is a relevant instance. Gould and Roberts (1981), in a substantive review which emphasises socio-motivational factors, pointed out the potential value of modelling as a medium for anxiety reduction. However, despite the obvious importance of this area, there have been relatively few research studies. The general conclusion from two studies cited in Gould and Roberts's (1981) paper was that young learners' fear of high-avoidance tasks was only significantly reduced by a combination of demonstration by a model and direct participation. The notion of direct

TIMING IN MODELLED MOVEMENT

A.

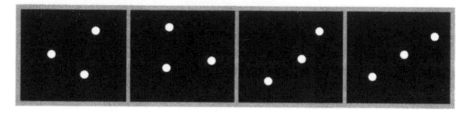

B.

C.

Figure 9.3 Spatio-temporal features of modelled movements. The subject observes a sequence of arm movements which lead to a throwing action modelled in point-light format. Prior testing had determined that participants' were equally competent under point-light and familiar-cue conditions. The kinematic spatio-temporal features of the model are predetermined

involvement, interaction or participation with a model whilst learning is a recurrent theme in the literature and will be returned to when other modelling variables are considered later.

In the main, motor skill instructors consider very carefully the qualities and appropriateness of the models that are to be part of a teaching strategy. Paradoxically, a highly skilled model can be a source of positive motivation for a learner, yet, at the same time, create a feeling of hopelessness relative to a demonstrated performance standard. Bandura (1977) hypothesised that observers attend more closely to models who are older, are highly skilled, control important resources and possess status-conferring symbols than models who lack these qualities. Several researchers have tested these propositions. For example, Landers and Landers (1973) examined the relationship between the social status of the model and the modelling of balance-ladder climbing. The results showed that participants who observed a skilled teacher performed better than those observing an unskilled teacher or peer. However, participants observing a skilled peer performed better than those who observed an unskilled teacher. This is thought to be because the unskilled teacher set an easily matched standard which prevented participants from attempting higher performance levels.

The notion of the competence or skill level of the model has been further examined in some more recent studies. The suggestion is that motor learning is a problem-solving process which involves the use of error information to adapt to a given standard (in the manner advocated by Adams (1971) in his closed-loop learning theory). From this perspective, it is suggested that observation of an unskilled model going through the learning process has a more potent effect than observation of a skilled model (Adams 1986). Research which has examined this proposition has produced equivocal results (see Lee and White 1990; McCullagh and Caird 1990; Pollock and Lee 1992) which may have much to do with the learning material (in these instances, knocking down plywood barriers and computer games) and the sensitivity of the measurements employed. These paradigms bear a close resemblance to those used in research on 'incidental motor learning' mentioned earlier (e.g. see Dickinson 1977, 1978; Crocker 1983). The general findings from these experiments lend some support to Adams's suggestion that observation of someone else learning

by kinematic analysis. Thus, the observer's response can be compared with that of the model. In this experiment, the spatial features of the model were held constant but the temporal features varied at three levels. Participants responded by producing similar spatial arrangement of the upper and lower arm segments as well as moving the arm at a similar velocity to the model. (Adapted from Williams, J.G. (1989b) 'Visual demonstration and movement production: effects of timing variations of a model's actions', *Perceptual and Motor Skills* 68: 891–6.)

is as effective as self-involved learning with the rider that this can occur whether learning is intended or not. The structure and style of much of the teaching and coaching in the motor domain (largely a group process) suggests that this is an area worthy of the attention of sports coaches and further sport science research.

Several studies have taken into account model gender as a motivational variable. Feltz and Landers (1977) found that men had a greater desire to compete with a teacher's performance than women participants. In studies of modelling with tasks which require the subject to move rapidly to reach and grasp an object (referred to as 'ball-snatch', see Gould and Roberts 1981), enhanced performance in men observing male models but no modelling effects for women participants was reported. They concluded that the modelling of motor performance is influenced by the interaction of model gender and the observer. Prior research on this topic (not specific to motor behaviour) concluded that boys have a tendency to acquire more of a male model's behaviour than girls have for modelling a woman model's behaviour (Grusec and Brinker 1972; Perry and Perry 1975).

Follow-up investigations of participants observing similar or dissimilar models making varying self-confidence statements in connection with a gymnastic skill showed enhanced performance in 'similar-model' participants relative to both 'dissimilar-model' and control participants. Participants in 'similar-no-talk' and 'similar-positive-talk' groups showed significantly better performance than those in 'dissimilar-negative-talk', 'dissimilar-no-talk', 'dissimilar-positive-talk' and 'no-model' groups (Gould and Roberts 1981).

Research in the general area of child socialisation processes has shown that children selectively imitate older models and same-age models, but rarely imitate children younger than themselves (Brody and Stoneman 1981). In the motor domain, McCullagh (1986) reported that participants aged 11 to 14 years who observed a 'high-status' model performed better on balance-ladder climbing than a group who observed a 'low-status' model. However, status was not implemented in the attentional phase of learning or the actual amount of the task that was ultimately learned. This conclusion renders it difficult to determine the precise nature of the general modelling effect as was indicated by the extensive *post hoc* reasoning in the paper.

Most motor skill learning situations, whether instructional or incidental, probably involve 'live' modelling conditions, whereas the requirements of experimental control have resulted in the use of televised or video models in most research studies. Televised or symbolised models have been found to be as effective as live models for the observational learning of a motor skill (Feltz, Landers and Raeder 1979; Maccoby and Sheffield 1961). In this context, an interesting observation arising from a quasi-experimental study of self-discovered learning of a gross motor sequence (triple-jump) (Williams 1979) was that of young adult participants who had freedom of choice (any one or combination of media) of a silent-video model, a verbal-video model, a silent-live model and a verbal-live model for learning the task, *all* of the participants spontaneously chose the verbal-live model option. Although the scale of this study limits generalisation, human interaction does appear to be an extremely important factor in modelling in spite of the many clever technical possibilities currently available through the use of various imaging devices. This area certainly seems worthy of further investigation. Earlier, general modelling research with young children indicated that human presence was not a significant factor; rather, the model, whether televised or live, served the purpose of presenting the events to which the participants were required to respond (Dubanoski and Parton 1971).

In summary, effective motor skill modelling is only likely to occur in the presence of positive motivation on the part of the learner. The results of research into a range of variables which affect motivation to learn through observation have important implications for modelling in sport skill acquisition and performance across the developmental range. Careful consideration of the findings serves to supplement coaching knowledge. There are fewer studies of motivational variables in the motor domain than might be expected. The interplay of model nurturance, gender, status, competence, task importance, and the production of movement during skill learning, are among numerous variables which should be the focus of future motor skill research. Extensions to completed research should determine whether stereotypical alterations have occurred as a result of contemporary sociocultural change connected with the role of women in sport.

Perception and representation

As indicated earlier, successful modelling is probably contingent upon the clarity with which the model's actions are perceived. A principal tenet of instruction is to enable the learner to establish as clear an idea as possible of the required action. In sports skill learning, the instructor mostly exploits human visual information processing faculties with the aid of verbal directions. The varied contributions to the text edited by Lumsdaine (1961) provide copious examples of inventive efforts to assist the learner's perception and communicate understanding of mechanical procedures through use of clever film editing and camera technology over thirty years ago. Despite staggering technological advance with respect to the presentation of images (models) of action which possess clear 'perceptual value' for teachers, instructors and coaches for assisting their students, such resources seem not to have been infused into the learning process to the extent that they might have been. Motor skill learning, especially in the important early phase, remains 'instruction' rather than 'action' dominant.

To date, the bulk of modelling research in the motor domain has sought to verify either theoretical propositions concerning the acquisition of the so-called 'conceptual representation' as the mediator of perception and action or the clarification of variables which could influence learning such as status of the model or verbal activity of the model. However, despite its obvious importance, the relationship between the learner's information gathering–interpretative processes and the type and source of information inherent in the model's action has received relatively scant attention from researchers. Furthermore, when this aspect of modelling has been the subject of research either the task/skill selected for study or the measurement system on which inferences are based have been woefully inadequate. Clearly, in studies of movement and actions there must be movement and action information for a learner to interpret and use. Also, the learner's attempts at producing movement can only be fully reflected in a comprehensive analysis of the essential features of the modelled action. This said, there has been more research on the action–perception aspects of modelling and the visual demonstration than has frequently been reported in the literature.

Kinematic demonstrations

A kinematic model of a given action displays spatio–temporal information about a body's motion without revealing the shape of the limbs. Such information is a higher derivative of movement displacement patterns; the point-light demonstrations shown by Johannson (1973) are examples of such models. These were produced by filming actors in the dark with light-reflectant markers attached at the major joints. The resultant movies are compelling expositions of the redundancy of the body's shape when recognising human actions. Point-light methodology as pioneered by Johannson has been vitally important in the advancement of knowledge concerning the perception of human and animal motion.

Research has shown that point-light demonstrations contain sufficient information for both accurate perception and production of motor action (Williams 1988; 1989a) and quite complex judgements of what people are doing in both everyday and athletic tasks (Bassili 1978; Hoenkamp 1978; Cutting and Kozlowski 1977; Poizner, Bellugi and Lutes-Driscoll 1981; Runeson and Frykholm 1981, 1983; Scully 1986, 1988). The results from these studies are sufficiently compelling to consider the application of kinematic information as an aid to perception within the modelling process. Williams (1989c) proposed that enhancement of a model's limbs by highlighting the linearity of the segments in a gymnastic vault would assist participants who were learning the skill to produce this aspect of form (straightness of legs) more effectively. In this case, the results did not support the prediction (perhaps because phase of learning was not adequately considered). Nonetheless, the principle of clarifying essential information in the model's action and thereby helping a learner to perceive affordances in the sense suggested by Gibson (1979), and discussed in greater detail in Chapter 6, should aid learning.

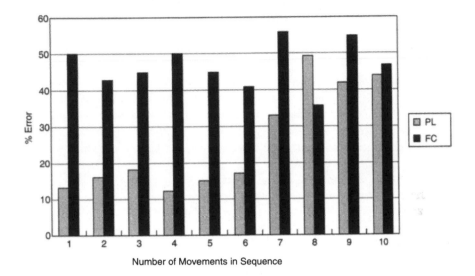

Figure 9.4 Observational learning of movement sequences: production under familiar-cue (FC) versus point-light (PL) conditions. Participants were required to observe sequences of arm movements on a video screen and produce what they had seen. The number of components (flexions/extensions at the elbow) in the sequence was varied from two to eight. As can be seen in the bar graph, performance under the two conditions is about equal when the number of to-be-remembered movements in these sequences was eight (beyond immediate memory span). The trends in these data suggest that as the information content of the to-be-remembered material increases, reduction of the modelled action to only the essential motion components (in this case with a dynamic point-light display) may facilitate memory for movement sequences. (Source: Williams, J.G. (1984) 'Movement imitation as perceptuo-motor coupling', unpublished manuscript.)

Memory for sequential components in a complex action pattern may be assisted when form information (the shape of the limbs) is eliminated and only kinematic information displayed to the learner. Williams (1985) showed that when the number of to-be-remembered components of an arm-action sequence exceeded six the potential benefits of clarifying the display, by including essential (kinematic) information only, began to accrue. The results of this study are highlighted in Figure 9.4.

It seems that further research is needed into the effects of manipulating the information inherent in a modelled display so as to clarify the learner's perception of movement and action. Recent advances in imaging technology render this a more plausible option than in the past (see suggestions offered by Berry 1991). Certainly, a more complete understanding of which aspects of a model's movement attracts a learner's attention and how learners perceive modelled action is necessary both for theoretical assertion and instructional strategy.

Narration

Despite the undoubted power of the human visuoperceptual motor system, it would be rather unusual in a formal instructional setting for a model's actions to be demonstrated and nothing said other than to request that the learner(s) attempt to produce what they saw. Even in 'informal' modelling situations, a learner usually attempts to elicit some verbal guidance from the model. It is evident that description, telling, directing and similar forms of verbalisation are crucially important in motoric modelling. Early researchers were acutely aware that 'narration' could play a key role in the development of effective visual aids for teaching complex sequences in industrial training (Sheffield and Maccoby 1961). Surprisingly, motor skills researcher have paid very little attention to variables associated with narration in their modelling research. Seldom, if ever, has it been reported exactly how narration was controlled, although this is almost certain to have occurred at some point and may well have affected results.

Narration can be used by both instructor and model. The medium may be in any combination of spoken words, text and symbolic form (e.g. arrows, action lines). It can be provided prior to or during modelling to prepare an observer for what they are about to see, to direct attention to cues or known key features of the learning material, to summarise what happened and to assist a learner to initiate or maintain continuity during movement production. Also, verbal instructions can be delivered within modelling in the form of a memorial strategy as per Gallagher and Thomas (1986).

A couple of research studies have pointed to some considerations when providing (or failing to provide) appropriate verbal directions during modelling. Daugs *et al.* (1986) found that in modelling a frame-by-frame static depiction of a gymnastic movement sequence many participants performed in the reverse of the intended direction. It was concluded from eye movement data, presented in Figure 9.5, that when observers are confronted with an unfamiliar movement pattern the display is scanned in a 'predominant direction' (left-to-right as per reading in Western cultures) which results in the pattern being produced in the left-to-right order. The application of either verbal directions accompanying the static depiction (in this case) or a dynamic model would have altered the outcome.

Williams (1989a) monitored the eye movements of young adult participants whilst they observed, then attempted to produce, a video-modelled throwing action. He was able to classify most of the participants into two predominant (preferred) viewing modes. Following this, directions were given to observe the model in a *counter-preferred* manner. As can be seen

Materials presented
to group I (assembled
left-to-right)

Materials presented
to group II (assembled
right-to-left)

Mean coefficients of scanning behaviour

sequence of pictures	task	mean CS	standard deviation	N*
left-to-right	learning	+ 0.63	0.15	23
	recognition	+ 0.64	0.23	23
right-to-left	learning	+ 0.35	0.47	21
	recognition	− 0.32	0.41	21

*Number of subjects with valid eye movement recordings

Distribution of subjects in learning task with respect
to preconceived categories of motor performance

sequence of pictures	motor execution of gymnastics movement			total number of subjects
	correct	reversed	disordered	
left-to-right	26	3	1	30
right-to-left	6	19	2	27

Figure 9.5 Scanning habits: observational learning of movement sequences and
actions from static depictions. In this study, the researchers first determined the visual scanning habits of the participants (see data in the
lower half of the illustration) then required them to observe and produce
action from the sets of static displays (gymnastic and hurdling sequences
which are often to be found in coaching manuals and similar material – top half of illustration). There was no problem at all with the
hurdling; however, the order of the gymnastic sequence which could
be produced in either of two ways was predominantly a function of
visual scanning mode. Adapted from Blischke, K. (1986) 'Memory
effects in motor learning by visual instructions', Proceedings of AIESEP
World Congress, Heidelberg, Germany.

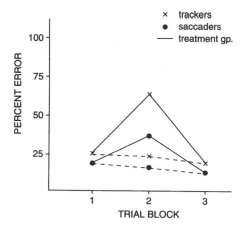

Figure 9.6 Effects of directed use of the eyes during modelling of arm movement sequences. Coaches and teachers often instruct players or students to attend to events in a particular way which can influence preferred viewing mode. This study examined the effects of disruption of preferred viewing mode. The eye movements of participants were monitored while they observed then produced sequences of arm movements. The participants were found to possess three predominant viewing modes: namely, saccadic, pursuit-tracking and mixed (combined sacccadic and pursuit movements during observation). Groups of saccades and trackers were then formed with matched controls. The experimental treatment was instruction which altered preferred viewing mode during observation prior to production of movement. As the illustration shows, the performance of both groups was seriously affected by the instructional treatment delivered in the second trial block, compared with controls (dotted plot).

in Figure 9.6, the instruction critically impaired movement production. This may be regarded as a rather brutal experimental manipulation; nonetheless, it served to illustrate the potential consequences when an instructor insists that a learner attends to a particular area or feature of modelled action.

The power of modelling lies largely in its clarity and rapidity of impact whilst avoiding the intricacies of language. Yet, in certain instances a word or phrase ('action prototype' in the language of Annett 1982) can be equally, and often more, effective in producing a desired action. There seems to be little doubt that the embodiment of verbal instruction in motoric modelling is complex. Further research is required if this important aspect is to be better understood by those who devise and implement instructional strategies for motor skill learning. The old adage that 'a picture is worth a thousand words' may have to be revised for those working in the motor domain!

Viewing angle and distance

Most experienced motor skills instructors are aware that the position from which a learner observes a visual demonstration by a model is important for several reasons. These include individual difference (laterality/dominance) as well as general perceptual/attentional factors. Also, there is a well established developmental effect for left–right transposition (hand movements) evident into late childhood (Wapner and Cerillo 1968). In practice, it is surprising how often this consideration is overlooked (perhaps because optimal orientation is actually quite difficult to arrange). The fact that so little research has been undertaken on this facet of modelling is even more surprising. A long time ago Roshal (1949, 1961) thoroughly researched several aspects of this problem (camera angle, 'real-' and 'slowed-time', disposition of body parts relative to the task, and participation or non-participation by the subject during observation) for the learning of knot tying through film modelling. His general conclusion was that a learner should observe the model's action from the same visual angle that he or she would experience when performing the skill. Also, that learner participation during viewing should be encouraged.

Of the few more recent studies, Jordan (1979) examined the effects of viewing orientation when learning dance steps. The analysis consisted of sequential, spatial and temporal performance measures. He concluded that learner orientation was a highly significant factor in both learning and performance; in this instance, observing the model from the rear or 'action' perspective produced the best results. Furthermore, participation in the action during exposure to the model exerted a powerful effect on learning which diminished when participation was delayed. Ishikura and Inomata, (1995a), who examined the effects of angle of model demonstration on memory for a collection of individual dance-style postures, found what they termed the 'subjective' angle ('action' viewpoint) to be the superior orientation. However, these findings were not substantiated by further research (Ishikura and Inomata 1995b). More recently, Ishikura and Inomata (1998), again with dance postures, have shown that 'rear angle' orientation in modelling may be superior. On this occasion, eye movement analysis was added to the paradigm and no differences in visual search behaviour were found between the 'frontal' and 'rear angle' viewpoints. In a similar vein, Ramsey (1995) studied the effects of viewing orientation whilst video modelling 'receiving' skill in novice field hockey players. There was a significant learning effect, but no differences were found between lateral, action and combined viewpoints in timing of ball–stick contact.

Participative behaviour during modelling, sometimes referred to as 'enactive mediation'; a form of non-verbal representation of information (see Hillix and Marx 1960; Berger, Smith-Irwin and Frommer 1970; Williams and Willoughby 1971; Williams 1987), will be considered in more detail in a subsequent section.

In summary, logical reasoning suggests that a learner stands to gain perceptual advantage by being positioned at both an optimal orientation to, and distance from, the action when modelling a movement pattern. Research completed to date on visual angle when modelling has yielded equivocal results. Instructors often wish that their charges possessed the 'zoom' capability of video cameras because the need for close-up and distant viewing can alter within the same modelling context. Sheffield and Maccoby (1961) were well aware of the potentially facilitative and disruptive effects on learning of relative distance from the display. Thus far, this variable seems to have been a 'blind spot' for motoric modelling research which should receive some attention in light of developments in modern imaging technology. Furthermore, the variable of distance from the model introduces a 'body-scaling' problem for the subsequent process of movement production (see Warren 1988). This aspect raises practical instructional issues and could form the basis of tackling such questions as 'How direct can modelling be?' which are germane to modelling theory.

Speed of model's action

Because of human information-processing limitations, modelled movement frequently has to be slowed (indeed static!) to be registered. This is difficult for a 'live' model, but slow-motion film or video permits this to be done. Roshal (1961) included this variable as part of his studies of film-mediated learning (knot tying of varied difficulty) and found films portraying normal continuity of action to be more effective except for the most difficult task.

An instructional consideration is the possible equivalence of slow motion and number of presentations of the demonstration. This issue was addressed by Fehres and Olivier (1986) in the study of a gymnastic movement pattern. They standardised duration of presentation and compared repetition and exposure speed. It was concluded that the speed reduction (fourfold slowing) improved performance because of enhanced visual perception of the action (improved visual intake and processing of spatial information).

A potential difficulty with altering the speed (usually slowing down) of a model's demonstration is that a learner may attune to the transmitted cadence. If timing is a vital element of the desired action this could be problematic. In a study which required participants to imitate a throwing action when the video model moved at varied speeds, Williams (1989b) showed that the timing of performance was most accurate when the timing which was most 'natural' for the object to be projected to appropriate areas of a target was observed. Participants altered their cadence in response to the velocity characteristics of the demonstration. Slowed demonstration is probably desirable when learning a relatively fast action in the early phase especially when the order of movements in a sequence has to be acquired (Williams 1986, 1987). However, motoric modelling should be supported by real-time observation because this permits the learner to develop a 'true' impression of what is to be done. This is necessary to get across the complex coherence of the spatio–temporal–kinetic structure of events which make up an action.

To return to the 'tongue-in-cheek' remark placed earlier in parenthesis, it is often forgotten that static depiction is a prominent way of demonstrating movement. This has been, and still is, widely used in motor skill instruction and general motoric modelling; few coaching manuals or instructional texts are without pictorial or schematic illustrations of action. Experience suggests that illustrations of this kind are frequently confusing and ambiguous (for a critical overview of the use of static and slow-motion displays during skill instruction, see Scully 1988). Few studies have examined this topic within the motor domain despite the fact that a substantial literature exists in the broader area of picture perception.

In this context, Daugs *et al.* (1985) and Blischke (1986) compared the production by adult participants from horizontally aligned, still row sequences of an 'unfamiliar' gymnastic movement (see Figure 9.4) which was presented to be 'read' either from left-to-right or right-to-left (and could be interpreted as a backwards movement from either presentation!). In keeping with typical visual scanning strategies, 87% of participants who viewed the left-to-right sequence performed correctly whereas 70% of those who used the right-to-left sequence performed the movement backwards (a highly significant difference ($p < 0.001$)). In further research, this group proceeded to compare the execution of the same gymnastic movement by adults and children who were instructed through variations of picture and text combinations. They concluded that pictures plus text instructions were superior to unimodal illustrations for both adults and children (nine years and above).

In a recently completed study which sought to examine the effectiveness of modelling on the acquisition of mechanically-safe lifting technique, Williams and Thompson (1994) combined a correct dynamic model with static depictions (vidi-prints) of key phases in the action. As a result of the instructional treatment, experimental participants (unlike controls) adapted their original, unsound lifting action to closely approximate the model's posture at the end of the instructional sequence and retained the more efficient action when reassessed fourteen days later.

Further research in this area is called for as it is seems unlikely that static models for the depiction of action will be entirely replaced by dynamic models for either formal or informal learning in the near future. Also, some optimal combination of dynamic and static depictions of action may well enhance the quality and speed of learning rather than either condition on its own.

Task type

Single demonstrations have been shown to be sufficient to convey the information necessary for the instant and correct performance of simple short tasks (Sheffield 1961). In a series of experiments which compared different types of tasks, Gould (1978) showed that modelling facilitated movement time on a speed-of-movement ball-snatch task and geometric construction-assembly task, but not on a rebound-ball-roll accuracy task. These findings for laboratory tasks (claimed to be representative of 'existing athletic skills') imply that the benefits derived from modelling treatments are probably task specific. As asserted in Social Cognitive Theory (e.g. Bandura 1986), tasks with a relatively high informational component produce modelling effects while those with a relatively low information content do not. However, as specification of the class and relative valence features displayed in the actions of a model and perceived by the modeller have yet to be delineated, confident statements await the findings of future research in this area.

In this context, Weeks (1992) pointed out that the bulk of modelling research has focused on skills in which coordinated control of the limbs as paced by the performer is the criterion rather than interceptive action which requires adaptation to changing environmental demands (skills at the 'closed' end of the skill continuum rather than 'open' end). His research studied an 'externally-paced' skill and reports evidence of a significant effect for perceptual modelling (as distinct from motoric, perceptuo–motor, and no-modelling) early in the acquisition of a coincidence–anticipation skill. However, by the end of the allocated practice period in this experiment, there were no significant performance differences between the experimental groups. This approach highlights the difficulty (perhaps futility) of attempting to understand modelling processes by means of a traditional experimental approach which seeks to differentiate function within a perception–action system that may well be inseparably integrated. The opinions of Paivio (1975), Weimer (1977), and Chase and Chi (1980) are worthy of consideration on this point.

Faced with the problem of designing appropriate instructional strategies, Sheffield (1961) introduced the idea of 'natural units' inherent in sequential action whereby the task was subdivided into natural units. He coined the term 'demonstration–assimilation span' (DAs) which is the largest unit of sequence within a task that the learner can store in memory and, subsequently, recall. Such a division is said to produce better conceptual representation because less information has to be processed by a learner (Carroll and Bandura 1982). Plainly, with complex action sequences such as those found in most sport skill learning, division of demonstration into DAs is perhaps a necessary instructional strategy. Within this process, the attainment of positive transfer between spans becomes an important consideration for modelling because of the need for coherence in producing a complete action sequence. This problem does not seem to have attracted the attention of motor skills researchers despite its clear significance for the categories of action which sports coaches routinely face.

Practice

It is self-evident that practice (repeating or rehearsing what was seen) exerts a profound influence upon learning. Motor skills instructors constantly manipulate practice in a variety of ways to achieve learning objectives. In what may be the most common form of modelling, echo-kinesis ('see then do'; see Prinz 1984), time elapses and events inevitably intervene between observation of the action and production of what was seen. Learners are faced with the problem of somehow retaining what they saw for both immediate and later recall. In the case of motoric modelling, it is supposed that this process is absolutely vital for the establishment of an appropriate 'cognitive representation' – the link between perception and action.

Both the passage of time and intervening events have an effect on memory for movement. Crucial information dissipates if nothing is done to facilitate retention. Older children and adults are known to use rehearsal strategies in order to remember (Flavell 1970; Kail 1979). As a general rule, researchers contend that the strategy used by a person to memorise what is to be learned influences the quality of subsequent movement production with quality of rehearsal being more important than the number of repetitions (e.g. Gallagher and Thomas 1984, 1986). There are many variants of rehearsal strategy and some of these are discussed below.

Motoric rehearsal

The usual sequence of events when modelling motor skills is for the learner to observe the skilled action which is to be learned and to follow this by moving their own body in such a way as to produce the desired action, then repeating (rehearsing) the movements a number of times. It has been suggested that this motoric rehearsal provides a means of translating a conception of action and kinematic characteristics into skilled action. The process is said to clarify symbolic representation by enhancing and channelling information (Carroll and Bandura 1985; Southard and Higgins 1987). It is interesting to note that Sheffield (1961) refers to the observation of a visual demonstration as a practice in itself. This use of the term could be taken to imply that he conceived of his analogy of a 'perceptual blueprint' as more direct (in the model's action) than those who have assumed it to be internally represented by the modeller.

Enactive mediation

This expression was introduced earlier and refers to the fact that, whilst modelling, learners find it extremely difficult to observe 'passively' when they know that they have to attempt to repeat what they saw. It seems that when the information-gathering system (attending, perceiving, remembering) is engaged, the coupling with the motor system is such that it is, in turn, 'coupled' to the model's action (see Jacobson 1932; Berry and Davis 1958; Berger, Smith-Irwin and Frommer 1970; Hatano, Miyake and Binks 1977). Recall that 'participation' by the learner has been a recurrent theme in this chapter. It is plausible that 'passive' observation in the sense that the observer watches, but does not move at all, may only appear to happen during modelling. However, Shea, Wright and Whitacre (1993), who examined practice effects in learning to control a dot of light moving around a screen using response keys, contend that 'actual' (motoric) and observational (cognitive) practice make unique contributions to skill acquisition.

Frequently a learner can be seen to 'shadow' or move synchronously with the actions of the model. Prinz (1984) refers to this behaviour as 'synkinesis' (see and do) in his two-way classification of ideo-motor action. If a lengthy period elapses between observation and production, learners often attempt a rudimentary, active reconstruction of what was observed then proceed to a full-scale attempt of the seen action. These strategies have been referred to as 'enactive mediation' and 'delayed motoric mediation' respectively and have been the subject of a limited amount of research (Roshal 1961; Berger et al. 1970; Williams and Willoughby 1971; Williams 1987). Depending on the complexity of the task and the velocity of the action, both kinds of physical practice have been found to enhance the quality of movement production when compared with passive observation. Enactive mediation may exert the effect of firmly establishing the action pattern through active involvement.

In a similar vein, Doody et al. (1985) reported improved performance in a task which required accurate timing of limb movement (displacing small barriers with the hand) by participants who were required to discriminate relevant environmental stimuli for the 'representation' of movement rather than passively watch a visual representation of the action. More recently, Carroll and Bandura (1987) have continued their research to find support for the prediction, suggested in Social Cognitive Theory (Bandura 1986), that the more firmly established a 'cognitive representation' of the task (in their case sequencing of arm movements), the better is subsequent production of the given pattern. It was reported that concurrent and delayed matching of the model's action (with or without visual monitoring by participants of their own response) enhanced the acquisition of serial ordering of components in the sequence and their retention throughout the course of the experiment. The results supported the prediction and, of course, added weight to the case for 'cognitive representation' as the perception-into-action catalyst.

Verbal rehearsal

Research into the effects of verbal rehearsal during modelling has shown that this variable produces significantly better modelling performance and retention of information in young and older children who used this strategy than in participants who did not (Weiss and Klint 1987; Housner 1984). This work suggests that verbalisation may be an integral part of the process of serial recall of movement information. As mentioned earlier, in the section on theory which discussed ideas advanced by Annett (1982, 1985, 1986), there are a number of possible combinations for the establishment of an appropriate action representation and verbal activity is among the likely contributors. The notion of 'action prototypes' as coined seems to be worthy of research as these are known to be liberally used during motor skill instruction.

Recently, Bandura and Carroll (1990) predicted that the number of presentations of the sequence by the model and verbal coding as a guide to action would, in combination, contribute to a more comprehensive cognitive representation which, in turn, would enhance the level of movement production. Once again the prediction was supported by the results. However, those who might be tempted to infuse these findings direct to instructional strategy would be wise to consider with care the task studied, measurement of the performance variable and the rationale for, and validity of, the measurement of the cognitive representation.

Imaginal rehearsal

Following a general finding from memory research that remembering is facilitated by imaginal or mental rehearsal, Finke (1986) has elaborated on a long-held view (Jacobson 1932; Paivio 1975) that mental imagery might facilitate perceptual processes by initiating neurological events equivalent to those occurring during overt performance. It is plausible that a learner's effort to retain then produce previously observed action would be aided by such a strategy. During research into the nature of the retention subprocess en route to Social Cognitive Theory, Bandura and Jeffrey (1973), in discussing problems encountered by participants who had been set the task of reproducing the more intricate versions of modelled configurations made with a stylus, suggested that reliance might be placed on ill-defined proprioceptive cues.

From the same research group, Gerst (1971), studying modelling of manual sign language, concluded that his results provided evidence of an influential role for imaginal mediators, particularly with respect to a positive link between imagery-producing effects of the stimulus material and accuracy of movement production. This has implications for the notion referred to earlier of aiding a learner's perception of the model through provision and enhancement of information which is vital to movement production.

Research by Housner (1984) found that adults spontaneously use imaginal processing strategies when required to observe then produce movement sequences. However, production of sequence accuracy was not enhanced when the participants were instructed to employ such strategies. In the same report, observers assessed as being 'high visual imagers' demonstrated recall accuracy superior to that of 'low visual imagers'. Wide individual differences in both reported and actual use of imagery are common knowledge. As Finke (1986) has shown for static images, a great deal of manipulation of an image is possible, but the quality of the image developed is dependent upon the subject's knowledge of the object. Likewise, 'quality of image' may not facilitate movement production.

As ever the notion of 'imagery' remains nebulous. A major problem for 'science' in this area is that the only people who have actually seen mental images are those who report having seen them! In the context of motoric modelling (and every other area which might be influenced by imagery), the topic warrants further investigation because of its possible elemental role in the perception–action process (see, Annett 1982, 1985; Whiting and den Brinker 1981). Such studies would inevitably include the consideration of individual difference, experiential and developmental variables, as well as type of imagery.

Temporal spacing and exposure to model

Although it is generally the case that learners observe a model prior to the practice of a skill (or an appropriate subcomponent), both the timing and amount of exposure to the model are significant instructional variables. Such issues were examined experimentally by researchers in the industrial–military training domain some time ago. For example, in the industrial skills area, Margolius, Sheffield and Maccoby (1961) tested the hypothesis that synchronisation (compared with asynchronisation) of demonstration to naturally occurring subdivisions of complex mechanical assembly task would facilitate learning. However, they observed no significant differences across their experimental manipulations. More recently, researchers with an interest in sports skills have investigated some aspects of these variables with a similar purpose (see Gould and Roberts 1981). Previously, Landers (1975) compared the effects of observing a model prior to, and midway through, practice on a balance-ladder task to test the assertion that spacing would be beneficial for the learner's attention and cue discrimination. The results supported their predictions with the group that received a demonstration both before and midway through practice being superior to the group that only received a demonstration prior to practice.

A variant of this theme is the number of showings of a demonstration which are required to bring about a modelling effect. The thrust of the argument is that some number beyond one is required for the learner to pick up the required information for movement production, but that diminishing returns result beyond a given number which may be fewer than many instructors believe (see discussion by McGuire 1961). Feltz (1982) embodied this variable into research on balance-ladder climbing as a possible interactant with age. She concluded that the number of showings of the modelled action is dependent upon the nature of the task and the length of the practice period (see also Martens *et al.* 1976). It is also expected that the phase of skill learning as well as developmental age would be important variables.

Williams (1984) found that the learning of the order of sub-movements in a relatively 'simple' throwing action sequence (video model lasting ten seconds) required some six demonstrations before accurate production was achieved by young adult participants. In practice, most instructors would probably consider this number of repeat showings to be unnecessary. Recall that earlier the potential perceptual advantage of slow motion over further repetitions of a model's action was discussed. Related to this topic is the issue of whether relatively high frequencies of exposure to a modelled action could detrimentally affect learning by interfering with cognitive processing. Hand and Sidaway (1992) addressed this issue in a study which examined relative frequency of observing a model prior to practice whilst learning a golf chip shot; prior to each practice trial, every fifth and every tenth were the experimental conditions. The results showed a significant trend in favour of greater modelling frequency.

Knowledge of performance and results

Knowledge of performance (KP) refers to information which becomes available to the learner as movement is made to achieve a particular goal as distinct from knowledge of results (KR) or outcome information. Both are important sources of information in motor learning and performance. As a general rule, it is accepted that more or less immediate and relevant information feedback is a potent learning variable. Arising from this, it might be supposed that information provided for a learner which directly depicts his or her actions relative to the model would be a very powerful learning variable indeed and one that researchers would be keen to explore. Thus far, this has not been the case. The provision of such feedback is quite difficult to contrive though less so nowadays with contemporary video technology. Carroll and Bandura (1982) examined this notion and concluded that the learning of a sequential motor task which involved moving the arms in positions outside of the learner's normal field of view was enhanced by simultaneous (concurrent visual) feedback relative to the model.

An extension of the idea introduced above is that of 'self-modelling' which emanates from research in the area of behaviour modification. This is defined as 'the behavioural change that results from the repeated observation of oneself on videotapes that show only desired target behaviours' (Dowrick and Dove 1980). These researchers used a self-modelling technique in an experiment with three spina bifida children whose swimming skills had reached a plateau. The participants' performance in the water was filmed and edited to produce instructional film based on positive behaviours only. The children's water skills improved significantly with repeated viewing of the edited tapes. A variant of this technique was used with positive effects in a single case study of a child learning to catch (Williams 1992). Lewis (1974) provides a review of various strategies. These findings imply that self-modelling is a potent form of observational learning centred on learners being more attentive and perceptive when practising their own positive behaviour.

Despite the fact that performers in many sports engage in self-modelling on an incidental basis (e.g. virtually all strength-training facilities and dance studios have mirrors and many athletes view video film of themselves and attempt to repeat their best efforts), there have been few controlled studies of self-modelling in the sports domain. An exception is a recent study by Winfrey and Weeks (1993) which looked at self-modelling in artistic gymnastic beam-balance performance. Although no significant differences were observed between control and self-modelling groups, the authors concluded that self-modelling enhances the athletes' ability to accurately assess performance relative to predetermined standards. Clearly, this is an area which warrants further research, particularly with respect to video modelling which appears to be ill-understood and under-utilised by coaches.

SUMMARY AND CONCLUSIONS

In this chapter we reviewed research and theory concerning the role of demonstrations in skill acquisition. Initially, we provided a review of contemporary theories of observational learning. The Social Cognitive Theory (formerly Social Learning Theory) put forward by Bandura (1986) appears to be the most comprehensive and coherent attempt to explain the constituent processes when people learn by observing the actions of others. The theory suggests that four components are crucial to the skill learning process: attention, retention, motor reproduction and motivation. However, although quite thorough in its exposition, Social Cognitive Theory lacks clarity with respect to the nature of perceiving whilst modelling and the link between perception and action, particularly the part played by 'symbolic representation'. These shortcomings have resulted in both suggested amendments and attempts at alternative explanations based on contemporary theorising on the visual perception of human movement (see Williams 1982, 1985; Prinz 1984; Scully and Newell 1985).

After outlining the main theoretical propositions, we then provided a comprehensive review of the empirical research work. In particular, we examined how selected variables such as developmental age, motivation, verbal cues, viewing angle and distance and the mode of presentation of demonstration impinge on the skill-learning process. It is clear that modelling and observational learning play a key role in the acquisition of sports skills. Finally, we examined how the effectiveness of demonstrations interacts with the type of task to be learnt and the organisation and mode of practice.

Although there now exists substantive and informative research on observational learning in sport, there are still many issues to be addressed and much work to be done. Our current understanding is tempered somewhat in light of the cautions and criticisms which have been signalled in this chapter. The exposition of modelling theory as it relates to motor skill learning and performance requires refinement in keeping with the findings of recent perception–action research. Replication and new research into aspects of learners' attention, perception and motoric enaction with that of the model are needed. Manipulations of crucial motion features in a model's action which enable a learner to perceive movement production affordances should be investigated further.

Regardless, at present the following general statement concerning the role of modelling in relation to motor skill learning can be made. An initial demonstration, either live or filmed, shown at natural speed and containing relevant visual and/or verbal cues helps a learner to understand the purpose of an action and the sequential organisation of movement subroutines. Further demonstrations of the same task, part way through practice, when used in conjunction with rehearsal strategies serve to enhance performance. Participation by a learner in the sense of movement which matches that of the model is a preferable strategy to passive observation except when constrained by the speed of the action. Novel tasks with a high informational display tend to produce stronger modelling effects. Finally, the status of the model must be considered along with the motivational, cognitive-representational and physical abilities of the learner.

Epilogue

In the nine chapters of this book we have considered many studies which highlight the nature and scale of the spatio–temporal demands on the sports performer. They have all emphasised the important role played by visual perception in helping athletes gear their actions to more or less dynamic environments. This is because the human performer has evolved to travel around the environment in different ways (e.g. walk, run, jump, dive, swim and hop) and to negotiate important objects (e.g. the arrival of a ball at an intercepting limb) and surfaces (e.g. the wall of the swimming pool for a tumble turn) along the way. The significant points that we have noted are that human actions always occur in a dynamic context and, more specifically, that skilled performance in sport consists of producing an appropriate balance between consistent (but not stereotyped) and flexible (but not random) movements. In order to produce just the right amount of persistence and change in movement patterns, sports performers need to perceive the spatio–temporal structure of the environment. As we have seen, there is little doubt that, without the capacity to detect and make sense of visual information from the environment, athletes would be unable to achieve the right blend of consistency and adaptability to successfully cope with complex tasks such as interceptive actions and locomotion in air, water and on land. What is needed now, from a sport perspective, is more empirical work to extend our understanding of the processes of perception and action, and, in particular, what coaches and teachers can do to help athletes develop important perceptual and movement skills as a basis for expertise in sport.

In this book we have outlined two broad approaches to the study of visual perception and their pertinence to many different aspects of sport performance, including the productions of actions, the recognition and identification of patterns in environmental information and relevant issues related to information management and practice organisation. In a recent review paper (i.e. Williams *et al.* 1992), we were content to alert the sport science community to the key issues under discussion in the motor–action systems debate. Since that time it is fair to say that concepts and theories in both camps have become more refined and there has been an increase in the number of researchers attempting to further our understanding of each specific theoretical framework. Also, since that time it is noticeable that there seems to have been a general acceptance of the difficulty in successfully resolving the debate and there have been a growing number of attempts to integrate criticisms as theoretical frameworks develop.

For example, cognitive theories of motor behaviour have been forced to reconsider the construct of mental representations, and many of the other symbolic tenets of the so-called 'computational hypothesis' (van Gelder, in press). In this respect, there are many who now believe that (non-symbolic) neural network modelling offers a more testable basis for understanding cognition. The underlying point is that many cognitive theorists now agree that an integration of psychological theory and the neurosciences offers a viable avenue for studying coordination and control of movements in dynamic environments (e.g. see the Lambda (λ) model of Feldman and Levin (1995)). On the other hand, ecological theorists have recently been attempting to develop their understanding of how intentions, cognitions, emotions and memories can be modelled within a dynamical systems framework. Moreover, there has been a greater emphasis on the thorny issues of learning and the acquisition of movement coordination.

Despite the strong philosophical traditions in these areas, there have been clear indications for some time of the general dissatisfaction with the polemics of the earlier debate. In the past few years, some commentators have advocated a pessimistic view of the possible integration of cognitive and ecological models (e.g. Abernethy and Sparrow 1992). Others have argued that it is too early in the developmental history of the ecological approach to dismiss such an integration, and that understanding the relationship between intentions and movement system dynamics represents a key task for researchers in the movement sciences (e.g. Davids *et al.* 1994; Summers 1992, 1998). In the context of sport, because of the highly specific and often artificial task constraints, the question has been posed whether a hybrid, integrated model is needed to account for the emergence of coordination in the movement system (e.g. Davids *et al.* 1994; Summers 1992).

A significant issue for future research to resolve concerns how much of movement coordination is due to self-organisation under constraint and how much is emergent due to the influence of intentional constraints. There are at least two main approaches to studying this problem, both of which have a strong theoretical and philosophical rational. These are: (i) the current attempts of movement scientists, such as Kelso and colleagues and Thelen and co-workers, to integrate intentionality within the dynamical systems framework and the efforts of cognitive scientists to incorporate dynamical modelling in the study of neural network models of cognition (see van Gelder, in press); and (ii) the cogently constructed, yet radical, arguments of Bongaardt (1996), based on a 'shifting focus', implying that more than one type of model may ultimately be needed to adequately describe the behaviour of a movement system *qua* complex system. The concept of 'shifting focus' refers to an approach which Bongaardt (1996) claims was originally introduced by Bernstein (1967). For Bongaardt (1996), the seeming incompatibility between many of the descriptions of the movement system is indicative of the way that the neuromotor system itself is organised. For Bernstein, coordination, exploration and planning are three interrelated processes which cannot be framed within one model. Quite simply, the argument is that in order to study movement behaviour one needs a 'shifting focus' between the three key processes, suggesting that more than one type of model is necessary to describe the behaviour at all levels of the movement system.

Whether it will be possible eventually to compare the viability of either approach remains open to question. Currently, the task of integrating intentionality into the dynamical systems framework is receiving a great deal of empirical attention. On the other hand, the 'shifting focus' theoretical perspective has a special pedigree that only someone of the stature of Bernstein (1967) could provide. In this respect, the coming years suggest that there may be many exciting developments in our theoretical understanding of perception and action. From what we have presented in this book, there is little doubt in our minds that sport-related tasks will represent most important vehicles for theoretical development. It is our hope that sport scientists will be able to play a part in these proceedings as we strive to gain a better understanding of human movement behaviour.

Notes

1 Indirect theories of perception and action

1 For example, without considering the system operation at the muscular and neural level, there are 28 degrees of freedom in the human arm.
2 In catching fly balls, for example, Brancazio (1985) has calculated that perturbations, such as wind resistance, may alter the flight characteristics of a ball by as much as 40%.
3 According to Edelman (1992), intentionality refers to our need to interact or negotiate or deal with significant objects in the environment. The term 'object' is used generically to refer to other people, animals, equipment and environmental properties, such as surfaces, gaps or brinks, which we are required to interact with during goal-directed behaviour. Important objects in a sport context obviously include projectiles, nets boundary markings, opponents, teammates, judges, referees, umpires, observers, forms of transportation including horses, cars and bicycles, and relevant equipment such as bats, rackets and other striking equipment. As Turvey (1986: 153) argues, 'intentionality is directedness towards objects'.
4 Recently, Bootsma and Peper (1992) have commented that Hubbard and Seng's (1954) data on swing duration and pitch velocity were 'not completely independent' (p. 294). They calculated that there was indeed a small slope of the regression line between ball speed and movement time during the batswing (2.42 ms). However, the data on swing duration seem remarkably constant given the imprecision in the measurement techniques employed by Hubbard and Seng (1954). The frame rates of 24 or 48 Hz used in filming batting performance will clearly result in some error in plotting the exact initiation point of the swing, given pitch speeds of between 142 and 187 kph.

3 The visual system hardware

1 The 'geography' of the visual region of the cerebral cortex is labelled in various ways in the research literature. Differences in terms seem to arise from the different experimental subjects (e.g. cat, monkey, human). Also, advances in neuroanatomy and neurophysiology have resulted in greater differentiation of target areas. For the purposes of this chapter the primary visual cortex, cortical area 17 and the striate cortex are equivalent.

5 Visual search strategy in sport

1 Although these systems measure eye movements, sports-based research has mainly been concerned with analysing the ocular fixations which separate eye movements (i.e. assessing visual point-of-gaze).

2 Further information is available from: NAC Incorporated 2–7, Nishi-Azabu. 1-Chome, Minato-Ku, Tokyo, Japan. Fax: +81 3 3479 8842.
3 Further information is available from: Applied Science Laboratories, 175 Middlesex Turnpike, Bedford, Massachusetts, 01730, USA. Fax: 617 275 3388.

Section B Introduction

1 Although a diversity of ideas exist to explain how coordinated patterns of movement emerge, we shall focus here on the commonalities that the theories share. Furthermore, it is our aim to avoid burdening the reader with the nuances underlining the subtle differences between these main theoretical strands. We will use the term 'ecological' to describe an approach which does not prioritise high-level, cognitive processes in explanations of human movement behaviour. In fact, as we shall see, influential ideas from paradigms of modern science are invoked to support the fundamental belief that information storage and representation do not figure strongly in lawful accounts of movement coordination in biological organisms.

6 Direct perception and action

1 For example, Weeks and Proctor (1991) have argued that the cognitive revolution over the last 40 years has resulted in considerable progress in understanding perception and action. However, their insistence on the success of the information processing approach brings to mind Dennett's (1991) criticism that cognitive explanations of human behaviour require some major assumptions by the scientist. Although Weeks and Proctor (1991) acknowledge that the 'approach afforded by the information processing framework provides only tentative explanations for behavioural phenomena' (p. 292), their argument is predicated on the notion that scientists interested in motor control and skill acquisition should be willing to 'evaluate the inclusion of mental representations "as if" they had construct validity' (p. 294).
2 This seems a consistent theme as the neurosciences unravel the mysteries of the CNS. Similar arguments at a monodisciplinary level, have been summarised by Morris *et al.* (1994) on the notion of motor programmes. They have argued that the representation in the CNS of movement programmes is difficult to reconcile with current neurological evidence on movement control. A whole range of problems (e.g. flexibility issues and context-conditioned action) have emerged which seriously question the idea that movements are stored in detail within the CNS (see also Davids *et al.* 1994). The basic point is that the dynamic nature of sport environments makes it difficult to rely on internal representations of specific movement sequences for the purposes of control.
3 Gibsonian theory is not just a theory of optical information, however. Other important sources of energy flows to support actions are auditory, haptic and proprioceptive. We have chosen to focus on optical information because of the orientation of this book.
4 In Chapter 3 on the hardware of the visual system, it was noted how current neurophysiological research is suggesting the existence of a number of distinct pathways in the cortex which are dedicated to information related to organismic needs such as perception and action (Milner and Goodale 1995).
5 A backward glance is a delicate stroke in which the player exploits the speed of a fast pitch delivery by deflecting the ball right in front of the stumps towards the boundary behind the wicket.

6 Note that bat displacement was measured in radians in this instance (and not metres per second as with linear motion) because the angular motion of the arm as it rotated around the shoulder joint was of interest.

7 The finding that the infants' timing behaviour became more precise and stable as the speed of the target object increased seems somewhat puzzling, given traditional notions of the development of computational precision with practice. However, as we shall see, the data are wholly consistent with the use of the tau margin information to provide time-to-contact information for the infants (see Lee and Young 1985). Lee and Young (1985) showed that the faster the relative speed at contact between an observer and an object to be caught, the more accurately the tau margin estimates actual time to contact.

8 We acknowledge the depth of understanding of Mark Scott who contributed greatly to the theoretical outline developed in this section.

9 The original ideas for this form of local tau originate from Lee and Young (1985). Their preferred term for this variant of local tau was 'spherical tau'. However, the equation they provided applies to non-spherical objects too, provided that the outline shape of the approaching object is not affected by a significant amount of rotation. We see no reason to disagree with the suggestion of Tresilian (1991) that the term 'Local Tau 2' can be used for this definition of tau.

10 Later identified as the standard deviation by Hay (1988).

11 These errors are significant given that only 2% of the total number of trials resulted in errors.

12 Luminous balls in a totally dark laboratory were used to isolate the informational support to that of the optical dilation rate of the image of the ball on the retina.

13 Defined on a within-task criterion measure as suggested by Whiting (1986).

14 Curiously, it was termed the 'tau strategy' (Lee and Reddish 1981; Lee *et al.* 1983) even though it is a strategy which does not require the pick-up of tau. The computational approach also assumes constant velocity and, for this reason, it has been argued that a better name would be the 'constant velocity' strategy (Tresilian 1991).

15 Judging relative distances is a fundamental requirement of the human species which receives a modern expression in sport and other more mundane activities. The evolution of smart perceptual mechanisms in humans for spatiotemporal judgements in relation to external objects may have its basis in the hunting techniques of the Palaeolithic age.

16 Acceleration came out as the best predictor of landing position of the dot for only three of the eleven subjects in that experiment. The data showed that subjects were able to detect acceleration but either did not or could not use it in their verbal judgements. More observers relied on information about the height that the dot rose to on screen and the duration of the simulation display.

17 McLeod and Dienes (1996) also pointed out that Chapman's influential modelling was based on subjects watching objects in parabolic flight. They asked whether the modelling was relevant to fielders required to catch a ball in the real world.

18 Although, here it is worth noting that Wann (1996) believes Tresilian (e.g. 1995) to be unnecessarily harsh when he argued that 'the old tau hypothesis is unable to account for skilled timing' (p. 233).

19 Tresilian (1994b: 343) points out that the average underestimate of reported Tc in these tasks is around 60% of Tc at the point of execution of the button press, with the SD of the estimates being 50%.

7 Information and dynamics

1 Typically, differential equations are used in the modelling because they capture the essence of change.
2 The landscape as a visual metaphor for the state space of a biological system was originally devised by the biologist Waddington (1954) to describe how evolutionary change could occur in a species. It has been introduced to the movement sciences by Thelen and colleagues.
3 For example, Beek and van Santvoord (1992) have demonstrated how skilled jugglers 'juggle with flair' by probing the common equation of juggling. This has been specified as the ratio of hand cycle time to ball cycle time which must on average equal the ratio of the number of hands to the number of balls being juggled. Satisfying this non-specific constraint required a fixed proportionality between the time taken by the hand to carry the ball and the total cycle time of a hand (with and without ball). Although, the value of 0.75 was argued as an attractor for juggling, expert jugglers could show off by varying this ratio to move hands more slowly or quickly in an intentional manner.
4 The exact temporal duration of ball flight was not made explicit by the authors although it seems to have been around 1500 ms, given the mean time for the one-handed catch by six subjects.
5 A major task for physicists is to discover the parameters which impose temporary spatio-temporal order on the microscopic components of a dynamical system. Usually they are parameters responsible for energy distributions surrounding the system. Some examples which spring to mind include: wind pressure on the molecular structure of a projectile; water pressure on flows in a pool; pheromones in insect nest-building; light rays reflecting from a ball approaching a fielder.
6 Possible exceptions occur in ball games when opponents may occlude sight of an approaching ball for a part of its flight towards the receiver. The wicket-keeper in cricket may need to resort to perceptual anticipation strategies when the bowler's delivery is occluded by the individual batting; the goalkeeper in soccer may use these processes when a defensive wall occludes a curling free kick; and the wide receiver in American football may have to perceptually anticipate part of the trajectory of a quarterback's pass in evading a running back.

8 The acquisition of movement coordination

1 The number of grasp errors may actually be an underestimate since committing a positional error could preclude the appearance of a grasp error. Elliott, Zuberec and Milgram (1994) concluded that a better analysis involves the proportion of grasp errors made only on trials when the hand was correctly positioned.

Bibliography

Abel, O. (1924) 'Eyes and baseball', *Western Optometry World* 12(1): 401–2.

Abernethy, B. (1981) 'Mechanisms of skill in cricket batting', *Australian Journal of Sports Medicine* 13: 3–10.

Abernethy, B. (1985) 'Cue usage in 'open' motor skills: A review of available procedures', in D.G. Russell and B. Abernethy (eds) Motor Memory and Control: Otago Symposium, Dunedin, New Zealand: Human Performance Associates.

—— (1987a) 'Anticipation in sport: A review', *Physical Education Review* 10: 5–16.

—— (1987b) 'Selective attention in fast ball sports: II Expert-novice differences', *Australian Journal of Science and Medicine in Sport* 19(4): 3–6.

—— (1987c) 'Selective attention in fast ball sports: I General principles', *Australian Journal of Science and Medicine in Sport* 19(4): 7–16.

—— (1988a) 'Dual-task methodology and motor skills research: Some applications and methodological constraints', *Journal of Human Movement Studies* 14: 101–32.

—— (1988b) 'Visual search in sport and ergonomics: Its relationship to selective attention and performer expertise', *Human Performance* 4: 205–35.

—— (1988c) 'The effects of age and expertise upon perceptual skill development in a racquet sport', *Research Quarterly for Exercise and Sport* 59(3): 210–21.

—— (1990a) 'Expertise, visual search, and information pick-up in squash', *Perception* 19: 63–77.

—— (1990b) 'Anticipation in squash: Differences in advance cue utilization between expert and novice players', *Journal of Sport Science* 8: 17–34.

—— (1993a) 'Attention', in R.N. Singer, M. Murphey and L.K. Tennant (eds) *Handbook of Research on Sport Psychology*, New York: Macmillan.

—— (1993b) 'Searching for the minimal essential information for skilled perception and action', *Psychological Research* 55: 131–8.

Abernethy, B. and Packer, S. (1989) 'Perceiving joint kinematics and segment interactions as a basis for skilled anticipation in squash', in C.K. Giam, K.K. Chook and K.C. Teh (eds) Proceedings of the 7th World Congress in Sport Psychology, Singapore: International Society of Sport Psychology.

Abernethy, B. and Russell, D.G. (1984) 'Advance cue utilisation by skilled cricket batsmen', *Australian Journal of Science and Medicine in Sport* 16(2): 2–10.

—— (1987a) 'Expert-novice differences in an applied selective attention task', *Journal of Sport Psychology* 9: 326–45.

382 Bibliography

—— (1987b) 'The relationship between expertise and visual search strategy in a racquet sport', *Human Movement Science* 6: 283–319.

Abernethy, B. and Sparrow, W. (1992) 'The rise and fall of dominant paradigms in motor behaviour research', in J.J. Summers (ed.) *Approaches to the Study of Motor Control and Learning*, Amsterdam: Elsevier Science.

Abernethy, B. and Wollstein, J.R. (1989) 'Improving anticipation in racquet sports', *Sports Coach* 12: 15–18.

Abernethy, B., Burgess-Limerick, R. and Parks, S. (1994b) 'Contrasting approaches to the study of motor expertise', *Quest* 46: 186–98.

Abernethy, B., Neal, R.J. and Koning, P. (1994a) 'Visual-perceptual and cognitive differences between expert, intermediate, and novice snooker players', *Applied Cognitive Psychology* 8: 185–211.

Abernethy, B., Thomas, K.T. and Thomas, J.T. (1993) 'Strategies for improving understanding of motor expertise (or mistakes we have made and things we have learned!)', in J.L. Starkes and F. Allard (eds) *Cognitive Issues in Motor Expertise*, Amsterdam: Elsevier Science.

Abernethy, B., Kippers, V., Mackinnon, L.T., Neal, R.J. and Hanrahan, S. (1997) *The Biophysical Foundations of Human Movement*, Champaign IL: Human Kinetics.

Abraham, F.D., Abraham, R.H. and Shaw, C.D. (1990) *A Visual Introduction to Dynamical Systems Theory for Psychology*, Santa Cruz: Aerial Press.

Abravanel, E., Levan-Goldschmidt, E. and Stevenson, M. (1976) 'Action imitation: the early phase of infancy', *Child Development* 47: 1032–44.

Ada, L., O'Dwyer, N.J. and Neilson, P.D. (1993) 'Improvement in kinematic characteristics and coordination following stroke quantified by linear systems analysis', *Human Movement Science* 12: 137–53.

Adams, J. (1986) 'Use of the model's knowledge of results to increase the observer's performance', *Journal of Human Movement Studies* 12: 89–98.

Adams, J.A. (1971) 'A closed-loop theory of motor learning', *Journal of Motor Behavior* 3: 111–50.

Adams, J.A., Gopher, D. and Lintern, G. (1977) 'Effects of visual and proprioceptive feedback on motor learning', *Journal of Motor Behaviour* 9: 11–22.

Adolphe, R.M., Vickers, J.N. and Laplante. G. (1997) 'The effects of training visual attention on gaze behaviour and accuracy: A pilot study, *International Journal of Sports Vision* 4(1): 28–33.

Alain, C. and Girardin, Y. (1978) 'The use of uncertainty in racquetball competition', *Canadian Journal of Applied Sports Sciences* 3: 240–3.

Alain, C. and Proteau, L. (1977) 'Perception of objective probabilities in motor performance', in B. Kerr (ed.) *Human Performance and Behaviour*, Banff, Alberta.

—— (1978) 'Etude des variables relatives au traitement de l'information en sports de raquette', *Canadian Journal of Applied Sports Sciences* 3: 27–35.

—— (1980) 'Decision-making in sport', in C.H. Nadeau, W.R. Halliwell, K.M. Newell and G.C. Roberts (eds) *Psychology of Motor Behavior and Sport*, Champaign IL: Human Kinetics.

Alain, C. and Sarrazin, C. (1990) 'Study of decision-making in squash competition: A computer simulation approach', *Canadian Journal of Sport Science* 15(3): 193–200.

Alain, C., Lalonde, C. and Sarrazin, C. (1983) 'A decision making model of squash competition', in H. Reider, H. Bos, H. Mechling and K. Reischle (eds) *Motor Learning and Movement Behavior: A Contribution to Learning in Sport*, Cologne: Hoffman.

Alain, C., Sarrazin, C. and Lacombe, D. (1986) 'The use of subjective expected values in decision making in sport', in D.M. Landers (ed.) *Sport and Elite Performers*, Champaign IL: Human Kinetics.

Alderson, G.J.K., Sully, D.J. and Sully, H.G. (1974) 'An operational analysis of one-handed catching task using high speed photography', *Journal of Motor Behavior* 6: 217–26.

Allard, F. (1982) 'Cognition expert performance and sport', in J.H. Salmela, J.T. Partington and T. Orlick (eds) *New Paths of Sport Learning and Excellence*, Ottawa, Ontario: Sport in Perspective.

Allard, F. (1993) 'Cognition expertise, and motor performance', in J.L. Starkes and F. Allard (eds) *Cognitive Issues in Motor Expertise*, Amsterdam: Elsevier Science.

Allard, F. and Burnett, N. (1985) 'Skill in sport', *Canadian Journal of Psychology* 39: 294–312.

Allard, F. and Starkes, J.L. (1980) 'Perception in sport: Volleyball', *Journal of Sport Psychology* 2: 22–33.

—— (1991) 'Motor-skill experts in sports, dance, and other domains', in K.A. Ericsson and J. Smith (eds) *Towards a General Theory of Expertise: Prospects and Limits*, Cambridge MA: MIT.

Allard, F., Deakin, J., Parker., S. and Rodgers, W. (1993) 'Declarative knowledge in skilled motor performance: Byproduct or constituent?', in J.L. Starkes and F. Allard (eds) *Cognitive Issues in Motor Expertise*, Amsterdam: Elsevier Science.

Allard, F., Graham, S. and Paarsalu, M.L. (1980) 'Perception in sport: basketball', *Journal of Sport Psychology* 2: 14–21.

Allport, D.A. (1980) 'Attention and Performance', in G. Claxton (ed.) *New Directions in Cognitive Psychology*, London: Routledge and Kegan Paul.

—— (1987) 'Selection for action: Some behavioral and neurophysiological considerations of attention and action', in H. Heuer and A.F. Sanders (eds) *Perspectives on Perception and Action*, Hillsdale NJ: Lawrence Erlbaum.

—— (1989) 'Visual Attention', in M.I. Posner (ed.) *Foundations of Cognitive Science*, Cambridge MA: MIT Press.

Anderson, J.R. (1982) 'Acquisition of cognitive skill', *Psychological Review* 89: 396–406.

—— (1983) *The Architecture of Cognition*, Cambridge MA: Harvard University Press.

—— (1987) 'Skill acquisition: Compilation of weak-method problem solutions', *Psychological Review* 94: 192–210.

—— (1990) *Cognitive Psychology and Its Implications*, 3rd edn, New York: W.H. Freeman.

—— (1992) 'Automaticity and the ACT theory', *American Journal of Psychology* 105(2): 165–80.

Anderson, D.I. and Sidaway, B. (1994) 'Coordination changes associated with practice of a soccer kick', *Research Quarterly for Exercise and Sport* 65(2): 93–9.

Annett, J. (1982) 'Motor learning: a cognitive psychological viewpoint', Proceedings of International Symposium on Research in Motor Learning and Movement Behaviour, Heidelberg, Germany.

—— (1985) 'Motor learning: a review', in H. Heuer, U. Kleinbeck and K.H. Schmidt (eds) *Motor Behavior: Programming, Control, and Acquisition*, Berlin: Springer-Verlag.

—— (1986) 'Some questions about imitation: notes for a workshop on movement imitation', Center for Interdisciplinary Research: Bielefeld, Germany.

Applegate, R.A. and Applegate, R.A. (1992) 'Set shot shooting performance and visual acuity in basketball', *Optometry and Vision Science* 69: 765–8.

Aronfreed, J. (1969) 'The problem of imitation', in H.W. Reese and L.P. Lipsitt (eds) *Advances in Child Development and Behavior*, vol. 4, New York: Academic Press.

Arutyunyan, G.H., Gurfinkel, V.S. and Mirskii, M.L. (1968) 'Investigation of aiming at a target', *Biophysics* 13: 536–8.

—— (1969) 'Organisation of movements on execution by man of exact postural task', *Biophysics* 14: 1162–7.

Austin, S. and Miller, L. (1994) 'Empirical study of the Sybervision golf video-tape', *Perceptual and Motor Skills* 74: 875–81.

Ayalon, A. and Ben-Sira, D. (1987) 'The mechanical changes during learning of a landing skill through various feedback methods', in G. de Groot, A.P. Hollander, P.A. Huijing and G.J. van Ingen Schenau (eds) *Biomechanics XI-B*, Amsterdam: Free University Press.

Bacon, S.J. (1974) 'Arousal and range of cue utilization', *Journal of Experimental Psychology* 102: 81–7.

Bahill, A.and LaRitz, T. (1984) 'Why can't batters keep their eyes on the ball?', *American Scientist* 72: 249–53.

Bainbridge, L. (1990) 'Verbal protocol analysis', in J.R. Wilson and E.N. Corlett (eds) *Evaluation of Human Work: A Practical Ergonomic Methodology*, London: Taylor and Francis.

Bakker, F.C., Whiting, H.T.A. and Brug, H. van der (1990) *Sport Psychology: Concepts and Applications*, Chichester: John Wiley.

Balan, C.M. and Davis, W.E. (1993) 'Ecological task analysis: An approach to teaching physical education', *Journal of Physical Education, Recreation and Dance*, November-December: 54–61.

Baldwin, J. M. (1920) [1906]*Mental Development in the Child and the Race*, New York: Macmillan.

Bandura, A. (1969) *Social Learning Theory*, London: Prentice-Hall.

—— (1971) *Psychological Modeling*, Chicago: Aldine-Atherton.

—— (1977) *Social Learning Theory*, Englewood Cliffs NJ: Prentice-Hall.

—— (1986) *Social Foundations of Thought and Action: A Social-Cognitive Theory*, New York: Prentice-Hall.

Bandura, A. and Jeffrey, R. (1973) 'Role of symbolic coding and rehearsal processes in observatioanl learning', *Journal of Personality and Social Psychology* 26: 122–30.

Barber, P.J. (1989) 'Executing two tasks at once', in A.M. Colley and J.R. Beech (eds) *Acquisition and Performance of Cognitive Skills*, Chichester: Wiley.

Bard, C. and Carriere, L. (1975) 'Etude de la prospection visuelle dans des situations problèmes en sports', *Mouvement* 10: 15–23.

Bard, C. and Fleury, M. (1976) 'Analysis of visual search activity during sport problem situations', *Journal of Human Movement Studies* 3: 214–22.

—— (1981) 'Considering eye movement as a predictor of attainment', in I.M. Cockerill and W.W. MacGillvary (eds) *Vision and Sport*, Cheltenham: Stanley Thornes.

Bard, C., Fleury, M. and Carriere, L. (1976) 'La stratègie perceptive et la performance motrice: Actes du septième symposium canadien en apprentissage psychomoteur et psychologie du sport', *Mouvement* 10: 163–83.

Bard, C., Fleury, M. and Paillard, J. (1990) 'Different patterns in aiming accuracy for head-movers and non-head-movers', *Journal of Human Movement Studies* 18: 37–48.

Bard, C., Guezennec and Papin, J.P. (1981) 'Escrime: Analyze de l'exploration visuelle', *Medicine du Sport* 15: 117–26.

Bard, C., Hay, L. and Fleury, M. (1985) 'Role of peripheral vision in the directional control of rapid aiming movements', *Canadian Journal of Psychology* 39(1): 151–61.

Bard, C., Fleury, M., Carriere, L. and Halle, M. (1980) 'Analysis of gymnastics judges visual search', *Research Quarterly for Exercise and Sport* 51: 267–73.

Bardy, B. (1993) 'Perception-action coupling in gymnastics: How do somersaulters control their orientation in space?', in S. Serpa, J. Alves, V. Ferreira and A. Paulo-Brito (eds) Proceedings of the 8th World Congress in Sport Psychology, Lisbon: ISSP.

Barfield, B. and Fischman, M. (1991) 'Control of ground-level ball as a function of skill level and sight foot', *Journal of Human Movement Studies* 19: 181–8.

Barmack, N.H. (1970) 'Dynamic visual acuity as an index of eye movement control', *Vision Research* 10: 1377–91.

Bartlett, F.C. (1932) *Remembering: A Study in Experimental and Social Psychology*, Cambridge, UK: Cambridge University Press.

Bassili, J.N. (1978) 'Facial motion in the perception of faces and emotional expression', *Journal of Experimental Psychology: Human Perception and Performance* 4: 373–9.

Baumeister, R.F. (1984) 'Choking under pressure: Self-consciousness and paradoxical effects of incentives on skilful performance', *Journal of Personality and Social Psychology* 46: 610–20.

Beals, R.P., Mayyasi, A.M., Templeton, A.E. and Johnson, W.L. (1971) 'The relationship between basketball shooting performance and certain visual attributes', *American Journal of Optometry and Archives of American Academy of Optometry* 48: 585–90.

Beek, P.J. (1989a) 'Timing and phase locking in cascade juggling', *Ecological Psychology* 3: 55–96.

—— (1989b) *Juggling Dynamics*, Amsterdam: Free University Press.

Beek, P.J. and Bingham, G. (1991) 'Task-specific dynamics and the study of perception and action: A reaction to von Hofsten (1989)', *Ecological Psychology* 3: 35–54.

Beek, P.J. and Meijer, O.G. (1988) 'On the nature of 'the' motor-action controversy', in O.G. Meijer and K. Roth (eds) *Complex Movement Behaviour: The Motor-Action Controversy*, Amsterdam: Elsevier Science.

Beek, P.J. and Santvoord, A.A. van (1992) 'Learning the cascade juggle: A dynamical systems analysis', *Journal of Motor Behavior* 24: 85–94.

Beek, P.J. and Wieringen, P.C.W. van (1994) 'Perspectives on the relation between information and dynamics: An epilogue', *Human Movement Science* 13: 519–34.

Beek, P.J., Peper, C.E. and Stegeman, D.F. (1995) 'Dynamical models of movement coordination', *Human Movement Science* 14: 573–608.

Beek, P.J., Rikkert, W.E. and Wieringen, P.C.W. van (1996) 'Limit cycle properties of rhythmic forearm movements', *Journal of Experimental Psychology: Human Perception and Performance* 22: 1077–93.

Bennett, S. and Davids, K. (1995) 'The manipulation of vision during the power-lift squat: Exploring the boundaries of the specificity of learning hypothesis', *Research Quarterly for Exercise and Sport* 66: 210–18.

—— (1996) 'Manipulating the informational constraints in one-handed catching: How generalisable is the specificity of learning hypothesis?', *British Psychological Society Sport and Exercise Psychology Section Newsletter* 5: 21–5.

Bennett, S., Davids, K. and Button, C. (1996) 'The specificity of learning hypothesis and one-handed catching', *Journal of Sports Sciences* 14: 21–2.

Berg, W.P. and Greer, N.L. (1995) 'A kinematic profile of the approach run of novice long jumpers', *Journal of Applied Biomechanics* 11: 142–62.

Berg, W.P., Wade, M.G. and Greer, N.L. (1994) 'Visual regulation of gait in bipedal locomotion: revisiting Lee, Lishman and Thomson (1982)', *Journal of Experimental Psychology: Human Perception and Performance* 20: 854–63.

Berger, S.M., Smith-Irwin, D., Frommer, G.P. (1970) 'Electromyographic activity during observational learning', *American Journal of Psychology* 83: 86–94.

Berman, A.M. (1995) 'Sports Vision for the Primary Care Practitioner', *Sports Vision* 11(2): 23–8.

Bernstein, N.A. (1967) *The coordination and regulation of movements*, Oxford: Pergamon Press.

Berry, D.S., Kean, K.J., Misovich, S.J. and Baron, R.M. (1991) 'Quantized displays of human movement', *Journal of Non-Verbal Behavior* 15: 81–97.

Berry, R.N. and Davis, R.C. (1958) 'Muscle responses and their relation to rote learning', *Journal of Experimental Psychology* 55: 188–94.

Bertalanffy, L. von (1950) 'The theory of open systems in physics and biology', *Science* 111: 23–9.

Beuter, A. and Duda, J.L. (1985) 'Analysis of the arousal/motor performance relationship in children using movement kinematics', *Journal of Sport Psychology* 7: 229–43.

Bingham, G.P. (1988) 'Task-specific devices and the perceptual bottleneck', *Human Movement Science* 7: 225–64.

Bingham, G.P., Schmidt, R.C. and Rosenblum, L.D. (1989) 'Hefting for a maximum distance throw: A smart perceptual mechanism', *Journal of Experimental Psychology: Human Perception and Performance* 15: 507–28.

Birch, H. and Lefford, A. (1967) 'Visual differentiation, intersensory integration and voluntary motor control', monograph of Society for Research in Child Development 32: 1–42.

Blischke, K. (1986) 'Memory effects in motor learning by visual instructions', Proceedings of AIESEP World Congress, Heidelberg, Germany.

Bloom, B.S. (1985) *Developing Talent in Young People*, New York: Random House.

Blumberg, M.S. and Wasserman, E.A. (1995) 'Animal mind and the argument from design', *American Psychologist* 50: 133–44.

Blundell, N.L. (1982) 'A multivariate analysis of the visual-perceptual attributes of male and female tennis players of varying ability levels', *Psychology of Motor Behaviour and Sport: Abstracts North American Society for the Psychology of Sport and Physical Activity*, University of Maryland.

Blundell, N.L. (1984) 'Critical visual-perceptual attributes of championship level tennis players', in M. Howell and B. Wilson (eds) Proceedings of the VII Commonwealth and International Conference on Sport, Physical Education, Recreation and Dance, University of Queensland, Brisbane, *Kinesiological Science* 7: 51–9.

Blundell, N.L. (1985) 'The contribution of vision to the learning and performance of sports skills: Part 1: The role of selected visual parameters, *Australian Journal of Science and Medicine in Sport* 17(3) 3–11.

Bongaardt, R. (1996) *Shifting Focus: The Bernstein Tradition in Movement Science*, Amsterdam: Free University Press.

Bootsma, R.J. (1988) 'The timing of rapid interceptive actions: Perception-action coupling in the control and acquisition of skill', PhD thesis, Amsterdam: Free University Press.

—— (1989) 'Accuracy of perceptual processes subserving different perception-action systems', *Quarterly Journal of Experimental Psychology* 41A: 489–500.

—— (1991) 'Predictive information and the control of action: What you see is what you get', *International Journal of Sport Psychology* 22: 271–8.

Bootsma, R.J. and Oudejans, R.R.D. (1993) 'Visual information about time-to-collision between two objects', *Journal of Experimental Psychology: Human Perception and Performance* 19: 1041–52.

Bootsma, R.J. and Peper, C.E. (1992) 'Predictive visual information sources for the regulation of action with special emphasis on catching and hitting', in L. Proteau and D. Elliott (eds) *Vision and Motor Control*, Amsterdam: Elsevier Science.

Bootsma, R.J. and Wieringen, P.C.W. van (1990) 'Timing an attacking forehand drive in table tennis', *Journal of Experimental Psychology: Human Perception and Performance* 16: 21–9.

Bootsma, R.J., Bakker, F.C., Snippenberg, F.J. van and Tdlohreg, C.W. (1992) 'The effects of anxiety on perceiving the reachability of passing objects', *Ecological Psychology* 4: 1–16.

Bootsma, R.J., Houbiers, M., Whiting, H.T.A. and Wieringen, P.C.W. van (1991) 'Acquiring an attacking forehand drive: The effects of static and dynamic environmental conditions', *Research Quarterly for Exercise and Sport* 62: 276–84.

Boutcher, S.H. (1992) 'Attention and athletic performance: An integrated approach', in T.S. Horn (ed.) *Advances in sport psychology*, Champaign IL: Human Kinetics.

Boutcher, S.H. and Zinsser, N. (1990) 'Cardiac deceleration of elite and beginning golfers during putting', *Journal of Sport and Exercise Psychology* 12: 37–47.

Bourgeaud, P. and Abernethy, B. (1987) 'Skilled perception in volleyball defense', *Journal of Sport Psychology* 9: 400–6.

Bower, T.G R., Broughton, J.M. and Moore, M.K. (1970) 'The coordination of visual and tactile input in infants', *Perception and Psychophysics* 8: 51–3.

Brancazio, P. J. (1985) 'Looking into Chapman's Homer: The physics of judging a fly ball', *American Journal of Physics* 53: 849–55

Brinkman, J.A. (1993) 'Verbal protocol accuracy in fault diagnosis', *Ergonomics* 36(11): 1381–97.

Broadbent, D.E. (1971) *Decision and Stress*, London: Academic Press

—— (1958) *Perception and Communication*, New York: Pergamon Press.

—— (1982) 'Task combination and selective intake of information', *Acta Psychologica* 50: 253–90.

Brody, G.H. and Stoneman, Z. (1981) 'Selective imitation of same-age, older and younger peer models', *Child Development* 52: 717–20.

Broker, J.P., Gregor, R.J. and Schmidt, R.A. (1993) 'Extrinsic feedback and the learning of kinetic patterns in cycling', *Journal of Applied Biomechanics* 9(2) 111–23.

Brown, B. (1972a) 'Dynamic visual acuity, eye movements and peripheral acuity for moving targets', *Vision Research* 12: 305–21.

—— (1972b) 'The effect of target contrast variation on dynamic visual acuity and eye movements, *Vision Research* 12: 1213–24.

Bruce, V., Green, P.R and Georgeson, M.A. (1996) *Visual Perception: Physiology, Psychology and Ecology*, 3rd edn, London: Lawrence Erlbaum.

Bruner, J.S. (1973) 'Organization of early skilled action', *Child Development* 44: 1–11.

Buckolz, E. Prapavesis, H. and Fairs, J. (1988) 'Advance cues and their use in predicting tennis passing shots', *Canadian Journal of Sports Sciences* 13: 20–30.

Bullock, D., Grossberg, S. and Guenther, F. (1996) 'Neural network modeling of sensory-motor control in animals', in H.N. Zelaznik (ed.) *Advances in Motor Learning and Control*, Champaign IL: Human Kinetics.

Bunge, M. (1967) *Scientific research. I: The Search for System*, Berlin: Springer-Verlag.

Burg, A. (1966) Visual acuity as measured by dynamic and static tests: A comparative evaluation, *Journal of Applied Psychology* 45: 460–6.

Burns, R.B. and Dobson, C.B. (1984) *Introductory Psychology*, Lancaster: MTP Press.

Burroughs, W.A. (1984) 'Visual simulation training of baseball batters', *International Journal of Sport Psychology* 15: 117–26.

Carlton, L.G. (1981) 'Visual information: The control of aiming movements', *Quarterly Journal of Experimental Psychology* 33A: 87–93.

Carello, C., Turvey, M.T., Kugler, P.N. and Shaw, R.E. (1984) 'Inadequacies of a computer metaphor', in M. Gazzaniga (ed.) *Handbook of Cognitive Neuroscience*, New York: Plenum Press.

Carpenter, R.H S. (1988) *Movements of the Eyes*, London: Plion.

Carroll, W.R. and Bandura, A. (1987) 'Translating cognition into action: the role of visual guidance in observational learning', *Journal of Motor Behavior* 19: 385–98.

—— (1982) 'The role of visual monitoring in observational learning of action patterns: making the unobservable observable', *Journal of Motor Behavior* 14(2): 153–67.

—— (1985) 'Role of timing of visual monitoring and motor rehearsal in observational learning of action patterns', *Journal of Motor Behavior* 17(3): 269–81.

—— (1990) 'Representational guidance of action production in observational learning: a causal analysis', *Journal of Motor Behavior* 22(1): 85–97.

Carson, R.C., Goodman, D., Kelso, J.A.S. and Elliott, D. (1995) 'Intentional switching between patterns of interlimb coordination', *Journal of Human Movement Studies* 27: 201–18.

Castiello, U. and Umiltá, C. (1988) 'Temporal dimensions of mental effort in different sports', *International Journal of Sport Psychology* 19: 199–210.

—— (1992) 'Orienting of attention in volleyball players', *International Journal of Sport Psychology* 23: 301–10.

Catina, P. (1995) 'Adaptations in the observer's cognitive representation in response to increased loading during modeling of a powerlifter's squatting action', unpublished MSc dissertation, West Chester University of Pennsylvania.

Chamberlin, C.J. and Coelho, A.J. (1993) 'The perceptual side of action: decision-making in sport', in J.L. Starkes and F. Allard (eds) *Cognitive Issues in Motor Expertise*, Amsterdam: Elsevier Science.

Chamberlain, C.J. and Lee, T. (1993) 'Arranging practice conditions and designing instruction', in R.N. Singer, M. Murphey and L.K. Tennant (eds) *Handbook of Research on Sport Psychology*, New York: Macmillan.

Chapman, S. (1968) 'Catching a baseball', *American Journal of Physics* 36: 368–70.

Charness, N. (1976) 'Memory for chess positions: Resistance to interference', *Journal of Experimental Psychology: Human Learning and Memory* 2: 641–53.

—— (1979) 'Components of skill in bridge', *Canadian Journal of Psychology* 33: 1–16.

Chase, W.G. and Chi, M.T.H. (1980) 'Cognitive skill: implications for spatial skill in large scale environments', in J. Harvey (ed.) *Cognition Social Behavior, and the Environment*, Potomac MD: Erlbaum.

Chase, W.G. and Ericsson, K.A. (1981) 'Skilled memory', in J.R. Anderson (ed.) *Cognitive Skills and Their Acquisition*, Hillsdale NJ: Lawrence Erlbaum.

Chase, W.G. and Simon, H.A. (1973a) 'The mind's eye in chess', in W.G. Chase (ed.) *Visual Information Processing*, New York: Academic Press.

—— (1973b) 'Perception in chess', *Cognitive Psychology* 4: 55–81.

Chi, M.T.H. and Rees, E.T. (1983) 'A learning framework for development', in M.T.H. Chi (ed.) *Contributions in Human Development*, vol. 9, Basel: S. Karger.

Christina, R.W., Barresi, J.V. and Shaffner, P. (1990) 'The development of response selection accuracy in a football linebacker using video training', *Sport Psychologist* 4: 11–17.

Churchland, P.M. (1989) *A Neurocomputational Perspective*, Cambridge MA: MIT Press.

Clark, J.E. (1995) 'On becoming skillful: Patterns and constraints', *Research Quarterly for Exercise and Sport* 66: 173–83.

Clarke, D. and Crossland, J. (1985) *Action Systems: An Introduction to the Analysis of Complex Behaviour*, London: Methuen.

Cobner, J. (1981) 'Auditory perception: A study of its contribution to motor learning and performance', *International Journal of Sport Psychology* 12(1): 75.

Cockerill, I.M. (1981) 'Peripheral vision and hockey', in I.M. Cockerill and W.W. MacGillivary (eds) *Vision and Sport*, Cheltenham: Stanley Thornes.

Cockerill, I.M. and Callington, B.P. (1981) 'Visual information processing in golf and association football', in I.M. Cockerill and W.W. MacGillivary (eds) *Vision and Sport*, Cheltenham: Stanley Thornes.

Cockerill, I.M. and MacGillivary, W.W. (eds) (1981) *Vision and Sport*, Cheltenham: Stanley Thornes.

Coelho, A. and Chamberlin, C.J. (1991) 'Decision-making in volleyball as a function of expertise', paper presented at meeting of North American Society for Psychology of Sport and Physical Activity, Asilmor CA, USA.

Coffey, B. and Reichbow, A.W. (1995) 'Visual performance enhancement in sports optometry', in D.F.C. Loran and C.J. MacEwen (eds) *Sports Vision*, Oxford: Butterworth Heinemann.

Cohen, J.D., Servan-Schreiber, D. and McClelland, J.L. (1992) 'A parallel distributed processing approach to automaticity', *American Journal of Psychology* 105(2): 239–69.

Coley, D. and McPherson, S.L. (1994) 'The influence of previewing a server prior to return of serve simulation tasks on decision making confidence and ability', *Journal of Sport and Exercise Psychology* 16: S42.

Committee on Vision of the National Research Council (1985) *Emergent Techniques for the Assessment of Visual Performance*, Washington DC: National Academy Press.

Connelly, J.G., Jr, Wickens, C.D., Lintern, G. and Harwood, K. (1987) 'Attention theory and training research', in Proceedings of 31st Annual Meeting of Human Factors Society, Santa Monica CA: Human Factors.

Cote, J., Salmela, J., Trudel, P., Baria, A. and Russell, S. (1995) 'The coaching model: A grounded assessment of expert gymnastic coaches' knowledge', *Journal of Sport and Exercise Psychology* 17: 1–17.

Cox, R.H. (1991) 'Relationship between stages of motor learning and kinesthetic sensitivity', *Journal of Human Movement Studies* 21: 85–98.

Craik, K.J.W. (1948) 'The theory of human control systems: II. Man as element in a control system', *British Journal of Psychology* 38: 142–8.

Crocker, P.R.E. (1983) 'Incidental and intentional motor learning', unpublished MSc thesis, Simon Fraser University, Canada.

Cutting, J.E. (1978) 'Generation of synthetic male and female walkers through manipulation of a biomechanical invariant', *Perception* 7: 393–405.

—— (1986) *Perception With an Eye For Motion*, Cambridge MA.: MIT Press.

Cutting, J.E. and Kozlowski, L. (1977) 'Recognising friends by their walk: Gait perception without familiarity cues', *Bulletin of Psychonomic Society* 9: 353–6.

Cutting, J. E., Proffitt, D. and Kozlowski, L. (1978) 'A biomechanical invariant for gait perception', *Journal of Experimental Psychology: Human Perception and Performance* 4: 357–72.

Damos, D.L. and Wickens, C.D. (1980) 'The identification and transfer of time-sharing skills', *Acta Psychologica* 46: 15–39.

Daugs, R., Blischke, K. and Olivier, N. (1986) 'Scanning habits and visuo-motor learning', Proceedings of the 3rd European Conference on Eye Movements, Amsterdam: Elsevier Science.

Davids, K. (1984) 'The role of peripheral vision in ball games: Some theoretical and practical notions', *Physical Education Review* 7: 26–40.

Davids, K. (1988) 'Developmental differences in the use of peripheral vision during catching performance', *Journal of Motor Behavior* 20(1): 39–51.

Davids, K. (in press) 'Skill acquisition and the theory of deliberate practice: It ain't what you do its the way that you do it!', *International Journal of Sport Psychology*.

Davids, K. and Bennett, S.J. (1994) 'How specific is the specificity of learning hypothesis?', in M. Audiffren and G. Minvielle (eds) *Psychologie des pratiques physiques et sportives*, Poitiers: University of Poitiers Press.

Davids, K. and Handford, C.H. (1994) 'Perception and action in sport: The practice behind the theories', *Coaching Focus* 26: 3–5.

Davids, K. and Stratford, R. (1989) 'Peripheral vision and simple catching: The screen paradigm revisited, *Journal of Sports Sciences* 7: 139–52.

Davids, K., Button, C. and Bennett, S.J. (in press) 'Modeling human movement systems in nonlinear dynamics: Intentionality and discrete movement behaviours', *Nonlinear Dynamics, Psychology and the Life Sciences*, in press.

Davids, K., Handford, C. and Williams, A.M. (1994) 'The natural physical alternative to cognitive theories of motor behaviour: An invitation for interdisciplinary research in sports science?', *Journal of Sports Sciences* 12: 495–528.

Davids, K., Palmer, D.R.P. and Savelsbergh, G.J.P. (1989) 'Skill level, peripheral vision and tennis volleying performance', *Journal of Human Movement Studies* 16: 191–202.

Davids, K., Bennett, S.J., Court, M., Tayler, M.A. and Button, C. (1997) 'The cognition-dynamics interface', in R. Lidor and M. Bar-Eli (eds) *Innovations in Sport Psychology: Linking Theory and Practice*, Netanya, Israel: ISSP.

Davids, K., Bennett, S.J., Handford, C.H., Jolley, L. and Beak, S. (1997) 'Acquiring coordination in interceptive actions: An ecological approach', in R. Lidor and M. Bar-Eli (eds) *Innovations in Sport Psychology: Linking Theory and Practice*, Netanya, Israel: ISSP.

Davis, W.E. (1988) 'An ecological approach to perceptual-motor learning', in R.L. Eason, T.L. Smith and F. Caron (eds) *Adapted Physical Activity: From Theory to Application*, 2nd edn, Champaign IL: Human Kinetics.

Day, L.J. (1980) 'Anticipation in junior tennis players', in J. Groppel and R. Sears (eds) Proceedings of International Symposium on Effective Teaching of Racquet Sports, Champaign IL: University of Illinois.

Deakin, J. and Allard, F. (1991) 'Skilled memory in expert figure skaters', *Memory and Cognition* 19: 79–86.

DeKlerk, L.F., Eernst, J.J. and Hoogerheide, J. (1964) 'The dynamic acuity of 30 selected pilots', *Aeromedica Acta* 9: 129–36.

DeLucia, P.R. (1991) 'Pictorial depth cues and motion-based information for depth perception', *Journal of Experimental Psychology: Human Perception and Performance* 17: 738–48.

DeLucia, P.R. and Warren, R. (1994) 'Pictorial and motion-based depth information during active control self-motion: Size-arrival effects on collision avoidance', *Journal of Experimental Psychology: Human Perception and Performance* 20: 783–98.

Dennett, D.C. (1991) *Brainstorms: Philosophical Essays on Mind and Psychology*, 2nd edn, Montgomery VT: Bradford Books.

Descartes, R. (1978) 'Meditations and passions of the soul', in E. Haldane and G. Ross (eds) *The Philosophical Works of Descartes*, vols I & II, Cambridge: Cambridge University Press.

Deutsch, J.A. and Deutsch, D. (1963) 'Attention: Some theoretical considerations', *Psychological Review* 70: 80–90.

Dickinson, J. (1977) 'Incidental motor learning', *Journal of Motor Behavior* 9: 135–8.

Dickinson, J. (1978) 'Retention of intentional and incidental motor learning', *Research Quarterly* 49: 437–41.

Diggles, V.A., Grabiner, M.D. and Garhammer, J. (1987) 'Skill level and efficacy of effector visual feedback in ball catching', *Perceptual and Motor Skills* 64: 987–93.

Dillon, J.M., Crassini, B. and Abernethy, B. (1989) 'Stimulus uncertainty and response time in a simulated racquet-sport task', *Journal of Human Movement Studies* 17: 115–32.

Ditchburn, R.W. (1973) *Eye movements and visual perception,* London: Oxford University Press.

Doody, S.G., Bird, A.M. and Ross, D. (1985) 'The effect of auditory and visual models on acquisition of a timing task', *Human Movement Science* 4: 271–81.

Dowrick, P.W. and Dove, C. (1980) 'The use of self-modeling to improve the swimming performance of spina bifida children', *Journal of Applied Behavior Analysis* 13: 51–6.

Dreyfus, H.L. and Dreyfus, S.E. (1986) 'Why skills cannot be represented by rules', in N.E. Sharkey (ed.) *Advances in Cognitive Science,* vol. I, Chichester: Ellis Horwood.

Dubanoski, R.A. and Parton, D.A. (1971) 'Effect of the presence of a model on imitative behavior in children', *Developmental Psychology* 4: 463–68.

Dupuy, C. and Ripoll, H. (1989) 'Analyse des stratégies visuo-motrices en escalade sportive', *Science et Motricité* 7: 19–26.

Easterbrook, J.A. (1959) 'The effect of emotion on cue utilization and the organization of behavior', *Psychological Review* 66: 183–201.

Edelman, G. (1987) *Neural Darwinism,* New York: Basic Books.

—— (1992) *Bright Air, Brilliant Fire: On the Matter of Mind,* New York: Penguin.

Egan, D.E. and Schwartz, B.J. (1979) 'Chunking in recall of symbolic drawings', *Memory and Cognition* 7: 149–58.

Egeth, H.E. and Yantis, S. (1997) 'Visual attention: Control, representation, and time course', *Annual Review of Psychology* 48: 269–97.

Elliott, B.C., Hardcastle, P.H., Burnett, A.F. and Foster, D.H. (1992) 'The influence of fast bowling and physical factors on radiologic features in high performance young fast bowlers', *Sports Medicine, Training and Rehabilitation* 3: 113–30.

Elliott, D. (1988) 'The influence of visual target and limb information on manual aiming', *Canadian Journal of Psychology* 41: 57–68.

Elliott, D., Zuberec, S. and Milgram, P. (1994) 'The effects of periodic visual occlusion on ball catching. *Journal of Motor Behavior* 2: 113–22.

Ells, J.G. (1973) 'Analysis of temporal and attentional aspects of movement control', *Journal of Experimental Psychology* 99: 10–21.

Emes, C., Vickers, J.N. and Livingston, L. (1994) 'Gaze control of children with high versus low motor proficiency', in *Adapted Physical Activity,* Tokyo: Springer Verlag.

Enns, J.T. and Richards, J.C. (1997) 'Visual attentional orienting in developing hockey players', *Journal of Experimental Child Psychology* 64: 255–75.

Ericcson, K.A. (1996) (ed.) *The Road to Excellence,* New Jersey: Lawrence Erlbaum.

Ericsson, K.A. and Charness, N. (1994) 'Expert performance: Its structure and acquisition', *American Psychologist* 49: 725–47.

Ericsson, K. A. and Chase, W. G. (1982) 'Exceptional memory', *American Scientist* 70: 607–15.

Ericsson, K.A. and Oliver, W.L. (1989) 'A methodology for assessing the detailed structure of memory skills', in A.M. Colley and J.R. Beech (eds) *Acquisition and Performance of Cognitive Skills*, New York: John Wiley.

Ericsson, K.A. and Simon, H.A. (1980) Verbal reports as data, *Psychological Review* 87: 215–51.

—— (1993) *Protocol Analysis: Verbal Reports as Data*, Cambridge MA: MIT Press.

Ericsson, K.A., Krampe, R.T. and Tesch-Römer, C. (1993) 'The role of deliberate practice in the acquisition of expert performance', *Psychological Review* 100: 363–406.

Eysenck, M.W. and Keane, M.T. (1995) *Cognitive Psychology: A Student's Handbook,* 2nd edn, London: Lawrence Erlbaum.

Fehres, K. and Olivier, N. (1986) 'The effects of videotaped repetitive presentations and slow-motion presentations on the acquisition of a complex motor skill', Proceedings of the AIESEP World Congress, Heidelberg, Germany.

Feldman, A.G. and Levin, M.F. (1995) 'Positional frames of reference in motor control. The origin and use', *Behavioural and Brain Sciences* 18: 723–806.

Feltz, D.L. (1982) 'The effects of age and number of demonstrations on modeling of form and performance', *Research Quarterly* 53(4): 291–96.

Feltz, D.L. and Landers, D.M. (1977) 'Information-motivational components of a model's demonstration', *Research Quarterly* 48(3): 525–33.

Feltz, D.L., Landers, D.M. and Raeder, U. (1979) 'Enhancing self-efficacy in high avoidance motor tasks: a comparison of modeling techniques', *Journal of Sport Psychology* 1: 112–22.

Festinger, L. (1971) 'Eye movement and perception', in P. Bach-y-Rita, C.C. Collins and J.E. Hyde (eds) *The Control of Eye Movements*, New York: Academic Press.

Finke, R.A. (1986) 'Mental imagery and the visual system', *Scientific American* 254: 76–83.

Fischman, M.G. and Mucci, W.G. (1989) 'The influence of a baseball glove on the nature of errors produced in simple one-handed catching', *Research Quarterly for Exercise and Sport* 60: 251–5.

Fischman, M.G. and Schneider, T. (1985) 'Skill level, vision and proprioception in simple catching', *Journal of Motor Behaviour* 17: 219–29.

Fitch, H. and Turvey, M.T. (1978) 'On the control of activity: Some remarks from an ecological point of view', in D. Landers and R. Christina (eds) *Psychology of Motor Behavior and Sport*, Champaign IL: Human Kinetics.

Fitch, H.L., Tuller, B. and Turvey, M.T. (1982) 'The Berstein perspective: III. Tuning of coordinative structures with respect to perception', in J.A. Scott Kelso (ed.) *Human Motor Behavior: An Introduction*, Hillsdale NY: LEA.

Fitts, P.M. and Posner, M.I. (1967) *Human Performance*, Belmont CA: Brooks/Cale.

Flavell, J.H. (1970) 'Developmental studies of mediated memory', in H.W. Reese and L.P. Lipsitt (eds) *Advances in Child Development and Behavior*, vol. 5, New York: Academic Press.

Fleishman, E. and Rich, S. (1963) 'Role of kinesthetic and spatial-visual abilities in perceptual-motor learning', *Journal of Experimental Psychology* 66: 6–11.

Fleury, M., Goulet, C. and Bard, C. (1986) 'Eye fixations as visual indices of programming of service return in tennis', *Psychology of Motor Behaviour and Sport* (abstract only), Champaign IL: Human Kinetics.

Fodor, J.A. and Pylyshyn, Z.W. (1981) 'How direct is visual perception? Some reflections on Gibson's "Ecological Approach"', *Cognition* 9: 139–96.

Forssberg, H. and Nashner, L. (1982) 'Ontogenetic development of postural control in man: Adaptation to altered support and visual conditions during stance', *Journal of Neuroscience* 2: 545–52.

Fowler, C.A. and Turvey, M.T. (1978) 'Skill acquisition: An event approach with special reference to searching for the optimum of a function of several variables', in G.E. Stelmach (ed.) *Information Processing in Motor Control and Learning*, New York: Academic Press.

Franks, I.M., Weicker, D. and Robertson, D.G. (1985) 'The kinematics, movement phasing and timing of a skilled action in response to varying conditions of uncertainty', *Human Movement Science* 4: 91–105.

French, K.E. and Nevett, M.E. (1993) 'The development of expertise in youth sport', in J.L. Starkes and F. Allard (eds) *Cognitive Issues in Motor Expertise*, Amsterdam: Elsevier Science.

French, K.E. and Thomas, J.R. (1987) 'The relation of knowledge development to children's basketball performance', *Journal of Sport Psychology* 9: 15–32.

French, K.E., Spurgeon, J.H. and Nevett, M.E. (1995) Expert-novice differences in cognitive and skill execution components of youth baseball performance, *Research Quarterly for Exercise and Sport* 66(3): 194–201.

Frey, P. W. and Adesman, P. (1976) 'Recall memory for visually presented chess positions', *Memory and Cognition* 4: 541–7.

Fuchs, A. (1962) 'The progression-regression hypothesis in perceptual-motor skill learning', *Journal of Experimental Psychology* 63: 177–92.

Fullerton, C. (1925) 'Eye, ear brain, and muscle tests on Babe Ruth', *Western Optometry World* 13(4): 160–1.

Gallagher, J.D. and Thomas, J.R. (1984) 'Rehearsal strategy effects on developmental differences for recall of a movement series', *Research Quarterly for Exercise and Sport* 55(2): 123–8.

—— (1986) 'Developmental effects of grouping and recoding on learning a movement series', *Research Quarterly for Exercise and Sport* 57: 117–27.

Gallway, T. and Kriegal, R. (1977) *Inner Skiing*, New York: Random House.

Gardner, J.J. and Sherman, A. (1995) 'Vision requirements in sport', in D.F.C Loran and C.J. MacEwen (eds) *Sports Vision*, Butterworth/Heinemann, Oxford.

Garland, D.J. and Barry, J.R. (1990) 'Sport expertise: the cognitive advantage', *Perceptual and Motor Skills* 70: 1295–1314.

—— (1991) 'Cognitive advantage in sport: The nature of perceptual structures', *American Journal of Psychology* 104: 211–28.

Gauthier, G.M., Semmlow, J.L., Vercher, C., Pedrono, C. and Obrecht, G. (1991) 'Adaption of eye and head movements to reduced peripheral vision', in R. Schmid and D. Zambarbieri (eds) *Oculomotor Control and Cognitive Processes*, New York: Elsevier Science.

Gelder, T. van (in press) 'The dynamical hypothesis in cognitive science', *Brain and Behavioural Sciences*

Gelder, T. van and Port, R.F. (1995) 'It's about time: An overview of the dynamical approach to cognition', in R.F. Port and T. van Gelder (eds) *Mind As Motion: Explorations in the Dynamics of Cognition*, Cambridge MA: MIT Press.

Gerst, M. (1971) 'Symbolic coding processes in observational learning', *Journal of Personality and Social Psychology* 19: 7–17.

Geurts, A.C.H. and T.W. Mulder (1994) Attention demands in balance recovery following lower limb amputation. *Journal of Motor Behavior* 26(2): 162–70.

Gibson, E.J. (1988) 'Exploratory behavior in the development of perceiving, acting, and acquiring knowledge', *Annual Review of Psychology* 39: 1–41.

Gibson, J.J. (1979) *An Ecological Approach to Visual Perception*, Boston MA: Houghton-Mifflin.

Gilhooly, K.J. and Green, A.J.K. (1989) 'Learning problem-solving skills', in A.M. Colley and J.R. Beech (eds) *Acquisition and Performance of Cognitive Skills*, Chichester: Wiley.

Glencross, D.J. (1978) 'Control and capacity in the study of skill', in D.J. Glencross (ed.) *Psychology and Sport*, Sydney: McGraw-Hill.

—— (1980) 'Response planning and organization of speed movements', in R.S. Nickerson (ed.) *Attention and Performance*, vol. VIII, Hillsdale, NJ: Lawrence Erlbaum.

Glencross, D. and Cibich, B. (1977) 'A decision analysis of games skills', *Australian Journal of Sports Medicine* 9: 72–5.

Glencross, D., Whiting, H.T.A. and Abernethy, B. (1994) 'Motor control, motor learning and the acquisition of skill: historical trends and future directions', *International Journal of Sport Psychology* 25: 32–52.

Goldfield, E. C. (1995) *Emergent Forms: Origins and Early Development of Human Action and Perception*, Oxford: OUP.

Goldman-Rakic, P. S. (1988) 'Topography of cognition: parallel distributed networks in the primate association cortex', *Annual Review of Neurosciences* 11: 137–56.

Goodale, M. A. (1993) Visual pathways supporting perception and action in the primate cerebral cortex, *Current Opinion in Neurobiology* 3: 578–85.

Goodale, M.A. and Milner, A.D. (1992) 'Separate visual pathways for perception and action', *Trends in Neuroscience* 15: 20–5.

Goodale, M.A. and Servos, P. (1996) 'Visual control of prehension', in H.N. Zelaznik (ed.) *Advances in Motor Learning*, Champaign IL: Human Kinetics.

Goodale, M.A., Milner, A.D., Jakobsen, L.S. and Carey, D.P. (1991) 'A neurological dissociation between perceiving objects and grasping them', *Nature* 349: 154–6.

Gopher, D. and Sanders, A.F. (1984) 'S-Oh-R: Oh stages! Oh resources!', in W. Prinz and A.F. Sanders (eds) *Cognition and Motor Processes*, Berlin/Heidleberg: Springer-Verlag.

Gordon, I. (1989) *Theories of Visual Perception*, Chichester: Wiley.

Gottsdanker, R.M. and Kent, K (1978) 'Reaction time and probability on isolated trials', *Journal of Motor Behavior* 10: 233–8.

Gould, D.R. (1978) 'The influence of motor task types on model effectiveness', unpublished doctoral dissertation, University of Illinois.

Gould, D.R. and Krane, V. (1992) 'The arousal-athletic performance relationship: Current status and future directions', in T.S. Horn (ed.) *Advances in Sport Psychology*, Champaign IL: Human Kinetics.

Gould, D.R. and Roberts, G.C. (1981) 'Modeling amd motor skill acquisition', *Quest* 33: 214–30.

Gould, J.D. (1973) 'Eye movements during visual search and memory search', *Journal of Experimental Psychology* 2: 399–407.

Goulet, C., Bard, C. and Fleury, M. (1989) 'Expertise differences in preparing to return a tennis serve: A visual information processing approach', *Journal of Sport and Exercise Psychology* 11: 382–98.

Graybiel, A., Jokl, E. and Trapp, C. (1955) 'Russian studies of vision in relation to physical activity and sports', *Research Quarterly* 26: 480–5.

Green, A.J. (1995) 'Verbal protocol analysis', *Psychologist* 8(3): 126–9.

Grieve, D.W. (1968) 'Gait patterns and the speed of walking', *Biomedical Engineering* 3: 119–22.

Grillner, S. (1975) 'Locomotion in vertebrates: Central mechanisms and reflex interaction', *Physiological Reviews* 55: 247–304.

Groner, R., McConkie, G.W. and Menz, C. (1985) *Eye Movements and Human Information Processing*, Amsterdam: Elsevier Science.

Groot, A.D. de (1965) *Thought and Choice in Chess*, The Hague, Netherlands: Mouton.

Grusec, J.E. and Brinker, D.B. (1972) 'Reinforcement for imitation as a social learning determinant with implications for sex-role development', *Journal of Personality and Social Psychology* 21: 149–58.

Guitton, D. and Volle, M. (1987) 'Gaze control in humans: Eye-head coordination during orienting movements to targets within and beyond the oculomotor range', *Journal of Neurophysiology* 58: 427–59.

Haken, H. (1983) *Synergetics, An Introduction: Non-Equilibrium Phase Transitions and Self-Organization in Physics, Chemistry, and Biology*, 2nd edn, Berlin: Springer-Verlag.

—— (1991) *Synergetics, Computers and Cognition*, Berlin: Springer.

Haken, H. and Wunderlin, A. (1990) 'Synergetics and its paradigm of self-organization in biological systems', in H.T.A. Whiting, O.G. Meijer and P.C.W. van Wieringen (eds) *The Natural Physical Approach to Movement Control*, Amsterdam: Free University Press.

Haken, H., Kelso, J.A.S and Bunz, H. (1985) 'A theoretical model of phase transitions in human hand movements', *Biological Cybernetics* 51: 347–56.

Hand, J. and Sidaway, B. (1992) 'Relative frequency of modeling effects on the performance and retention of a motor skill', *Research Quarterly for Exercise and Sport* Suppl. 63(1): A57–8.

Handford, C. and Williams, A.M. (1992) 'Expert-novice differences in the use of advance visual cues in volleyball blocking', *Journal of Sports Sciences* 9(4): 443–4.

Handford, C., Davids, K., Bennett, S. and Button, C. (1997) 'Skill acquisition in sport: Some applications of an evolving practice ecology', *Journal of Sports Sciences* 15(6): 621–40.

Harcum, E. R. (1975) *Serial Learning and Para-Learning*, New York: Wiley.

Harrington (1964) *The Visual Fields*, St Louis MO: Mosby.

Harris, C.M. (1989) 'The ethology of saccades: a non-cognitive model', *Biological Cybernetics* 60: 401–10.

Harris, C.M., Hainline, L., Abramov, I., Lemerise, E. and Camenzuli, C. (1988) 'The distribution of fixation durations in infants and naive adults', *Vision Research* 28: 419–32.

Hartfield, B.D., Landers, D.M. and Ray, W.J. (1984) 'Cognitive processes during self-paced motor performance: An electroencephalographic profile of marksmen', *Journal of Sport Psychology* 6: 42.

Hartfield, B.D., Landers, D.M. and Ray, W.J. (1987) 'Cardiovascular-CNS inter-actions during a self-paced, intentional state: Elite marksmanship performance', *Psychophysiology* 24: 542–9.

Haskins, M.J. (1965) 'Development of a response-recognition training film in tennis', *Perceptual and Motor Skills* 21: 207–11.

Hasse, H. and Mayer, H. (1978) 'Optische orientierungsstrategien von fechtern (Strategies of visual orientation of fencers)', *Leistungssport* 8: 191–200.

Hatano, G., Miyake, E. and Binks, M. (1977) 'Performance of expert abacus oper-ators', *Cognition* 5: 57–71.

Hatze, H. (1976) 'The complete optimization of a human motion', *Mathematical Biosciences* 28: 99–135.

Hay, J.G. (1988) 'Approach strategies in the long jump', *International Journal of Sport Biomechanics* 4: 114–29.

Hay, J.G. and Koh, T.J. (1988) 'Evaluating the approach in horizontal jumps', *International Journal of Sport Biomechanics* 4: 372–92.

Hayes, J.R. (1985) '*The Complete Problem Solver*, 2nd edn, Hillsdale NJ: Lawrence Erlbaum.

Haywood, K.M. (1984) 'Use of the image-retina and eye-head movement visual systems during coincidence-anticipation performance', *Journal of Sports Sciences* 2: 139–44.

Heijden, A.H.C. van der (1986) 'On selection in vision', *Psychological Research* 48: 211–19.

—— (1990) 'Visual information processing and selection', in O. Neumann and W. Prinz (eds) *Relationships Between Perception and Action*, Berlin/Heidelberg: Springer-Verlag.

—— (1992) *Selective Attention in Vision*, London: Routledge, Chapman and Hall.

Held, R. and Schlank, M. (1959) 'Adaption to disarranged eye-hand coordina-tion in the distance-dimension', *American Journal of Psychology* 72: 603–5.

Helmholtz, H. von (1925) *Treatise on Psychological Optics* (English language version translated and edited by J.P. Southall), Rochester NY: Optical Society of America.

Helsen, W. and Pauwels, J.M. (1988) 'The use of a simulator in evaluation and training of tactical skills in football', in T. Reilly, A. Lees, K. Davids and W.J. (eds) *Murphy Science and Football*, London: E. & F.N. Spon.

—— (1992) 'A cognitive approach to visual search in sport', in D. Brogan and K. Carr (eds) *Visual Search*, vol. II, London: Taylor and Francis.

—— (1993) 'The relationship between expertise and visual information processing in sport', in J.L. Starkes and F. Allard (eds) *Cognitive Issues in Motor Exper-tise*, Amsterdam: Elsevier Science.

Herbert, E.P. and Landin, D. (1994) 'Effects of a learning model and augmented feedback on tennis skill acquisition', *Research Quarterly for Exercise and Sport* 65(3): 250–7.

Hick, W.E. (1952) 'On the rate of gain of information', *Quarterly Journal of Experimental Psychology* 4: 11–26.

Hill, W.F. (1963) *Learning: A Survey of Psychological Interpretations*, London: Methuen.

—— (1965) *Learning: A Psychological Interpretation*, Oxford: Blackwell.

Hillix, W.A. and Marx, M.H. (1960) Response strengthening by information and effect. *Journal of Experimental Psychology* 60: 97–102.

Hitzeman, S.A. and Beckerman, S.A. (1993) 'What the literature says about sports vision', *Optometry Clinics* 3(1) 145–59.

Hoenkamp, E. (1978) 'Perceptual cues that determine the labelling of human gait', *Journal of Human Movement Studies* 4: 59–69.

Hoffman, L.G., Polan, G. and Powell, J. (1984) 'The relationship of contrast sensitivity functions to sports vision', *Journal of American Optometry Association* 55(10): 747–52.

Hoffman, L.G., Rouse, M. and Ryan, J.B. (1980) 'Dynamic visual acuity: a review', *Journal of American Optometric Association* 52: 883–7.

Hofsten, C. von (1983) 'Catching skills in infancy', *Journal of Experimental Psychology: Human Perception and Performance* 9: 75–85.

—— (1987) 'Catching', in H. Heuer and A. Sanders (eds) *Perspectives on Perception and Action*, Hillsdale NJ: Lawrence Erlbaum.

Holyoak, K.J. (1991) 'Symbolic connectionism: Toward third-generation theories of expertise', in K.A. Ericsson and J. Smith (eds) *Towards a General Theory of Expertise: Prospects and Limits*, Cambridge: Cambridge University Press.

Horak, F.B. and Nashner, L.M. (1986) 'Central programming of postural movements: Adaptation to altered support-surface configurations', *Journal of Neurophysiology* 55: 1369–81.

Houlston, D.R. and Lowes, R. (1993) Anticipatory cue-utilisation processes amongst expert and non-expert wicketkeepers in cricket, *International Journal of Sport Psychology* 24: 59–73.

Housner, L.D. (1984) 'Role of imaginal processing in the retention of visually-presented sequenced motoric stimuli', *Research Quarterly for Exercise and Sport* 55(1): 24–31.

Housner, L.D. and French, K.E. (1994) 'Future directions for research on expertise in learning, performance, and instruction in sport and physical activity', *Quest* 46: 241–6.

Howarth, C., Walsh, W.D. Abernethy, B. and Snyder, C.W. Jr (1984) 'A field examination of anticipation in squash: Some preliminary data', *Australian Journal of Science and Medicine in Sport* 16: 7–11.

Hoyle, F. (1957) *The Black Cloud*, London: William Heineman.

Hubbard, A.W. and Seng, S.N. (1954) 'Visual movements of batters', *Research Quarterly of American Association of Health and Physical Education* 25: 42–57.

Hubel, D. H. (1982) 'Exploration of the Primary Visual Cortex, 1955–78', (Nobel Lecture) *Nature* 299: 515–24.

—— (1988) *Eye, Brain, and Vision*, New York: W. H. Freeman.

Hubel, D.H. and Wiesel, T.N. (1977) 'Functional architecture of Macaque monkey visual cortex', (Ferrier Lecture), *Proceedings of Royal Society, London* B 198: 1–59.

Hubel, D.H. and Wiesel, T.N. (1979) 'Brain Mechanisms of Vision', *Scientific American* 241: 130–44.

Hughes, C. (1994) *The Winning Formula*, London: William Collins.

Hughes, C. (1995) *The Football Association Book of Tactics and Skills*, London: Queen Anne Press.

Hyman, R. (1953) 'Stimulus information as a determinant of reaction', *Journal of Experimental Psychology* 45: 188–96.

Imwold, C. H. and Hoffman, S. J. (1983) 'Visual recognition of a gymnastics skill by experienced and inexperienced instructors', *Research Quarterly for Exercise and Sport* 54: 149–55.

Ingen Schenau, G.J. van (1989) 'From rotation to translation: Constraints on multi-joint movements and the unique action of bi-articular muscles', *Human Movement Science* 8, 301–37.

Isaacs, L.D. (1981) 'Relationship between depth perception and basketball shooting performance over a competitive season', *Perceptual and Motor Skills* 53: 554.

Isaacs, L.D. and Finch, A.E. (1983) 'Anticipatory action of beginning and intermediate tennis players', *Perceptual and Motor Skills* 57: 451–4.

Ishikura, T. and Inomata, K. (1995a) 'Effects of angle of model-demonstration on learning of motor skill', *Perceptual and Motor Skills* 80: 651–8.

—— (1995b) 'A study comparison between rear and looking-glass model-demonstration conditions on modeling of a sequential motor task', *Japanese Journal of Physical Education* 38: 397–405.

—— (1998) 'Effects of reversal processing strategy of model demonstration on learning of motor skill', *Perceptual and Motor Skills*, in press.

Jackson, M. (1986) 'Sportspersons use of postural cues in rapid decision making', in J. Bond and J.B. Gross (eds) *Sports Psychology: Australia 1983*.

Jacobson, E. (1932) 'Electrophysiology of mental activities', *American Journal of Psychology* 44: 677–94.

James, W. (1890) *The Principles of Psychology*, vols 1 and 2, New York: Holt.

Jeannerod, M. (1993) 'A theory of representation-driven actions', in U. Neisser (ed.) *The Perceived Self: Ecological and Interpersonal Sources of Self-Knowledge*, Cambridge: Cambridge University Press.

Jeannerod, M. and Marteniuk, R.G. (1992) 'Functional characteristics of prehension: From data to artificial neural networks', in L. Proteau and D. Elliot (eds) *Vision and Motor Control*, Amsterdam: Elsevier Science.

Johansson, G. (1973) 'Visual perception of biological motion and a model for its analysis', *Perception and Psychophysics* 14: 201–11.

—— (1975) 'Visual motion perception', *Scientific American* 232(6): 76–88.

Jones, C.M. and Miles, T.R. (1978) 'Use of advance cues in predicting the flight of a lawn tennis ball', *Journal of Human Movement Studies* 4: 231–5.

Jonides, J. (1981) 'Voluntary versus automatic control over the mind's eyes movement', in J. Long and A. Baddeley (eds), *Attention and Performance*, vol. IX, Hillsdale NJ: Lawrence Erlbaum.

Jonides, J., Naveh-Benjamin, M. and Palmer, J. (1985) 'Assessing automaticity', *Acta Psychologica* 60: 157–71.

Jordan, F. (1979) 'Meaningful motor learning and cognitive-motor structure: the experimental facilitation of imitation learning of a complex motor task', unpublished MEd., University of Sydney, Australia.

Jordan, M.I. (1990) 'Motor learning and the degrees of freedom problem', in M. Jeannerod (ed.) *Attention and Performance*, vol. XIII, Hillsdale NJ: Lawrence Erlbaum.

Jordan, M.I. and Rosenbaum, D.A. (1989) 'Action', in M.I. Posner (ed.) *Foundations of Cognitive Science*, Cambridge, MA: MIT Press. *Journal of Motor Behaviour* 6(1): 11–16.

Just, M.A. and Carpenter, P.A. (1976) 'Eye fixations and cognitive processes', *Cognitive Psychology* 8: 441–80.

Kahneman, D. (1973) *Attention and Effort*, Englewood Cliffs NJ: Prentice Hall.

Kail, R. (1979) 'Use of strategies and individual differences in children's memory', *Developmental Psychology* 16: 251–5.

Kaiser, M.K. and Mowafy, L. (1993) 'Optical specification of time-to-passage: Observer's sensitivity to global tau', *Journal of Experimental Psychology: Human Perception and Performance* 19: 1028–40.

Kamp, J. van der, Vereijken, B. and Savelsbergh, G.J.P. (1996) 'Physical and informational constraints in the coordination and control of movements', *Corpus, Psyche and Societas* 3: 102–18.

Kandel, E.R., Schwartz, J.H. and Jessell, T.M. (1991) *Principles of Neural Science*, 3rd edn, New York: Prentice-Hall.

Kantowitz, B.H. (1974) 'Double stimulation', in B.H. Kantowitz (ed.) *Human Information Processing: Tutorials in Human Performance and Cognition*, New York: Wiley.

Kauffman, S.A. (1993) *The Origins of Order: Self-organisation and Selection in Evolution*, New York: Oxford University Press.

—— (1995) *At Home in the Universe: The Search for Laws of Complexity*, London: Viking.

Kawato, M. (1993) 'Optimization and learning in neural networks for formation and control of coordinated movement', in D.E. Meyer and S. Kornblum (eds) *Attention and Performance. Vol. XIV: Synergies in Experimental Psychology, Artificial Intelligence and Cognitive Neuroscience* Cambridge MA: MIT Press.

Kay, B. (1988) 'The dimensionality of movement trajectories and the degrees of freedom problem: A tutorial', *Human Movement Science* 7: 343–64.

Keele, S.W. (1968) 'Movement control in skilled motor performance', *Psychological Bulletin* 70: 387–403.

—— (1973) *Attention and Human Performance*, Pacific Palisades CA: Goodyear.

Keele, S.W. and Hawkins, H. (1982) 'Exploration of individual differences relevant to high skill level', *Journal of Motor Behavior* 14: 3–23.

Kelso, J.A.S. (1981) 'Contrasting perspectives on order and regulation in movement', in J. Long and A.Baddeley (eds) *Attention and Performance*, vol. IX, Hillsdale NJ: Lawrence Erlbaum

—— (1984) 'Phase transitions and critical behavior in human bimanual coordination', *American Journal of Physiology: Regulatory, Intergrative and Comparative Physiology* 15: R1000–4.

—— (1992) 'Theoretical concepts and strategies for understanding perceptual-motor skill: From informational capacity in closed systems to self-organization in open, nonequilibrium systems', *Journal of Experimental Psychology (General)* 121: 260–1.

—— (1994) 'The informational character of self-organized coordination dynamics', *Human Movement Science* 13: 393–41.

—— (1995) *Dynamic Patterns: The Self-Organization of Brain and Behavior*, Cambridge: MIT Press.

—— (1997) 'Relative timing in brain and behaviour: Some observations about the generalised motor program and self-organized coordination dynamics', *Human Movement Science* 16: 453–60.

Kelso, J.A.S. and Ding, M. (1993) 'Fluctuations, intermittency, and controllable chaos in biological coordination', in K.M. Newell and D.M. Corcos (eds) *Variability and Motor Control*, Champaign IL: Human Kinetics.

Kelso, J.A.S. and Jeka, J.J. (1992) 'Symmetry-breaking dynamics in human inter-limb coordination. *Journal of Experimental Psychology: Human Perception and Performance*, 18, 645–.

Kelso, J.A.S. and Schoner, G. (1988) Self-organization of coordinative movement patterns', *Human Movement Science* 7: 27–46.

Kelso, J.A.S., DelColle, J.D. and Schoner, G. (1990) 'Action-perception as a pattern formation process', in M. Jeannerod (ed.) *Attention and Performance*, Hillsdale NJ: Erlbaum.

Kelso, J.A.S., Ding, M. and Schoner, G. (1993) 'Dynamic pattern formation: A primer', in L.B. Smith and E. Thelen (eds) *A Dynamic Systems Approach to Development: Applications*, Cambridge, MA: MIT Press.

Kelso, J.A.S., Putnam, C.A. and Goodman, D. (1983) 'On the structure of human interlimb coordination', *Quarterly Journal of Exeprimental Psychology* 35A: 347–75.

Kelso, J.A.S., Southard, D. and Goodman, D. (1979) 'On the coordination of two-handed movements', *Journal of Experimental Psychology: Human Perception and Performance* 5: 229–38.

Kelso, J.A.S., Buchanan, J.J., DeGuzman, G.C. and Ding, M. (1993) 'Spontaneous recruitment and annihilation of degrees of freedom in biological coordination', *Physics Letters* A179: 364–71.

Kelso, J.A.S., Holt, K.G., Rubin, P. and Kugler, P.N. (1981) 'Patterns of human interlimb coordination emerge from the properties of non-linear, limit cycle oscillatory processes: Theory and data', *Journal of Motor Behavior* 13: 226–61.

Kimura, D. (1993) *Neuromotor Mechanisms in Human Communication*, Oxford: Oxford University Press.

Kluka, D.A., Love, P.A. Hammack, G. and Wesson, M.D. (1996) 'The effect of a visual skills training program on selected female intercollegiate volleyball athletes', *International Journal of Sports Vision* 3: 1.

Kluka, D.A., Love, P., Sanet, R., Hillier, C., Stroops, S. and Schneider, H.M. (1995) 'Contrast sensitivity function profiling: By sport and sport ability level, *International Journal of Sports Vision* 2(1): 5–16.

Kramer, A.F., Coles, M.G.H. and Logan, G.D. (1996) *Converging Operations in the Study of Visual Selective Attention*, Washington DC: American Psychological Association.

Kugler, P.N. (1986) 'A morphological perspective on the origin and evolution of movement patterns', in M. Wade and H.T.A. Whiting (eds) *Motor Development in Children: Aspects of Coordination and Control*, Dordrecht: Martinus Nijhoff.

Kugler, P. N. and Turvey, M.T. (1987) *Information, Natural Law, and the Self-Assembly of Rhythmic Movement*, Hillsdale NJ: Lawrence Erlbaum.

Kugler, P.N., Kelso, J.A.S. and Turvey, M.T. (1980) 'On the concept of coordinative structures as dissipative structures: I. Theoretical Lines of Convergence', in G.E. Stelmach and J. Requin (eds) *Tutorials in Motor Behavior*, Amsterdam: Elsevier Science.

—— (1982) 'On the control and co-ordination of naturally developing systems', in J.A.S. Kelso and J.E. Clark (eds) *The Development of Movement Control and Co-ordination*, Chichester: Wiley.

Kugler, P.N., Shaw, R.E., Vincente, K.J. and Kinsella-Shaw, J. (1990) 'Inquiry into intentional systems: Issues in ecological physics', *Psychological Research* 52: 98–121.

Lacquiniti, F. and Maioli, C. (1989a) 'The role of preparation in tuning anticipatory and reflex responses during catching', *Journal of Neuroscience* 9: 134–48.

—— (1989b) 'Adaptation to suppression of visual information during catching', *Journal of Neuroscience* 9: 149–59.

Land, M.F. and Fernald, R.D. (1992) 'The evolution of the eyes', *Annual Review of Neurosciences* 15: 1–29.

Landers, D.M. (1982) 'Arousal, attention, and skilled performance: Further considerations', *Quest* 33: 271–83.

—— (1975) 'Observational learning of a motor skill: temporal spacing of demonstrations and audience presence', *Journal of Motor Behavior* 7(4): 281–7.

Landers, D.N. and Landers, D.M. (1973) 'Teachers versus peer models: effects of model's presence and performance level', *Journal of Motor Behavior* 5(3): 129–39.

Landers, D.M., Wang, M.Q. and Courtet, P. (1985) 'Peripheral narrowing among experienced and inexperienced rifle shooters under low- and high-time stress conditions', *Research Quarterly for Exercise and Sport* 56: 122–30.

Landers, D.M., Christina, B.D., Hartfield, L.A., Doyle, L.A. and Daniels, F.S. (1980) 'Moving competitive shooting into the scientists' lab', *American Rifleman* 128: 36–7, 76–7.

Landers, D.M., Han, M., Salazar, W., Petruzzello, S.J., Kubitz, K.A., Gannon, T.L. (1994) 'Effects of learning on electroencephalographic and electrocardiographic patterns in novice archers', *International Journal of Sport Psychology* 25: 313–30.

Laszlo, J. I. and Bairstow, P.J. (1985) *Perceptual-Motor Behaviour: Developmental Assessment and Therapy*, Eastbourne UK: Holt, Rinehart and Winston.

Latash, M. (1993) *Control of Human Movement*, Champaign IL: Human Kinetics.

Latash, M.L. (1996) 'The Bernstein problem: How does the central nervous system make its choices?', in M.L. Latash and M.T. Turvey (eds) *Dexterity and Its Development*, Mahwah NJ: LEA.

Le Plat, J. and Hoc, J.M. (1981) 'Subsequent verbalizations in the study of cognitive processes', *Ergonomics* 24: 743–56.

Leavitt, J.L. (1979) 'Cognitive demands of skating and stick handling in ice hockey', *Canadian Journal of Applied Sports Sciences* 4: 46–55.

Lee, D.N. (1976) 'A theory of visual control of braking based on information about time-to-collision', *Perception* 5: 437–59.

—— (1978) 'The functions of vision', in H. Pick and E. Saltzman (eds) *Modes of Perceiving and Processing Information*, Hillsdale NJ: Lawrence Erlbaum.

—— (1980a) 'Visuo-motor coordination in space-time', in G.E. Stelmach and J. Requin (eds) *Tutorials in Motor Behavior*, Amsterdam: Elsevier Science.

—— (1980b) 'The optic flow field: The foundation of vision', *Philosophical Transactions of the Royal Society of London* B290: 169–79.

—— (1990) 'Getting around with light and sound', in R. Warren and A.H. Wertheim (eds) *Perception and Control of Self-Motion*, Hillsdale NJ: LEA.

Lee, D.N. and Aronson, E. (1974) 'Visual proprioceptive control of standing in human infants', *Perception and Psychophysics* 15: 529–32.

Lee, D.N. and Lishman, R. (1975) 'Visual proprioceptive control of stance', *Journal of Human Movement Studies* 1: 87–95.

Lee, D.N. and Reddish, P.E. (1981) 'Plummeting gannets: A paradigm of ecological optics', *Nature* 293, 293–4.

Lee, D.N. and Young, D.S. (1985) 'Visual timing of interceptive action', in D. Ingle, M. Jeannerod and D.N. Lee (eds) *Brain Mechanisms and Spatial Vision*, Dordrecht: Martinus Nijhoff.

Lee, J.R. and Zeigh, D.S. (1991) *The Neurology of Eye Movements*, Philadelphia: F.A. Davies.

Lee, T. and White, M.A. (1990) 'Influence of an unskilled model's practice schedule on observational motor learning', *Human Movement Science* 9: 349–67.

Lee, T.D. and Swinnen, S.P. (1993) 'Three legacies of Bryan and Harter: Automaticity, variability and change in skilled performance', in J.L. Starkes and F. Allard (eds) *Cognitive Issues in Motor Expertise*, Amsterdam: Elsevier Science.

Lee, D.N., Lishman, J.R. and Thompson, J.A. (1982) 'Regulation of gait in long jumping', *Journal of Experimental Psychology: Human Perception and Performance* 8: 448–59.

Lee, D.N., Young, D.S., Reddish, P.E., Lough, S. and Clayton, T.M.H. (1983) 'Visual timing in hitting an accelerating ball', *Quarterly Journal of Experimental Psychology* 35A: 333–46.

Legge, D. (1965) 'Analysis of visual and proprioceptive components of motor skill by means of a drug', *British Journal of Psychology* 56: 243–54.

Leifer, A.D., Collins, W.A., Gross, B.M., Taylor, P., Andrews, L. and Blackmer, E. (1971) 'Developmental aspects of variables relevant to observational learning', *Child Development* 42: 1509–16.

Levin, M. and Feldman, A.G. (1995) 'The gamma model for motor control: More than meets the eye', *Behavioral and Brain Sciences* 18: 786–98.

Lewis, S.A. (1974) 'A comparison of behavior therapy techniques in the reduction of avoidance behavior', *Behavior Therapy* 5: 648–55.

Livingston, M.B. and Hubel, D.H. (1987) 'Psychophysical evidence for separate channels for the perception of form, color, movement, and depth', *Journal of Neuroscience* 7: 3418–68.

Logan, G.D. (1988) 'Toward an instance theory of automisation', *Psychological Review* 95: 492–527.

—— (1985) 'Skill and automaticity: relations, implications, and future directions', *Canadian Journal of Psychology* 39: 367–86.

Long, G.M. and Crambert, R. (1990) 'The nature and basis of age-related changes in dynamic visual acuity', *Psychology and Aging* 5: 138–43.

Long, G.M. and Penn, D.L. (1987) 'Dynamic visual acuity: normative functions and practical implications', *Bulletin of Psychonomic Society* 25, 253–6.

Long, G.M. and Riggs, C.A. (1991) 'Training effects on dynamic visual acuity with free-head viewing', *Perception* 20: 363–71.

Long, G.M. and Rourke, D.A. (1989) 'Training effects on the resolution of moving targets dynamic visual acuity', *Human Factors* 31: 443–51.

Loran, D.F.C. and MacEwen, C.J. (eds) (1995) *Sports Vision*, Oxford: Butterworth Heinemann.

Low, F.N. (1943) 'The peripheral visual acuity of 100 subjects', *American Journal of Physiology* 140: 83.

—— (1946) 'Some characteristics of peripheral visual performance', *American Journal of Physiology* 146: 573.

Lumsdaine, A.A. (1961) *Student Response in Programmed Instruction*, Washington DC: National Research Council.

—— (1962) 'Experimental research on instructional devices and materials', in R. Glaser (ed.) *Training Research and Education*, New York: Wiley.

Lyle, J. and Cook, M. (1984) 'Non-verbal cues and decision-making in games', *Momentum* 9: 20–5.

Maccoby, N. and Sheffield, F. (1961) 'Combining practice with demonstrations in teaching complex sequences: summary and interpretation', in A.A. Lumsdaine (ed.) *Student Response in Programmed Instruction*, Washington DC: National Research Council.

Mackworth, N.H. (1976) 'Ways of recording line of sight', in R.A. Monty and J.W. Senders (eds) *Eye Movements and Psychological Processes*, Hillsdale NJ: Lawrence Erbaum.

Magill, R.A. (1993) *Motor Learning Concepts and Applications*, Oxford: Brown and Benchmark.

—— (1994) *Motor Learning: Concepts and Applications*, 4th edn, Dubuque IA: WCB Publishers.

Mahoney, M.J. and Avener, A. (1977) 'Psychology of the elite athlete: An exploratory study', *Cognitive Therapy and Research* 1: 135–41.

Majeres, R.L. and Timmer, T. (1981) 'Imitation preference as a function of motor competence', *Perceptual and Motor Skills* 52: 175–80.

Margolius, G.J., Sheffield, F.D. and Maccoby, N. (1961) 'Timing of demonstration and overt practice as a function of task organisation', in A.A. Lumsdaine (ed.) *Student Response in Programmed Learning*, Washington DC: National Research Council.

Marr, D. (1982) *Vision*, New York: W.H. Freeman.

Marr, D. and Poggio, T. (1976) 'Cooperative computation of stereo disparity', *Science* 194: 283–7.

Marteniuk, R.G. (1976) *Information Processing in Motor Skills*, New York: Holt, Rinehart and Winston.

Marteniuk, R.G. and MacKenzie, C.L. (1980) 'A preliminary theory of two-handed coordinated control', in G.E. Stelmach and J. Requin (eds) *Tutorials in Motor Behavior*, Amsterdam: Elsevier Science.

Marteniuk, R.G., MacKenzie, C.L. and Baba, D.M. (1984) 'Bimanual movement control: Information processing and interaction effects', *Quarterly Journal of Experimental Psychology* 36A: 335–65.

Martens, R. (1987) *Coaches Guide to Sport Psychology*, Champaign IL: Human Kinetics.

Martens, R., Burwitz, L. and Zuckerman, J. (1976) 'Modeling effects on motor performance', *Research Quarterly* 47(2): 277–91.

Martens, R., Burton, D., Vealey, R., Bump, L. and Smith, D. (1990) 'The development of the Competitive State Anxiety Inventory-2 (CSAI-2)', in R. Martens, R.S. Vealey and D. Burton (eds) *Competitive Anxiety In Sport*, Champaign IL: Human Kinetics.

Maschette, W. (1980) 'The use of advance cues during high-speed skilled performance', *Sports Coach* 4(1): 10–12.

Massaro, D. (1975) *Experimental Psychology and Information Processing*, Chicago: Rand McNally College Processing.

Masson, M.E.J. (1990) 'Cognitive theories of skill acquisition', *Human Movement Science* 9: 221–39.

Massone, L. and Bizzi, E. (1989) 'A neural network model of limb trajectory formation', *Biological Cybernetics* 61: 417–25.

Masters, R.S.W. (1992) 'Knowledge, Knerves and Know-how: The role of explicit versus implicit knowledge in the breakdown of a complex motor skill under pressure', *British Journal of Psychology* 83: 343–58.

Matsuo, T. and Kasai, T. (1994) 'Timing strategy of baseball-batting', *Journal of Human Movement Studies* 25: 253–69.

McClelland, J.L. (1989) 'Parallel distributed processing: Implication for cognition and development', in R.G.M. Morris (ed.) *Parallel Distributed Processing: Implications for Psychology and Neurobiology*, Oxford: Clarendon Press.

McCullagh, P. (1986) 'Model status as a determinant of observational learning and performance', *Journal of Sport Psychology* 8: 319–31.

McCullagh, P. and Caird, J.K. (1990) 'Correct and learning models and the use of model knowledge of results in the acquisition and retention of a motor skill', *Journal of Human Movement Studies* 18: 107–16.

McCullagh, P., Weiss, M.R. and Ross, D. (1989) 'Modeling considerations in motor skill acquisition and performance: an integrated approach', in K.B. Pandolf (ed.) *Exercise and Sports Sciences Reviews*, 17: 475–513, Baltimore: Williams and Wilkins.

McDonald, P.V., Emmerik, R.E.A. van and Newell, K.M. (1989) 'The effects of practice on limb kinematics in a throwing task', *Journal of Motor Behaviour* 21(3): 245–64.

McDonald, P.V., Oliver, S.K. and Newell, K.M. (1995) 'Perceptual-motor exploration as a function of biomechanical and task constraints', *Acta Psychologica* 88: 127–66.

McGuire, W.J. (1961) 'Some deleterious effects on a perceptual-motor skill produced by an instructional film: massing effects, interference, and anxiety', in A.A. Lumsdaine (ed.) *Student Responses in Programmed Instruction*, Washington DC: National Research Council.

McKenzie, I. (1992) *The Squash Workshop*, Marlborough, Wilts UK: Crowood Press.

McLeod, P. (1977) 'A dual-task response modality effect: Support for multi-processor models of attention', *Quarterly Journal of Experimental Psychology* 29: 651–67.

—— (1987) 'Visual reaction and high-speed ball games', *Perception* 16: 49–59.

McLeod, P. and Dienes, Z. (1993) 'Running to catch the ball', *Nature* 362: 23.

—— (1996) 'Do catchers know where to go to catch the ball or only how to get there?', *Journal of Experimental Psychology: Human Perception and Performance* 22: 531–43.

McLeod, P. and Jenkins, S. (1991) 'Timing, accuracy and decision time in high-speed ball games', *International Journal of Sport Psychology* 22: 279–95.

McLeod, R.W. and Ross, H.E. (1983) Optic-flow and cognitive factors in time to collision estimates', *Perception* 12: 417–23.

McLeod, P. McLaughlin, C. and Nimmo-Smith, I. (1985) 'Information encapsulation and automaticity: Evidence from the visual control of finely timed actions', in M.I. Posner and O. Marin (eds) *Attention and Performance*, vol. XI, Amsterdam: Elsevier Science.

McMorris, T. and Graydon, J. (1996) 'Effect of exercise on the decision-making performance of experienced and inexperienced soccer players', *Research Quarterly for Exercise and Sport* 67: 109–14.

McPherson, S.L. (1993a) 'Knowledge representation and decision-making in sport', in J.L. Starkes and F. Allard (eds) *Cognitive Issues in Motor Expertise*, Amsterdam: Elsevier Science.

—— (1993b) 'The influence of player experience on problem solving during batting preparation in baseball', *Journal of Sport and Exercise Psychology* 15: 304–25.

—— (1994) 'The development of sport expertise: Mapping the tactical domain', *Quest* 46: 223–40.

McPherson, S.L. and French, K.E. (1991) 'Changes in cognitive strategies and motor skill in tennis', *Journal of Sport and Exercise Psychology* 13: 26–41.

McPherson, S.L. and Thomas, J.R. (1989) 'Relation of knowledge and performance in boys' tennis: Age and expertise', *Journal of Experimental Child Psychology* 48: 190–211.

Meijer, O.G. (1988) *The Hierarchy Debate: Perspectives for a Theory and History of Movement Science*, Amsterdam: Free University Press.

Meijer, O.G., Wagenaar, R.C. and Blankendaal, F.C.M. (1988) 'The hierarchy debate: Tema con variazioni', in O.G. Meijer and K. Roth (eds) *Complex Movement Behaviour: 'The' Motor-Action Controversy*, Amsterdam: Elsevier Science..

Mendoza, L. and Schollhorn, W. (1993) 'Training of the sprint start technique with biomechanical feedback', *Journal of Sports Sciences* 11: 25–9.

Merigan, W.H. and Maunsell, J. H. R. (1993) 'How parallel are the primate visual pathways?', *Annual Review of Neurosciences* 16: 369–402.

Michaels, C.F. and Beek, P. (1995) 'The state of ecological psychology', *Ecological Psychology* 7: 259–78.

Michaels, C.F. and Carello, C. (1981) *Direct Perception*, Englewood Cliffs NJ: Prentice-Hall.

Michaels, C.F. and Oudejans, R.R.D. (1992) 'The optics of catching fly balls: Zeroing out optical acceleration', *Ecological Psychology* 4: 199–222.

Milgram, P. (1987) 'A spectacle-mounted liquid-crystal tachistoscope', *Behavior Research Methods, Instruments and Computers* 19: 449–56.

Miller, J. (1982) 'Discrete versus continuous stage models of human information processing: In search of partial output', *Journal of Experimental Psychology: Human Perception and Performance* 8(2): 273–96.

Miller, D.M. (1960) 'The relation between some visual perceptual factors and the degree of success realised by sport performances (doctoral dissertation, University of Southern California), *Dissertation Abstracts International*, 21: 1455A (University Microfilms No. 60–4484).

Miller, J. W. and Ludvigh, E. J. (1957) 'An analysis of certain factors involved in the learning process of dynamic visual acuity for 1000 naval aviation cadets', NSAM-574, Naval School of Aviation Medicine, Pensacola FL, USA.

—— (1962) 'The effect of relative motion on visual acuity', *Survey of Ophthalmology* 7: 83–116.

—— (1964) 'Some effects of training on dynamic visual acuity', NSAM-567, Naval School of Aviation Medicine, Pensacola FL, USA.

Miller, N.E.. and Dollard, J. (1941) *Social Learning and Imitation*, New Haven: Yale University Press.

Millsagle, D.G. (1988) 'Visual perception, recognition recall and mode of visual search control in basketball involving novice and experienced basketball players', *Journal of Sports Behavior* 11: 32–44.

Milner, A.D. and Goodale, M.A. (1993) 'Visual pathways to perception and action', in T.P. Hicks, S. Molotchnikoff and T. Ono (eds) *The Visually Responsive Neuron: From Basic Neurophysiology to Behaviour. Vol. 95: Progress in Brain Research*, Amsterdam: Elsevier Publishing.

—— (1995) *The Visual Brain In Action*, Oxford: Oxford University Press.

Montagne, G. and Laurent, M. (1994) 'The effects of environmental changes on one-handed catching', *Journal of Motor Behavior* 26: 237–46.

Moran, A.P. (1996) *The Psychology of Concentration in Sports Performers: A Cognitive Analysis*, London: Acadmic Press.

Morris, G.S.D. and Kreighbaum, E. (1977) 'Dynamic visual acuity of varsity women volleyball and basketball players', *Research Quarterly* 48: 480–3.

Morris, M.E., Summers, J.J., Matyas, T.A. and Iansek, R. (1994) 'Current status of the motor programme', *Physical Therapy* 74: 738–48.

Morrison, T.R. (1980) 'A review of dynamic visual acuity', NAMRL, Monograph 28, Naval Aerospace Medical Research Laboratory, Pensacola FL, USA.

Mosston, M. (1981) *Teaching Physical Education*, New York: Merrill.

Mowbray, G.H. and Rhoades, J.D. (1959) 'On the reduction of choice reaction-times with practice', *Quarterly Journal of Experimental Psychology* 11: 16–23.

Muchisky, M., Gershkoff-Cole, L., Cole, E. and Thelen, E. (1996) 'The epigenetic landscape revisited: A dynamic interpretation', in C. Rovee-Collier and L.P. Lipsitt (eds) *Advances in Infancy Research*, vol. 10, Norwood NJ: Ablex.

Nakagawa, A. (1982) 'A field experiment on recognition of game situations in ball games: In the case of static situations in rugby football', *Japanese Journal of Physical Education* 27: 17–26.

Nakayama, K. (1985) 'Biological image processing: A review', *Vision Research* 25: 625–60.

Navon, D. and Gopher, D. (1979) 'On the economy of the human processing system', *Psychological Review* 86: 214–55.

Neisser, U.N. (1967) *Cognitive Psychology*, New York: Appleton Press.

Neumaier, A. (1982) 'Untersuchung zur funktion des blickverhaltens bei visuellen wahrnehmungsprozessen im sport (An investigation of the function of looking in visual perception processes in sport)', *Sportswissenschraft* 12: 78–91.

Neumann, O. (1985) 'The limited capacity hypothesis and the functions of attention', report no. 23, Research Group on Perception and Action at the Center for Interdisciplinary Research, Bielfield University, Germany.

—— (1987) 'Beyond capacity: A functional view of attention', in H. Heuer and A.F. Sanders (eds) *Perspectives on Perception and Action*, Hillsdale NJ: Lawrence Erlbaum.

—— (1990) 'Visual attention and action', in O. Neumann and W. Prinz (eds) *Relationships Between Perception and Action*, Berlin: Springer-Verlag.

Neumann, O. and Prinz, W. (eds) (1990) *Relationships Between Perception and Action: Current Approaches*, Berlin: Springer-Verlag.

Neumann, O., Heijden, A.H.C. van der and Allport, D.A. (1986) 'Visual selective attention: Introductory remarks', *Psychological Research* 48: 185–8.

Newell, A. (1980) 'Physical symbol systems', *Cognitive Science* 4: 135–83.

Newell, A. and Simon, H. (1976) 'Computer science as empirical enquiry: Symbols and search', *Communications of the Association for Computing Machinery* 19: 113–26.

Newell, K.M. (1985) 'Coordination, control and skill', in D. Goodman, R.B. Wilberg and I.M. Franks (eds) *Differing Perspectives in Motor Learning, Memory, and Control*, Amsterdam: Elsevier Science.

—— (1986) 'Constraints on the development of coordination', in M. Wade and H.T.A. Whiting (eds) *Motor Development in Children: Aspects of Coordination and Control*, Dordrecht: Martinus Nijhoff.

—— (1996) 'Change in movement and skill: Learning, retention and transfer', in M.L. Latash and M.T. Turvey (eds) *Dexterity and its Development*, Mahwah NJ: LEA.

Newell, K.M. and Emmerik, R.E.A. van. (1989) 'The acquisition of coordination: Preliminary analysis of learning to write', *Human Movement Science* 8: 17–32.

—— (1990) 'Are Gesell's developmental principles general principles for the acquisition of coordination?', in J. Clark and J. Humphrey (eds) *Advances in Motor Development Research*, vol. III, New York: AMS Press.

Newell, K.M. and McDonald, P.V. (1991) 'Practice: a search for task solutions', in R. Christina and H.M. Eckert (eds) *American Academy of Physical Education Papers, Enhancing Human Performance in Sport: New Concepts and Developments*, Champaign IL: Human Kinetics.

—— (1994) 'Learning to coordinate redundant biomechanical degrees of freedom', in S. Swinnen, H. Heuer, J. Massion and P. Casaer (eds) *Interlimb Coordination. Neural, Dynamical and Cognitive Constraints*, New York: Academic Press.

Newell, K.M. and Walter, C.B. (1981) 'Kinematic and kinetic parameters as information feedback in motor skill acquisition', *Journal of Human Movement Studies* 7: 235–54.

Newell, K.M., Sparrow, W.A. and Quinn Jr., J.T. (1985) 'Kinetic information feedback for learning tasks', *Journal of Human Movement Studies* 11: 113–23.

Newell, K.M., Kugler, P.N., Emmerik, R.E.A. van and McDonald, P.V. (1989) 'Search strategies and the acquisition of coordination', in S.A. Wallace (ed.) *Perspectives on the Coordination of Movement*, Amsterdam: Elsevier Science.

Newell, K.M., Scully, D.M., Tenenbaum, F. and Hardiman, S. (1989) 'Body scale and the development of prehension', *Developmental Psychobiology* 22: 1–13.

Nisbett, R.E. and Wilson, T.D. (1977) 'Telling more than we can know: Verbal reports on mental processes', *Psychological Review* 84: 231–59.

Norman, D.A. (1968) 'Toward a theory of memory and attention', *Psychological Review* 75: 522–36.

—— (1969) *Memory and Attention*, New York: Wiley.

—— (1976) *Memory and Attention*, 2nd edn, Chichester: Wiley.

Nougier, V., Azemar, G. and Stein, J.F. (1992) 'Covert orienting to central visual cues and sport practice relations in the development of visual attention', *Journal of Experimental and Child Psychology* 54: 315–33.

Nougier, V., Ripoll, H. and Stein, J.F. (1989) 'Orienting of attention with highly skilled athletes', *International Journal of Sport Psychology* 20: 205–23.

Nougier, V. Stein, J.F. and Bonnel, A.M. (1991) 'Information processing in sport and orienting of attention', *International Journal of Sport Psychology* 22: 307–27.

Ogle, K.N. (1964) *Researches in Binocular Vision*, New York: Hafner.

Oudejans, R.R.D., Michaels, C.F., Bakker, F. and Davids, K. (1996) 'Catching in the dark', *British Psychological Society Sport and Exercise Psychology Section Newsletter* 5: 19–21.

Paillard, J. (1980) 'The multi-channeling of visual cues and the organisation of a visually guided response', in G.E. Stelmach and J. Requin (eds) *Tutorials in Motor Behaviour*, Amsterdam: Elsevier Science.

Paillard, J. (1982) 'The contribution of peripheral and central vision to visually guided reaching', in D.J. Ingle, M.A. Goodale and R.J.W. Mansfield (eds) *Analysis of Visual Behaviour*, Cambridge MA: MIT Press.

Paillard, J. (1985) 'The contribution of peripheral and central vision to visually guided reaching', in D.J. Ingle, M.A. Goodale and J.W. Mansfield (eds) *Analysis of Visual Behaviour*, MIT: MIT Press.

Paillard, J. and Amblard, B. (1985) 'Static versus kinetic visual cues for processing spatial relationship', in D.J. Ingle, M. Jeannerod and D.N. Lee (eds) *Brain Mechanisms and Spatial Vision*, Series D: no. 21, Dodrecht: Martinus Nijhoff.

Paivio, A. (1975) 'Neomentalism', *Canadian Journal of Psychology* 29: 263–91.

Palmer, A. and Dobereiner, P. (1986) *Arnold Palmer's Complete Book of Putting*, New York: Antheneum.

Papin, J.M., Metges, P. and Amalberti, R. (1984) 'Use of NAC eye mark by radiologists', in A. Gale and F. Johnson (eds) *Theoretical and Applied Aspects of Eye Movements Research*, Amsterdam: Elsevier Science.

Parasuraman, R. (1984) 'Sustained attention in detection and discrimination', in R. Parasuraman and D.R. Davies (eds) *Varieties of Attention*, New York: Academic Press.

Parker, H. (1981) 'Visual detection and perception in netball', in M. Cockerill and W.W. MacGillivary (eds) *Vision and Sport*, Cheltenham: Stanley Thornes.

Parker, S.G. (1989) 'Organization of knowledge in ice hockey experts', unpublished master's thesis, University of New Brunswick (cited in Allard and Starkes 1991).

Parton, D. (1976) 'Learning to imitate in infancy', *Child Development*, 47: 14–31.

Pashler, H. (1996) *The Psychology of Attention*, Cambridge MA: MIT Press.

Patrick, J. and Spurgeon, P. (1978) 'The use of body cues in the anticipation of the direction of a ball', paper presented at 19th International Congress of Applied Psychology, Munich, Germany.

Pattee, H. (1979) 'Complementation vs reduction as an explanation of biological complexity', *American Journal of Physiology* 5: 241–6.

Paull, G. and Glencross, D. (1997) 'Expert perception and decision making in baseball', *International Journal of Sport Psychology* 28: 35–56.

Peper, C.L.E., Bootsma, R.J., Mestre, D. and Bakker, F.C. (1994) 'Catching balls: How to get the hand to the right place at the right time', *Journal of Experimental Psychology: Human Perception and Performance* 20: 591–612.

Perry, D.G. and Perry, L.C. (1975) 'Observational learning in children: effects of sex of model and subject's sex role behavior', *Journal of Personality and Social Psychology* 31: 1083–8.

Petrakis, E. (1986) 'Visual observation patterns of tennis teachers', *Research Quarterly for Exercise and Sport* 57(3): 254–9.

—— (1987) 'Analysis of visual search patterns of dance teachers', *Journal of Teaching in Physical Education* 6(2): 149–56.

Pew, R.W. (1966) 'Acquisition of hierarchical control over the temporal organization of a skill', *Journal of Experimental Psychology* 71: 764–71.

Piaget, J. (1951) *Play, Dreams, and Imitation in Childhood*, New York: Norton.

Pinel, J.P.J. (1993) *Biopsychology*, London: Allyn and Bacon.

Planer, P.M. (1994) *Sports Vision Manual*, Harrisburg PA: International Academy of Sports Vision.

Poggio, G.F. and Poggio, T. (1984) 'The analysis of stereopsis', *Annual Review of Neurosciences* 7: 379–412.

Poizner, H., Bellugi, U. and Lutes-Driscoll, V. (1981) 'Perception of American sign language in dynamic point-light displays', *Journal of Experimental Psychology: Human Performance and Perception* 7: 430–40.

Pollock, B. and Lee,T. (1992) 'Effects of the model's skill level on observational motor learning', *Research Quarterly for Exercise and Sport* 63: 25–9.

Port, R.F. and Gelder, T. van (1995) (eds) *Mind as Motion: Explorations in the Dynamics of Cognition*, Cambridge MA: Bradford Books/MIT Press.

Posner, M.I. and Keele, S.W. (1969) 'Attention demands of movements', *Proceedings of 16th Congress of Applied Psychology*, Amsterdam: Swets and Zeitlinger.

Posner, M.I. and Raichle, M.E. (1994) (eds) *Images of Mind*, New York: Scientific American Library.

Posner, M.I and Snyder.C. (1975) 'Facilitation and inhibition in the processing of signals', in P. Rabbit and S. Dornic (eds) *Attention and Performance*, vol. V, London: Academic Press.

Posner, M.I., Snyder, C.R. and Davidson, B.J. (1980) 'Attention and the detection of signals', *Journal of Experimental Psychology* (General) 109: 160–74.

Postman, L. (1964) 'Short-term memory and incidental learning', in A.W. Melton (ed.) *Categories of Human Learning*, New York: Academic Press.

Poulton, E.C. (1957) 'On prediction in skilled movements', *Psychological Bulletin* 54: 467–78.

—— (1965) 'Skill in fast ball games', *Biological Affairs* 31: 1–5.

Prigogine, I. and Stengers, I. (1984) *Order Out of Chaos*, New York: Bantam Books.

Prinz, W. (1984) 'Ideo-motor action', Report No. 5, Research Group on Perception and Action, Center for Interdisciplinary Research, University of Bielefeld, Germany.

Proctor, R.W. and Dutta, A. (1995) *Skill Acquisition and Human Performance*, California: Saga Publications.

Proctor, R. and Reeve, T.G. (eds) (1990) *Stimulus-Response Compatibility: An Integrated Perspective*, Amsterdam: Elsevier Science.

Proteau, L. (1991) 'Extensive practice in a manual aiming task: A test of the specificity of learning hypothesis', unpublished paper cited in L. Proteau (1992) 'On the specificity of learning and the role of visual information for movement control', in L. Proteau and D. Elliott (eds) *Vision and Motor Control*, Amsterdam: Elsevier Science.

—— (1992) 'On the specificity of learning and the role of visual information for movement control', in L. Proteau and D. Elliott (eds) *Vision and Motor Control*, Amsterdam: Elsevier Science.

Proteau, L. and Alain, C. (1983) 'Strategie de decision en fonction de l'incertitude de l'evenement: I. Latence de la decision', *Canadian Journal of Applied Sports Sciences* 8: 63–71.

Proteau, L. and Cournoyer, J. (1990) 'Vision of the stylus in a manual aiming task: The effects of practice', *Quarterly Journal of Experimental Psychology* 42B: 811–28.

Proteau, L. and Dugas, C. (1982) 'Strategie de decision d'un groupe de jouers de basketball Inter-Universitaire', *Canadian Journal of Applied Sports Sciences* 7: 127–33.

Proteau, L. and Laurencelle, L. (1983) 'Strategie de decision: Effet de la probabilitie des evenements et du temps accorde sur le temps de reaction au choix et sur le temps de mouvement', *Canadian Journal of Applied Sports Sciences* 8: 54–62.

Proteau, L., Marteniuk, R. and Lévesque, L. (1992) 'A sensorimotor basis for motor learning: Evidence indicating specificity of practice', *Quarterly Journal of Experimental Psychology* 44A: 557–75.

Proteau, L., Levesque, L., Laurencelle, L. and Girouard, Y. (1989) 'Decision making in sport: The effect of stimulus-response probability on the performance of a coincidence-anticipation task', *Research Quarterly for Exercise and Sport* 60: 66–76.

Proteau, L., Marteniuk, R., Girouard, Y. and Dugas, C. (1987) 'On the type of information used to control and learn an aiming movement after moderate and extensive training', *Human Movement Science* 6: 181–99.

Ramsey, B. (1995) 'Effects of viewing orientation on modeling of field hockey receiving skill in the early phase of learning', unpublished MSc dissertation, West Chester University of Pennsylvania.

Reed, E.S. (1982) 'A outline theory of action systems', *Journal of Motor Behavior* 14: 98–134.

—— (1988) 'Applying the theory of action systems to the study of motor skills', in O.G. Meijer and K. Roth (eds) *Complex Movement Behaviour: 'The' Motor-Action Controversy*, Amsterdam: Elsevier Science.

Regan, D.M. (1986) 'The eye in ball games: Hitting and catching', *Proceedings of Conference on Vision and Sport*, Haarlem: De Vriesborch.

Regan, D. and Beverley, K.I. (1978) 'Looming detectors in the human visual pathway', *Vision Research* 18: 415–521.

Regan, D.M., Beverley, K. and Cynader, M. (1979) 'The visual perception of motion in depth', *Scientific American* 241: 122–33.

Regan, D., Erkelens, C.J. and Collewijn, H. (1986) 'Necessary conditions for the perception of motion in depth', *Investigations in Ophthalmology and Visual Science* 27: 584–97.

Regan, D., Frisby, J.P., Poggio, G.F., Schor, C.M. and Tyler, C.W. (1990) 'The perception of stereodepth and stereomotion: Cortical mechanisms', in *Visual Perception: The Neurophysiological Foundations*, New York: Academic Press.

Remington, R.W. (1980) 'Attention and saccadic eye movements', *Journal of Experimental Psychology: Human Perception and Performance* 6: 726–44.

Requin, J., Riehle, A. and Seal, J. (1993) 'Neuronal networks for movement preparation', in D.E. Meyer and S. Kornblum (eds) *Attention and Performance, XIV: Synergies in Experimental Psychology, Artificial Intelligence and Cognitive Neuroscience*, Cambridge MA: MIT Press.

Riccio, G.E. (1993) 'Information in movement variability about the qualitative dynamics of posture and orientation', in K.M. Newell and D.M. Corcos (eds) *Variability and Motor Control*, Champaign IL: Human Kinetics.

Riccio, G.E. and Stoffregren, T.A. (1988) 'Affordances as constraints on the control of stance', *Human Movement Science* 7: 265–300.

Ripoll, H. (1988) 'Analysis of visual scanning patterns of volleyball players in a problem solving task', *International Journal of Sport Psychology* 19: 9–25.

—— (1989) 'Uncertainty and visual search strategy in table tennis', *Perceptual and Motor Skills* 68: 507–12.

—— (1991) 'The understanding-acting process in sport: The relationship between the semantic and the sensorimotor visual function', *International Journal of Sport Psychology* 22: 221–43.

Ripoll, H., Bard, C. and Paillard, J. (1986) 'Stabilization of head and eyes on target as a factor in successful basketball shooting', *Human Movement Science* 5: 47.

Ripoll, H., Fleurance, P. and Cazeneuve, D. (1987) 'Analysis of the visual strategies involved in the execution of forehand and backhand strokes in table tennis', in J.K. O'Regan and A. Levy-Schoen (eds) *Eye Movements: From Physiology to Cognition*, Amsterdam: Elsevier Science.

Ripoll, H., Kerlirzin, Y., Stein, J.F. and Reine, B. (1995) 'Analysis of information processing, decision making, and visual strategies in complex problem solving sport situations', *Human Movement Science* 14(3): 325–49.

Ripoll, H., Papin, J.P., Guezennec, J.Y., Verdy, J.P. and Philip, M. (1985) 'Analysis of visual scanning patterns of pistol shooters', *Journal of Sport Science* 3: 93–101.

Ritzdorf, V. (1983) 'Antizipation in sportspiel-dargestelt am beispiel des tennis-grundschlangs (Anticipation in sport: investigation of the tennis ground stroke)', *Leistungssport* 13: 5–9.

Roach, N.K. and Burwitz, (1986) 'Observational learning in motor skill acquisition: the effect of verbal directing cues', in J. Watkins and L. Burwitz (eds) *Sports Science: Proceedings of VIII Commonwealth and International Conference on Sport, Physical Education, Dance, Recreation, and Health*, London: E & F Spon.

Roberton, M.A. (1993) 'New ways to think about old questions', in L.B. Smith and E.A. Thelen (eds) *A Dynamic Systems Approach to Development*, Cambridge MA: Bradford Books/MIT Press.

Robertson, S. and Elliott, D. (1996) 'Specificity of learning and dynamic balance', *Research Quarterly for Exercise and Sport* 67: 69–75.

—— (1997) 'The influence of skill in gymnastics and vision on dynamic balance', *International Journal of Sport Psychology* 4: 361–8.

Robertson, S., Collins, J., Elliott, D. and Starkes, J. (1994) 'The influence of skill and intermittent vision of dynamic balance', *Journal of Motor Behavior* 26: 333–9.

Rockwell, T. (1972) 'Skills, judgement and information acquisition in driving', in T.W. Forbes (ed.) *Human Factors in Highway Traffic Safety Research*, New York: Wiley.

Rose, D.J. and Christina, R.W. (1990) 'Attention demands of precision pistol-shooting as a function of skill level', *Research Quarterly for Exercise and Sport* 61: 111–13.

Rosenbaum, D.A. (1991) *Human Motor Control*, San Diego CA: Academic Press.

Rosengren, K.S., Pick, H.L. and Hofsten, C. von (1988) 'Role of visual information in ball catching', *Journal of Motor Behaviour* 20: 150–64.

Roshal, S.M. (1949) 'Effects of film-mediated perceptual-motor learning with varying representations of the task', unpublished doctoral dissertation, Pennsylvania State University.

—— (1961) 'Film-mediated learning with varying representation of the task: viewing angle, portrayal of demonstration, motion, and student participation', in A.A. Lumsdaine (ed.) *Student Response in Programmed Instruction*, Washington DC: National Research Council.

Ruch, T.C. (1965) 'Vision', in T.C. Ruch and H.D. Patton (eds) *Physiology and Biophysics*, Philadelphia: Saunders.

Rugg, M.D. and Coles, M.G.H. (1995) *Electrophysiology of Mind: Event-Related Brain Potentials and Cognition*, Oxford: Oxford University Press.

Rumelhart, D.E. (1989) 'The architecture of the mind: A connectionist approach', in M.I. Posner (ed.) *Foundations of Cognitive Science*, Cambridge MA: MIT Press.

Rumelhart, D.E. and McClelland, J.L. (eds) (1986) *Parallel Distributed Processing*, Cambridge MA: MIT Press.

Rumelhart, D.E. and Todd, P.M. (1993) 'Learning and connectionist representations', in *Attention and Performance, XIV: Synergies in Experimental Psychology, Artificial Intelligence and Cognitive Neuroscience*, Cambridge MA: MIT Press.

Runeson, S. (1977) 'On the possibility of "smart" perceptual mechanisms', *Scandinavian Journal of Psychology* 18: 172–9.

—— (1985) 'Perceiving people through their movements', in B. Kirkcaldy (ed.) *Individual Differences in Movement*, London: MTP Press.

Runeson, S. and Frykholm, G. (1981) 'Visual perception of lifted weight', *Journal of Experimental Psychology: Human Perception and Performance* 7: 733–40.

—— (1983) 'Kinematic specification of dynamics as an informational basis for person-and-action perception: expectation, gender recognition and deceptive intention', *Journal of Experimental Psychology* (General) 112: 585–615.

Russell, S.J. and Salmela, J.H. (1992) 'Quantifying expert athlete knowledge', *Journal of Applied Sport Psychology* 4: 10–26.

Russo, J.E., Johnson, E.J. and Stephens, D.L. (1989) 'The validity of verbal protocols', *Memory and Cognition* 17, No. 759–747.

Salazar, W., Landers, D.M., Petruzzello, S.J., Crews, D.J., Kubitz, K. and Han, M.W. (1990) 'Hemispheric asymmetry, cardiac response, and performance in elite archers', *Research Quarterly for Exercise and Sport* 61: 478–9.

Salmela, J.H and Fiorito, P. (1979) 'Visual cues in ice hockey goaltending', *Canadian Journal of Applied Sports Sciences* 4: 56–9.

Salmoni, A.W. (1989) 'Motor skill learning', in D.H. Holding (ed.) *Human Skills*, 2nd edn, Chichester: Wiley.

Sanders, A.F. and Houtmans, M.J.M. (1985) 'Perceptual processing modes in the functional visual field', *Acta Psychologica* 58: 251–61.

Sanderson, D.J. and Cavanagh, P.R. (1990) 'Use of augmented feedback for the modification of the pedalling mechanics of cyclists', *Canadian Journal of Sport Science* 15(1): 38–42.

Sanderson, F.H. (1981) 'Visual acuity and sports performance', in I.M. Cockerill and W.W. MacGillivary (eds) *Vision and Sport*, Cheltenham: Stanley Thornes.

Sanderson, F.H. and Whiting, H.T.A. (1978) 'Dynamic visual acuity: A possible factor in catching performance', *Journal of Motor Behavior* 10: 7–14.

Sardinha, L.F. and Bootsma, R.J. (1993) 'Visual information for timing a spike in volleyball', in S. Serpa, J. Alves, V. Ferreira and A. Paulo-Brito (eds) *Proceedings of 8th World Congress in Sport Psychology*, Lisbon: ISSP.

Savelsbergh, G.J.P. (1990) *Catching Behaviour: From Information-Processing to Ecological Psychological Explanation*, Amsterdam: Free University.

Savelsbergh, G.J.P. and Bootsma, R.J. (1994) 'Perception-action coupling in hitting and catching', *International Journal of Sport Psychology* 25: 331–43.

Savelsbergh, G.J.P. and Emmerik, R.E.A. van (1992) 'Dynamic interactionism: From co-regulation to the mapping problem', *Human Movement Science* 11: 443–51.

Savelsbergh, G. J. P. and Whiting, H.T.A. (1988) 'The effect of skill level, external frame of reference and environmental changes on one-handed catching', *Ergonomics* 31: 1655–63.

Savelsbergh, G.J.P., Wimmers, R., Kamp, J. van der and Davids, K. (1998a) 'The development of movement control and coordination', in M.L. Genta, B. Hopkins and A.F. Kalverboer (eds) *Basic Issues in Developmental Biopsychology*, Dordrecht: Kluwer.

—— (1998b) 'The visual guidance of catching', *Experimental Brain Research* 93: 146–56.

Savelsbergh, G.J.P., Whiting, H.T.A., Burden, A.M. and Bartlett, R.M. (1992) 'The role of predictive visual temporal information in the coordination of muscle activity in catching', *Experimental Brain Research* 89: 223–8.

Savelsbergh, G.J.P., Whiting, H.T.A., Pijpers, J.R. and Santvoord, A.M.M. van (1993) 'The visual guidance of catching', *Experimental Brain Research* 93: 146–56.

Scheerer, E. (1986) 'Pre-evolutionary conception of imitation', in G. Eckhardt, W. Bringmann and L. Sprung (eds) *Contributions to the History of Developmental Psychology*, Paris: Mouton.

Schiff, W. (1965) 'Perception of impeding collision: A study of visually directed avoidant behavior', *Psychological Monographs: General and Applied* (No. 604) 79: 11.

Schiff, W. and Detwiler, M.L. (1979) 'Information used in judging impending collision', *Perception* 8: 647–58.

Schiff, W. and Oldak, R. (1990) 'Accuracy of judging time-to-arrival: Effects of modality, trajectory, and gender', *Journal of Experimental Psychology: Human Perception and Performance* 16: 303–16.

Schmidt, R.A. (1975) 'A schema theory of discrete motor skill learning', *Psychological Review* 82: 225–60.

—— (1982) *Human Motor Behavior: An Introduction*, Hillsdale NJ: Erlbaum.

—— (1987) 'The acquisition of skill: Some modifications to the perception-action relationship through practice', in H. Heuer and A.F. Sanders (eds) *Perspectives on Perception and Action*, Hillsdale NJ: Lawrence Erlbaum.

—— (1988) *Motor Control and Learning: A Behavioural Emphasis*, 2nd edn, Champaign IL: Human Kinetics.

—— (1991) *Motor Learning and Performance: From Principles to Practice*, Champaign IL: Human Kinetics.

Schmidt, R.A. and White, J.L. (1972) 'Evidence for an error detection mechanism in motor skills: A test of Adams' closed-loop theory', *Journal of Motor Behavior* 4: 143–53.

Schmidt, R.A. and Young, D.E. (1991) 'Methodology for motor learning: a paradigm for kinematic feedback', *Journal of Motor Behaviour* 23(1): 13–24.

Schmid, R.A. and Zambarbieri, D. (1991) 'Strategies of eye-head coordination', in R. Schmid and D. Zambarbieri (eds) *Oculomotor Control and Cognitive Processes*, New York: Elsevier Science.

Schmidt, R.C. and Fitzpatrick, P. (1996) 'Dynamical perspective on motor learning', in H.N. Zelaznik (ed.) *Advances in Motor Learning and Control*, Champaign IL: Human Kinetics.

Schmidt, R.C., Carello, C. and Turvey. M.T. (1990) 'Phase transitions and critical fluctuations in the visual coordination of rhythmic movements between people', *Journal of Experimental Psychology: Human Perception and Performance* 16: 227–47.

Schmidt, R.C., Treffner, P.J., Shaw, B.K. and Turvey, M.T. (1992) 'Dynamical aspects of learning an inter limb rhythmic movement pattern', *Journal of Motor Behaviour* 24(1): 67–83.

Schneider, G.E. (1969) 'Two visual systems: Brain mechanisms for localization and discrimination are associated with tectal and cortical lesions', *Science* 163: 895–902.

Schneider, K., Zernicke, R.F., Schmidt, R.A. and Hart, T.J. (1989) 'Changes in limb dynamics during the practice of rapid arm movements', *Journal of Biomechanics* 22: 805–17.

Schneider, W. and Detweiler, M. (1988) 'The role of practice in dual-task performance: Toward workload modeling in a connectionist/control architecture', *Human Factors* 30: 539–66.

Schneider, W., Dumais, S.T. and Shiffrin, R.M. (1984) 'Automatic and control processing and attention', in R. Parsaurrman and R. Davies (eds) *Varieties of Attention*, Orlando FL: Academic Press.

Schoner, G. (1994) 'Dynamic theory of action-perception patterns: The time-before-contact paradigm', *Human Movement Science* 13: 415–40.

Scott, M.A., Li, F.-X. and Davids, K. (1997) 'Expertise and the regulation of gait in the approach phase of the long jump', *Journal of Sports Science* 15(6): 597–605.

Scott, M.A., Williams, A.M. and Davids, K. (1993) 'Perception-action coupling in Karate Kumite', in S. Valanti and J. Pittenger (eds) *Studies in Perception and Action*, vol. II, Hillsdale NJ: Lawrence Erlbaum.

Scully, D.M. (1986) 'Visual perception of technical execution and aesthetic quality in biological motion', *Human Movement Science* 5: 185–206.

—— (1988) 'Visual perception of human movement: the use of demonstrations in teaching motor skills', *British Journal of Physical Education Research Supplement* 4: 12–14.

Scully, D.M. and Newell, K.M. (1985) 'Observational learning and the acquisition of motor skills: towards a visual perception perspective', *Journal of Human Movement Studies* 11: 169–86.

Sekuler, R. and Blake, R. (1990) *Perception*. New York: McGraw-Hill.

Shadbolt, N. (1988) 'Models and methods in cognitive science', in M.F. McTear (ed.) *Understanding Cognitive Science*, Chichester: Ellis Horwood.

Shallice, T. (1964) 'The detection of change and the perceptual-moment hypothesis', *British Journal of Statistical Psychology Record* 17: 113–35.

—— (1978) 'The dominant action system: An information processing approach to consciousness', in K.S. Pope and H.H. Muller (eds) *The Stream of Consciousness*, New York: Plenum.

Shank, M.D. and Haywood, K.M. (1987) 'Eye movements while viewing a baseball pitch', *Perceptual and Motor Skills* 64: 1191–7.

Shapley, R. (1990) 'Visual sensitivity and parallel retinocortical channels', *Annual Review of Psychology* 41: 635–58.

Sharp, R.H. (1992) *Acquiring skill in sport*, Eastbourne UK: Sports Dynamics.

Sharp, R.H. and Whiting, H.T.A. (1974) 'Exposure and occluded duration effects in a ball-catching skill', *Journal of Motor Behaviour* 6(3): 139–47.

—— (1975) 'Information processing and eye movement behaviour in ball catching skill, *Journal of Human Movement Studies* 1: 124–31.

Shaw, R. and Bransford, J. (1977) 'Introduction: Psychological approaches to the problem of knowledge', in R. Shaw and J. Bransford (eds) *Perceiving, Acting, and Knowing: Toward an Ecological Psychology*, Hillsdale NJ: Lawrence Erlbaum.

Shaw, R.E. and Alley, J.R. (1985) 'How to draw learning curves: Their use and justification', in T.D. Johnston and A.T. Pietrewicz (eds) *Issues in the Ecological Study of Learning*, Hillsdale NJ: Erlbaum.

Shea, C., Wright, D. and Whitacre, C. (1993) 'Actual and observational practice: unique perspectives on learning', *Research Quarterly for Exercise and Sport* 64 (Suppl. A79).

Sheffield, F.D. (1961) 'Theoretical considerations in the learning of complex sequential tasks from demonstrations and practice', in A.A. Lumsdaine (ed.) *Student Response in Programmed Instruction*, Washington DC: National Research Council.

Sheffield, F.D. and Maccoby, N. (1961) 'Summary and interpretation of research on organizational principles in constructing filmed demonstrations', in A.A. Lumsdaine (ed.) *Student Response in Programmed Instruction*, Washington DC: National Research Council.

Sherman, A. (1980) 'Overview of research information regarding vision and sports', *Journal of American Optometric Association* 51: 661–6.

Shiffrin, R.M. and Schneider, W. (1977) 'Controlled and automatic human information processing: II Perceptual learning, automatic attending, and a general theory', *Psychological Review*, 84: 127–90.

Shik, M.L. and Orlovsky, G.N. (1976) 'Neurophysiology of locomotor automatism', *Physiological Reviews* 56: 465–501.

Silva, J.M. and Hardy, C.J. (1984) 'Precompetitive affect and athletic performance', in W.F. Straub and J.M. Williams (eds) *Cognitive Sport Psychology*, Ithaca NY: Sports Science Associates.

Simpson, J.I. (1984) 'The accessory optic system', *Annual Review of Neuroscience* 7: 13–41.

Singer, R.N. (1980) 'Motor behavior and the role of cognitive processes and learner strategies', in G.E. Stelmach and J. Requin (eds) *Tutorials in Motor Behavior*, Amsterdam: Elsevier Science.

Singer, R.N. and Gerson, R.F. (1981) 'Task classification and strategy utilization in motor skills', *Research Quarterly for Exercise and Sport* 52: 100–16.

Singer, R.N., Cauraugh, J.H., Chen, D., Steinberg, G.M. and Frehlich, S.G. (1996) 'Visual search, anticipation, and reactive comparisons between highly-skilled and beginning tennis players', *Journal of Applied Sport Psychology* 8: 9–26.

Singer, R.N., Cauraugh, J.H., Chen, D., Steinberg, G.M., Frehlich, S.G. and Wang, L. (1994) 'Training mental quickness in beginning/intermediate tennis players', *Sport Psychologist* 8: 305–18.

Sivak, B. and Mackenzie, C. L. (1992) 'The contributions of peripheral vision and central vision to prehension', in L. Proteau and D. Elliott (eds) *Vision and Motor Control*, Amsterdam: Elsevier Science.

Sluckin, W. (1970) *Early Learning in Man and Animals*, London: Unwin.

Smith, M.D. and Chamberlin, C.J. (1992) 'Effects of adding cognitively demanding tasks on soccer skill performance', *Perceptual and Motor Skills* 75: 955–61.

Smith, L.B. and Thelen, E. (eds) (1993) *A Dynamic Systems Approach to Development: Applications*, Cambridge MA: MIT Press.

Smyth, M.M. and Marriot, A.M. (1982) 'Vision and proprioception in simple catching', *Journal of Motor Behavior* 15: 237–61.

Smythies, J. (1996) 'A note on the concept of the visual field in neurology, psychology, and visual neuroscience', *Perception* 25: 369–71.

Soest, A.J. van and Beek, P.J. (1996) 'Perceptual-motor coupling in the execution of fast interceptive actions', *Corpus, Psyche et Societas* 3: 92–101.

Solomon, H., Zinn, W.J. and Vacroux, A. (1988) 'Dynamic stereoacuity: A test for hitting a baseball?', *Journal of the American Optometric Association* 59: 522–6.

Solso, R.L. (1995) *Cognitive Psychology*, 4th edn, Boston: Allyn and Bacon.

Souliere, D. and Salmela, J.H. (1982) 'Indices visuels, stress temporel et performance motrice au volleyball', in J.H. Salmela J.T. Partington and T. Orlick (eds) *New Paths of Sport Learning and Excellence*, Ottawa, Ont.: Sport in Perspective.

Southard, D. and Higgins, T. (1987) 'Changing movement patterns: effects of demonstration and practice', *Research Quarterly for Exercise and Sport* 58(1): 77–80.

Sparks, D.L. and Mayes, L.E. (1990) 'Signal transformations required for the generation of saccadic eye movements', *Annual Review of Neuroscience* 13: 3309–36.

Sperling, G.A. (1963) 'A model of visual memory tasks', *Human Factors* 5: 19–31.

Spoorns, O. and Edelman, G.M. (1993) 'Solving Bernstein's problem: A proposal for the development of coordinated movement by selection', *Child Development* 64: 960–81.

Stager, P. and Angus, R. (1978) 'Locating crash sites in a simulated air-to-ground visual search', *Human Factors* 20: 453–66.

Starkes, J.L. (1987) 'Skill in field hockey: The nature of the cognitive advantage', *Journal of Sport Psychology* 9: 146–60.

—— (1993) 'Motor experts: Opening thoughts', in J.L. Starkes and F. Allard (eds) *Cognitive Issues in Motor Expertise*, Amsterdam: Elsevier Science.

Starkes, J.L. and Allard, F. (1993) *Cognitive Issues in Motor Expertise*, Amsterdam: Elsevier Science.

Starkes, J. L. and Deakin, J. (1984) 'Perception in Sport: a cognitive approach to skilled performance', in W.F. Straub and J.M. Williams (eds) *Cognitive Sport Psychology*, Lansing NY: Sport Science Associates.

Starkes, J.L. and Lindley, S. (1994) 'Can we hasten expertise by video simulations?', *Quest* 46: 211–22.

Starkes, J.L., Allard, F., Lindley, S. and O'Reilly, K. (1994) 'Abilities and skill in basketball', *International Journal of Sport Psychology* 25: 249–65.

Starkes, J. L., Deakin, J. M., Lindley, S. and Crisp, F. (1987) 'Motor versus verbal recall of ballet sequences by young expert dancers', *Journal of Sport Psychology* 9: 222–30.

Starkes, J.L., Edwards, P., Dissanayake, P. and Dunn, T. (1995) 'A new technology and field test of advance cue usage in volleyball', *Research Quarterly for Exercise and Sport* 66(2): 162–7.

Steier, D.M. and Mitchell, T.M. (eds) (1996) *Mind Matters: A Tribute to Allen Newell*, London: Lawrence Erlbaum.

Stelmach, G.E. and Hughes, B. (1983) 'Does motor skill automation require a theory of attention?', in R.A. Magill (ed.) *Memory and Control of Action*, Amsterdam: Elsevier Science.

Sternberg, R.J. (1996) 'Costs of expertise', in K.A. Ericsson (ed.) *The Road to Excellence: The Acquisition of Expert Performance in the Arts and Sciences, Sports and Games*, New Jersey: Lawrence Erlbaum Associates.

Stone, J., Dreher, B. and Leventhal, A. (1979) 'Hierarchical and parallel mechanisms in the organization of visual cortex', *Brain Research Review* 1: 345–94.

Stroud, J. (1955) 'The fine structure of psychological time', in H. Quastler (ed.) *Information Theory and Psychology*, New York: Free Press.

Stroup, F. (1957) Relationship between measurements of field motion perception and basketball ability in college men', *Research Quarterly* 28: 72–6.

Stubbs, D. (1976) *Student Response in Programmed Instruction*, Washington DC: National Research Council.

Sugden, D.A. and Connell, R. (1979) 'Information processing in children's motor skills', *Physical Education Review* 2: 123–40.

Summers, J.J. (1977) 'The relationship between the sequencing and timing components of a skill', *Journal of Motor Behavior* 9: 49–59.

—— (1992) (ed.) *Approaches to the Study of Motor Control and Learning*, Amsterdam: Elsevier Science.

—— (1998) 'Has ecological psychology delivered what it has promised?', in J.Piek (ed.) *Motor Control and Skill: A Multidisciplinary Perspective*, Champaign IL: Human Kinetics.

Swinnen, S.P. (1990) 'Interpolated activities during the knowledge of results delay and post-knowledge of results interval: Effects of performance and learning', *Journal of Experimental Psychology: Learning, Memory, and Cognition* 16: 692–705.

—— (1994) 'Motor control', *Encyclopedia of Human Behavior* 3: 229–43.

Swinnen, S.P., Beirinckx, M.B., Meugens, P.F. and Walter, C.B. (1991) 'Dissociating the structural and metrical specifications of bimanual movement', *Journal of Motor Behavior* 23: 263–79.

Swinnen, S.P., Schmidt, R.A., Nicholson, D.E. and Shapiro, D.C. (1990) 'Information feedback for skill acquisition: Instantaneous knowledge of results degrades learning', *Journal of Experimental Psychology: Learning, Memory, and Cognition* 16: 706–16.

Takeuchi, T. (1993) 'Auditory information in playing tennis', *Perceptual and Motor Skills* 76: 1323–8.

Tayler, M.A. and Davids, K. (1997) 'Catching with both hands: An evaluation of neural cross-talk and coordinative structure models of bimanual coordination', *Journal of Motor Behavior* 29: 254–62.

Tayler, M.A., Burwitz, L. and Davids, K. (1994) 'Coaching perceptual strategy in badminton', *Journal of Sports Sciences* 12: 213.

Taylor, G. (1992) *Soccer Training Can Be Fun*, London: Hamlyn.

Tenenbaum, G. and Bar-Eli, M. (1995) 'Personality and intellectual capabilities in sport psychology', in D.H. Saklofske and M. Zeidner (eds) *International Handbook of Personality and Intelligence*, New York: Plenum.

Tenenbaum, G, Levy-Kolker, N., Bar-Eli, M. and Weinberg, R. (1994) 'Information recall of younger and older skilled athletes: The role of display complexity, attentional resources and visual exposure duration', *Journal of Sports Sciences* 12: 529–34.

Tenenbaum, G., Levy-Kolker, N., Sade, S., Liebermann, D.G. and Lidor, R. (1996) 'Anticipation and confidence of decisions related to skilled performance', *International Journal of Sport Psychology* 27: 293–307.

Thelen, E. (1983) 'Learning to walk is still an "old" problem: A reply to Zelazo (1983)', *Journal of Motor Behavior* 15: 139–61.

—— (1995) 'Motor development: A new synthesis', *American Psychologist* 50: 79–95.

Thelen, E. and Smith, L.B. (1994) *A Dynamic Systems Approach to the Development of Cognition and Action*, Cambridge MA: MIT Press.

Thiffault, C. (1980) 'Construction et validation d'une measure de la rapidite de la pensée tactique des joueurs de hockey sur glace', in C.H. Nadeau, W.R. Haliwell, K.M. Newell and G.C. Roberts (eds) *Psychology of Motor Behaviour and Sport*, Champaign IL: Human Kinetics.

Thomas, J.R, French, K.E. and Humphries, C.A. (1986) 'Knowledge development and sport skill performance: Directions for motor behavior research', *Journal of Sport Psychology* 8: 259–72.

Thorpe, R. (1996) 'Telling people how to do things does not always help them learn', *Supercoach* 8: 7–8.

Tienson, J.L. (1990) 'An introduction to connectionism', in J.L. Garfield (ed.) *Foundations of Cognitive Science: The Essential Readings*, New York: Paragon House.

Todd, J.T. (1981) 'Visual information about moving objects', *Journal of Experimental Psychology: Human Perception and Performance* 7: 795–810.

Tootell, R. (1982) 'Deoxyglucose analysis of retinotopic organization in the primate striate cortex', *Science*, 218: 902–4.

Trachtman, J.N. (1995) 'Accommodative microfluctuations: diagnosis and treatment with biofeedback. a pilot investigation', *International Journal of Sports Vision* 2(1): 36–44.

Trachtman, J.N. and Kluka, D.A. (1993) 'Future trends in vision as they relate to peak performance in sport', *International Journal of Sports Vision*, 1–7.

Treisman, A. (1964) 'Selective attention in man', *British Medical Bulletin* 20: 12–16.

—— (1985) 'Preattentive processing in vision', *Computer Vision, Graphics, and Image Processing* 31: 156–77.

—— (1988) 'Features and objects: Fourteenth Bartlett Memorial Lecture', *Quarterly Journal of Experimental Psychology* 40A(2): 201–37.

Tresilian, J.R. (1990) 'Perceptual information for the timing of interceptive action', *Perception* 19: 223–39.

—— (1991) 'Empirical and theoretical issues in the perception of time to contact', *Journal of Experimental Psychology: Human Perception and Performance* 17: 865–76.

—— (1993) 'Four questions of time to contact: A critical examination of research on interceptive timing', *Perception* 22: 653–80.

—— (1994a) 'Approximate information sources and perceptual variables in interceptive timing', *Journal of Experimental Psychology: Human Perception and Performance* 20: 154–73.

—— (1994b) 'Perceptual and motor processes in interceptive timing', *Human Movement Science* 13: 335–73.

—— (1995) 'Perceptual and cognitive processes in time-to-contact estimation: Analysis of prediction-motion and relative judgement tasks', *Perception and Psychophysics* 57: 231–45.

Trevarthen, C.B. (1968) 'Two mechanisms of vision in primates', *Psychologische Forschung* 31: 299–337.

Turvey, M.T. (1977) 'Preliminaries to a theory of action with reference to vision', in R. Shaw and J. Bransford (eds) *Perceiving, Acting and Knowing: Toward an Ecological Psychology*, Hillsdale NJ: Erlbaum.

—— (1986) 'Intentionality: A problem of multiple reference frames, specificational information, and extraordinary boundary conditions on natural law', *Behavioral and Brain Sciences* 9: 153–5.

—— (1990) 'Coordination', *American Psychologist* 45: 938–53.

—— (1992) 'Ecological foundations of cognition: Invariants of perception and action', in H. Pick, P. van den Broek and D. Knill (eds) *Cognition: Conceptual and Methodological Issues*, Dordrecht: Kluwer.

Turvey, M.T. and Fitzpatrick, P. (1993) 'Commentary: Development of perception-action systems and general principles of pattern formation', *Child Development* 64: 1175–90.

Turvey, M.T. and Kugler, P.N. (1984) 'An ecological approach to perception and action', in H.T.A. Whiting (ed.) *Human Motor Actions: Bernstein Re-assessed*, Amsterdam: Elsevier Science.

Turvey, M.T., Fitch, H. and Tuller, B. (1982) 'The Bernstein Perspective: I. The problem of degrees of freedom and context-conditoned variability', in J.A.S. Kelso (ed.) *Human Motor Behavior: An Introduction*, Hillsdale NJ: LEA.

Tyldesley, D. and Whiting, H.T.A. (1975) 'Operational Timing', *Journal of Human Movement Studies* 1: 172–7.

Tyldesley, D.A., Bootsma, R.J. and Bomhoff, G.T. (1982) 'Skill level and eye movement patterns in a sport orientated reaction time task', in H. Rieder, H. Mechling and K Reischle (eds) *Proceedings of an International Symposium on Motor Behaviour: Contribution to Learning in Sport*, Cologne: Hofmann.

Ungerleider, L. G. and Mishkin, M. (1982) 'Two cortical visual systems', in D.J. Ingle, M.A. Goodale and R.J.W. Mansfield (eds) *Analysis of Visual Behavior*, Cambridge MA: MIT Press.

Vereijken, B. (1991) *The Dynamics of Skill Acquisition*, Amsterdam: Free University Press.

Vereijken, B. and Whiting, H.T.A. (1990) 'In defence of discovery learning', *Canadian Journal of Sports Science* 15: 99–106.

Vereijken, B., Emmerik, R.E.A. van, Whiting, H.T.A. and Newell, K.M. (1992) 'Free(z)ing degrees of freedom in skill acquisition', *Journal of Motor Behaviour* 24(1): 133–42.

Vickers, J.N. (1988) 'Knowledge structures of elite-novice gymnasts', *Human Movement Science* 7: 4–72.

—— (1992) 'Gaze control in putting', *Perception* 21: 117–32.

—— (1996) 'Control of visual attention during the basketball free throw', *American Journal of Sports Medicine* 24(6): S93–7.

—— (1996) 'Visual control when aiming at a far target', *Journal of Experimental Psychology: Human Perception and Performance* 22(2): 1–13.

Vickers, J.N. and Adolphe, R.M. (1997) 'Gaze behaviour during a ball tracking and aiming skill', *International Journal of Sports Vision* 4(1): 18–27.

Vickers, J.N. Canic, M., Abbott, S. and Livingston, L. (1988) 'Eye movements of elite ice hockey players', Proceedings of Canadian Society for Psychomotor Learning and Sport Psychology Conference, Collingwood, Canada.

Vogt, S. (1986) 'A frequency coding model applied to movement imitation', paper presented at Workshop on Movement Imitation, Center for Interdisciplinary Research, University of Bielefeld, Germany.

Waddington, C.H. (1954) *The Integration of Gene-controlled Processes and its Bearing on Evolution.* Proceedings of the 9th International Congress of Genetics (Caryologia suppl.)

Waldrop, M.M. (1992) *Complexity*, London: Viking.

Wallace, S.A. (1996) 'Dynamic pattern perspective of rhythmic movement: An introduction', in H.N. Zelaznik (ed.) *Advances in Motor Learning and Control*, Champaign IL: Human Kinetics.

Wang, M.Q. and Landers, D.M. (1988) 'Cardiac responses and hemispheric differentiation during archery performance: A psychophysiological investigation of attention, unpublished manuscript, Arizona State University, Tempe AZ.

Wann, J.P. (1996) 'Anticipating arrival: Is the tau margin a specious theory?', *Journal of Experimental Psychology: Human Perception and Performance* 22: 1031–48.

Wapner, S. and Cerillo, L. (1968) 'Imitation of a model's hand movements: Age changes in transposition of left-right relations', *Child Development* 39: 887–94.

Warren, W.H. (1988) 'Action Modes and laws of control for the visual guidance of action', in O.G. Meijer and K. Roth (eds) *Complex Movement Behaviour: 'The' Motor-Action Controversy*, Amsterdam: Elsevier Science.

—— (1990) 'The perception-action coupling', in H. Bloch and B.I. Bertenthal (eds) *Sensory-Motor Organizations and Development in Infancy and Early Childhood*, Dordrecht: Kluwer.

Warren, W.H., Young, D.S. and Lee, D.N. (1986) 'Visual control of step length during running over irregular terrain', *Journal of Experimental Psychology: Human Perception and Performance* 12: 259–66.

Webster's New Collegiate Dictionary (1977) Springfield MA: Merriam.

Weeks, D. (1992) 'A comparison of modeling modalities in the observational learning of an externally-paced skill', *Research Quarterly for Exercise and Sport* 63: 373–80.

Weeks, D. and Proctor, R. (1991) 'Ecological and process approaches to skill acquisition', *Journal of Human Movement Studies* 20: 291–6.

Weimer, W.B. (1977) 'A conceptual framework for cogniitve psychology: motor theories of the mind', in R. Shaw and J. Bransford (eds) *Perceiving, Acting, and Knowing*, Hillsdale NJ: Erlbaum.

Weinberg, R.S. and Hunt, V.V. (1976) 'The interrelationships between anxiety, motor performance and electromyography', *Journal of Motor Behaviour* 8: 219–24.

Weiss, M.R. (1983) 'Modeling and motor performance: a developmental perspective', *Research Quarterly* 54(2) 190–7.

Weiss, M.R. and Klint, K.A. (1987) '"Show and tell" in the gymnasium: An investigation of developmental differences in modeling and verbal rehearsal of motor skills', *Research Quarterly for Exercise and Sport* 58: 234–41.

Welford, A.T. (1952) 'The "psychological refractory period" and the timing of high-speed performance: A review and a theory', *British Journal of Psychology* 43: 2–19.

White, P.A. (1988) 'Knowing more about what we can tell: Introspective access and causal report accuracy 10 years later', *British Journal of Psychology* 79: 13–45.

White, R. W. (1959) 'Motivation reconsidered: The concept of competence', *Psychological Review* 66: 297–330.

Whiting, H.T.A. (1968) 'Training in a continuous ball-throwing and catching task', *Ergonomics* 11: 375–82.

—— (1969) *Acquiring Ball Skill: A Psychological Interpretation*, London: Bell

—— (1970) 'An operational analysis of a continuous ball throwing and catching task', *Ergonomics* 13: 445–54.

—— (1979) 'Subjective probability in sport', in G.C. Roberts and K.M. Newell (eds) *Psychology of Motor Behavior and Sport*, Champaign IL: Human Kinetics.

—— (1986) 'Isn't there a catch in it somewhere?', *Journal of Motor Behaviour* 18: 486–91.

—— (1988) 'Imitation and the learning of complex cyclical actions', in O.G. Meijer and K. Roth (eds) *Complex Motor Behaviour: 'The' Motor Systems: Action Systems Controversy*, Amsterdam: Elsevier Science.

Whiting, H.T.A. and Brinker, B. den (1981) 'Image of the act', in J.P. Das, R.F. Mulcahy and A.E. Wall (eds) *Theory and Research in Learning Disabilities*, New York: Plenum.

Whiting, H.T.A. and Sanderson, F.H. (1974) 'Dynamic visual acuity and performance in a catching task, *Journal of Motor Behavior* 6: 87–94.

Whiting, H.T.A. and Savelsbergh, G.J.P. (1992) 'An exception that proves the rule!', in J. Requin and G.E. Stelmach (eds) *Tutorials in Motor Behavior*, vol. II, Amsterdam: Elsevier Science.

Whiting, H.T.A. and Sharp, R.H. (1974) 'Visual occlusion factors in a discrete ball catching task', *Journal of Motor Behaviour* 6(1): 11–16.

Whiting, H.T.A, Alderson, G.J.K. and Sanderson, F.H. (1973) 'Critical time intervals for viewing and individual differences in performance of a ball-catching task', *International Journal of Sport Psychology* 4: 155–6.

Whiting, H.T.A., Bijlard, M.J. and Brinker, B.P.L.M. den (1987) 'The effect of availability of a dynamic model on the acquisition of cyclical action', *Quarterly Journal of Experimental Psychology* 39A: 43–59.

Whiting, H.T.A., Gill, E.B. and Stephenson, J.M. (1970) 'Critical time intervals for taking in flight information in a ball-catching task', *Ergonomics* 13: 265–72.

Whiting, H.T.A., Savelsbergh, G.J.P. and Faber, C.M. (1988) 'Catch questions and incomplete answers', in A.M. Colley and J.R.Beech (eds) *Cognition and Action in Skilled Behaviour*, Amsterdam: Elsevier Science.

Wierda, M. and Maring, W. (1993) 'Interpreting eye movements of traffic participants', in D. Brogan, A. Gale and K. Carr (eds) *Visual Search*, vol. II, London: Tayler and Francis.

Wickens, C.D. (1980) 'The structure of attentional resources', in R. Nickerson and R. Pew (eds) *Attention and Performance*, vol. VIII, Hillsdale NJ: Lawrence Erlbaum.

—— (1984) 'Processing resources in attention', in R. Parasuraman and R. Davies (eds) *Varieties of Attention*, New York: Academic Press.

—— (1989) 'Attention and skilled performance', in D.H. Holding (ed.) *Human Skills*, Chichester: Wiley.

—— (1992) *Engineering Psychology and Human Performance*, 2nd edn, Illinois: Harper Collins.

Wickstrom, R.L. (1983) *Fundamental Motor Patterns*, 3rd edn, Philadelphia: Lea and Febiger.

Widmaier, H. (1983) 'Zur psychologie des volleyballspielers: Aufmerksmkeit, motivation, angst und kohasion', *Leistungssport* 13(6) 19–22.

Wieringen, P.C.W. van (1988) 'Kinds and levels of explanation: Implications for the motor systems versus action systems controversy', in O.G. Meijer and K. Roth (eds) *Complex Movement Behaviour: 'The' Motor Systems-Action Systems Controversy*, Amsterdam: Elsevier Science.

Wiese-Bjornstal, D.M. and Weiss, M.R. (1992) 'Modeling effects on children's form kinematics, performance outcome, and cognitive recognition of a sport skill: an integrated perspective', *Research Quarterly for Exercise and Sport* 63:, 67–75.

Wightman, D.C. and Lintern, G. (1985) 'Part-task training for tracking and manual control', *Human Factors* 27: 267–83.

Wilberg, R.B. (1972) 'A suggested direction for the study of motor performance by physical educators, *Research Quarterly* 43: 387–93.

Williams, A.M. and Burwitz, K. (1993) 'Advance cue utilization in soccer', in T. Reilly, J. Clarys and A. Stibbe (eds) *Science and Football*, vol. II, London: E & FN Spon.

Williams, A.M. and Davids, K. (1994) 'Eye movements and visual perception in sport', *Coaching Focus* 26: 6–9.

—— (1995) 'Declarative knowledge in sport: a byproduct of experience or a characteristic of expertise?', *Journal of Sport and Exercise Psychology* 17(3): 259–75.

—— (1997) 'Assessing cue usage in performance contexts: a comparison between eye movement and verbal report methods', *Behavioral Research Methods, Instruments, and Computers* 29: 364–75.

—— (1998a) 'Motor expertise in sport', in H. Steinberg (ed.) *What Sport Psychologists Do*, British Psychological Society, Leicester.

—— (1998b) 'Visual search strategy, selective attention and expertise in soccer, *Research Quarterly for Exercise and Sport* 69(2): 111–29.

Williams, A.M. and Elliott, D. (1997) 'Visual search strategy in karate kumite: A function of experience and anxiety', in R. Lidor and M. Bar-Eli (eds) *Innovations in Sport Psychology: Linking Theory and Practice*, Netanya, Israel: ISSP.

Williams, A.M., Davids, K. and Burwitz, L. (1994) 'Ecological validity and visual search research in sport', *Journal of Sport and Exercise Psychology* S16: 22.

Williams, A.M., Singer, R.N. and Weigelt, C. (1998) 'Visual search strategy in "live" on-court situations in tennis: an exploratory study', in A. Lees and I.W. Maynard (eds) *Science and Rackets*, vol. II, London: E & FN Spon.

Williams, A.M., Davids, K., Burwitz, L. and Williams, J.G. (1992) 'Perception and action in sport', *Journal of Human Movement Studies* 22: 147–204.

—— (1993a) 'Visual search and sports performance', *Australian Journal of Science and Medicine in Sport* 22: 55–65.

—— (1993b) 'Cognitive knowledge and soccer performance', *Perceptual and Motor Skills* 76: 579–93.

—— (1994) 'Visual search strategies of experienced and inexperienced soccer players, *Research Quarterly for Sport and Exercise* 65(2): 127–35.

Williams, J.G. (1979) 'Self-discovered learning of a complex coordinative skill', unpublished research report, Brentwood College, England.

—— (1982) 'Observational motor learning: some input and output characteristics', paper presented at Annual Conference of North American Society for Psychomotor Learning and Sports Psychology, Edmonton, Canada.

—— (1984) 'Movement imitation as perceptuo-motor coupling', unpublished manuscript.

—— (1985) 'Movement imitation: some fundamental processes', unpublished PhD thesis, University of London, UK.

—— (1986) 'Perceiving human movement: A review of research with implications for the use of the demonstration during motor learning', *Physical Education Review* 9(1): 53–8.

—— (1987) 'Visual demonstration and movement production: effects of motoric mediation during observation of a model', *Perceptual and Motor Skills* 65: 825–6.

—— (1988) 'Perception of a throwing action from point-light demonstrations', *Perceptual and Motor Skills* 67; 273–4.

—— (1989a) 'Motor skills instruction, visual demonstration and eye movements', *Physical Education Review* 12(1): 49–55.

—— (1989b) 'Visual demonstration and movement production: effects of timing variations of a model's actions', *Perceptual and Motor Skills* 68: 891–6.

—— (1989c) 'Effects of kinematically enhanced video-modeling on improvement of form in a gymnastic skill', *Perceptual and Motor Skills* 69: 473–4.

—— (1992) 'Effects of instruction and practice on ball catching skill: single-subject study of an eight-year-old', *Perceptual and Motor Skills* 76: 392–4.

—— (1993) 'Motoric modeling: research and theory', *Journal of Human Movement Studies* 25: 237–79.

Williams, J.G. and Horn, R.R. (1995) 'Exercise intensity effects on peripheral perception of soccer player movement', *International Journal of Sports Vision* 2(1): 22–8.

Williams, J.G. and Thompson, H. (1994) 'Effects of video-modeling on posture whilst learning to lift a weighted box', *Journal of Human Movement Studies* 27: 117–29.

Williams, J.M. and Thirer, J. (1975) 'Vertical and horizontal peripheral vision in male and female athletes and non-athletes', *Research Quarterly* 46: 200–205.

Winfrey, M.L. and Weeks, D.L. (1993) 'Effects of self-modeling on self-efficacy and balance beam performance', *Perceptual and Motor Skills* 77: 907–13.

Williams, M.L. and Willoughby, R.H. (1971) 'Observational learning: the effects of age, task difficulty, and observer's motoric rehearsal', *Journal of Experimental Child Psychology* 12: 146–56.

Woods, D.L. (1990) 'The physiological basis of selective attention: Implications of event-related potential studies', in J.W. Rohrbaugh, R. Parasurasman and R. Johnson (eds) *Event-Related Brain Potentials*, New York: Oxford University Press.

Worrell, B.E. (1996) 'The impact of specialized sports vision testing and therapy on baseball batting averages', *International Journal of Sports Vision* 3: 1.

Wright, D.L., Plesants, F. and Gomez-Meza, M. (1990) 'Use of advanced cue sources in volleyball', *Journal of Sport and Exercise Psychology* 12: 406–14.

Wright, R.A. and Ward, L.M. (1994) 'Shifts in visual attention: An historical and methodological overview', *Canadian Journal of Experimental Psychology* 48(2): 151–66.

Yando, R., Seitz, V. and Zigler, E. (1978) *Imitation: A Developmental Perspective*, London: Wiley.

Yantis, S. and Jonides, J. (1990) 'Abrupt visual onsets and selective attention: Voluntary versus automatic allocation', *Journal of Experimental Psychology: Human Perception and Performance* 16: 121–34.

Yarbus, A.L. (1967) *Eye Movements and Vision*, New York: Plenum Press.

Yates, F.E. (1979) 'Physical biology: A basis for modeling living systems', *Journal of Cybernetics and Information Science* 2: 57–70.

Zani, A. and Rossi, B. (1991) 'Cognitive psychophysiology as an interface between cognitive and sport psychology', *International Journal of Sport Psychology* 22: 376–98.

Zanone, P.G. and Kelso, J.A.S. (1994) 'The coordination dynamics of learning: theoretical structure and experimental agenda', in S. Swinnen, H. Heuer, J. Massion and P. Casaer (eds) *Interlimb Coordination-Neural, Dynamical and Cognitive Constraints*, New York: Academic Press.

Zeki, S. (1993) *A Vision of the Brain*, Oxford: Blackwell Scientific.

Zinn, W.J. and Solomon, H. (1985) 'A comparison of static and dynamic stereoacuity', *Journal of the American Optometric Association* 56: 712–15.

Index

Entries marked in *italic* refer to figures.